McGraw-Hill Series in Political Science
JOSEPH P. HARRIS, *Consulting Editor*

An Introduction to the Law of Nations

McGRAW-HILL SERIES IN POLITICAL SCIENCE

JOSEPH P. HARRIS, *Consulting Editor*

✦ ✦ ✦

AN INTRODUCTION
TO THE LAW OF NATIONS

Oscar Svarlien

PROFESSOR OF HISTORY AND POLITICAL SCIENCE
UNIVERSITY OF FLORIDA

McGRAW-HILL BOOK COMPANY, INC.

New York   Toronto   London

1955

To
Jeanne and John

Preface

The years of our century are marked by revolutionary forces in human society on every level from the family to the community of nations, and that which once seemed remote and peripheral is now of central importance. The action taking place in the arena of international relations, therefore, is very often of the greatest concern to the individual citizen, whose main desire and most fervent hope is to live out his life in peaceful pursuit of those values which his own culture has determined. But it is a paradox of our age that, though the relationship between man and the material universe has become more precise and, in many respects, more advantageous, the relations between man and man and among the nations are marked by an empiricism as detestable as it is false. Nationalism, which in the nineteenth century was associated with liberalism in political philosophy, is now more often aligned with movements of reaction which insist on cultural uniformity and deny the rights of ethnic and religious minorities. The ideal of collective security is withering in the heat of power politics, and the law of nations, like many other institutions, is in a state of crisis. Such are the affairs of the world at the time of this writing; yet to the student of international law there never was a greater challenge or a more inviting opportunity.

This introductory volume to the law of nations is the outgrowth of long experience in teaching this subject to college students on both the undergraduate and the graduate level. It is not meant to be a definitive treatise or a reference book for the expert, and the author lays no claim to having presented "the whole of the argument." It is hoped, however, that this book may be found an interesting and useful guide to the student who is just beginning his study of international law.

Experience over many years has led the author to the conclusion that the so-called "case method" of instruction, without the parallel use of a basic text providing an orientation to the whole subject, is unsatisfactory. It fails to give the student a sense of synthesis and an appreciation of the historical development of the law of nations, which is so essential to its understanding. A better approach to the learning process in this field, it would seem, is a combination of the text and case-book method. This opinion is, indeed, supported by recent discussions in the American Society of International Law. It is the hope of the author, therefore, that this volume will, to some extent at least, meet the need for an up-to-date introductory text which may conveniently be used in combination with many of the excellent case-books now available.

A special effort has been made to give the subject a certain unity and a larger appeal by organizing the material, as far as possible, around a central theme, which is the *community of nations*. Because of the voluminous nature and the complexity of the subject, as well as limited time and space, the most difficult task has been the selection of topics to be treated. In this respect an orthodox pattern has been followed, though a great deal more space is devoted to the historical background and to the development of international-legal theory than is usually found in modern texts. A greater emphasis has also been given such topics as the continental shelf doctrine, air law, the development of regionalism in international organization, and the individual in international law than is generally the case in a treatise of this kind. Attempts have been made, wherever possible, to treat each topic, first, in the light of its history; second, in that of its law; and finally, in terms of modern trends and developments. It is hoped that this method of treatment will not only be found helpful as a guide to the contemporary law, but also provide an appreciation of its classic origins and a more intimate acquaintance with some of the great masters of the past, who have contributed so much to the literature which laid the foundations of the law of nations.

It is the pleasure of the author to acknowledge his debt to those who have labored before him. Extensive use has been made of the Lauterpacht editions of Oppenheim's *International Law*; of Charles Cheney Hyde's *International Law Chiefly as Interpreted and Applied by the United States*; Charles G. Fenwick's *International Law*; and J. L. Brierly's little classic *The Law of Nations*. Heavy reliance has also been placed on numerous special treatises and monographs and on periodical literature in the field. The monumental *Digests* of Hackworth and Moore have been of invaluable help, as has Manley O. Hudson's *World Court Reports* and *International Legislation*.

To his many friends and colleagues, who have been helpful along the way, the author's eternal thanks: to William G. Carleton, who on many occasions encouraged the enterprise; Manning J. Dauer, who read several chapters in typescript and from whose able and very candid suggestions much benefit was derived; David L. Dowd, who was especially helpful in matters involving French sources. Others who have read portions of the manuscript and made valuable suggestions are John G. Eldridge, E. Ashby Hammond, Paul Lamont Hanna, Ross Y. Koen, Ralph E. Page, Arthur W. Thompson, and George Elliott Wolff. But perhaps the most immeasurable contribution was made by one of the author's closest friends and most respected colleagues, Donald E. Worcester, who by various means of intimidation forced the submission of the first part of the manuscript to the publisher and hounded the author ever after until it was finally completed. Special mention is also due Mrs. Margaret D. Duer, Head Librarian of Circulation in the University of Florida Library, whose kind cooperation will always be remembered, and Mrs. Ila R. Pridgen, Law Librarian, for her friendly and efficient service. Last, but not the least worthy of recognition, are the author's own students, who in innumerable ways have contributed to this volume.

There are many others who have added their friendly council and who have demonstrated a strange confidence in the author's ability to see the job through to the last period. Among these his good wife has been long suffering and has kept the faith.

OSCAR SVARLIEN

Contents

PART TWO
THE FUNCTION OF STATES IN INTERNATIONAL LAW

United States—Matters Pertaining to the States of the Union—Treaties and the Charter of the United Nations—Specialized Agencies—Negotiation and Ratification of Treaties—Ratification of Treaties in the United States—Essentials of Validity—Treaty Interpretation—*Pacta Sunt Servanda*—Modification and Termination of Treaties—The Effect of War upon Treaties.

Diplomatic Negotiation—Good Offices and Mediation—The *Dogger Bank Case*—Arbitration—Arbitral Procedure—The Court of Judicial Arbitration—The International Prize Court—The Central American Court of Justice—A World Court of Justice—The United States and the Permanent Court of Justice—The United Nations and Pacific Settlement of Disputes—The International Court of Justice—Evaluation of the Court in the Settlement of Disputes.

The Great Schism and the North Atlantic Treaty Organization: The Failure of Collective Security—Soviet Theory of International Law—The Great Problem—The North Atlantic Treaty Organization. The American and Soviet Security Systems: The Organization of American States—American Regionalism and the United Nations—The Rio Pact of 1947—The Soviet System of Collective Security. Toward a United Europe: The Western European Union—The Council of Europe—The European Coal and Steel Community—The European Defense Community—A European Political Community. Other Consolidations and the Uniting for Peace Resolutions: Uniting for Peace—ANZUS—The Arab League—The Mutual Defense Assistance Agreement between the United States and Japan of 1954.

PART FIVE

HOSTILE RELATIONS BETWEEN NATIONS

The Nature of Modern War—Legal Limitations upon the Right to Wage War—A Summary of Certain Rules of Belligerent Operations—General Effects of the Outbreak of War—The Effect of War upon Private Citizens and Subjects—Enemy Aliens—Enemy Property and Economic Warfare—The Effect of War upon Contracts—Civil War—*Bellum Justum* and *Bellum Legale*.

The Evolution of the Law of Neutrality: The Evolution of Traditional Neutrality—The Second Hague Conference of 1907—The London Declaration—Contraband of War—The Doctrine of Continuous Voyage—Blockade—Visit and Search. Neutrality, Total War, and Collective Security: Departure from Traditional Neutrality in the United States—Neutrality and the Doctrine of Necessity—Neutrality and Collective Security. Conclusion.

The Legal Nature of Occupation—Administration of Occupied Territory—The Legal Status of "War Treason"—The Legal Status of War Rebellion—

Military Occupation and the Transfer of Property—German Practice During the Second World War—The Taking of Hostages—Certain Problems in Connection with Friendly Occupation—The Attitude of the United States. Recent Developments: Allied Occupation of Germany—The Treaty of Peace with Japan—Agreement Concerning NATO Forces—United States-United Kingdom Mutual Defense Agreement.

A New Conception—War Criminals Are Warned—The Establishment of the Nuremberg Tribunal—The Procedure—Definitions of Crimes and the Law of the Charter—The Great Controversy—Crimes against Peace—War Crimes—The Legality of the Tribunal—Crimes against Humanity—War Crimes and the United Nations—The Meaning of Nuremberg.

PART SIX
THE INDIVIDUAL IN INTERNATIONAL LAW

The Failure of Positivism—Nationality—How Nationality Is Acquired—Expatriation—Dual Nationality—Stateless Persons—Statelessness and the International Law Commission—Extradition.

The Classical Origins of Natural Law—The Pursuit of Happiness—Human Rights and the United Nations Charter—The Universal Declaration of Human Rights—A United Nations Bill of Rights—The European Convention on Human Rights—A Turn in the Road.

PART ONE

Concerning the International Community

CHAPTER 1

Sovereignty and the
International Community

It is becoming more and more apparent that the system of national states, which reached its greatest height in the nineteenth century, is now passing through a period of severe crisis. The conflict between the forces of nationalism, on the one hand, and those of a world unitarianism looking to a federation of the peoples and the parliament of man, on the other, is perhaps basic to this age.

Modern nationalism has its genesis in the French Revolution, while the strongest arguments for "One World" are to be found in the results of the technological advances which have taken place in the last hundred years. The manner in which the conflict between these divergent forces is to be resolved will determine the shape of things to come, and it constitutes a problem which is of central importance to international law and politics. A paradoxical situation is presented, however, in the fact that, though the increased interdependence of nations requires a more advanced international organization, an attitude of mind conducive to the kind of cooperation that would maintain peace with justice is not yet present. The community of nations, which is the most essential prerequisite to effective law, is in a primitive state of development.

Nationalism was a unifying and integrating force at the opening of modern times, when the fragments of medieval Europe were gathering into larger political and territorial units under the aegis of royal absolutism. Thus, the political anarchy of the Middle Ages gave way to the modern state with an enlarged territorial sovereignty. With the passing of time, the power of kings was often limited by constitutionalism and, indeed, sometimes lost through republicanism, while nationalism not only remained but tended to become more extreme, especially in the last fifty years. Thus the nation-state "which had been based upon a unifying, centralizing principle became in the twentieth century an element of division

3

and disintegration." [1] But the first half of the present century has been an age of wars and revolutions, destructive in their total effect of both ideas and techniques that are so essential to the perpetuation of nationalism. It cannot be denied that the sentiment of nationality is a force of incalculable strength and may continue to be the greatest impediment to world cooperation for a long time to come. Yet, there are discernible tendencies in the operation of the present state system which are indicative of a pathological condition and may ultimately lead to the eclipse of the national state.

The Sixteenth-century Concept of Sovereignty. By the time of the Protestant Reformation, monarchs rose to claim absolute power by the grace of God, and monarchy was fast becoming the usual type of government in the countries of Western Europe.

This monarchial absolutism was justified and defended by such political philosophers as Jean Bodin (1530–1596), who published a famous treatise known as the *Six livres de la république* [2] in 1576. The *Republic* [3] of Bodin was inspired by the general anarchy which prevailed in France in the sixteenth century as a result of the Wars of Religion. It presented the views of the *Politiques*, who sought to promote peace and order by placing the royal power above that of political parties and religious sects. [4] In his eagerness to strengthen the royal hand, and thus to promote national unity, Bodin arrived at the central conception of his philosophy—the doctrine of absolute sovereignty.

Though it has been said of Bodin's political philosophy that it is a mixture of the old and the new—that it is neither medieval nor modern—his works exerted a vast influence upon his contemporaries, especially in those countries where the power of kings had become great. Sovereignty, which he defined as *supreme power over citizens and subjects, unrestrained by the laws,* is a concept which has had a profound effect on political thought even in our own times and is reflected in such notions as the abstract and fictitious personality of the state. In the sixteenth and seventeenth centuries sovereignty was believed to reside in the person of the king. Thus, if Louis XIV really had said, *"L'état, c'est moi,"* he would not merely have been using clever and witty language, but would have been giving utterance to a maxim which in his day was widely accepted. It should be noted, however, that the concept of sovereignty, which saw its first clear definition in the writings of Bodin and was carried to its

---

[1] Nicholas Doman, *The Coming Age of World Control* (1943), p. 5.

[2] A larger Latin edition of this work was published in 1586.

[3] The word *république* in the title of this work meant "realm" or "government," in this case one which was actually monarchial in form.

[4] George H. Sabine, *A History of Political Theory* (1945), p. 399.

most ludicrous extreme in Hobbes [5] a century later, was prompted by the forces of history. It was the distillation of a great sentiment for peace in an age of almost constant war—a desire for order in a time of revolution. But in later times, when constitutional government began to curb the powers of monarchial absolutism, new theories of sovereignty were to emerge.

The Social-contract Theory. Though the trend in the sixteenth century was unmistakably in the direction of royal absolutism, there was a considerable body of political thought, even then, which opposed the extension of the monarch's power. A famous tract, written over a pseudonym [6] two hundred years before the Declaration of American Independence, entitled *Vindiciae contra tyrannos*,[7] was to become the basis for political reforms in France to the time of the Revolution of 1789. The point of view expounded in this pamphlet, though it was somewhat medieval in tone,[8] became the central theme which was later expanded into the social-contract theory of the state. Even though this theory could be used in defense of absolutism, as in Hobbes and Spinoza, it was more frequently employed in the literature of the seventeenth and eighteenth centuries to establish limitations upon the royal power and as a justification for revolution.

Historians have often pointed to the seventeenth century as the most remarkable in the modern age. It was a time when thinkers were more conscious than they had been since the days of classic Greek philosophy, of the "whimsicality of unsupported habit, of the insignificance of mere inherited position, and of the uncouthness of force without intelligence." [9]

Important discoveries in mathematics and physics had a profound effect upon the intellectual climate, and it now seemed possible to begin the building of a new world in which reason rather than providence should be the guide.

The scientific turn of mind for which the seventeenth century is distinguished was clearly reflected in the contemporary development of legal and political theory, with a shifting emphasis from a preoccupation with

[5] According to Bodin, the only restrictions upon sovereignty were the Commandments of God and the immutable law of nature. Thomas Hobbes (1588–1679), on the other hand, would not admit even these restrictions upon sovereignty.

[6] Stephanus Junius Brutus, who is believed by many to have been Philippe Duplessis-Mornay. See Ernest Barker, "The Authorship of the *Vindiciae contra tyrannos*," *Cambridge Historical Journal*, vol. 3 (1930), pp. 164–181.

[7] Published in the year 1576.

[8] The *Vindiciae*, like the Magna Charta, was in some ways a reactionary document. It stood for the rights (or ancient privileges) of towns, provinces, and classes as against the leveling effect of royal power. "The spirit of the *Vindiciae* was not democratic but aristocratic"—Sabine, *op. cit.*, p. 383. But like the Great Charter of 1215, it was to prove of inestimable value as a justification for later developments.

[9] Sabine, *op. cit.*, p. 431.

the rights of states to a genuine concern for the individual in his relationship to the body politic. The new ideological structure was to be erected upon the foundations of self-evident propositions grounded in natural law. In this new scheme, the individual, with his interests, enterprise, desire for happiness and advancement, and above all with his reason, "appeared to be the foundation on which a stable society must be built." [10] And if, indeed, there existed in human nature an unchangeable core, it was reasonable to assume that a political society could be created based on the eternal laws of nature which no prince could defy with impunity. According to seventeenth-century philosophy, man rather than society was primary. It was this concept of the individual which was to become "the most marked and the most persistent quality of the theory of natural law, and the clearest differentia of the modern from the medieval theory." [11] Among the most influential exponents of this school of thought in the seventeenth century was the English philosopher John Locke (1632–1704), who wrote his essays on government in defense of the Parliamentary party, and whose main task it had been to justify the Glorious Revolution of 1688–1689. According to Locke, the original state of nature was one in which peace and reason prevailed, and though prepolitical it was not presocial.[12] Neither was it a lawless state, as all men were governed by natural law.

The importance of the social-contract theory in the overthrow of absolutism and the substitution of popular sovereignty for the rule of kings cannot easily be overestimated. In the late eighteenth century it was to serve as a justification for revolutions both in Europe and America. Out of these events new forces were set in motion which, as we shall see, came to have a profound effect upon the development of international law in the nineteenth century.

The Idealistic Theory. Plato, who held that the state is the only means through which the individual can reach the noblest ends of his existence, may perhaps be classed as the founder of the idealistic theory of sovereignty. In modern times this theory of the state has been greatly elaborated by the German philosophers, especially those of the late eighteenth and early nineteenth centuries.

With the Germans the state became an end in itself. It could do no wrong, and revolt against it was never justified. Such men as Nietzsche, Treitschke, and Bernhardi argued that the power of the state could not be contained and that war is not only necessary but desirable. German idealism in political philosophy was largely a reaction against eighteenth-

---

[10] *Ibid.*, p. 432.
[11] *Ibid.*, p. 433.
[12] Raymond G. Gettell, *History of Political Thought* (1924), p. 255.

century rationalism, deriving its chief inspiration from the writings of Rousseau. It was for the most part an anti-intellectual approach to the problems of human society, seeking a "higher truth" not through science and reason but rather through metaphysical intuition and a mystical faith in the infallibility of the general will. In the language of Professor Sabine: "Rousseau's philosophy emphasized the aggrandizement of a group, the satisfactions of participation, and the cultivation of the non-rational." [13] This, in a sense, was the beginning of the romantic movement which dominated the greater part of the nineteenth century.

German idealism in political philosophy came to a climax with Georg Wilhelm Friedrich Hegel (1770–1831), whose most famous exposition in the realm of political theory is found in *The Philosophy of Right* which was published in 1821. Hegel, along with many other Germans who felt themselves humiliated by the defeat at Jena, came to the conclusion that the only road to the restoration of *Macht und Ehre* was through the medium of a powerful state—for "the state," said Hegel, "is the march of God in the world." [14]

International law, according to Hegel, arises out of the mutual relations of independent states. "But because the relations of states to one another has sovereignty as its principle, they are so far in a condition of nature one to the other. Their rights have reality not in a general will, which is constituted as a superior power, but in their particular will." [15] Thus we see that states in their external relations, according to Hegel, are free, equal, and independent, subject to no law outside their own will. The ordinary rules of morality were held to have no application in international relations, and treaties should be observed only so long as their enforcement is of advantage to the state. Prolonged peace was believed to lead to internal corruption, while successful war would unify and strengthen the state. The influence upon contemporary political thought of such writers as Hegel, Fichte, Nietzsche, and Treitschke should not be underestimated, and the tenacity with which political theorists have clung to the concept of state sovereignty may be attributed in large measure to the inspiration of German political thought in the nineteenth century.

The survival of the concept of state sovereignty has had unfortunate effects upon the development of the theory of international law. Writers in this field have been faced with the dilemma of explaining how any law can be binding upon sovereign states, which by the very fact that they

---

[13] *Op. cit.*, p. 592.

[14] G. W. F. Hegel, *The Philosophy of Right*, as reprinted in *Readings in Recent Political Philosophy*, edited by Margaret Spahr, p. 189.

[15] *Ibid.*, p. 203.

are sovereign can be subject to no law.[16] It is obvious that the doctrine of the "natural and inalienable rights of man," so dear to the philosophers of the eighteenth century, has been transmuted in the last hundred and fifty years into a principle of "fundamental rights of states."

It should be noted that, though the eighteenth-century concept of the "rights of man" has been fundamental in the development of individual freedom and political democracy in certain parts of the world, its corollary, the doctrine of "fundamental rights of states," has been a disruptive and disintegrating force in international relations. What is most needed in a modern society of states is not greater freedom of action on the part of the members, but a stronger social bond between them, and rather than insistence upon rights, a reminder of their mutual obligations.[17] Finally, it might be said that this doctrine is, in effect, a denial of the possibility of a real international order, as the "fundamental rights of states" are held to be an integral part of their very nature. Thus we see that this concept, which was derived from eighteenth-century rationalism and perverted by the philosophers of the nineteenth century, was the more dangerously effective as it rested its major tenets on a fixed order of nature.

Distinction between External and Internal Sovereignty. One of the major difficulties in international law springs from the fact that states have been regarded as no less sovereign in their external or international relations than within their respective territorial jurisdictions. The theory of sovereignty which arose in early modern times, however, was mainly concerned with the internal aspects of the state. Its purpose was to substitute for the anarchy of the Middle Ages a unity within, which it was believed could be achieved through the centralized rule of an absolute monarch. But in later times, as we have already indicated, there was, as a result of the decline of absolutism, a certain disintegration at the center of internal sovereignty. This is evidenced by such phenomena as constitutionalism, federalism, and theories of pluralism. It is in its external aspect, however, that the concept of sovereignty has broken down most completely under the impact of compelling forces in an interdependent world.

The traditional concept of external sovereignty would imply that there are no restrictions to which states may be subjected in their mutual relations. Yet, their behavior in the international community shows clearly that they are interdependent, and that numerous rules and restrictions govern their conduct. In 1932 the Permanent Court of International Justice in an advisory opinion concerning the Polish nationals in Danzig stated, in effect, that international obligations cannot be avoided by

[16] J. L. Brierly, *The Law of Nations* (1949), p. 39.
[17] *Ibid.*

the invocation of constitutional law.[18] In this connection it is of interest to note that the Constitution of the Republic of France, which was submitted to the people and approved by popular vote on September 29, 1946, provided that the French Republic, in conformity with the rules of international law, would not resort to war "with a view to conquest" nor employ its forces "against the liberty of any people." Furthermore, that on "condition of reciprocity," France would consent to such limitations of sovereignty as are necessary "to the organization and defense of peace." [19]

Thus, we see in our time a great nation, compelled by the forces of historic necessity, recognize in her Constitution the need for limitations of sovereignty in order to strengthen the international community and the rule of law.

A number of writers on international law have long admitted the possibility of a state not being fully sovereign.[20] They conceived of sovereignty as a collection of powers, some of which could be taken away without destroying the state.[21] Furthermore, they held that in an international community no nation could be wholly independent. The very existence of international-legal rules binding upon states, their domestic legislation to the contrary notwithstanding, lends a certain primacy to international law and negates the claim on the part of states to absolute sovereignty in the area of external relations.[22] Thus, external sovereignty can no longer be regarded as a fixed and irreducible quantity, but rather as a variable which is perhaps altogether dependent upon the potential of power.

There is in international-legal theory a profound contradiction, which constitutes a very great impediment to the development of the law of nations. It is a basic problem, and its solution is essential to the establishment of a world community in which all peoples may find a greater measure of security under the aegis of effective law. The great difficulty, as we have noted earlier, stems from the fact that the doctrine of state sovereignty constitutes a central proposition in international-legal theory. Even in the United Nations, the "Organization is based on the principle of the sovereign equality of all its Members," [23] and nothing contained in

[18] *Permanent Court of International Justice Advisory Opinion*, Feb. 4, 1932, ser. A/B, no. 44, p. 24. See also the *Free Zones Case, PCIJ Order*, Dec. 6, 1930, ser. A, no. 24, p. 12. Also the Court's opinion concerning the *Greco-Bulgarian Communities, PCIJ Advisory Opinion*, July 31, 1930, ser. B, no. 7, p. 32.

[19] *M.I.T. Publications in International Affairs . . . A Selection of Current Readings*, no. II (June, 1947), p. 170.

[20] See J. J. Moser, *Beitraege zu dem neuesten europaeischen Voelkerrecht* (1777–1780), and G. F. de Martens, *Précis du droit des gens moderne de l'Europe* (1788).

[21] Gettell, *op. cit.*, p. 421.

[22] Oppenheim-Lauterpacht, *International Law* (1947), vol. I, p. 119.

[23] Art. 2, par. 1, of the Charter.

the Charter "shall authorize the United Nations to intervene in matters which are essentially within the domestic jurisdiction of any state or shall require the Members to submit such matters to settlement under the present Charter." [24] It is generally recognized, however, that any so-called "fully sovereign state," [25] through its treaty-making capacity, may voluntarily impose certain limitations upon the exercise of its sovereignty. The degree of sovereignty or independence which a state may in fact enjoy is, as we have suggested above, not so much a resultant of law as it is the product of the industrial and military power at its disposal at a given time. But from a strictly legal point of view, independence may mean that states are to be free from outside intervention, but only to the extent that this freedom is not limited by international law.

With respect to the principle of independence, the Permanent Court of International Justice, in an advisory opinion regarding the *Nationality Decrees Issued in Tunis and Morocco* (1923), held that the League of Nations in its capacity "to make such recommendations as are deemed just and proper in the circumstances with a view to the maintenance of peace must, at a given point, give way to the equally essential interest of the individual State to maintain intact its independence in matters which international law recognizes to be solely within its jurisdiction." [26] The Court, however, admitted that whether a certain matter is or is not within the exclusive jurisdiction of a state is essentially a relative question, largely dependent upon the development of international relations. In a strictly legal sense, it is determined by existing treaties as interpreted in the light of the general law of nations. In such a case the matter at issue ceases to be one solely within domestic jurisdiction and, according to the Permanent Court, "enters the domain governed by international law." [27] Thus it may be concluded that once a state has limited its sovereignty by treaty, its independence is restricted by international law to the extent of this limitation. We shall return to this topic for a more detailed consideration in a later chapter.

The Theory of Divisible Sovereignty. In the sixteenth and seventeenth centuries there appears to have been general agreement among political theorists to the effect that sovereignty could not be divided.[28] As we have

---

[24] Art. 7 of the Charter.

[25] This phrase, often employed by publicists, seems to imply that sovereignty may be measured in degrees, and that states may exist which are not, in the fullest sense of the term, sovereign. The logical difficulty inherent in this assumption is plain, yet it is an inevitable consequence of an obvious attempt to bring the earlier theory into line with the compelling realities of contemporary international relations.

[26] *PCIJ Advisory Opinion* (1923), ser. B, no. 4, p. 24.

[27] *Ibid.*, p. 26.

[28] Oppenheim-Lauterpacht, *op. cit.*, p. 117.

seen, the sovereign power was then believed to have had its seat in the person of the monarch, and the distinction between the king and the state was not always clear. But in the eighteenth century, when ideas of popular sovereignty rose in opposition to absolutism and the unitary state was challenged by decentralized federalism, the effect upon political and legal theory was salutary.

In the United States the so-called "division of powers" between the states and the federal union was eloquently defended by Hamilton, Jay, and Madison in the *Federalist Papers*, and later no less ably denied by John C. Calhoun in his *Disquisition on Government*. The American War between the States and the establishment of federal states in Switzerland and Germany gave a new impetus to this great controversy, which continued to be debated throughout the remainder of the century, even to the present day.

"It is difficult," wrote Madison, "to argue intelligibly concerning the compound system of government in the United States without admitting the divisibility of sovereignty." [29] But according to Calhoun, sovereignty is by its very nature indivisible, and a state must be fully sovereign or it is not a state in the true meaning of that term. Yet, according to Oppenheim, "as there can be no doubt about the fact that there are semi-independent States in existence, it may well be maintained that sovereignty is divisible." [30]

It seems obvious that much of the confusion surrounding this whole question is largely a result of repeated attempts to adjust an old theory to new facts. The classic conception of sovereignty with its inevitable corollary—the equality of states—bears little relationship to the realities of the twentieth century. Sovereignty in an external sense can well be regarded as synonymous with independence, which tends to be proportional to the potential of power. But this is not the whole story, for it is also true that the development of a community of nations, whether it be on a regional or a universal level, must inevitably lead to the progressive reduction of the external sovereignty of states. The mere fact, however, that there are "semi-independent States in existence" does not constitute evidence of the divisibility of sovereignty as such, but rather that this property in the state requires some qualification. This, as we have already stated, is due primarily to two factors: (1) the overshadowing power of other states, and (2) the voluntary relinquishment of sovereignty by individual states in favor of a larger community.

Law and the Community. While in the nineteenth century the discussion centered on whether sovereignty could be divided or not, the main

[29] James Madison, *Works*, vol. IV, p. 394.
[30] Oppenheim-Lauterpacht, *op. cit.*, p. 118.

question which now confronts both law and politics is how far sovereignty, as seen through the internal law of the state, can be reconciled with the development and function of international law and organization.[31]

The shortcomings of the doctrine of sovereignty in the external relations of states would undoubtedly have been made apparent much earlier but for the fact that it has resulted in a whole series of other doctrines. These doctrines have been carefully constructed by theorists in international law, with the result that they not only have acquired a standing of their own, but have contributed toward the perpetuation of the original concept— the external sovereignty of states.[32] International jurists have called into being the principle of inherent limitations upon the judicial process in cases involving states. This, in turn, has given rise to the doctrine of so-called nonjusticiable disputes. In this way a differentiation between two categories of international disputes was arrived at—the legal and the political. The first of these is held to be justiciable, while the second is not. We shall have more to say on this point in a later chapter.

Notwithstanding the disintegrating effect of outmoded doctrines of sovereignty, a multiplicity of problems which can be met successfully only by collective action continue to demonstrate the need for further consolidation in the direction of a more effective world community. Among these perhaps the most compelling is the universal desire for peace and security.

"At the basis of every community," wrote Elihu Root to Colonel House in 1918, "lies the idea of organization to preserve peace. Without that idea really active and controlling there can be no community of individuals or of nations." [33]

Professor Hans Morgenthau, on the other hand, speaks of an "iron law" in international politics, from which no nation has ever been immune, and contends that legal obligations must yield to national interests. He objects to the evaluation of a particular foreign policy in terms of international law or abstract standards of morality.[34] This, indeed, would seem to deny the existence of a world community and the consequent validity of its law. But even Cicero fancied a *civitas gentium*; and Victoria in his unforgettable lessons at Salamanca in the sixteenth century justified the existence of a law of nations on the ground that the world as a whole could be considered, in a sense, a single state. As early as 1612 Suarez, in his *Tractatus de legibus ac deo legislatore*, spoke of the unity of the human race. Hugo Grotius, who has been called the "father of international law," wrote of an

[31] *Ibid.*, pp. 118–119.
[32] H. Lauterpacht, *The Function of Law in the International Community* (1933), p. 4.
[33] Alfred Zimmern (ed.), *Modern Political Doctrines*, pp. 271–272.
[34] *In Defense of the National Interest: A Critical Examination of American Foreign Policy* (1951), p. 144.

appetitus societatis—a gregarious propensity of the human race—which he found rooted in the rational qualities of mankind.

Regarding the relationship of law to organization for the preservation of peace, there are two points of view. These turn on the question of which has priority, law or organization.[35] It may well be true, as Professor Brierly suggests, that there "has to be order before law can even begin to take root and grow." [36] Thus it would appear that *law is effective in direct proportion to the degree a community is present.* It makes no difference whether the individual is an American, an Englishman, a Frenchman, or a Russian, he is most aware of community within the orbit of his own culture, and he tends to judge the merits of civilization by the standards of his own people.

It is quite likely that a better understanding of international law, both as to its nature and function, can be gained when it is realized that it is primarily a result rather than a cause. Law, whether municipal or international, is a social science which derives its validity from a dominant consensus. It is not like flying buttresses of external support, but rather like lines of force emanating from the center of social gravity. These, like their counterparts in the physical world, must fall within the base in order to lend equilibrium to the structure of politics.

In view of the rather meager development of community consciousness on a universal basis, it is unlikely that we shall realize the dream of One World soon. Yet, the future for world law and organization is far from hopeless. It is simply a matter of building the edifice, stone upon stone, from firmly laid foundations. If one takes an historic view of the problem, there is great cause for optimism. The story is one of extension of community consciousness in ever-widening circles, from such microscopic beginnings as the innumerable feudal principalities of Europe to the present community of the Anglo-American world. To say that enough interdependence, common interest, and cultural affinity has already developed among the English-speaking peoples to constitute a community within which future wars are not likely to occur may not be too farfetched a statement. It may well be that the next step in the creation of a more permanent order in the world will be in the direction of regionalism without losing sight of the ultimate goal which must be a federation of the world. But if the "parliament of man" is yet far in the future, let it be a challenge rather than a cause for despondency, for "all excellent things," said Spinoza, "are as difficult as they are rare."

[35] J. L. Brierly, *The Outlook for International Law* (1944), p. 73.
[36] *Ibid.*, p. 74.

CHAPTER 2

A Survey of Various Plans
for World Organization

There is considerable evidence that nationalism was not an unknown emotion even in ancient times. The Old Testament is replete with examples of such a sentiment among the Hebrew people, and it is indeed difficult to read the philosophical and poetic writings of the early Greeks without noting a strong undertone of nationalism. Even Plato thanked the gods that he was born a Greek and not a barbarian.

But if we find evidences of nationalism in the ancient world, it can also be demonstrated that even in those times there were forces and ideas at work moving in the direction of a larger unity both of mankind and of nations. Early attempts at such unity came to a climax with the creation of the Roman Empire, which for many centuries enforced law and peace throughout most of the then known world. The Christian religion, with its equalitarian doctrines of the universal brotherhood of all men, became a new force for world unity in the latter days of the Roman millennium. Thus the idea of a universal Church and state was the bequest of Rome to medieval Europe and dominated the intellectual life of that continent to the days of the Reformation.

By the end of the fifteenth century the principle of nationality was rather well established in England and was rapidly taking form in the Iberian Peninsula and in France. These examples of the building of the modern state were, as we have already seen, a unifying process. But the sanguinary wars which attended this unification gave rise to larger and more universal concepts of organization. The Italian poet Dante, in his *De monarchia*, had made an elaborate argument for some sort of world state. Weary of the fraternal strife among princes and cities, he advocated a supreme monarch and a universal law. Thus modern internationalism, looking to a larger unity, came into being as a reaction to the constant warfare which accompanied the advent of the modern state.

In all periods of crises, as in the present age, when impending disaster looms before us through the inadequacy of existing international institutions, the minds of men have often turned in their search for security to various projects for "a more perfect union." Ideas and plans for world organization are not new. They did not originate with the United World Federalists or other contemporary groups who advocate a union now of the English-speaking world or a federation of the Atlantic nations. Ideas of this kind are exceedingly old. And it is important to appreciate that their embodiment in contemporary institutions is not the result of a sudden inspiration but is the labor of accumulated time. In the following pages of this chapter, therefore, an attempt will be made to illustrate the antiquity of such ideas by presenting a historical survey of some of the more important plans for world organization which have been advanced from time to time for the sake of peace.

The Grand Design. At first, European statesmen, in an effort to establish peace, borrowed an idea familiar to medieval Italy, namely, the establishment of an equilibrium among the great powers. But this device proved an unstable means to world order. The problem of religious conflict between Protestants and Catholics aggravated the situation and required serious attention, lest the nations so lately unified be rent apart by civil conflict.

It was conditions such as these that gave rise to a bold idea, since known as the "Grand Design" and associated with the French king Henry IV and his minister Sully.[1] This plan for peace proposed mutual toleration by the various religious groups, and a confederation of Western Europe containing 15 states, some monarchial and others republican. This confederation would be presided over by the Emperor, but its common affairs would be administered by a council of 64 delegates, who would represent the member states. Perhaps the most interesting provision of the whole scheme was that disputes between the states were to be settled by the council, supported by an international army and navy.

The Plans of William Penn and the Abbé de Saint-Pierre. In the latter part of the seventeenth century, when Louis XIV was preoccupied in a devastation of Europe, William Penn in a famous essay[2] proposed the establishment of a European Parliament,[3] empowered to hear international disputes. The representation in this body by the sovereignties of Europe should be in proportion to their respective national income, and the states

---

[1] Maximilien de Béthune, duc de Sully, Minister of Finance and confidant of Henry IV, would have us believe that the plan was conceived by the monarch himself, perhaps at the instigation of Queen Elizabeth of England. See Sylvester John Hemleben, *Plans for World Peace through Six Centuries* (1943), p. 31.
[2] *Essay towards the Present and Future Peace of Europe* (1693).
[3] This assembly was to be called "the Sovereign or Imperial Dyet, Parliament or State of Europe" and would meet annually or at least every two or three years.

which should refuse to submit their differences to arbitration or fail to abide by the awards would be subjected to collective action by the other states.

Somewhat later, in 1713, the Abbé de Saint-Pierre, secretary to the French plenipotentiary at the Peace of Utrecht, advocated a perpetual alliance among the sovereigns of Europe.[4] He too favored the creation of an international congress with delegates from the member states. A fund was to be provided over which the congress would have control. A further function of the congress was to define the cases in which common action should be taken against offending states.

The Projects of Rousseau, Kant, and Bentham. Jean Jacques Rousseau, who was greatly influenced by the Abbé de Saint-Pierre, also suggested a Federation of Europe.[5] He had little faith, however, in the willingness of the absolute monarchies of his day to subordinate their independence and submit to an international army. Rousseau, therefore, came to the melancholy conclusion that such federation as he had in mind for Europe could be formed only through war and revolution.

The German philosopher Immanuel Kant, at the close of the eighteenth century, wrote a notable essay *On Perpetual Peace* [6] in which he stipulated the establishment of representative republican institutions in every country as a condition for peace. He also advocated the creation of a law of nations based on a federation of free states and world citizenship for their populations. He was of the opinion that war would finally be eliminated for economic reasons and that natural law would someday emerge supreme to guarantee the peace.

The British utilitarian philosopher Jeremy Bentham was vitally interested in the development of international law and bitterly condemned secret diplomacy. In his *Fragments of an Essay on the Principles of International Law* [7] he suggested the establishment of an international court, the emancipation of colonial dependencies, and the codification of the law of nations. He did not favor the use of force against a recalcitrant state, believing that public opinion would exert sufficient pressure provided the press remained free.

[4] *Projet de traité pour rendre la paix perpétuelle.* Saint-Pierre's plan was drawn up in the form of a treaty ready for the signatures of the sovereigns of Europe. It was divided into three parts: (1) fundamental articles, (2) important articles, and (3) useful articles.

[5] To his abstract of Saint-Pierre's *Projet* Rousseau later added *Jugement sur la paix perpétuelle,* which was a criticism of the scheme of Saint-Pierre. This was an independent work and was not published until six years after Rousseau's death.

[6] *Zu einem ewigen Frieden.*

[7] In vol. II of *The Works of Jeremy Bentham,* published under the direction of John Browning (Edinburgh, 1843, 11 vols.), there are four essays on international law, published from Bentham's original manuscripts of the period 1786–1789.

Since Bentham's plan remained unpublished for many years, it had no influence upon the events of the time. The two features of his proposal which are of special interest to us and which are worthy of notice are, first, the confidence expressed in the force of public opinion, and secondly, the advocacy of an international court.[8]

The Plan of Saint-Simon and Augustin Thierry. At the end of the Napoleonic Wars there was a genuine desire for peace. This sentiment was not least evident among the French, and it found its expression in a brochure, published in Paris in October, 1814, of which Claude Henri, comte de Saint-Simon, and Augustin Thierry were the joint authors. This little pamphlet of 112 pages was entitled *The Reorganization of European Society*.[9] It called not only for a parliament for each nation in Europe, but for a general representative body in which all the states would be represented. It was proposed that the general European parliament be given the power of an international court to adjudicate the differences which, from time to time, would arise among the member states.

At the head of this European organization there was to be a king, although the method of his selection was not made clear. The general parliament was to be fashioned on the English model, with two houses—a house of deputies and a house of peers. The king would appoint the latter, while the deputies were to be elected by vote of the literate populations. It was proposed that a common parliament be established at once by France and England, since these countries already had a representative system of government. Other nations would be added as they qualified for membership. It was the firm opinion of Saint-Simon that this system, once established, would be the best possible for Europe and that it would preserve the peace.

The Plan of William Ladd. The desire for peace was not confined to Europe. In the United States, in 1828, the American Peace Society was founded by William Ladd, who in 1840 proposed the establishment of a congress of nations to adjust international differences and promote peace without resort to arms. In his essay,[10] Ladd presented a plan in two parts: first, there was to be a congress of ambassadors from the various states; second, a court of nations was to be established for the arbitration and adjudication of international disputes.

The theory of the equality of states was given due recognition in the plan of William Ladd. Though each nation could send as many repre-

[8] Hemleben, *op. cit.*, p. 87.
[9] *De la Réorganisation de la société européenne ou de la nécessité et des moyens de rassembler les peuples de l'Europe en un seul corps politique en conservant à chacun son indépendance nationale.*
[10] *An Essay on a Congress of Nations for the Adjustment of International Disputes without Resort to Arms.*

sentatives to the congress as it liked, each would have no more than one vote. One of the first tasks of the congress would be the consideration of the law of nations, and no principle would be accepted unless it had the unanimous consent of the member states and the ratification of their governments. The congress, furthermore, was forbidden to interfere in the domestic affairs of states and was to limit itself strictly to their international relations. Aside from a general reconsideration of international law, the main functions of the congress would be to define the rights of belligerents and neutrals; to agree on measures useful to mankind in time of peace; and finally to establish a court of nations.

As indicated above, the second part of the *Essay* was devoted to a consideration of an international court. It was to be established by the assembly, or congress, with as many members as this body should decide. The court was to take cognizance only of such cases as were referred to it by the parties to a dispute. Whenever treaties and laws should fail in establishing the point at issue, the court was directed to apply principles of equity and justice. For the successful operation of this ambitious project, Ladd, like Bentham, relied altogether on the force of public opinion.

The plan of William Ladd was widely circulated in the United States and was published in England, where it had a considerable influence on the peace movement. The project was introduced by Ladd's disciple, Elihu Burritt, at a series of peace conferences. [11] The Ladd plan was more immediately influential than any of the earlier projects for the reason that it was less radical in its conception. It recognized the equality and independence of states, while many of the earlier schemes tended to submerge the individual nations in an international organization with considerable power—projects which required a departure from the habitual standards of conduct. In this respect the plan of William Ladd was somewhat more realistic.

The Plan of William Jay. Another American plan for world organization was proposed in 1842 by William Jay. This project contemplated special provisions in future treaties to the effect that all disputes between the parties to such arrangements should be submitted for arbitration, rather than be resolved by force of arms. Jay also was of the opinion that war could in time be eliminated by the force of public opinion and by various institutions and agencies which would be created gradually to cope with international problems. He favored the establishment of an international court to adjudicate disputes between nations; and though he recognized the proposal as too advanced for the thinking of the time,

[11] Conferences of Brussels (1848), Paris (1849), Frankfort (1850), and London (1851).

he nevertheless hoped that it could be accomplished by gradual steps in man's eternal search for security.

The Proposal of Gustave de Molinari. In the same manner that Hugo Grotius had been impelled by the cruelty of war to lend his powerful intellect to the cause of peace, so Gustave de Molinari was inspired to produce a notable biography of the Abbé de Saint-Pierre.[12] He had been greatly disturbed by the destruction and suffering caused by the Crimean War, and in a famous preface to the work on Saint-Pierre, he presented his own views regarding world organization. He based his argument on the proposition that war was the concern not only of the belligerents, but of all nations.

De Molinari contended that nations, like individuals, could not survive standing alone in a hostile world. It was therefore necessary to create a union of states—a *concert universel*—for the sake of survival. Such a union would have the power to interpret international law and to settle disputes among the member states, rather than to allow each to enforce its own *droit de guerre*. As a result of such a system of collective security, disarmament would be possible.

De Molinari pointed out that two-thirds of the European budgets were devoted to the preparation for future wars and to the payments of debts incurred by past conflicts. To insure security by such means, he contended, required the payment of a premium which far exceeded the risk. Even though De Molinari realized that it would take much time and patience to establish the *concert universel* and to thus remove the danger of war, he looked with confidence to a future which would see its ultimate achievement.

Johann Caspar Bluntschli's Confederation of Europe. In the year 1878, a plan for the Organization of a European Union of States [13] was proposed by Johann Caspar Bluntschli, a professor at the University of Heidelberg. He argued that the fundamental problem in establishing a European union was to preserve the independence and freedom of the individual states.

The confederation proposed by Bluntschli would consist of 18 selected states whose independence would be preserved. There was to be an international legislature composed of two houses—a united council and a senate. The first of these would consist of delegates representing the member states, the 6 great powers having two votes each and the 12 lesser nations only one vote each. The senate would constitute representatives of the

---

[12] Published in Paris in 1857.
[13] *Die Organisation des europäischen Statenvereines.* This plan forms the third part of Chap. XII in his *Gesammelte kleine Schriften: Aufsätze über Recht und Staat* (1879), vol. I.

various peoples, and its members were to be elected by the national parliaments. In the senate, as in the united council, the voting strength of the members would be unequal. Here the great powers would have 8 or 10 votes each, while the small states were to have 4 or 5 votes each. The term of the president of the council was to be one year, and the office would rotate among the great powers. The project called for the enactment of a code of international law, and to create such a code would be the chief function of the united council and the senate.

Political questions which might involve the independence of the member states were to be entrusted to the council, while questions of less importance were to be placed before administrative bureaus, though under the direction of the council. In certain cases where sanctions were needed in the execution of a decision, the matter would be handled by a collegium of the great powers. In most cases, however, the implementation of decisions would be left to the states individually.[14]

Bluntschli did not claim that his plan, even if put into operation, would necessarily eliminate war. This, even to him, was a goal far in the future.

The Plan of James Lorimer. In his work *The Institutes of the Law of Nations*,[15] James Lorimer presented what was the most noteworthy project for world organization in the nineteenth century. He advocated the establishment of an international government which would be independent of the various national governments and which would act as the "guardian of the freedom of all national governments." [16] Lorimer also proposed a general reduction in armaments. The risk of war would be greatly reduced, he contended, by the limitation of "combustible matter" in each community, and the consequent relief from heavy tax burdens would promote prosperity and direct the attention of the people toward peaceful occupations.

Lorimer was of the opinion that closer association among the peoples of the world would lead to common interests, which in turn would produce a will to mutual concessions and general cooperation. He recognized that his plan for international government was bound to meet with great opposition from the military classes, who would see in disarmament a reduction of the importance of their profession. Opposition was also expected from the old-style diplomatists, but this he believed could more easily be overcome by giving them positions as officials in the international government.

[14] For a more complete discussion of the Bluntschli plan, see Hemleben, *op. cit.*, pp. 116–118.

[15] James Lorimer, *The Institutes of the Law of Nations*, published in Edinburgh and London in 1884.

[16] Quoted by Hemleben in *op. cit.*, p. 119.

Lorimer's project called for a multilateral treaty to be negotiated in two parts as follows: [17]

I. An undertaking by the parties to reduce, simultaneously and proportionally, their national forces to the limit which they may reciprocally recognize as necessary for municipal purposes, but so as to preserve the *relative* power to each state unchanged.

II. An undertaking to establish a government for international purposes exclusively, consisting of a legislature, judicature, executive, and exchequer.

The legislative branch of this international government would consist of two houses—a senate and a chamber of deputies. Each of the six great powers was to be represented by 5 senators and 15 deputies; the lesser states, by numbers proportional to their international importance as determined by the great powers. The senators were to be appointed for life without remuneration, and each would have one vote. The deputies were appointed as determined by the individual states and were to receive a salary of £1,000 for each session; like the senators, the deputies would have one vote each. There would also be a bureau of 15 members, which would be composed of 5 senators and 10 deputies. This bureau was to have at least one representative from each of the great powers. The president of this international government was to be elected by the bureau from among its own members. Constantinople was to be the permanent home for the organization. If this was not found satisfactory, Geneva was suggested. In any case, the ultimate place of its location was to be declared international property. Meetings were to be held in the autumn of each year. The assembly would not be competent to discuss national or domestic questions, though civil wars were to be within the jurisdiction of the assembly.

The international court was to consist of two departments—one criminal and the other civil. The judges, 15 in number, were to be appointed by the bureau with at least one from each of the six great powers. In civil cases judgments were to be determined by a majority vote of all the judges. All questions of public international law could be taken directly to the international court, while matters involving private international law could only reach this tribunal by appeal from the municipal courts. The bureau was to appoint an attorney general, who would act as public prosecutor of international crimes.

Lorimer's plan also provided for men or money to be contributed by the member states to enable the organization to enforce its enactments

[17] "Opinion of Mr. Lorimer, Professor in the University of Edinburgh, on the Question of Disarmament," *Documents Respecting the Limitation of Armaments, Laid before the First Hague Peace Conference of 1899 by the Government of the Netherlands* (1916), p. 279.

and decrees. There was to be a small standing force at the seat of the international government. These troops were to be under the orders of the president, who was made responsible for his acts to the international legislature. This army was to be paid by the organization, the money being derived by a special tax levied by the member states upon their citizens. The amount of the tax levied in each state was to be proportional to the number of its representatives in the international legislature. All the financial affairs of the organization, however, were to be under the management of the bureau.

That the ideas of James Lorimer, concerning the ways and means to a lasting peace, were not without influence on the practical affairs of his time is evidenced by the fact that the government of the Netherlands presented his opinions concerning the question of general disarmament at the Peace Conference at The Hague in 1899.

Proposals for the Avoidance of War by James Bryce. The tragic consequences of the First World War made a profound and widespread impression, and many came to agree with Lord James Bryce who said, "If we do not try to end war, war will end us. . . ." [18] As a result, a number of plans for world organization to preserve the peace were formulated by various groups in a number of countries.

In the year 1915, a group in England, presided over by Lord Bryce, came forward with a scheme which took for its starting point a number of international agreements generally known as the "Bryan treaties." These agreements, which had been concluded between the United States and a number of other countries, provided that disputes of whatever nature which ordinary diplomacy failed to adjust, and where recourse was not had to arbitration, were to be submitted to a permanent commission for investigation and report. A further provision of these treaties was to the effect that, while the matter giving rise to the dispute was under investigation by the commission, no hostile action was to be taken by the contracting parties.[19]

The Bryce plan provided that justiciable disputes be referred to an arbitral tribunal, in cases where settlement could not be achieved by diplomatic means. In such cases the parties to the controversy must agree to abide by the award of the tribunal. Justiciable disputes were defined

[18] Viscount James Bryce, Introduction to Viscount Grey *et al., The League of Nations* (1918, 1919), p. 18.

[19] According to the Bryan treaties, a period of one year was to elapse before hostilities could begin. It was expected that this period of time would cool the anger of the disputants and create a mood that would be receptive to the report of the commission. See the *Treaties for the Advancement of Peace between the United States and Other Powers Negotiated by the Honorable William J. Bryan, Secretary of State of the United States,* with an Introduction by James Brown Scott (1920).

as embracing "disputes as to the interpretation of a treaty, as to any question of international law, as to the existence of any fact which, if established, would constitute a breach of any international obligation, or as to the nature and extent of the reparation to be made for any such breach." [20] Whether or not a dispute was justiciable was to be decided by the court.

The Bryce plan also provided for the establishment of a permanent council of conciliation which would have the function of preventing as well as settling nonjusticiable controversies between states. It was further provided that powers signatory to the organization should be pledged to take action against any state who would take up arms against another without first submitting the matter at dispute to the council or court for settlement. The nature of the action taken by the members of the organization against an offending state might be economic sanctions, but military pressures were not to be excluded.

The outstanding merits of this program, according to Lord Bryce himself, were first, that the union was to be world-wide in scope; second, that it bound the signatory states to submit their disputes to an impartial body for peaceful settlement before having recourse to arms; third, that it established an international body which could deal in an impartial manner with contentious questions.[21]

The British League of Nations Society. With a program somewhat similar to the Bryce plan, the British League of Nations Society was organized the same year. The Society was "founded to advocate an Agreement among civilized States, which will serve as a basis for permanent peace among them, by providing for the Peaceful Settlement of Disputes, for Mutual Defense, and the Observance of Treaties and International Law." [22] The program of this organization also distinguished between justiciable and nonjusticiable disputes. Controversies of the first category were to be referred to the Permanent Court of Arbitration at The Hague or some other tribunal, the decisions or awards to be final. The disputes of nonjusticiable classification were to be placed in the hands of a council of inquiry, which was to be representative of the member states in the League. In this plan, as in the proposals of Lord Bryce, there was to be collective action against any state violating the peace before the available means for pacific settlement of disputes had been exhausted.

The American League to Enforce Peace. One of the most influential organizations at the time of the First World War was the American League to Enforce Peace. It had its official beginning when a meeting of about 300 men was called in Philadelphia on June 17, 1915, to organize

---

[20] Quoted by Hemleben, *op. cit.*, p. 141.
[21] *Ibid.*, p. 143.
[22] *Ibid.*

an association whose main object would be the prevention of future wars.

The League to Enforce Peace had for its first objective the promotion of an international conference of the powers by which a treaty to establish a league of nations could be agreed upon. Its second objective was to persuade all political parties in the United States to adopt the principles of the League, and to urge that the Congress of the United States as well as the several state legislatures adopt resolutions in favor of such international organization as was proposed by the League. Thirdly, there was a moral or educational objective, "to implant the principles of the League in the minds and consciences of the American People as deeply as the Monroe Doctrine." [23]

The association proposed that the United States join in a league of nations which would bind the signatories to a policy similar to that contained in the Bryan treaties. It called for a court of justice and a council of conciliation. The court would handle all disputes between states which were of a justiciable character, while the council would deal with matters involving national policy and "vital interests." No provisions were made, however, to enforce the decisions of the court or the council. Only under one condition could the league resort to force, namely, if a member state should resort to arms before submitting a dispute to arbitration.

After the defeat of Germany in the First World War, the League to Enforce Peace expanded its program, the terms of which were adopted by the organization on November 23, 1918. The substance of its provisions was as follows: (1) A tribunal was to be established to handle justiciable disputes. (2) The competence of such a court was not to be dependent upon the assent of the parties to the dispute, and the decisions were to be enforceable. (3) Questions which were not of a justiciable nature would be mediated by a council of conciliation. (4) An administrative organization was to be established to look after matters of common interest and care for backward regions. Peaceful change was recognized as preferable to repression for the sake of maintaining the *status quo*. (5) A representative congress of nations was to formulate and codify international law and to consider any matter which might disturb the peace of the world and impede the progress of the human race. (6) There was to be an executive organ to act in all cases where the peace was endangered, and the rules of international law were not to be defeated for lack of unanimity. (7) No military alliances either of a defensive or of an offensive nature were allowed, and all treaties were to be made public. (8) Aggression was to be met with "such an overwhelming economic and military force that it will not be attempted." [24]

[23] *Ibid.*, p. 148.   [24] *Ibid.*, p. 158.

A CONCLUDING COMMENT

In the preceding paragraphs of this chapter only a few of a multitude of plans for international organization have been summarized. The list could, of course, be greatly lengthened, but it is felt that the catalogue is sufficiently extensive to permit a lesson to be drawn. It was Montesquieu who said: "One must not always finish a subject so completely as to leave nothing for the reader to do. The object is not to make others read but to make them think." [25]

Of the various plans which we have described, each failed in its time and ultimate purpose; yet a residue of the ideas they embodied always survived. Such instrumentalities of collective security as the League Covenant and the Charter of the United Nations are indebted for much of their inspiration and substance to the dreamers of earlier times. It should be noted also that in international organization, as in the natural sciences, the most substantial achievements are often the products of many minds.

There is little reason to doubt that deeply embedded in human nature is a strong desire for order and permanence, security and peace. But to achieve these ends political organization is necessary. With the development of nationalism in modern times, reinforced by the concept of sovereignty, such political and legal organization tended to become coterminous with the national state.[26] Yet with the development of modern means of transportation and communication, trade and commerce between nations, the need for law and order in a world society of states became more and more pressing. But as we have so strongly emphasized above, the development of an effective legal order is in turn dependent upon the existence of a community among the nations. The terms *society* and *community*, as used in this treatise, should not be regarded as synonymous. As Georg Schwarzenberger has pointed out, the members of a community are united in spite of their individual existence, while in a society they are isolated even though parties to the association.[27]

To argue that community is the essential prerequisite to effective international law is not to deny the intricate nature of the problem, but rather to recognize its immense complexity. For it should be clearly understood

[25] *De l'Esprit des lois.*

[26] As early as 1877 Funck-Brentano and Albert Sorel could write: "Eternal peace is contradictory to the principle of independence and sovereignty of states which is the foundation of the law of nations"—quoted in Nicholas Doman, *The Coming Age of World Control* (1943), p. 11.

[27] *Power Politics* (1951), p. 35. See also Thomas I. Cook, "Theoretical Foundations of World Government," *Review of Politics*, vol. 12 (1950), pp. 41 ff.

that community in itself is one of the most elusive concepts in the whole area of the social sciences. It is the product of multifarious group relationships and is conditioned and influenced not only by the factors of environment but by the inscrutable nature of man.[28]

The most powerful single barrier to the establishment of a world community is, of course, the rigidity of the present state system. The separate states, through their efforts to self-perpetuation, resist amalgamation and instead concentrate on those elements in their make-up which tend to set them apart in categories of uniqueness, both with respect to each other and in their relationships to the whole complex of international organization. This was all well and good in the days of the sailing vessel and the windmill, but in this brave new world of jet propulsion and atomic energy such behavior of states presents not alone a grave danger to world peace, but a menace to the survival of our civilization.

The forces of external nature have been far easier to subdue than the inner drives of man, which are often motivated by selfish desires for wealth, power, and security. Yet, because of a superior intelligence, he, unlike the lower animals, is able to weigh the means against the ends of desire. It is quite possible, therefore, that someday we shall learn at last that the noblest goals presented in life are as elusive as the proverbial pot of gold at the end of the rainbow, and that what is most to be desired in our earthly existence is really the means by which we live.

In the plans for international organization presented in this chapter there are certain common features in structure and function and a common goal, which is eternal peace. As we have already indicated, most, if not all, of these ideas were embodied in the League of Nations after the First World War, and now in the United Nations Organization. Significantly, the main purpose of these organizations, however, was not to achieve peace but rather *to maintain peace and security* by providing the means for pacific settlement of international disputes. But according to the United Nations Charter: "The Organization is based on the principle of the sovereign equality of all its Members." [29] Thus, in the letter of the law, at least, does the concept of sovereignty survive. The international-legal theory manifested in the Charter would seem to show little progress in more than three centuries since Henry IV of France and the Grand Design.

[28] According to Immanuel Kant: "When we consider the perverseness of human nature, which shews itself unveiled and unrestrained in the relations of nations with each other, where it is not checked, as in a state of civilization, by the coercive power of the law, one may well be astonished that the word right has not yet been totally abolished from war-politics as a pedantic word, and that a state has not yet been found bold enough openly to profess this doctrine"—*Perpetual Peace* (1939), p. 19.

[29] The Charter of the United Nations, Art. 2, par. 1.

In view of the state of affairs in the world at the time of this writing, it may be safest to conclude this chapter in the words of Jean Jacques Rousseau: "If, in spite of all this, the project remains unrealised, that is not because it is Utopian. It is because men are mad, and because to be sane in a world of madmen is in itself a kind of madness." [30]

[30] From his *Plan for European Federation.*

CHAPTER 3

From the Westphalian Peace to the Declaration of London

In the society of states which came into being in Europe at the end of the Middle Ages, no political superior was recognized. In theory sovereigns were equal, and in the formulation as well as execution of policy each regarded his own interest without concern for the rest. Under these conditions conflict was inevitable, and the only arbiter was the force of arms. In course of time numerous efforts were made to resolve the disputes of nations by pacific means, and as we have seen in the preceding chapter, ingenious plans for international organization were advanced in order to avoid the horrors of war. But human beings are slow to undertake changes in behavior and to create new institutions. They are by and large creatures of habit and attached to the familiar *status quo*. Only when conditions become unbearable will an effort be made to abandon the old. Generally speaking, "change is a gradual, almost imperceptible process."[1]

Inasmuch as treaties and custom are among the chief sources of the law of nations, it might be well at this point to take a brief look at some of the more important multilateral agreements which today constitute the great body of international law. Such a survey, it is hoped, will in some measure provide the historical perspective so necessary to an appreciation of a growing international community and the development of its law.

THE PERIOD 1648–1856

The Peace of Westphalia. At the end of the Thirty Years' War (1618–1648) the powers of the Continent met at Osnabrück and Münster for more than three years to negotiate the peace. This assembly has sometimes been referred to as the "first European congress,"[2] and the peace

---

[1] Verner Levi, *Fundamentals of World Organization* (1950), p. 9.
[2] Arthur Nussbaum, *A Concise History of the Law of Nations* (1947), p. 86.

itself, for at least a century, remained the framework of international organization in Europe. Amos S. Hershey has said of the Westphalian peace that "it gave to Europe a sort of international constitution which remained the basis of its public law down to the French Revolution." [3] But the balance of power which was fixed by the Peace of Westphalia was unstable at best, and before the end of the century it was to collapse under the aggressive policies of Louis XIV. The intermittent struggle between England and France for colonial supremacy in the period from 1688 to 1815 has been referred to by the historian Seeley as the "Second Hundred Years' War." [4] The final result of this contest for power, which was sometimes interrupted by periods of peace, was not only the acquisition by England of the major French colonies, but also the establishment of British maritime supremacy for more than a century, which was to have a significant effect upon the development of international law.

The Peace of Utrecht. As compared with conditions in the sixteenth and seventeenth centuries, the eighteenth century presented a picture of relative stability. In the Peace of Utrecht (1713), which ended the War of the Spanish Succession, one can see the beginning of a new era in international relations. The principle of the balance of power was believed to be the only key to a lasting peace. Thus it was announced that the peace and tranquillity of Christendom could best be restored through the "just balance of power [*justum potentiae equilibrium*], which is the best and most solid foundation of mutual friendship and of lasting accord." [5] This principle of the Peace of Utrecht was to remain the basic element in European international relations to the time of the Napoleonic Wars.

The French Revolution. The most important political event in the eighteenth century was the French Revolution, which gave rise to a new legal development in France. This was later to make itself felt in most of the continent of Europe, as the ideas of the Revolution were spread in the course of the Napoleonic Wars and during the era which followed the Corsican adventurer. The influence of the French was not alone reflected in the municipal legislation of many countries but had a profound effect upon the theory of international law as well. The famous *Declaration of the Law of Nations* [6] which was submitted to the Convention in 1795 by the Abbé Grégoire is, in this respect, illustrative of the ideology of the Revolution in spite of the fact that it was never adopted. The parallelism between this document and the earlier *Declaration of the*

[3] Amos S. Hershey, *The Essentials of International Public Law and Organization* (1927), p. 69.
[4] *Expansion of England* (1883), lecture II, pp. 24–29.
[5] Quoted by Nussbaum in *op. cit.*, p. 126.
[6] *Déclaration du droit des gens.*

Rights of Man [7] is believed to derive from a common inspiration in natural law.[8]

The National Assembly of 1789 and later the Convention had sought to lay down certain broad principles of international law, some of which the Abbé Grégoire incorporated in his famous declaration. Among these are found the principles of nonintervention and the renunciation of wars of conquest.[9] The democratic forces which were set in motion by the French Revolution are illustrated by the introduction of the plebiscite as a condition for territorial annexation. Even though papal rule in the enclave of Avignon had been destroyed by revolution, annexation of this territory by the National Assembly of France in 1791 was made consequent upon the will of the people. This is perhaps the first instance in modern history where the principle of self-determination is recognized.[10]

The Convention in a decree of May 25, 1793, made a significant contribution to the law of war by providing for reciprocal treatment of sick and wounded prisoners as a matter of "justice and humanity." [11] The Provisional Executive Council of the Republic, during the French occupation of Belgium in 1792, issued a decree opening the Scheldt to navigation in accordance with "the principles of the law of nature." But this right, curiously enough, was to apply only to the riparian states.[12]

As we have intimated earlier, the greatest single result of the French Revolution regarding international relations is the incalculable force of modern nationalism which was then set in motion. The fraternal spirit which was born of revolution gave to the French nation its *élan vital* and to Europe a new era. The nineteenth century, which, in one sense, does not begin until the Congress of Vienna or end until the establishment of the League of Nations, has become known in modern history as the "Age of Nationalism." During this same period positivism became dominant in international legal theory, and a romantic conception of the state began more and more to undermine the rational basis for the rights of man.

The general transformation of political ideas both in Europe and America which came as a result of the French Revolution certainly had a significant, though indirect, influence upon the development of international law, but one which is exceedingly difficult to measure.

The Congress of Vienna. The development of positive international

---

[7] *Déclaration des droits de l'homme et du citoyen* of 1789.

[8] Nussbaum, *op. cit.*, p. 132.

[9] *Ibid.*

[10] See p. 33 for earliest recognition of this principle by treaty.

[11] Nussbaum, *op. cit.*, pp. 132–133.

[12] The river Scheldt, in accordance with the provisions of the Peace of Westphalia (1648), had been closed by the Dutch.

law was given a considerable impetus by the work of the Congress of Vienna, especially by its Final Act of June 9, 1815. Aside from redrawing the map of Europe, the treaty concerned itself with general problems of international law. It established the various categories of diplomatic envoys [13] and came to an agreement upon the general principles which were to govern the navigation of international rivers. Another important matter with which the Final Act of the Treaty of Vienna was concerned was the suppression of the slave trade. Though the British government tried to obtain an outright prohibition of this traffic in human merchandise, it was unable to obtain more than a condemnation of the practice. England, however, was to continue her humanitarian efforts, and as a result a great number of treaties were negotiated culminating in the General Act of the Anti-Slavery Conference of Brussels in 1890.

Among the political acts of the Congress of Vienna, we might mention the union of Norway and Sweden, and that of Holland and Belgium, as well as the reorganization and neutralization of Switzerland; the establishment of the German Confederation of 39 states, and the restoration, in general, of the old dynasties, not only in Germany and Italy, but in the Iberian Peninsula and France as well.

The Holy and Quadruple Alliances. In the year 1815, the Emperors of Austria and Russia, with the King of Prussia, formed what has been known as the Holy Alliance, by which they pledged themselves to apply the precepts of Christianity to the affairs of nations both in internal and external matters, "as being the only means of consolidating human institutions and remedying their imperfections." [14]

More important, perhaps, than this sentimental effort was the renewal of the Quadruple Alliance in the same year and by the same powers plus England. In Article VI of this treaty it was decided "to renew, at fixed intervals, . . . meetings consecrated to great common objects, and . . . the examination of such measures as . . . shall be judged most salutary for the peace and prosperity of the Nations and for the maintenance of the peace of Europe." [15]

The Concert of Europe. The Quadruple Alliance marks the beginning of the so-called Concert of Europe, which was organized to suppress the forces of revolution and maintain the treaties so recently signed in the old Austrian capital. It was an attempt on the part of the great powers to maintain the *status quo* as established by the reactionary Congress of Vienna. In 1818 France joined the Alliance, but this pentarchy soon began

[13] An appendix, amended by the Protocol of Aix-la-Chapelle in 1818, to the Final Act gives a classification of the diplomatic envoys which has persisted to the present day.

[14] From the Preamble to the Act of the Holy Alliance, Sept. 26, 1815.

[15] Quoted by Hershey in *op. cit.*, p. 85.

to show significant weaknesses, as both France and England failed to sign the Troppau Protocol [16] in 1820. At Aix-la-Chapelle, in 1818, a declaration was made by the powers of Europe to the effect that it was their "unalterable determination never to swerve from the strictest observance of the principles of the Law of Nations, either in their relations with one another or with other States."

The Monroe Doctrine. In the New World, the Napoleonic Wars and the ensuing Metternich System had repercussions which were to outlast both the Holy Alliance and the pentarchy. Spanish preoccupation in Europe as a result of Napoleon's invasion of the Iberian Peninsula, and the temporary dethronement of the Bourbon dynasty, were to signal the start of the wars of independence in Latin America. The mere fact that a number of new states emerged in Central and South America was in itself a phenomenon of great importance to international law. Moreover, it was to give rise to another significant event in modern history—the promulgation of the Monroe Doctrine.

At the Congress of Verona in 1822, the question of intervention in an effort to restore Spanish power in Latin America had been discussed. This move was cause for alarm in the young republic of the United States. Accordingly, President Monroe, in a message to Congress in 1823, declared the firm opposition of his country to any such moves as were contemplated at Verona. The language of this message, since known as the Monroe Doctrine, runs in part as follows: [17]

In the wars of the European powers, in matters relating to themselves, we have never taken any part, nor does it comport with our policy so to do. It is only when our rights are invaded or seriously menaced that we resent injuries or make preparation for our defense. With the movements in this hemisphere we are of necessity more intimately connected, and by causes which must be obvious to all enlightened and impartial observers. The political system of the allied powers is essentially different in this respect from that of America. . . . We owe it, therefore, to candor and to the amicable relations existing between the United States and those powers to declare that we should consider any attempt on their part to extend their system to any portion of this hemisphere as dangerous to our peace and safety. With the existing colonies or dependencies of any European power we have not interfered, and shall not interfere. But with

[16] The Protocol of Troppau was an attempt to extend to all Europe the Carlsbad decrees, which had effectively put an end to the development of free institutions in Germany. The Protocol declared that the "States which have undergone a change of government due to revolution, the results of which threaten other States, *ipso facto*, cease to be members of the European Alliance, and remain excluded from it until their situation gives guaranties for legal order and stability. If, owing to such alterations, immediate danger threatens other States, the Powers bind themselves, by peaceful means, or if need be by arms, to bring back the guilty State into the arms of the Great Alliance."

[17] John Bassett Moore, *Digest of International Law*, vol. VI, p. 402.

the Governments who have declared their independence and maintained it, and whose independence we have, on great consideration and on just principles, acknowledged, we could not view any interposition for the purpose of oppressing them, or controlling in any other manner their destiny, by any European power in any other light than as a manifestation of an unfriendly disposition toward the United States.

Some writers have held the Monroe Doctrine to be in violation of international law on the grounds that it goes beyond the right of self-preservation. But the right of the United States to pursue a policy in international relations along the lines drawn in the message of President Monroe has never been challenged by any nation on legal grounds.[18] Article XXI of the Covenant of the League of Nations gave a somewhat qualified recognition to the doctrine by a provision that "regional understandings like the Monroe Doctrine, for securing the maintenance of peace," would not be affected in their validity by the Covenant. Though the Monroe Doctrine may be said not to run counter to international law, it is very doubtful that it can be considered a part of the real substance of the law outside the Western Hemisphere. In the development of continental regionalism, of which there are some indications at the present time, and which we shall deal with in a later chapter, the Monroe Doctrine has undoubtedly played a major role as far as the Western world is concerned.

The Peace of Paris, 1856. The European Concert of great powers broke down in the middle of the nineteenth century as a result of the Crimean War. The Treaty of Paris, which ended the struggle, is of considerable importance in the development of the positive law of nations. According to the terms of this treaty, Turkey was admitted to the community of states, and international law was thereby extended beyond the nations of Christian Europe. The Paris treaty also neutralized the Black Sea and established an International Commission of the Danube. The work of this Commission was to prove fairly successful and lasted until the end of the Second World War. This treaty was, furthermore, the first in which recognition was given to the principle of self-determination of peoples, as evidenced by the reorganization of Walachia and Moldavia in accordance with the wishes of the populations involved.

Of special importance to the development of international law was a separate instrument from the rest of the treaty of 1856, the so-called Declaration of Paris. By its terms privateering was abolished, and except for contraband of war, enemy goods were regarded as covered by the neutral flag. Conversely, neutral goods, with the exception of contraband, were declared not liable to capture under an enemy's flag, and finally, it was

---

[18] It is true that both England and Russia protested the clause barring any further colonization, but no such colonization was ever attempted after 1823.

declared that blockade in order to be binding must be effective. There can be no doubt that this document represented a notable gain of neutral rights as against those of belligerents. But the century that has transpired since the famous declaration was made has seen many changes in the techniques of warfare, the total effect of which has been to render this instrument, along with much else in the law of war and neutrality, quite meaningless and ineffectual.

The original signatories of the Declaration of Paris were the powers represented at the Peace Conference of 1856. These were France, England, Austria, Russia, Sardinia, Turkey, and Prussia. The states not represented were invited to sign later, and most of them did so before the end of the year. Japan became a signatory in 1866, and Spain gave notice of her adhesion at the Hague Conference of 1907. Though the United States, Mexico, and some smaller states never signed the Declaration of Paris,[19] its provisions were generally observed until the outbreak of the First World War.

THE DEVELOPMENT FROM 1856 TO 1914

A Half Century of Progress. The years that intervened between the Peace of Paris in 1856 and the outbreak of the First World War saw greater progress in the development of the positive law of nations than had been the case in all previous time. It was an era of congresses and conferences, prompted by the compelling needs for cooperation among the nations in a world which was becoming increasingly interdependent. Innumerable international unions, bureaus, and commissions were established, and these in turn began to develop a kind of legislation, and what may be called international administrative law.

Though it is true that this period was one of growing nationalism, which saw the unification of such nations as Italy and Germany, it was also an age of international organization in which the peoples of many lands sought to build international institutions in order to promote their common welfare. It was a time, according to Professor Hershey, in which "the older conceptions of sovereignty and independence were yielding to ideals of solidarity and interdependence."[20]

First Steps in Codification of the Law of Land Warfare. It was in the year 1863 that the American government published the *Instructions for the Government of Armies of the United States in the Field*.[21] These rules

---

[19] The United States did not have a large navy in 1856, and for that reason objected especially to the provision in the declaration of 1856 which abolished privateering.

[20] Hershey, *op. cit.*, p. 89

[21] These *Instructions*, issued at the request of the War Department, were known as "General Order No. 100."

of land warfare were prepared by Dr. Francis Lieber, a German veteran of Waterloo, who later came to America and became professor of political science in the Columbia University Law School. The *Instructions* are regarded as definitive on the usages of civilized warfare, and today they form the basis of a number of military codes.

A year later, at the initiative of Switzerland, the so-called Geneva Convention for the Amelioration of the Condition of the Wounded in War was concluded. This convention, which provided for the neutralization of medical personnel and supplies, is now superseded by the Second Geneva Convention of 1929 and the Convention of 1949. In the Declaration of St. Petersburg, a large number of states renounced, in case of war among themselves, the use of any "projectile of less weight than 400 grammes which is explosive, or is charged with fulminating or inflammable substances."

When we come to consider the law of war and neutrality, in a later section of this work, we shall see how futile such resolutions proved to be in the face of the technological revolution, which among other things greatly transformed the techniques of warfare. New weapons of such unimaginable horror were soon to be introduced that any declaration on the part of nations to refrain from the use of dumdum bullets would appear as a joke.

At the Brussels Congress in 1874, a code of land warfare was formulated, and though it was never ratified, it was generally observed. It was based, for the most part, on the American *Instructions* and was later to become a basis for the code of The Hague in 1899. The Brussels Conference was attended by delegates from 15 European countries. The United States, however, did not take part and the states of Latin America were not invited.

The Congo Conference of Berlin. Another important law-making conference in the nineteenth century was the Congo or West African Conference, which met in Berlin in the year 1884–1885. Among the accomplishments of this conference was the recognition of the Congo Free State. It was also agreed that trade and travel should be free within the Congo Basin and that the nations should "strive for the suppression of slavery, and especially of the negro slave trade." [22] The neutrality of the Congo territories was to be respected, and the signatories agreed to preserve reasonable order in the territories which were occupied by them, as well as to notify one another of any future occupation of any portion of the coast of Africa or of the establishment of any new protectorate in the Dark Continent.

The General Act of the Congo Conference was signed by the leading

[22] Art. VI of the General Act of the Conference of Berlin Concerning the Congo.

maritime powers, including the United States of America. President
Cleveland, however, neglected its submittal to the Senate and the act was
never ratified. Later, the General Act was supplemented by the Brussels
Agreement of 1890, which finally abolished the slave trade. It also restricted the importation and sale of spirituous liquors, firearms, and
ammunition in a certain defined zone of Africa.

International Unions. As stated above, the period since 1850 was characterized by a multiplicity of international congresses and saw the establishment of a great number and variety of international unions. Beginning
with the first International Sanitary Conference, which was held in Paris
in 1851, a long list of official congresses were convened to deal with all
kinds of subjects, such as statistics, sugar duties, weights and measures,
monetary matters, international postal and telegraphic correspondence,
navigation of rivers, submarine cables, protection of industrial property,
railroad transportation, international copyright, customs duties, protection
of labor, international arbitration, and suppression of the traffic in women
and children.

Many of these unions are endowed with permanent organs of legislation and administration. The conferences and congresses which are held
from time to time may be looked upon as the legislative apparatus, while
the commissions and bureaus are the organs of administration. As a result
of this development in international organization, a new branch of jurisprudence has developed, namely, international administrative law.
Though this branch of law is outside the compass of this treatise, it is
mentioned because of its steadily growing importance in the general field
of international relations.

International Arbitration. With the Jay Treaty of 1794 between the
United States and Britain, the principle of international arbitration as a
means to settlement of international disputes was revived. It was not,
however, until the arbitration, by the Geneva Tribunal in 1872, of the
American claims against England in the case of the *Alabama* that this
method of settling international disputes was to prove a great practical
success. Since the arbitration of the famous *Alabama* claims, a vast number of arbitration treaties have been negotiated by many nations, and a
Permanent Court of International Arbitration has been established. We
shall have occasion to deal with the whole question of arbitration more
fully and specifically in a later chapter.

The First Peace Conference at The Hague in 1899. The Russian Czar
called the First Hague Conference, which met on May 18, 1899, to seek,
"by means of international discussion, the most effectual means of insuring
to all peoples the benefits of a real and durable peace, and above all, of
putting an end to the progressive development of the present armaments."

The conference, however, soon found that an agreement on reduction of armaments could not be obtained, and accordingly it devoted its attention to the secondary purpose for which it had been convened, namely, the preservation of peace.

The conference resulted in the establishment of three international conventions, two of which have been of such great practical significance that "they may well be called codes. . . ." [23] The first in importance is undoubtedly the Convention for the Pacific Settlement of International Disputes, which established a Permanent Court of Arbitration. This Court was to function in the arbitration of "questions of a legal nature, and especially in the interpretation or application of International Conventions. . . ." [24] In order to "encourage the development of arbitration," the signatory powers to this convention also agreed on a set of rules, applicable to arbitral procedure.

The convention with respect to the laws and customs of war on land, though it contains a number of gaps even as amended by the second Hague Peace Conference of 1907, is nevertheless among the more important lawmaking treaties. This convention, which was based on the work of the Brussels conference of 1874, "represents a model the very existence of which teaches that codification of parts of the Law of Nations is practicable." [25] The third convention of the first Hague Peace Conference related to the adaptation of the Geneva convention of 1864 to naval warfare. It declared against the dropping of explosives from balloons and the use of asphyxiating or deleterious gases, as well as the use of the so-called dumdum bullets.

The Second Peace Conference at The Hague, 1907. Again at the invitation of the Russian government, an international conference was held at The Hague for the purpose of promoting the cause of peace. The delegates from the various countries assembled on June 15, 1907, to consider the following main items on the agenda:

1. Improvements in the convention relative to the pacific settlement of international disputes as regards the Court of Arbitration and the International Commissions of Inquiry

2. Additions to the convention of 1899 relative to the laws and customs of warfare on land

3. Framing a convention relative to the laws and customs of maritime warfare

4. Additions to the convention of 1899 for adapting to maritime warfare the principles of the Geneva convention of 1864

[23] Oppenheim-Lauterpacht, *International Law* (1947), vol. I, p. 56.
[24] From Art. XVI of the "Convention for the Pacific Settlement of International Disputes." M. D. A. R. von Redlich, *The Law of Nations* (1937), appendix I, p. 524.
[25] Oppenheim-Lauterpacht, *op. cit.*, p. 56.

The question of limitation of armaments was not given a place on the program, though Great Britain had insisted strongly that it be taken up for consideration. The failure of England in this respect was largely due to the opposition of Germany, Austria-Hungary, and Japan. The United States was more successful in pressing for a modification of the Drago Doctrine. This doctrine had reference to the practice of armed intervention by European powers in South America for the purpose of collecting debts. At the beginning of the present century this question had become an acute issue in international as well as in domestic politics. In 1902, when the combined fleets of Great Britain, Germany, and Italy blockaded Venezuela for the purpose of enforcing contractual and other claims against that state, the foreign minister of Argentina, Dr. Drago, formulated a declaration to the effect that "a public debt cannot give rise to the right of intervention, and much less to the occupation of the soil of any American nation by any European power." [26] The United States took a special interest in this matter, because of its obvious connection with the Monroe Doctrine. The result was the adoption of a convention by the second Hague conference in which the contracting powers agreed not to have recourse to armed force for the recovery of contract debts claimed from the government of one country by the government of another as being due its nationals. This agreement, however, was conditioned upon the willingness of the debtor state to reply to an offer to arbitrate and, having agreed to arbitration, to abide by the award.

The second Hague conference produced no less than 13 conventions, 3 of which were modifications of those adopted by the conference of 1899 and 10 of which were entirely new agreements. The new conventions, with the exception of one which related to the limitation on the use of force for collection of contract debts and another concerning the opening of hostilities, were devoted to the regulation of neutrality and warfare on land and sea.

The London Conference of 1908–1909. One of the conventions of the second Hague Peace Conference related to the establishment of an international prize court. The uncertainty of what law the court would apply in its interpretation of the phrase "general principles of justice and equity" was a question which aroused a great deal of concern, particularly in Britain. The laws of naval warfare, especially those relating to neutrals, were rather unsettled, and some jurists were of the opinion that the court should be left free to develop new law on all disputed points.[27] Such a solution of the matter was, however, strongly opposed by public opinion.

---

[26] Charles G. Fenwick, *International Law* (1948), p. 295.
[27] Pearce A. Higgins and John C. Colombos, *The International Law of the Sea* (1943), p. 315.

Thus, in order to fix certain rules for the court, the British government sent invitations to a number of states on February 27, 1908, to send delegates to a conference in London. The countries invited were Austria-Hungary, France, Germany, Italy, Japan, Russia, Spain, and the United States. Later an invitation was sent to Holland, as it was proposed that the international prize court should have its seat in The Hague.

The conference met on December 4, 1908. On February 26, 1909, its work was completed with the signing of the Declaration of London by the representatives of the powers present. This declaration concerning the laws of naval warfare is composed of no less than 70 articles, grouped under the following headings: blockade in time of war; contraband of war; unneutral service; destruction of neutral prizes; transfer to a neutral flag; enemy character; convoy; resistance to search; compensation; and final provisions. This was the first attempt in history to codify the law of prize, and is therefore regarded as a landmark even though it was never ratified.

CHAPTER 4

Legal Organizations since Versailles

The outbreak of the First World War marks the beginning of a new era in the history of warfare. The old conception that war is a contest between belligerent states, each using its armed forces against the enemy, while others, not involved in the dispute, might repose in impartial neutrality, was greatly undermined by the experience of the war. To the conventional arms of land and sea, the air forces were added, and the technological revolution gave rise to new techniques, which rendered the Geneva and Hague conventions regarding the conduct of war obsolete. Science and industry became the handmaidens of a total war that soon engulfed whole populations, and because of the increased interdependence of nations, neutrality lost much of its meaning. The optimistic notion, subscribed to by so many at the turn of the century, that man had at last become too civilized to resort to destructive arms for the settlement of international disputes was rudely shattered by the cataclysmic upheaval of a world war. Nevertheless, the conclusion of hostilities gave rise to new hopes and to the commencement of a new and radical development in international law and organization.

While the First World War was still in progress, the governments of both England and France took steps toward the establishment of a new legal order designed to preserve the peace, for this was "the war to end war." But it was from the United States that the real initiative in this matter was to come.[1] In a message to Congress on January 8, 1918, President Wilson presented a program for world peace in Fourteen Points. These included, among other things, the abandonment of secret diplomacy; the realization of the freedom of the seas; the self-determination of nations; limitations of armaments; and as a final point, the establishment of a League of Nations. The famous Fourteen Points along with four subsequent speeches,[2] by the President, and eight diplomatic notes ex-

[1] Frede Castberg, *Folkerett* (1948), p. 43.
[2] These speeches were an address to the Congress on Feb. 11, 1918; a speech at Baltimore on Apr. 6, 1918; an address at Mount Vernon on July 4, 1918; and an

40

changed between the governments of the United States and Germany in the months of October and November, 1918, were formally accepted by the Allies and Germany as the legal basis for both the armistice and the peace.

The Treaty of Versailles. The Paris peace conference met in its first plenary session on January 18, 1919. But as the delegates from the Allied and Associated Powers gathered in the French capital, the general situation in Europe was far from favorable to calm and dispassionate deliberation. The tide of revolution had engulfed the Russian Empire, and the economic and social conditions in Germany and Austria, as well as in the countries of Eastern and Southeastern Europe were such as to require swift and drastic action, if what remained of the institutions of the past were to be rescued from the chaos of the present.

On June 28, 1919, after more than five months of hard work, the treaty of peace with Germany was signed in the famous Hall of Mirrors at Versailles. Because of the importance of this document in the public international law of this century, it might be well at this point to summarize briefly some of its more important provisions.

According to its terms, Alsace-Lorraine was restored to France, and Germany was "forbidden to maintain or construct any fortifications either on the left bank of the Rhine or on the right bank to the west of a line drawn fifty kilometers to the east of the Rhine." This area in the Rhineland was thus to be completely demilitarized; and in case of any violation of this article of the treaty, Germany was to be regarded as having acted in a way "calculated to disturb the peace of the world." [3]

As compensation for the destruction of French coal mines by the Germans in the last days of the war, the treaty provided that the coal of the Saar Basin be given to France. The government of the Saar, however, was to be under the administration of a commission of the League of Nations for a period of fifteen years. At the end of that time the inhabitants of the Saar were to determine, by popular vote, their future political status. [4]

Other significant provisions of the treaty were the restoration of Poland as an independent state with a "corridor" to the sea; the establishment of the Free City of Danzig under the government of a High Commissioner appointed by the League; [5] the loss to Germany of her overseas possessions;

---

address in New York on Sept. 27, 1918. For the texts of these addresses, see H. W. V. Temperley (ed.), *A History of the Peace Conference of Paris* (6 vols., 1920–1924), vol. I, pp. 431–448.

[3] Arts. 42–44 of the Treaty of Versailles.

[4] In 1935 the eligible voters (those who were resident in the Saar at the time of the signing of the Versailles treaty) voted to return to German sovereignty.

[5] Poland, however, was to conduct the foreign relations of the Free City and was to enjoy the use of its port facilities.

and the creation of international commissions for the regulation of navigation on such international rivers as the Rhine, Oder, Elbe, and Danube.

The treaty further declared that "Germany accepts the responsibility of herself and her allies for causing all the loss and damage to which the Allied and Associated Powers and their nationals have been subjected as a consequence of the war imposed upon them by the aggression of Germany and her allies." Accordingly, heavy reparations were imposed on Germany.[6] In an attempt to forestall a similar adventure in the future, Germany was deprived of her general staff, and her Army was limited to 100,000 men including no more than 4,000 officers. The treaty also provided that the enlistment of officers must be for a minimum period of twenty-five consecutive years, and that of privates for no less than twelve.

The reduction of Germany's naval establishment was equally drastic. No submarines were allowed, and the entire sea strength was limited to 6 battleships, 6 light cruisers, 12 destroyers, and 12 torpedo boats. The entire naval personnel was limited to 15,000 men, including no more than 1,500 officers. The periods of enlistment were to be the same for officers and sailors respectively as those provided for the Army. No person in the merchant marine was to receive naval training, and Germany was to be allowed no air forces.

Another significant provision of the Treaty of Versailles had to do with the punishment of war criminals. It was stipulated that Germans who had committed crimes in violation of the law and customs of war should be subjected to trial before the courts of the victorious powers. In the end, however, the whole matter was left to the German courts, with results far from satisfactory. Yet, as a precedent for the trial of war criminals at Nuremberg, following the Second World War, this provision of the Versailles treaty acquired a new importance.

The League of Nations. Though the Congress of Paris had been concerned, in the main, with the dictation of a victor's peace to the vanquished,[7] a significant attempt was made to deal with the international anarchy which prevailed in the world by the establishment of a League of Nations. A proposal to establish such an institution for the purpose of preserving the peace was made to the Inter-Allied Conference at Paris on January 25, 1919. After a resolution had been adopted by the conference, a commission, with President Wilson at the head, was created to draft a "constitution" for the organization.[8]

The Covenant of the League of Nations was drafted in ten days, and

[6] The amount of reparations was to be fixed by a Reparations Commission.

[7] Carlton J. H. Hayes, *A Political and Social History of Modern Europe* (1932), p. 797.

[8] Pitman B. Potter, *An Introduction to the Study of International Organization* (1948), p. 240.

after certain revisions had been made, it was adopted by the conference. On June 28, 1919, the Covenant was first signed as Part I of the Treaty of Versailles. The term *covenant* was used in order to give the instrument a somewhat higher standing than a mere treaty and yet not so exalted a one as that of a *constitution*—a term proposed and later rejected.[9]

Structurally, the League was composed of the member states, an Assembly, a Council, and a Secretariat. In addition to these elements there were a fluctuating number of commissions and conferences operating under the authority of the Assembly or the Council or both. A number of international organizations, some of which had been established long before 1919, became linked to the League in varying degrees. Under separate statutes were created a Permanent Court of International Justice and the International Labor Organization.

Functionally, the League sought to attain the two major ends for which it had been established, namely, the promotion of international cooperation and the achievement of peace and security.[10] In the first decade of its existence, the League met with considerable success in the realization of these aims, but in the years following 1930 to the outbreak of the Second World War, its feeble efforts to stem the tide of power politics in Europe and Asia could only result in dismal failure.

The Kellogg-Briand Pact. In the year 1928 a dramatic effort was made, through the Pact of Paris or, as it is more commonly known, the Kellogg-Briand Pact, to unite "the civilized nations of the world in a common renunciation of war as an instrument of their national policy."

Though there were no specific references in the Pact of Paris to the obligations of nations under the League Covenant, it nevertheless bore a spiritual kinship to the League.[11] But in its idealistic aim to banish war from the earth it was no less a failure than the League of Nations. Thus, in 1931, when the storm broke over the Manchurian plain and Secretary Stimson declared that the United States could not recognize any agreement or situation brought about in violation of the Kellogg-Briand Pact, his voice was alone in a wilderness.

Humanitarian Efforts. Notwithstanding the weaknesses of such institutions of peace as the League of Nations and the Pact of Paris, the period between the two world wars was far from barren with regard to the growth and development of the positive law of nations.

In this period, considerable progress was made in the international law of communications. As examples, we might mention the multilateral convention of 1923 which sought to establish a degree of uniformity in the

[9] *Ibid.*, p. 242.
[10] See Preamble to the Covenant of the League of Nations.
[11] Arthur Nussbaum, *A Concise History of the Law of Nations* (1947), p. 251.

technical regime of international railways, and the multilateral Convention for the Regulation of Aerial Navigation of 1919.

In the field of social and humanitarian problems, the work of the League and its agencies was perhaps most conspicuously successful. Its fight against epidemic and contagious diseases; the suppression of the traffic in opium and other dangerous drugs; the international control of traffic in women and children; and the aid to political and other refugees are notable examples.

The Norwegian diplomat, scientist, and explorer Dr. Fridtjof Nansen played a major role in the humanitarian efforts of the League in his capacity as High Commissioner. He was the author of a new international document, the so-called "Nansen passport," by which stateless persons could travel from one country to another, and his work on behalf of the League in Russia and Armenia, in the alleviation of famine and the placement of refugees, constitutes a brilliant chapter in the history of international humanitarianism.[12]

The Pan American Union. In the year 1890, under the auspices of the United States, the International Union of American Republics was founded. This organization, which since 1910 has been known as the Pan American Union, is the central organ in the inter-American system.

The Pan American Union is directed by a Governing Board which is composed of one delegate from each of the 21 American republics.[13] The Chairman of the Board is elected for one year and is not eligible for immediate reelection. The Governing Board elects the Director General of the Union, whose term of office is ten years. Among the functions of the Pan American Union is the preparation of agendas for inter-American conferences, and the publication of reports and other documents relative to its activities.

Aside from the Pan American Union itself, there are about thirty-five administrative agencies, some of which operate through permanent secretariats, while others function by means of correspondence among their members.[14] The work of these agencies, however, is not well coordinated, as their duties often overlap and duplicate each other.

The Pan American Union became a "league of nations" for the Americas, through which means a large number of multilateral treaties were prepared. Among the many conventions so far concluded is the famous Anti-War Pact of Nonaggression and Conciliation, or, as it is often called, the Saavedra-Lamas Treaty. The Argentine Republic provided the initi-

[12] In order to promote justice and humanity, the International Labor Organization was established by Part XIII of the Treaty of Versailles.

[13] The Dominion of Canada is not a member of the Pan American Union.

[14] Charles G. Fenwick, *International Law* (1948), p. 206.

ative for the treaty, which was signed at Rio de Janeiro in 1933. This agreement not only supplements the Kellogg-Briand Pact but also elaborates the Monroe Doctrine. It provides for inter-American solidarity against foreign aggression, a policy which proved very effective in the Second World War, and the effect of which was to strengthen the Pan American Union.

Other inter-American conventions, worthy of mention here, are the Convention on Private International Law, or "Code Bustamante" of 1928; a Convention of Rights and Duties of States in the Event of Civil Strife, concluded in the same year; and a Convention on the Rights and Duties of States, signed in 1933. There were other treaties dealing with such subjects as political asylum, the status of aliens, aviation, and extradition. It should be noted, however, that in spite of the vast number of treaties and conventions concluded under the aegis of the Pan American Union, the total effect of it all has not been very impressive. Like the treaties concluded under the League of Nations, the inter-American agreements were often not enforced and more often not ratified by the various states. We shall have more to say about the Pan American Union and the inter-American regional system in another connection.

The Permanent Court of International Justice. The interwar period was one of significant development in international judicial administration. An outstanding achievement of this era was the establishment, in accordance with Article 14 of the League Covenant, of the Permanent Court of International Justice. This judicial institution came into being in 1921, when a majority of the members of the League of Nations ratified the Statute of the Court. The magnificent Peace Palace at The Hague became the home of the Court, which was composed of 15 judges appointed for a term of nine years. Unlike the Permanent Court of Arbitration, established in 1899, it gave to international law a central position, and the parties to litigation could have no influence on the composition of the Court. In cases, however, where members of the bench were of the nationality of the contesting parties, extra judges were added.

With regard to the competence of the Court, Article 36 of the Statute provided that its jurisdiction should include "all cases which the parties refer to it and all matters specially provided for in Treaties and Conventions in force." According to Article 38, the Court was to apply [15]

1. International Conventions, whether general or particular, establishing rules expressly recognized by the contesting States;
2. International custom, as evidence of a general practice accepted as law;
3. The general principles of law recognized by civilized nations;

[15] Art. 59 provided that "the decision of the Court has no binding force except between the parties and in respect of that particular case."

4. Subject to the provisions of Article 59, judicial decisions and the teachings of the most highly qualified publicists of the various nations, as subsidiary means for the determination of rules of law.

This provision shall not prejudice the power of the Court to decide a case *ex aequo et bono*, if the parties agree thereto.

The Statute of the Permanent Court of International Justice also contained an "optional clause" with regard to

compulsory . . . jurisdiction of the Court in all or any of the classes of legal disputes concerning:

(*a*) The interpretation of a Treaty.

(*b*) Any question of International Law.

(*c*) The existence of any fact which, if established, would constitute a breach of an international obligation.

(*d*) The nature or extent of the reparation to be made for the breach of an international obligation.[16]

Of the 11 cases which actually came before the Court under the "optional clause," there were only four in which the contesting parties agreed on the point of jurisdiction.[17] Perhaps the most important question brought before the Permanent Court of International Justice under this "clause" was the East Greenland Case, involving a territorial dispute between Norway and Denmark. The judgment in this case, which was handed down on April 5, 1933, in favor of Denmark, constitutes an important contribution to the doctrine of acquisition of territory by means of occupation.[18]

Though the "optional clause" was largely a failure as a means to compulsory jurisdiction, it should be noted that hundreds of international agreements provided for the exclusive jurisdiction of the Permanent Court in cases defined by the terms of such treaties. The first such case to come before the Permanent Court was that of the S.S. *Wimbledon* in 1923. The Court assumed jurisdiction under the Treaty of Versailles and found that the German authorities on March 21, 1921, were wrong in refusing the *Wimbledon* access to the Kiel Canal.[19] In the case of the *German Settlers in Poland*,[20] the Permanent Court was asked by the Council of the League of Nations to give an advisory opinion as to whether or not the German settlers, who had concluded *Rentengutsvertraege* with the Prussian state, were entitled to execution of such con-

[16] Art. 36 of the Statute.

[17] Nussbaum, *op. cit.*, p. 268.

[18] See pp. 170–171.

[19] Manley O. Hudson, *Cases and Other Materials on International Law* (1936), p. 475.

[20] Manley O. Hudson, *World Court Reports*, vol. I, p. 208.

tracts by the Polish government. The Court held in favor of the German settlers, on the ground that "private rights acquired under existing law do not cease on a change of sovereignty."

Another advisory opinion was handed down by the Court in 1931.[21] The question at issue involved the projected establishment of a customs union between Austria and Germany, in which it was held, by a vote of 8 to 7, that such a union would be in violation of Austrian obligations under the financial agreement of 1922.

The advisory activities of the Court, however, were held to be of a quasi-judicial character. This is illustrated by the fact that, when the Council of the League of Nations asked for an advisory opinion in the Russo-Finnish dispute over Eastern Karelia, the Court refused to hand down an opinion.[22] The reason for this refusal was the categorical objections of Russia to any interference by the Court which, it was contended, had no jurisdiction. Yet, it should be noted that a body of legal experts, such as the Permanent Court, needs no "jurisdiction" merely to hand down an advisory opinion.

The function of the Court in its advisory capacity proved to be rather important, however. The Council of the League, which was a political body, was spared thereby many difficult and embarrassing decisions. Though the Council could not be bound by an advisory opinion of the Court, it is of interest to note that such an opinion was never rejected.[23]

The San Francisco Conference. Even while the guns of the Second World War roared and men died on battlefields around the world, the United Nations Conference on International Organization opened at San Francisco. In 1945 as in 1918, the President of the United States took the lead in the establishment of an institution for world peace. When the Conference convened on April 25, 1945, Franklin D. Roosevelt was dead. But his idealistic spirit, which would free men everywhere in the world from fear and want, as well as from the tyranny over their minds, was not without influence in the deliberations of the Conference.

Three important lessons from the experience with the League of Nations proved to be of significance in the negotiations at San Francisco First, it was felt that the General Assembly and the Security Council in the new Organization should be given separate powers and functions. This had not been the case with the League, where the functions of the two main organs were virtually identical. Second, it was felt that the

[21] *Austro-German Customs Union Case, PCIJ Advisory Opinion,* ser. A/B, no. 41 (1931).

[22] *The Eastern Karelia Case, PCIJ Advisory Opinion,* ser. B, no. 5 (1923); Hudson, *World Court Reports,* vol. I, p. 190.

[23] J. L. Brierly, *The Law of Nations* (1949), p. 218.

United Nations, unlike the League, ought to be given some executive powers, especially in matters involving peace and security. Third, it was felt that the rule of unanimity which had prevailed under the Covenant of the League should be abandoned for some form of majority rule even in substantive matters.

A crucial problem throughout the negotiations both at Dumbarton Oaks and in San Francisco concerned the voting procedure in the new Organization. The experience of the League of Nations had shown that the unanimity rule was a major obstruction to the making of necessary decisions for the preservation of international peace. Thus, the question of voting procedure in the Security Council was one of the more sharply debated issues at San Francisco. The final outcome, however, was to the effect that there should be three levels of voting: (1) In matters of procedure, such as whether or not a controversy between states may be taken up for discussion, a decision can be made by any seven members of the Security Council. (2) In matters of substance, such as whether an investigation of a controversy is to be made and a decision rendered, seven votes are needed, including all the five permanent members. (3) To enforce a decision also requires seven votes, but all the permanent members must be among the seven even if they are parties to the dispute. Thus any one of the so-called "big five" powers—the United States, the Soviet Union, Great Britain, China, and France—can veto any punitive action against either itself or its allies.

In order to avoid the overlapping of powers and functions, for which the League had been notorious, each of the main organs of the United Nations was to be given its distinctive duties within the proper framework of interrelation. Thus, though the General Assembly and the Security Council are concerned with the problems of peace and security, their powers are coordinate in the sense that neither has authority over the other.

The Security Council. The main responsibility for maintaining peace and security is lodged with the Security Council. This body is composed of the "big five" as permanent members, and six other member states, elected by the General Assembly for a period of two years. The Security Council, however, is given no powers or functions in matters relating to the promotion of the general welfare. These are within the exclusive province of the General Assembly, or under its authority in the Economic and Social Council and the Trusteeship Council.

The real basis for the security arrangement under the Charter must, of course, be found in the obligations assumed by the member states. The most fundamental of these is the obligation to "refrain in their international relations from the threat or use of force in any manner inconsistent with the Purposes of the Organization." [24] In accordance with Article 33 of the Charter, the member states are bound "to seek a solution by negotiation, enquiry, mediation, conciliation, arbitration, judicial settlement, resort to regional arrangements, or other peaceful means of their own choice," in disputes "the continuance of which is likely to endanger the maintenance of international peace and security."

Though the United Nations Organization is given a number of specific powers and the authority to act in the adjustment of disputes of an international character, most of these powers are lodged in the Security Council. It should also be noted that the member states, according to Article 25 of the Charter, have agreed "to accept and carry out the decisions of the Security Council."

According to Article 43, all members of the Organization undertake to make available, on the call of the Security Council, "armed forces, assistance and facilities, including rights of passage, necessary for the purpose of maintaining international peace and security." However, "the numbers and types of forces, their degree of readiness and general location, and the nature of the facilities and assistance to be provided" were to be governed by special agreements to be concluded later and "subject to ratification by the signatory states in accordance with their respective constitutional processes."

The General Assembly. Though the General Assembly is far less important than the Security Council as an organ for the maintenance of peace and security, it nevertheless has certain rather important functions under the Charter.[25] Under Articles 10 and 11, the Assembly is free to discuss any questions or any matters within the scope of the Charter or relating to the powers and functions of the various organs under the Charter, and, more specifically, to "discuss any questions relating to the maintenance of international peace and security brought before it by any Member of the United Nations, or by the Security Council." The Assembly is also free to make recommendations relative to these matters either to the states concerned or to the Security Council. In cases, however, where the Security Council is "exercising" the functions assigned to it by the Charter with respect to a given dispute, the Assembly can make no recommendations unless it is asked to do so by the Council.

The problem of domestic jurisdiction is involved in the powers and functions of both the Security Council and the General Assembly. According to Article 2, paragraph 7, "Nothing contained in the present Charter

[24] Art. 2 of the Charter of the United Nations.

[25] It should be noted, however, that because of the unanimity rule regarding the "big five" in the Council, the General Assembly has assumed a greater importance in the determination of policy than its position under the Charter would indicate. See summary at the end of this chapter.

shall authorize the United Nations to intervene in matters which are essentially within the domestic jurisdiction of any state or shall require the Members to submit such matters to the settlement under the present Charter; but this principle shall not prejudice the application of enforcement measures under Chapter VII." [26]

The Economic and Social Council. With a view to the creation of stability and well-being, so necessary for peaceful international relations, the United Nations shall promote:

(*a*) higher standards of living, full employment, and conditions of economic and social progress and development;

(*b*) solutions of international economic, social, health, and related problems; and international cultural and educational cooperation; and

(*c*) universal respect for, and observance of, human rights and fundamental freedoms for all without distinction as to race, sex, language, or religion.[27]

In pursuance of these objectives the Economic and Social Council was established as one of the six principal organs of the United Nations. It was believed that the peace of the world could best be made secure through an agency of preventive measures, calculated to reduce the strains and stresses in international relations that so often in the past have led to war. The Economic and Social Council was designed as an instrument to achieve these ends, and its functions are described in Article 62 of the Charter as follows:

(1) The Economic and Social Council may make or initiate studies and reports with respect to international economic, social, cultural, educational, health, and related matters and may make recommendations with respect to any such matters to the General Assembly, to the Members of the United Nations, and to the specialized agencies concerned.

(2) It may make recommendations for the purpose of promoting respect for, and observance of, human rights and fundamental freedoms for all.

(3) It may prepare draft conventions for submission to the General Assembly, with respect to matters falling within its competence.

(4) It may call, in accordance with the rules prescribed by the United Nations, international conferences on matters falling within its competence.

In addition to these functions it is the task of the Economic and Social Council to coordinate the activities of existing international unions and, if desirable, bring them under the aegis of the United Nations.[28] Each

---

[26] Chap. VII of the Charter has to do with the removal of threats to the peace and the suppression of breaches of the peace.

[27] Art. 55 of the Charter.

[28] It should be noted that a large part of the work of the Economic and Social Council is carried out through a multiplicity of commissions, such as the Commissions on Human Rights, Social Questions, Economics and Employment, Transport and Communication, and Narcotic Drugs, to mention only a few. The ECOSOC also serves

of the 18 members of the Economic and Social Council has one vote, and decisions arrived at by a majority of the members present and voting.[29]

The Trusteeship Council. It is provided in Article 75 of the Charter that the United Nations shall establish under its authority an international trusteeship system for the administration and supervision of such territories as may be designated through subsequent individual agreements. Its main objectives are (1) to further international peace and security; (2) to promote the political, economic, social, and educational advancement of the inhabitants of the trust territories, and their progressive development toward self-government; (3) to encourage respect for human rights and for fundamental freedoms for all without distinction as to race, sex, language, or religion, and to encourage recognition of the interdependence of the peoples of the world; and (4) to ensure equal treatment in social, economic, and commercial matters for all members of the United Nations and their nationals.[30]

The composition of the Trusteeship Council is very different from that of the Mandates Commission under the League of Nations. In the latter case the members were not representatives of governments, and a majority not even nationals of the mandatory states. The Trusteeship Council is made up of states which are members of the United Nations and each has one vote.[31] It is provided, however, that the total number of representatives in the Trusteeship Council must be large enough to be equally divided between those members of the United Nations which administer trust territories and those which do not.[32]

The United Nations Charter distinguishes between ordinary trust territories and the so-called strategic areas. With respect to the latter, the strategic requirements of defense make it necessary that they should be under the supervision of the Security Council. The ultimate responsibility for the trusteeship system, as far as nonstrategic areas are concerned, however, rests with the General Assembly. The decisions of the Trusteeship Council are made by a majority of its members present and voting.

The Secretariat. The chief administrative officer of the United Nations is the Secretary-General, who is appointed by the General Assembly upon

---

in a consultative and coordinating capacity with reference to a large number of specialized agencies, among which we may mention the United Nations Educational, Scientific, and Cultural Organization (UNESCO), the Food and Agricultural Organization (FAO), the International Monetary Fund (Fund), the International Bank for Reconstruction and Development (Bank), the International Civil Aviation Organization (ICAO), the International Labor Organization (ILO), the World Health Organization (WHO), and the International Telecommunication Union (ITU).

[29] Art. 67. [30] Art. 76.
[31] Art. 89. [32] Art. 86.

the recommendation of the Security Council for a period of five years. The Secretary-General may bring to the attention of the Security Council any matter which in his opinion may threaten the maintenance of international peace and security, and must make an annual report to the General Assembly on the work of the Organization. The Secretary-General and other members of the Secretariat must in the performance of their duties refrain from any action which might reflect on their position as international officials responsible only to the Organization.[33] It is likewise incumbent upon each member of the United Nations to respect the international character of the Secretary-General and the staff and not seek to influence them in the discharge of their responsibilities. The entire staff of the Secretariat is appointed by the Secretary-General under regulations established by the General Assembly, and due regard is given to the importance of recruiting the staff on as wide a geographical basis as possible.[34]

The International Court of Justice. Based largely upon the Statute of the Permanent Court of International Justice, but made an integral part of the United Nations Organization, is the "World Court," known officially as the International Court of Justice. This institution, like its predecessor, has its seat in The Hague. It is composed of 15 justices, all from different countries, who are elected for a term of nine years by concurrent action of the General Assembly and the Security Council.

The jurisdiction of the Court comprises all cases which the parties refer to it and all matters specially provided for in the Charter of the United Nations or in treaties and conventions in force. But as provided in Article 34, paragraph 1, of the Statute, "only states may be parties in cases before the Court."

The states which are parties to the Statute may at any time make declarations to the effect that

they recognize as compulsory *ipso facto* and without special agreement, in relation to any other state accepting the same obligation, the jurisdiction of the Court in all legal disputes concerning:

a. the interpretation of a treaty;

b. any question of international law;

c. the existence of any fact which, if established, would constitute a breach of an international obligation;

d. the nature or extent of the reparation to be made for the breach of an international obligation.[35]

[33] Art. 100.

[34] Art. 101.

[35] Art. 36, par. 2, of the Statute. The following states, at the time of this writing, are accepting compulsory jurisdiction of the International Court of Justice: Australia, Belgium, Bolivia, Brazil, Canada, China, Colombia, Denmark, Dominican Republic,

The Statute also provides that the International Court of Justice shall have competence in cases where treaties and conventions still in force provide for reference to a tribunal instituted by the League of Nations or to the Permanent Court of International Justice. It should also be noted that considerable progress is being made toward the extension of the Court's jurisdiction by specific provisions in a number of international instruments. In the American Treaty on Pacific Settlement, signed by the 21 American republics at Bogota, April 30, 1948, for example, "the High Contracting Parties declare that they recognize, in relation to any other American State, the jurisdiction of the Court as compulsory *ipso facto*, without the necessity of any special agreement so long as the present Treaty is in force, in all disputes of a juridical nature" [36] concerning the four categories enumerated in Article 36, paragraph 2, of the Statute of the International Court of Justice. Significant provisions concerning resort to the Court were also included in a series of Economic Cooperation Agreements concluded in June and July of 1948 between the United States and a number of European countries.[37]

The International Court of Justice is open to states that are not parties to the Statute, upon conditions which are laid down by the Security Council, subject to special provisions of treaties in force.[38] But in no case may the parties be placed in a position of inequality before the Court.[39] The conditions by which such a state may gain access to the Court were laid down by the Security Council in a resolution of October 15, 1946. The resolution runs in part as follows: [40]

(1) The International Court of Justice shall be open to a State which is not

---

El Salvador, France, Guatemala, Haiti, Honduras, India, Israel, Liberia, Liechtenstein, Luxembourg, Mexico, Netherlands, New Zealand, Nicaragua, Norway, Pakistan, Panama, Paraguay, Phillippines, Sweden, Switzerland, Thailand, Turkey, Union of South Africa, United Kingdom, United States of America, and Uruguay. Of these 36 states, most have limited the commitment regarding compulsory jurisdiction to a period of five years, and many (especially the larger states) have stipulated certain very significant qualifications. It is interesting also to note that not a single state within the Soviet world has seen fit to accept compulsory jurisdiction of the International Court of Justice under any conditions.

[36] Art. XXXI of the Treaty.

[37] Manley O. Hudson, "The Twenty-seventh Year of the World Court," *American Journal of International Law*, vol. 43 (1949), p. 19.

[38] All members of the United Nations are *ipso facto* parties to the Statute of the International Court of Justice (Art. 93 of the Charter). This follows from the fact that the Statute of the Court is an integral part of the Charter of the United Nations. It will be remembered, by way of contrast, that a state who became a party to the Covenant of the League of Nations did not thereby also become a party to the Statute of the Permanent Court of International Justice, as the Covenant and the Statute in those days were quite separate instruments.

[39] Art. 35 of the Statute.

[40] *ICJ Yearbook 1949–50*, pp. 35–36.

a party to the Statute of the International Court of Justice, upon the following conditions, namely, that such State shall previously have deposited with the Registrar of the Court a declaration by which it accepts the jurisdiction of the Court, in accordance with the Charter of the United Nations and with the terms and subject to the conditions of the Statute and Rules of the Court, and undertakes to comply in good faith with the decision or decisions of the Court and to accept all the obligations of a Member of the United Nations under Article 94 of the Charter.

(2) Such declaration may be either particular or general. A particular declaration is one accepting the jurisdiction of the Court in respect only of a particular dispute or disputes which have already arisen. A general declaration is one accepting the jurisdiction generally in respect to all disputes or of a particular class or classes of disputes which have already arisen, or which may arise in the future.

A State, in making such a general declaration, may, in accordance with Article 36, paragraph 2, of the Statute recognize as compulsory, *ipso facto*, and without special agreement, the jurisdiction of the Court, provided, however, that such acceptance may not, without explicit agreement, be relied upon vis-a-vis States parties to the Statute, which have made the declaration in conformity with Article 36, paragraph 2, of the Statute of the International Court of Justice.

The original declarations made under the terms of this resolution are to be kept in the custody of the Registrar of the Court, and certified true copies are transmitted to the states parties to the Statute of the International Court of Justice. Copies are also transmitted to states which have deposited declarations in conformity with the resolution, and to the Secretary-General of the United Nations. All questions as to the validity or the effect of a declaration made under the terms of the resolution shall be decided by the Court, but the Security Council reserves the right to rescind or amend it.

All questions before the International Court of Justice are decided by a majority of the judges present, and in the event of a tie the President of the Court or the judge who acts in his place casts the deciding vote.[41] The decisions of the Court have no binding force except between the parties in each individual case, but every judgment must contain the reasons upon which it is based. The judgment of the Court is final and without appeal, but in the event of dispute as to its meaning and scope the Court will provide elucidation at the request of any party.[42] An application for revision of a judgment may be made only as a result of the discovery of new material facts which have bearing on the case, and which were unknown to both the Court and the party in question when the judgment

[41] Art. 55 of the Statute.
[42] Art. 60 of the Statute.

was given, provided such ignorance was not due to negligence.[43] No application for revision may be made, however, after a lapse of ten years from the date of the judgment.

The International Court of Justice may give an advisory opinion on any legal question submitted in accordance with the Charter of the United Nations. Questions in regard to which advisory opinions are asked must be laid before the Court by means of a written request containing an exact statement of the question itself accompanied by all documents likely to throw light upon the matter. It is specifically provided in Article 96 of the Charter that the General Assembly or the Security Council may request the International Court of Justice to give an advisory opinion on any legal question. And it is further provided in paragraph 2 of the same article that other organs of the United Nations and specialized agencies may also request advisory opinions of the Court with regard to legal questions arising within the scope of their activities, provided they are authorized to do so by the General Assembly.

In December, 1946, the United Nations Assembly recommended that member states grant diplomatic privileges and immunities to the judges and the Registrar of the Court; furthermore, that agents and counsel of parties before the Court and assessors, witnesses, and experts should be granted such privileges and immunities as might be necessary for the independent exercise of their functions. Accordingly, in June of 1950, the International Court of Justice issued *laissez-passer* to the judges and to the Registrar and other officials of the Court.

The Legal Status of the United Nations. On December 3, 1948, the General Assembly of the United Nations adopted a resolution which was communicated to the Registry of the International Court of Justice at The Hague. This action was prompted by a series of tragic events which had befallen agents of the United Nations engaged in the performance of their duties.[44] The resolution embodied two specific questions regarding which an advisory opinion was asked and ran, in part, as follows:

The General Assembly

Decides to submit the following legal questions to the International Court of Justice for an advisory opinion:

I. In the event an agent of the United Nations in the performance of his duties suffering injury in circumstances involving the responsibility of a State, has the United Nations, as an Organization, the capacity to bring an international claim against the responsible *de jure* or *de facto* government with a view

[43] Art. 61, par. 1, of the Statute.
[44] This action of the Assembly was inspired by the assassination of Count Folke Bernadotte and of others serving the United Nations in Palestine. See *Everyman's United Nations* (1952), p. 271.

to obtaining the reparation due in respect to the damage caused (*a*) to the United Nations, (*b*) to the victim or the person entitled through him?

II. In the event of an affirmative reply on point I (*b*), how is action by the United Nations to be reconciled with such rights as may be possessed by the State of which the victim is a national?

The Court's opinion, of which the English version is authoritative, was delivered on April 11, 1949. The question of whether or not the United Nations possessed "international personality" in the sense of being "an entity capable of availing itself of obligations incumbent upon its Members" was explored by the Court. As this question is "not settled by the actual terms of the Charter," the Court undertook to "consider what characteristics it was intended thereby to give to the Organization" as follows:

The subjects of law in any legal system are not necessarily identical in their nature or in the extent of their rights, and their nature depends upon the needs of the community. Throughout its history. the development of international law has been influenced by the requirements of international life, and the progressive increase in the collective activities of States has already given rise to instances of action upon the international plane of certain entities which are not States.

The Court then endeavored to assay the nature of the Organization in terms of the United Nations Charter. One of the aspects relied upon was its capacity to conclude agreements with the member states, which shows that it "occupies a position in certain respects in detachment from its Members." Reference was also made to the convention of 1946 on the Privileges and Immunities of the United Nations, which could operate only "upon the international plane and as between parties possessing international personality." The main provisions of this Convention [45] are as follows:

The United Nations shall possess juridical personality;

Its property and assets shall enjoy immunity from legal process except when that immunity is waived;

The premises and the archives of the United Nations shall be inviolable and its property and assets shall be free from all direct taxes and customs duties;

In regard to its official communications, the United Nations shall enjoy treatment in the territory of each Member state which is no less favorable than that accorded by the government of that Member to any other government;

The representatives of Members, officials of the United Nations, and experts on missions of the United Nations shall enjoy such privileges and immunities as are necessary for the independent exercise of their functions; and

The United Nations may issue United Nations *laissez-passer* to its officials

[45] For full text of this Convention, see *Official Records of the First Part of the First Session of the General Assembly* (Jan. 10–Feb. 14, 1946), pp. 644–650.

which shall be recognized and accepted as valid travel documents by the Member states.

The International Court of Justice, therefore, concluded that the United Nations is an international person—but not a state and still less a "super-state"—and that it is a subject of international law capable of possessing rights and duties and having the "capacity to maintain its rights by bringing international claims." Thus in reply to question 1 the Court said: "The United Nations as an Organization has the capacity to bring an international claim against the responsible *de jure* or *de facto* government with a view to obtaining the reparation due in respect of the damage caused to the United Nations." With respect to question 2, the Court answered in part as follows: "When the United Nations as an Organization is bringing a claim for reparation for damage caused to its agent, it can only do so by basing its claim upon a breach of obligations due to itself."

The importance of the advisory opinion related above, from the point of view of legal theory, lies chiefly in the fact that no longer can international personality be confined to states. Though this doctrine had been tacitly recognized since the days of the League of Nations, its legality had not previously been authoritatively established. We shall return to this question again in a later chapter.

CONCLUDING OBSERVATIONS

To the panoramic survey presented in this chapter a few concluding observations may be added in order to make clear the significance of international institutions in a modern society of states. In this connection it is important to remember our earlier distinction between the terms *society* and *community*. International organization is ineffectual in many respects, not only because its development is inadequate to the needs, but also because a real sense of community among nations is, as yet, a feeble emotion, especially when pitted against the forces of nationalism. Yet, the reality of the existence of such a community, however primitive, is difficult to deny, and as we have seen in an earlier chapter, the concept of a *civitas gentium* is of great antiquity.

An outstanding result of modern technical development is not only greater interdependence of nations, but new methods of diplomacy. Less than a century ago, it was the common practice of states to conduct their external affairs almost exclusively through the agency of legation and on a bilateral basis. Today, however, a variety of international institutions have become useful instrumentalities for the conduct of foreign relations.

This new method is largely the result of a shrinking world where the national interest of individual states cannot, in many cases, be separated from the common welfare of a larger community. This development, which began about the middle of the nineteenth century, has led to the establishment of many institutions which, "while they cannot yet be regarded as giving a 'constitution' to the international society, may not unfairly be described as a beginning of its constitutional law." [46]

It should be noted, however, that an international organization such as the United Nations is in no manner a supragovernment in relation to its members. Rather it is an association of states which exist primarily for the purpose of facilitating peaceful relations among the members. Thus, it is "probably not so much the beginnings of an international 'government,' though the term is often convenient, as a substitute for one." [47]

If in contemporary international organization we seek those elements which in municipal law are classified according to functions as the legislature, the executive, and the judiciary, we shall find only forms without the substance of power. This is so because in the international society there is no central authority to furnish such a substance. Even though we may speak of certain multilateral treaties as lawmaking in character, there is no international legislature with the authority to enact laws which are binding upon a community of nations. Nevertheless, hundreds of treaties classified as legislative in nature do exist and are constantly being enacted through the medium of conferences and congresses. This process was, of course, greatly stimulated by the establishment of the League of Nations, and more recently through the operations of the United Nations Organization. Article 24 of the Charter provides that the Security Council shall act on behalf of the member states in order to maintain international peace and security; while according to Article 25: "The members of the United Nations agree to accept and carry out the decisions of the Security Council in accordance with the present Charter." Clearly, these two articles of the Charter confer upon the Security Council of the United Nations far greater powers than have ever before been given to an international body. According to Brierly: "They constitute the most far-reaching of the innovations which the Charter has introduced into international organization." [48]

Neither is there in the international society a central organ of law enforcement. There is no executive in the municipal sense of that term. The two situations, however, are really not analogous, as an international police action suggests the application of overwhelming force by the community against a relatively weak lawbreaker. But, as we have seen, the

[46] Brierly, *op. cit.*, p. 86.
[47] *Ibid.*   [48] *Ibid.*, p. 102.

sense of international community is feeble, and the lawbreaker may indeed command preponderant force. In spite of this it would be incorrect to say that international law is not law in the true meaning of that term, nor is there totally lacking the means by which its observance may be secured. States not only recognize the rules of the law of nations as binding in innumerable treaties and conventions, but constantly emphasize the existence of such a law. And now, under the Charter of the United Nations, the greater part of mankind is pledged "to establish conditions under which justice and respect for obligations arising from treaties and other sources of international law can be maintained." [49]

Apart from a rudimentary apparatus of international legislation and administration there are, as we have seen, special institutions designed for the arbitration and adjudication of disputes between nations. Among these are the Permanent Court of Arbitration and the International Court of Justice. In the Charter the latter is described as "the principal judicial organ of the United Nations." [50] Among the functions of the Court, as defined in Article 38 of the Statute, is that of deciding "in accordance with international law such disputes as are submitted to it." It is futher provided that "in the event of a dispute as to whether the Court has jurisdiction, the matter shall be settled by the decision of the Court." [51] The distinction which is frequently drawn between legal and political questions, or justiciable and nonjusticiable disputes, is really quite tenuous and lacks any objective criterion. It may be said, therefore, that the jurisdiction of the Court in any case is determined by the willingness of the parties to submit the dispute for adjudication rather than by the substantive nature of the cause.

In the interstate system which in the language of the Charter of the United Nations is "based on the sovereign equality of all its members," a great many topics suitable for international government tend to be confined to the domestic jurisdiction of states. The League of Nations and the United Nations are nevertheless notable attempts to provide a permanent institutional framework for an international society. As of this moment, however, it is not possible to maintain in all situations that an alternative to the rule of force is to be found in existing international institutions.

In spite of the considerable power vested in the Security Council by the Charter of the United Nations, its effectiveness as an instrument of collective action for the solution of international problems has to a large extent been neutralized through lack of agreement among the great

[49] Preamble to the Charter of the United Nations.
[50] Art. 1 of the Statute of the International Court of Justice.
[51] Art. 36 (6) of the Statute.

powers. But because of the relative impotence of the Security Council, the General Assembly of the United Nations has gradually assumed a position of greater importance in the formulation of policy than had been at first anticipated. One of the problems which has occupied the attention of the General Assembly from the beginning is the regulation of armaments and, in this connection, international control of atomic energy. Accordingly, in its first session of 1946 an Atomic Energy Commission was established by the Assembly.[52] Aside from its concern with the control of atomic energy, the Assembly has also devoted much time to the formulation of principles for the control of general armament. While the prerogatives of the Security Council in this field could not be disregarded, the Assembly has nevertheless been quite effective both in securing the acceptance of certain basic principles and in exerting a stimulating influence on the Security Council.[53]

In this connection we might mention a number of resolutions which at various times have been passed by the Assembly. In 1947 a resolution was adopted by the General Assembly condemning all forms of propaganda designed or likely to provoke or encourage violation of the peace.[54] In 1948 the Assembly made an appeal to the great powers to proceed to a final settlement of the war and to create a world order under law dedicated to peace, security, and general well-being.[55] In 1949 a resolution entitled "Essentials of Peace" was adopted by the General Assembly, setting forth the basic principles required to ensure a lasting peace.[56] Other resolutions along this line are the "Duties of States in the Event of the Outbreak of Hostilities," [57] and the "Peace through Deeds" resolution.[58] But most illustrative of the growing influence of the Assembly is the so-called "Uniting for Peace" resolution [59] of 1950, which

Resolves that if the Security Council, because of lack of unanimity of the permanent members, fails to exercise its primary responsibility for the maintenance of international peace and security in any case where there appears to be a threat to the peace, breach of the peace, or act of aggression, the General Assembly shall consider the matter immediately with a view of making appro-

[52] Resolutions Adopted by the General Assembly during the First Session from January 10 to February 14, 1946, United Nations Document A/64 (July 1, 1946), p. 9.

[53] See Leland M. Goodrich, "Development of the General Assembly," *International Conciliation*, no. 471 (May, 1951), p. 255.

[54] *Official Records of the Second Session of the General Assembly* (Sept. 16–Nov. 29, 1947), Resolutions, p. 14.

[55] *Official Records of the Third Session . . . Part I . . .* Resolutions, p. 15.

[56] *Official Records of the Fourth Session . . .* Resolutions, p. 13.

[57] *Official Records of the Fifth Session . . .* Resolutions, pp. 12–13.

[58] *Ibid.*, pp. 13–14.

[59] *Ibid.*, pp. 10–12.

priate recommendations to Members for collective measures, including in the case of the breach of the peace or act of aggression the use of armed force when necessary, to maintain or restore international peace and security. If not in session at the time, the General Assembly may meet in emergency special session within twenty-four hours of the request therefor. Such emergency special session shall be called if requested by the Security Council on the vote of any seven members, or by a majority of the Members of the United Nations.

It may be argued, therefore, that while the Charter of the United Nations gives a wide range of discretionary powers to the Security Council, it also recognizes the existence of a legal order among nations, and the General Assembly has become more and more responsible for the development of that order. Thus, the provision in the Charter which empowers the General Assembly of the United Nations to initiate studies and make recommendations "encouraging the progressive development of international law and its codification," is taking on a new significance. With the growing importance of the Assembly, that of the Security Council will be correspondingly reduced. But since the Security Council is the chief instrumentality through which the great powers exercise a preponderant influence within the United Nations, a reduction in the powers of the Council must inevitably detract from the importance of the "big five" in the Organization. While the General Assembly is far from being a world legislature, it is nevertheless performing quasi-legislative functions for which it has taken primary responsibility.

CHAPTER 5

The Nature and Origins
of International Law

A DEFINITION OF THE LAW OF NATIONS
AND ITS CLASSICAL ORIGINS

The law of nations, or international law, has been variously defined by the publicists.[1] Lack of uniformity in this respect is not surprising when we consider the wide discrepancy which exists in the emphasis of sources from which the law is derived.[2] Generally speaking, it might be said that *public international law is that body of customs, rules, and principles which are recognized as binding upon all states and other international persons in their mutual relations.* As a branch of jurisprudence it has been distinguished from private international law, or conflict of laws, which concerns the right of individuals who are involved in varying systems of

[1] According to Sir Henry Maine: "The Law of Nations is a complex system, composed of various ingredients. It consists of general principles of right and justice, equally suited to the conduct of individuals in a state of natural equity, and to the relations and conduct of nations, of a collection of usages, customs and opinions, the growth of civilization and commerce, and a code of positive law"—*International Law* (1883), p. 33.

According to William E. Hall: "International law consists in certain rules of conduct which modern civilised states regard as being binding on them in their relations with one another with a force comparable in nature and degree to that binding the conscientious person to obey the laws of his country, and which they also regard as being enforceable by appropriate means in case of infringement"—*International Law* (1924), p. 1.

According to J. L. Brierly: "The Law of Nations, or International Law, may be defined as the body of rules and principles of action which are binding upon civilized states in their relations with one another"—*Law of Nations* (1949), p. 1.

According to Emmerich de Vattel: "The Law of Nations is the science of the rights which exist between Nations or States, and of the obligations corresponding to these rights"—*Le Droit des gens* (1758), Fenwick's translation (1916), pp. 3, 4.

[2] Among the earlier writers greater weight was given to doctrines of natural law, whereas in more recent literature custom and treaties are regarded as the main sources of international law.

municipal law. Such involvement may be illustrated by conflicts and disputes which arise in connection with domicile, marriage, divorce, wills, validity of contracts, and other matters where states as such are not directly involved. In the *Serbian Loans Case* [3] of 1929, the Permanent Court of International Justice drew a less clear distinction by saying that the rules of private international law "may be common to several States and may even be established by international conventions or customs, and in the latter case may possess the character of true international law governing the relations between States. But apart from this, it has to be considered that these rules form part of municipal law."

Dualists versus Monists. There are two schools of legal theory—dualist and monist—concerning the distinction between the law of nations and municipal law. According to the dualists, international law and municipal law may be differentiated as follows: For its sources, international law looks to custom and treaties evolved in a society of states, while the main sources of municipal law are found in custom and legislation grown up and enacted by the lawmaking authority within the state's jurisdiction. Whereas the law of nations regulates the relations between member states in an international society, municipal law concerns individual citizens in their relations both to each other and to the state. In international law there is no central executive authority to compel observance of its norms, but in municipal law individual citizens are subjected by the power of the state. For these reasons, according to the dualist theory, international law can never operate as the law of the land save through municipal custom or statutory enactment. There can be no such thing, for example, as a self-executing treaty; enabling legislation would be required in every case in order to make the provisions of an international agreement operative upon persons and corporations within the state.

The monistic theorists,[4] on the other hand, deny that any essential difference exists as to the subjects of international and municipal law. They contend that in both instances it is individual persons who in the final analysis are regulated by the law. "Like all law," says Hans Kelsen, "international law is a regulation of human conduct. . . . it is men to whom international law entrusts the responsibilities for order." [5] Monistic doctrine furthermore asserts that international law is not without commanding authority, and that, far from being essentially different from

[3] Ser. A, nos. 20/21, p. 41; Manley O. Hudson, *World Court Reports*, vol. II, p. 371.
[4] See the works of such publicists as Bourquin, Kelsen, Kunz, Scelle, Verdross, and Wright.
[5] Hans Kelsen, "Théorie générale du droit international public," *Académie de droit internatonal, Recueil des cours*, vol. 42 (1932), pp. 142 ff. Translated by Manley O. Hudson in *Cases and Other Materials on International Law* (1936), p. 13. See also Kelsen's *Allgemeine Staatslehre* (1925), pp. 121–124.

municipal law, it must be regarded as a part of the same juristic conception.[6]

The Doctrine of Incorporation. The doctrine that international law is to be regarded as part of the law of the land has had a long and continuous support in Anglo-American jurisprudence.[7] In the famous case of *West Rand Central Gold Mining Co. v. The King*[8] Lord Alverstone agreed with the proposition laid down by Lord Robert Cecil that "International Law is part of the law of England." He said:

It is quite true that whatever has received the common consent of civilised nations must have received the assent of our country, and that to which we have assented along with other nations in general may properly be called International Law, and as such will be acknowledged and applied by our municipal tribunals when legitimate occasion arises for those tribunals to decide questions to which doctrines of International Law may be relevant.

Five years earlier, in the United States, the same doctrine was given forceful expression by Justice Gray when he said: "International law is part of our law, and must be ascertained and administered by the courts of justice of appropriate jurisdiction, as often as questions of right depending upon it are duly presented for their determination."[9] Likewise in *Hilton v. Guyot*[10] the Supreme Court of the United States held that "international law, in its widest and most comprehensive sense . . . is part of our law, and must be ascertained and administered by the courts of justice as often as such questions are presented in litigation between man and man, duly submitted to their determination. . . ."

But according to Judge Atkin, in *Commercial Estates Co. v. Board of Trade*,[11] "International law as such can confer no rights cognizable in the municipal courts. It is only in so far as the rules of international law are recognized as included in the rules of the municipal law that they are allowed in the municipal courts to give rise to rights or obligations."[12]

The so-called "doctrine of incorporation,"[13] which in the eighteenth

[6] Oppenheim-Lauterpacht, *International Law* (1947), vol. I, pp. 36–37.
[7] "It is an ancient doctrine of the Anglo-American common law that the law of nations is incorporated in and in some sense forms part of the national law"—Edwin D. Dickinson, "Changing Concepts and the Doctrine of Incorporation," *American Journal of International Law*, vol. 26 (1932), pp. 239–259.
[8] [1905] K.B. 391.
[9] United States Supreme Court, 1900. *Paquete Habana and The Lola*, 175 U.S. 677.
[10] 159 U.S. 113 (1895).   [11] [1925] 1 K.B. 271, 295.
[12] Cf. Pitman B. Potter, "Relative Authority of International Law and National Law in the United States," *American Journal of International Law*, vol. 19 (1925), p. 315; Quincy Wright, "International Law in Its Relation to Constitutional Law," *ibid.*, vol. 17 (1923), p. 234.
[13] This refers to the notion that international law was an integral part of municipal law.

century had been so generally accepted, underwent a marked change in the nineteenth century under the impact of positivism. The reason was that in the eighteenth century juridical concepts of the law of nations were dominated by natural law, while in the nineteenth the norms of this branch of jurisprudence came to be regarded more and more as having their foundations in usage sanctioned by consent.[14]

Indeed, in its modern version, the doctrine is essentially like the modern Anglo-American doctrine underlying the so-called conflict of laws or private international law. It means simply that the national law governing matters of international concern is to be derived, in the absence of a controlling statute, executive decision, or judicial precedent, from such relevant principles of the law of nations as can be shown to have received the nation's implied or express assent.[15]

Though it is true that the doctrine of incorporation was first formulated in Anglo-American countries, it is at the present time by no means confined to England and the United States. Courts in France, Belgium, and Switzerland have for a long time taken the same position, and in the years following the First World War a number of countries wrote the doctrine of incorporation into their constitutions. Article 4 of the Weimar Constitution, for example, provided that "the universally recognized rules of international law are valid as binding constituent parts of German Federal Law."[16]

Treaties and Custom. As we have already indicated, the sources of the law of nations are found mainly in *treaties* and *custom*. As regards treaties, it is necessary to differentiate between those which are lawmaking in character and those which are not. A lawmaking treaty is a multilateral arrangement, or *traité-loi*, which has the effect of setting up certain legal norms for the conduct of states in their mutual intercourse. In contradistinction to the lawmaking treaty is the so-called *traité-contrat*, or contract treaty. This, as a rule, is a bilateral treaty dealing with problems which are of special interest to the participating powers, while a lawmaking treaty is of more universal interest and multilateral. As examples of lawmaking treaties we have the Declaration of Paris of 1856; the Hague conventions of 1899 and 1907; the Kellogg-Briand or Paris Peace Pact of 1928; the Geneva convention of 1929; and, most conspicuous of all, the Charter of the United Nations. We shall have occasion to explain these and other treaties more fully in another chapter.

Coming back to the second main source of international law, which is *custom*, we note that the various states in many of their mutual relations have adopted certain standard practices. In international law, as in

---

[14] Dickinson, *op. cit.*, p. 239.   [15] *Ibid.*, p. 260.
[16] Oppenheim-Lauterpacht, *op. cit.*, p. 41n.

other human affairs, things which are done in a certain way over a long period of time without successful challenge tend to become more or less fixed, and we have a general usage based on custom. A good example illustrating the force of custom as a basis for international law is the extraterritorial rights and privileges extended by all civilized states to foreign diplomats who are lawfully within their borders. It should be understood, however, that custom as a source of international law must not be confused with mere frequency or habit of conduct. "Custom is that line of conduct which the society has consented to regard as obligatory." [17]

In order for a state to be bound by international custom, it is not necessary that such a state should itself have been a party to the development of the custom. This is especially well illustrated in the cases of new states which, when recognized, become members of the international community and *ipso facto* subjects of the customary law of nations. If, however a state should, during the time in which a certain custom in international law is being formed, claim for itself the right not to adhere to the custom thus developed, but should, on the contrary, engage in a different practice, such a state could not be forced to comply with the customary law established by the other states. This principle may be illustrated by the fact that, though a large number of states have accepted the customary "marine league" as the measure of their territorial waters, other states have protested this custom over a long period of time and have maintained a greater distance for the measure of the so-called maritime belt. The states which refuse to agree to the "3-mile limit" cannot be forced to comply on the ground that this distance, which was the range of eighteenth-century cannon, is a custom which rests on a better foundation than the claim of a "4-mile limit" or some other distance.[18]

Comity of Nations. Custom in international law must not be confounded with *comitas gentium* or the comity of nations. Comity consists of certain rules of "politeness, convenience, and good will." [19] It is according to the practice of comity, for example, that diplomatic envoys are exempted from payment of customs duties. Comity is not a source of international law, but rules of comity may in time, and often do, become part of the law of nations. English and American courts have tended not to make a very clear distinction between comity and law; they have often used the term *international comity* where the term *international law* ought to have been applied. In *Russian Socialist Federated Soviet Republic v. Cibra-*

[17] John Westlake, *International Law* (1910), vol. I, p. 14.
[18] Frede Castberg, *Folkerett* (1948), p. 9. See also the *Anglo-Norwegian Fisheries Case.*
[19] Oppenheim-Lauterpacht, *op. cit.*, p. 32.

rio,[20] the Court said: "Comity may be defined as that reciprocal courtesy which one member of the family of nations owes to the others. . . . Rules of comity are a portion of the law that they [the courts] enforce."

Judicial Decisions. Another source of international law is the decisions of judicial tribunals. These would include municipal as well as international courts. Among the decisions and awards which have been of importance in this connection are those of the courts of arbitration, international commissions of inquiry, prize courts, mixed tribunals, the Court of Arbitration at The Hague, the Permanent Court of International Justice, and its successor the present International Court of Justice.

Judicial decisions and arbitral awards, though important as sources of the law of nations, should not be overestimated as such. In the Anglo-Saxon world a great deal of deference is shown to judicial opinions, some of which contain obiter dicta, and decisions are very often given a more extended application than they deserve.[21] It is the opinion of the author that too heavy reliance is often placed upon the study of cases, while not enough attention is given to the great and basic principles which have emerged through usage and custom. The forces of history, which have shaped the modern law of nations, have been largely neglected as a key to its development.

In view of what has been said so far, it might perhaps be concluded that the doctrine of incorporation, which in the eighteenth century was accepted without challenge, has lost some of its force under the impact of modern nationalism. Yet, the proposition that international law cannot operate as a part of municipal law without express legislation would seem to run contrary to the juristic practice of most nations. The practice is so general and the case law on this point so extensive as to warrant the conclusion that international law is indeed to be regarded as a part of the law of the land, and that this is a principle of positive law.

Roman Origins of International Law. Even though the present system of international law is generally regarded as having had its origin with the rise of the modern state in the sixteenth and seventeenth centuries, its earliest foundations are to be found in the ancient world. In this respect, the influence of Roman law is of special significance. It is a tribute to the legal genius of Rome that the primitive law of the city-state was capable of such expansion and refinement as the great world empire should in time require. A brief review, therefore, of certain juristic conceptions which were familiar to the Roman world, and in which the earliest rudiments of international law are found, might be helpful. In this

[20] 235 N.Y. 255, 139 N.E. 259 (1923).
[21] Amos S. Hershey, *The Essentials of International Public Law and Organization* (1927), pp. 26–27.

way we shall be able to appreciate the antiquity of ideas even in the relatively modern science of the law of nations.

The very phrase "law of nations" is itself derived from the Latin term *jus gentium*, of which it is a literal translation.[22] It became the fashion among writers on international law to employ the highly refined terminology of Roman law, not only because it offered the most precise juristic tool, but because Latin continued to be the language of learning both in Europe and America until the triumph of philosophic radicalism in the nineteenth century.[23]

The original *jus civile* was a crude and archaic system of law in early Rome—a system which, like the common law of England, failed to keep pace with the growth of empire. It provided no legal remedies in cases involving foreigners, in spite of the fact that many alien tribes had been subjected to Roman power. But by 242 B.C. a special magistrate known as *praetor peregrinus* was instituted, and under his direction judges were appointed to take care of any litigation in which one or both parties were foreigners. As a result of this procedure new and liberal rules evolved, while the archaic forms of *jus civile* were gradually abandoned. In time this new branch of the law, known as *jus gentium*, came to be generally applied, even in cases where only Roman citizens were involved, and is today regarded as the classic core of the Roman legal system.[24] A distinction, however, should be drawn between what might be called the "historical" and the "philosophical" *jus gentium*. While in a historical sense *jus gentium* is the result of a certain expansion—a liberal and progressive adaptation—of the municipal law of Rome, its philosophical justification was bound to produce enlargements of this conception. Here the influence of Greek philosophy should not be overlooked, particularly that of the Stoics, which found many followers among the Romans. It is in the Greek tradition that the idea of natural law first appears. Cicero did much to popularize Greek philosophy in his own country, with the

[22] Arthur Nussbaum, *A Concise History of The Law of Nations* (1947), pp. 18–19.
[23] Elie Halévy, in *La Formation du radicalisme philosophique*, describes the ideas associated with the English utilitarians in the early nineteenth century as "philosophic radicalism." See *The Growth of Philosophic Radicalism*, translated by Marry Morries (1928).
[24] See Nussbaum, *op. cit.*, pp. 16–19. It should be made clear, however, that, though *jus gentium* was later translated as "the law of nations," it was private rather than public law, and can in no sense be regarded as equivalent to what we now call "international law." It is also of interest to note that, though the term "law of nations" had its origin in the Latin phrase *jus gentium*, it was more recently derived from the French title of Vattel's famous work *Droit des gens* which was published in 1758. Likewise the term "international law," first used by Jeremy Bentham in 1780, is a translation of the phrase *juris inter gentes* used by Richard Zouche as part of the title of his famous manual, *Juris et judicii fecialis, sive juris inter gentes et quaestionum de eodem explicatio* (1650), *Classics of International Law.*

result that *jus naturale* became an important element in the Roman system of jurisprudence. Inasmuch as *jus gentium* was regarded by the Romans as consisting of very general principles of law and justice having a universal application, it was easily identified with *jus naturale,* and the two terms soon became synonymous in Roman law.

The Medieval Conception. During the Middle Ages the notion of natural law was further developed, and the Church was impelled to give it a place in the doctrinal system. In the writings of such men as St. Thomas Aquinas, the law of nature became identified with the law of God, and thus acquired an authority far superior to that of man-made ordinances. It is not strange, therefore, that in the later Middle Ages, when the modern nation-states began to take shape, a clash should develop between the protagonists of absolute sovereignty and the divine right of kings on the one side, and the defenders of a *civitas gentium* and a universal Church on the other side.

The medieval conception of natural law, though largely determined by its classical foundations, was nevertheless profoundly modified by the impact of Christian theology. It should also be remembered that the human mind is most susceptible to contemporary forces and for this reason tends to reflect the experience of its own time. It is not surprising, therefore, that the medieval philosopher, living in an age of almost imperceptible change, could pursue his search for eternal truth with a confidence which to modern man seems almost naïve. But for us as for them a rational universe seems to be a necessary postulate. The difference, therefore, between our thought and theirs "is mainly that we have different ways of regarding the world and human society." [25] In spite of the groundwork that was laid in ancient and medieval times, it was not until the latter part of the sixteenth century that the law of nations was considered worthy of special attention as a field of study. Though it is true that medieval authors had frequently been concerned with special topics which would fall within the general ambit of international law, much of what they wrote was closely bound up with theology and ethics. So profound was the influence of the medieval mind that it was not until the eighteenth century that international law was fully refined and separated from its theological admixture.

A BRIEF SURVEY OF CLASSICAL AUTHORS

Grotius, in his famous treatise *De jure belli ac pacis,* wrote:

The proof of the law of nations is similar to that of unwritten municipal law; it is found in unbroken custom and the testimony of those who are skilled in it.

[25] Brierly, *op. cit.,* p. 22.

The law of nations, in fact, as Dio Chrysostom well observes "is the creation of time and custom." And for the study of it the illustrious writers of history are of the greatest value to us.

Without wishing to exaggerate the importance of writers and publicists, it might be pointed out that they are, in the main, impartial in their judgments. "They are witnesses of the sentiments and usages of civilized nations, and the weight of their testimony increases every time their authority is invoked by statesmen, and every year that passes without the rules laid down in their works being impugned by the avowal of contrary principles." [26] In the *Paquete Habana and The Lola* case,[27] Justice Gray, in delivering the opinion of the United States Supreme Court, called attention to the fact that there was "no treaty, and no controlling executive or legislative act or judicial decision," and that, therefore, recourse must be had "to the works of jurists and commentators, who by years of labor, research and experience, have made themselves peculiarly well acquainted with the subjects of which they treat. Such works are resorted to by judicial tribunals, not for the speculations of their authors concerning what the law ought to be, but for trustworthy evidence of what the law really is." [28] The writers of texts in the field of international law usually consider international relations from the broad point of view, and some have taken into consideration the main streams of history as well as the juridical and ethical elements of the problem. Though pure theory in the field of international law cannot be considered as a valid source in and of itself, it is nevertheless true that when such theoretical principles are adopted by a large number of states in their intercourse with one another, the theory will through this process have become a substantive part of the law of nations. "The work of writers may continue to play a part in proportion to its intrinsic scientific value, its impartiality and its determination to scrutinize critically the practice of states by reference to legal principle." [29]

The meaning and scope of international law is a matter of dispute among the authorities. Opinion is divided, in the main, between two schools of thought: the rationalistic or philosophical school on the one hand, and the positivist or historical school on the other. The first group is largely concerned with rules and principles which *ought* to be observed in international relations, while the positivists are interested only in those norms and regulations which *are* generally observed and which are founded on lawmaking treaties and other positive agreements entered into by the various states.

[26] Quoted by Justice Gray in the *Paquete Habana and The Lola* case.
[27] 175 U.S. 677 (1900).   [28] *Ibid.*
[29] Oppenheim-Lauterpacht, *op. cit.*, p. 32.

Many of the early writers on international law were especially concerned with the law as it ought to be. Their main purpose was to search out and define certain axiomatic truths, which were believed to repose in a universal law of nature. The fact that Roman law was regarded as a *ratio scripta* throughout most of Europe at the beginning of modern times was to have a profound effect upon the development of international law. Furthermore, the close connection which existed between Roman law and the law of the Church tended to reinforce the authority of the former. Thus it is not surprising that the early writers on international law, most of whom were trained not only in Roman law but in canon law as well, should find in both these a certain guide to the basic principles of the law of nations.

Franciscus de Victoria (1480–1546). In the second quarter of the sixteenth century Franciscus de Victoria [30] was professor of theology at the famous University of Salamanca. His lectures, which were published posthumously, contained two series which are of special interest to students of international law. One is called *Relectiones de indis* and the other is titled *De jure belli hispanorum in barbaros*. In these works, Victoria inquired into the just causes of making war, and examined at length the foundations and extent of Spanish rights and authority as a result of discovery and conquest of vast dominions beyond the seas. He was especially concerned with the relations between the Spaniards and Indians. His work is remarkable for its fearless defense of the rights of the Indians and for its humanitarian views on war. In a passage from the third section of his lecture *On the Indians* Victoria tells us that "there are many things . . . which issue from the law of nations, which, because it has a sufficient derivation from natural law, is clearly capable of conferring rights and creating obligations." Thus, with Victoria the real source of the law of nations is to be found in natural law.

It appears that Victoria, resting his arguments upon the tenets of natural law, was the first to advocate freedom of the seas.[31] He is also given credit as the originator of the terms "offensive" and "defensive" warfare, which in later times have proved so troublesome to both statesmen and scholars. He did not regard offensive war as unjust, however, as this would depend upon the nature of its cause.[32] This famous theologian of

---

[30] An alternative and equally correct spelling of the name is Vitoria.

[31] In this connection another Spanish writer famous in the early literature of international law, Ferdinand Vasquez (1509–1566) who published his *Illustrum controversarium* in three books in 1564, should be mentioned. He challenged the right of the Italian city-states to close the Adriatic and Ligurian Seas to foreign commerce and presented some of the first great arguments in favor of the freedom of the seas.

[32] Nussbaum, *op. cit.*, pp. 62–63. The differentiation between just and unjust wars is of Roman origin, and in each case it was determined by the justice or injustice of the

Salamanca, who was of a conservative disposition and a staunch defender of monarchy by divine right, nonetheless displayed a remarkable humaneness in an age of barbarism, and it is perhaps safe to say that among authorities on international law in the sixteenth century, Victoria was the most distinguished.

The importance of this Spanish scholastic is evidenced by the following resolution passed by the Seventh International Conference of American States at Montevideo on December 23, 1933:

> The Seventh International Conference of American States, *Resolves*, to recommend that a bust of the Spanish Theologian, Francisco de Victoria, be placed in the Headquarters of the Pan American Union, in Washington, as a tribute to the professor of Salamanca who, in the sixteenth century, established the foundations of modern international law.

Francisco Suarez (1548–1617). Another among the more important of the early Spanish writers on the subject of the law of nations was Francisco Suarez, who advanced a theory of international law in which he distinguished between the law of nature and *jus gentium*. He conceived of a community of nations and insisted upon the existence of a law which all nations ought to obey.[33] Suarez produced three large tomes on legal and political philosophy. The first of these is entitled *On Laws and God as Legislator* [34] published in 1612. This work is of special interest to students of international law. Suarez conceived of a universal society of states, "but these states when standing alone are never so self-sufficient that they do not require some mutual assistance, association, and intercourse. . . ." [35] Thus we see that Suarez recognized the interdependence of states and the need for law to govern their mutual relations. One of the most important principles in the legal philosophy of Suarez is that of *good faith*. Though a serious effort was made by this Spanish theologian and jurist to separate the law of nature from the law of nations, he held that the relationship between the law of nature and *jus gentium* is very intimate. With regard to treaties, Suarez contended that, as far as their form was concerned and the procedure involved in their making, both would be classified as in the area of *jus gentium*. But the observance of a treaty or contract after it has been drawn up is a matter of *good faith*—a principle of natural law.[36]

Albericus Gentilis (1552–1608). With Albericus Gentilis international

---

cause. In the modern revival of this concept, however, just and unjust wars are classified in terms of their defensive or offensive nature.

[33] Raymond G. Gettell, *History of Political Thought* (1924), p. 188.

[34] *Tractatus de legibus ac Deo legislatore.*

[35] Suarez, as quoted by James Brown Scott in his *Law, the State and the International Community* (1939), vol. I, pp. 559–560.

[36] *Ibid.*, p. 566.

law reached an advanced stage of development. Gentilis was perhaps the first of the early writers to clearly separate international law from ethics and theology and to treat this subject as a branch of jurisprudence.[37] Gentilis was an Italian Protestant who had to flee his native land to escape religious persecution. He came to England and was appointed Regius Professor of Civil Law at Oxford in the year 1588. The writings of Gentilis show a marked departure from the doctrine of the law of nature and nations as it had been developed by the Spanish jurists, whom we have already mentioned. It is for this reason that some writers have considered him to be the founder of the positivist school.[38]

Gentilis enriched his works by the use of illustrative examples drawn from the practice of states in their interrelations and by reference to contemporary opinion and events. He preferred historical investigation to abstract reasoning and syllogistic argumentation. He discussed the nature of war and, among other things, its effects on persons and property. Much attention was also given to the matter of treaties. With regard to treaties, Gentilis sought to apply the theory of international law to the problems of his time and was to have a profound influence on Grotius, the famous Dutchman whom we shall consider next.

Hugo Grotius (1583–1645). Huig de Groot, poet, philosopher, mathematician, theologian, and jurist, is better known to our generation by his Latinized name, Grotius, and as the father of international law. Grotius was born in the town of Delft, Holland, in 1583; and because of the remarkable genius which he displayed even in his childhood, was referred to as "the miracle of Holland." Grotius received the degree of Doctor of Laws from the University of Orleans at the age of fifteen, and in 1599, when he was only sixteen years old, he took his oath as advocate before the courts at The Hague. But the legal profession did not hold much appeal for Grotius. "What time wasted," he wrote, "which might be better devoted to philosophy, history, or letters!" Yet he could not avoid the challenge of his time.

The Dutch East India Company was engaged in armed conflict with Portugal, and in a prize case involving the captured galleon *Catharina*, Grotius was retained by the Company as its attorney. In this connection he began to explore the whole question of the theory of prize, and as a result he laid the foundation for the great opus which was to come from his pen some years later.

Few men in history have written more voluminously than Grotius or been interested in a wider range of subjects. He became widely known in his own time for his poems and dramas, as well as for his historical, legal,

[37] Brierly, *op. cit.*, p. 19.
[38] Hershey, *op. cit.*, pp. 73–74.

and theological dissertations. Yet, in spite of this impressive record in letters and science, it is unlikely that the name Hugo Grotius would have been known by many outside his native land but for the fact that he also happened to be the author of *De jure belli ac pacis*. This work in three books was published in June, 1625. The challenge which had impelled Grotius to write this great dissertation was the fanatical contest in which the powers of Europe were then engaged, namely, the Thirty Years' War. This great carnage made a deep impression on Grotius, and in the preface to his famous work on the *Law of War and Peace* he wrote as follows: [39]

Throughout the Christian world I observed a lack of restraint in relation to war, such as even barbarous races should be ashamed of; I observed that men rush to arms for slight causes, or no cause at all, and that when arms have once been taken up there is no longer any respect for law, divine or human; it is as if, in accordance with a general decree, frenzy had openly been let loose for the committing of all crimes.

The effect of the great treatise was immediate and profound. In the Peace of Westphalia, its leading principles were recognized, and became the very foundation of the new order of Europe which in 1648 was established by the treaties of Osnabrück and Münster. By the close of the seventeenth century, *De jure belli ac pacis* had been translated into all the leading languages of the world, and by the middle of the eighteenth century no fewer than 45 Latin editions had appeared. Grotius readily admits his indebtedness to those who labored before him—particularly Gentilis. "But no previous writer," he says, "has treated the whole of the argument, and those who have written on parts thereof have so treated them that they have left much to the industry of others."

Grotius, like his predecessors and many who followed him, started with the proposition that there is a universal and immutable law of nature, and that this law constitutes a very substantial part of the law of nations. Since the law of nature had application to individuals as well as to states, it might perhaps be inferred that Grotius would, to the extent that natural law is a part of international law, hold the latter to have application not only to states but to individuals as well.

In opposition to Hobbes, who held that there could be no universal standard of justice and that utility or expediency is the true test of law,[40] Grotius maintained that there is an essential morality and divine justice in the nature of things, and that nations as well as men ought to be governed by this universal principle. He also held that international relations, besides being subject to the law of nature, were governed by *jus gentium*,

[39] *De jure belli ac pacis libri tres*, in *Classics of International Law*, translation by Francis W. Kelsey, *Prolegomena*, p. 20.
[40] Gettel, *op. cit.*, p. 190.

which had been established by consent of the community of nations. Thus we see in Grotius, as well, an attempt at separation of the law of nature from *jus gentium.* Moreover, *jus gentium,* which to the Romans was a common law of nations, was to Grotius the established rules of custom which had come into being by the common and tacit consent of the states, which are members of the international community.

Richard Zouche (1590–1660). Another prolific writer on the subject of the law of nations in the seventeenth century was Richard Zouche, a successor of Gentilis as professor of civil law [41] at Oxford and judge of the Admiralty Court. Twenty-five years after Grotius had published his *De jure belli ac pacis,* Zouche also published a work entitled *Jus et judicium feciale, sive jus inter gentes.* This has been called "the first manual of international law."[42] He is believed to have been one of the first to use the phrase *jus inter gentes,* which with Bentham gave rise to the term, "international law." Though Zouche did not abandon the law of nature as a basis for international law, he nevertheless emphasized the precedents which had been established in the intercourse of states and saw in these the stuff of which the law of nations is made. It is for this reason that he must be classed with Gentilis as one of the founders of the positivist school, i.e., the group of writers who, as we have seen, regard the practice of states in their mutual relations as the true source of international law. Zouche, moreover, was the first writer on the law of nations to make a clear division between the law of war and the law of peace and to give the latter the greater prominence.

The Three Schools of the Eighteenth Century. The distinction between natural law, as treated by Grotius and the Spanish theologians already mentioned, and the customary or "positive" law, as treated by such writers as Gentilis and Zouche, gave rise in the seventeenth and eighteenth centuries to three different schools among the writers on international law.[43] These were the "naturalists," the "positivists," and the "Grotians." The first of these is sometimes known as the "pure-law-of-nature school," the second as the "historical school," and the third as the "eclectics." [44]

The Naturalists. The foremost exponent of the naturalists was Samuel von Pufendorf (1632–1694), who was the first professor of the law of nature and nations at the University of Heidelberg. Among the writings of Pufendorf, there are three works of special interest to the student of international law: (1) *Elementa jurisprudentiae universalis,* 1666; (2) *De jure naturae et gentium,* 1672; (3) *De officio hominis et civis juxta legem naturalem,* 1673.

---

[41] "Civil law" in England at this time had reference to the law of nations.
[42] Georges Scelle, *Fondateurs du droit international,* p. 322.
[43] Oppenheim-Lauterpacht, *op. cit.,* p. 90.
[44] Hershey, *op. cit.,* p. 72.

Pufendorf started with the proposition that the law of nations is wholly, but no more than, a part of the law of nature. He denied that custom and treaties could ever be sources of international law. It was the opinion of Pufendorf that no war could be considered justified unless all means to a peaceful settlement had first been exhausted. But his most striking doctrine was that in the prosecution of war no mercy should be shown, as it would only delay the return of the natural state of peace. Thus, according to Pufendorf, there should be no laws of war.[45] Professor Brierly contends that the law of nature as conceived by Pufendorf is something very different from the *jus naturale* in Roman law. It is, he says, "a natural law in a new and debased form of a law supposed to be binding upon men in an imaginary *state of nature*." [46]

A famous follower of Pufendorf was Christian Thomasius (1655–1728). Thomasius distinguished between the science of law and morals and between natural and positive law. He also separated the natural rights of man from the legal rights acquired through man-made laws. Other writers on international law who may be classified as belonging to the naturalists are the Englishman Thomas Rutherford, who published his *Institutes of Natural Law* in 1754; Jean Jacques Burlamaqui, a native of Geneva who was the author of a work called *Principes de droit de la nature et des gens;* and the French diplomatist De Rayneval, who wrote a work titled *Institutions de droit de la nature et de gens.* If space permitted this list could, of course, be lengthened, but we must now go on to consider some of the more outstanding proponents of the positivist school.

The Positivists. The positivist or historical school of international law could perhaps be divided into two groups—the extremists and the moderates. The first of these would go so far as to deny the existence of natural law and would maintain that the law of nations is made up wholly of custom and treaties. The moderates, on the other hand, would not go quite so far. They would admit the existence of the law of nature as an element of international law but would contend that this is a very minor element and that the great body of the law derives from the subjective will of the state, as manifested in well-established custom and lawmaking treaties. In the seventeenth century the positivists were of minor importance, but in the eighteenth century leading exponents of this doctrine such as Bynkershoek, Moser, and Martens exerted an influence which was to have a profound effect upon the thinking in the field of international law for some time to come.

Cornelius van Bynkershoek (1673–1743). Bynkershoek is one of the most illustrious names in the legal history of Holland, and though he never

---

[45] William Seagle, *The History of Law* (1946), p. 357.
[46] Brierly, *op. cit.*, p. 28.

wrote a complete treatise on the law of nations, he is nevertheless considered to be one of its founders. His great fame in the field of international law rests on three books which he wrote dealing with various parts of this law.[47]

According to Bynkershoek the basis of international law is custom and treaties commonly consented to by the various states. He is also chiefly responsible for the principle of the so-called marine league as the measure of the territorial waters of states, as he set forth the proposition that territorial dominion should end where the effective range of arms ends; [48] and it so happened that in the early eighteenth century the range of cannon was about three miles. Bynkershoek, in his *Quaestiones juris publici*, also gave sanction to the practice of issuing an ultimatum before engaging in active war.[49] It was Bynkershoek, too, who pointed out that "as customs change, so the law of nations changes.[50]

Johan Jacob Moser (1701–1785). Moser was perhaps the most prolific writer in all German history—he is said to have written more than 500 volumes. His work on *Völkerrecht* was published between 1777 and 1780 in 12 octavo volumes, plus two supplementary works of 8 volumes. Moser tells us in the introduction to his *Versuch*, or essay, that he is interested only in the actual law of nations, i.e., the practice which determines their international relations. The law of nations, according to Moser, is to be found in custom and treaties—not in the law of nature but in the experience of men and nations. Though Moser has perhaps been overrated by some writers, one cannot deny that this remarkable scholar holds a prominent place in the development of the modern law of nations.

Georg Friedrich von Martens (1756–1821). Martens is the last important writer in the field of the law of nations in the eighteenth century. His main work in international law, *Précis de droit des gens moderne de l'Europe fondé sur les traités et l'usage*, appeared in the memorable year 1789. Along with being a great exponent of the positivist point of view, Martens is also credited with being the author of the first case book on the law of nations. He preferred to write in French rather than in German, and not the least of his merits is to be found in his clear and elegant style. His *Précis* came to be considered by many as the best systematic treatment of the law of nations up to the end of the eighteenth century and for long afterward.

The Grotians or Eclectics. The third school of international jurists

[47] *De dominio maris*, 1702; *De foro legatorum*, 1721; and *Quaestionum juris publici libri duo*, 1737.

[48] *De dominio maris*, edited by James Brown Scott in Scott's *Classics of International Law*, with a translation by Magoffin, 1923.

[49] George Crafton Wilson, *Handbook of International Law* (1939), p. 260.

[50] *Quaestiones*, book I, chap. 12, quoted by Brierly, *op. cit.*, p. 29.

and writers occupies a middle position between the naturalists and the positivists. This group has followed Grotius in preserving the distinction between natural law and positive law. Though Grotius was inclined to give the greater weight to the law of nature, his followers have tended to treat natural law and the positive law of custom and treaties as of about equal importance.[51] The two greatest representatives of this school in the eighteenth century were Christian Wolff (1679–1754) and Emmerich de Vattel (1714–1767).

Wolff, who was professor at the University of Halle, enjoyed an enviable reputation for his great learning, not only in Germany but throughout all Europe. Though he began as professor of mathematics and philosophy, he became interested in the law of nations and wrote voluminously on this subject. His chief work is *Institutiones juris naturae et gentium*, which was published in 1750. Wolff saw in the international community a *civitas maxima* or a superstate which stood above the component member states.

Emmerich de Vattel was a Swiss who in 1758 wrote his main thesis on *Le droit des gens: ou, Principes de la loi naturelle appliqués à la conduite et aux affaires des nations et des souverains.* According to Vattel there are two kinds of law, the *voluntary* and the *necessary* law, both found in the law of nations. The first is that part of international law which consists of custom and treaties, while the second part constitutes natural law. Vattel started his excursion into the field of international law as an interpreter of the abstruse Wolff. Yet, as he proceeded in his task, he found it necessary to present the work in the light of his own philosophy and knowledge. The result is that the influence of Vattel's work upon the nature of international law is second only to that of Grotius. He rejected the Wolffian fiction of the *civitas maxima* as a foundation for international law but accepted the doctrine of the *state of nature* as understood in the eighteenth century.

The rationale upon which Vattel based his theory of the equality of states is to be found in the eighteenth-century idea of natural law. He held that, since states were made up of men and all men were by nature free and equal, it would follow that sovereign states should be regarded as free persons living together in a state of nature. The doctrine of the equality of states was one of Vattel's cardinal principles—"strength and weakness produce in this regard no distinction." [52]

In the early nineteenth century, Vattel became a kind of oracle to diplomats and statesmen. This development was due in part to the many

---

[51] Oppenheim-Lauterpacht, *op. cit.*, p. 93; also Hershey, *op. cit.*, p. 76.

[52] Quoted from the Introduction to *Le droit des gens* by Vattel, in Brierly, *op. cit.*, p. 30.

legal problems of an international nature which came as a result of the Napoleonic Wars. Another reason for his vast popularity is the fact that he was the author of one of the latest systematic treatises on the law of nations.

Vattel's fame in the United Sates has been graphically depicted by Edwin D. Dickinson, who has shown that, in cases before American courts in the period 1789–1820, Vattel was cited as an authority far more frequently than Grotius, Pufendorf, or Bynkershoek. In his introduction to the Carnegie edition of Vattel, published in 1916, the French professor De Lapradelle wrote: "Grotius had written the international law of absolutism, Vattel has written the international law of political liberty." Though this statement is true, it does little more than acknowledge that each wrote in the spirit of his own time.

PART TWO

The Function of States in International Law

CHAPTER 6

International Persons

The meaning in law of the term *person* is somewhat different from its ordinary connotation. We are here concerned with the capacity to stand in court or in judgment, the capacity to be a party to a legal action, and the ability to sue and be sued. An entity having these qualifications is often referred to as a *subject* of the law.

Although in municipal law both corporations and individuals, generally speaking, have the status of legal persons, in international law only states have in the past been so regarded. Recent developments, however, both in general theory and in the positive law of nations, tend to show that international legal capacity is no longer confined to states, but may sometimes be enjoyed by organizations of various kinds as well as by individuals. In this chapter, therefore, we shall not only examine the legal position of the state in the international community, but also inquire into the juridical position of certain entities other than states.

TYPES OF STATES

Inasmuch as the state is the most important international person, it seems logical to begin this section with a brief analysis of its nature and function in the general scheme of international law. In the first place, the state is an institution established by the group as a means to certain ends, the most important of which are the enforcement of law and order within its boundaries and the independence of its people in relation to other nations. The state is, nevertheless, only one of many institutions, and its function in human affairs is limited, though not to the same degree in all times and places. It cannot be denied, for example, that in this age the state has achieved a new importance as regards both service and control, and that other institutions, therefore, tend to be obscured by the shadow of its power. Yet, this phenomenon is more apparent in the internal regime of states than in their external relations. In the latter case they are limited by each other, as an increased interdependence operates to reduce their external sovereignty.

Before going on to a consideration of the various types of states, it may be well to review briefly the conditions which are essential to a state, i.e., the elements of its constitution. According to generally accepted political theory the existence of a state is dependent on the following conditions: (1) There must be a *people*. A people is an aggregate of individual human beings who live together in a community. (2) There must be a *territory*, which means a definite area of the earth's surface upon which the population is permanently settled. A nomadic people cannot, therefore, constitute a state. (3) There must also be a *government*, i.e., an apparatus for the making and enforcement of laws. (4) Finally, there must be *sovereignty*, i.e., relative independence from external control and the power to enforce laws within the state's jurisdiction. The doctrine of sovereignty, as we have already indicated, played a major role over many centuries in the formulation of the basic principles of the law of nations.

The Doctrine of Equality. The proposition that all states are equal is derived from the doctrine of sovereignty as elaborated by eighteenth-century rationalism. Equality was conceived as a "natural" right of states, and the reasoning was as follows: In prepolitical times man was believed to have lived in a "state of nature" in which all were free and equal. Similarly, the states, which were believed to be fully sovereign and thus subject to no authority outside their own will, were considered to exist in a "state of nature" with "fundamental rights" including that of complete equality.

The doctrine of equality, thus derived, has had a profound effect upon the theory of international law and is undoubtedly responsible for a great deal of the confusion which exists at the present time in the teachings of those who have attempted to reconcile an outmoded legal theory with the actual facts and practice of international relations. For in spite of assertions to the contrary, states are unequal by all conceivable tests which can be applied: They are unequal not only in size, population, resources, state of the arts, and in power, but it would be at variance with the facts even to contend that they are always equal in legal rights.

In international law, certain states are classified as dependent or not fully sovereign, such as protectorates and trusteeships, as well as different types of colonial status. Historically, we must also take into account the legal restrictions which were imposed on certain nations on the ground that they were too weak and primitive in organization to be responsible for the full discharge of their duties under international law. As examples we might mention the Turkish capitulations and the system of exterritorial rights in China.

Following both world wars a number of countries had treaties imposed upon them regarding the treatment of minorities, while others were transformed into *de facto* protectorates as a result of heavy pressure exerted by powerful neighbors. Under the Covenant of the League of Nations the great powers enjoyed a legal superiority over the lesser states, and the same is true under the Charter of the United Nations. It should be noted also that the conditions under which a state not party to the Statute of the International Court of Justice may have access to the Court "shall, subject to the special provisions contained in treaties in force, be laid down by the Security Council." [1] It is added, to be sure, that "in no case shall such conditions place the parties in a position of inequality before the Court." [2]

It seems clear, therefore, that states have certain legal rights with reference to other international persons and the community of nations as a whole. But it would be incorrect to assume that those rights are equal. Nevertheless all states are entitled to equal protection of whatever legal rights they possess. Thus, the weakness of a state cannot serve as an excuse in law for the denial of such rights. [3]

Dependent States. International law is primarily concerned with the external relations of independent states, but does not exclude from consideration those states which, to a greater or less degree, are dependent on other nations. There are in the world today between sixty and seventy states, all of which in a theoretical sense are independent. They are recognized as members of the international community and are abstractly conceived to be separate juridical entities or *persons*, subject to the rules and regulations of the law of nations. Such states are held to be fully capable of meeting their obligations to the society of nations by possessing the needed competence both in internal and external affairs.

The dependent states, on the other hand, are those which are under *suzerainty* or *protection* of other nations. It is very difficult, indeed, to give a precise juristic signification of these terms, as the degree of dependency on the one side and control on the other may vary greatly according to the terms of treaties by which the relationship between such states is fixed. This rule was laid down in 1923 by the Permanent Court of International Justice as follows: [4]

The extent of the powers of a protecting State in the territory of a protected State depends, first, upon the treaties between the protecting State and the protected State establishing the Protectorate, and, secondly, upon the conditions under which the Protectorate has been recognized by third Powers as against

---

[1] Art. 35, par. 2, of the Statute. [2] *Ibid.*
[3] J. L. Brierly, *The Law of Nations* (1949), pp. 91–92.
[4] *Tunis-Morocco Nationality Decrees, PCIJ Advisory Opinion*, ser. B, no. 4: Manley O. Hudson, *World Court Reports*, vol. I, p. 143.

whom there is an intention to rely on the provisions of these Treaties. In spite of common features possessed by Protectorates under international law, they have individual legal characteristics resulting from the special conditions under which they were created, and the stage of their development. . . .

Even though dependent states, as the term implies, operate under reduced sovereignty,[5] it would certainly be incorrect to say that they are devoid of any legal position in an international sense and that they are not members of the community of nations. On the contrary, such states enjoy many rights and fulfill numerous obligations of international persons. They frequently send representatives, such as consuls, abroad to conclude commercial and other agreements with foreign nations; and their monarchs have often been accorded the immunities and courtesies which, according to international law, are granted to such dignitaries.[6] These, and similar facts, would seem to lead to the conclusion that "not-full sovereign States are in some way or other International Persons and subjects of International Law."[7]

It should be noted that the terms "suzerainty" and "protectorate" are less and less frequently used in the terminology of diplomats. The same can be said for the "mandate," which came into existence, and likewise died, with the League of Nations. New types of subservient states, however, have come into being, especially since the Second World War. Among these may be mentioned the trusteeships,[8] which took the place

[5] In *Parounak v. Turkey*, the Anglo-Turkish Mixed Arbitral Tribunal said, in regard to the British protectorate in Cyprus in 1914: "It is generally recognized in international law that there is no single and uniform type of protectorate, and that each case must be taken by itself. In every case, however, the protectorate involves in general a certain change in the sovereign rights of the protected State, inasmuch as it confers upon the protecting State not only the conduct of the international relations but also various rights concerning the regulation of the domestic affairs of the protected State, such as military command, administration of justice, levying of taxes, etc. . . . It is typical of agreements establishing protectorates that they often allow to subsist the more or less nominal sovereignty of the protected State, while transferring the real power into the hands of the protecting State." *Annual Digest* (1920–1930), Case No. 11.

[6] In *Statham v. Statham and Gaekwar of Baroda* the decision of the British court was based on a certificate from the India Office to the effect that the "Gaekwar of Baroda has been recognized by the Government of India as a ruling chief governing his own territories under the suzerainty of His Majesty. . . . But, though His Highness is thus not independent, he exercises as ruler of his State various attributes of sovereignty. . . ." The court found that this residue of sovereignty was sufficient to exempt the Gaekwar from the jurisdiction of the British courts: "His Highness by international law is not capable of being made a co-respondent in a suit for dissolution of marriage in the High Court of England. . . ." Great Britain, Probate, Divorce and Admiralty Division, [1912] P. 92.

[7] Oppenheim-Lauterpacht, *International Law* (1947), vol. I, p. 115.

[8] The trusteeship arrangement is more comprehensive than the system of mandates associated with the League of Nations. Art. 73 of the Charter of the United Nations,

of the old mandates, and the so-called "satellite" states of Eastern Europe. The last-named are in a position not very different from that of *de facto* protectorates. Legally these states are independent of external control, but actually they are subjected to a variety of pressures from their powerful neighbor in the East, the result of which is that their independence is more fictitious than real.

It might also be pointed out that far-reaching economic and political control has at times been exercised by the United States over nominally independent countries in Central America and the West Indies. In the present century a number of these states have been under American military government, and in cases where native governments were allowed to function officially, the actual control was often in the hands of Americans. Another illustrative example of this type of dependency is Egypt, which in the period from 1882 to 1914 could certainly be classified as a *de facto* protectorate of Great Britain.[9]

Neutralized States. States whose independence and neutrality are guaranteed for all future time by treaty are known as "neutralized" states. In the last century there were three such states in Europe, namely, Switzerland, Belgium, and the Grand Duchy of Luxembourg. Today, however, only Switzerland can be classified in this category, as the neutrality of both Belgium and Luxembourg was violated by the Germans in 1914, and no new convention has since returned those countries to their former status. The Swiss, on the other hand, have been able to maintain a precarious neutrality for more than a hundred years.

The British Commonwealth of Nations. Before the First World War the Dominions [10] of Australia, Canada, New Zealand, and British South Africa did not enjoy international status. From the point of view of international law they were mere colonial possessions of the mother country, and their behavior in the international community a mere reflection of the independence of Great Britain. Though the Dominions were often parties to international administrative unions and could enter into certain treaty arrangements with other states, they were not considered to be subjects of international law. Legally, it was held that the treaty-making power resided in the British state, which in turn delegated portions of that power for certain purposes to the colonies.

---

for example, contains a "declaration" with reference to "territories whose peoples have not yet attained a full measure of self-government," and leaves to the members of the United Nations the administration of such territories and the promotion of the well-being of their inhabitants.

[9] Brierly, *op. cit.*, p. 95.

[10] This term is often used generally, with regard to Australia, Canada, New Zealand, and South Africa, though South Africa is officially a Union and Australia a Commonwealth.

During the first decade following the war several steps were taken which culminated in the Statute of Westminster, 1931. By this arrangement the Dominions were given full autonomy and equality of status in the Commonwealth with Britain herself. The Statute clearly sets forth that in the future no laws or resolutions passed by the Dominion parliaments shall be made inoperative on the ground that they are repugnant to the laws of England. Future acts of the British Parliament would not extend to the Dominions, and any British legislation which might still be in force could be repealed by the Dominion parliaments. It is true that the equality of status which the Dominions enjoy under the Statute of Westminster has not always brought forth equality of functions with the mother country. Especially is this true in diplomatic and consular representation. Yet, the legal right to full international personality on the part of the Dominions is beyond question. It is clear then that since the advent of the Statute of Westminster, the Dominions are fully independent states and as such they are charged with the responsibilities, and enjoy the rights and privileges, of full members of the international community. But what is the position of the Commonwealth as a whole? The legal bonds of union are here so loose as to defy any known classification as a state. It is not a confederation, because there are no articles or treaty to unite legally the member states; nor is there any government which is common to all of them. Neither is it a personal union, because such a relationship requires that there should be two or more crowns united in the same person. The Commonwealth, when taken as a unit, is not even a state, because it lacks government, which is one of the essential elements of statehood. The most that can be said, perhaps, is that the Commonwealth is a community held together by the bonds of common origin, sentimental traditions, and solidarity of interest.

The Holy See. The Italian annexation of the Papal States in 1870 put an end to the temporal power of the Holy See, which had then been exercised for more than 1,100 years. As a result of the extinction of its territory, the Papacy ceased to be a state according to international law. Pius IX proclaimed himself a "prisoner in the Vatican" and refused to accept the terms of the Law of Papal Guarantees, which had been enacted by the Italian parliament in May of 1871. By the terms of this law, the Pope and his successors were guaranteed the possession of the Basilica of St. Peter, the Vatican and Lateran Palaces, as well as the villa of Castel Gandolfo. Within this area the Holy Father was given complete authority. In addition, an annual sum of $645,000 was offered the Pope as an indemnity for the loss of his temporal possessions. In the period between 1870 and 1929, however, the Pope never left the Vatican, and continued to refuse the terms of Italy's unilateral action for more than half a century.[11]

Finally, on February 11, 1929, a treaty [12] between the Holy See and the Kingdom of Italy was signed by whose terms the Vatican City was constituted as a territory under the sovereignty of the Holy See. Article 4 of the treaty states that the "sovereignty and exclusive jurisdiction over the Vatican City, which Italy recognizes as appertaining to the Holy See, precludes any intervention therein on the part of the Italian Government and any authority other than that of the Holy See." [13] In Article 24 of the same treaty, the Holy See made a declaration to the effect that "it desires to remain and will remain aloof from rivalries of a temporal nature between other States and from international congresses convened to deal with them, unless the contending parties make a joint appeal to its mission of peace." The right was reserved by the Holy See, however, to "exercise its moral spiritual influence." [14]

The Lateran Treaty returned the Holy See to the society of nations, but it is difficult to decide, in terms of international law, whether the statehood in this case is vested in the Holy See or in the Vatican City. Some writers have even contended that the effect of the treaty was to create two international persons instead of one—the Vatican City and the Holy See—and that the only point of dispute was whether the union between the two was personal or real. A more accurate view, perhaps, would be that the Lateran Treaty, by the constitution of the Vatican City, did create a new state and that the incumbent of the Holy See is its head. The main significance of this treaty in the law of nations is due to the fact that international personality is here seen to repose in an entity pursuing objects on the whole so different from those of national states.[15]

States as International Persons. It is traditional among writers on the law of nations to limit international juristic personality to states alone. Thus states are considered to be the *subjects* of international law, while individuals are held to be its *objects*. This conception is undoubtedly de-

[11] In practice both the Pope and foreign states took advantage of the Italian Law of Guarantees. Some states sent special envoys to the Papacy, and papal nuncios were sent abroad. The Holy See also concluded several concordats during this period. In 1934, a case was decided by the Supreme District Court of Bavaria in which the decision was based on the theory that concordats had the same internal validity as treaties: *In re A Nun's Dress, Annual Digest* (1933–34), Case No. 176.

[12] The so-called Lateran Treaty.

[13] For the original text of the treaty, see *Acta apostolicae sedis* (1929), vol. 21, p. 209; *Trattati e convenzioni*, vol. 39, p. 62.

[14] For English translation of the main points of the treaty, see Manley O. Hudson, *Cases and Other Materials on International Law* (1936), pp. 37–38.

[15] On this point see Josef D. Kunz, "The Status of the Holy See in International Law," *American Journal of International Law*, vol. 46 (1952), pp. 308–314.

rived from the juristic theory of the state itself, for it is obvious that unless the state is conceived as an entity quite apart from the people such a proposition would have no meaning.

In recent years, however, a number of outstanding publicists in the field of international legal theory have placed this dogma in serious question. Georges Scelle refers to the traditional view of the state "as an anthropomorphic abstraction, historically responsible for the unreal character and the paralysis of the traditional science of the law of nations." [16] Léon Duguit denies both the sovereignty and the personality of the state.[17] Only human beings can have personality, according to Duguit, and to attribute such to the state is not only an absurd but a harmful fiction. Another unorthodox theorist is the Dutch jurist Hugo Krabbe, who opposes the rationalistic point of view and contends that the state is a creature of law.[18] We might also mention the famous contemporary jurist Hans Kelsen, who has spoken most unequivocally on the relation of the state to the law of nations: "International law regulates the mutual behavior of States; but this does not mean that international law imposes duties and confers rights only upon States, not upon individuals."[19] Thus, according to Kelsen, the traditional opinion that states are the only subjects of international law and that individuals are not is in error.

It would seem clear that, as the nature of international relations changes, the law which governs those relations must change also. And as the British jurist Sir John Fischer Williams has pointed out, it "is obvious that international relations are not limited to relations between states." [20] If this be true, it would not be correct to say that international personality is confined to states and that only states are subjects of the law of nations. It seems clear that, at the present stage of development in international relations, it would not be in conformity with either theory or practice to say that the state is without personality. But the personality is a juristic one, and all states have such a personality under the law of nations. Legal or juristic personality is an artificial creation of law, through which the rights of real persons may be secured.

[16] "Une abstraction anthropomorphique, historiquement responsable du caractère fictif et de la paralysie de la science traditionelle du droit des gens"—*Règles générales du droit de la paix, 46 Hague recueil des cours* (1933), vol. IV, p. 343.
[17] See *Manuel du droit constitutionnel* (1911); *Transformations du droit public* (1913), translated as *Law in the Modern State* by F. and H. Laski.
[18] *Die Lehre der Rechtssouveränität* (1906), translated as *The Modern Idea of the State* by G. H. Sabine and W. J. Shepard.
[19] Hans Kelsen, *General Theory of Law and State*, translated by Anders Wedberg (1946), p. 342.
[20] *Aspects of Modern International Law* (1939), p. 18.

INTERNATIONAL PERSONS OTHER THAN STATES

Corporate Bodies as International Persons. If we assume that the state is a human institution, created by man for the satisfaction of certain needs, and that among its several capacities is that of international personality, it does not necessarily follow that it is the only organ or entity possessing such a character. The state is undoubtedly the most important of international persons, and its legal capacity is vastly greater than that of any other. Yet, there is a large amount of historical evidence which leads to the conclusion that it would be an error to say that international personality is exclusively confined to states. There is no doubt that the category of international legal personality can be greatly enlarged, and that this is gradually being done, thus giving to the norms of the law of nations a much wider application. It may be safe to assume, therefore, that those entities which are admitted to the international legal system are, in fact, persons of international law. There is nothing unusual in the suggestion that a state may delegate some of its functions to other units or organizations.

The Final Act of the Treaty of Vienna in 1815 established the Central Commission for the Navigation of the Rhine with comparable powers. These organizations, therefore, could well be considered to have possessed a certain degree of international personality. The Treaty of Paris of 1856, for example, provided for the creation of the European Commission of the Danube with legislative, administrative, and judicial powers.[21] In this regard, we might also mention the convention of November 8, 1884, between Germany and the International Congo Corporation. According to Article V of this agreement, it became incumbent upon Germany "to recognize the flag of the Congo Corporation as that of a friendly State." [22]

It is interesting to note that the International Court of Justice in an advisory opinion of April 11, 1949,[23] has recognized the United Nations as "an international person," but this, said the Court, was not tantamount to saying that it is a "state" or a "superstate." The functions and rights of the United Nations, according to the Court, "can only be explained on the basis of the possession of a large measure of international personality and the capacity to operate upon an international plane." [24] It is at present the supreme type of international organization, and it could not carry out the intentions of its founders if it were devoid of "international personality." [25] Thus, it would appear that international jural personality is not

[21] See Tenekides, *L'Individu dans l'ordre juridique international* (1933), p. 84.
[22] Frede Castberg, *Folkerett* (1948), p. 29.
[23] *ICJ Reports* (1949), p. 174.
[24] *Ibid.*, p. 179.   [25] *Ibid.*

confined to states but may include certain corporate bodies and organizations as well. The position of the League of Nations, in this respect, was never so well defined, though most jurists held that it possessed some corporate capacity: [26] It supervised mandated territories; made agreements with Switzerland, on whose soil it had its headquarters; administered property; and made contracts as a corporate body.[27] In view of these facts, the League might be said to have performed functions which ordinarily are associated with international persons.

Concerning legal personality, the Charter of the United Nations is far more explicit than the Covenant of the League. Articles 24, 26, 41, and 42 clearly attribute legal powers and responsibilities to the United Nations; while Article 104 states that "the Organization shall enjoy in the territory of each of its Members such legal capacity as may be necessary for the exercise of its functions and the fulfillment of its purposes." It should be noted that in the advisory opinion, already mentioned, the International Court of Justice went beyond these articles of the Charter. According to the opinion, the United Nations not only has jural personality but is entitled to bring claims against any government, *de jure* or *de facto*, which may be responsible for any injury suffered by the Organization or its agents or both. Note, however, that when the United Nations as such is bringing a claim for damages done to its agents, "it can only do so by basing its claim upon a breach of obligations due to itself." [28]

Individuals as Persons in International Law. As we have seen in the preceding section, certain corporate entities, apart from states, may under certain circumstances possess international personality in a legal sense. But what is the position of individual human beings in this respect? Is it in conformity with the facts to make the categorical assertion that under no circumstances can individuals be considered as subjects of the law of nations? "Man," writes Pasquale Fiore, "must be considered as a person of the *Magna civitas*; as such he is a subject of law in his relations with international law." [29] Though this statement was written before the First World War, and though it rests on a much firmer positive foundation today than was the case then, it is still an assertion which requires some elaboration.

The existence of important norms in international law, which impose certain obligations and confer certain rights upon individuals, cannot be denied. The law in regard to piracy is such a norm. All maritime states

[26] See Quincy Wright, "The Jural Personality of the United Nations," *American Journal of International Law*, vol. 43 (1949), p. 510.

[27] Quincy Wright, *Mandates under the League of Nations* (1930), pp. 364 ff.

[28] *ICJ Reports* (1949), p. 188.

[29] *International Law Codified and Its Legal Sanction*, translated from the Italian by Edwin M. Borchard (1918), p. 108.

have the authority under international law to capture, on the high seas, individuals who are guilty of piratical acts and to punish them. It is important to note here that it is individuals who are obligated to refrain from committing acts of piracy, the nature of which is defined in international law.[30] Though municipal statutes may provide for the punishment,

it is an offense against the law of nations; and as the scene of the pirate's operations is the high seas, which is not the right or duty of any nation to police, he is denied the protection of the flag which he may carry, and is treated as an outlaw, as an enemy of all mankind—*hostis humani generis.* . . .[31]

We might also mention the breach of blockade, i.e., the unlawful ingress or egress of vessels in spite of declared and legal blockade. Such acts are considered to be violations of general international law. But the sanctions provided are directed not against the state to which the owner of the vessel or cargo belongs, but rather against the property of private individuals.[32] The person legally responsible for the delict in such a case would be the owner of vessel and cargo.[33] Similar analogies can be made with respect to the international-legal norms affecting contraband of war. In such cases as well, the sanctions are directed not against the state but against individuals.

Furthermore, it is of interest to notice that individuals may at times be subjects of the positive law of nations. According to Article 2 of the International Convention for the Protection of Submarine Telegraph Cables, signed in Paris in 1884, it is stipulated that "the breaking or injury of a submarine cable, done willfully or through culpable negligence . . . shall be a punishable offense, but the punishment inflicted shall be no bar to a civil action for damages." The states party to the convention are obligated under its terms to provide specific sanctions for violations and to execute such sanctions against private persons. Thus the national courts, in cases which arise under this convention, do in fact execute international law, "even if they apply their national law at the same time."[34] The presence of a municipal law does not remove the obligation on the part of an individual to refrain from a delict determined by international law.

[30] In 1926 the subject of piracy engaged the attention of the League of Nations. The Committee of Experts on the Progressive Codification of International Law appointed a subcommittee on the question of piracy. In the report of this subcommittee (C. 196, M. 70. 1927. V. p. 116) piracy was defined as follows: "According to international law, piracy consists in sailing the seas for private ends without authorization from the government of any State with the object of committing depredations upon property or acts of violence against persons."
[31] John Bassett Moore, Justice, in the Lotus Case, *PCIJ Publications*, ser. A, no. 10; Hudson, *World Court Reports*, vol. II, p. 23.
[32] Kelsen, *op. cit.*, p. 345.
[33] *Ibid.*
[34] *Ibid.*, pp. 346–347.

Another rather striking example of individual responsibility under international law is the abortive Washington treaty of 1922, relating to the use of submarines. According to Article 3 of this treaty, any person in the service of a state who violates the terms of the treaty, whether or not he is under the orders of a governmental superior, "shall be deemed to have violated the laws of war and shall be liable to trial and punishment as if for an act of piracy and may be brought to trial before the civil or military authorities of any Power within the jurisdiction of which he may be found." Here again the personal and material element of the delict is determined by positive international law, and sanction is provided by the authorization of states to punish the offending individual.[35]

The contention that individuals may at times be subjects of the law of nations is further strengthened by the fact that agreements have been entered into from time to time in which individuals appear to be parties. A notable example is the treaty relative to Napoleon Bonaparte's abdication, signed in Paris on April 11, 1814. Austria, Prussia, and Russia were the parties of one side while Napoleon himself was the party of the other side. This treaty must be considered as a valid instrument, subject to the rules and interpretation of the law of nations.[36]

The prize-law convention of the Second Hague Conference, 1907, though it was never ratified, is of theoretical interest in this connection. The convention included, among other things, the stipulation that private individuals might bring suit against a foreign state before the international prize court. We might also mention the Central American Court of Justice which was established in 1907. This Court, before it was abolished in 1918, handled a number of important cases and was given wide jurisdiction, including the right to hear suits brought by individuals against states.[37]

Finally we must mention individual responsibility for war crimes, crimes against peace, and crimes against humanity, which in view of the Tokyo and Nuremberg trials has greatly strengthened the hypothesis of individual obligations under the law of nations. But since this matter is of an extremely controversial nature, it will be left to a later chapter for more complete discussion.

International Persons and the International Court of Justice. Though international personality cannot be confined to states alone, it is nevertheless true that only states may be parties in cases before the International Court of Justice.[38] But the reason that entities apart from states do not have a *locus standi* before this Court is perhaps more political than it is

[35] *Ibid.*, p. 347.   [36] Castberg, *op. cit.*, p. 29.
[37] Linden A. Mander, *Foundations of Modern World Society* (1947), p. 846.
[38] Art. 34, par. 1, of the Statute of the Court of International Justice.

juridical.[39] There were determined but unsuccessful efforts made at San Francisco to amend Article 34 of the Statute, in order to allow intergovernmental organizations to appear as parties before the Court. In accordance with Articles 34 and 66 of the new Statute, however, such organizations may in relevant cases furnish information to the Court. They may also request advisory opinions from the Court if authorized to do so by the General Assembly.[40]

For the sake of caution, a postscript should be added to what has been said so far regarding the status of corporate entities and individuals in international law. Though it is true that corporations and certain international organizations as well as private individuals may at times and under certain circumstances possess the capacity of international legal persons, such a condition is an exception rather than a rule. It is clear that international legal norms, for the most part, are concerned with the rights and duties of states. By and large, therefore, it is correct to say that states are the subjects of international law and that individuals, generally, are its objects. According to the terms of most treaties, it is only states who can bring action under the law of nations, and the fact that the language of international agreements may point in another direction is not in itself decisive. Yet, in view of actual practice, particularly in recent times, it would not be correct to make the categorical assertion that only states are, or can be, subjects of the law of nations. The present trend in the development of positive international law seems to point in the direction of a wider scope, through which organizations and individuals to an increasing extent are given legal personality along with states.

[39] Philip C. Jessup, *A Modern Law of Nations* (1948), p. 25.
[40] Art. 96 of the Statute of the International Court of Justice.

CHAPTER 7

Recognition of States and Governments

There are few subjects in the classification of international law more interesting and at the same time more difficult than the general topic of recognition. Here, perhaps to a greater extent than elsewhere in the entire area of our discipline, law and policy are closely intertwined. As a consequence of this fact, there has been considerable disagreement among authorities regarding the general nature, as well as the various aspects, of recognition. Some have contended that recognition, though productive of certain legal results, is a matter of policy; while others have attempted to show that it is essentially a part of international law and that this is no less true as regards the "primary aspect of its function" than "in the matter of some of its incidental consequences." [1]

Distinction between State and Government. In order to avoid a great deal of confusion as we study the material contained in this chapter, it is necessary to note clearly the distinction between the state and its government. As we have already seen, the term *state* is a generic expression of a people's political and legal organization within a territorial space with relative independence. Though *government* is an integral part of the state, the two are not synonymous. But because the power of the state is exercised through its government the two terms are often confused. Another factor which has contributed to the perplexity is the tendency on the part of many writers to classify states according to their various types of government. But inasmuch as all states contain the necessary elements—territory, population, government, and sovereignty—a classification of states, in a strict sense, would seem impossible. As the political and legal nature of a state is determined by its governmental organization, any attempt at classification of states can be little more than a classification of governments. It should thus be borne in mind that while governments vary greatly both in organization and function, the basic elements of states are everywhere the same.

Recognition of States. According to strict positivist theory, the real basis

[1] H. Lauterpacht, *Recognition in International Law* (1947), Preface, p. v.

for the law of nations is found in the common consent of the states which make up the international community. Furthermore, recognition is a necessary prerequisite to membership in the society of states and to the attainment of international personality. According to Oppenheim, "A State is, and becomes, an International Person through recognition only and exclusively." [2] In this view, therefore, recognition is the process by which a political community becomes a member of the society of nations and acquires personality in international law.[3] But when the identity of a state has been established and its position in the world community fixed, its international personality continues to exist regardless of changes in its internal organization and government. In the case of the *Lehigh Valley Railroad Co. v. State of Russia* [4] it was held that even if "a foreign State refuses the recognition of a change in the form of government of an old State, this latter does not thereby lose its recognition as an international person," and further that "the State is perpetual and survives the form of its government."

It is a matter of controversy among writers whether recognition is declaratory or constitutive in nature, i.e., whether a state is created through the act of recognition or had a previous existence. The greatest weight of authority in this matter seems to rest with the opinion that states may and, in fact, do exist without the benefit of recognition.[5] Japan, for example, was certainly endowed with all the elements of statehood long before 1854, when relations with the Western world were formally established. The same can be said for Turkey before 1856, when by the Treaty of Paris that country was permitted "to participate in the public law and concert of Europe." [6] In such cases, therefore, recognition is surely not of constitutive effect. On the other hand, it might perhaps be argued that the recognition of Poland and Czechoslovakia in 1918 through the instrumentality of the Treaty of Versailles was of constitutive nature. Thus it might be said that recognition is always declaratory in that it confirms the

[2] Oppenheim-Lauterpacht, *International Law* (1947), vol. I, p. 121.

[3] This view is sometimes referred to as *constitutive*, as opposed to the so-called *declaratory* theory of recognition. For an able exposition of the latter, see Ti-Chiang Chen, *The International Law of Recognition* (1951), edited by L. C. Green.

[4] 21 F.2d 396 (1927).

[5] Art. 3 of the convention signed at Montevideo Dec. 26, 1933, states that "the political existence of the State is independent of recognition by the other States. Even before recognition the State has the right to defend its integrity and independence, to provide for its conservation and prosperity, and consequently to organize itself as it sees fit, to legislate upon its interests, administer its services, and to define its jurisdiction and competence of its courts. The exercise of these rights has no other limitation than the exercise of the rights of other States according to international law"—*U.S. Treaty Series*, no. 881.

[6] It should be noted, however, that numerous treaties had been entered into between a number of European nations and the Ottoman Empire long before 1856.

existence of a state and recognizes its legal position in the international community. But it may also, at times, be constitutive in so far as it has the effect of actually creating a state where none existed before.

Recognition of Governments. It is obvious that the recognition of a new state also involves the recognition of the government which happens to be in power at the time. It is perhaps this circumstance, more than any other, that is responsible for the confusion concerning the distinction between the recognition of states and the recognition of governments. In reality, very different considerations are involved in the two types of recognition, and they should therefore be clearly distinguished.

In the first place, it will be remembered that the recognition of a state, once established, is perpetual or coterminous with the state's existence. Secondly, it is possible to recognize the existence of an old state without recognizing its government. The United States, though it failed to accord recognition to the Soviet government for a period of sixteen years after the Revolution of 1917, did not thereby deny the existence of the Russian state during the same period.[7] The recognition of a government, on the other hand, is not perpetual in time, as a change in government may result in nonrecognition. It should be clearly understood, however, that breaking off diplomatic relations is not tantamount to derecognition of a government.

A consideration of importance with regard to recognition is the manner by which the government in question has come into being. If a state were to change its form of government, let us say from a monarchy to a republic, and such change should take place in a peaceful and constitutional way, the mere fact that a change of government took place would scarcely be a valid reason for denying recognition. But, on the other hand, should such a government be established by means not constitutional, such as by revolution, by a *coup d'état,* or by any other event constituting a break in its legal continuity, the matter of recognition might be complicated by the attitude of other states.

As to whether or not recognition of states and governments is at any time and under certain conditions mandatory under the law of nations, there is profound controversy among legal scholars. As we have already seen, an authority like Lauterpacht holds that recognition is not a phenomenon to be left within the precarious orbit of politics but is something which under certain requisite conditions becomes a matter of right and duty under international law.[8] It should be said, in order to avoid misunderstanding, that Lauterpacht admits we are not in a position to say

[7] *Oetjen v. Central Leather Co.,* 246 U.S. 297 (1918).
[8] For a complete exposition of this view see Lauterpacht, *op. cit.*

there is a clear and uniform practice of states in support of the legal view of recognition.[9]

Brierly, on the other hand, holds that "the granting of recognition . . . is a political rather than a legal act" [10] and shows how states may grant or withhold recognition as circumstances may dictate in order to promote national policy. An illustration of such a practice is found in the case of American recognition of the Republic of Panama in 1903 only three days after its secession from Colombia.[11]

In this same connection, it might be worthwhile to look briefly at a memorandum of March 8, 1950, prepared under the direction of the Secretary-General of the United Nations and presented to the President of the Security Council. The memorandum concerned the problem of recognition raised by the demands of the Chinese Communist government for the seats occupied by the Nationalist government of China in the various organs of the United Nations. It contains, *inter alia*, the following paragraph: [12]

The recognition of a new State, or of a new government of an existing State, is a unilateral act which the recognizing government can grant or withhold. It is true that some legal writers have argued forcibly that when a new government, which comes into power through revolutionary means, enjoys a reasonable prospect of permanency, the habitual obedience of the bulk of the population, other States are under a legal duty to recognize it. However, while States may regard it as desirable to follow certain legal principles in according or withholding recognition, the practice of States shows that the act of recognition is still regarded as essentially a political decision, which each State decides in accordance with its own free appreciation of the situation.

The same memorandum also states that, in the view of a number of legal scholars, recognition through the free choice of states should be replaced by collective recognition through an international organization such as the United Nations. The fact remains, however, that the various states have refused to accept any such rule. The memorandum further points out that to establish the rule of collective recognition by the United Nations would require either an amendment of the Charter or a multilateral treaty including all the members of the United Nations.[13]

The Attitude of the United States. The traditional policy of the United States concerning the matter of recognition has been guided by *de facto* considerations. That is to say, the practice in the past has been to grant

[9] *Ibid.*, p. 78.
[10] Brierly, *op. cit.*, p. 131.
[11] *Ibid.*, p. 125.
[12] As quoted by Quincy Wright in *American Journal of International Law*, vol. 44 (1950), p. 548.
[13] *Ibid.*

recognition to any government, regardless of its origin, which could demonstrate its capacity to govern, and without regard to the so-called principle of "legitimacy." This criterion for recognition was expressed in 1792 by Thomas Jefferson, who as Secretary of State sent a letter of instructions to Gouverneur Morris regarding this country's attitude toward the revolutionary government of France. Jefferson wrote in part as follows: "It accords with our principles to acknowledge any government to be rightful which is formed by the will of the nation substantially declared." [14] In later instructions relating to the same matter, Jefferson wrote: [15]

We surely can not deny to any nation that right whereon our own Government is founded—that every one may govern itself according to whatever form it pleases, and change these forms at its own will; and that it may transact its business with foreign nations through whatever organ it thinks proper, whether king, convention, assembly, committee, president, or anything else it may choose.

The above statement has often been referred to as authoritative of the American position relative to the recognition of new governments. In 1848 Secretary Buchanan said: [16]

In its intercourse with foreign nations the Government of United States has, from its origin, always recognized *de facto* governments: We recognize the right of all nations to create and reform their political institutions according to their own will and pleasure. We do not go beyond the existing government to involve ourselves in the question of legitimacy. It is sufficient for us to know that a government exists, capable of maintaining itself, and then its recognition inevitably follows. . . .

Concerning the *coup d'état* of Louis Napoleon of 1851, Secretary Webster wrote to William Cabell Rives, American minister to France, in part as follows: [17]

From President Washington's time down to the present day it has been a principle, always acknowledged by the United States, that every nation possesses the right to govern itself according to its own will, to change institutions at discretion, and to transact its business through whatever agents it may think proper to employ.

The criterion for recognition outlined above was followed, generally, throughout the nineteenth century, but a clear departure from this prac-

[14] John Bassett Moore, *A Digest of International Law*, vol. I, p. 120.
[15] *The Writings of Thomas Jefferson*, edited by Ford, vol. VI, p. 199, quoted in Moore, *op. cit.*, p. 120.
[16] Moore, *op. cit.*, p. 124.
[17] *Ibid.*, p. 126. For more material relative to the recognition policy of the United States see Goebel, in *Columbia University Studies*, vol. 66 (1915), no. I, *passim;* Charles Cheney Hyde, *International Law* (1945), vol. I, pp. 3344–3345; and Moore, *op. cit.*, pp. 119–163.

tice was first initiated by President Wilson, when in 1914 the United States refused to recognize the Huerta regime in Mexico on the ground that it constituted a mere military despotism. "Cooperation," said Wilson, "is possible only when supported at every turn by the orderly processes of government based upon law, not upon arbitrary or irregular force." [18] Another factor, which has acquired substantive importance in American policy with respect to recognition, is that of *willingness,* as well as capacity, on the part of the foreign state to "protect American interests" located within its jurisdiction. Thus during the Harding administration, the United States withheld recognition of the Obregon regime in Mexico from January 1, 1920, to August 31, 1923, because satisfactory assurances were lacking regarding protection of American interests.

The most complete departure from the earlier policy was evidenced by the reluctance on the part of the United States to recognize the government of the Soviet Union, following the revolution of 1917.[19] In justification of this policy, Secretary Hughes, on March 21, 1923, made the following pronouncement: [20]

The fundamental question in the recognition of a government is whether it shows ability and a disposition to discharge international obligations. Stability, of course, is important; stability is essential. Some speak as though stability was all that was necessary. What, however, would avail mere stability if it were stability in the prosecution of a policy of repudiation and confiscation? In the case of Russia we have a very easy test in a matter of fundamental importance, and that is of good faith in the discharge of international obligations. I say that good faith is a matter of essential importance because words are easily spoken. Of what avail is it to speak of assurances, if valid obligations and rights are repudiated and property confiscated?

It is obvious, from what has been said already, that the policy of the United States concerning recognition has undergone a sharp change since the end of the last century. The mere presence of a *de facto* government, secure and stable, is no longer sufficient reason for granting recognition. To be sure, such conditions are still regarded as essential, but in addition the regime must be such as to assure the protection of our property and nationals within its jurisdiction. Thus in matters of recognition the evolution of American policy has been in the direction of a formula more heavily weighted with politicial considerations [21] than was the case in

[18] G. H. Hackworth, *Digest of International Law* (1940), vol. I, p. 181.
[19] Recognition by the United States of the Soviet regime was finally effected on Nov. 16, 1933.
[20] *American Journal of International Law,* vol. 17 (1923), p. 296.
[21] In 1948 the United States recognized the new state of Israel within hours of its declaration of independence. In this connection Warren R. Austin, the American representative to the United Nations Security Council, asserted the political character of

earlier times when the presence of a *de facto* government was generally regarded as sufficient.

The Estrada Doctrine. In 1930 the Mexican government evolved a practice concerning recognition, which clearly rests on political considerations and yet is sustained by jural arguments.[22] The practice resulted from a set of instructions, formulated by Genaro Estrada, Secretary of Foreign Affairs, to the diplomatic representatives of Mexico. The basis for the instructions were to be found in the historic experience of Mexico herself, and their substance was as follows: Mexico would no longer give any expression concerning recognition of governments which might have come into power by *coups d'état* or by revolutions. It was felt that the policy of recognition now in general practice was presumptuous in that it assumes the right to determine the legal capacity of a foreign regime, and that this is in fundamental conflict with the principle of state independence. In practice, therefore, the Mexican government would simply, in cases of mere change of government in a foreign country with which she mantains diplomatic relations, continue its diplomatic representation without any statement of opinion as to the origin and nature of the new government. If, however, other matters and circumstances, aside from mere change in the government, should cause offence to Mexico, her diplomats would be recalled.

It might be noted here that the Estrada Doctrine of recognition clearly assumes that diplomats are accredited to states rather than to governments. It also recognizes the clear proposition of international law that states have a continuous existence, whereas governments do not.

Is Recognition Legal or Political in Nature? At this point it becomes necessary to return to the question of whether recognition is a legal rather than a political act. It seems obvious that, though recognition may be a declaration of capacity rather than a contractual arrangement or a political concession,[23] a distinction should be made between its motivation and its results. It might be admitted, for example, that political considerations are of paramount importance when a decision is made to grant or withhold recognition, without denying the legal consequences of whatever action is taken.

That recognition can be used as a political weapon has long since been

---

recognition in unmistakable terms: "I should regard it as highly improper for me to admit that any country on earth can question the sovereignty of the United States of America in the exercise of that high political act of recognition of the *de facto* status of a state. Moreover I would not admit here, by implication or by direct answer, that there exists a tribunal of justice or of any other kind, anywhere, that can pass upon the legality or the validity of that act of my country."

[22] Philip C. Jessup, *A Modern Law of Nations* (1948), p. 60.

[23] Oppenheim-Lauterpacht, *op. cit.*, p. 143.

discovered, and the history of international relations is replete with examples of such a practice. The practice of states in this matter indicates that recognition, in the primary aspect of its function at least, is a political rather than a legal act.

It has been contended that states are entitled to recognition on the basis of a right to enjoy the benefits of membership in the international community, if they meet the conditions laid down in the law of nations. That states have such a right to recognition, is certainly not supported by the evidence of history. Furthermore, the corollary of such a right would be an obligation to extend recognition to any political community which by the standards of international law could be said to constitute a state. That such an obligation exists, except perhaps in natural-law theory, cannot be satisfactorily demonstrated. With respect to the recognition of new states and governments, therefore, no valid basis can be found for the contention that it is primarily a legal rather than a political act.

There are two tests which may be applied to a new government in order to determine whether recognition is indicated: (1) stability, and (2) capacity and willingness to fulfill its obligations under the law of nations. It is quite possible that the determination of the absence or presence of a *de facto* control, on the part of the government seeking recognition, can be accomplished on a quasi-legal basis. But the second test, which involves the question of willingness to observe international law regarding such matters as the protection of foreign persons and property, is essentially subjective, and can scarcely be resolved apart from political considerations.

We may say, therefore, that recognition is a process which is both political and legal in nature. Its initiation is deeply affected by the current policy of the recognizing states, while its completion and results are to a very large extent legal. It is very difficult indeed to separate law from policy in this particular phase of international relations.

Distinction between *De Facto* and *De Jure* Recognition. Recognition *de facto* has a somewhat indefinite connotation. In an earlier time the expression was used by the monarchies of Europe in opposition to recognition *de jure divino* in order to stigmatize republican forms of government.[24] At present, however, *de facto* recognition can best be understood in terms of its provisional nature. It simply means that one state recognizes the government of another state as an authority in fact, with undisputed control within the territorial limits of that state. The question of whether or not such a government has arrived at its power by legal means is immaterial. It is significant also that *de facto* recognition is often accorded for practical reasons, such as for the purpose of maintaining trade

[24] Jessup, *op. cit.*, p. 57.

relations with foreign countries; but it is never accompanied by formal diplomatic intercourse.

Recognition *de jure*, on the other hand, is complete and involves full and normal diplomatic relations. It may be *express* in that it takes place by formal exchange of notes in pursuance of preliminary conversations between authorized representatives of the states involved. If, for example, it is a question of recognizing a new government of an old state, such as the recognition of the Soviet government of Russia by the United States on November 16, 1933, a note may be dispatched by the government of the first state to the government of the second, expressing a desire to establish normal diplomatic relations and to exchange ambassadors. The government of the second state will upon receipt of such a note transmit an answer to the government of the first, expressing its happiness over the opportunity to establish such relations and to exchange ambassadors.[25] Recognition *de jure* is also sometimes *tacit* in that it may come about as a result of any act which implies the intention of recognizing a new state or government. An example would be the conclusion of a bilateral treaty which has the effect of comprehensively regulating the relations between the two states.[26]

Recognition of Insurgents. Under certain conditions the scope and character of a civil conflict may not call for a formal recognition of the insurgent faction as a belligerent. But in order to protect their persons and property, other states may establish contact with a revolutionary group, which might happen to be in control of considerable territory. Whenever such a recognition of *de facto* authority is accorded a revolutionary faction by a foreign state, for the sake of protection of its property and nationals, the rebellion does thereby acquire the status of insurgency. In order that intercourse between the insurgents and the state recognizing the insurgency may continue to their mutual advantage, the legitimate government might be asked to refrain from closing the ports of the territory occupied by the insurgents unless accompanied by effective blockade.[27] Care must be taken by such states as may maintain close contact with the insurgents, to avoid recognition of belligerency by implication.

Recognition of Belligerents. In order to justify recognition of belligerency there must exist a state of public war. In cases of armed conflict between recognized and independent states the matter is clear, even though there may not have been a formal declaration of war. On the other hand,

[25] See the Exchange of Notes, Washington, Nov. 16, 1933, Department of State Publication 528.

[26] Oppenheim-Lauterpacht, *op. cit.*, p. 143.

[27] See *Spanish Government v. North of England Steamship Company*, where it was held that a blockade instituted by an insurgent group is not a blockade in a legal sense. 54 T.L.R. 852 (1938).

in cases of insurrection by a revolutionary group against the legal authority of an established state, the conditions required to constitute a public war may or may not be present. It is generally held, however, that if a *de facto* political organization has been established by the revolutionists, able to conduct military and naval operations in conformity with the laws of war, and if the legitimate government, on its part, is exercising the belligerent rights of visit, search, and blockade, a state of public war does in fact exist.[28] Unless these conditions obtain, recognition of belligerency must be considered an unlawful intervention in the internal affairs of the state affected by civil strife. Refusal to extend recognition of belligerency in the presence of public war is contrary to the principles and precedents of international law.[29]

Here again it should be noted that authorities differ. A number of writers consider recognition of belligerency a political rather than a legal question. Norman J. Padelford, in his penetrating study, *International Law and Diplomacy in the Spanish Civil Strife*, holds that the law of nations in its present development does not require recognition of belligerency, even in cases where public war exists.[30] Though there may be some dispute as to whether recognition of belligerency is motivated by political considerations or governed by international law, there can be little doubt as to the nature of its effect. It is fairly certain that such recognition gives the insurgent community and the parent state the same international status with respect to the prosecution of the war. One may say, therefore, that recognition of belligerency has the effect of creating a new international entity possessing all the rights and obligations of independent states with respect to the conduct of armed conflict.[31]

An Internal View of Recognition. So far we have been dealing with recognition in its external aspect, seeking to define its position in international law *per se*. But its function cannot be fully understood without some knowledge of the relationship between recognition and the internal functions of government and politics. It is important to note, for example, that recognition of a new state or government is uniformly regarded as an act reserved to the political departments rather than to the courts of law. As the Supreme Court of the United States has clearly stated: [32]

[28] Moore, *op. cit.*, pp. 165–205, *in re* the Latin American States.
[29] Oppenheim-Lauterpacht, *op. cit.*, Vol. II, p. 198.
[30] See the Havana convention of Feb. 20, 1928, with respect to the duties and rights of states in the event of civil strife, Manley O. Hudson, *Legislation*, vol. IV, p. 2416.
[31] Arnold Raestad, "La reconnaissance internationale des nouveaux états et des gouvernements," *Revue de droit internationale et de législation comparée*, vol. 18 (1936), pp. 257–263.
[32] *Jones v. United States*, 137 U.S. 202.

Who is the sovereign, *de jure* or *de facto,* of a territory, is not a judicial, but a political, question, the determination of which by the legislative and executive departments of any government conclusively binds the judges, as well as all other officers, citizens, and subjects of that government. This principle has always been upheld by this court, and has been affirmed under a great variety of circumstances.

Aside from the fact that recognition is a prerogative of the executive department rather than of the judicial branch of government, it is more often than not a question of internal politics. It is obviously outside the scope of this treatise to examine the results of party politics with respect to recognition or the influence of pressure groups. But it should be noted that the political aspect, which we have shown to weigh so prominently in the whole question of recognition, is not confined to external functions alone, but is very often reflected in the internal politics of a nation.

Retroactive Effect of Recognition. It has come to be a well-established rule in international law that once a government is recognized the effect is retroactive.[33] This means that all the acts of the recognized government from the beginning of its existence are legal and valid and therefore cannot be assailed in the courts of the recognizing states. In the case of *Oetjen v. Central Leather Co.*[34] the Supreme Court of the United States interpreted the principles of international law to mean that "when a government . . . is recognized by the political department of our government as a *de jure* government of the country in which it is established, such recognition is retroactive in effect and validates all the actions and conduct of the government so recognized from the commencement of its existence."

In the matter of retroactive effect, there seems to be no clear distinction between *de jure* and *de facto* recognition. This point was first decided by the English courts in *Aksionariornoye Obchestvo v. James Sagor & Company.*[35] It was held in that case, reversing the decision of the court below, that the acts of a foreign government which is recognized *de facto* by the government of Great Britain, are not only valid but have retroactive effect. Lord Justice Bankes, in answer to the argument that, according to American precedent, only *de jure* recognition was given retroactive effect, held that in this case no such distinction could be made.

It would appear, however, that under certain circumstances the retroactive effect of recognition is subject to modification. This is well illustrated in the case of *Gdynia Ameryka Linie Zeglugowe Spolka Akcyjna v.*

---

[33] This is especially true in Anglo-American practice.
[34] 246 U.S. 297 (1918).
[35] This case is often cited as *Luther v. Sagor,* L.R. [1921] 3 K.B. 532.

Boguslawski and Another,[36] in which the House of Lords upheld the decision of the court below [37] concerning the retroactive effect of British recognition of the Provisional Polish Government of National Unity on midnight, July 5/6, 1945. The plaintiffs were Polish seamen who sued for sums of money allegedly due them from the defendant Polish owner of the vessel on which they served. The action was based on a contract made on behalf of the plaintiffs by the Warsaw government, which in 1940 escaped from Poland to become a government-in-exile in London and was recognized as the *de jure* government of Poland up to July 5/6, 1945. But on June 28, 1945, the Polish Government of National Unity had been established in Lublin, and, as we have seen, it was recognized by the British at midnight, July 5/6, 1945. The question to be answered was whether or not recognition of the Lublin government had retroactively invalidated the actions of the Warsaw government with respect to Polish vessels and crews outside their country while this government-in-exile was still the recognized regime of Poland. According to the Lords, although from June 28, 1945, the new Polish government was the *de facto* government of metropolitan Poland, retroactive effect could not be given outside of Poland to any of its acts so long as the old government was recognized. Even assuming, said the Court, that the British government's recognition of the Lublin regime dated back to June 28, 1945, this could have no effect outside Poland in the interval between June 28 and July 5/6. Thus, the decision of the Court of Appeal of June 15, 1950,[38] was upheld by the Lords.

Recognition by International Organizations. In the days of the League of Nations two questions arose with respect to recognition of states and governments: (1) Was recognition a prerequisite of membership in the League? (2) Did such admission constitute recognition? It is necessary, of course, to distinguish between the recognition of a member by the League of Nations in its corporate capacity and recognition by the individual states constituting the League. It is obvious that admission of a

[36] [1952] 2 All Eng. 470.

[37] [1950] 2 All Eng. 355.

[38] [1950] 2 All Eng. 355. In this decision Judge Denning made the following observation: "In the ordinary way, of course, our Courts do give retroactive effect to the recognition of a Government, in that we recognize the acts of that Government within its proper sphere to have been lawful, not merely from the time of recognition but antecedently from the time that it was an effective government. . . . The retroactive effect must, however, be confined to acts of the Government within its proper sphere, that is to say, acts with regard to persons and property in the terriory over which it exercised effective control (*Banco de Bilbao v. Sancha*, [1938] 2 K.B. 176); or acts with regard to ships which are registered there and whose masters attorn to them: the *Arantzazu Mendi* [1939] A.C. 256; 63 Ll. L. Rep. 89. Just as the new Government only gains its right to recognition by its effective control, so also the extent of retroactivity is limited to the area of its effective control."

certain state to the League of Nations *ipso facto* constituted recognition of that state by the League as a corporate body, as it would be absurd to admit to membership an entity the existence of which was not recognized.[39]

As to whether or not recognition of a new member by the League was contingent upon previous recognition by the states already members, the answer seems to be in the negative. Argentina, Belgium, and Switzerland, for example, were members of the League from 1934 to 1939, yet none of these recognized the government of the Soviet Union. This leads us to the answer of the second question, namely, whether admission to the League was tantamount to implied recognition by the states already in the League. The mere fact that Soviet Russia was made a member of the League of Nations in 1934 did not imply recognition *de jure* on the part of the above-mentioned states. It seems clear, therefore, that simultaneous membership in an international organization is not to be regarded as a substitute for recognition by states individually and independently.[40]

It should be noted also that political entities other than states may be recognized for the purpose of membership in international agencies and organizations. The Ukrainian Soviet Socialist Republic and the Byelorussian Soviet Socialist Republic, though not states in the accepted sense of international law, are nevertheless recognized as separate entities for the purpose of membership in intergovernmental agencies. As we have already seen, international personality, which until recently was believed to attach to states only, has now acquired a wider connotation.

Collective Recognition. As we have noted earlier in this chapter, a

---

[39] Hans Aufricht, "Principles and Practices of Recognition by International Organizations," *American Journal of International Law*, vol. 43 (1949), p. 680.

[40] *Ibid.* It must be pointed out, however, that this whole matter is extremely controversial. In *Soviet Union v. Luxembourg and Saar Co.* it was held that "the recognition of one State by another need not necessarily take the form of an express recognition; it can also be implied, for instance, when as in the present case, two States conclude a treaty or are parties to international agreements creating reciprocal obligations. The Union of Soviet Socialist Republics was, on September 18, 1934, admitted to the League of Nations, of which Luxembourg is also a Member. It is true that the delegate of Luxembourg in the Assembly of the League of Nations refrained from voting on the question of the admission of the Union of Soviet Socialist Republics, but, according to Article 1, paragraph 2, of the Covenant of the League, every State whose admission is supported by a vote of two-thirds of the Assembly becomes a Member of the League. It is clear that the decision of the majority binds also those who have not voted in favour of the admission or who may even have voted against it. Article 10 of the Covenant imposes on Members of the League the obligation to insure each other's territorial integrity and political independence. The obligation thus assumed can have no meaning except as between States which recognise each other, and it follows therefore that the admission of the Union of Soviet Socialist Republics into the League of Nations implies the recognition by Luxembourg of the Soviet Government, the only lawful authority in that State." Luxembourg, Commercial Tribunal (1935), *Annual Digest* (1935–1937), Case no. 33.

number of legal scholars have advocated the theory of collective recognition.[41] But if this process is to be substituted for the present system, the independence of states must be further reduced in the political integration of a world community. Those who propose collective recognition contend that such practice is not altogether absent in the experience of states. Lauterpacht gives as examples the recognition of Greece in 1830 by the Treaty of London, that of Belgium by the Treaty of London in 1831, that of some of the Balkan states by the Berlin Treaty of 1878, that of the Congo in the Berlin treaty of 1885, and that of Albania by the Conference of London in 1913, as well as the various instances of "collective recognition" of the new states following the First World War.[42]

The examples cited above are of doubtful value as illustrations of collective recognition. The best that can be said for them is that they may possibly be indicative of a trend or tendency in the direction of international concert in the matter of recognition. But even this is doubtful. It is imperative that a clear distinction be made between *simultaneous recognition* and *collective recognition*. The examples cited by Professor Lauterpacht are excellent illustrations of the former rather than the latter. Recognition through the instrumentality of a treaty or joint declaration is not a recognition by the group, but rather a recognition by each individual member of the group simultaneously.[43]

Collective recognition contemplates an international body such as the General Assembly of the United Nations in which might be vested the power to recognize new states and governments. The issue might be resolved by majority vote, making compliance with the results mandatory upon all the members of the Organization. Of this type of recognition no examples can be found in the long history of international relations. The only type of collective recognition so far developed is the recognition extended by an international body such as the United Nations to an individual state or other political entity for the sole purpose of membership. It is very possible, however, that the forces of technology and commerce, which have done so much to reduce the true independence of states, will some day make collective recognition not only desirable but necessary.

[41] See Lauterpacht, *op. cit.*, for an able exposition of this view.
[42] *Ibid.*, pp. 68–69.
[43] For contrary view, see Herbert W. Briggs, "Community Interest in the Emergence of New States: The Problem of Recognition," *American Society of International Law, Proceedings*, 1950, pp. 169–181.

CHAPTER 8

State Succession

In the preceding chapter a differentiation was made between state and government. If this distinction is kept clearly in mind, the succession of states and its ramified legal consequences will be better understood. Remember, therefore, that while governments may come and go, states have a certain continuity.

During the years from 1791 to 1875 the French state experienced, in succession, various forms of government. These ranged from monarchy to republic and from republic to empire, then back again to monarchy, republic, empire, and again to republic. But through it all the French state remained as an international person with the same rights and obligations under the law of nations.[1]

This principle of state continuity was recognized by the Supreme Court of the United States in the case of the *Sapphire*,[2] when it was held that the deposition of Napoleon III in no way affected the suit brought in his name to obtain damages, the reasoning being that it was the French state which had suffered the losses and that this state continued to exist. The same can be said regarding the various changes in the Russian government after 1917. The transition from an empire to a federation of republics, the R.S.F.S.R., and later to the larger union of the U.S.S.R. did not affect the corporate character of the Russian state. "A State," says Oppenheim, "remains one and the same International Person in spite of changes in its headship, in its dynasty, in its form, in its rank and title, and in its territory."[3]

There are changes which affect the international personality of states, but these involve the destruction of the state itself, throughout all or part of its former territorial space, and the substitution of a new jural personality for the old. The process thus involved is called state succession.

The Extinction and Succession of States. The term *continuity* as used

---

[1] Charles G. Fenwick, *International Law* (1948), p. 158.
[2] 11 Wall. 164 (1871).
[3] Oppenheim-Lauterpacht, *International Law* (1947), vol. I, p. 148.

above is of relative significance only, as even states do not abide forever. It should be remembered that the international personality with which a state is endowed cannot be projected in time beyond the period of the state. There are various causes of state extinction, such as the merger of one with another, the breaking up of a state into several new ones, and annexation by conquest. The Congo Free State lost its independence by merger with Belgium in 1908, as did Korea in 1910 when it became part of Japan, and Montenegro when it joined the Kingdom of the Serbs, Croats, and Slovenes after the First World War. Conquest is, of course, one obvious cause of state extinction. In this manner the Orange Free State and the South African Republic were absorbed by Great Britain in 1901.

It is immaterial by what means old states are extinguished; new states will always take their place in the same territory and among the same people. "A succession of International Persons occurs," says Oppenheim, "when one or more International Persons take the place of another International Person, in consequence of certain changes in the latter's condition." [4] The important legal question which emerges in connection with the displacement of one state by another is the determination of the extent to which rights and obligations devolve upon the succession state. It seems fairly clear that no general rule can be laid down that will cover every contingency in this matter. State succession is another subject on which the literature of international law offers divided, if not confusing, counsel.

Much of the uncertainty which surrounds the whole question of state succession may be attributed to a failure to define terms precisely. As J. Mervyn Jones has pointed out, the very phrase "state succession" is in itself misleading. It may be used to denote succession in fact, as well as succession in law.[5] *The displacement of one state by another in a given territory is a succession in fact; while a succession in law is the juridical substitution, in such circumstances, of one state for another.*

Some writers are of the opinion that no rights and obligations can survive the extinction of an international person, while others hold that such devolution of rights and duties upon the succession state does indeed take place. In the remaining part of this chapter we shall explore the question of juridical succession of states with regard to such things as treaties, debts, contracts, torts, and public and private property.

Succession with Regard to Treaties. The main principle governing treaty obligations is grounded on the proposition that treaties are of a "personal" rather than a "real" character. Thus, rather than being purely

[4] *Ibid.*, p. 151.
[5] J. Mervyn Jones, "State Succession in the Matter of Treaties," *The British Year Book of International Law*, vol. 24 (1947), p. 360.

territorial phenomena, they are attached to the state as such and are valid only so long as the state exists. Therefore, no succession can take place with regard to rights and duties set forth in treaties. Thus, cession of territory by one state to another, as a general rule, has no effect upon the rights and obligations set forth in treaties to which these states are parties. There are, however, certain exceptions to this principle. According to consistent practice extending over so long a period as to raise "an irresistible presumption of law," [6] treaties which relate to the area ceded or annexed may be regarded as no longer valid. This was the view taken by both Britain and the United States concerning the effect of the annexation of Algiers by France in 1831. The United States was also of the same disposition regarding the annexation of Nassau, Frankfurt, and Hanover by Prussia, as well as the unification of Italy and the British annexation of South Africa.

It might be pointed out also that, if a state's territorial integrity is guaranteed by treaty and such a state should subsequently acquire territory much exposed to attack, the treaty of guarantee might fall, in accordance with the principle of *rebus sic stantibus*, as the conditions under which the treaty was first made have greatly changed. This, however, is clearly a matter of treaty law rather than state succession. Another exception to the general rule that cession and annexation of territory have no effect on existing treaties results from the fact that treaties of a certain type are attached to the territory and cannot be separated from it. An example of this would be a treaty which defines the boundary between two states. As an illustration, we might mention the treaty of 1826, fixing the boundary between Norway and Russia in the Finnmark-Petsamo district. This treaty not only survived the cession of the Petsamo district by Russia to Finland in 1920, but also the reversal of this process in 1944, when Petsamo again became Russian territory.

Treaties setting up international servitudes may, under certain circumstances, survive the succession of states. The convention of March 30, 1856, involving Great Britain, France, and Russia, which was attached to the Treaty of Paris of the same date, is an example. By this convention Russia was bound not to fortify the Aaland Islands. Later, a committee of jurists, appointed by the Council of the League of Nations, took the view that the convention of 1856 was also binding on Finland, because its stipulations constituted a part of the public law of Europe. [7] In a subsequent convention of October 20, 1921, Finland assumed a specific obligation not to fortify the islands.

---

[6] *Ibid.*, p. 362.
[7] See League of Nations, *Official Journal*, October, 1920, spec. suppl., no. 3, pp. 17–19.

Since servitudes are territorial in character they are not extinguished through the process of state succession. They are "rights inherent in the object with which they are connected," [8] i.e., rights *in rem*, which remain valid even though ownership of the territory to which they belong may change. Servitudes, according to Dr. Reid, "establish a permanent legal relationship of territory to territory, unaffected by change of sovereignty in either of them, and terminable only by mutual consent, by renunciation on the part of the dominant state, or by consolidation of the territories affected." [9]

In cases where several states combine to form a single international person, such as a federal union, all treaties to which these states were parties can no longer stand. The same principle also obtains when, as a result of the dissolution of an old state, several new states are formed. It was precisely this construction which was applied by the Austrian authorities following the First World War. The old Austrian state was considered as nonexistent, and the rights and obligations contained in treaties to which this state had been a party did not devolve upon the new Austrian republic or any of the other succession states.[10] It should be noted here, however, that certain provisions were inserted into the peace treaties of St. Germain and the Trianon, continuing in force such multipartite conventions as had special application to these states. With respect to bilateral treaties, a right was reserved by the Allied and Associated Powers to designate the agreements which they might desire to revive or continue in force.[11]

Succession with Regard to Debts. The question of whether the contractual obligations concerning debts devolve upon succession states is not altogether clear, as the international practice in this respect is far from uniform. It is fairly certain, however, that there is no fixed rule under the law of nations which makes it mandatory for succession states to assume contractual obligations of the former state, either in whole or in part.[12] If a general rule can be stated relative to this matter, it would be that questions of this nature are usually settled by treaty arrangements.

There are cases, to be sure, in which succession states have assumed obligations regarding debts. Prussia, for example, in annexing the duchies of Schleswig-Holstein in 1866 also acquired their debts. In the same year, Italy assumed as much of the papal debts as was proportionate to the revenues of the conquered Romagna. But the United States, after the Spanish-American War of 1898, refused to accept responsibility for any portion of

[8] Oppenheim-Lauterpacht, *op. cit.*, p. 493.
[9] Helen Dwight Reid, *International Servitudes in Law and Practice* (1932), p. 25.
[10] Frede Castberg, *Folkerett* (1948), pp. 65–66.
[11] Jones, *op. cit.*, p. 368.
[12] Llewellyn Pfankuchen, *A Documentary Textbook in International Law* (1940), p. 335.

the Spanish debt, even that which was secured by Cuban revenues; nor was Cuba, herself, allowed to assume such obligations.[13] In the famous case of *West Rand Central Gold Mining Company v. the King*[14] the Court[15] decided that there is no principle in international law by which the annexing state becomes responsible, in the absence of express stipulations to that effect, for the financial obligations incurred by the annexed territory before such annexation took place.

There are, however, in the history of international relations a great many cases in which such obligations have been assumed by succession states through the medium of special treaty provisions. Following are a few examples: By the Treaty of Lausanne (Art. 10), 1912, Italy undertook to make payments on the public debt of Turkey with respect to the provinces of Tripolitana and Cyrenaica. Likewise by the Treaty of Versailles, 1919, a portion of the Imperial debt of Germany was assumed by the state to which any of the *Reich's* territory was ceded.[16] Following the First World War, the dissolution of the Austro-Hungarian Empire resulted in a division of its former territory between a number of succession states. The treaty of St. Germain, 1919, provided that each of the states to which any of the territory of the former monarchy was transferred, including Austria, should assume a portion of the debt of the former monarchy existing on July 28, 1914. The apportionment was to be made by the Reparation Commission.[17] The same treaty further provided that the public debt of Bosnia and Herzegovina was to be regarded as the debt of a local area and not as a part of the former empire as a whole.[18] By the Treaty of Lausanne, July 24, 1923, the Ottoman public debt was distributed among the various succession states, including Turkey. Even the states which had benefited by Turkish territory after the Balkan Wars of 1912–1913 were included in this apportionment.[19]

Many more examples could, of course, be cited to indicate how frequently succession states have assumed the debts of extinct states—or,

[13] See *ibid.*, p. 335. The reasons advanced by the United States for refusing the assumption of Cuban debts were that these debts consisted of a "mass of Spanish obligations and charges" and were "in no sense created by Cuba as a province or department of Spain or by the people of the island." These debts, it was contended, had been contracted "for the purpose of supporting a Spanish army in Cuba," and "from no point of view can the debts . . . be considered as local debts of Cuba or as debts incurred for the benefit of Cuba"—See John Bassett Moore, *Digest of International Law*, vol. I, pp. 351–385.

[14] [1905] 2 K.B. 391.

[15] British Court of the King's Bench Division, Lord Averstone, Chief Justice.

[16] It should be noted that, inasmuch as Germany had refused to assume any portion of the French debt in 1871, France, according to Art. 254 of the Treaty of Versailles, was exempt from payment of any German debts with respect to Alsace-Lorraine.

[17] Art. 203.   [18] Art. 204.

[19] Arts. 46–57.

in cases of partial succession, a portion thereof commensurate with the territory acquired. We repeat, therefore, what was said earlier, that no general principle can be found in the law of nations which makes the assumption of debts mandatory upon the succession state, and that such matters are for the most part governed by specific treaty provisions.

The Effect of State Succession upon Private Rights. The general rule in international law with respect to private rights, especially those of property, seems to be that such rights are unaffected by succession. In a leading case, *United States v. Percherman*,[20] the Court [21] held that

> the modern usage of nations, which has become law, would be violated; that sense of justice and of right which is acknowledged and felt by the whole civilized world would be outraged if private property should be generally confiscated. The people change their allegiance; their relation to their ancient sovereign is dissolved; but their relations to each other, and their rights of property remain undisturbed.

The rights of private property, according to John Marshall, are of so basic and fundamental a nature that they cannot be disturbed by the mere succession of states. He held, for example, that even if the treaty by which Florida was ceded to the United States had not contained special provisions, safeguarding the property rights of individuals, such rights would still remain undiminished. In *United States v. Soulard*,[22] the famous Chief Justice contended that "the United States, as a just nation, regards this stipulation (viz., that the inhabitants of the Louisiana cession should be protected in their property rights)[23] as the avowal of a principle which would have been equally sacred, though it has not been inserted in the contract." In the case of *Chicago, Rock Island & Pacific Railway Company v. McGlinn*,[24] the Court held:

> It is a general rule of public law, . . . that whenever political jurisdiction and legislative power over any territory are transferred from one nation or sovereign to another, the municipal laws of the country, that is, laws which are intended for the protection of private rights, continue in force until abrogated or changed by the new government or sovereign. By the cession, public property passes from one government to the other, but private property remains as before, and with it those municipal laws which are designed to secure its peaceful use and enjoyment.

[20] 7 Pet. 51, 86 (1833). For abridged versions of this case see L. B. Evans, *Cases on American Constitutional Law* (1942), p. 320, or J. B. Scott, *Cases on International Law* (1922), p. 99.

[21] United States Supreme Court, Marshall, Chief Justice.

[22] 4 Pet. 511 (1830).

[23] In the treaty by which Louisiana was ceded to the United States, it was provided (Art. III) that the inhabitants should be "maintained and protected in the free enjoyment of their liberty, property, and the religion which they profess."

[24] 114 U.S. 542; 29 L. Ed. 270.

Those laws, however, which "are political in their nature, and pertain to the prerogatives of the former government, immediately cease upon the transfer of sovereignty." [25]

The Effect of Succession upon Concessions and Contracts. Legal opinion regarding the validity, in cases of succession, of concessions by which the annexed state may have created private as well as public rights is again without consistency. The Transvaal Concessions Commission of 1901, appointed by the British government to inquire into concessions of mixed public and private rights granted by the former South African Republic, held that a state which has annexed another is not legally bound by any contracts made by the state which has ceased to exist, and that no court of law has jurisdiction to enforce such contracts if the annexing state refuses to recognize them. The United States, however, recognized as valid any Spanish contracts and concessions in Cuba, Puerto Rico, and the Philippines, which were of a purely local nature and in the exclusive interest of the islands.[26]

A whole series of European treaties concerning cession of territory contain specific provisions for the fulfillment of contracts by the succession state, even though these contracts had been entered into by the former state. In a treaty of October 17, 1797, between Austria and France, signed at Campoformio, it was provided (Art. XII) that "all sales or conveyances, all obligations contracted, either by the cities or by the government or civil and executive authorities of the countries heretofore Venetian for the maintenance of the French and German armies up to the date of this treaty, shall be confirmed and considered as valid." In the Treaty of Paris, May 30, 1814, it was stipulated (Art. XXX) that "the sums due for all works of public utility on the Rhine and in the departments separated from France by virtue of this treaty, not yet completed or completed after December 31, 1812, shall be charged to the future owners of the territory and will be liquidated by the Commission entrusted with the liquidation of the debt of the two countries." [27] The Treaty of Zurich, November 10, 1859, between France, Austria, and Sardinia declared (Art. VIII) that the Sardinian government succeeded "to the rights and obligations growing out of contracts duly entered into by the Austrian administration for the ends of the public interests especially concerning the ceded territory." Likewise by the Treaty of London, 1864, to which Britain, France, Russia, and Greece were parties, and by which Britain renounced her protectorate over the Ionian Islands, Greece undertook "to assume all the engagements and contracts legally concluded" by the government of the Islands or by

---

[25] J. W. Griggs, Attorney General, in Moore, *op. cit.*, p. 310.
[26] See Moore, *op. cit.*, p. 406.
[27] Georg Friedrich de Martens, *Nouveau recueil de traités . . . de l'Europe . . . depuis 1808 jusqu'à présent* (1818), vol. II, p. 12.

the protecting power in its behalf, as well as pensions and other compensations due to various individuals. The treaty between Austria and Italy, signed at Vienna October 3, 1866, provided (Art. VIII) that "the government of H. M. the King of Italy succeeds to the rights and obligations growing out of contracts formally entered into by the Austrian administration for purposes of public interest especially relating to the ceded country." By a special treaty between France and Germany, signed at Frankfort December 11, 1871, it was provided (Art. XIII)[28] that the German government

recognizes and confirms concessions for roads, canals, and mines granted either by the French Government or by the Departments or Municipalities of the ceded territory. The same will apply to contracts made by the French Government, Departments or Municipalities relative to the leasing or exploitation of the State, Departmental or Municipal properties situated in the ceded territory.

The German Empire becomes subrogated to all the rights and burdens growing out of the concessions granted by the French Government. . . .

As regards pecuniary or other obligations which these conditions imposed on the ceded Departments and Municipalities, the Government of the Empire will see to it that they are strictly performed in behalf of the concessionaries, lessors or contractors.

Perhaps the most authoritative statement we have concerning the effect of state succession on private rights is to be found in the advisory opinion handed down by the Permanent Court of International Justice in 1923 relative to *The German Settlers in Poland.*[29] The Council of the League of Nations requested the advisory opinion in an effort to ascertain (1) whether a certain law enacted by Poland on July 14, 1920, would involve the international obligations of Poland, and (2) whether, should this question be answered in the affirmative, Poland's action was in conformity with its international obligations. The effect of the Polish statute would be to dispossess German settlers holding lands under contracts *(Rentengutsvertraege)* granted by the Prussian Colonization Commission before November 11, 1918, if *Auflassung* (transfer of title) had not taken place before that date. Poland contended that *Auflassung* could be withheld. Furthermore, Poland refused to recognize any leases of Prussian properties granted before the armistice.

With reference to point 1 above, the Court found that international obligations were indeed involved, and as to point 2, it found that the position adopted by the Polish government was not in conformity with such obligations.

[28] See Moore, *op. cit.*, pp. 385–414.
[29] *PCIJ Publications*, ser. B, no. 6; Manley O. Hudson, *World Court Reports*, Vol. I, p. 208.

The Rights to Office. The question of whether the right to office and the emoluments therefrom survive state succession was finally answered by the United States Supreme Court in 1908 in the famous case of *O'Reilly de Camara v. Brooke*.[30] Antecedent to this case had been an unsuccessful appeal to the government of the United States and a dismissal by the United States District Court.

It happened that, in the year 1728, Don Sebastian Calvo de la Puerta had bought at public auction the office of *alguacil mayor,* or high sheriff, of the city of Havana, Cuba. The office which he had thus purchased from the Crown of Spain was declared to be perpetual and inheritable, and in due time it descended to the Countess of O'Reilly y Buena Vista. Among the duties of this office was the inspection of meat in return for fees, proportionate to the number of cattle butchered at the slaughterhouse in Havana. In 1895 Dr. Don Gustavo Gallet Duplessis purchased half interest in this office for the satisfaction of a private debt. But during the military occupation of Havana by the United States in 1898, the Countess of Buena Vista and Dr. Duplessis were denied the rights and duties of their office and its emoluments.[31] They then appealed to the government of the United States, contending that the office was property, and that as such it was protected by Article VIII of the treaty of December 10, 1898, and by international law. It was further argued, in behalf of the petitioner, that the rights to the office in question rested on a personal contract with Spain, still valid, as it had not been assumed by the United States in the treaty of peace.

Elihu Root, then Secretary of War for the United States, decided that the office of sheriff of Havana did not constitute a perpetual franchise: [32]

The fact that the Spanish Crown permitted an office to be inherited or purchased does not make it any the less an office the continuance of which is dependent upon the sovereignty which created it. . . . The petitioner has been deprived of no property whatever. The office, right, or privilege which she had acquired by inheritance was in its nature terminable with the termination of the sovereignty on which it depended.

When the matter finally came before the Supreme Court of the United States in 1908, Justice Holmes, writing for the majority, expressed agreement with the Secretary of War (Root) that "the plaintiff had no property that survived the extinction of the sovereignty of Spain." [33] It was not established to the satisfaction of the Court that the alleged rights and

---

[30] 209 U.S. 45 (1908).

[31] By order of General Brooke, later ratified by both the President and the Congress of the United States.

[32] Moore, *op. cit.,* pp. 428–429.

[33] *O'Reilly de Camara v. Brooke,* 209 U.S. 45 (1908).

emoluments in connection with the office constituted hereditaments independent of their source. Thus the rights were held to be nonexistent as against the government of the United States, and by failure to establish these conditions, the plaintiff's case came to an end.

The conclusion to be drawn from this case is, of course, that the right to office with its attendant emoluments does not survive state succession. Though this may be readily admitted, the elimination here of the factor of private property rights is less convincing. But would it not have been impossible for a municipal court to invalidate the act of one of its country's generals (in this case, General Brooke), especially when this act had subsequently been ratified by both the Executive and Congress? What might have been the decision could this case have come before the World Court?

Torts and State Succession. The question of whether a tort, or wrong, transfers *ipso facto* to the succession state is one which may be unequivocally answered in the negative. There is no rule of international law making it mandatory upon a succession state to assume responsibility for a delict committtted by a predecessor.[34] A leading case on this point is the *Claim of Robert E. Brown*,[35] decided by the United States–Great Britain Claims Arbitration of 1923.

The background of this claim was as follows: In 1902, following England's annexation of the Republic of South Africa, the United States presented a claim in behalf of Robert E. Brown, an American mining engineer who had been denied the right to stake out mining claims in South Africa and who alleged that an injustice had been done him by the refusal of the courts to grant him redress. The views of the British government with respect to this matter were set forth by Lord Lansdowne in a note to the American ambassador on November 4, 1903, in which he said: [36]

His Majesty's Government are unable to find that it has ever been admitted that a conquering State takes over liabilities of this nature, which are not for debts, but for unliquidated damages. . . . It has never so far as His Majesty's government are aware been laid down that the conquering State takes over liabilities for wrongs which have been committed by the Government of the conquered country and any such contention appears to them to be unsound in principle.

By special agreement of August 18, 1910, between the United States and Britain, a claims arbitration tribunal was established to which the American claim in the amount of £330,000 was submitted. In its award of November 23, 1923, the tribunal held that Brown had indeed suffered

[34] See Oppenheim-Lauterpacht, *op. cit.*, p. 156; also Pfankuchen, *op. cit.*, p. 338.
[35] Nielsen's Report (1926), p. 187.
[36] Green Haywood Hackworth, *Digest of International Law* (1940), vol. I, p. 560.

"a real denial of justice" at the hands of the South African Republic but that no liability "passed to or was assumed by the British Government."

Later the same tribunal handled the *Hawaiian Claims*, which arose as a result of torts suffered by British subjects at the hands of the authorities of the Hawaiian Republic before the latter's annexation by the United States. The British contended that the Brown case could not serve as a precedent here, as the facts and circumstances were essentially different. The main argument advanced was that the Hawaiian Republic had come to an end by voluntary cession, while conquest was involved in the case of South Africa. In rejecting this contention and disallowing the claims the tribunal said: [37]

We are unable to accept the distinction contended for. In the first place, it assumes a general principle of succession to liability for delict, to which the case of succession of one state to another through conquest would be an exception. We think there is no such principle. It was denied in the Brown Case and has never been contended for to any such extent. The general statements of writers, with respect to succession to obligations, have reference to changes of form of government, where the identity of the legal unit remains, to liability to observe treaties of the extinct state, to contractual liabilities, or at most to quasi-contractual liabilities. Even here, there is much controversy. The analogy of universal succession in private law, which is much relied on by those who argue for a large measure of succession to liability for obligations of the extinct state, even if admitted (and the aptness of the analogy is disputed), would make against succession to liability for delicts. Nor do we see any valid reason for distinguishing termination of a legal unit of International Law through conquest from termination by any other mode of merging in, or swallowing up by, some other legal unit. In either case the legal unit which did the wrong no longer exists, and legal liability for the wrong has been extinguished with it.

Succession with Respect to Public Property. International legal practice indicates that succession obtains in all cases where public property is involved, i.e., in cases of public enterprise with ownership vested in the state such as public buildings and funds. These will, by succession, become the property of the new state. This principle has taken on added importance in this age of ever-widening public ownership of the means of economic production. It should be noted, however, that succession carries with it all the obligations as well as all the rights with which such public property is invested. This principle may be illustrated by a case which came before the High Court of Chancery in 1865.[38]

It happened that during the American War between the States an agreement had been entered into between the defendant Prioleau, a member

---

[37] *Hawaiian Claims*, Nielsen's Report (1926), pp. 85, 160–161.
[38] *United States of America v. Prioleau* (2 Hem. & M. 559); see also 35 L.J. Ch. (n.s.) 7.

of a Liverpool firm, and McCrae, who was an agent for the government of the Confederacy, regarding the building of eight ships to be used by McCrae in the shipment of cotton from the Confederate States. The cargoes were to be consigned to Prioleau, to be sold by him according to specific instructions. The proceeds were to be used, in part, to pay for the construction and, in part, for the cost of operation of the vessels, which would be transferred to McCrae upon completion of payment. The purchase money was to be 20 per cent in addition to the construction costs. In due time about £40,000 worth of cotton was shipped from Galveston to Havana, where it was delivered to the firm of Prioleau, and subsequently reshipped to England in the *Aline,* one of the eight vessels mentioned above. It also appeared from the evidence in this case that Prioleau's firm, Fraser & Company, had incurred expenses in sailing the ships amounting to £20,000. Following the war, the United States government laid claim to the cotton on the ground that it had been the public property of the now defunct Confederacy.

The questions to be decided were (1) whether the United States was entitled to the cotton and (2) if so, whether such acquisition would be subject to the agreement between the defendants and the former Confederacy. With respect to the first point, it was held that since the cotton had been acquired by the *de facto* government of the Confederate States, it was public property to which the United States was entitled by the law of nations. Concerning the second point, however, the court was of the opinion that such transfer of public property could not be made without regard to agreements made with the former government.

The conclusion to be drawn is that, though succession with respect to public property takes place, substitution cannot occur without regard to claims which might arise as a result of agreement with the former state.[39] It was in accordance with this principle of law that the United States, in consequence of Germany's absorption of Austria in 1938, sent a note to the government of the succession state, which read in part as follows:[40]

It is believed that the weight of authority clearly supports the general doctrine of international law founded upon obvious principles of justice that in case of absorption of a State, the substituted sovereignty assumes the debts and obligations of the absorbed State, and takes the burdens with the benefits.

[39] See the case of *Virginia v. West Virginia*, 220 U.S. 1 (1911). Here the United States Supreme Court held that the constitution of West Virginia did, in effect, amount to a contract between Virginia and West Virginia: "Therefore West Virginia must be taken to have promised to Virginia to pay her share, whoever might be the persons to whom ultimately the payment was to be made."
[40] Charles Cheney Hyde, *International Law* (1947), vol. I, p. 419.

CHAPTER 9

The Rights and Duties of States

The subject of rights and duties of states has attracted considerable attention on the part of both jurists and publicists during the last century and a half. It has frequently been the subject of discussion and resolution by international organizations and scientific institutions interested in the development and codification of international law.[1]

One of the most important single drafts, judged from the attention it has attracted, is that prepared on the initiative of Dr. James Brown Scott and adopted by the American Institute of International Law in 1916 under the name Declaration of the Rights and Duties of Nations. The American Institute draft has been widely discussed both officially and unofficially. Secretary of State Hughes in 1923 stated that the declaration "embodies the fundamental principles of policy of the United States in relation to the Republics of Latin America."[2] This draft also served as a precedent for the Convention on Rights and Duties of States signed at Montevideo in 1933, and was presented to the United Nations Conference on International Organization at San Francisco in 1945.

Another significant draft is the International Law of the Future: Postulates, Principles and Proposals, which was prepared by some two hundred jurists, under the chairmanship of Manley O. Hudson, and which in 10 principles laid down specific duties of states.

As we have seen in an earlier chapter, conditions upon which states are admitted, through the process of recognition, to membership in the international community are their willingness and capacity to meet certain responsibilities and obligations to other nations and peoples. We have also seen that the exclusive force which is attendant upon the sovereignty of states within their respective territorial jurisdictions is tempered by minimum standards of international law. Hence, states are responsible not only for their official acts which may affect other members of the inter-

[1] For a compilation of the texts of the most important of these unofficial precedents, see appendix A, nos. 13–19, A/CN. 4/2, Dec. 15, 1948, p. 139.
[2] *American Journal of International Law*, vol. 19 (1925), p. 336.

national community, but also for the acts of private persons within their dominions. It is true that states have certain fundamental rights as international persons, but as with private individuals, in their relation to each other, those rights have their corollaries of obligations to the whole community.

Hans Kelsen, in a closely analytical essay [3] concerning the Draft Declaration on the Rights and Duties of States prepared by the International Law Commission of the United Nations in 1949, has called attention to "an incontestable primacy" of duty over right and to the norms of international law which impose duties upon states and by so doing "confer rights upon others." For this reason, according to Kelsen, "If the duties are correctly formulated, the formulation of the corresponding rights is superfluous." [4] In the present chapter, therefore, we shall consider the rights and duties of states as opposite sides of the same coin, but we shall contemplate the side of duties at greater length than the side of rights.

The State's Right to Existence. One of the most fundamental rights of man is that of self-preservation. The same can be said for states, who are juridical persons in an international community. According to Article 1 of the Draft Declaration prepared by the International Law Commission, "Every State has the right to independence" and to a free choice of its own form of government. [5]

It is, of course, true, as we have said earlier, that independence is an essential characteristic of the state, and for this reason the correctness of the statement that "every State has a right to independence" has been questioned on the basis of its logic. [6] "Independence and territorial as well as personal supremacy are not rights," says Oppenheim, "but recognised and therefore protected qualities of States as International Persons." [7] It is perhaps more nearly correct, therefore, to say that states have a right to their continued existence as members of the family of nations. Thus the first concern of a state is undoubtedly the integrity of its personality, and its preservation the most fundamental right; for upon this all other rights are dependent.

The Duty of Nonintervention. It is obvious that the *right* of a state to exist as a juridical person in the international community imposes the

---

[3] Hans Kelsen, "The Draft Declaration on Rights and Duties of States, Critical Remarks," *American Journal of International Law*, vol. 44 (1950), pp. 259–276.
[4] *Ibid.*, p. 264.
[5] For the text of the Draft Declaration on Rights and Duties of States, see Report of the International Law Commission covering its First Session, Apr. 12–June 9, 1949. General Assembly, *Official Records, 4th Session*, supp. no. 10 (A/925), pp. 7 ff.; also *The American Journal of International Law*, vol. 44 (1950), supp., pp. 15–21.
[6] See Kelsen, *op. cit.*, p. 267.
[7] Oppenheim-Lauterpacht, *International Law* (1947), vol. I, p. 255.

corelative *duty* of nonintervention in both the internal and external affairs of another state. That sovereign states are free to take any action necessary to self-preservation is a principle which under the law of nations is regarded as axiomatic. But this right must be strictly construed, for no state may lawfully violate the rights of other sovereignties on the basis of vague and general allegations that its existence is threatened by acts taking place exterior to its own frontiers. The German contention in 1914, therefore, that her violation of the Belgian Neutralization Treaty of 1839 was an act of necessity for self-preservation can find no reasonable support either in law or in fact. The argument of self-preservation can be used as justification for infringement of the rights of other states only when the danger is real and immediate and can be averted by no other means.

This principle was laid down in classic language by the American Secretary of State in connection with the *Caroline* affair. Daniel Webster demanded not only an apology from the British for their violation of American territory, but reparations as well, unless Her Majesty's Government could "show a necessity for self-defense, instant, overwhelming, leaving no choice of means, and no moment for deliberation." [8]

Intervention has sometimes been justified on the ground that citizens of one state have been denied ordinary justice within the jurisdiction of another.[9] Though states are obliged to meet minimum standards of international law in this respect, it is not altogether clear what those standards are,[10] nor has it been possible to reconcile conflicting ideas of justice in various nations.

The collection of public debts has also given rise to armed intervention by one state against another. In this connection the *Venezuelan Preferential Claims Arbitration* [11] is a notorious example of how the nations who used force were given an advantage over those who sought to settle the matter by wholly peaceful means. The arbitration had its origin in a controversy which arose over certain pecuniary claims of the subjects of

[8] W. E. Hall, *International Law* (1924), pp. 323–324.
[9] George Grafton Wilson, *Handbook of International Law* (1939), p. 59.
[10] The kernel of it is found in the proposition that a certain minimum of fair treatment is due to foreigners and that the failure on the part of a state to grant this is tantamount to a denial of justice. According to Stowell: "When an alien is unable to secure from the authorities of the receiving state that minimum of security of life and property to which he is entitled under international law, he is 'denied justice.'"
According to Fenwick: "Some writers have gone so far as to deny that there is any such minimum or 'international standard of justice'; holding that each state, in the exercise of its sovereign rights, is privileged to maintain its own methods of procedure. If they are observed, the alien can have no complaint and the state of which he is a national can have no ground of intervention in his behalf"—*International Law* (1948), p. 277.
[11] James Brown Scott, *The Hague Court Reports* (1916), p. 55.

Great Britain, Germany, and Italy against the Republic of Venezuela. Because the controversy could not be settled through diplomatic negotiations, Great Britain, on December 11, 1902, ordered a blockade of the Venezuelan ports. Two days later Venezuela offered to submit the question at issue to arbitration. This offer was ignored, and Germany and Italy joined Britain in the blockade.

At the same time eight other nations, including the United States, also had claims against Venezuela, which had been the subject of negotiations, but no forcible measures had been employed by these nations to secure settlement of the debts.

After the blockade had been put into effect, Venezuela sent a representative to Washington with full powers to negotiate a settlement with representatives of the creditor states. It was proposed by Venezuela that 30 per cent of the customs collected each month at the ports of La Guaira and Puerto Cabello be set aside for the adjustment of the claims. This was accepted by the claimant nations, and an assignment of the revenues mentioned was made in their favor. The blockading powers of Britain, Germany, and Italy took the position, however, that they should be given a priority of payment. It was this question which came before the Hague Court for arbitration in 1904, and it was decided that the blockading powers of Great Britain, Germany, and Italy were entitled to preferential treatment in the payment of the debts as set aside from the revenues mentioned above.[12]

---

[12] In a letter which bears the date of Dec. 29, 1902, Luis M. Drago, Minister for Foreign Affairs of the Republic of Argentina, presented to the Department of State of the United States a proposition with respect to the collection of public debts, since known as the "Drago Doctrine," as follows: "The only principle which the Argentine Republic maintains, and which it would, with great satisfaction, see adopted, in view of the events in Venezuela, by a nation that enjoys such great authority and prestige as does the United States, is the principle, already accepted, that there can be no territorial expansion in America on the part of Europe, nor any oppression of the peoples of this continent, because an unfortunate financial situation may compel some one of them to postpone the fulfillment of its promises. In a word, the principle which she would like to see recognized is that the public debt cannot occasion armed intervention, nor even the actual occupation of the territory of American nations, by a European power."

The "Drago Doctrine" is reflected in the first article of the Convention Respecting the Limitation of the Employment of Force for the Recovery of Contract Debts approved by the Second Conference of The Hague in 1907. This article reads as follows: "The contracting powers agree not to have recourse to armed force for the recovery of contract debts claimed from the government of one country by the government of another country as being due to its nationals. This undertaking is, however, not applicable when the debtor state refuses or neglects to reply to an offer of arbitration, or, after accepting the offer, prevents any compromise from being agreed on, or, after the arbitration, fails to submit to the award."

American states, in recent years, have come to look with disfavor upon intervention

Intervention in Civil War. Situations which frequently have led to intervention are those of civil conflict. The norms of the law of nations do not, however, sanction such intervention, even on invitation by one or the other of the belligerent factions. Such intervention on behalf of the insurgents would constitute a violation of an established state, and on the side of the legally constituted regime it would imply a doubt as to the ability of a *de facto* government to maintain itself. Thus for one state to judge the merits of the internal conflict in another is without sanction in international law.[13]

The American republics, who have had much experience in these matters, adopted a Convention on the Duties and Rights of States in the Event of Civil Strife. According to the terms of this convention, signed in Havana in 1928, it was agreed that the contracting parties should use all means at their disposal to prevent their nationals from participating in the civil strife of neighboring states; furthermore, that rebel forces crossing their frontiers should at once be interned.

One of the most infamous examples of intervention in a civil war is illustrated by the events in Spain in the tragic years from 1936 to 1939. From the outbreak of the insurrection, men and materials of war of foreign origin, and for the benefit of both sides, poured across the frontiers of that unhappy Iberian land. It should be noted, however, that a number of European nations, in an effort to prevent a general war, sought to establish an international nonintervention control system. To this end an international committee was set up in London to supervise and coordinate the system of nonintervention. But under the steadily increasing pressures of power politics all legal efforts to prevent, or even control, intervention in the Spanish civil war collapsed. According to Norman J. Padelford, who has done the most comprehensive study on international law and diplomacy with reference to the Spanish civil war: "The most that may be said for the system is that it probably reduced the total amount of intervention which would have taken place without it, and that it perhaps was instrumental in preventing the civil strife from becoming international war."[14]

It is a regrettable but salient fact that, in actual practice, intervention tends to become a matter of policy rather than of law, and it has never

---

regardless of the nature of the question at issue. The governments which took part in the Inter-American Conference for the Maintenance of Peace at Buenos Aires, on Dec. 23, 1933, signed a protocol affirming as a fundamental principle that "no State has the right to intervene in the internal or external affairs of another."

[13] Wilson, *op. cit.*, p. 62.

[14] Norman J. Padelford, *International Law and Diplomacy in the Spanish Civil Strife* (1939), p. 120.

been very difficult to find plausible reasons to justify an act of intervention. President McKinley, in a special message to the Congress of the United States on April 11, 1898, listed four reasons for his country's intervention in the Cuban civil war: [15]

First. In the cause of humanity and to put an end to the barbarities, bloodshed, starvation, and horrible miseries now existing there, and which the parties to the conflict are either unable or unwilling to stop or mitigate. It is no answer to say this is all in another country, belonging to another nation, and is therefore none of our business. It is specially our duty, for it is right at our door.

Second. We owe it to our citizens in Cuba to afford them that protection and indemnity for life and property which no government there can or will afford, and to that end to terminate the conditions that deprive them of legal protection.

Third. The right to intervene may be justified by the very serious injury to the commerce, trade, and business of our people, and by the wanton destruction of property and devastation of the island.

Fourth, and which is of the utmost importance. The present condition of affairs in Cuba is a constant menace to our peace, and entails upon this government an enormous expense. . . .

The Charter of the United Nations, in its restrictions of arbitrary use of force, clearly condemns intervention as a measure of self-help. Article 2, paragraph 4, provides that "all Members shall refrain in their international relations from the threat or use of force against the territorial integrity or political independence of any state. . . ." Even the United Nations as a collective body may not intervene in the internal affairs of its members. According to Article 2, paragraph 7, "Nothing contained in the present Charter shall authorize the United Nations to intervene in matters which are essentially within the domestic jurisdiction of any state. . . ." It is also provided, in Article 4 of the Draft Declaration of the International Law Commission of the United Nations, 1949, that "every State has the duty to refrain from fomenting civil strife in the territory of another State, and to prevent the organization within its territory of activities calculated to foment such civil strife." [16]

The Right to Equality. The whole structure of international law since the days of Hugo Grotius has rested very largely upon the doctrine of a legal equality of sovereign states. More than a century and a half ago Chief Justice Marshall wrote concerning the case of *The Antelope*: [17] "No principle of general law is more universally acknowledged than the perfect equality of nations. . . . A right, then which is vested in all by

[15] John Bassett Moore, *Digest of International Law*, vol. VI, pp. 219–220.
[16] For the full text of the Draft Declaration with critical remarks, see Kelsen, *op. cit.*
[17] 10 Wheat. 66 (1825).

the consent of all, can be divested only by consent. . . . As no nation can prescribe a rule for others, none can make a law of nations." [18]

In an earlier chapter, we attempted to show that the dictum of state equality is a proposition akin to a legal fiction and inconsistent with the hard facts of international relations. "Dear to the hearts of the smaller nations," wrote Jackson H. Ralston, "is the dogma and delusion of equality." [19] Though the actual practice of states has very largely destroyed the foundation of a "perfect equality," writers have been reluctant to part with this classical concept of international legal theory. And if the pressure of positive facts has forced some to abandon the old positions, the retreat has been in good order, and the defensive technique one of division and redefinition of certain concepts in an earlier doctrine. In 1920 Edwin D. Dickinson wrote: [20]

> Equality before the law is absolutely essential to a stable society of nations. If it is denied, the alternatives are universal empire or universal anarchy. Equality of capacity for rights, on the other hand, is not essential to the reign of law. Strictly speaking, it has never been anything more than an ideal in any system of law.

In 1935 the Permanent Court of International Justice made a distinction between *equality in fact* and *equality in law* as follows: [21]

> It is perhaps not easy to define the distinction between the notions of equality in fact and equality in law; nevertheless, it may be said that the former notion excludes the idea of merely formal equality; that is indeed what the Court laid down in its Advisory Opinion of September 10th, 1923, concerning the case of the *German Settlers in Poland* (Opinion No. 6), in which it said that: "There must be equality in fact as well as ostensible legal equality in the absence of discrimination in the words of the law."
>
> Equality in law precludes discrimination of any kind; whereas equality in fact may involve the necessity of different treatment in order to attain a result which establishes an equilibrium between different situations.

Among the principles set forth in Article 2 of the Charter of the United Nations is "the sovereign equality of its Members." Yet, as we have seen, the composition of the Security Council seems to violate this principle by giving to five of the greater powers permanent seats, while the other six are nonpermanent members. Furthermore, the provision in the Charter that there must be unanimity among the "big five" on all substantive

[18] It is interesting to note that this decision was handed down only two years after the promulgation of the Monroe Doctrine.
[19] *A Quest for International Order* (1941), p. 61.
[20] *The Equality of States in International Law* (1920), p. 335.
[21] *Minority Schools in Albania*, PCIJ Advisory Opinion, ser. A/B, no. 64 (1935), p. 19.

matters has the effect of relatively reducing the power of the "small six." This arrangement can hardly be said to exemplify the equality of states, even in so general a law as the Charter of the United Nations.

The same situation prevailed under the Covenant of the League of Nations, where all the members were given equality in the Assembly but not in the more important Council. The latter body was composed of the so-called great powers who were given permanent seats, while the lesser states enjoyed only occasional representation. Other historic examples of inequality, recognized by the public law of nations, were the notorious Turkish capitulation treaties and treaties giving exterritorial rights to a number of Western nations in the Far East.[22] It can also be demonstrated that treaties of peace in almost every age have imposed upon the vanquished conditions which have tended to place them in a position of inequality with respect to the victors. But in spite of all this, according to the law, all states are equal for some purposes but not for all.

Duty to Seek Pacific Settlement of Disputes. Jurists and publicists have often pointed to the successful arbitration of the *Alabama* claims in 1872 as a propitious beginning of a concerted movement for peaceful settlement of disputes between nations. But of greater legal importance, because of its multilateral character, is the Hague Convention for the Pacific Settlement of International Disputes of July 29, 1899, as it was amplified by the second Peace Conference of 1907. This convention, according to Professor Manley O. Hudson, "still stands as a great charter of pacific settlement . . . and has served as a convenient aid in many periods of international stress and strain." [23]

The principal contribution of the Hague conferences, however, was made in the field of arbitration. Before 1899 arbitral law and procedure was sporadic and *ad hoc*. As a result many difficulties were encountered with respect to both the organization of tribunals and the reception of awards.[24] The most noteworthy accomplishment of the Hague Peace Conference of 1899 was the creation of a Permanent Court of Arbitration. This institution has a rather feeble structure, consisting as it does of a mere panel of judges who have never met as a body in the Court's entire history. Each member state may appoint four jurisconsults to this panel, and from these a tribunal of arbitration may be set up by the parties to a given dispute. The only "permanent" feature of the Court is the Bureau, consisting of a Secretary-General with a small staff. In the more than fifty years of the Court's existence a large number of disputes have been set-

---

[22] These servitudes have at last succumbed to overwhelming pressures of nationalism in both the Near East and the Far East.

[23] "By Pacific Means," addresses delivered at the Fletcher School of Law and Diplomacy, Tufts College, March, 1935, p. 6.

[24] *Ibid.*, p. 9.

tled through its agency and in no case has a state refused to abide by or carry out an award. Thus it may be said that the record of the Permanent Court of Arbitration has been such as to inspire much confidence in the Court as an institution and in arbitration as a means to the pacific settlement of disputes between nations.

The tradition of The Hague, however, was not sufficient to evaporate the storm clouds that settled over Europe in 1914. But when at length the smoke of battle lifted and more than 10 million persons had lost their lives as a result of the war, there was a moment's resolve by an exhausted world to find more secure means to a lasting peace. By Article 12 of the Covenant of the League of Nations, 59 states agreed that "if there should arise between them any dispute likely to lead to rupture, they will submit the matter either to arbitration or judicial settlement or to enquiry by the Council." Article 15 of the Covenant made it an obligation to submit questions of controversy to the League Council, if not to arbitration or judicial settlement in accordance with Article 13.[25]

By Article 2 of the Pact of Paris, "the High Contracting Parties agree that the settlement or solution of all disputes or conflicts of whatever nature or of whatever origin they may be, which may arise among them, shall never be sought except *by pacific means.*"

But as we have already seen, neither the League nor the Kellogg-Briand Pact nor the Courts of Arbitration and Justice were able to avert a new catastrophe. "By the light of a perverted science," a second world war within a generation brought death and destruction. But in the spring of 1945, while the bombs were yet falling, 50 nations met in San Francisco to provide new guards for their collective security, and their great resolution is set forth in the Preamble to the Charter of the United Nations.

The duty of states to settle their differences by pacific means is clearly set forth in Article 33 of the Charter as follows:

1. The parties to any dispute, the continuance of which is likely to endager the maintenance of international peace and security, shall, first of all, seek a solution by negotiation, enquiry, mediation, conciliation, arbitration, judicial settlement, resort to regional agencies or arrangements, or other peaceful means of their own choice.

2. The Security Council shall, when it deems necessary, call upon the parties to settle their disputes by such means.

[25] Art. 13, par. 1, provided that "the Members of the League agree that whenever any dispute shall arise between them which they recognize to be suitable for submission to arbitration or *judicial settlement,* and which can not be satisfactorily settled by diplomacy, they will submit the whole subject matter to arbitration or judicial **settlement.**"

In the remaining five articles of Chapter VI of the Charter there is further elaboration of the means by which pacific settlement of international disputes may be secured. It may be noted, however, that these provisions are based on a series of precedents in international legislation through a period of more than a hundred years and therefore constitute no radical innovation in the positive law of nations.

The Duty to Abide by Treaty Obligations. Treaties, like custom, are law-creating facts and are binding upon the contracting parties. Thus one of the most ancient principles of international law is *pacta sunt servanda*. "The rule that compacts must be kept," writes Lauterpacht, "is certainly one of the bases of the legal relations between the members of any community." [26] Thus it becomes the duty of every state to carry out in good faith all obligations assumed through the agency of international agreements. "It is a truism," writes Brierly, "to say that no international interest is more vital than the observance of good faith between states, and the 'sanctity' of treaties is a necessary corollary." [27]

The Eighth International Conference of American States in 1938, in its *Declaration of American Principles*, stated that "respect for and the faithful observance of treaties constitute the indispensable rule for the development of peaceful relations between States. . . ." [28] In 1942, the Inter-American Juridical Committee [29] submitted to the governments of states which are members of the Pan American Union a resolution reaffirming certain fundamental principles of international law. Article IV of this Resolution provides in part as follows: "Good faith, which is a sacred principle of international law, should govern the relations of States. Mutual trust in the pledged word is an essential condition of the peaceful cooperation of States. Treaty obligations, freely and voluntarily entered into, must be faithfully observed." [30] In a Draft Declaration of the Rights and Duties of American States, the Governing Board of the Pan American Union in 1946, in very much the same language, proclaimed that treaties must be in the nature of open covenants "and must be faithfully observed." [31]

There can be little doubt that the principle of sanctity of treaties finds

[26] *The Function of Law in the International Community* (1933), p. 273.
[27] *The Law of Nations* (1949), p. 240.
[28] *Preparatory Study Concerning a Draft Declaration on the Rights and Duties of States*, A/CN. 4/2, Dec. 15, 1948, p. 143.
[29] This was created by a resolution of the Third Meeting of the Ministers of Foreign Affairs, held at Rio de Janeiro in 1942, as an agency of the inter-American codification machinery.
[30] *American Journal of International Law*, vol. 27 (1943), pp. 21–24.
[31] *Draft Declaration of the Rights and Duties of American States. Formulated in Accordance with Resolution IX of the Inter-American Conference on Problems of War and Peace, and Submitted to the Governments of the American Republics by the Governing Board of the Pan American Union* (1946).

ample support in the general law of nations. But as a counterpoise to the doctrine of *pacta sunt servanda* stands the *clausula rebus sic stantibus*. We shall have occasion to deal with these and other questions in connection with the general topic of treaties in a later chapter.

The Right to Self-defense. As we have already seen, the right of a state to existence is one of the most elemental in international law. From this there follows not only a duty of nonintervention, but also a right to self-defense. The right of states to collective and individual self-defense against armed attack finds strong support in the Charter of the United Nations. But such measures taken by any of the members of the Organization "shall not in any way affect the authority and responsibility of the Security Council . . . to take at any time such action as it deems necessary in order to maintain or restore international peace and security." [32]

Though it would be quite impossible both on moral and legal grounds to deny a nation's right to self-defense, it must be admitted that this principle of international law has not infrequently been used as a justification for the breach of peace. Thus the most flagrant aggression may in the eyes of the nation who commits it take on a defensive character and find justification as a preventive measure against attack. There are no reliable legal criteria to determine with certainty who first created the conditions or set the forces in motion which precipitated the conflict. The questions of responsibility for starting unprovoked and aggressive wars, therefore, are usually answered by political rather than by judicial decisions.

It should be noted also that the argument of "military necessity" in time of war looks for its logical basis to the principle of the right to self-defense. On these grounds belligerent states have often sought to justify armed attacks on neutrals. Thus on April 9, 1940, the *Wehrmacht*, without the slightest warning, attacked the neutral kingdoms of Denmark and Norway. The German government attempted to justify its action before the world on the basis of a military necessity, and the Danes still remembered the battle of Copenhagen.

[32] Art. 51 of the Charter.

CHAPTER 10

The Responsibility of States

Now, as we have seen, states, both in relation to each other and with respect to the international community, have not only rights but duties. In this chapter it is our task to explore the related topic of state *responsibility*, i.e., the implied obligation on the part of a state to repair damages resulting from an offense committed within its jurisdiction and against another member of the community of nations.

There can no longer be any doubt that responsibility, in this sense, is a fundamental principle of international law.[1] In the *Carthage Case*[2] the Court of Arbitration at The Hague said: "Considering that, in case a Power should fail to fulfill its obligations, whether general or special, to another Power, the establishment of this fact, especially in an arbitral award, constitutes in itself a serious penalty." While responsibility as a principle of the law of nations is very generally admitted, there is disagreement among the authorities as to its specific application. The reason for this is to be found largely in a confusion of the principle itself and the procedure of enforcement.

Responsibility is apparent at the moment an act of commission or omission causing injury to another member of the international community takes place within the jurisdiction of any state. Even though diplomatic action may not be appropriate, or reparation demandable, until the state has refused its obligation to render justice, responsibility is always present "if an internationally illegal act may be imputed to the state."[3] It should be noted, however, that it is incumbent upon the injured party in any case to exhaust all local remedies before any diplomatic interposition is justifiable. But it is certainly not true to say that only in cases where diplomatic action is called for does responsibility exist.

Original and Vicarious Responsibility. There are two kinds of state responsibility which should be distinguished from each other. The one is

[1] Clyde Eagleton, *The Responsibility of States in International Law* (1928), p. 21.
[2] James Brown Scott, *The Hague Court Reports* (1916), p. 329.
[3] Eagleton, *op. cit.*, p. 23.

original and the other *vicarious*. With regard to the first, responsibility is assumed by the state for its official acts, while in the second case it is responsibility of states for acts other than their own. Thus, any acts of individuals if done at the command of the state would fall within the purview of original responsibility. On the other hand, responsibility for acts committed by the state's own officials, if unauthorized, would be of a vicarious nature, provided they did not fall within the scope of normal duties.

The neglect on the part of a state of its legal duties to the community of nations constitutes an international delinquency, for which responsibility is "especially grave." [4] A state is, in general, liable for any damage done to another member of the international community, even if caused by an act not specifically authorized. That is to say, if the wrong is done by some official of the state and, though unauthorized, falls within the normal scope of duties,[5] this would clearly be an example of original responsibility and would ordinarily require the payment of compensation by the delinquent state. If, on the other hand, the injury is due to an act of some irresponsible individual who has no official capacity, the responsibility of the state having jurisdiction over such individual is of a vicarious character. In the latter case an apology by the state responsible, and punishment of the wrongdoer, are usually all that is required. But failure on the part of a state to make the proper adjustments for whatever wrong is done constitutes an international delinquency, and the vicarious responsibility is *ipso facto* transmuted into original responsibility.[6]

Responsibility for Acts of State Officials. As we have already seen, states are juridical persons in an international community who can be made articulate only through their legally constituted officials. "Since the State is an abstract entity, it must, in order to find expression, provide itself with organs wherewith to exercise its powers." [7] Thus, when a state invests authority in an individual, the acts of that individual become acts of state with the attendant responsibility under the law of nations.

In this connection, we are reminded of the *East Greenland Case* [8] and the Ihlen Declaration. Relative to the long-standing controversy between Denmark and Norway over sovereignty in East Greenland, the Norwegian Minister for Foreign Affairs, Mr. Ihlen, on July 22, 1919, made a declaration to the Danish Minister saying that the Norwegian government would not make any difficulty in the settlement of the East Greenland question.

---

[4] Oppenheim-Lauterpacht, *International Law* (1947), vol. I, p. 306.
[5] *Ibid.*   [6] *Ibid.*
[7] League of Nations, *Committee of Experts for the Progressive Codification of International Law*, Questionnaire No. 4, "Responsibility of States for Damages Done in their Territories to the Persons or Property of Foreigners," p. 8.
[8] *PCIJ Judgment*, Apr. 5, 1933, ser. A/B, no. 53, pp. 69–72; Manley O. Hudson, *World Court Reports* (1938), vol. III, pp. 148, 190–192.

Though the statement was made as a *quid pro quo* to a Danish promise to lay no impediments in the way of Norwegian claims to Svalbard, it was to prove of unforeseen significance in the adjudication of the *East Greenland Case* in 1933. The Permanent Court of International Justice went on to say: [9]

The declaration which the Minister for Foreign Affairs gave on July 22nd, 1919, on behalf of the Norwegian Government, was definitely affirmative: 'I told the Danish Minister today that the Norwegian Government would not make any difficulty in the settlement of this question.'

The Court considers it beyond all dispute that a reply of this nature given by the Minister for Foreign Affairs on behalf of his Government in response to a request by the diplomatic representative of a foreign Power, in regard to a question falling within his province, is binding upon the country to which the Minister belongs.

In the *Massey Case* [10] the question was raised as to whether the acts of so-called minor officials would involve responsibility of the state. The case concerned William B. Massey, an American citizen, who was killed by a Mexican at Palo Blanco, Vera Cruz. The murderer was arrested but later escaped through the negligence of the jailer, and the claim was predicated on the failure of Mexico to administer adequate punishment for the murder of Massey. In the Mexican brief the contention was advanced that a state is not responsible for the delinquency of a minor officer if the act is disapproved and the official in question is at once punished, as was the case here. An award in the amount of $15,000 was nevertheless granted Gertrude Parker Massey, and Nielsen, writing for the Commissioners, justified the decision, in part, on the following grounds:

I believe that it is undoubtedly a sound general principle that, whenever misconduct on the part of any such persons, whatever may be their particular status or rank under domestic law, results in the failure of a nation to perform its obligations under international law, the nation must bear the responsibility for the wrongful acts of its servants.

The award in this case was based, in the main, on Article I of the convention of September 8, 1923, which stipulated that the Claims Commission should pass upon "all claims for losses or damages originating from acts of officials or others acting for their Government and resulting in injustice." Such an expedient is the more legitimate when the confused state of the law on this subject is taken into consideration. It means, how-

[9] Green H. Hackworth, *Digest of International Law*, vol. V, pp. 32–33.
[10] *United States (G. P. Massey Claim) v. United Mexican States*, United States–Mexico General Claims Commission, 1927, *Opinions of Commissioners* (1927), p. 228; Herbert W. Briggs, *The Law of Nations: Cases, Documents, and Notes* (1952), p. 680.

ever, that this decision of the Claims Commission, concerning the responsibility of a state for acts of minor officials, should not be taken as illustrative of the general law of nations on this subject.[11]

Whether the action of a minor official involves a breach of his country's international obligations and thus creates a situation of responsibility, must, in the final analysis, depend upon the facts and circumstances in each particular case. But the conclusion which emerges from the decision in a large number of claims cases is such as to challenge the suggestion that state responsibility should be proportional to the rank of the offending officer.[12] Rather it goes to show that the character of the offense is a criterion more frequently employed in the fixing of state responsibility.

Responsibility for the Acts of Private Persons. According to the Grotian theory, a state could become responsible for the acts of its individual members only through complicity; i.e., through command, advice, aid, encouragement, and especially *patientia et receptus*. With the development of transportation and communication in more recent times the area of responsibility was widened in practice, and this in turn necessitated modification in the earlier theory. Accordingly a new concept was introduced to the effect that states were prima facie responsible for all acts taking place within their territories. But a distinction was made between what we have called *original* and *vicarious* responsibility. Some theorists have argued that the state cannot be held responsible for the act of an individual as such, but only for the failure to properly punish the offender, provided the act is illegal in an international sense.[13]

The responsibility of states in connection with the acts of private persons is predicated upon territorial jurisdiction rather than upon the bond of nationality. Thus a state, though not responsible for the acts of its own *nationals* abroad, may very well be held accountable for the behavior of *aliens* within its own boundaries.[14]

As we have seen, sovereign states enjoy exclusive force within their respective territorial jurisdictions, but this in turn entails a corresponding

---

[11] A. H. Feller, *The Mexican Claims Commissions 1923–1934: A Study in the Law and Procedure of International Tribunals* (1935), pp. 140–141.

[12] Charles Cheney Hyde, *International Law* (1945), vol. II, pp. 928–929.

[13] In a letter of May 22, 1929, to the Preparatory Committee of the Conference for the Codification of International Law, held in The Hague in 1930, the Secretary of State of the United States gave expression to the following views: "The State is not responsible for the wrongful acts of individuals. . . . It is only where State officials fail after opportunity to use due diligence to prevent the injury and there is no local redress that State responsibility arises. The State is not a guarantor of successful prevention, although it must exercise due diligence to preserve order, prevent crime and confer reasonable protection to the person and property of foreigners. A delinquency on the part of the State, independent of the act of a private citizen, is essential to raise responsibility"—Hackworth, *op. cit.*, pp. 654–655.

[14] Eagleton, *op. cit.*, pp. 77–78.

responsibility to the whole of the international community. According to William Edward Hall: [15]

A state must not only itself obey the law, but it must take reasonable care that illegal acts are not done within its dominion. Foreign nations have a right to take acts done upon the territory of a state as being *prima facie* in consonance with its will. . . . Hence it becomes necessary to provide by municipal law, to a reasonable extent, against the commission by private persons of acts which are injurious to the rights of other states, and to use reasonable vigour in the administration of the law so provided.

Treatment of Aliens. The acts of individuals which most frequently raise the question of state responsibility are those which do harm to aliens. It is in this connection also that rules and procedure for the determination of responsibility have been most carefully worked out.[16] In general, it has been said that the duty which a state owes to aliens within its jurisdiction is the same treatment and protection accorded its own citizens. This principle has sometimes been stated in negative terms as follows: "Ordinarily (i.e., in the absence of special privileges conferred by treaty or municipal law) foreigners are not entitled to a greater degree of protection or better guarantees of justice than are afforded to a State's own citizens or subjects." [17]

It is doubtful, indeed, that the obligation of a state in its treatment of aliens can be correctly described merely in terms of equality with citizens. Still less defensible is the proposition that aliens are not entitled to a greater degree of protection than that accorded citizens or subjects. Though these criteria of obligation may be sufficient in a majority of cases, they are not the ultimate test. For though a state may set whatever standards it chooses for its own people, the treatment of aliens must in the final analysis be governed by minimum standards of international law. In the *Neer Case*,[18] decided by the Mexican Claims Commission in 1926, it was held:

(first) that the propriety of governmental acts should be put to the test of international standards, and (second) that the treatment of an alien, in order to constitute an international delinquency, should amount to an outrage, to bad faith, to willful neglect of duty, or to an insufficiency of governmental action so far short of international standards that every reasonable and impartial man would readily recognize its insufficiency. Whether the insufficiency

[15] *A Treatise on International Law* (1924), pp. 64–65.
[16] Eagleton, *op. cit.*, pp. 82–83.
[17] Amos S. Hershey, *The Essentials of International Public Law and Organization* (1927), p. 254.
[18] United States–Mexico General Claims Commission, 1926, *Opinions of Commissioners* (1927), p. 71; Briggs, *op. cit.*, p. 613.

proceeds from the deficient execution of an intelligent law, or from the fact that the laws of the country do not empower the authorities to measure up to international standards, is immaterial.

Thus it is implied that a state is allowed to discriminate between citizens and aliens so long as the position of the latter does not fall below what is reasonably regarded as acceptable international standards. On the other hand, a state cannot justify its conduct toward a foreigner by reference to the fact that its own citizens are no better off than he.

Thus, in the *Roberts Case* [19] of 1927, the Commissioners held that the

facts with respect to equality of treatment of aliens and nationals may be important in determining the merits of a complaint. But such equality is not the ultimate test of the propriety of the acts of authorities in the light of international law. That test is, broadly speaking, whether aliens are treated in accordance with ordinary standards of civilization.

Clyde Eagleton, who is among the foremost authorities on the subject of state responsibility, has pointed out that though discrimination against aliens, "in the matter of justice," is not permissible under the law of nations, it is, on the other hand, quite possible that the standards of this law may actually require discrimination in their favor. Yet, it is most difficult to determine what the minimum standards of international law are with respect to this problem.

From the exclusive control and jurisdiction of states within their respective territories, there follows the assumption of responsibility for all acts taking place within the boundaries of any state that are illegal under the law of nations. In actual practice, however, this principle is tempered to some degree by the rules of *due diligence* and *local redress.*

The Rule of Local Remedies. The rule that all local remedies must be exhausted before diplomatic interposition is permissible is, from the point of view of procedure, the most important rule in the application of the doctrine of state responsibility.[20] It follows from the principle of exclusive territorial jurisdiction that an alien is subject to the laws of the country in which he resides. But the responsibility of the state for the alien's protection and fair treatment is not thereby reduced. If, however, the protective system of the state fails and if the alien should, as a consequence, suffer an injustice, he must exhaust all local remedies before it becomes legally defensible to call into play the protective apparatus of his own state. It should be noted, however, that local remedies may serve a double capacity: (1) they are the means by which damages are obtained, and (2)

[19] *U.S.A. (Harry Roberts) v. United Mexican States, Opinions of Commissioners* (1927), p. 100.
[20] Eagleton, *op. cit.*, p. 95.

if insufficient, they give rise to state responsibility. Thus, it is apparent that responsibility on the part of a state is contingent not only upon the failure to provide local redress, but upon a sufficiency of such remedies as well.

It goes without saying that opportunities for local redress, for a wrong suffered, differ widely throughout the world. In countries where the standards of justice are primitive and governments unstable, local remedies, even if fully utilized, may prove insufficient in terms of accepted standards of civilization. A condition of this nature has often provided a plausible excuse for diplomatic, and even military, intervention by states to protect their nationals abroad. It is, of course, possible that in some cases economic and political interests were the prime movers setting in motion a "punitive expedition."

Among the states who have suffered most from this inconvenience are those of Latin America. As might be expected, therefore, a number of jurists in that part of the world have searched high and low for legal grounds to prevent intervention in behalf of aliens within their territories. They have sought to limit the right of interposition to those cases where access to the courts are actually denied, thus eliminating the question of a particular standard of justice. On this basis rests the famous Calvo Doctrine.[21]

The Calvo Doctrine. As the Calvo Doctrine has thrown the whole question of state responsibility with respect to local redress into controversy, it merits a brief explanation here. During the latter part of the nineteenth century, a number of Latin American states adopted a policy of writing into contracts with aliens the so-called Calvo clause. It provided that any disputes under such contracts were to be settled by the local courts and in conformity with local law, and that the alien who was party to such a contract should not invoke the diplomatic interposition of his own government. In a section of the Constitution of Mexico dealing with the ownership of property, the Calvo Doctrine is apparent. It stipulates that the nation may grant the same rights to foreigners as to citizens,

provided they agree before the Secretariat of Foreign Relations to consider themselves as nationals in respect to such property, and accordingly not to invoke the protection of their Government in matters relating thereto; under penalty in case of non-compliance, of forfeiture to the nation of property so acquired.[22]

The case law as it has emerged from the decisions of arbitration tribunals and claims commissions is somewhat uncertain with respect to the

[21] *Ibid.*, p. 104.
[22] Hackworth, *op. cit.*, p. 636.

Calvo clause. In the *Orinoco Steamship Company Case* [23] the umpire upheld the Calvo clause by deciding that the parties, having chosen their court, must accept its decision as final. The United States, however, protested the validity of the award, with the result that the case was later submitted to the Permanent Court of Arbitration at The Hague, where it was decided that rejection of the American claim in the first instance was unwarranted. The *North American Dredging Company Case,*[24] decided by the Claims Commission in 1926, concerned a claim against Mexico for alleged breach of contract. Included in the contract was a clause to the effect that the employees of the company should be "considered as Mexicans" in all matters relating to the fulfillment of the contract. They were "deprived of any right as aliens," and under no conditions, in the language of the contract, "shall the intervention of foreign diplomatic agents be permitted." The Claims Commission decided, however, that though an alien may make such a promise, he "can not deprive the government of his nation of its undoubted right of applying international remedies to violations of international law committed to his damage."

As we have seen, the Calvo Doctrine finds its legal support in the proposition that a state has exclusive jurisdiction over all persons, alien and citizen, within its dominions. Thus the controversy regarding this doctrine is one of degree rather than principle. But the United States has never receded from the position that a citizen's right to ask protection does not depend upon the local laws. It has maintained, on the other hand, that such a right is dependent upon the laws of his own country, "and that the limits of diplomatic protection are fixed by international law without possibility of restriction by municipal legislation." [25] The United States has also taken the position that though an individual may voluntarily resign the right to his country's protection, he cannot by so doing reduce, in the slightest degree, the right of a state under the law of nations to protect its nationals abroad.

Responsibility for Mob Action. The question of whether a state may be held responsible (i.e., liable to pay damages) for losses suffered as a result of mob violence is one of the most controversial in international law. It is

[23] *Orinoco Steamship Co. (United States) v. Venezuela* (1903); J. H. Ralston, *International Arbitral Law and Procedure* (1910), p. 72. See also the same case before the Hague Permanent Court of Arbitration (1910), Scott, *op. cit.,* p. 226; M. M. Whiteman, *Damages in International Law* (3 vols., 1937–1943), vol. II, p. 1134.

[24] *United States (North American Dredging Co.) v. United Mexican States,* United States–Mexico General Claims Commission, 1926, *Opinions of Commissioners* (1927), p. 21; Manley O. Hudson, *Cases and Other Materials on International Law* (1936), p. 1109; C. G. Fenwick, *Cases on International Law* (1951), p. 236. For comment, see also F. S. Dunn, *Diplomatic Protection of Americans in Mexico* (1933), pp. 406 ff.

[25] Edwin Borchard, *The Diplomatic Protection of Citizens Abroad; or, The Law of International Claims* (1915), p. 845.

suggested by some writers that the loss of life and property to aliens as a result of mob violence cannot result in the fixation of state responsibility because of the extraordinary strain put upon the resources of a country in time of such emergency. It is argued that mob violence belongs in the category of *force majeure*, for which no state can be held accountable. But it is contended, on the other hand, that to say "an injury occurred as the result of mob action . . . is not enough, in itself, to eliminate or fix responsibility." [26]

The official attitude of the United States on the question of responsibility for mob action against aliens is marked by an astonishing inconsistency. If arguments advanced by the United States in behalf of her own nationals are taken as a criterion, the conclusion will emerge that responsibility for losses suffered by aliens as a result of mob action must rest with the state having jurisdiction. On the other hand, if her contentions in reply to claims directed against herself are examined, the answer is clearly a denial of state responsibility in such cases.[27]

One of the most notorious examples of the latter attitude is exhibited in connection with the Rock Springs riot, which took place in the Territory of Wyoming on September 2, 1885. On this occasion, an armed and lawless mob drove the Chinese inhabitants from the town of Rock Springs, with the result that 28 were killed and 15 were more or less seriously wounded. The property of the Chinese in an estimated value of nearly $150,000 was either destroyed or appropriated by the rioters. The Chinese minister in Washington asked that the subjects of the Celestial Empire "be fully indemnified for all losses and injuries they had sustained; and that suitable measures be adopted to protect the Chinese residing in Wyoming and elsewhere in the United States from similar attacks." [28] He went on to point out that, in like cases in China, the United States had asked reparations for as trivial a sum "as $73.00 stolen from American Citizens." [29] Secretary Bayard in a long but hopeless argument attempted to refute the contentions of the Chinese note and denied "all liability to indemnify individuals." Nevertheless, the details of the case are such as to leave no doubt of American responsibility under the law of nations, and at length the Congress of the United States made an appropriation sufficient to cover the damage.

A change in the official attitude of the United States with respect to this matter seems to have developed since the turn of the century. The new line of approach to the whole question of responsibility may be traced to a morning of March, 1891, when 11 Italians were killed by a mob in New

---

[26] Eagleton, *op. cit.*, pp. 125–126.   [27] *Ibid.*, p. 132.
[28] John Bassett Moore, *Digest of International Law*, vol. VI, p. 823.
[29] *Ibid.*, p. 825.

Orleans. The outrage occasioned a sharp diplomatic tilt with Italy, resulting in the payment by the United States of damages amounting to 125,000 francs. In the note which accompanied the payment, Secretary Blaine observed that while the injury "was not inflicted directly by the United States, the President nevertheless feels that it is the solemn duty, as well as the great pleasure, of the National Government to pay a satisfactory indemnity." [30]

At this point one might indeed ask: What are the principles of international law, most generally accepted, with regard to the question of state responsibility for mob violence against aliens? The most authoritative view seems to be that a state cannot be held responsible for losses sustained by foreigners within its jurisdiction, provided due diligence was exhibited by the authorities in the state concerned. In other words, the state must make every effort to apprehend and punish the wrongdoers, and the courts must be open to the alien for purpose of claiming damages. It is presumed, however, that individuals who freely enter the territory of another state must take the consequences of riots and insurgency along with other calamities.[31] In the *Gelbtrunk Case* [32] it was held that an alien must be considered as having "cast in his lot" with the citizens or subjects of the state in which he resides. The governing principle of law is well summarized by Richard Olney, American Secretary of State, in the following: [33]

The general position is that the responsibility of an established government for acts committed by rioters or insurgents depends upon the failure of the constituted authorities to exercise due diligence for protection of alien property when in a position to protect it and the imminence of danger is known.

This principle has been reinforced in later pronouncements by the Department of State, as the two examples which follow clearly illustrate.

In the year 1906, the International Harvester Company of America suffered certain property losses in the Russian city of Odessa in consequence of mob action. In its answer to an inquiry by the company relative to the possibility of collecting indemnities from the Russian government, the Department of State said that "a nation, as well as an individual, is not ordinarily liable for consequences arising from a sudden and unforeseen event which it could neither prevent nor control." [34]

[30] *Ibid.*, p. 840.
[31] Oppenheim-Lauterpacht, *op. cit.*, p. 333.
[32] United States–El Salvador Claims Arbitration, 1902, *U.S. Foreign Relations* (1902), p. 877; Hudson, *Cases*, p. 1075; Briggs, *op. cit.*, p. 713.
[33] Mr. Olney, Secretary of State, to Messrs. Lauman and Kemp (Jan. 13, 1896), 207 Ms. Dom. Let. 146, in Moore, *op. cit.*, p. 967.
[34] Hackworth, *op. cit.*, p. 657.

During internal disturbances in Cuba in 1933, an American citizen suffered loss of property as a result of burning and looting by a mob. The Department of State in declining to present a claim said: [35]

From the evidence produced it would seem that these depredations were committed by an irresponsible mob entirely out of control. In the circumstances the case would seem to come within a well established principle of international law that governments are not responsible for losses sustained by aliens on account of acts of mobs or insurgents out of control and where no negligence is attributable to the established government either before or after the acts resulting in the losses.

Responsibility for Claims Based on Contracts. As surplus capital accumulated in the industrial countries of the West during the nineteenth century, enterprise found its way to other lands where great wealth lay buried in the earth and cheap labor stood waiting. This development led to a variety of contractual arrangements not only between citizens of different states, but between governments and aliens as well.

Contracts between individuals of different states are in their adjudication a matter of private international law and can occasion no question of responsibility unless local remedies fail. If local redress is denied, however, responsibility emerges in terms of denial of justice.[36] The great majority of contract cases which have come before claims commissions and international tribunals for settlement are concerned with concessions of various kinds granted by a state to aliens operating within its jurisdiction. There are two schools of thought with respect to the handling of controversies resulting from contracts between the citizens of one state and the government of another. It is argued, on the one hand, that hazardous investments should be discouraged; that those who make them usually do so with full knowledge of the risks, and in the expectation of exceptionally large returns; furthermore, that "it is an inherent qualification of all sovereignties that no proceedings for the execution of a judgment may be instituted or carried out against it." [37] This latter point is well illustrated in *Dexter & Carpenter v. Kunglig Jaernvaegsstyrelsen*,[38] in which the United States Circuit Court of Appeals, Second District, held in 1930 that mere consent "to be sued does not give consent to a seizure or attachment of the property of a sovereign government."

It is precisely this principle of international law, coupled with the fact that no sovereign may be sued without his own consent, that has given

[35] Ms. Department of State, file 437.11 Ramirez, Myrtle Giefers/14, in Hackworth, *op. cit.*, p. 658.
[36] Eagleton, *op. cit.*, p. 158.
[37] Hershey, *op. cit.*, pp. 261–262.
[38] 43 F.2d 705; also Hudson, *Cases*, p. 547.

rise to the point of view of what may be called the interventionist school. This group argues that the only way an alien can obtain redress in claims, based upon contracts with a sovereign state, is for his own government to intervene diplomatically in his behalf. They further contend that, on the basis of equal sovereignty, "the injured state has as much right to enforce payment as has the respondent state to refuse it." [39] It would seem that this theory lies dangerously close to the "doctrine of protection" of which John Bassett Moore, in his dissenting opinion in the *Lotus Case*,[40] wrote as follows:

> It is evident that this claim is at variance not only with the principle of the exclusive jurisdiction of a State over its own territory, but also with the equally well settled principle that a person visiting a foreign country, far from radiating for his protection the jurisdiction of his own country, falls under the dominion of the local law and, except so far as his government may diplomatically intervene in case of a denial of justice, must look to that law for his protection.

As we have seen in an earlier section of this chapter, the "Calvo clause" in contracts was designed to prevent the appeal by aliens to their home governments for diplomatic intervention in their behalf. Though this doctrine is not devoid of controversy, it has, nevertheless, been upheld in a number of decisions by arbitration tribunals and mixed claims commissions.[41]

It should be observed, however, that the question is not so much whether a state has a right to intervene in behalf of its nationals as it is on what grounds such intervention may proceed and what procedure is to be followed. It seems clear that in a case where all local remedies have been exhausted and justice denied, diplomatic interposition is justified. This principle seems well established in international law and has frequently been asserted by the United States. On July 25, 1858, Lewis Cass, then Secretary of State, wrote to Lamar, minister to Central America, as follows: [42]

> The United States believe it to be their duty, and they mean to execute it, to watch over the persons and property of their citizens visiting foreign countries, and to intervene for their protection when such action is justified by existing circumstances and by the law of nations. . . . Wherever their citizens may go through the habitable globe, when they encounter injustice they may appeal to the Government of their country, and the appeal will be examined into with a view to such action in their behalf as it may be proper to take.

[39] Eagleton, *op. cit.*, p. 159; see also Hershey, *op. cit.*, p. 261.
[40] Hudson, *World Court Reports*, vol. II, p. 82.
[41] Charles G. Fenwick, *International Law* (1948), p. 293.
[42] Moore, *op. cit.*, p. 723.

It is doubtful, indeed, that in the present day the United States, though a vastly more powerful nation than it was in 1858, would address a similar note to Nicaragua.

Denial of Justice. It is a well-established principle of international law that aliens are subject to the laws of the state in whose jurisdiction they may be found. Thus if they violate the laws, they are subject to punishment, while if they suffer injury to person or property, redress must first be sought in terms of local remedies. On the other hand, though states have the right to impose their laws upon aliens residing within their boundaries, they also have the correlative duty, under the law of nations, to see to it that justice is not denied. If this duty has been complied with, the responsibility of the state cannot ordinarily be called into question.[43]

As we have already seen, these principles are not in themselves absolute but are contingent upon minimum standards of international law. As Commissioner Nielsen wrote in the *Neer Case*, "A strict conformity by authorities of a government with its domestic law is not necessarily conclusive evidence of the observance of legal duties imposed by international law, although it may be important evidence on that point."[44] It is clear that the so-called "presumption of conformity" will fall whenever denial of justice is shown.[45] It should be noted that the rule which compels the alien to seek local redress for a wrong suffered bears the implication of competence on the part of the judicial apparatus in the state concerned. That is, it must be sufficient to the protection of the substantive rights of aliens under international law.

In the determination of an international delinquency deriving from the denial of justice, the important thing is not to show a failure to comply with domestic law and procedure but rather to prove that the resultant protection has been inadequate in terms of international standards of justice.[46] Two well-settled principles of international law have developed in connection with judicial protection of aliens: first, a minor irregularity in judicial procedure where an alien is involved does not of itself engage the responsibility of the state; second, a state cannot be held accountable for a faulty judicial decision, provided the error does not infringe a rule of international law.[47]

An examination of the work of publicists reveals a great deal of disagreement as to the precise meaning of the term "denial of justice." Some,

[43] Alwyn V. Freeman, *The International Responsibility of States for Denial of Justice* (1938), pp. 73–74.
[44] U.S. *(Pauline Neer) v. Mexico, Opinions,* p. 77.
[45] Freeman, *op. cit.,* p. 76.
[46] *Ibid.,* p. 81.
[47] *Ibid.,* p. 82.

especially Latin-American jurists, have taken the narrow or procedural
view to the effect that denial of justice must be limited to a simple refusal
of access to the courts. Others take the broad view and include within
the compass of the term any wrong committed against aliens by any organ
whatever of the state.

The narrow view was given expression in the *Fabiani Case* [48] when the
arbitration tribunal held that denial of justice simply meant the refusal of
judicial authorities to exercise their functions. Likewise, in an advisory
opinion handed down by the Supreme Court of Peru, in the case of
Cantero-Herrera v. The Canevaro Co.,[49] the Court said that in order to
make the claim "denial of justice" conform to the "principles and usages
of international law, it is necessary . . . that the denial of justice be
manifest or *notorious*, that is, that the hearing which the foreigner claims,
or the recourse which he interposes, has been denied him. . . ."

In the *Claim of Robert E. Brown*, [50] however, an extremely broad interpretation of the concept "denial of justice" was given expression by the
international tribunal:

We are persuaded that on the whole case, giving proper weight to the cumu-
lative strength of the numerous steps (legislative and judicial) taken by the
Government of the South African Republic with the obvious intent to defeat
Brown's claims, a definite denial of justice took place. . . . All three branches
of the government conspired to ruin his enterprise.

The same position was taken in the *El Triunfo Co. Case*.[51] This arbitration involved the unlawful cancellation of a concession, and loss of
property through the enactment of executive decrees. The Tribunal
declared, *inter alia*, that "it is not the denial of justice by the courts alone
which may form the basis for reclamation against a nation, according
to the rules of international law." Again in the *Mariposa Claim* [52] the
question before the Commission was whether there had been "a denial
of justice in the case, that is to say, whether there has been any official
act which results in a clear injustice for which there is no redress under
local law."

The narrow view has been criticized because it tends to eliminate the
criterion of an international standard of justice, which is beyond amendment by local law. Conversely, the liberal interpretation is unacceptable

[48] *France v. Venezuela* (1896), Moore, *Arbitrations*, p. 4877.
[49] McNair-Lauterpacht, *Annual Digest* (1927–1928), Case no. 149.
[50] United States–Great Britain Claims Arbitration, 1923, Nielsen's Report (1926),
p. 187.
[51] Special Arbitration Tribunal of the United States and El Salvador, *U.S. Foreign
Relations* (1902), p. 870. Also Scott, *Cases* (1922), p. 123.
[52] American and Panamanian General Claims Arbitrations, Hunt's Report (1934),
p. 555.

to many, as it makes "denial of justice" coterminous with the general notion of responsibility for wrongs suffered by aliens at the hands of any agency of the state.[53]

Nationality of Claimant. The first essential of an international claim is proof that the claimant is entitled to the protection of the state whose assistance is invoked. Aside from special cases involving alien seamen and aliens serving in the armed forces—and even here some confusion exists—it is a well-settled principle that the right to protect is confined to nationals of the protecting state. It may be laid down as a general rule that any break in the national ownership of a claim, as by assignment or change in nationality of the claimant, defeats the claim. Thus, until the claimant's right to protection by the state whose aid is invoked has been established, there is no need to consider either the facts or the law in order to determine the existence of a just grievance against a foreign state.[54]

In the adjustment of international claims there are two distinct stages: (1) the diplomatic presentation of the claim by the government of the injured national as well as the determination of its validity and amount; and (2) the distribution of the award among those entitled to receive it. Under the present rules of law it is probably correct to say that the first of these stages comes within the purview of international law and procedure, while the second stage, that of distribution of awards is a matter of municipal law.[55]

It should be observed that the right of diplomatic protection is not a personal right of the claimant but exists in favor of one state as against another. It is a privilege which a state may extend or withhold in behalf

[53] See Freeman, *op. cit.*, p. 105.

[54] The General Claims Commission, United States and Mexico, established under the convention of Sept. 8, 1923, stated: "Nations of course do not make a practice of pressing diplomatic reclamations of persons other than their own nationals. . . . It [the Commission] realizes, of course, that the nationality of claimants is the justification in international law for the intervention of a government of one country to protect persons and property in another country, and, further, that by the jurisdictional articles of the Convention of September 8, 1923, namely, Articles I and VII, each Government is restricted to the presentation of claims in behalf of its own nationals." From the *Opinions of the Commissioners* (1929), pp. 6, 7; Hackworth, *op. cit.*, p. 802.

Basis for Discussion No. 28 of the Preparatory Committee for the 1930 codification conference at The Hague reads in part as follows: "A State may not claim a pecuniary indemnity in respect of damage suffered by a private person in the territory of a foreign State unless the injured person was its national at the moment when the damage was caused and retains its nationality until the claim is decided."

[55] In his opinion of Aug. 14, 1912, the Solicitor for the Department of State of the United States said, concerning the distribution of the Alsop Award, that the distribution to private claimants "is a matter not of international law, but of municipal law which embodies the rules and principles governing and controlling private, personal and property rights." Hackworth, *op. cit.*, p. 763.

of its nationals under the rules of the law of nations. The mere fact that a private person or corporation declines the protection of its government cannot deprive the state of its legal right to extend diplomatic protection in behalf of such person or corporation.[56] This principle, however, is not always consistently applied. In the case of *The Tattler*,[57] for example, it was held that the conditions agreed to by the Canadian authorities and the private owner, for the release of an American vessel, should be allowed to stand, though it was objected that the agreement was not binding upon the government of the United States. "In this case," said the Tribunal, "the only right the United States Government is supporting is that of its national, and consequently in presenting this claim . . . it can rely on no legal ground other than those which would have been open to its national."

In 1926, the same Tribunal handed down an award in the case of *Cayuga Indians*.[58] The facts of this case were briefly as follows: The State of New York had agreed in treaties of 1789, 1790, and 1795 to pay an annuity to the Cayuga Nation in return for certain lands ceded by the Indians. During the War of 1812, a certain group of the Cayugas migrated to Canada, with the result that no payment had been made to them since 1810. On repeated occasions, the Cayugas had asked the British government to press their claim with the United States. Nothing was done, however, until 1899 when the British brought the matter to the State Department's attention in Washington.

When the case finally came up for arbitration in 1926, the American agent contended that the long delay on the part of the British in bringing the claim constituted laches and that therefore it should not be entertained by the Tribunal. An award was nevertheless handed down in favor of the Cayugas, largely based on considerations of equity, *ex aequo et bono*, "that have repeatedly been invoked by the courts where strict regard to the legal personality of a corporation would lead to inequitable results." Accordingly, a sum of $100,000 was awarded, not to the Indians directly, of course, but to the British who had presented the claim in their behalf. The Tribunal significantly observed that in cases of this kind

[56] In instructions to claimants contained in the "Application for the Support of Claims against Foreign Governments" (October, 1924), issued by the Department of State of the United States, it was stated: "The Government of the United States can interpose effectively through diplomatic channels only on behalf of itself, or of claimants (1) who have American nationality (such as citizens of the United States, including companies and corporations), . . . or (2) who are otherwise entitled to American protection in certain cases (such as certain classes of seamen on American vessels, members of the military and naval forces of the United States, etc.). . . ." Hackworth, *op. cit.*, p. 812.

[57] United States–Great Britain Claims Arbitration, 1926, Neilsen's Report, p. 490.

[58] *Ibid.*, p. 307.

"courts have not hesitated to look behind the legal person and consider the human individuals who were the real beneficiaries."

It might be suggested that procedure in claims cases, where private claims are involved, could be made far less confusing if individual persons were allowed to present their own claims before appropriate tribunals. This would mean the formulation of legal principles with respect to the prosecution of claims which could more nearly meet the demands of justice. Thus, for the present formula, by which the state is fictitiously regarded as the injured party in all claims cases, one might better substitute the principle of individual rights, where no injury has been suffered by the state itself. This notion, though it runs counter to the generally accepted theory, would not constitute a radically new departure in international relations. The Central American Court of Justice in its day recognized the *locus standi* of individuals. The same was true of the mixed arbitral tribunals set up following the First World War.

The Measure of Reparation. The principal legal consequences of an international delinquency are payment of reparations to those who have suffered damage. Generally such reparations take two possible forms: (1) *restitutio in integrum*, i.e., the restoration of things as they were before the wrong was committed; and (2) *dommages-intérêts*, or economic compensation, either in lieu of restoration, which may be impossible, or as a complement to restoration, as the mere reestablishment of facts antecedent to the injury may not be sufficient to repair the damage actually done.[59]

It is, said the umpire in the *Lusitania Case*,[60]

a general rule of both the civil and common law that every invasion of a private right imports an injury, and that for every such injury the law gives a remedy. . . . It is variously expressed as 'compensation,' 'reparation,' 'indemnity,' 'recompense.' . . . The remedy should be commensurate with the loss, so that the injured party may be made whole.

Beyond this it is impossible to lay down any general rule, except to say that the amount and kind of reparation will depend on the circumstances of each individual case. There are, of course, a number of instances in which a formal apology on the part of the delinquent state may be all that is required.[61] A distinction would naturally be made between the type of reparation demanded for injuries of a premeditated and malicious nature, and those which arise as a result of culpable negligence.[62]

[59] Freeman, *op. cit.*, p. 573.
[60] Mixed Claims Commission, United States and Germany, Opinion in the *Lusitania Case*, Nov. 1, 1923, *Report and Decisions* (1925), p. 17.
[61] Oppenheim-Lauterpacht, *op. cit.*, p. 319.
[62] *Ibid.*, p. 320.

Should the delinquent state refuse reparations for the wrong done, a right would thereby be created in favor of the injured party to take any measures consistent with international obligations to pacific settlement of disputes. Among the questions which the Permanent Court of Arbitration in The Hague is competent to handle is "the nature or extent of the reparation to be made for the breach of an international obligation." [63]

In death cases, the right of action derives from the loss sustained by the claimant, not by the state.[64] The basis of damages is "not the physical or mental suffering of the deceased, or his loss, or the loss of his estate, but the losses resulting to claimant from his death." [65] Therefore, the problem in such cases is how to fix a reparation that will adequately compensate the claimants. The formula employed by Judge Parker in the *Lusitania Claims* was threefold: (1) estimate of the amount the decedent would have contributed to the claimant had he not been killed; (2) the pecuniary value of the services the deceased would have rendered to the claimant; and (3) reasonable compensation for the mental suffering and shock the claimant may have sustained as a result of such loss of life. In *United States (Janes Claim) v. Mexico* [66] it was held that the damage caused by the failure on the part of the Mexican authorities to punish the murder of Janes, an American national in Mexico, should be measured in terms of the grief and indignity suffered by the relatives of the deceased. In an opinion concurring in the award, but on different grounds, Commissioner Nielsen defended the condonation theory of liability. "Assuredly," he wrote, "the theory repeatedly advanced that a nation must be held liable for failure to take appropriate steps to punish persons who inflict wrongs upon aliens, because by such failure the nation condones the wrong and becomes responsible for it, is not illogical or arbitrary." [67]

The Permanent Court of International Justice, in a *Case Concerning Certain German Interests in Upper Silesia*,[68] has held that "a principle which seems to be established by international practice and in particular by the decisions of arbitral tribunals—is that reparation must, as far as possible, wipe out all the consequences of the illegal act and reestablish the situation which would, in all probability, have existed if that act had not been committed." The Court went on to say, however, that

the reparation due by one State to another does not . . . change its character by reason of the fact that it takes the form of an indemnity for the calculation

[63] Art. 36 of the Statute.   [64] *Ibid.*
[65] *Ibid.*
[66] United States–Mexico General Claims Commission, 1926, *Opinions of the Commissioners* (1927), p. 108.
[67] *Ibid.*, pp. 123 ff.   [68] *PCIJ Judgment*, ser. A, no. 7.

of which the damage suffered by a private person is taken as the measure. The rules of law governing the reparation are the rules of international law in force between the two States concerned, and not the law governing relations between the State which has committed a wrongful act and the individual who has suffered the damage.

The rights of the individual who has suffered damage through their infringement are always in a different plane from the rights of the state. But the rights of the state may indeed be infringed by the same illegal act. The damage suffered by the individual, therefore, is never identical in kind with that of the state. It can only "afford a convenient scale for the calculation of the reparation due to the State." [69]

There is also the question as to whether damages awarded as a result of violation of international law are punitive or merely compensatory in nature. Judge Parker addressed himself to this point in the *Lusitania Case* [70] as follows:

In our opinion, the words exemplary, vindictive, or punitive as applied to damages are misnomers. The fundamental concept of "damage" is satisfaction, reparation for a *loss* suffered; a judicially ascertained compensation for wrong. . . . The industry of counsel has failed to point us to any money award by an international arbitral tribunal where exemplary, punitive, or vindictive damages have been assessed against one sovereign nation in favor of another presenting a claim in behalf of its nationals.

It is true that international tribunals have been reluctant to award so-called indirect damages against states and have held that punitive reparations cannot be so awarded. Nevertheless, it should be remembered that the arbitrators have very often been bound in this regard by the terms of the *compromis d'arbitrage*.

With respect to the damage and destruction of property, it is equally difficult to state a general rule of measurement. Arbitral tribunals have sometimes based compensation on presumed profits which might have been realized but for the damage inflicted. But in other cases they have been content to award reparations commensurate with the intrinsic value of the property lost. [71] It may be said that the whole question of whether indirect as well as direct damages are to be awarded is controversial, or at least uncertain. In the *Irene Roberts Case,* [72] however, Commissioner Bainbridge pointed out that under certain circumstances "well established rules of international law fix a liability beyond that of compensa-

[69] *Ibid.*

[70] Mixed Claims Commission, United States–Germany (1923), *Decisions and Opinions*, pp. 25–27.

[71] See Eagleton, *op. cit.*, p. 197.

[72] J. H. Ralston, *Venezuelan Arbitrations* (1904), p. 145.

tion for the direct losses sustained." In the *Alabama Claims Case*,[73] however, it was held that "prospective earnings cannot properly be made the subject of compensation, inasmuch as they depend in their nature upon future and uncertain contingencies." Likewise, in the *Dix Case*,[74] the Arbitrators said: "International as well as municipal law denies compensation for remote consequences, in the absence of deliberate intention to injure."

Extinctive Prescription. A question which has frequently been raised in connection with claims cases is whether the principle of extinctive prescription has application in international law, i.e., whether the legal basis for various reparations and claims is dissipated by the efflux of time. A leading case concerning this matter is that of *Italy (Gentini) v. Venezuela*,[75] in which it was contended on behalf of Venezuela that the Italian claim in the amount of 3,900 bolivars must be considered barred by prescription. Italy, on the other hand, insisted that the principle of laches had no application in international law and based her argument upon the findings of the Permanent Court of Arbitration in the *Pious Fund Case*.[76] The United States had argued in this case that "it has never yet been held in international tribunals" that a claim brought before them could be defeated by reason of the existence of domestic statutes of limitation, "such statutes having no authority whatsoever over international courts." The Court agreed substantially with this argument and adopted almost verbatim the position taken by the United States.

But it would be incorrect to interpret the decision in the *Pious Fund Case* as a denial of the principle of prescription in international law. According to Ralston, Umpire in the *Gentini Case*: [77] "The Permanent Court of Arbitration has never denied the principle of prescription, a principle well recognized in international law, and it is fair to believe it will never do so."

It is desirable that the application of this doctrine should remain flexible in the manner of laches, rather than narrowed to fixed periods of time. It is a well-established principle that no state may invoke its municipal legislation or even its constitution to avoid international obligations. It has been repeatedly affirmed by jurists and publicists that there exist in the society of nations certain minimum standards of conduct, and that failure on the part of states to live up to these standards must necessarily result in international liability.

[73] United States–Great Britain Claims Arbitration, 1872, *Papers Relating to the Treaty of Washington*, vol. III, p. 49; Hudson, *Cases*, p. 1335.
[74] Ralston, *Venezuelan Arbitrations*, p. 9.
[75] Italy-Venezuela Mixed Claims Commission, 1903, Ralston's Report, p. 724.
[76] Scott, *Hague Court Reports*, p. 3.
[77] Ralston's Report, p. 724.

PART THREE

Territorial Problems

CHAPTER 11

State Territory

As we have already seen, one of the requisite elements of the state is *territory*. But the conception of territory has undergone many changes since the dawn of the law of nations. Even as late as the seventeenth century the Roman-medieval theory prevailed, by which state territory was regarded, more or less, as private property of the monarch. Thus we find that Grotius and his followers looked to the Roman law of property for the legal basis of state territory. At the present time the rules of Roman property law are no longer applicable to the acquisition of territory by states, but the fact that these principles were once regarded as primary is not without significance, for certain traces have been left from them which the tide in the affairs of nations has failed to obliterate. Yet the rules which govern acquisition and loss of state territory must be derived from the practice of states and not from Roman law. In this chapter we shall attempt to describe territory in terms of its various subdivisions.

How the Territory of a State Is Defined. *The territory of a state is composed of all the land and water surface within its boundaries and jurisdiction, all the earth and water below this surface, and all the air above it.* It will be remembered that territory is an essential element of the state and that no state can exist without it. As we have already seen, when the Papacy was forced to give up the remainder of its territory in 1870, by the Sardinian conquest of Rome, it lost thereby its identity as a state. It is generally agreed, however, that this "missing link" was supplied by the Lateran Treaty of 1928 when a portion of the lost territory was restored and made independent of the kingdom of Italy. Vatican City, thus established, is undoubtedly a state, though its territory is very small. The same may be said for the principalities of Monaco and Liechtenstein, as well as the Republic of San Marino. The requisite of state territory is not that it be large or small but rather that it be a "definite portion of the surface of the globe which is subject to the sovereignty of the State." [1]

The importance of territory lies in the fact that within its boundaries

[1] Oppenheim-Lauterpacht, *International Law* (1947), vol. I, p. 407.

the state exercises supreme authority. This would seem to suggest that in the same territory only one sovereignty can operate at any one time. This, however, is not in conformity with historic experience and contemporary practice, as many examples of condominium may be found, i.e., territories over which sovereignty is exercised by two or more states conjointly. As an example, we might mention the Duchies of Schleswig-Holstein and Lauenburg which from 1864 to 1866 were under the condominium of Austria and Prussia.[2] Another illustration is found in the treaty of August 6, 1914, by which the New Hebrides were placed under the condominium of France and England.[3] Likewise in the peace treaties of 1919 it was provided that joint sovereignty was to be exercised by the Allied and Associated Powers over certain territories ceded to them by the Central Powers until a final disposition should be made of such territories.[4]

In certain instances of territorial administration a state may exercise sovereignty which, in a strictly legal sense, is vested elsewhere. Thus the Turkish island of Cyprus from 1878 to 1914 was actually under British administration.[5] A similar situation obtained in the case of Austro-Hungarian rule in the Turkish provinces of Bosnia and Herzegovina in the period from 1878 to 1908. Though sovereignty was, for all practical purposes, exercised by the Dual Monarchy during this time, the legal seat of such power was located in the Turkish state. In the *Case concerning the Lighthouses in Crete and Samos*[6] of October 8, 1937, the Permanent Court of International Justice held that Turkey could properly grant and renew concessions regarding these islands and that, notwithstanding the wide autonomy which these territories enjoyed, sovereignty rested with Turkey in 1913. The question might well be raised at this point: How far can a juristic conception be stretched? Manley O. Hudson, in a dissenting opinion in the *Lighthouses Case*,[7] spoke of "a ghost of hollow sovereignty" which could not be permitted to obscure the realities of a situation.

There are also in the history of international relations a number of cases in which territory has been leased by one state to another, though the lessor did not thereby lose sovereignty over the territory in question. By

[2] *Ibid.*, p. 409.

[3] See also the Treaty of Alliance between Great Britain and Egypt of 1936, *Treaty Series*, no. 6 (1937), Cmd. 5360.

[4] See Art. 99 of the Treaty of Versailles concerning Memel, and Arts. 53 and 74 of the Treaty of Trianon with respect to Fiume.

[5] Cyprus was annexed outright by Great Britain on Nov. 5, 1914. See *Revue générale de droit international public*, vol. 21 (1914), pp. 510–512. By Art. 20 of the Treaty of Lausanne this annexation was recognized by Turkey.

[6] *PCIJ Judgment*, ser A/B, no. 71.

[7] *Ibid.*, p. 127.

such process China, in 1898, transferred certain territories to European powers.[8] It is true that for practical purposes such leases amount to territorial cessions, yet in a strictly legal sense the title and basic sovereignty is retained by the lessor. Furthermore, it is possible for such leases to expire. As an example we might mention the lease of the Lado Enclave by Great Britain to the Congo Free State in 1894, which was rescinded in 1906.

A most curious situation in this regard is that of the respective legal relationships of the United States and the Republic of Panama to the so-called Canal Zone. In 1903 the Panamanian Republic transferred to the United States a strip of territory 10 miles wide for the purpose of constructing, administering, and defending the Panama Canal. The best opinion seems to be that though all the sovereignty is exercised by the grantee in this case, the grantor retains, in a strictly legal sense, the territorial property. In the case of the *Luckenbach Steamship Company v. United States* [9] the Supreme Court held that the ports of the Canal Zone were foreign ports within the meaning of a United States statute. A corollary to this is a decision in 1930 by the Panamanian Supreme Court in which it was held that, in relation to Panama, the Canal Zone was not to be considered as foreign territory.[10]

Various Parts of State Territory. Aside from the land which lies within the boundaries of a state, the national waters—and, in cases of nations by the sea, the territorial waters—must be included under the general conception of territory. In addition to this we may also classify the regions which lie below the surfaces of land and water, as well as the air above them, as parts of the state's territory.

It is important to distinguish clearly between the waters which lie within the state and those which are adjacent to its borders. In the first case the waters are *national*, while in the second they are *territorial*. The national waters include lakes, rivers, and canals, as well as certain bays. Such waters are, from the standpoint of strict law, in a category no different from the land itself. Territorial waters, on the other hand, are in a somewhat different legal classification and comprise portions of certain gulfs, bays, and straits together with the waters which lie between the low-water mark and a line parallel to the shore located some distance at sea. The waters that intervene between this line and the low-water mark are sometimes referred to as the *marine belt* or the *marginal seas*. There is no universally accepted rule as to the width of the territorial waters,

[8] Kiaochow was leased to Germany; Wei-Hai-Wei and the land opposite the island of Hong Kong, to Great Britain; Kuang-Chou Wan, to France; and Port Arthur, to Russia.

[9] 280 U.S. 173 (1930).

[10] *Annual Digest* (1927–1930), Case no. 51.

though many nations have taken the measure to be one marine league or a distance of 3 miles.[11]

The Sea Bed and Its Subsoil. The same technological development in the last half century that made the atmosphere of the earth a useful medium of transportation and wireless communication has also made it possible for man to reach into the region which lies deep beneath the floor of the sea. One of the factors which has brought the sea bed and its subsoil within the focus of international legal considerations is the need for replenishment of the world's relatively limited oil reserves. Thus a great deal of attention has been devoted by prospectors and engineers to the possibility of locating and exploiting oil-bearing strata in the subsoil of ocean beds. In this connection a number of interesting questions have arisen, to which the law of nations must sooner or later provide the answers.

It is generally acknowledged that the littoral state may exercise certain rights with respect to the sea bed and subsoil that lie beneath its territorial waters.[12] But what is the situation regarding these regions when they are located below the waters of the open sea? Some writers have pointed to a difference in legal status between the sea bed and its subsoil,[13] while other writers have held that no such differentiation can be

---

[11] In 1930 a conference was held at The Hague on the codification of international law. The powers were unable, however, to come to any agreement on a convention relative to the "territorial sea." The questionnaire sent out preparatory to this conference revealed a variety of opinions as to "the breadth of the territorial waters under the sovereignty" of the littoral state. "According to the majority, the breadth is three nautical miles. No reply disputes that territorial waters include such a three mile belt. . . . The breadth proposed in some replies is four miles (e.g., by Sweden), in others six (e.g., Italy) or eighteen (e.g., Portugal)." *Report of the Preparatory Committee, League of Nations Document*, C. 74. M. 39. 1929. V, p. 33.

See also the case of the *Elida* (*Entscheidungen des Oberprisengerichts*, p. 9) in which it was held by the Imperial Supreme Prize Court of Germany that "heretofore, the maritime boundary of states has been generally recognized in theory and practice as being three nautical miles distant from the coast. Originally, it was based on the carrying distance, corresponding to the gunnery technique of those times, of ships' and coast guns. It is true that now-a-days this reason is no longer applicable. Here, however, the axiom *cessante ratione non cessat lex ipsa* applies, and although numerous proposals and opinions have been put forward with regard to a different delimitation of the national waters, it cannot be asserted that any other method has in practice met with the general concurrence of the maritime States"—translation from the German as published in the *American Journal of International Law*, vol. 10 (1916), p. 916.

But see also the judgment of the International Court of Justice in the *Anglo-Norwegian Fisheries Case* of Dec. 18, 1951, pp. 164–166.

[12] Jonkheer P. R. Feith, *Rights to the Sea Bed and Its Subsoil*, International Law Association (Brussels Conference, 1948).

[13] "A clear distinction must be drawn between the bed of the sea and its subsoil. As regards the former, the better opinion appears to be that it is incapable of occupation by any State and that its legal status is the same as that of the waters of the open sea above it. The same reasons for maintaining it unappropriated in the interests

made.[14] All authorities agree, however, that the ocean floor subsoil outside the territorial waters is a *res nullius*, a no man's land, open to occupation by anyone who is able to overcome the physical, as well as technical, difficulties standing in the way. On the other hand, there is much controversy concerning the status of the sea bed or sea floor as such. At times the bed of the sea, like its subsoil, has been regarded as a *res nullius*; at other times, like the ocean itself, it has been considered a *res communis omnium* or a *res extra commercium*.[15] It might be pointed out that exploitation of both the bottom and the subsoil of the sea has been carried on in various times and places, and the rights thus acquired have often been recognized by the law of nations.[16] In this connection a number of treaties have been entered into by the states whose interests were involved.[17]

The Continental Shelf Doctrine. On September 28, 1945, the President of the United States, Harry S. Truman, issued two very important proclamations. The first of these has reference to the sea bed and its subsoil, while the second extends the jurisdiction of the United States beyond the 3-mile limit with regard to fisheries.

The language of the first proclamation runs in part as follows:

Whereas it is the view of the Government of the United States that the exercise of jurisdiction over the natural resources of the subsoil and sea bed of the continental shelf by the continuous nation is reasonable and just, since the effectiveness of measures to utilize or conserve these resources would be contingent upon cooperation and protection from the shore, since the continental shelf may be regarded as an extension of the land-mass of the coastal nation and thus naturally appurtenant to it, since these resources frequently form a seaward extension of a pool of deposit lying within the territory, and since self-protection compels the coastal nation to keep close watch over activities off its shores which are of the nature necessary for utilization of these resources; . . . Having concern for the urgency of conserving and prudently utilizing its natural resources, the Government of the United States regards the natural resources of the subsoil and sea bed of the continental shelf beneath the high seas but continuous to the coasts of the United States as appertaining to the United States,

of the freedom of navigation apply, with equal force, to the bed of the sea"—A. P. Higgins and C. J. Colombos, *The International Law of the Sea* (1943), p. 54.

[14] See Oppenheim-Lauterpacht, *op. cit.*, p. 575. For the same opinion, see also Westlake, *International Law*, 2d ed., vol. I, pp. 190 and 203; Smith, *Great Britain and the Law of Nations*, vol. II, pt. I, p. 122; Verdross, *Die Verfassung der Völkerrechtsgemeinschaft*, p. 220.

[15] For authoritative treatment of this question, see Sir Cecil Hurst, "Whose Is the Bed of the Sea?" *The British Year Book of International Law* (1923–24), pp. 34–43.

[16] Feith, *op. cit.*

[17] For a list of such treaties see the Report of the League of Nations Committee of Experts for the Progressive Codification of International Law, March–April, 1927, p. 125.

subject to its jurisdiction and control. In cases where the continental shelf extends to the shores of another State, or is shared with an adjacent State, the boundary shall be determined by the United States and the State concerned in accordance with equitable principles. The character as high seas of the waters above the continental shelf and the right to their free and unimpeded navigation are in no way thus affected.

The second proclamation calls attention to the inadequacy of present arrangements for the "conservation and protection of fishery resources," located along the coasts of the United States. It proposes to establish conservation zones, "explicitly bounded," either by unilateral action on the part of the United States or by agreements with other states. It is made clear, however, that the character of the conservation areas as high seas and the right to their free navigation will remain unimpeded.[18]

Though these proclamations are interesting in themselves and may in the future be of great significance in determining the norms of the law of nations,[19] the theory of the continental shelf is nevertheless not a new invention. A Spanish writer, as early as 1916, urged that the territorial waters be made coterminous with the continental shelf in order to protect important food species of fish.[20]

At the same time and for the same reason Argentine writers expressed great interest in the continental shelf.[21] It was in 1916 also that the imperial government of Russia proclaimed as part of the empire's territory certain uninhabited islands in the arctic on the ground that they formed "the northern continuation of the Siberian continental shelf." [22] The Soviet government reasserted this claim in 1924.[23] Professor José Léon Suarez, who in 1927 served as reporter to the Sub-Committee for Exploitation of the Resources of the Sea in the preliminary proceedings to the Hague Codification Conference, argued that "there is no stable, permanent and convenient solution except to adopt the rule of the continental shelf with some modifications according to circumstance."

[18] For a critical analysis of both proclamations in terms of present international law, see E. Borchard, "Resources of the Continental Shelf," *American Journal of International Law*, vol. 40 (1946), p. 53; also J. W. Bingham, "The Continental Shelf and the Marginal Belt," *ibid.*, p. 173. See also Charles B. Selak, Jr., "Recent Developments in High Seas Fisheries Jurisdiction under the Presidential Proclamation of 1945," *ibid.*, vol. 44 (1950), pp. 670–681.

[19] "Six States have followed the example in the last three years, with certain notable modifications of their own, and it appears not improbable that the principle thus put forward may gain increasing acceptance in international practice"—Richard Young, "Recent Developments with Respect to the Continental Shelf," *American Journal of International Law*, vol. 42 (1948), p. 849.

[20] See League of Nations Document C. 196. M. 70. 1927. V. (1927), p. 63.

[21] S. R. Storni, *Intereses argentinos en el mar* (1916), p. 38 ff.; see also J. L. Suarez, *Diplomacia universitaria americana* (1918), pp. 174, 180 ff.

[22] Young, *op. cit.*, pp. 849–850.   [23] *Ibid.*, p. 850.

The treaty of February 26, 1942, between the United Kingdom and Venezuela concerning the submarine areas of the Gulf of Paria, may also be regarded as a significant precedent to subsequent claims by a number of states to the territory of the continental shelf. The waters which separate British Trinidad from Venezuela are about thirty-five miles wide and very shallow, but petroleum deposits are reported to exist in the subsoil of this sea bed. By the treaty of 1942 each state will recognize "any rights of sovereignty or control which have been or may hereafter be lawfully acquired" by the other over submarine areas on their respective sides of an arbitrary boundary line. By an Order in Council of August 6, 1942, Great Britain annexed the submarine areas on the Trinidad side of the boundary, while Venezuela took similar action on her side of the Parian Gulf.[24]

Only a month after President Truman's famous proclamation concerning the continental shelf, the President of Mexico followed suit by asserting that for the purpose of conserving the resources for "the welfare of the nation, the continent and the world," the Mexican government would claim the right of jurisdiction, protection, and control over the continental shelf contiguous to its recognized territory. In order to implement this proclamation certain proposals were made by the Executive to amend the constitution of the republic. Article 42, for example, would be altered to include the continental shelf as part of Mexico's territory, as well as the waters which cover this shelf to a depth of 200 meters at low tide.

Argentina, which because of her large continental shelf has a special interest in this matter, soon followed the example of the United States and Mexico. Thus, on October 11, 1946, the President of the Argentine Republic issued a decree declaring that the submarine shelf and its superincumbent waters are "subject to the sovereign power of the nation." Likewise, on May 1, 1947, Nicaragua proclaimed by congressional action sovereignty over the continental shelf adjacent to her shores. Two months later, the President of Chile proclaimed "national sovereignty" over the submarine shelf and the epicontinental waters for a distance seaward of 200 miles. On August 1 of the same year, Peru made a similar declaration, and a year later Costa Rica.[25] On November 26, 1948, a British Order in Council declared the boundaries of the Bahamas to "include the area of the continental shelf which lies beneath the sea contiguous to the coasts" of the colony. On the same day a similar Order was issued with reference to "the coasts of Jamaica, including its dependencies."[26]

With these examples and precedents we must end this section, as space

[24] *Ibid.*
[25] For more detail, see *ibid.*, pp. 849–857.
[26] See Orders in Council (1948), Statutory Instruments 2574 and 2575.

does not permit a more detailed history. But perhaps enough has been said to justify the tentative conclusion that a discernible trend is now in progress, particularly in the New World, to include the continental shelf within the territory of states. As to the extent of the territorial or marginal seas, it seems rather obvious that the eighteenth-century concept of the marine league is, in terms of modern problems of national defense, wholly inadequate. Would it not, therefore, be both logical and proper to extend the territorial waters to the edge of the continental shelf or to a depth of 100 fathoms, and in all cases to a minimum of 12 nautical miles?

Rivers. The territorial aspect of rivers which are located within the boundaries of a state is in no wise different from the land itself. The rule of both theory and practice is to the effect that rivers are part of the territory of the riparian state.[27] Rivers which originate and flow their entire course within the territory of one and the same state are known as *national rivers*. In countries such as the British Isles, Australia, and New Zealand, all the rivers would obviously come within this category. The same would be true of most rivers flowing in large countries such as the United States and the Soviet Union. In a second classification are the so-called *boundary rivers*, of which the Rio Grande and Rio de la Plata are examples. In the third place are *seminational rivers*,[28] so called because only part of their course can be located within the boundaries of any one state. Aside from the three types already mentioned, there is yet another group known as *international rivers*.[29] In this latter classification are rivers which, because of their importance as highways of commerce, are open to navigation by merchant ships of all nations in time of peace in accordance with existing international conventions.

With respect to the right of navigation on national rivers, the Grotian proposition that innocent passage must be granted is not in conformity with the recognized practice of states. Neither does the law of nations, as it exists today, support the assertion by Bluntschli that rivers which are navigable from the sea must be open, in time of peace, to all nations.[30] The same is true of seminational and boundary rivers, where the sovereign rights and the power to control navigation and other matters pertaining to such rivers rest exclusively with the riparian states. With regard to international rivers, the situation is wholly different. But even here no

[27] Oppenheim-Lauterpacht, *op. cit.*, p. 420.

[28] Other terms have been used to denote this category, such as *not-national, plurinational,* and *multinational rivers.*

[29] The classification of rivers into the categories of *national, boundary, seminational,* and *international* is identical with the terminology employed by Oppenheim, with one exception: Where we have used the term *seminational,* Oppenheim uses *not-national rivers.* See Oppenheim-Lauterpacht, *op. cit.*, pp. 420–421.

[30] *Ibid.*, p. 421.

legal rights, apart from those of the riparian states, can or do exist in the absence of special treaties and conventions.

Interior Seas and Lakes. From the point of view of territory, inland seas and lakes are no different from the land itself. Thus if such bodies of water are surrounded by the territory of the same state, the matter is simple. Like the rivers which flow their entire course wholly within the territory of the same state, lakes and seas thus surrounded by land come within the classification of national waters, and the jurisdiction of the state within which they are located is as complete as over the land. The fact that the water of certain inland seas or lakes may be salt is in this connection of no importance.[31] If, however, the waters of such seas or lakes are enclosed by the land of two or more states, the rule, in the absence of treaty arrangements to the contrary, is that they form proportionate parts of the territories of the states concerned.[32] Examples of lakes which are located wholly within the territory of the same state are the Great Salt Lake in the United States and the lakes Ladoga and Onega, which are Russian. Among the inland bodies of water that are surrounded by the land territory of more than one state, we may mention the American Great Lakes and the Caspian Sea.

Gulfs and Bays. With regard to the territorial definition of gulfs and bays, there seems to be considerable controversy among the authorities. It is fairly certain, however, that the waters of a gulf or bay, enclosed by the land territory of one and the same state and a line drawn from one headland to the other where the distance between them is no more than 10 miles, are to be considered as the national waters of the littoral state. Such a line drawn between the headlands must, therefore, be regarded as a continuation of the shoreline,[33] and its perpendicular seaward, for a distance of at least 3 nautical miles, as the width of the maritime belt.

The rules we have stated in the preceding paragraph with respect to the territorial definition of bays are not without exceptions. The most important of these, and the only one with which we need be concerned here, is that of the so-called *historic* bays. The fact that uninterrupted dominion over certain bays has been exercised by the littoral state for a considerable period of time has created a historic basis for territorial claims recognized as valid under the law of nations. In accordance with this principle, the

---

[31] John Bassett Moore, *Digest of International Law*, vol. I, p. 669.
[32] *Ibid.*
[33] See *Commonwealth v. Manchester*, 152 Mass. 230; 25 N. E. 113; 9 L.R.A. 236; 23 Am. St. Rep. 820 (1890). But see also the judgment of the International Court of Justice in the *Anglo-Norwegian Fisheries Case* of Dec. 18, 1951. Here the so-called headland theory was recognized, with the application of base lines 44 miles in length. The Court refused to accept the contention that there existed a rule in international law delimiting the length of base lines to 10 miles.

United States has always claimed as part of its maritime territory the bays of Chesapeake and Delaware, as well as other inlets of the same character.[34] France considers the Bay of Cancale as within its territorial waters, even though the distance across at the entrance is 17 miles. Great Britain holds the Bay of Conception to be territorial, a claim which was supported by the Privy Council in *Direct United States Cable Co. v. The Anglo-American Telegraph Co.*[35] Though the Lords were guided in their decision by a British statute of 1819,[36] they were not unmindful of the principles of international law in so far as they were applicable to the question at issue. Even such a great body of water as the Hudson Bay, which has an area of about 580,000 square miles, is in its entirety claimed by Canada as part of that country's territory, though its width at the entrance is no less than 50 miles.

The Base-lines System. On September 28, 1949, the United Kingdom filed an application with the Registry of the International Court of Justice asking that the Norwegian royal decree of July 12, 1935, regarding the delimitation of a fisheries zone off the Norwegian coast be tested as to its legality under the law of nations. Norway's position was to the effect that the extent of her territorial sea should be measured by perpendiculars drawn from the outer islands in the *skjaergaard*,[37] and from base lines drawn between these islands as well as between the headlands of certain bays.

The judgment in this case was rendered on December 18, 1951, and was completely in favor of the Norwegian position. The Court pointed out that "although it is true that the act of delimitation [of coastal waters] is necessarily a unilateral act, because only the coastal State is competent to undertake it, the validity of the delimitation with regard to other States depends upon international law."[38] Another fundamental consideration, according to the judgment in this case, is the "more or less close relationship existing between certain sea areas and the land formations which divide and surround them."[39] The Court went on to say that "it is

[34] See Moore, *op. cit.*, p. 735.
[35] L. R. 2 App. Cas. 394 (1877).   [36] 59 Geo. III, c. 38.
[37] *The skjaergaard* is a generic term for the islands and rocks which form a belt along the Norwegian coast. According to the Court: "Since the mainland is bordered in its western sector by the 'skjaergaard,' which constitutes a whole with the mainland, it is the outer line of the 'skjaergaard' which must be taken into account in delimiting the belt of Norwegian territorial waters. This solution is dictated by geographic realities"—fisheries case, Judgment of Dec. 18, 1951, *ICJ Reports*, 1951, p. 128.
[38] *Ibid.*, p. 132.
[39] *Ibid.*, p. 133. In this connection, see also the *Grisbadarna Case*, Tribunal of the Permanent Court of Arbitration, 1909, J. B. Scott, *The Hague Court Reports* (1916), p. 127. In that case it was held "in conformity with the fundamental principles of the law of nations, both ancient and modern . . . , [that] the maritime territory is an essential appurtenance of the land territory. . . ."

the land which confers upon the coastal State a right to the waters off its coasts." [40] Thus the relevant question regarding the choice of base lines was actually whether the sea areas lying inside these lines were so closely connected with the land domain as to be reasonably treated as internal waters.[41]

In a final consideration going beyond purely geographical factors, the Court recognized the "economic interests peculiar to a region, the reality and importance of which are clearly evidenced by a long usage." [42]

On the bases of these criteria, the Court rejected all submissions to the contrary, and found by 10 votes to 2 that "the method employed for the delimitation of the fisheries zone by the Royal Norwegian Decree of July 12th, 1935, is not contrary to international law." It likewise found, by 8 votes to 4, that "the base-lines fixed by the said Decree in application of this method are not contrary to international law." [43]

The fact that Norway, along with the other Scandinavian states, is claiming a 4-mile belt for its territorial waters was not a matter at issue in this case, as this point was conceded by Great Britain.[44] Therefore, that this claim will ever be contested in the future is highly unlikely.[45] It is of the greatest importance that though the Norwegian royal decree of July 12, 1935, had reference only to the delimitation of a fisheries zone, the Court went on to decide the actual delimitation of territorial waters as such. "There can be no doubt," said the Court, "that the zone delimited by this decree is none other than the sea area which Norway considers to be her territorial sea. That is how the Parties argued the question and that is the way in which they submitted it to the Court for decision." [46] This should not, however, be taken as an indication that all objective criteria for the delimitation of territorial waters have been displaced by the subjective discretion of each coastal state. On the contrary, the Court definitely states that "the delimitation of sea areas has always an international aspect; it cannot be dependent merely upon the will of the coastal State as expressed in its municipal law." [47]

Another important conclusion to be drawn from this case is that the base-line method of delimitation of territorial waters is in conformity with existing international law and that no rule is valid which would

[40] *Judgment, ICJ Reports* (1951), p. 133.
[41] Jens Evensen, "The Anglo-Norwegian Fisheries Case and Its Legal Consequences," *American Journal of Internation Law* vol. 46 (1952), p. 623.
[42] *Judgment, ICJ Reports* (1951), p. 133.
[43] Manley O. Hudson, "The Thirtieth Year of the World Court," *American Journal of International Law* vol. 46 (1952), p. 26.
[44] *Judgment, ICJ Reports* (1951), p. 126.
[45] See Evensen, *op. cit.*, p. 628.
[46] *Judgment, ICJ Reports* (1951), p. 125.
[47] *Ibid.*, p. 132.

limit the length of such base lines to 6 or 10 miles. Even Sir Arnold Mc-Nair, in his dissenting opinion, admitted that no such rule can be said to exist under the law of nations. It may be said, therefore, that there exists no fixed maximum as to the length of such lines which may be drawn between islands and headlands. On the other hand, geographic, economic, and historical factors may determine, in each individual case, the use of this method as well as the length of such base lines, and hence the area of both the internal and external seas belonging to any state.

Straits. Straits which divide the land territory of one and the same state are in all cases territorial, provided their width does not exceed 6 nautical miles. But in cases where the opposite shores of straits are those of different states, the territory of each will extend 3 miles from the low-water mark in the direction of the other. If, however, the straits are so narrow as to make such measures overlap, the general rule is that the boundary shall be a line located midway between the opposite shores, unless it is otherwise fixed by treaty.[48] It is a matter of controversy whether straits which are more than 6 miles wide, yet narrow enough to be commanded by coastal guns, are to be considered as national territory. A majority of writers seem to think that waters thus defensible do in fact constitute part of the territory of the littoral state, while a minority—among them the famous authority Westlake—take a contrary view.

Historically, we know that states have laid claim to whole oceans as part of their territory, supposedly on the basis of discovery and exploration. In his *Mare liberum,* that first great argument for the freedom of the seas, Grotius advanced the proposition that no nation could make the open sea a part of its territory, as effective occupation was impossible. Though this contention was denied by the learned Selden in the latter's *Mare clausum,* history was on the side of the renowned Dutchman. Yet, the notion that the territorial claims of states could not extend to the high seas was not generally accepted until the eighteenth century. It was Bynkershoek, another famous jurist of the Netherlands, who first suggested that the maritime territory of states should terminate with the range of land-based cannon, which in the early eighteenth century was approximately 1 marine league, i.e., 3 nautical miles.

According to Oppenheim, "It would seem that claims of states over

[48] See the Act of 1928 (18 & 19 Geo. 5, c. 23) approving the agreement between Great Britain and the Sultan of Johore of Oct. 19, 1927; the boundary line between the territorial waters of Singapore and Johore shall follow the center of the deep-water channel in Johore Strait. See also the Anglo-American treaty of June 15, 1846, regarding the Straits of Luis de Haro and Juan de Fuca and the arbitral award relating to Portland Canal of Oct. 20, 1903, between Great Britain and the U.S., adopting the middle line and rejecting the American arguments based on the *thalweg.* Higgins and Colombos, *op. cit.,* p. 125.

wider straits than those which can be commanded by guns from coast batteries can no longer be upheld." [49] The present author, however, is of the opinion that though the range of coastal guns may at one time have been a valid criterion for the measure of territorial waters, it is no longer acceptable. Recent technological developments have shown the factor of gun range too unstable and indeed too unpredictable as a standard in this regard. It would seem, therefore, that the only reasonable solution can be found in a linear measure which can be agreed upon and fixed quite independently of the range of modern weapons.

Were we to accept the criterion implied by Oppenheim, it might logically follow that Norway could claim as part of her territorial waters the open seas intervening between Magerö and Svalbard. Similarly, it might well be that Portugal could consider as part of her territory that portion of the south Atlantic which lies between her own shores and the Canary Islands. This could go on almost ad infinitum and is obviously impossible. It is not unreasonable, however, to maintain, as some do, that the maritime belt should be widened beyond the present more or less universally accepted 3-mile limit to some greater distance. If, for example, this distance should be extended to a minimum of 12 miles, it would be possible for a State whose territory was located on opposite sides of a strait 24 miles wide to claim its waters as territorial. In any case, to preserve the freedom of the seas, it is obviously necessary to arrive at the territorial demarcation of states by means other than gun range.

Territorial Air. With the development of aerial transportation in the present century, the air territory of states has acquired a new significance. As we have already said, the airspace above the land and water surfaces of any state is the exclusive property of that state and of its inhabitants. From this follows the right on the part of states and peoples to exploit the atmospheric space located over their respective territories, not only with regard to its chemical resources, but also with regard to its usefulness as a medium of transportation and communication.

Since the utility of the aerial space in these respects did not become apparent until recently, customary law on the subject was necessarily lacking. As a result a number of theories relating to the territorial air were advanced by jurists and writers in the field of international law. According to some authorities, the airspace in its entirety was to be considered analogous to the high seas, thus common and free to all. Others argued that the atmosphere be divided into an upper and lower zone, the first being free like the oceans and the second territorial in the same sense as the marginal seas.

With the coming of the First World War it became apparent that none

[49] Oppenheim-Lauterpacht, *op. cit.*, p. 463.

of these theories was practical, and a number of states hastened to claim complete sovereignty over the air superincumbent on their land and water territories. The Aerial Navigation or International Flying Convention, which was signed at Paris on October 13, 1919, confirmed this as the law by stating that "every Power has complete and exclusive sovereignty over the air space above its territory." [50] In almost identical language, the Convention on International Civil Aviation, signed at Chicago November 1, 1944, which has been described as the "constitution for the postwar global air world," reaffirms the principle of sovereignty complete and exclusive on the part of states in the atmospheric space which lies over their respective land and sea territories.[51]

[50] See M. O. Hudson, *International Legislation,* vol. I, p. 359.
[51] See *Final Act and Related Documents of the International Civil Aviation Conference,* Department of State Publication 2282.

CHAPTER 12

Territorial Acquisition and Loss

Since time immemorial man has contended against man and nation against nation for possessions in the earth. We find therefore, in the historic annals of the human race many interesting and heroic accounts of explorers and soldiers whose exploits increased the domains of their native lands by discovery and conquest.

Among the various modes by which states acquire territory, in conformity with the law of nations, occupation and cession are the most important. The history of occupation may be divided into three periods: (1) Before the sixteenth century territorial acquisition was based in the main upon papal grants. (2) During the sixteenth and seventeenth centuries the British, French, and Dutch, who refused to recognize the papal grants to Spain and Portugal, based their respective claims upon discovery and occupation. (3) It was not until the eighteenth century that the principle of "effective occupation" became firmly established. This last doctrine was put into practice in connection with the partition of Africa in the last half of the nineteenth century.

Cession is a derivative mode of territorial acquisition, for the most part a result of purchase and conquest, but defined by treaty provisions. Whatever the motivating cause of cession, there is a fiction in the law which maintains that all cessions are voluntary, even though imposed by the force of conquest. It should be noted, however, that because of the glaring disparity in such cases between law and ethics, numerous attempts have been made by publicists, and even by some statesmen when politically expedient, to consider such territorial acquisition illegal and to refuse recognition of any changes in the *status quo* which are brought about by armed aggression. We shall have more to say on this point in a later chapter.

Among other methods by which the domain of a state may be increased, we might mention subjugation, prescription, and accretion. Our task in this chapter will be to define and illustrate the various modes of territorial

169

acquisition and loss by reference both to the theory and the practice of states.

Discovery and Occupation. According to Vattel:

All men have an equal right to things which have not yet come into the possession of anyone, and these things belong to the person who first takes possession. When, therefore, a Nation finds a country uninhabited and without an owner, it may lawfully take possession of it, and after it has given sufficient signs of its intention in this respect, it may not be deprived of it by another Nation.[1]

Though it is an established norm in international law that territory may be acquired by any state as a result of discovery and occupation, its practical significance is less today than in former times. The surface of the earth has already been conquered by intrepid explorers of many lands, and the world needs least of all a new Columbus. Yet the law which governed the occupations of former times is not without application in the present, especially with regard to such problems as boundary disputes. It should be noted, however, that though the principles of law are fairly clear, much difficulty is encountered in its application to facts which may have accumulated for many centuries.[2] This is very well illustrated in the famous *East Greenland Case*,[3] decided by the Permanent Court of International Justice in 1933, where it became necessary to apply the existing law to events that took place nearly a thousand years ago.

In view of the fact that the East Greenland dispute is considered by some authorities the leading case on territorial acquisition by occupation, a synopsis is given of its main facts. It began in 1931 with a Norwegian proclamation announcing occupation of certain parts of East Greenland. Denmark, claiming sovereignty over the whole of Greenland, and acting under the optional clause of the Statute, asked the Permanent Court to declare the Norwegian proclamation illegal under the law of nations. Norway's claim was based on the assumption that since the areas in question were uninhabited, they constituted for all practical purposes *terra nullius*, capable of occupation.

The Court in its decision of April 5, 1933, pointed out that two factors are involved in the acquisition of title by occupation, namely, "the intention or will to act as sovereign, and some actual exercises or display of authority." In other words, the Court was saying that what is needed to sustain territorial claims of this kind is effective occupation. The Court

[1] E. de Vattel, *Le droit des gens*, edition of 1758, book I, secs. 207–208. Fenwick's translation, *Classics of International Law*, No. 4, 1916.

[2] J. L. Brierly, *The Law of Nations* (1949), p. 143.

[3] *PCIJ Judgment* (1933), ser A/B, no. 53, p. 22; M. O. Hudson, *World Court Reports*, vol. III, p. 151.

was satisfied on the basis of evidence that, from the year 1721 to 1931, Danish claims to sovereignty over the whole of the island had never been challenged by any other nation. The arctic and inaccessible nature of Greenland made it unreasonable to demand a continuous and vigorous exercise of authority. The absence of any rival claim to the territory in question, or any other part of the island, was given considerable weight by the Court; there could be no doubt of the intention or will on the part of Denmark to act as a sovereign. As to the second factor, that of "exercise or display of authority," the Court held that in the absence of any rival claims by other states only a relatively slight manifestation of authority was required.

The existence of numerous legislative and administrative acts having purported application to the whole of Greenland, as well as a number of treaties in which this state of affairs was recognized, tended to strengthen the case of the Kingdom of Denmark. In view of these things, the Permanent Court of International Justice held that the area claimed by Norway was not in 1931 *terra nullius*, capable of acquisition by occupation.

Though it is correct to say that mere discovery of new territory is not in itself enough to establish valid claims, it does nevertheless qualify the strict rule of "effective occupation" in that it gives to the discoverer an "inchoate title" to the territory in question. That is to say, it gives to the state of discovery an option to establish effective occupation within a reasonable time.

A famous case dealing with the legal significance of discovery is the *Island of Palmas Arbitration* of 1928 [4] between the United States and the Netherlands. The island of Palmas or Miangas, which lies about halfway between the Cape of San Augustin on Mindanao in the Philippines and the northernmost island of Nanusa in what was then the Netherlands East Indies, was claimed by the United States following the Spanish-American War. The United States rested its claim principally on the Treaty of Paris of December 10, 1898, by which the island of Palmas had allegedly been acquired through the Spanish cession. The main point to be decided was whether the island of Palmas, at the time of the conclusion of this treaty, was part of the Spanish or the Netherlands domain. "It is evident," said the Arbitrator, Huber, "that Spain could not transfer more rights than she herself possessed."

It was admitted by both parties to the dispute that the law of nations has undergone profound modifications between the end of the Middle Ages and the end of the nineteenth century with respect to rights of discovery and territorial acquisition of uninhabited regions or those inhabited by savages or semicivilized peoples. It was also agreed by both disputants

[4] J. B. Scott, *Hague Court Reports*, 2d series, p. 84.

that "a juridical fact must be appreciated in the light of the law contemporary with it, and not of the law in force at the time when a dispute in regard to it arises or falls to be settled." Thus the effect of discovery by Spain was to be determined by those rules of international law which were in force in the first half of the sixteenth century, when the Spanish explorers made their appearance in the Sea of Celebes.

Even if the view is taken that mere discovery, without any attempt at temporary or continuous occupation, is sufficient to establish title, one question still remains: Did such sovereignty exist at the *critical date*, i.e., the moment of the conclusion of the treaty of Paris? This question obviously had to be answered in terms of the law of nations as understood in the late nineteenth century. But the law ever since the middle of the eighteenth century had laid down the principle that territorial claims can rest only on *effective occupation*, i.e., that the state claiming the territory must be in a position to offer certain guarantees to other states and their nationals. The Court of Arbitration, therefore, held that "discovery alone without any subsequent act, cannot at the present time suffice to prove sovereignty over the Island of Palmas." Thus while the title originally acquired by Spain was inchoate, it had not been converted into a definitive title by effective occupation within a reasonable time.

Another case illustrative of the manner in which territory may be acquired by occupation is the *Clipperton Island Arbitration of 1931*.[5] This arbitration was in pursuance of an agreement of March 2, 1909, and involved a dispute between France and Mexico regarding the sovereignty over Clipperton Island. There were two questions which had to be answered in this case: (1) Was there any basis for the claim that Clipperton Island belonged to Mexico before the French proclaimed sovereignty? (2) If no foundation in law and fact could be found to substantiate the Mexican claim, then had France proceeded to an effective occupation by satisfying all the conditions required by the law of nations?

After having answered the first question in the negative, the Arbitrator addressed himself to the remaining and disputed question of whether or not the alleged French occupation was of a nature that could be deemed "effective" in terms of contemporary international law. It was held that, by immemorial usage having the force of law, it is necessary to the claim of sovereignty that occupation be *actual* rather than *nominal*. "This taking of possession consists in the act, or series of acts, by which the occupying State reduces to its possession the territory in question and takes steps to exercise exclusive authority there." Since the island was considered *territorium nullius,* the Arbitrator saw no reason to invoke the provisions

[5] M. O. Hudson, *Cases and Other Materials on International Law* (1936), pp. 358–361.

of the Act of Berlin of 1885, which required that occupation be accompanied by the exercise of authority sufficient to safeguard acquired rights. Furthermore, the French proclamation of sovereignty over Clipperton was dated November 17, 1858, a fact which rendered the subsequent Act of Berlin inapplicable. As to the question of proper notification on the part of the French government, the Arbitrator held that the publication in a Honolulu journal of the fact that sovereignty over Clipperton Island had been assumed by France, and the communication of the accomplishment to the government of Hawaii by the French Consulate, were sufficient under the then existing law. Here again the special provisions relative to such notification contained in Article 34 of the Act of Berlin were held to be without application. On the basis of these main premises, the Arbitrator arrived at the conclusion that "Clipperton Island was legitimately acquired by France on November 17, 1858."

Territorial Claims in the Arctic. As a result of the development of air transportation, the frigid "ends of the earth" are no longer exclusive to polar bears and penguins. It was not geography but the hazards of climate that made the polar regions remote. Before the advent of aircraft, the frozen sea formed a barrier between two worlds, a barrier that for all practical purposes was impassable to man. But modern science and technology have changed all this, and lent a new significance to the geographic truth that over the arctic ice fields lies the shortest route between Washington and Moscow. It is the strategic rather than the economic importance of this ice-filled sea that has inspired new territorial claims to "lands and islands," both known and unknown, which lie within the region.

Of special interest in this connection are the claims of the Dominion of Canada and those of the Soviet Union, based upon the so-called "sector principle." By the application of this principle, each of these states claims sovereignty within an area circumscribed by a base line connecting the meridians of longitude marking the limits of its easterly and westerly frontiers and the projection of those meridians to their final intersection at the North Pole.[6] Though the "sector principle" has found favor in Canada, it has been somewhat informally expressed and has been consciously reinforced by the attempted exercise of administrative control.[7]

A more formal assertion to territorial claims has been made by Russia. On April 15, 1926, the Presidium of the Central Executive Committee of the U.S.S.R. issued a decree [8] proclaiming as

[6] Charles Cheney Hyde, *International Law* (1945), vol. I, p. 349.
[7] Edwin D. Dickinson, *Cases and Materials on International Law* (1950), pp. 185–186.
[8] See Lakhtine, "Rights over the Arctic," *American Journal of International Law*, vol. 24 (1930), pp. 703–709.

part of the territory of the Union of Soviet Socialistic Republics all lands and islands already discovered, as well as those which are to be discovered in the future, which at the moment of the publication of the present decree are not recognized by the Union of Soviet Socialistic Republics as the territory of any foreign state, and which lie in the Northern Frozen Ocean north of the coast of the Union of Soviet Socialistic Republics up to the North Pole, within the limits between the meridian longitude 32° 4′ 35″ east from Greenwich, which passes along the eastern side of Vaida Cay through the triangular mark on the Kekurski Cape, and the meridian longitude 168° 49′ 30″ west from Greenwich, which passes along the middle of the strait which separates Ratmanoff and Krusenstern Islands from the group of Diomede Islands in the Behring Straits.

Russia has also sought to strengthen her claims in the arctic by explorations and by setting up at least a minimum of administrative control.[9]

Gustav Smedal has pointed out the comparative advantage to Canada and the Soviet Union in the application of the so-called "sector principle," as these nations have long coastlines along the Arctic Sea.[10]

The most authoritative position with regard to the acquisition of territory seems to be that sovereignty cannot be gained over any portion of a *territorium nullius* by such relatively simple expedients as the establishment of radio stations or scientific observation posts. Such activities on the part of states, though not in themselves sufficient to establish title, are nevertheless not without importance as means to that end. "A wireless station is, for instance, an excellent point of support to a colonization."[11] This is especially true if such outposts are given police powers sufficient to control the areas in question and thus to bring them under the authority of the state. Furthermore, the scientific knowledge gained from such expeditions may indeed facilitate permanent settlement.

It should be noted also that any acts on the part of states, though not in themselves an expression of sovereignty, may in case of future disputes regarding territorial claims be of decisive importance. This is especially true in cases where the court is not bound by strict law but is free to seek the most equitable solution.[12] In the *Grisbadarna Case*,[13] for example, the Permanent Court of Arbitration based its decision in part on the following facts and circumstances: [14]

(a) The circumstance that lobster fishing in the shoals of Grisbadarna has

[9] Dickinson, *op. cit.*, p. 186.
[10] Gustav Smedal, *Acquisition of Sovereignty over Polar Areas* (Oslo, 1931; translated by C. Meyer), p. 62.
[11] G. H. Hackworth, *Digest of International Law*, vol. I, p. 406.
[12] See Smedal, *op. cit.*, p. 39.
[13] Between Norway and Sweden, decided Oct. 23, 1909. See J. B. Scott, *The Hague Court Reports* (1916), pp. 122 and 487.
[14] *Ibid.*, p. 130.

been carried on for a much longer time, to a much larger extent, and by a much larger number of fishermen by the subjects of Sweden than by the subjects of Norway.

(b) The circumstance that Sweden has performed various acts in the Grisbadarna region, especially of late, owing to her conviction that these regions were Swedish, as, for instance, the placing of beacons, the measurement of the sea, and the installation of a lightboat, being acts which involved considerable expense and in doing which she not only thought that she was exercising her right but even more that she was performing her duty; whereas Norway, according to her own admission, showed much less solicitude in this region in these various regards.

Territorial Claims in the Antarctic. Discovery and exploration in and around the antarctic continent have lately given rise to conflicting territorial claims by many nations. Great Britain has laid claim to a very large portion of the antarctic region. While these claims are based largely on discovery and exploration, the "sector theory" seems to have been made use of in some cases, especially in connection with the Falkland Island and Ross Dependencies. Argentine and Chilean claims appear to be based in part on the "sector principle" and in part on certain explorations and administrative acts. The Norwegian claim to the coast of the antarctic continent which lies between the Falkland Islands and Australian Dependencies, as well as to the territory situated within this coast and its adjacent waters, seems to rest primarily on discovery. An attempt at some sort of administrative control was certainly indicated by the fact that Norway's Ministry of Justice was authorized to take the necessary steps concerning the exercise of police authority in the region.

The United States has refused to recognize territorial claims in polar regions which are based merely on discovery and the formal taking of possession. The French claim to Adélie Land, which was initially based on discovery, the territory being by decrees placed under the authority of the colonial government of Madagascar, was not recognized as valid by this country. In this connection the Department of State of the United States instructed the American ambassador to transmit a note to the French Minister of Foreign Affairs in terms as follows: [15]

My Government understands that France bases its claims to the territory in question on the discovery of the coast of the region by the distinguished French explorer, Admiral Dumont d'Urville, in 1840; on the subsequent publication of the facts of his discovery and the action taken by him in connection therewith; and on the decrees of March 27, 1924, November 21, 1924, and April 1, 1938. So far as my Government is aware, Admiral Dumont d'Urville did not even land on the coast claimed for France by him, nor has any French citizen

[15] Hackworth, *op. cit.*, p. 460.

visited the area south of the 60th parallel south latitude and between the 136th and 142nd meridian east longitude since then.

While my Government believes that it is unnecessary at this time to enter into any detailed discussion of the subject, nevertheless, in order to avoid misapprehension, I am instructed to inform your Excellency that in the light of established principles of international law the United States Government cannot admit that sovereignty accrues from mere discovery.

On January 29, 1934, a note was addressed to the Secretary of State of the United States by the British ambassador in Washington, concerning the second Byrd expedition to the antarctic. His Majesty's Government of New Zealand had become alarmed by certain news reports to the effect that a United States Post Office was to be established at Admiral Byrd's base camp. It was also understood that special stamps for use in antarctica had been issued by the government of the United States, and that certain members of the expedition had been duly sworn in to act as postmasters in Little America. The note went on to say: [16]

While His Majesty's Government in New Zealand recognize that some allowance must be made for the absence of ordinary postal facilities in the Ross Dependency, they would point out that if a United States post office were to be officially established in the dependency, or if the United States Government were to sanction the use of United States postage stamps there without permission from the sovereign Power, such acts could not be regarded otherwise than as infringing the British sovereignty and New Zealand administrative rights in the dependency as well as the laws there in force.

The reply from the government of the United States ran in part as follows: [17]

It is understood that His Majesty's Government in New Zealand bases its claim of sovereignty on the discovery of a portion of the region in question. While it is unnecessary to enter into any detailed discussion of the subject at this time, nevertheless, in order to avoid misapprehension, it is proper for me to say, in the light of long established principles of international law, that I can not admit that sovereignty accrues from mere discovery unaccompanied by occupancy and use.

An interesting question which has arisen with regard to territorial claims in polar regions is whether the peculiar geographic and climatic conditions in those areas require modifications in the ordinary tests of effective occupation. It would seem reasonable, however, that if there are to be certain relaxations of legal requirements for territorial claims because of special conditions, such changes in the law can have no gen-

[16] *Ibid.*, p. 456.
[17] *Ibid.*, p. 457.

eral application. "The relaxation should be confined to the waiving of settlement as a necessary condition for the perfecting of a right of sovereignty, provided a claimant state may establish that by some other process it is in a position to exercise control over what it claims as its own." [18] It will be remembered, in this connection, that in the *East Greenland Case,* the Permanent Court of International Justice held that Denmark could not be expected to exercise continuous and vigorous authority over all Greenland because of the rigorous climate and the inaccessible nature of that arctic island.

In the event that great natural resources should be discovered in the antarctic regions and further advancement in technology should make their exploitation profitable, it would most certainly be necessary to resolve the conflicting territorial claims in this frozen continent. It is also reasonable to expect that whatever is done in this regard in the south polar regions will serve as precedents for the solution of similar problems in the arctic. The present author is of the opinion, however, that any attempt to alter the formula of *effective occupation* because of special geographic and climatic conditions can be of only dubious value. It would seem that any territorial title, whether based on original discovery or the "sector principle," in the absence of effective occupation, would tend to widen rather than bridge the gap between reality and law.

Conquest and Subjugation. When as a result of the application of force the territory of one state is brought under the control of another, the term most frequently used to describe the phenomenon is *conquest.* But "conquest alone," says Oppenheim, "does not *ipso facto* make the conquering State the sovereign of the conquered territory, although such territory comes through conquest for the time under the sway of the conqueror." [19] The territory thus conquered is regarded as in a state of military occupation, and the legal transfer of sovereignty must await the formal annexation by the conquering state. If all the territory of the vanquished state is annexed, the process is known as *subjugation.* But should only a portion of the territory be involved in the transfer and the defeated state be allowed to exist as an international person, the result is termed *cession.*

The distinction between conquest and subjugation, however, is illustrated by the eclipse of the German state authority following the destruction of her armies in 1945 by the military forces of the Allies. By joint declaration of January 5, 1945, the United States, Great Britain, France, and the Soviet Union assumed supreme authority over all German terri-

[18] *Ibid.,* p. 453. See also Charles Cheney Hyde, "Acquisition of Sovereignty over Polar Areas," *Iowa Law Review,* vol. 19 (1934), pp. 293–294.

[19] L. Oppenheim-Lauterpacht, *International Law* (1947), vol. I, p. 518.

tory, and the functions of local as well as central government in the former *Reich*. But it was expressly stated that such assumption of power was not tantamount to annexation and that the future boundaries of Germany would be fixed later. Thus, the assumption of full authority within Germany by the powers mentioned above could not legally have been distinguished from subjugation but for the express disclaimer of annexation.[20]

Though it is generally true, as stated above, that subjugation involves the annexation of the whole territory of the vanquished state, it is, of course, possible that only a portion of the territory of such a state would be involved. This would be the case if, at the end of a war, in the absence of a treaty of cession, a conquered state should submit, without protest, to territorial appropriation by the victor. It is clear, however, that no legal transfer of title can take place so long as the war is in progress. "For annexation of conquered enemy territory, whether of the whole or of part, confers a title only after a *firmly established* conquest, and so long as war continues conquest is not firmly established." [21]

The legality, under any and all circumstances, of the acquisition of territory through conquest and subjugation is, in view of recent legal developments, open to question. But we shall reserve this debate to a later chapter.

Territorial Cession. Cession is a bilateral transaction by which territorial sovereignty is transferred by one state to another. It has been classified as a derivative mode of acquisition, as title to such territory is always derived from the state that was the previous owner. History is replete with examples of territorial acquisition and loss through this means, and its legality under the law of nations is unquestioned. Whatever the provisions of municipal law may be with respect to cession, they are without direct effect upon the established rules of international law. Yet, it is true that in cases where municipal rules contain constitutional restrictions with regard to the cession of territory, any act by the agents of the state in contravention of such constitutional provisions cannot stand. Nevertheless, under certain circumstances such action on the part of state agents may create international obligations.

In order for cession to have legal effect, the subjects involved in the transaction must be international persons. Thus cessions made by tribal chiefs, private persons, and corporations have no standing in international law. The same would be true if the parties to a territorial transfer were

---

[20] *Ibid.*, p. 520. In this connection see Hans Kelsen in *American Journal of International Law*, vol. 39, pp. 518–526.

[21] Oppenheim-Lauterpacht, *op. cit.*, p. 522.

states not yet recognized as members of the international community. On the other hand, if the cession is made to an established international person by a state not yet recognized as a member of the family of nations, the transfer is legal on the ground that the grantor, through the treaty of cession, becomes, in some respects, a member of the community of states.[22] Though it is possible for a state to cede a portion of its territory to another, it should be noted that this does not apply to the marginal seas apart from the land. The maritime belt is held to be an inalienable appurtenance of the land, and as such it cannot be ceded independently.

It would appear that the consent of the inhabitants of a territory to be ceded is not required to make the transaction legal, though Grotius was of the opposite opinion.[23] In recent years, however, a certain vindication of the Grotian view is evidenced by the fact that territorial cessions have often been conditioned upon the popular will as expressed in plebiscites. Though this principle for determining territorial cession had been forgotten by diplomats and condemned by legal publicists, it was revived with the First World War together with the formula of "self-determination of nations." In connection with American-Danish negotiations relative to the cession of the Virgin Islands to the United States, a Danish *contre-projet* read in part as follows: [24]

The United States Government will be aware from previous negotiations respecting the questions now at issue that a cession of these islands which from olden times have belonged to the Danish Crown will only seem justifiable to Danish public opinion if the Danish public feel convinced that both the islands and their inhabitants will gain by the union with the United States. . . . This point of view manifested itself during the previous negotiations in the wish that the inhabitants of the islands might, through voting, be given an opportunity of expressing themselves respecting the contemplated cession.

On June 9, 1916, Secretary Lansing replied by informing the American minister to Denmark that "this Government regrets that it cannot favor submitting the question of transfer of the islands to a vote of the inhabitants." [25] The result was that Denmark dropped her demand that the cession be made dependent on a popular referendum.

Though the United States opposed a plebiscite in the case of the Danish West Indies, in 1916, it was President Wilson who became the greatest

[22] *Ibid.*, p. 499.
[23] Hugo Grotius, *De jure belli ac pacis*, book II, chap. vi, sec. 4.
[24] Minister Egan to Secretary Lansing, no. 240 (Apr. 27, 1916), Ms. Department of State, file 711.5914/56.
[25] Mr. Lansing to Mr. Egan, no. 110 (June 9, 1916), Ms. Department of State, file 711.5914/59.

champion of this principle in connection with a number of territorial problems following the First World War. In an address before the United States Senate on January 22, 1917, he said: [26]

And there is a deeper thing involved than even equality of right among organized nations. No peace can last, or ought to last, which does not recognize and accept the principle that governments derive all their just powers from the consent of the governed, and that no right anywhere exists to hand peoples about from sovereignty to sovereignty as if they were property.

It is quite certain, however, that the present norms of international law do not require that cessions shall be accompanied by a manifestation of the will of the people in the territory involved. No compulsion in this regard can be said to exist in the general law, apart from treaty commitments by individual states. An example is the Treaty of Versailles, by which a number of states were bound to consult the will of the inhabitants of certain territories which were to be shifted from one sovereignty to another. But as the law of nations widens its scope to include individuals as well as states under its aegis, cession of inhabited territory might well become contingent upon the people's will.

Title by Prescription. Prescription in international law may be defined as the acquisition of territory by adverse possession over an extended period. It is not a settled question whether this mode of acquisition is original or derivative. Some hold that it is derivative on the assumption that a former owner did in fact exist, while others contend that the mode is original on the ground that the title is derived, not from the former owner directly, but from a set of facts created by his presumed abandonment of the territory. As to the length of time required to justify the presumption of abandonment there is no agreement among the authorities.

Grotius, who rejected the *usucaptio* in Roman law, nevertheless derived from this practice "immemorial prescription for the Law of Nations." [27] He argued that if the doctrine of prescription were without application as between nations the most unfortunate conclusion would follow, namely, "that controversies concerning kingdoms and the boundaries of kingdoms, are never extinguished by the lapse of time; which not only tends to disturb the minds of many and perpetuate wars, but is also repugnant to the common sense of mankind." [28] As to the length of time required to achieve title by adverse holding, Grotius held "that a possession beyond memory, not interrupted, nor disturbed by appealing to an arbitrator, absolutely transfers dominion." [29] Others have pointed out that "mere

[26] *Congressional Record*, vol. 54, pt. 2, p. 1742.
[27] Oppenheim-Lauterpacht, *op. cit.*, p. 526.
[28] For the original text, see Grotius, *op. cit.*, chap. IV, sec. 1.
[29] For original text, see *ibid.*, sec. 9.

lapse of time, independent of legislation or positive agreement, cannot of itself either give or destroy title. . . . It creates a presumption equivalent to full proof. But it differs from proof in this, that proof is *conclusive* and final, whereas presumption is conclusive only until it is met by counter-proof, or a stronger counter-presumption." [30]

On the other hand, the famous Emmerich de Vattel, who wrote in the eighteenth century, held that . . . "it becomes necessary to admit prescription founded on length of time as a valid and incontestable title." [31] Phillimore is likewise of the opinion that there "is a lapse of time after which one state is entitled to exclude every other from property of which it is in actual possession." [32] "Title by prescription," says Hall, "arises out of the long-continued possession, where no original source of proprietary right can be shown to exist, or where possession in the first instance being wrongful, the legitimate proprietor has neglected to assert his right, or has been unable to do so." [33]

In addition to the opinions of publicists, we might also call attention to a number of cases which have come before the Supreme Court of the United States and which have turned in their decision upon the principle of prescription. In *Rhode Island v. Massachusetts* [34] it was held that "for the security of rights, whether of states or of individuals, long possession under a claim of title is protected." In *Indiana v. Kentucky* [35] the Court called attention to "a principle of public law universally recognized, that long acquiescence in the possession of territory and in the exercise of dominion and sovereignty over it, is conclusive of the nation's title and rightful authority." In *Louisiana v. Mississippi* [36] the Supreme Court, resting on precedent, said that exercise of dominion and sovereignty within the disputed territory should be accepted as conclusive. In the case of *Maryland v. West Virginia* [37] the controversy related to the true location of a portion of their common boundary. Maryland rested its case on the Charter granted by Charles I, on June 20, 1632, to Lord Baltimore, while West Virginia relied on the long-continued practice of regarding the so-called "Deakins" line as the boundary. The Court, citing previous cases and publicists, refrained from laying down a general rule, but said: "In this case we think a right, in its nature prescriptive, has arisen, prac-

[30] John Bassett Moore, *Digest of International Law,* vol. I, p. 293.
[31] Vattel, *op. cit.,* book II, chap. XI, sec. 149.
[32] *International Law,* vol. I, p. 303.
[33] *A Treatise on International Law* (1924), p. 143. Among other famous authorities who have upheld prescription in international law are Dana, Heineccius, Wolff, Mably, Bynkersoek, Rutherford, Wheaton, and Burke.
[34] 4 How. 591, 639 (1846).
[35] 136 U.S. 479 (1890).
[36] 202 U.S. 1, 53–54 (1906).
[37] 217 U.S. 1, 41, 44–45 (1910). For final decree, see *ibid.,* 577.

tically undisturbed for many years, not to be overthrown without doing violence to principles of established right and justice equally binding upon States and individuals."

Though our argument has by no means been exhausted, enough has been said to indicate, fairly conclusively, that the acquisition of title by prescription is recognized as valid in both the theory and practice of international law. It is very possible, as Fenwick has suggested, that had prescription as a means to title been confined to uninhabited territories no dispute would have arisen regarding its validity. It was only when this principle became an impediment to the aspirations of dismembered states, such as Poland, or confirmed the *status quo* of irredentas, as in the Austro-Italian disputes, that it began to fracture against the rocks of nationalism.[38]

Accretion, Erosion, and Avulsion. By erosion and accretion, the territory of states may be slowly lost and gained respectively; while avulsion has reference to a sudden change in the channel of a stream, which in many cases may present certain problems with respect to boundaries.

The natural phenomenon of accretion is of two kinds: by *alluvion,* i.e., by the washing up of sand or soil, to form solid ground; and by *dereliction,* as when the sea falls below the usual water mark. Erosion is the gradual eating away of the land by currents, winds, or tides. Both accretion and erosion are of minor importance as modes of territorial gain and loss and deserve no extended treatment here. It is sufficient to note that, whatever territory may be gained by one process or lost through the other, such losses and gains are recognized as valid under the law of nations.

Avulsion, on the other hand, is a phenomenon in nature which frequently has given rise to boundary disputes where the dividing line is a turbulent river. It is a process by which a stream may suddenly change its course, thus shifting land from one of its banks to the other. A number of boundary cases in which accretion, erosion, and avulsion have given rise to controversy have in course of time been decided by the Supreme Court of the United States.

One of the most illustrative and interesting of these is *Louisiana v. Mississippi.*[39] The facts were as follows: For nearly a hundred years gradual erosion had taken place on the Mississippi side and gradual accretion on the Louisiana shore of the Mississippi River. As a result of

[38] Charles G. Fenwick, *International Law* (1948), pp. 357–358.
[39] 282 U.S. 458 (1931). See also *New Orleans v. United States,* 10 Pet. 662, 717; (1836) *Jefferis v. East Omaha Land Co.,* 134 U.S. 178, 189 (1890); *Nebraska v. Iowa,* 143 U.S. 359, 361, 367, 370 (1892); *Missouri v. Nebraska,* 196 U.S. 23, 34–36 (1904); *New Mexico v. Texas,* 275 U.S. 279, 301–302 (1927); *Arkansas v. Tennessee,* 246 U.S. 158, 173 (1918); *Oklahoma v. Texas,* 260 U.S. 606, 636–637 (1923).

this alluvial action the great stream moved gradually and imperceptibly in a northeasterly direction for a distance of about six miles. In the year 1912–1913 a sudden avulsion took place by which the river cut a new channel separating from Louisiana a large portion of the land which that state had earlier gained by accretion. A bill was brought in the Supreme Court of the United States in 1928 to locate the interstate boundary at this point.

One might suppose that, since the land in question had originally been lost to Mississippi by the process of erosion, its return by avulsion would be allowed to stand. Not so, however, for the law knows no poetic justice. The case was decided in February, 1931, and it was held that the changes which took place between 1823 and 1912–1913 were due to gradual erosions and accretions and that the land thus shifted belonged to the state of Louisiana. In other words, when a river which is the boundary between two states changes its course gradually due to erosion and accretion, the boundary continues to follow the main channel of the river. But the change which occurred in 1912–1913 was due to avulsion, and therefore the boundary was not changed but remained in the middle of the old river bed.

Likewise, in *Arkansas v. Tennessee* [40] the Supreme Court held as follows:

It is settled beyond the possibility of dispute that where running streams are the boundaries between States, the same rule applies as between private proprietors, namely, that when the bed and channel are changed by the natural and gradual processes known as erosion and accretion, the boundary follows the varying course of the stream; while if the stream from any cause, natural or artificial, suddenly leaves its old bed and forms a new one, by the process known as an avulsion, the resulting change of channel works no change of boundary, which remains in the middle of the old channel, although no water may be flowing in it, and irrespective of subsequent changes in the new channel.

As a final example of how some of the natural processes described above become important in questions of international law, we call attention to the case of *The Anna*. [41] It was during the war between Great Britain and Spain in 1805 that the disposition of the Spanish vessel *Anna* was decided by a British prize court. The *Anna* had been captured by a British privateer near the mouth of the Mississippi, and the United States claimed the ship on the ground that the capture had taken place within its territorial waters. Lord Stowell gave judgment in favor of the United

[40] 246 U.S. 158, 173 (1918).
[41] 5 C. Rob. 373, 385 c. (1805).

States because the place of capture, though more than 3 marine miles from the coast, was well within that distance from islands which had drifted into the sea. These islands, formed by alluvial action, Lord Stowell held to be the "natural appendages of the coast on which they border and from which indeed they are formed."

CHAPTER 13

The Open Sea and Territorial Waters

The oceans which cover nearly three-quarters of the earth have long been the highroads of commerce between nations. Though it is now universally recognized that the high seas are not susceptible to territorial appropriation and that they are free to the navigation of all nations, this principle was not always so firmly established.

It is true that in antiquity and in the early Middle Ages the oceans were regarded as open to the commerce of all peoples. According to Ulpian and Celsus, the sea and air are by nature free to all mankind. But in the late Middle Ages and early modern times, the nations of Europe began to lay claims to the adjacent seas and to exercise authority over their waters. Venice and Genoa, respectively, claimed the Adriatic and Ligurian Seas, while Sweden and Denmark divided the Baltic between them. Great Britain was considered sovereign in the Narrow Seas and claimed proprietary rights in the North Sea and over large portions of the Atlantic. In the late fifteenth century, the Iberian kingdoms advanced their dominion over land and sea in two hemispheres, and their disputed claims were at length settled by Pope Alexander VI in the bull *Inter Caetera*. Thus the New World was divided between the Spanish and Portuguese, and while the whole of the Pacific, as well as the Gulf of Mexico, was regarded as parts of the Spanish domain, the Atlantic and Indian Oceans were claimed by Portugal.

Britain, however, blind to obvious inconsistency, stoutly protested the pretentious claims of Spain and Portugal and sent her bold navigators into the Spanish seas. When the Spanish ambassador, Mendoza, protested the intrusion of the British in the Pacific, his representations were rejected by Queen Elizabeth in terms that gave her the honor of being among the first in modern times to advocate freedom of the seas. She refused to admit any Spanish rights to close the seas to navigation and trade, "seeing the use of the sea and air is common to all," and that "neither nature nor public use and custom permitteth any possession thereof."

It was in 1604, nearly thirty years after Elizabeth's famous answer to

Mendoza, that a young advocate of The Hague, retained by the Dutch East India Company as its attorney in the prize case *Catharina*, presented an argument [1] which was to have an immediate and profound effect upon the theory of international maritime law.

Mare Liberum versus Mare Clausum. In the year 1602, the Dutch East India Company was organized for the purpose of extending the trade of the Netherlands to the exotic lands of the Far East. It was inevitable that conflict should develop between the Dutch and the Portuguese, as the latter asserted monopolistic claims to the East Indian trade and, as we have already seen, sovereignty over the Indian Ocean. An event which was to have significant repercussions in the development of international legal theory was the capture by the Dutch in 1602 of the treasure-laden Portuguese galleon *Catharina*, for it was in connection with the ensuing prize case that Hugo Grotius began his study on the law of prize and delivered his first great argument on the freedom of the seas.

It was Spain rather than Portugal that was at war with the Netherlands when the *Catharina* was captured, but in 1609 the conflict was suspended by the Truce of Antwerp. During the long negotiations, the Spanish had sought a renunciation by the United Provinces of all rights to trade both in the East and West Indies. It was to refute these unjustified claims that Grotius published, in a separate pamphlet, Chapter XII of the *Law of Prize*,[2] concerned mainly with the freedom of the seas, under the title *Mare liberum*.

In this famous dissertation, Grotius contended that it was an ordinance of nature that "one people should supply the needs of another" and justified freedom of trade by the fact that not every place and country is supplied with all the necessaries of life. As Virgil sang long ago: "Not every plant on every soil will grow." [3] Grotius agreed with Seneca that nature's greatest service to mankind was so to have distributed the resources of the world that commerce between the nations became a necessity. "I shall base my argument," he wrote, "on the following most specific and unimpeachable axiom of the Law of Nations, called the primary rule or first principle, the spirit of which is self-evident and immutable, to wit: Every nation is free to travel to every other nation, and to trade with it." [4]

Grotius advanced the proposition that all things which cannot be effectively occupied or taken into permanent possession are *ipso facto* free to all nations. This assertion he supported by reference to the great authorities both in his own time and of antiquity. He quoted Ovid as saying,

[1] See Introductory Note by James Brown Scott to Ralph van Deman Magoffin's translation of Grotius' work on *The Freedom of the Seas,* pp. vi and vii.

[2] *De jure praedae.*

[3] *Georgics* II, 109 (Dryden's translation, II, 154).

[4] Grotius, *Mare liberum*, the Magoffin translation edited by Scott, p. 7.

"Nature has made neither sun nor air nor waves private property; they are public gifts," and Seneca to the effect that "every path was free, all things were used in common." [5] Thus Grotius arrived at the conclusion that the open sea cannot become the private property of anyone, since nature has decreed that its use is common to all. "Hence it follows, to speak strictly, that no part of the sea can be considered as the territory of any people whatsoever. . . . It is clear, therefore, to everyone that he who prevents another from navigating the sea has no support in law." [6]

Grotius' great argument set forth in *Mare liberum* was soon answered by jurists in other lands. In his *Advocatio hispanica,* which appeared in 1613, Gentilis defended the claims of both England and Spain to the open sea, and in a work called *De dominio maris,* published in the same year, William Welwood also came to England's defense. In 1618, the learned British jurist John Selden wrote the most famous rejoinder of all to the thesis advanced by Grotius. It was significantly given the title *Mare clausum sive de dominio maris,* but it was not published until 1635. [7] In 1651 another book appeared in England in opposition to the Grotian thesis. It was a tract by Sir John Boroughs entitled *The Sovereignty of the British Seas Proved by Records, History, and the Municipal Laws of this Kingdom.* The rather sharp reaction provoked by the arguments in *Mare liberum* was not, however, confined to English publicists. In defense of Venetian claims to sovereignty in the Adriatic, Paolo Sarpi in 1676 published a book entitled *Del dominio del mare adriatico.* But of the many arguments in defense of the right of states to claim sovereignty over the seas, the most famous was that of Selden. It was by command of King Charles I that *Mare clausum* was published in 1635, and the king was so well impressed by its arguments that he made attempts, through his ambassador in the Netherlands, to have the author of *Mare liberum* punished for his audacity.

Gradual Triumph of the Grotian Thesis. It is difficult, indeed, for our generation to appreciate fully the novelty of the argument advanced in *Mare liberum* and the boldness of its author. For in 1609, we must remember, there was scarcely a principle more firmly established than that of maritime sovereignty. Though some progress was made, even in the seventeenth century, toward free navigation of the seas, it was occasioned more by the universal desire for profitable trade than by the cogency and logic in the thesis of Hugo Grotius. But aside from a general acceptance of free navigation by the end of the century, the principle of national sovereignty over the seas persisted.

[5] *Ibid.,* pp. 24 and 28.
[6] *Ibid.,* pp. 34 and 44.
[7] An English edition was published in 1652.

Throughout the eighteenth century a number of jurists and publicists continued to formulate principles of law with regard to the open sea. The most prominent of these was the Dutchman Cornelius Van Bynkershoek, who in 1702 published a standard work titled *De dominio maris*.[8] In this dissertation a position less extreme than that of Grotius was maintained. "It is possible," wrote Bynkershoek, "for the sea to be brought under sovereignty as completely as anything else in the world, and yet there is no sea today that is held under the control of any one ruler, except where the land happens to dominate it." [9] He admitted, however, that ancient Rome, both in fact and in law, exercised sovereignty over the Mediterranean, for here the occupation, for all practical purposes, was effective. With respect to the open sea at the time he was writing, Bynkershoek arrived at two main conclusions: (1) that occupation is essential to ownership, and (2) that anything which is so constituted by nature that it may serve all without prejudice to any is, and of right ought to be, used in common. The main contribution of Bynkershoek to modern international law, however, was his conception of the maritime belt.

When Grotius wrote his *Mare liberum* in 1609, he held that the shore was a part of the sea and, like the adjacent waters, common to all mankind. He did concede, however, that occupation of the shore was possible and, if done without inconvenience to other people, also permissible. But if any portion of the shore should be appropriated for the purpose of constructing certain installations, the property rights thus acquired would be coterminous with the occupation. "For just as a wild animal, if it shall have escaped and thus recovered its natural liberty, is no longer the property of its captor, so also the sea may recover its possession of the shore." [10]

Some years later, in his great masterpiece, *De jure belli ac pacis*, Grotius had occasion to deal with this subject again in the light of a greater experience "and with the moderation which comes with years." [11] In this work, Grotius arrives at the conclusion that certain parts of the sea may be considered as belonging to the land. "A portion of the sea," he wrote, "also may be occupied by him who possesses the land on each side: although it be open at one end, as a bay, or at both, as a strait; provided it be not such a portion of the sea as is too large to appear part of the land." [12] It remained for Bynkershoek to supply the method by which

[8] English translation by Magoffin with Introduction by Scott, *Classics of International Law.*
[9] *Ibid.*, p. 29.
[10] Grotius, *op. cit.*, p. 30.
[11] See Introduction by James Brown Scott to Bynkershoek's *De dominio maris*, the Magoffin translation, *Classics of International Law*, p. 19.
[12] *Ibid.*

territorial jurisdiction over the marginal seas could be effectively acquired. He suggested that cannon placed on the shore should be the means to territorial acquisition in the adjacent seas and that the range of such guns should determine the outer boundary of territorial waters.[13] Thus since the range of cannon in the eighteenth century was about one marine league, this distance seaward from low-water mark came to be accepted generally as the width of the so-called maritime belt.

Other writers such as G. F. de Martens, Azuni, and Vattel followed the lead of Grotius and Bynkershoek in advocating the freedom of the seas, and by the end of the first quarter of the nineteenth century it became a principle universally recognized both in theory and practice.[14]

A Definition of the Open Sea. In the preceding paragraphs of this chapter, we have attempted to give a historic résumé of certain legal theories concerning the territorial functions of the sea. Before going on, some sort of definition as to the meaning of the term "open sea"—or as it is sometimes called, the "high seas"—might be in order. Higgins and Colombos, in an authoritative treatise,[15] have defined the high seas as "so much of the ocean as is exterior to a line running parallel with the shore and some distance therefrom." According to Oppenheim, the open sea "is the coherent body of salt water all over the greater part of the globe, with the exception of the maritime belt and the territorial straits, gulfs, and bays, which are part of the sea; but not parts of the open sea." [16] Thus the great oceans of the world outside the generally accepted 3-mile limit clearly come within the definition of "high seas." The same may be said of other bodies of salt water, such as the Black Sea, which are connected with the great oceans by navigable straits open to all nations, even if such a connection with the sea is a part of the territorial waters of one or more littoral states.[17] The fact that such inland seas may be closed to free navigation in time of war does not change their legal character.[18]

The Meaning of Freedom of the Seas. As we have already seen, the thesis advanced by Grotius in *Mare liberum* and further elaborated by a number of writers in the eighteenth century became at the end of the

---

[13] See Wyndham L. Walker, "Territorial Waters: The Cannon Shot Rule," *The British Year Book of International Law*, vol. 22 (1945), pp. 210–231, where it is suggested that the cannon-shot rule antedates Bynkershoek. But see also Philip C. Jessup, *The Law of Territorial Waters and Maritime Jurisdiction* (1927), pp. 5–6.

[14] Oppenheim-Lauterpacht, *International Law* (1947), vol. I, p. 537.

[15] A. P. Higgins and C. J. Colombos, *The International Law of the Sea* (1943), p. 37. See also John Bassett Moore, *Digest of International Law*, vol. II, p. 885.

[16] Oppenheim-Lauterpacht, *op. cit.*, p. 538.

[17] *Ibid.*

[18] The line of demarcation between the seas which are open and those which are territorial is yet in some instances rather indefinite. See J. L. Brierly, *The Law of Nations* (1949), p. 224.

Napoleonic Wars a universally accepted principle of international law. In Thomas C. Wade's *Introduction* to Sir John Boroughs' *Sovereignty of the British Seas*,[19] we find the following conclusion:

Throughout the writings of the later jurists of all countries we find a steady progress toward the principle of the absolute freedom of the sea. By the nineteenth century this freedom had become axiomatic. The controversy had come to be of only historical interest, as an illustration of an obsolete theory and an example of the evolution of legal thought and international practice. The high sea, therefore, is now free to all.

According to Oppenheim: "The term 'Freedom of the Open Sea' indicates the rule of the Law of Nations that the open sea is not, and never can be, under the sovereignty of any State whatever." [20]

While there is a general consensus among authorities that the exterritorial seas are free, international jurists are not in agreement as to the legal basis of this doctrine. In general, there are two schools of thought on this matter: one which holds that the open sea is free because it belongs to no one (*res nullius*), and another which maintains that the oceans are the property of all (*res communis*).

It is argued in favor of the first view that sovereignty is absent on the high seas, and in behalf of the second that they are the common highway of commerce.[21] The French authority Fauchille is of the opinion that the Latin terms *res nullius* and *res communis* are inapplicable in this connection. He points out that to say the oceans are *res nullius* is tantamount to saying they are capable of occupation by anyone, which is not in conformity with either theory or practice. On the other hand, to regard the high seas as *res communis* is to maintain a common ownership, which in turn implies the possibility of partition and thus a return to individual state sovereignty over respective portions of the open sea. According to Fauchille, therefore, one should go no further than to say that the usage of the sea remains eternally open to all nations. The Greek jurist Nicolas Politis, however, is of the opinion that the doctrine of *res communis,* when applied to the high seas, is more in conformity with "the positive conception of the solidarity on which are grounded all modern international relations." [22]

The present author is inclined to agree with Fauchille that as a basis for the legal position of the open sea the term *res nullius* is unacceptable for the reasons given above. But he can see no difficulty in the designation

[19] 1920 edition, pp. 1–29.
[20] Oppenheim-Lauterpacht, *op. cit.,* p. 540.
[21] See Higgins and Colombos, *op. cit.,* pp. 52–53.
[22] *Annuaire,* vol. 32 (1925), pw 526), quoted by Higgins and Colombos in *op. cit.,* p. 53

res communis, by which it is understood that ownership in the open sea is a common ownership by all states, and that its use as a highway of commerce is *ipso facto* free to all. He holds, furthermore, that this common ownership is so mingled in the substance of the sea as to make any separation of the parts impossible from the point of view of practice and theory alike.

The Institute of International Law, at its Lausanne Conference in 1927, agreed on a declaration which constitutes an excellent summary of the present conception of international legal experts: [23]

The principle of the freedom of the sea implies specially the following consequences: (1) freedom of navigation on the high seas, subject to the exclusive control in the absence of a convention to the contrary, of the State whose flag is carried by the vessel; (2) freedom of fisheries on the high seas, subject to the same control; (3) freedom to lay submarine cables on the high seas; (4) freedom of aerial circulation over the high seas.

Article 1 of the draft entitled "Laws of Maritime Jurisdiction in Time of Peace," adopted by the International Law Association at its Vienna Conference in 1926, states that "for the purpose of securing the fullest use of the seas, all States and their subjects shall enjoy absolute liberty and equality of navigation, transport, communications, industry and science in and on the seas," while Article 13 provides that "no State or group of States may claim any right of sovereignty, privilege or prerogative over any portion of the high seas or place any obstacle to the free and full use of the seas." [24]

The Law of the Sea. In an address to the Congress of the United States, President Wilson said: "International law had its origin in the attempt to set up some law which would be respected and observed upon the seas, where no nation had right of dominion and where lay the free highways of the world." [25] It is clearly established, though the high seas are exterior to the sovereignty of states, that this region is not without law. It is imperative, for the sake of protection of persons and property, that anarchy should not be allowed to obtain in the open sea. Accordingly, a large number of international conventions have been concluded, setting down certain rules and regulations relating to such topics as safety, salvage, rules of the road, submarine cables, fisheries, and the suppression of the slave trade.

Among such arrangements we might mention the conventions concluded under the auspices of the International Maritime Committee, on the unification of the law in regard to collisions, and of the law respecting

[23] *Annuaire,* vol. 34 (1927), p. 339.   [24] Report 34, pp. 101 ff.
[25] G. H. Hackworth, *Digest of International Law,* vol. II, p. 655.

assistance and salvage at sea. The latter was amplified by the Treaty of Montevideo relating to salvage by aircraft at sea. Other conventions relate to shipowners' liability, and to the carriage of goods by sea (the York-Antwerp rules adopted by the International Law Association in 1890 and repeatedly revised, the Hague rules of 1921, and the Brussels conventions of 1924). In addition, there are numerous instruments relating to safety on the high seas, such as the convention for the safety of life at sea concluded in 1914 and revised in 1929; the International load-line convention of 1930, and the convention of 1930 concerning manned lightships not on their stations. Various other conventions, such as the International Radiotelegraph Convention, the International Convention for the Protection of Submarine Cables, and numerous conventions relating to the slave trade, constitute a substantial part of international maritime law.

Apart from the provisions contained in such conventions, the following rules of the law of nations are universally recognized: (1) Every maritime state must establish regulations regarding the use of its flag by merchant ships and furnish official vouchers giving authority for its use. (2) Every state has the authority, under the law of nations, to take punitive measures against foreign vessels making unauthorized use of its flag. (3) Every state has jurisdiction over all ships flying its flag, even when such ships are on the high seas. (4) Every state has the right to seize pirates on the high seas and to punish them, on the ground that pirates are enemies of the human race, *hostes humani generis.*

The Territorial Sea. In our discussion of state territory an attempt was made to describe the so-called territorial waters or maritime belt. Here we shall seek to define its legal position in terms of generally accepted law.

Questions relating to territorial waters have provoked much controversy among international-legal publicists. The result is that the literature on this subject is full of divergent views and opinions leading to uncertain conclusions. Nor does one find in the practice of states a consistent pattern that can serve as guide. It is quite possible, therefore, to take various positions with respect to the extent of territorial waters and the jurisdiction within them and to be able to support them all with fairly numerous illustrations. Yet it would be incorrect to conclude from this that there are no rules of law regarding this subject. According to Jessup: "Such a conclusion is unjustified and is the result of a limited perspective of a very wide field." [26]

Notwithstanding the universally recognized principle of the freedom of the seas, there is along the coasts of maritime states a portion of water which is considered a continuation of the land and therefore subject to the jurisdiction of the littoral state. The reasons which justify such exten-

[26] Jessup, *op. cit.,* p. v.

sion of sovereignty into the adjacent sea may be summarized as follows: (1) the security of the littoral state demands that it should have exclusive control over the marginal seas adjacent to its shores; (2) for the protection of its commercial and political interests, the littoral state must have the right to inspect foreign ships entering its territorial waters; (3) the economic interests demand that exclusive enjoyment of the products of the sea be regarded as a right of the littoral state.[27]

A real basis for jurisdiction in the marginal sea, aside from the justifications given above, is difficult to arrive at from the literature of publicists. Some hold to the actual ownership or *dominium* theory, while others take the view that sovereignty in the marginal sea is of a limited nature, but sufficient to confer jurisdiction upon the littoral state.[28] "There is an embarrassing abundance of contradictory opinions of text writers . . . and a varying and conflicting practice by States on this subject." [29]

The famous French authority de Lapradelle has taken the view that the littoral state is neither the owner nor the sovereign in the marginal seas but merely possesses a "bundle of servitudes" over them; [30] while such authorities as Westlake, Hall, and Oppenheim are of the opinion that the waters of the marginal belt are under the complete sovereignty of the adjacent state.

The present author considers the marginal seas, which lie between the national waters and the high seas in a belt of uncertain width, as a part of the territory of the littoral state.[31] Even though the marginal sea is considered as a part of the state's territory, he sees no difficulty in admitting a distinction, as suggested by Philip C. Jessup, between *jurisdiction* and *control* on the part of the littoral state with respect to those waters. Such a distinction is especially useful in dealing with innocent passage, a principle well established in international law. Jurisdiction, according to Jessup, connotes "the power of courts to adjudicate," while control is taken "to mean the power of administrative or executive officers to govern the actions of individuals or things." [32] To further illuminate this distinction it is suggested that a ship in the territorial waters of a foreign state, exercising the right of innocent passage, is generally immune from the jurisdiction, i.e., court processes of the littoral state, while at the same time subject to its control, as in the matter of sanitation, navigation, etc.[33]

In the Air Navigation Convention of 1919, the territory of states was

---

[27] Higgins and Colombos, *op. cit.*, p. 58.
[28] *Ibid.*, p. 59.   [29] *Ibid.*, p. 60.
[30] *Revue générale de droit international public*, vol. 5, pp. 264–284 and 309–347.
[31] He is of the opinion that the distance from low-water mark to the outer boundary of the territorial sea should for all purposes be no less than 12 sea miles.
[32] Jessup, *op. cit.*, p. xxxiii.
[33] *Ibid.*

defined as including the marginal sea, and in the preparatory work to the Hague Codification Conference of 1930 the same view was expressed. Likewise, the American Institute of International Law did not hesitate to claim for the American republics "the right of sovereignty over territorial waters." [34]

In this connection, an interesting though a rather indefinite conclusion was reached by the Institute of International Law at its Paris conference in 1894, when it was resolved that states do not have "an ownership" but nevertheless "a right of sovereignty over its territorial waters." [35] In the Stockholm conference of 1928, a resolution was adopted saying that "States enjoy the sovereignty of their territorial waters." [36] The International Law Association, in its draft convention on the laws of maritime jurisdiction in time of peace, elected to base the conception of territorial waters on a "right of jurisdiction" only.[37]

Further illustrations of the uncertain and inconsistent views with respect to the rights of states in territorial waters seem unnecessary. Enough has been said to indicate that on this topic it is indeed difficult to lay down a hard and fast rule.

Innocent Passage. The right of the merchant ships of one state to pass through the territorial waters of another is a principle solidly fixed in international law. Since this rule of the customary law could not easily be reconciled with territorial sovereignty in the marginal seas, it became a source of much confusion regarding the legal status of territorial waters. The right of innocent passage seems to have had its origin in an effort to adjust territorial sovereignty to the freedom of the seas. In this connection two questions present themselves: (1) To what extent are foreign vessels in territorial waters subject to the authority of the littoral state? (2) Do warships or other public vessels have a right to innocent passage through the territorial waters of a foreign state? Neither of these questions can be definitively answered at the present time, as considerable disagreement is found among jurists and publicists. Certain general rules are, however, discernible with respect to both of these problems, and it is with these we are concerned here.

In dealing with the first question, which had reference to the authority of the littoral state over foreign vessels, it is helpful to employ the terminology introduced by Jessup. It will be remembered that he made a distinction between jurisdiction and control in the marginal seas. In these terms the following rule may be formulated: A foreign ship, not in the

---

[34] *American Journal of International Law,* special supplement to vol. 20 (1926), pp. 318 ff.

[35] Higgins and Colombos, *op. cit.,* p. 61.

[36] *Ibid.*

[37] Report 34 (1926), p. 101 (art. 5), Vienna Conference.

category of a public vessel, has the right to innocent passage through the territorial waters of any state and is subject to the executive or administrative control of such a state, but generally speaking not to its jurisdiction. Warships, on the other hand, do not enjoy a legal right to innocent passage under the law of nations. As Elihu Root has said: "Warships may not pass without consent into this zone, because they threaten. Merchant-ships may pass and repass because they do not threaten." [38] The same view is held by William Edward Hall, who states that "this right of innocent passage does not extend to vessels of war." [39] But when such public ships are once within the territorial waters of a foreign state, the administrative authority of this state must be respected by the ships' officers and crews. This being the case, the law may perhaps be stated as follows: A warship or any other public vessel, when in foreign waters, is exempt from the jurisdiction of the littoral state. But its officers and crew cannot ignore the laws of the foreign state, as if such public vessel constituted a territorial enclave of the country whose flag it flies.[40]

There can be little doubt that ships of all categories are subject to a certain amount of control by the authorities of the state in whose territorial waters they may be found. As to whether the littoral state has jurisdiction over foreign vessels in the marginal seas, the answer is dependent upon a variety of circumstances. The general rule seems to be that in cases where the act is confined to the ship without the slightest repercussion in any part of the territory of the littoral state, jurisdiction resides in the state whose flag the ship flies. If, on the other hand, the act is of such nature as to disturb the port, the people, or any part of the territory of the state in whose adjacent waters the ship is found, jurisdiction resides in the littoral state.[41]

As we have already said, the right of merchant ships of one state to pass through the territorial waters of another, known as the right of innocent passage, is now generally recognized by all nations. The Institute of International Law in resolutions adopted at Stockholm in 1928, declared that merchant vessels have the right of innocent passage through the territorial sea. Such vessels are, however, subject to the laws and regulations enacted by the littoral state and, in cases of violation, amenable to its jurisdiction.[42]

The principle of innocent passage, now so well established in international law, may also be regarded as an extension of the freedom of the seas into those waters which clearly lie within the territorial boundaries

[38] Elihu Root, Argument in *Proceedings* (North Atlantic Coast Fisheries Arbitration), vol. XI, p. 2006.
[39] W. E. Hall, *Treatise on International Law* (1924), p. 198.
[40] *Ibid.*, p. 245.
[41] See *The Wildenhus Case* 120 U.S. 1 (1887).
[42] Higgins and Colombos, *op. cit.*, p. 211.

of states. For if the security of states demands that its territory should extend into the sea to a line parallel with the coast and at least 3 marine miles distant from low-water mark, innocent passage through those waters must be allowed to the ships of all nations in time of peace in order to give reality to the freedom of the seas. Such *passage*, however, must not be confused with a right to enter a port or roadstead. "No nation need allow this, although all States do allow it under certain conditions and with certain exceptions." [43]

As we have indicated in an earlier chapter, the waters of rivers, certain bays, ports, and harbors are in the category of *national* rather than *territorial* waters. Within these waters no right of innocent passage can be said to exist under the law of nations. Thus the legal status of foreign ships is not the same in harbors and roadsteads that it is when such vessels are merely exercising innocent passage through the marginal or territorial seas. Just precisely what the difference is has never been made clear.

A great many writers maintain that, as a matter of law, foreign merchant vessels when in port are subject to the jurisdiction of the littoral state. Others hold that exemption from jurisdiction must be granted to foreign merchant ships in ports and roadsteads, as a matter of right and not merely on the basis of comity.[44]

In view of such conflicting authority, we can only present the tentative conclusion here that ships in foreign ports cannot claim, as a matter of law, any right to immunity from the jurisdiction of local courts. The comity of nations seems to require, however, that acts which pertain strictly to the ship and its crew on board and which do not disturb the peace of the port are within the jurisdiction of the state whose flag the ship flies.

Some of the points we have raised here regarding jurisdiction on the high seas and in territorial waters will be further developed in the next chapter, where the main emphasis will be placed upon the practice of states rather than upon the history and theory of international maritime law.

[43] Oppenheim-Lauterpacht, *op. cit.*, p. 448.
[44] Jessup, *op. cit.*, pp. 144–145.

CHAPTER 14

Maritime Law and Jurisdiction

Over many centuries the peoples of the world have developed through usage a common law of the sea. Though the modern law is derived very largely from municipal legislation and international conventions, we must also count among its sources ancient custom and the early maritime codes. The rules which governed the seagoing commerce of the Mediterranean through long ages were in time collected and are known to us as the Rhodian Sea Laws. It is believed that this code dates from the eighth century. Other maritime codes of importance are those which grew out of the revival of trade in Western Europe following the Crusades. Among these we might mention the Rolls of Oléron, which are believed to have derived from the judgments of a maritime court of the island of Oléron, near Bordeaux.[1] A collection of the Rolls was made in the twelfth century, and the principles set forth in these judgments were soon accepted as the international maritime law of Western Europe and were not without influence even in the Mediterranean. Another such code was the *Tabula Amalfitana*, which had its origin in Amalfi, Italy, in the tenth century; while in the fourteenth century we find such collections of maritime law as the *Consolato del Mare* of Barcelona, and the *Leges Wisbuenses* of Wisby on the island of Gothland.

With the expansion of overseas trade in modern times, there has been a massive development of international maritime law. In this chapter we shall attempt to show how this body of law has come about and to describe and illustrate its main principles.

A Merchant Vessel on the Open Sea. Let us begin by considering the legal position of a ship at sea, located at any point outside the territorial waters of any state. If such a vessel is on a lawful mission and authorized to sail under the flag of an existing state, it is regarded as being under the jurisdiction of that state. It should be clearly understood, however, that this jurisdiction has no territorial basis, though the opposite assumption has erroneously been maintained by some writers and jurists. The doctrine

[1] A. P. Higgins and C. J. Colombos, *International Law of the Sea* (1943), p. 25.

which attributes territoriality to ships at sea has no foundation save in fiction and metaphor. According to Westlake, "the territorial character impressed on the ship by its flag is a fiction as accurate for purposes of jurisdiction as a fiction can ever be," [2] but there is something so disconcerting about a fictitious foundation. We prefer, therefore, to adhere to the position taken by Higgins and Colombos who, in discussing the legal regime of merchant ships, say that the "jurisdiction which a State may lawfully exercise over vessels flying its flag on the high seas is a jurisdiction over persons and property of its citizens; it is not a territorial jurisdiction." [3]

It should be clearly understood that jurisdiction on the open sea is closely connected with the flag under which the ship is sailing, and that the laws which govern the ship, its crew and passengers, are the municipal laws of the flag state. This doctrine was well defined by the Anglo-American Claims Commission in 1926 as follows: [4]

It is a fundamental principle of international maritime law that, except by special convention or in time of war, interference by a cruiser with a foreign vessel pursuing a lawful avocation on the high seas is unwarranted and illegal and constitutes a violation of the sovereignty of the country whose flag the vessel flies.

The right of merchant ships to sail under the flags of existing states is a right which derives from municipal rather than from international law. In the *Muscat Dhows* award,[5] handed down by the Hague Permanent Court of Arbitration in 1905, it was held that "it belongs to every sovereign to decide to whom he will accord the right to fly his flag and to prescribe the rules governing such grants. . . ." International law does, however, impose upon states the duty to invest their ships with nationality as a requisite for the enjoyment of the freedom of the seas. The fact that the conditions required by various states differ is of no real significance. It is enough that all ships are by some means invested with nationality and thus entitled under the law of nations to sail on the high seas. In addition, a condition generally required under municipal law is the registration of the ship in its home port, and a certificate in the hands of the owner to the effect that all the necessary formalities have been complied with.

The Ship's Papers. It is a requirement under international law that all maritime states should supply their ships with certain papers which, aside from the flag, serve as means of identification. As to the nature of these

[2] John Westlake, *International Law* (1913), vol. I, p. 179.
[3] Higgins and Colombos, *op. cit.*, p. 185.
[4] Nielsen's Report (1926), pp. 479–480.
[5] James Brown Scott, *The Hague Court Reports* (1916), p. 96.

papers there is no prescription, and the laws of the various states differ. Generally, however, ships are provided with the following papers:

1. A document known variously as a *passport, sea letter,* or *sea brief,* showing the nationality of the vessel
2. The *muster roll,* being a list of the ship's crew, their nationality, etc.
3. The *logbook,* which contains a full record of the voyage
4. The *bills of lading,* which are written memoranda given by the master of the vessel to the shippers, acknowledging the receipt in "good order" of the goods on board ship, and agreements to deliver them to the consignees in the same "good order," unless prevented by the dangers of the sea
5. The *manifest of cargo,* showing in detail the nature of the cargo for the facility of customs officers
6. In cases of chartered ships, the *charter party,* a contract by which a shipowner lets an entire ship or a part of it to a merchant for a monetary consideration

The question of whether a ship is entitled to the flag it is flying and carries the proper papers is one to be determined by the courts of the flag state. On this point, one of the most famous cases is that of *The Virginius,*[6] a vessel which in 1873 was engaged in the service of the Cuban insurgents, and captured on the high seas by a Spanish man-of-war. The *Virginius* was flying the flag of the United States and was fraudulently registered as an American ship. In the subsequent dispute with Spain concerning the affair of the *Virginius,* President Grant, in a special message on January 5, 1874, said among other things: "If her papers were irregular or fraudulent, the offense was one against the laws of the United States, justiciable only in their tribunals."[7]

Common Rules of Navigation. Though it is fairly certain that the internal regime of a ship on the high seas is under the exclusive jurisdiction of the state whose flag it flies, its external behavior, which may affect other nations, is governed by international maritime law.

In order to promote the safety of persons and property at sea, the maritime nations of the world were compelled to come to some common agreement regarding the rules of navigation. The uniformity in these rules existing today has been achieved largely through identical municipal regulations and to a lesser degree through the medium of international conventions.

In the second half of the nineteenth century, there was a tendency on the part of most states to copy British law with respect to the rules of maritime navigation. The rules were set forth in such legislation as the

[6] John Bassett Moore, *Digest of International Law,* vol. II, pp. 895 and 980.
[7] *Ibid.,* p. 900.

Merchant Shipping Amendment Act of 1862 and the Merchant Shipping Acts of 1873 and 1894. Moreover, the Commercial Code of Signals which was published by Britain in 1857, was soon adopted by other maritime states. The Washington conference of 1889, in which 18 maritime states took part, made certain recommendations regarding rules for the prevention of collisions and for revision of the Code of Signals. Subsequent changes in these rules by Great Britain were later adopted by most of the other maritime powers. The recommendations of the Washington Radiotelegraph Conference in 1927 resulted in a new edition of the International Code of Signals, which became effective in 1934. At the same time an international committee, whose task it would be to keep the Code up to date, was established in London under the direction of the Board of Trade.

Thus we see that the maritime states of the world, compelled by mutual needs and a common desire to protect persons and property, have through close cooperation in legislation as well as by means of international conventions created a legal regime of the open sea. In the case of *The Scotia*,[8] which came before the United States Supreme Court as early as 1871, it was held with respect to the applicable law that "whatever may have been its origin, whether in the usages of navigation or in the ordinances of maritime States, or in both, it has become the law of the sea only by the concurrent sanction of those nations who may be said to constitute the commercial world."

Collisions on the High Seas. In 1910 a conference of the maritime powers was held in the Belgian capital which resulted in two important conventions. One had to do with the law pertaining to collisions, while the other related to assistance and salvage at sea. Since that time the rules of law with respect to collisions have been clear enough, but the question of who has jurisdiction in such cases is still far from settled. On this matter there are many conflicting rules and claims. France, for example, claims jurisdiction if the damaged ship is of French nationality and, under certain special circumstances, even if both ships are foreign. Italy goes further still by claiming jurisdiction in all cases of collision, provided the accidents took place nearest an Italian port.

The United States and Great Britain base their claims to jurisdiction in cases of collision on the presence of the ship of the defendant party within their respective territories at the time the suit for damages is brought.[9] Such extensive claims to jurisdiction are based on the theory that a collision on the open sea is a matter *communis juris,* and thus justi-

[8] 14 Wall. 170.
[9] L. Oppenheim-Lauterpacht, *International Law* (1947), vol. I, pp. 552–553.

ciable in the courts of any nation.[10] In the case of the *Belgenland*,[11] which came before the United States Supreme Court in 1885, Justice Bradley in delivering the opinion said: "The same principles would seem to apply to the case of destroying or injuring a ship, as to the saving it. Both, when acted on the high seas between persons of different nationalities, come within the domain of the general law of nations, and are *prima facie* proper subjects of enquiry in any Court which first obtains jurisdiction of the rescued or offending ship at the solicitation in justice of the meritorious or injured party." Likewise, in *The Buenos Aires Case*,[12] the United States Circuit Court of Appeals said that "the procedure will be in accordance with the law of the United States."

The *Lotus* Case. Regarding collisions on the high seas, the case of *The Lotus*[13] is one of the most celebrated in international law. The facts were briefly as follows: Just before midnight on August 2, 1926, the Turkish collier *Boz-Kourt* was sunk on the high seas as a result of a collision with the French steamship *Lotus,* en route to Constantinople. Eight of the *Boz-Kourt's* company perished, but the remaining ten were rescued and were on board the *Lotus* when it arrived in Constantinople the next day. An enquiry was held by the Turkish police, which led to the arrest, not only of the captain of the sunken *Boz-Kourt,* but also of Lieutenant Demons, first officer of the *Lotus,* during whose watch the collision had taken place. The case was first heard in the Criminal Court of Stamboul on August 28, and on that occasion Lieutenant Demons submitted that the Turkish courts had no jurisdiction. This objection was overruled, and on September 15 a judgment was handed down by the Criminal Court, sentencing Lieutenant Demons to eighty days' imprisonment and a fine of 22 Turkish pounds.

The action of the Turkish judicial authorities gave rise to many diplomatic representations on the part of the French government, protesting the arrest of Demons, seeking his release, or at least the transfer of the case from the Turkish to the French courts. As a result of these protestations, the government of the Turkish Republic, in a declaration of September 2, 1926, indicated that "it would have no objection to the reference of the conflict of jurisdiction to the Court at The Hague." Accordingly, the case came before the Permanent Court of International Justice in 1927.

The main question to be determined was "whether or not the principles

[10] *Ibid.*, p. 553.   [11] 114 U.S. 355, 367, 369.
[12] 5F.2d 425.
[13] *PCIJ Publications* (1927), ser. A, no. 10; M. O. Hudson, *World Court Reports,* vol. II, p. 23.

of international law prevent Turkey from instituting criminal proceedings against Lieutenant Demons under Turkish law." "It is certainly true," said the Court, "that—apart from certain special cases which are defined by international law—vessels on the high seas are subject to no authority except that of the state whose flag they fly." Furthermore, because of the absence of territorial sovereignty on the high seas, "no State may exercise any kind of jurisdiction over foreign vessels upon them." The Court went on to say, however, that "it by no means follows that a State can never in its own territory exercise jurisdiction over acts which have occurred on board a foreign ship on the high seas." But here the reasoning is based upon the legal fiction that a ship on the high seas is to be regarded as a bit of the territory of the state whose flag it flies. It is upon this proposition, which the Court regarded as a "corollary of the principle of the freedom of the seas," that the whole decision in this case rests. From this it was made to follow that the collision which resulted in the *Boz-Kourt's* sinking constituted a delict committed in Turkish territory. In the language of the Court, "there is no rule of international law prohibiting the State to which the ship on which the effects of the offence have taken place belongs, from regarding the offence as having been committed in its territory and prosecuting, accordingly, the delinquent."

In exploring the question of whether, with respect to criminal proceedings arising out of collision cases as such, rules can be found to exist in international law giving exclusive jurisdiction to the flag state, the Court admitted divided opinion but arrived at a negative answer. The reasoning on this point was as follows:

The offence for which Lieutenant Demons appears to have been prosecuted was an act—of negligence or imprudence—having its origin on board the Lotus, whilst its effects made themselves felt on board the Boz-Kourt. These two elements are, legally, entirely inseparable, so much so that their separation renders the offence non-existent. Neither the exclusive jurisdiction of either State, nor the limitations of the jurisdiction of each to the occurrences which took place on the respective ships would appear calculated to satisfy the requirements of justice and effectively to protect the interests of the two States. It is only natural that each should be able to exercise jurisdiction and to do so in respect of the incident as a whole. It is therefore a case of concurrent jurisdiction. . . .

Dissenting Opinions in the *Lotus Case*. It is an interesting fact that in the judgment of the *Lotus Case* the Court divided 6 to 6, thus making it necessary for the President to cast the deciding vote for the conclusion as given above. This procedure was in conformity with Article 55 of the Court's Statute. The dissenting judges, in separate opinions, gave reasons for their failure to agree with the majority of the Court. Let us, therefore, examine the points at issue, and let the authority of the dissenting jurists bear upon each.

In the first place, are all things which are not prohibited by the law of nations *ipso facto* permissible to the various states? This was, indeed, the contention of Turkey, as justification for extending the application of her criminal law beyond her national frontiers. The Court in its judgment held this view to be substantially correct. On this point Judge Loder, in his dissent, asserted that the criminal law of a state "*cannot* extend to offences committed by a foreigner in foreign territory," as the jurisdiction of one state is without effect in the territory of another.[14] He admitted, however, that this rule is subject to exception in cases where offenses are committed by foreigners abroad, "in so far as they are directed against the State itself or against its security or credit." [15] Clearly, the offense of which Lieutenant Demons was accused cannot reasonably be construed as falling within this exception.

Though John Bassett Moore agreed with the majority of the Court that there is no universally recognized rule in international law giving exclusive jurisdiction over vessels on the high seas to the flag state, he denied the application of municipal law to foreigners outside the territorial bounds of the enacting state. It was on this point, precisely, that he dissented from the judgment of the majority. He likewise rejected the so-called "doctrine of protection" [16] as a valid basis for extraterritorial application of municipal law. Thus, he held [17] that the criminal proceedings which had resulted in the conviction of Lieutenant Demons, under Article 6 of the Turkish Penal Code,

were in conflict with the following principles of international law:

(1) that the jurisdiction of a State over the national territory is exclusive;

(2) that foreigners visiting a country are subject to the local law, and must look to the courts of that country for their judicial protection;

(3) that a State cannot rightfully assume to punish foreigners for alleged infractions of laws to which they were not, at the time of the alleged offence, in any wise subject.

[14] Hudson, *op. cit.*, p. 47.   [15] *Ibid.*, p. 48.

[16] This doctrine is to the effect that a person of one country, when traveling in the territory of another, carries with him the legal regime of his own state. Thus anyone with whom he has contact may be subjected to the laws of the country from which such a traveler hails. "It is evident," says J. B. Moore, "that this claim is at variance not only with the principle of the exclusive jurisdiction of a State over its own territory, but also with the equally well-settled principle that a person visiting a foreign country, far from radiating for his protection the jurisdiction of his own country, falls under the dominion of the local law and, except so far as his government may diplomatically intervene in case of a denial of justice, must look to that law for his protection." See Hudson, *op. cit.*, p. 82.

[17] Hudson, *op. cit.*, p. 83.

The Principle of Objective Jurisdiction. The next point of controversy in the *Lotus Case* is whether or not the so-called principle of "objective jurisdiction" has application. It should be noted that this doctrine is based upon a territorial foundation without which it cannot exist. It rests on the assumption that the place where the result of an act is produced is the place where it was committed. This is a legal fiction which can be said to have a certain justification in cases where the initiation and the effect are so closely connected as to be inseparable and therefore must be considered as parts of the same act. An example would be the firing of a bullet from one side of a frontier at some person on the opposite side, thus causing an injury within a jurisdiction other than the one in which the offender is physically present.

It is immediately apparent that unless one accepts the proposition that ships on the high seas, for certain purposes of jurisdiction, are as portions of the territory of the flag state, there is no foundation for objective jurisdiction. That is not to say that if the territorial fiction is attributed to such vessels, objective jurisdiction must follow *ipso facto*. Though Judge Loder in his dissenting opinion admitted that "the vessel *Boz-Kourt* must be regarded as Turkish territory," [18] he nevertheless discarded the principle of "objective jurisdiction" as without validity in this case. This he did on the ground that the French officer in charge of the navigation of the *Lotus* "had never set foot on board the *Boz-Kourt*, had no intention of injuring anyone," and that "no such intention is imputed to him." [19] It is clear that this reasoning is somewhat weak. According to Judge Moore, "It is opposed to authority and is obsolete and obviously fallacious, in the case of manslaughter as well as in other cases." [20] Inasmuch as the principle of objective jurisdiction rests upon territoriality, it has, in the view of the present author, no application in this case. As we have indicated earlier in this chapter, the practice of attributing territoriality to ships at sea is at best but a legal fiction. More reasonable is the conclusion arrived at by Lord Finlay, who in his dissenting opinion addressed himself to this point as follows: [21]

Turkey's case is that the crime was committed in Turkish territory, namely, on a Turkish ship on the high seas, and that the Turkish Courts therefore have a territorial jurisdiction. A ship is a movable chattel, it is not a place; when on a voyage it shifts its place from day to day and from hour to hour, and when in dock it is a chattel which happens at the time to be in a particular place. The jurisdiction over crimes committed on a ship at sea is not of a territorial nature at all.

[18] *Ibid.*, p. 48.   [19] *Ibid.*, p. 49.
[20] *Ibid.*, p. 76.
[21] *Ibid.*, p. 59.

It seems obvious, therefore, that the judgment in the *Lotus Case* is based very largely on the fictitious proposition that a merchant vessel on the open sea is, for purposes of jurisdiction, to be considered as a portion of the territory of the flag state. This was the starting point which led to the inevitable conclusion of concurrent jurisdiction. But this premise, as Lord Finlay pointed out in his dissent, was indeed "a new and startling application of a metaphor. . . ." [22]

Needless to say, a reaction to the judgment in the *Lotus Case* was not long in coming. In January, 1929, the League of Nations received a communication from the International Association of Mercantile Marine Officers, expressing grave concern as to the possible implications from this decision of the Permanent Court of International Justice. Would not the principle of concurrent jurisdiction, if allowed to stand, involve marine officers in double jeopardy? This question was considered by the International Maritime Committee at its Antwerp Conference in 1930 and again in Oslo in 1933. The result was the adoption by the Committee, at its Paris Conference in May of 1937, of a draft convention with provisions to the effect that, in cases of collisions or other accidents on the high seas, arrest and prosecution of responsible officers could take place only through the authorities and under the laws of the flag state. [23]

As to the present law on this point, it seems to have been well summarized by Lord Finlay in his dissenting opinion of the *Lotus Case* as follows: [24]

> The practice with regard to crimes committed at sea has been that the accused should be tried by the courts of the country to which his ship belongs, with the possible alternative of the courts of the country to which the offender personally belongs, if his nationality is different from that of the ship. There has been only one exception: pirates have been regarded as *hostes humani generis* and might be tried in the courts of any country.

The Doctrine of Hot Pursuit. It is a well-recognized principle in the customary law of nations that a vessel which has committed an offense within the territorial waters of a foreign state may be pursued onto the high seas and there captured. Such pursuit, however, is permissible only if begun while the offending ship is still within territorial waters or has just entered the high seas, and provided the chase is not interrupted but continuous.

In the case of *The Ship North v. The King*,[25] the Supreme Court of

---

[22] *Ibid.*, p. 58.

[23] P. Demeur, "Les projets de Conventions adoptés par la Conférence de Paris du Comité Maritime International," *Revue de droit international et de législation comparée*, vol. 19 (1938), pp. 886–897.

[24] Hudson, *op. cit.*, p. 58.   [25] 37 Can. Sup. Ct. 385.

the Dominion of Canada held that "when a vessel within foreign territory commits an infraction of its laws . . . she may be immediately pursued into the open seas beyond the territorial limits and there taken." The court went on to say, quoting Hall's *International Law*,[26] that "this can only be done when the pursuit is commenced while the vessel is still within the territorial waters or has only just escaped from them."

The principle of hot pursuit seems to rest upon the following rationale: The right, on the part of states, to territorial jurisdiction is unquestioned under the law of nations. But if this right is to be unimpaired, acts of control or jurisdiction which commence inside territorial waters must be allowed outside those waters in every case where an unbroken connection can be shown to exist between the beginning and the end of the act. Unless states, under certain circumstances, are permitted to complete regulatory acts outside the 3-mile limit, territorial jurisdiction would, for all practical purposes, be ineffectual.

Merchant Vessels within the Waters of a Foreign State. When a private ship leaves the open sea and enters the territorial waters of a foreign state, its legal regime is modified by the judicial and administrative authority of the local sovereign. As we have already seen, the term *territorial waters* has reference to a portion of the sea located between low-water mark and a line parallel to the coast. The great maritime powers have generally considered the location of this line to be 3 nautical miles from shore. Within this marginal sea the territorial sovereignty of the littoral state is exclusive, though subject to the limitation of *innocent passage.*

The right to make use of the territorial sea of a foreign state as a thoroughfare between points which lie outside its waters is known as *innocent passage,* and as indicated in the preceding chapter, it is a right well established in international law. It is, however, incumbent upon any ship, while in the territorial waters of a foreign state, to observe all local regulations as to navigation, sanitation, pilotage, etc., and to avoid any act which might in any way disturb the peace and tranquillity of the territorial sea. Thus, a ship in passage through the coastal waters of a foreign state, though generally immune to court processes, is nevertheless subject to the administrative control of the littoral state. The draft convention which emerged from the Hague Codification Conference of 1930 provides that merchant vessels passing through the territorial waters of a foreign state shall enjoy immunity from investigation and arrest by reason of any crimes commited on board, except in the following cases: [27]

(1) if the consequences of the crime extend beyond the vessel, or

[26] 4th ed., p. 267.
[27] Higgins and Colombos, *op. cit.,* p. 211.

(2) if the crime is of a kind to disturb the peace of the country or the good order of the territorial sea, or

(3) if the assistance of the local authorities has been requested by the master of the vessel or by the Consul of the country whose flag the vessel flies.

One of the most famous cases with respect to jurisdiction over foreign vessels in territorial waters is that of the *Franconia*,[28] which came before the English Court of Crown Cases Reserved in the year 1876. The case arose as a result of a collision between a German ship *Franconia* and the British steamer *Strathclyde* about two miles off the coast of Dover. The *Strathclyde* was sunk, and one of its passengers, an English woman, was lost. As a result Keyn, the master of the *Franconia*, was indicted for manslaughter and convicted in the Central Criminal Court of England. But the question of jurisdiction was reserved to the appellate court, where the issue became a *cause célèbre*. The Court of Crown Cases Reserved came to the conclusion on various grounds that the Central Criminal Court was without jurisdiction in the case. Six of the thirteen judges, however, in minority opinions, expressed the view that the sea within a 3-mile zone adjacent to the coast was part of the territory of Britain. An analysis of the various opinions reveals that a majority of the Court actually held this view and that the case turned not on the question of territory but on whether the local courts had jurisdiction in the absence of specific legislation. That Parliament had the right to confer such jurisdiction was admitted by a majority of the Court, and it was a minority of the 13 judges who held that no such right could be found under the law of nations.

The judgment in *Regina v. Keyn* served to call attention to the unsatisfactory nature of British legislation with respect to jurisdiction over the territorial sea. As a result of this situation, the Territorial Waters Jurisdiction Act [29] was passed by Parliament in 1878. Section 7 of this act provides that "any part of the open sea within one marine league of the coast measured from low water-mark shall be deemed to be open sea within the territorial waters of Her Majesty's dominions."

Merchant Vessels in Foreign Ports. When a merchant vessel enters a foreign port, its legal regime is compromised by the authority of the local sovereign. Not even the principle of innocent passage is here present to modify the paramount control of the littoral state. Certain general rules with respect to criminal matters have developed, and adjustments have been made through custom and treaties, giving to the flag state a limited jurisdiction over its vessels in foreign ports and over their crews.

[28] *Regina v. Keyn*, L.R. 2 Ex. D. 63 (1876).
[29] 41 & 42 Vict., c. 73.

They are of a nature as follows: In cases of crimes committed on the high seas, jurisdiction remains with the state to which the ship belongs, even though, subsequent to the commission of such crime, the first port of entry is foreign. The current practice in cases of this kind seems to be for the master of the ship to report the facts of the case to the consul of his country, and for the local courts to refuse jurisdiction.[30] With respect to crimes committed on merchant ships in foreign ports, rules of comity seem to require that jurisdiction rests with the state whose flag the ship flies, except in cases where the tranquillity of the port is disturbed, and except where treaties in force provide otherwise.

The law and practice of the United States with respect to the exercise of civil and criminal jurisdiction over foreign ships and their crews in American waters, and over ships flying the flag of the United States in foreign ports, was given by the Counselor for the Department of State in reply to an inquiry by the British ambassador on March 23, 1914. It reads in part as follows: [31]

This Government, while conceding on the one hand that, when one of its vessels visits the port of another country for the purpose of trade, it is amenable to the jurisdiction of that country and is subject to the laws which govern the port it visits so long as it remains unless it is otherwise provided by treaty, has, on the other hand, on a number of occasions, made clear its views to the effect that, by comity, matters of discipline and all things done on board which affect only the vessel or those belonging to her and do not involve the peace or dignity of the country or the tranquillity of the port should be left by the local government to be dealt with by the authorities of the nation to which the vessel belongs, as the laws of that nation or the interests of its commerce may require.

The *Wildenhus Case*. The above statement of the American position regarding jurisdiction over vessels in foreign ports was taken quite verbatim from the judgment in the *Wildenhus Case*,[32] which was handed down by the Supreme Court of the United States in 1887. Inasmuch as this case is of a leading character in the establishment of American law and practice regarding jurisdiction over foreign vessels in our ports, a closer inspection of the facts and of the decision of the Court will be helpful.

On October 6, 1886, the Belgian steamer *Noordland* was lying at the dock in Jersey City when below its decks a murder took place. The tragedy resulted from an affray between Joseph Wildenhus and one Fijens, as a result of which Fijens was killed. Both were Belgian subjects and both members of the ship's crew. Wildenhus was arrested, and

---

[30] Higgins and Colombos, *op. cit.*, p. 199.
[31] G. H. Hackworth, *Digest of International Law*, vol. II, p. 209.
[32] 120 U.S. 1.

along with him two other members of the *Noordland*'s crew were taken into custody by the police authorities of Jersey City as material witnesses.

On March 9, 1880, a convention between the United States and Belgium had been concluded which provided, *inter alia*, that with respect to the "internal order of the merchant vessels of their nation . . . , the local authorities shall not interfere, except when the disorder that has arisen is of such nature as to disturb tranquillity and public order on shore or in the port, or when a person of the country, or not belonging to the crew, shall be concerned therein."

Accordingly, the Belgian consul for New York and New Jersey attempted to secure the release of Wildenhus and his companions by application for a writ of habeas corpus before the Circuit Court of the United States for the District of New Jersey. The application was denied and the case appealed to the Supreme Court.

In conformity with Sections 751 and 753 of the Revised Statutes, the courts of the United States may issue writs of habeas corpus which shall extend to prisoners who are in custody "in violation of the constitution or a law or treaty of the United States." The only question for the Court to decide with regard to this appeal, therefore, was whether these prisoners were held in violation of the convention between the United States and Belgium to which we have referred above. "It is part of the law of civilized nations," said the Court, "that, when a merchant vessel of one country enters the ports of another for purposes of trade, it subjects itself to the law of the place to which it goes, unless, by treaty or otherwise, the two countries have come to some different understanding or agreement. . . ."

The treaty governing the present case clearly provided that the authorities of each State "shall not interfere" in the internal regime of the merchant vessels of the other, "except when the disorder . . . disturb the tranquillity and public order on shore or in the port. . . ." In order to determine whether the Belgo-American convention of 1880 had been violated by the police authorities of Jersey City as charged by the Belgian consul, it became incumbent upon the Court to decide whether the crime committed on board the *Noordland* was of such nature as to come within the exception clause of the treaty. In deciding the case the Court held that felonious homicide is a crime of a nature so grave as to disturb the public repose and that therefore no violation of the treaty existed. The judgment of the lower court was accordingly affirmed.

The Application of Prohibition Laws in American Ports. The Eighteenth Amendment to the Constitution of the United States, Section 1, provided that "the manufacture, sale or transportation of intoxicating liquors within, the importation thereof into, or the exportation thereof from the United States and all territories subject to the jurisdiction thereof for beverage purposes," was prohibited after one year from the date of its ratification. In pursuance of the amendment, Congress, on October 28, 1919, passed the National Prohibition Act, often referred to as the Volstead Act. This statute was similar in its provisions to the Amendment, but more specific. It provided for liberal construction "to the end that the use of intoxicating liquor as a beverage may be prevented." It became effective with the ratification of the Eighteenth Amendment.

Following the enactment of this law a number of steamship companies sought to prevent its application with regard to stores of liquors carried on shipboard while within the territorial limits of the United States. But in the case of *Cunard Steamship Company v. Mellon* [33] the Supreme Court of the United States held that the Eighteenth Amendment and the Prohibition Act alike were applicable "to merchant ships, either domestic or foreign" when within the territorial limits of the United States, and likewise had no application outside those limits. The only exception was "liquor in transit through the Panama Canal or on the Panama Railroad." The Court further went on to say that a

merchant ship of one country voluntarily entering the territorial limits of another subjects herself to the jurisdiction of the latter. The jurisdiction attaches in virtue of her presence, just as with other objects within those limits. During her stay she is entitled to the protection of the laws of that place and correlatively is bound to yield obedience to them. Of course, the local sovereign may out of considerations of public policy choose to forego the exertion of its jurisdiction or to exert the same in only a limited way, but this is a matter resting solely in its discretion. . . .[34]

Application of the provisions of the La Follette Seaman's Act of 1920 to foreign ships within the territorial waters of the United States caused considerable difficulty with respect to foreign labor contracts. Nevertheless, in the case of *Strathearn Steamship Company v. Dillon* [35] the Supreme Court of the United States held that the provisions of the act were not limited to American seamen but applied with equal force to foreign ships when within the territory of the United States. Thus the right as well as the effect of American legislation can in no way be conditioned by foreign contracts.

Civil Jurisdiction over Vessels in Foreign Ports. It can be said without equivocation that merchant ships in foreign ports are fully subject to the

[33] 262 U.S. 100 (1923).

[34] Enforcement in accordance with this decision was acquiesced in by the British government in the face of "no grounds for protest." But by treaty in 1924, Great Britain secured exemption from seizure of liquor stores on their ships in the territorial waters and ports of the United States.

[35] 252 U.S. 348. (1920).

local jurisdiction in civil cases. Thus actions *in rem* may be brought by the nationals of any state with the view of attaching a ship in port, and likewise civil suits *in personam* may be maintained against the officers and crews of such ships.[36]

The exercise of this civil jurisdiction, where those who are concerned are all citizens of the same foreign state and the cause of action occurred on or with regard to the ship, is not imperative, but discretionary, and the courts from motives of convenience or international comity will not take jurisdiction without the assent of the consul of the country to which the ship belongs, where the controversy involves matters arising beyond the territorial jurisdiction . . . or relates to differences between the master and the crew, or the crew and the shipowners.[37]

In the case of *The Thorgerd*[38] the United States District Court sustained a motion by the Norwegian consul general in New York to dismiss a libel filed by a member of its crew for injuries suffered on board. This action was taken by the Court in view of the fact that both the libelant and the owners of the ship were Norwegian. There seemed to be no good reason, in the opinion of the Court, for assumption of jurisdiction against the protest of the Kingdom of Norway.

Involuntary Entrance into Foreign Ports. There is one condition under which merchant vessels in foreign ports may claim total immunity from the local jurisdiction, namely, when their presence there is due to *force majeure*.[39] Thus if a ship is driven into a foreign port by a storm, is taken there by mutineers, or is seeking refuge for vital repairs and stores, "international customary law declares that the local state shall not take advantage of its necessity." [40] Even a ship which carries contraband, when entering a foreign port as a result of *force majeure*, is exempt from the jurisdiction of the local sovereign. In the case of *The Creole*,[41] which was decided by the United States–Great Britain Claims Arbitration in 1885, it was held that growing out of the right to navigate the oceans is "the right to seek shelter or enter the ports of a friendly power in case of distress or any unavoidable necessity." The fact that *The Creole* was carrying a cargo of slaves when, because of mutiny, she was forced into the port of Nassau, did not give grounds for intervention by the local authorities, even

---

[36] Charles G. Fenwick, *International Law* (1948), p. 315.
[37] Hackworth, *op. cit.,* p. 232.
[38] 11 F.2d 971 (E.D.N.Y. 1926); *Annual Digest* (supplementary volume, 1919–1942), Case No. 63.
[39] Philip C. Jessup, *Law of Territorial Waters and Martitime Jurisdiction* (1927), p. 194.
[40] *Ibid.,* p. 194.
[41] Report of the Decisions, p. 241; M. O. Hudson, *Cases and Other Materials on International Law* (1936) p. 621.

though such cargo was contraband in all British possessions. Among the "rights sanctioned by the law of nations," said the Umpire in this case, are the rights "to seek shelter in case of distress or other unavoidable circumstances, and to retain over the ship, her cargo, and passengers, the laws of her own country." [42]

The case of *Kate A. Hoff, Administratrix, etc. (United States v. Mexico)*, decided by the General Claims Commission in 1929, involved the *Rebecca*, an American vessel, which was forced by stormy weather into the Mexican port of Tampico. The master of the *Rebecca* was arrested for bringing goods into Mexico without the proper papers, and the ship and cargo was sold by order of the Mexican court. The General Claims Commission established the fact that the vessel when it sailed into the port of Tampico was in a crippled condition and that there had been no intention to circumvent Mexican custom laws. Accordingly, the award was made in favor of the claimants. The Commission said: "The enlightened principle of comity which exempts a merchant, at least to a certain extent, from the operation of local laws has been generally stated to apply to vessels forced into port by storm, or compelled to seek refuge for vital repairs or for provisioning, or carried into port by mutineers." [43]

Thus, it may be said, with a fair degree of certainty, that the rights, powers, and privileges which a state may exert over its territorial waters are for all practical purposes no less than its dominion over the land.[44] The only limitations by which this statement may be qualified are the rights of foreign ships to innocent passage and to seek shelter in distress.

---

[42] It should be noted that the national Prohibition Act in the United States, while it was in force, did not apply to merchant vessels which were forced into port by distress or by inevitable necessity.

[43] *Opinions of the Commissioners* (1929), pp. 174, 177; Hackworth, *op. cit.*, pp. 280–281.

[44] Jessup, *op. cit.*, p. 208.

CHAPTER 15

The Airspace and Aerial Navigation

The earth's atmosphere is a vast ocean which the remarkable development in science and technology has rendered navigable to man. The progress which has been made in aeronautical engineering in the first half of this century has given rise to new problems regarding the juridical nature of the *airspace* superincumbent on land and sea. These problems are the more difficult because in this area no customary law exists to serve as guide, unless it be the international law of the sea.

In 1909, only six years after the Wright brothers had made their historic flight at Kitty Hawk, Louis Blériot, a French pilot, crossed the English Channel in a heavier-than-air craft. From this day on, the security of international boundaries could no longer be achieved by means of land fortifications, or exclusively by land and naval armaments. Man had conquered a new element. This development in human history could not escape certain far-reaching consequences even in the realm of international legal theory.[1]

Before Blériot's famous exploit, the French government, because of promiscuous flights of balloons over the continent of Europe, had decided to call an international conference on aviation. By the time this conference met in Paris in 1910, not only balloons but heavier-than-air craft presented a variety of regulatory problems. Because of a sharp conflict between the mutually exclusive principles of "a right to fly" and "complete sovereignty" in the airspace on the part of the subjacent state, no agreement was possible except on certain technical points. These included such things as uniform registration of aircraft, certificates of navigability, and pilots' licenses.

---

[1] In this chapter only such material as can properly be classified as public international air law has been included. It should be noted, however, that a large body of private air law has come into being since the first conference on private air law held in Paris in 1925. It was then that the *Comité International Technique d'Experts Juridiques Aeriens* was established. The Second International Diplomatic Conference on Private Air Law was held in Warsaw in 1929. Others are the Rome conference of 1933, the Brussels conference of 1938, and the Rome conference of 1952.

213

The absence of custom and practice as a basis for air law resulted in the evolution of a number of theories with respect to rights of states in the superincumbent airspace. These theories may be briefly summarized as follows: (1) that the atmosphere, like the high seas, is incapable of occupation and therefore free; (2) that, analogous to the maritime belt, the lower portions of the airspace are considered territorial, while an upper and unlimited zone is free and open to all; (3) that according to an ancient maxim,[2] the airspace to an unlimited height is under the complete sovereignty of the subjacent state; (4) that the sovereignty of the airspace, like that in the marginal seas, is subject to innocent passage for foreign aircraft. But as innocent passage does not apply to foreign warships in the territorial seas, it would also be denied foreign military aircraft in the territorial air.[3]

Such theoretical speculation regarding aerial navigation was, however, interrupted by the First World War. The practice which prevailed during the period of hostilities tended to establish the principle that sovereignty in the airspace belongs exclusively to the subjacent state.[4] It is quite clear that the relationship which the airspace bears to the territory beneath is not the same as that existing between sea and land, "and statesmen have not been blind to the difference."[5] Thus practical necessity has forced a general acceptance of the theory that a state is sovereign in the airspace over its land and sea territories.[6]

By the end of the second decade of the present century it became obvious that the "flying machine" was here to stay. But if the prediction of Lord Tennyson that the heavens would "fill with commerce" was to be made a reality, it became imperative that the nations of the world should mutually agree upon certain rules regarding international aerial navigation. In this connection there are two competing interests which the law must seek to reconcile as far as possible: (1) that of the subjacent state in its own security, and (2) that of all states in the greatest possible freedom of communication and transportation.[7]

The Question of Sovereignty. In the preamble of the Aerial Navigation Convention of 1919,[8] the participating powers recognized the progress of aerial navigation and expressed the desire "to encourage the peaceful intercourse of nations by means of aerial communications." Furthermore,

---

[2] *Cujus est solum ejus est usque ad coelum et ad inferos.* (He who owns the soil owns everything above and below.)

[3] See Oppenheim-Lauterpacht, *International Law* (1947), vol. I, pp. 469–470.

[4] G. H. Hackworth, *Digest of International Law*, vol. IV, p. 358.

[5] Charles Cheney Hyde, *International Law* (1947), p. 586.

[6] See sec. 1107 (i) (3) of the Civil Aeronautics Act of 1938, Stat. L. 973.

[7] J. L. Brierly, *The Law of Nations* (1949), p. 183.

[8] *League of Nations Treaty Series,* vol. XI, p. 173; M. O. Hudson, *International Legislation,* vol. I, p. 359.

they said that the establishment of universal regulations would be to the interest of all. This was the first general convention for the regulation of international aerial navigation, and it constitutes with its amending protocols a substantial part of international public law in the field of aerial transportation. It recognizes that every state has complete and exclusive sovereignty in the airspace [9] above its territory and territorial waters. The language in this respect is clear and unmistakable and, in view of its substantive reiteration in later agreements, must be considered as a fairly accurate statement of the law on this point. "Right or wrong," wrote J. M. Spaight in the very same year, "the principle has been established that states control the *atmosphere* over their territories." [10] Thus with the conclusion of the Aerial Navigation Convention, signed in Paris on October 13, 1919, the sovereignty theory, mentioned above, was fully recognized. "This new principle of International law," wrote Spiropoulos, "established as the result of the custom adhered to through the World War, has found its sanction in modern aerial jurisprudence." [11]

In addition to the treaty law establishing the principle of sovereignty in the airspace on the part of the subjacent state, there is of course municipal legislation. Examples of such enactments are the British Air Navigation Act of 1920 [12] and, in the United States, the Air Commerce Act, 1926, as amended June 23, 1938.[13] According to the preamble of the British act, "full and absolute sovereignty and rightful jurisdiction of His Majesty extends, and has always extended, over the air superincumbent on all parts of His Majesty's dominions and the territorial waters adjacent thereto. . . ." Section 6(*a*) of the American statute provides: "The United States of America is hereby declared to possess and exercise complete and exclusive national sovereignty in the airspace above the United States, including the airspace above all inland waters and the airspace above those portions of the adjacent marginal high seas, bays, and lakes, over which by international law or treaty or convention the United States exercises national jurisdiction." [14]

Innocent Passage and Prohibited Transport. While the principle of

[9] It seems reasonable to conclude that the term "airspace," as contemplated by the convention, did not extend beyond the atmosphere.

[10] See Clement L. Bouve, "The Development of International Rules of Conduct in Air Navigation," *Air Law Review*, vol. 1 (1930), p. 1. Italics added.

[11] *Ibid.*

[12] 10 & 11 Geo. V, c. 80.

[13] 52 Stat. L. 1028, 49 U.S.C.A. sec. 176.

[14] The terms "air" and "airspace," as used in the British and United States statutes respectively, should, we think, be interpreted to mean the atmospheric space and therefore do not apply to the region which lies beyond the earth's atmosphere and sometimes referred to as "outer space." This "outer space," should, in the opinion of the present author, be regarded as *res communis* and should include all the natural satellites of the earth.

innocent passage with respect to foreign merchant ships in territorial waters is well established by the law of nations, the same cannot be said to apply to foreign commercial and private planes in the territorial air. This is so because a variety of problems are necessarily presented, in connection with aerial flights over the subjacent territories of foreign states, that are not encountered in ordinary maritime navigation. These problems spring from the general fact that surface vessels in the territorial seas are subjected to geographical limitations of movement which do not apply to freely moving aircraft. For the reason of national security, which is here implied, and because every state has complete and exclusive sovereignty in the airspace over its land and sea territories, the principle of innocent passage does not apply to foreign aircraft in the same manner that it applies to merchant ships in the territorial waters. In practice, however, innocent passage of foreign aircraft is allowed, subject to certain limitations, as provided by a number of international conventions.

The second article of the Aerial Navigation Convention of 1919 provides that each contracting state undertakes in time of peace to accord "freedom of innocent passage above its territory to the aircraft of the other contracting States." The right is reserved, however, "in time of war or for reasons of public safety," to deny passage of aircraft of any nation over certain portions of territory.[15] But the aircraft of every contracting state may cross the airspace of every other such state, provided in each case the planes follow the routes fixed by the subjacent power.[16] For reasons of general security, such planes, if ordered to do so by the state over whose territory they may be flying, must land at whatever aerodrome is designated by that power.[17] It was also provided that the establishment of international airways should be subject to the consent of the states flown over. This provision was changed, however, by the Protocol of June 15, 1929, which states that "every contracting State may make conditional upon its prior authorization the establishment of international airways and the creation and operation of regular international air navigation lines, with or without landing, in its territory." According to Article 16 of the Paris Convention of 1919, cabotage, i.e., intranational traffic, is reserved to aircraft of the territorial state.

Foreign aircraft are not allowed in international aerial navigation to transport explosives, arms, and munitions of war, nor are they permitted to carry such articles between any two points within the same state. The

---

[15] Art. 3.
[16] Art. 15.
[17] *Ibid.*

carriage or use of photographic apparatus by foreign aircraft may also be regulated or prohibited by any state.[18]

The provisions of the Paris convention, some of which we have summarized above, were closely followed in the Ibero-American Convention on Aerial Navigation, signed in Madrid on November 1, 1926, and in the Havana Convention on Commercial Aviation which was incorporated in the Final Act of the Sixth International Conference of American States in 1928. Article 4 of the Havana convention, for example, provides that "each contracting State undertakes in time of peace to accord freedom of innocent passage above its territory to private aircraft" [19] of the other contracting states. But each state has the right to prohibit "for reasons which it deems convenient in the public interest, the flight over fixed zones of its territory by the aircraft of the other contracting States." [20]

The Aerial Navigation Convention of 1919, like the later Havana agreement, defines "public aircraft" as military in character or those which are exclusively employed in the state service, such as customs and police. All state aircraft, however, which do not come within this classification are to be treated as private aircraft and therefore are subject to all the provisions of the convention. No military aircraft may fly over or land in the territory of any of the contracting states without special authorization to do so. But if such authorization is given, a military aircraft shall enjoy, in principle, the same privileges which are customarily accorded to foreign ships of war.[21]

The International Commission for Air Navigation. The Paris convention of 1919 established a permanent International Commission under the direction of the League of Nations.[22] Its main function was to receive and make proposals to amend the convention and its technical annexes; to collect information bearing on air navigation and publish maps; also to give its opinion on questions which the states may submit for examination. By a majority of three-fourths of the total possible vote, the Commission may amend the annexes, but it can only recommend modification in the convention itself. Disputes which might arise in connection with the interpretation of the convention were to be referred to the Permanent Court of International Justice. In 1929, the International Commission

[18] Art. 27 of the Aerial Navigation Convention of 1919.

[19] Private aircraft are defined as those which are not military or naval and those which are not employed exclusively in the state service, such as posts, customs, and police (Art. 3). For text of this convention see Hudson, *op. cit.*, vol. IV, p. 2354.

[20] Art. 5 of the Havana convention of 1928.

[21] Art. 32.

[22] Art. 34 as amended in 1923. The connection between the International Commission and the League of Nations constituted a stumbling block for ratification by the United States.

called a conference of the signatory powers to propose a protocol of amendments and thus remove the objections of certain states which had failed to ratify or adhere to the convention.[23]

The International Civil Aviation Convention of 1944 and the ICAO. The Second World War was not yet over when the International Civil Aviation Conference met in Chicago on November 1, 1944. At this conference no fewer than 54 nations were represented.[24] Although conflicting viewpoints with respect to a number of issues could not be reconciled, the conference was productive of a convention, three separate agreements, and several resolutions and recommendations. In this section we shall consider some of the main features of the Convention on International Civil Aviation as well as the function of the International Civil Aviation Organization or, as it is so frequently abbreviated, the ICAO.

The Chicago Convention on International Civil Aviation has been described as the "constitution" of the global air world.[25] It is a very comprehensive agreement of 22 chapters and 96 articles, covering every phase of civil aviation.[26] In addition to the main convention, separate agreements on transit and transport were signed. One of these, the International Air Services Transit Agreement (also known as the "two freedoms document"), provides that the contracting states shall enjoy the following freedoms with respect to scheduled international air services: (1) to fly across each other's territory without landing, and (2) to land for nontraffic purposes, i.e., for refueling and repairs. It is further provided that the services rendered by one contracting state to another, in connection with such stops, must be just and reasonable. The agreement [27] also stipulates that in situations causing injustice and hardship the con-

[23] Though the United States failed to ratify the convention of 1919, its government furnished important information to assist the International Commission for Air Navigation in carrying out the function for which it was created (see Hackworth, *op. cit.*, pp. 363–364). It should be noted that the Paris convention of 1919 had, in its original form, many objectionable features: (1) nonsignatory states were subjected to special conditions; (2) the parties to the convention attempted to monopolize international air traffic by refusing to the nonsignatory powers access to the airspace over their territories; and (3) the states represented in the International Commission for Air Navigation did not enjoy equal voting rights. All these features have since been eliminated. See the Amending Protocols of Oct. 27, 1922; of June 30, 1923; and of Dec. 11, 1929.

[24] Among these were included all the United Nations except the Soviet Union, which at the last moment decided not to participate. The present membership in the International Civil Aviation Organization, created by the convention of 1944, was raised to 59 when the United Kingdom of Libya became a member as of Febr. 28, 1953.

[25] Charles G. Fenwick, *International Law* (1948), p. 411.

[26] For complete text see Hudson, *op. cit.*, vol. IX, pp. 168–210.

[27] For the full text, see *ibid.*, pp. 229–231.

tracting parties may call for investigation by the International Civil Aviation Organization.

The International Air Transport Agreement,[28] sometimes referred to as the "five-freedoms document," provides that each contracting state grants to the other contracting states the following freedoms of the air in respect to scheduled international air services: (1) to fly across its territory without landing; (2) to land for nontraffic purposes; (3) to put down passengers, mail, and cargo taken on in the territory of the state whose nationality the aircraft possesses; (4) to take on passengers, mail, and cargo destined for the territory of the state whose nationality the aircraft possesses; (5) to take on passengers, mail, and cargo destined for the territory of any other contracting state and the privilege to put down passengers, mail, and cargo coming from any such territory.

Like the Paris convention of 1919, the Chicago convention asserts in its very first article that "every State has complete and exclusive sovereignty over the airspace above its territory," and in Article 2 this territory is defined as being "the land areas and territorial waters adjacent thereto under the sovereignty, suzerainty, protection and mandate of such State."

The convention is applicable only to civil aircraft,[29] and each contracting state agrees not to use civil aviation for any purpose inconsistent with the aims of the convention.[30] It was also agreed that the aircraft of the contracting states which were not engaged in regular international air services should have the right to nonstop transit and to land for nontraffic purposes without prior permission to do so—this, however, to be subject to the right of each state to *require* landing.[31] The convention further recognized the right of each state to reserve to itself the monopoly of cabotage[32] and stated that the country of registration is to determine the nationality of the aircraft.[33]

An aircraft cannot be validly registered in more than one state, although its registration may be changed from one state to another,[34] and every aircraft engaged in international navigation must be furnished with its appropriate nationality and registration marks.[35] It is further provided that every aircraft of the contracting states shall carry the following documents: certificates of registration and airworthiness; the appropriate licenses for each member of the crew; and a logbook. If the aircraft is equipped with radio, it must also carry a radio license, and if it carries passengers, their names and places of embarkation and destination. In

[28] For text, see *ibid.*, pp. 232–236.
[30] Art. 4.
[32] Art. 7.
[34] Art. 18.

[29] Art. 3.
[31] Art. 5.
[33] Art. 17.
[35] Art. 20.

cases where cargo is carried, a manifest is required.[36] Munitions and
implements of war may not be carried over the territory of any of the
contracting states without special permission to do so.[37]

The second part of the Chicago convention of 1944 deals with the International Civil Aviation Organization, an institution which was created
by the convention itself.[38] The ICAO functions through an Assembly, a
Council, a President of the Council, and a Secretary-General. In addition
there are various commissions, and committees. The Assembly includes
all members of the Organization, each of which has one vote. It is convened by the Council annually. The Assembly decides the policy of the
Organization, determines the budget, and deals with any question not
specifically referred to the Council. The Council, consisting of 21 states
as designated by the Assembly, meets in virtually continuous session. It
carries out the directives of the Assembly, elects its own President, and
appoints the Secretary-General of the Organization. The Council also
creates standards for international air navigation and collects, examines,
and publishes information regarding such matters. It may also act, if requested by the countries concerned, as a tribunal for the settlement of
disputes arising in connection with international civil aviation. The
Council is assisted in its work by an Air Navigation Commission and by
committees on air transport, legal matters, joint support of air navigation
services, and financial matters. The Secretary-General functions as the
chief executive officer of the Organization and appoints the staff of the
Secretariat. The ICAO has its headquarters in Montreal but maintains
five field offices which serve as liaison between the Organization and the
various member states.[39]

The aims and objectives of the Organization are to develop the principles and techniques of international air navigation; also, to foster the
planning and development of international air transport so as to [40]

(*a*) Insure the safe and orderly growth of international civil aviation throughout the world;

(*b*) Encourage the arts of aircraft design and operation for peaceful purposes;

(*c*) Encourage the development of airways, airports, and air navigation
facilities for international civil aviation;

[36] Art. 29.   [37] Art. 35.
[38] Actually, however, the ICAO, as such, did not come into being until Apr. 4, 1947,
thirty days after the convention had been ratified by the required 26 states. A Provisional International Civil Aviation Organization (PICAO) had been functioning in
the meantime under an agreement drawn up by the Chicago conference.
[39] North American Office at headquarters in Montreal, the South American Office in
Lima, the European and African Office in Paris, the Middle East Office in Cairo, and
the Far East and Pacific Office in Melbourne.
[40] Art. 44 of the convention.

(*d*) Meet the needs of the peoples of the world for safe, regular, efficient and economical air transport;

(*e*) Prevent economic waste caused by unreasonable competition;

(*f*) Insure that the rights of contracting States are fully respected and that every contracting State has a fair opportunity to operate international airlines;

(*g*) Avoid discrimination between contracting States;

(*h*) Promote safety of flight in international air navigation;

(*i*) Promote generally the development of all aspects of international civil aeronautics.

It is further provided that the Organization shall enjoy in the territory of each contracting state such legal capacity as may be necessary for the performance of its functions. "Full juridical personality shall be granted wherever compatible with the constitution and laws of the state concerned." [41]

Inasmuch as the Chicago convention supersedes both the Paris convention of 1919 and the Havana Convention on Commercial Aviation of 1928, it was made incumbent upon each contracting state to denounce the Paris and Havana conventions if party to either.[42]

Since August, 1945, when the PICAO Interim Council met for the first time, the ICAO and its earlier provisional organization have been instrumental in bringing about concerted action by the nations of the world in the organization and maintenance of facilities and services which are vital to international air navigation. Among these are patterns for meteorological services, traffic control, communications, radio beacons, and other facilities required for safe international air transport.[43] At the first regional air navigation meeting for the North Atlantic, it was proposed to establish weather stations in the North Atlantic Ocean in order to supply meteorological information to aircraft flying in that region. As a result, 10 member states of the ICAO at a special conference in September, 1946, agreed to maintain 13 ocean weather stations at specified points in the North Atlantic. In addition to meteorological information, these stations provide navigation aids, communications facilities, as well as search and rescue facilities throughout the region. At a later conference, held in London in the early spring of 1949, the agreement of 1946, in the light of accumulated experience, was substantially revised.

In order to ensure "the highest practicable degree of uniformity in

[41] Art. 47. [42] Art. 80.

[43] In this connection the ICAO has found it advantageous to cooperate closely with other international agencies such as the International Meteorological Organization (IMO); the International Telecommunications Union (ITU); the World Health Organization (WHO); and other organizations whose work and facilities are especially useful to the ICAO. See Eugene Pepin, "ICAO and Other Agencies Dealing with Air Regulation," *Journal of Air Law and Commerce*, vol. 19 (1952), pp. 156–163.

regulations, standards, procedures, and organization in relation to aircraft, personnel, airways and auxiliary services in all matters in which such uniformity will facilitate and improve air navigation," [44] the ICAO has adopted 14 sets of standards and recommended practices, known as "annexes to the convention." [45] These, however, include only a small part of the material that will ultimately be needed under their titles.[46] The 14 annexes which have been in effect since January 1, 1951, have laid down standards for the following:

1. Personnel licensing—indicating the technical requirements and experience necessary for pilots and aircrews flying on international routes

2. Aeronautical maps and charts—providing specifications for the production of all maps and charts required in international flying

3. Rules of the air—including general flight rules, instrument flight rules, and right-of-way rules

4. Dimensional practices—providing for progressive measures to improve air-ground communications

5. Meteorological codes—specifying the various systems used for the transmission of meteorological information

6. Operation of aircraft in scheduled international air services—governing flight preparation, aircraft equipment, and maintenance, and, in general, the manner in which aircraft must be operated to achieve the desired level of safety on any kind of route

7. Aircraft nationality and registration marks

8. Airworthiness of aircraft

9. Facilitation of international air transport—to simplify customs, immigration, and health inspection regulations at border airports

10. Aeronautical telecommunications—dealing with the standardization of communications systems and radio air-navigation aids

11. Air-traffic services—dealing with the establishment and operation of air-traffic control, flight information, and alerting services

12. Search and rescue—dealing with the organization to be established

[44] Art. 37 of the convention.

[45] "(*a*) The adoption by the Council of the Annexes described in Article 54, subparagraph (1), shall require the vote of two-thirds of the Council at a meeting called for that purpose and shall then be submitted by the Council to each contracting State. Any such Annex or any amendment of an Annex shall become effective within three months after its submission to the contracting States or at the end of such longer period of time as the Council may prescribe, unless in the meantime a majority of the contracting States register their disapproval with the Council.

"(*b*) The Council shall immediately notify all contracting States of the coming into force of any Annex or amendment thereto."

(Art. 90 of the International Civil Aviation Convention of 1944.)

[46] Pepin, *op. cit.*, p. 153.

by states for the integration of facilities and services necessary for search and rescue

13. Aircraft accident inquiry—dealing with the promotion of uniformity in the notification of, investigation of, and reporting on aircraft accidents

14. Aerodromes—dealing with the physical requirements, lighting, and marking of international aerodromes

Since the adoption of the first group of annexes in 1948, almost all the standards have been revised in order to adapt their provisions to the development of new techniques in air transport. The provisions contained in the annexes are to be implemented by the contracting states as prescribed in the various articles of Part I of the Chicago convention.[47] In adopting each annex, the Council urged the contracting states to introduce the text of the ICAO into their national regulations. Any state, however, which finds it impractical to adjust its national regulations to such international standard or procedure need not conform but must notify the ICAO as to the difference between its own practice and that established by the international standard.[48] But the Council is, of course, desirous of limiting the number and extent of such differences, and in a resolution of April 13, 1948, it made the recommendation that "where a Contracting State finds it necessary to depart from the ICAO text, it limit such departure to an absolute minimum"; and that "in any regulations or other publications based upon ICAO standards or recommendations, Contracting States indicate conspicuously their relationship to the ICAO text and the extent of substantive effect of any differences between the national text and its ICAO prototype." [49]

Many member states have progressively simplified their procedures,

[47] Part I of the convention is entitled "Air Navigation."

[48] Art. 38.

[49] Quoted by Pepin in *op. cit.*, pp. 153–154. Annexes are not the only form by which international air regulations are promulgated by the ICAO. Aside from these are the complementary "Procedures for Air Navigation Services" (PANS), "Regional Supplementary Procedures" (SUPPS), and "Specifications." Among the "Procedures" which have been issued and are in force, the following may be listed:

Aerodromes, Air Routes and Ground Aids, Doc. 4478–COM/501/1
Communications Codes and Abbreviations, Doc. 6100–COM/504/1
Radiotelephony Procedures, Doc. 7181–COM/546
Abbreviations of Place Names, Doc. 6919–COM/532
Abbreviations of Aeronautical Authorities, Services Aircraft Operating Agencies, Doc. 6938–COM/534
Aeronautical Information Services, Doc. 7106–AIS/501
Rules of the Air and Air Traffic Serv., Doc. 4444–RAC/501/1
Instrument Approach-to-land, Doc. 7087–OPS/585
Specifications for Meteorological Services for International Air Navigation Services, Doc. 7144–MET/521
Regional Supplementary Procedures, Doc. 7030

in conformity with ICAO recommendations, respecting such matters as clearance of passengers, baggage, cargo, and mail carried by aircraft. These measures have reduced considerably the time required for the handling of passengers at international airports. Agreements and contracts concluded by the member states or by air lines in those states are registered with the ICAO, and municipal aviation laws are likewise filed by the Organization.[50] A large number of studies on technical and legal questions relating to international aviation have been completed by the ICAO relating to such matters as aircraft accidents and means of reducing them, as well as the costs and charges for international air mail. The legal studies done by the ICAO include registration of aircraft by non-nationals; certificates of airworthiness for the international delivery of newly constructed aircraft; the liability of the air carrier to passengers and shippers of goods; liability for damages caused by aircraft to persons and property on the surface; and aerial collisions and aviation insurance. The ICAO continually collects, analyzes, and publishes statistical information relating to international aviation services. It issues a wide range of technical publications, including operational standards, regional manuals, and multilanguage glossaries, as well as the *ICAO Monthly Bulletin,* which contains a review of the Organization's current activities.

CONCLUSION

At the beginning of this chapter, we called attention to the importance of the earth's atmosphere as a highway of commerce in an age of aerial navigation. Of the various branches of technology in the last half century, the progress of aeronautical engineering has perhaps contributed most to the interdependence of peoples; with us, it is units of time, rather than of linear measure, that best describe the distance from New York to Paris. But international aerial navigation could not proceed without certain rules and regulations. Though it may be premature to speak of a universal body of law in the area of international aviation, common principles which emerge from existing conventions may be indicative of certain trends.

On the whole there are few principles which we can say are firmly established as a result of this international legislation. But the following may be listed as illustrative of the present law: (1) states are sovereign in the airspace over their respective land and sea territories; (2) freedom of innocent passage is accorded upon compliance with national and

---

[50] By January, 1952, approximately 1,000 agreements and contracts had been registered, and an extensive collection of texts of national laws and regulations had been assembled by the ICAO.

international regulations, though this freedom cannot be said to exist as a matter of general law; (3) guarantees must be given by the operators of foreign aircraft as to (*a*) identification and airworthiness, and (*b*) the competence of pilots; (4) reservations are often made by the states flown over, in the interest of national and public safety, and for the protection of commercial interests; (5) reciprocity of treatment is generally accorded contracting states.

But in view of recent advances in the science of aeronautics, a great many new problems have arisen to which the law, as yet, has provided no satisfactory answers. In this age of rocket propulsion, travel in outer space may indeed be possible. What legal implications might arise, for example, from the building of artificial satellites in this outer space, and what mortal danger to the freedom of the human race?

Though the present law grants to the subjacent state sovereignty in the airspace, it should not be inferred from this that such sovereignty is without limitations. Furthermore, as we have suggested above, the airspace must be considered as coterminous in all directions with the earth's atmosphere. There is certainly nothing in the existing law to warrant any other conclusion. Thus there are two main questions to which the law must eventually provide the answers: (1) What are the limitations, if any, upon the sovereignty of the subjacent state in the *airspace*? (2) What is the legal status of *outer space*?

The answer to the first of these questions, we think, is to some degree found in existing treaties. As regards the second, there is—at this time, at least—not even a partial answer. We suggest, therefore, that a page be lifted from international maritime law and that the *outer space* be considered as analogous to the open sea. In this manner, all the outer space, as it stretches indefinitely outward beyond the earth's atmosphere, and including all the natural satellites of this planet, can be regarded as *res communis*, the common property of all nations. This would mean that the outer space, as we have defined it above, would be free to all mankind and therefore incapable of occupation and control except as a result of collective action, and for peaceful purposes, through effective international organization. This, indeed, would not preclude the building of space stations, should the technical difficulties be overcome. But this could only be done for peaceful purposes, such as the control of climatic conditions in certain parts of the world, and only if in the opinion of enlightened and reasonable men the benefits to the human race would outweigh the cost of such projects.

PART FOUR

Diplomatic Relations

CHAPTER 16

Agencies of Foreign Affairs

As we have seen, the state becomes articulate both internally and externally through its government. If there can be no state without a government, it is no less certain there can be no government without a chief executive as its highest organ. In monarchies and most republics the chief of state is a single person, such as a king or a president, while in countries like Switzerland and the Soviet Union, the executive is plural. But even in the latter cases, in order to facilitate the function of the executive organ, it becomes necessary to operate through a single head. In Switzerland, for example, it is the President of the *Bundesrath* who signs laws and treaties and receives foreign diplomats, and in the U.S.S.R., it is not the Presidium of the Supreme Soviet who performs these functions, but its President. It would not be correct, however, to say that these men are heads of state, in the ordinary meaning of that term. In an indirect sense, at least, a head of state seems necessary under the law of nations, as, indeed, no state could exist without it. The title and organization of the executive organ is, nevertheless, a matter for each sovereign state to determine and lies entirely outside the province of international law.

The Legal Position of Heads of State. The position of heads of state in international legal theory bears little relationship to the contemporary practice in many countries and can be understood only in terms of certain historic origins. It derives from the days when the monarch was unlimited and absolute, and his person frequently regarded as synonymous with the state itself. Though monarchy was at one time universal throughout the civilized world, it has gradually given way in the last two hundred years to other forms of government. But where the institution still survives, the power of kings which was once so awesome has generally been limited by constitutional law and practice to a degree of almost complete impotence. Thus the President of the United States is vastly more powerful in his executive capacity than is Her Britannic Majesty.

The limitation of actual power in the chief executive whether he be prince or president, is a matter of domestic rather than international law.

The fact yet remains that any act by the titular head of a nation, or in his name, is considered an act of state for which responsibility cannot be avoided under the law of nations. Whether the chief of state has arrived at his position through the legal-constitutional process, or is a mere usurper of power, is from the point of view of international law immaterial. In any case, the state is legally bound by his acts.[1] The legal position of a nation's chief executive, however, is no longer derived from his own person, but from the rights and duties of the state of which he is the titular head. The honors and immunities due a sovereign, therefore, are merely reflections of the legal position which the state he represents enjoys in the international community.

Monarchs. It is in his capacity as chief representative of the state that the king becomes a sovereign himself, and this fact is recognized by the law of nations. Though in the light of municipal law the positions of sovereigns differ greatly, in terms of international law they are regarded as equals. It is, nevertheless, true that since states are sovereign they have the right to give to their respective heads whatever title they wish. Thus, according to the German Constitution of 1871, the king of Prussia was given the additional title of German Emperor, and in 1877 the British monarch became Emperor or Empress of India. But no foreign state is obliged to recognize such titles. Peter the Great in 1701 assumed the title of Emperor of Russia, but his exalted rank was not recognized by some of the great powers until half a century later.

Monarchs are entitled by international law to certain predicates. Thus, a king or emperor is addressed as "Your Majesty"; a grand duke, as "Your Royal Highness"; while the Pope is given the predicate of *Sanctitas*. Such titles as *Rex Catholicus,* used by the kings of Spain since 1496, and *Defensor Fidei,* used by the British monarch since 1521, are not, however, recognized by the law of nations.[2]

In consequence of the monarch's character as a sovereign, his home state has the right to demand that certain ceremonial honors be accorded him when traveling abroad, that proper measures be taken for the protection of his person, and that he be granted certain exterritorial rights in conformity with the principle *par in parem non habet imperium.*[3] Thus, the house in which he may take up his residence becomes inviolate in the same manner as his country's embassy or legation. Even if a criminal should take refuge within the precinct of the monarch's residence, an arrest by the local authorities could not there take place without permis-

[1] Oppenheim-Lauterpacht, *International Law* (1947), vol. I, p. 676.
[2] *Ibid.*, p. 250n.1.
[3] Among equals no one has superiority.

sion. If the attitude of a foreign prince is such, however, as to obstruct the course of justice, the local government has the right to demand that he leave the country.

Though the courts are open to a foreign monarch as a matter of comity, he cannot be made a defendant without his own consent. In *Mighell v. Sultan of Johore*,[4] the British Court of Appeal said that "the foreign sovereign is entitled to immunity from civil proceedings in the Courts of any other country, unless upon being sued he actively elects to waive his privilege and to submit to the jurisdiction." Even if the king should assume an ordinary name and travel through a country incognito, he could not thereby be deprived of his immunity from legal process. It is true that a foreign sovereign may voluntarily elect to submit to the jurisdiction of the local courts, but that he intends to waive his rights of immunity "by taking an assumed name cannot be inferred." [5]

If a sovereign owns immovable property, such as a landed estate, in a foreign country, immunity from local jurisdiction does not ordinarily extend to the land. It is subject to the authority and jurisdiction of the state in which it is located save during such periods as the foreign sovereign may make his residence there. Some countries do not, however, recognize immunity from civil action if the involvement stems from acts done by the sovereign in his private capacity. The rationale underlying this point of view is to the effect that whatever immunity the sovereign enjoys derives from his state, to be sure, but only through the medium of official acts. The more general theory is that any act of a monarch, whether done in public or private capacity, cannot be subject to the jurisdiction of another state, as the very person of the ruler is sovereign as long as he remains the titular head of his nation.[6] Such immunity, however,

---

[4] Great Britain, Court of Appeal, 1893. [1894] 1 Q.B. 149; M. O. Hudson, *Cases and Other Materials on International Law* (1936), p. 504.

[5] Hudson, *loc. cit.*

[6] But according to Jack B. Tate, Acting Legal Adviser to the Department of State, in a letter of May 19, 1952, to the Acting Attorney General: "A study of the law of sovereign immunity reveals the existence of two conflicting concepts of sovereign immunity, each widely held and firmly established. According to the classical or absolute theory of sovereign immunity, a sovereign cannot, without his consent, be made a respondent in the courts of another sovereign. According to the newer or restrictive theory of sovereign immunity, the immunity of the sovereign is recognized with regard to sovereign or public acts (*jure imperii*) of a state, but not with respect to private acts (*jure gestionis*)." Further, according to Mr. Tate: "There is agreement by proponents of both theories, supported by practice, that sovereign immunity should not be claimed or granted in actions with respect to real property (diplomatic and perhaps consular property excepted) or with respect to the disposition of the property of a deceased person even though a foreign sovereign is the beneficiary." See William W. Bishop, Jr., "New United States Policy Limiting Sovereign Immunity," *American Journal of International Law*, vol. 47 (1953), pp. 93–106.

is coterminous with the period of the sovereign's rule. Thus, the kings of yesterday, who for one reason or another have abdicated their thrones, when traveling or residing abroad can claim none of the rights, honors, and immunities they once enjoyed as heads of state.

The Chief Executive of Republics. In a republic, the people as a whole represent the sovereignty of the state, and as we have seen, the chief executive may consist of a body of individuals, as in Switzerland, or of one man, as in the United States of America. In any case the head of state, whether its constitution is singular or plural, represents the country in its foreign relations. But in a republic, the chief executive is not regarded as a sovereign but is himself a citizen of the state he represents. Curious custom requires that monarchs address each other as "brothers," while presidents of republics are merely their "friends." Though a republic may claim for its head such homage as is due to the dignity of the nation, it cannot demand those ceremonies and honors reserved for kings.[7] This, however, does not prevent states from according to presidents of republics the same honors monarchs receive. Thus, in 1918, when President Wilson visited England, he was celebrated in the manner of a sovereign prince.

Authoritative opinion differs as to the legal position of heads of republics when abroad. This is especially true as regards the question of exterritoriality. It has been argued by some that a state may not claim for its president those exterritorial rights and immunities accorded to kings. But the realities of the present century have greatly undermined this position, as republics have multiplied and thrones in increasing number have been made vacant. Others admit that heads of republics in their official capacity are entitled to the same privileges and immunities as are the sovereign princes, but they deny this endowment to presidents when traveling abroad as private persons having no official functions to perform in behalf of their country. A third group of theorists would admit of no distinction regarding exterritoriality between official heads of state. Their argument is based on the proposition that all states are equal regardless of the constitution of their governments, and for that reason no distinction can logically be made between heads of state, who in any case merely reflect the dignity, rights, and duties of equal sovereignties in a community of nations. With respect to exterritoriality, Oppenheim sees no good reason for making such distinction between presidents and kings.[8]

The President of the United States. The institution of the presidency in the United States of America is of such importance in foreign relations as to deserve special mention here. According to the Constitution, direction of external affairs is vested in the President, subject, in certain matters,

[7] See Oppenheim-Lauterpacht, *op. cit.,* pp. 680–681.
[8] *Ibid.,* p. 681.

to the approval of the Senate.[9] In *United States v. Curtiss-Wright Export Corporation* [10] Justice Sutherland, writing for the Supreme Court, had this to say concerning the position of the President in the nation's foreign affairs:

Not only, as we have shown, is the federal power over external affairs in origin and essential character different from that over internal affairs, but participation in the exercise of the power is significantly limited. In this vast external realm, with its important, complicated, delicate and manifold problems, the President alone has the power to speak or listen as a representative of the nation. He *makes* treaties with the advice and consent of the Senate; but he alone negotiates. Into the field of negotiation the Senate cannot intrude; and Congress itself is powerless to invade it. As Marshall said in his great argument of March 7, 1800, in the House of Representatives, "The President is the sole organ of the nation in its external relations, and the sole representative with foreign nations."

The importance of the presidential office in American foreign affairs was given equal emphasis by Thomas Jefferson, when as Secretary of State he wrote, on November 22, 1793, to Edmond C. Genêt, the French minister, informing him concerning the function of the President in relations of the United States with foreign countries: "He," said Jefferson, "being the only channel of communication between this country and foreign nations, it is from him alone that foreign nations or their agents are to learn what is or has been the will of the nation." [11] It is clear, therefore, that the proper channel for a foreign government to follow if it wishes to communicate with the United States is through the President of the republic or through his agent, the Secretary of State.[12]

Departments of Foreign Affairs. Because of the multitude and complexity of problems confronting states in their international relations, a vast apparatus has been created in every country to facilitate the administration of its foreign affairs. Thus we find that today practically all negotiations with foreign nations take place through the agency of a department of foreign affairs. At the head of such a department stands a

---

[9] According to Art. II, sec. 2, par. 2, of the Constitution the President "shall have Power, by and with the Advice and Consent of the Senate, to make Treaties, provided two-thirds of the Senators present concur; and he shall nominate, and by and with the Advice and Consent of the Senate, shall appoint Ambassadors, and other public Ministers and Consuls, Judges of the Supreme Court, and all other Officers of the United States, whose Appointments are not herein otherwise provided for, and which shall be established by Law."

[10] 299 U.S. 304 (1936); C. Gordon Post, Frances P. DeLancy, and Fredryc R. Darby, *Basic Constitutional Cases* (1948), p. 253.

[11] *American State Papers, Foreign Relations*, vol. I, p. 184; see also John Bassett Moore, *Digest of International Law*, vol. IV, pp. 680–682.

[12] Charles Cheney Hyde, *International Law* (1947), vol. II, p. 1216.

secretary or minister, who is a member of the cabinet and is responsible to the chief executive for his official conduct. The position of the foreign minister at home is fixed by municipal law, but in his conduct of affairs with other nations the impingement of international law is necessarily felt. Thus it can be said that the machinery for foreign relations is a matter of municipal legislation. "But the moment that machinery goes into action, it manifests itself in the international sphere, where many of its effects are subject to the requirements and limitations of international law." [13]

The minister of foreign affairs is the chief of his department to whom diplomatic and consular officers are responsible. It is he who personally, or through his agents, carries on negotiations with foreign countries, and as we have seen, any acts done by the foreign minister in his official capacity entail responsibility on the part of the state he represents.[14] The department of foreign affairs is also considered the most authoritative source of information regarding certain matters in the category of external relations. It is the practice of British courts, for example, to ascertain whether a foreign state or government is recognized by their own country by referring the matter to the Foreign Office.[15] A pronouncement by the Foreign Office with respect to such questions as the sovereign status of a foreign ruler,[16] the termination of a state of war,[17] and whether some individual is entitled to diplomatic status [18] is binding upon the courts in Britain. The presumption, however, is that the courts will draw the proper legal conclusions from the facts thus supplied by the Foreign Office. On the other hand, American courts have been inclined to accept conclusions of the Department of State, even on matters of legal substance, as binding.

An example of such substantive question of law would be whether a claim to immunity by some foreign state or government is well founded. In *Ex parte Republic of Peru*,[19] the Supreme Court of the United States laid down the rule that a foreign government may present its claim of immunity either to the court or to the Department of State. In the latter

---

[13] Elmer Plischke, *Conduct of American Diplomacy* (1950), pp. 25–26.

[14] A notorious example is the Ihlen Declaration, which is discussed in Part II, pp. 134–135.

[15] See *Luther v. James Sagor & Co.* (Great Britain, Court of Appeal, 1921), 3 K.B. 532; *The Gagara* (same Court, 1919), Probate 95; *The Annette* (Great Britain, Probate, Divorce, and Admiralty Division, 1919), Probate 105.

[16] *Mighell v. Sultan of Johore* (Great Britain, Court of Appeal, 1893), 1 Q.B. 149; *Duff Development Co. v. Government of Kelantan* (Great Britain, House of Lords, 1924), A.C. 797.

[17] *Janson v. Driefontein Consolidated Mines* (1902), 2 A.C 500.

[18] *Engelke v. Musmann* (Great Britain, House of Lords), A.C. 433 [1928].

[19] 318 U.S. 578 (1943).

case, the court is bound by the Department's decision as presented by the Attorney General. Likewise, in the case of *The Ucayali*[20] the same court said that once the Department of State has declared a foreign public vessel to be immune to local jurisdiction, the courts may not take any action so "as to embarrass the executive arm of the government in conducting foreign relations." In *Republic of Mexico v. Hoffman*,[21] decided by the United States Supreme Court in 1945, Chief Justice Stone wrote: [22]

Every judicial action exercising or relinquishing jurisdiction over the vessel of a foreign government has its effect upon our relations with that government. Hence it is a guiding principle in determining whether a court should exercise or surrender its jurisdiction in such cases. . . . [In any case, the] courts should not so act as to embarrass the executive arm in its conduct of foreign affairs. . . .

It is therefore not for the courts to deny an immunity which our government has seen fit to allow, or to allow an immunity on new grounds which the government has not seen fit to recognize.

It may be said, therefore, that in the United States the courts have, generally speaking, been guided by what the Department of State has considered in a given case to be the best public policy in the conduct of foreign affairs. French practice in this regard is even more derogatory of the judicial function. There the executive department has often been relied on by the courts even for the interpretation of treaties,[23] and the principle of public policy more often than law has guided the courts where foreign interests have been involved. In 1925, for example, the Court of Appeal of Aix refused to give effect to a Soviet decree of January 20, 1918, whereby the Russian merchant marine was nationalized, because the effect of the decree ran counter to French national policy. This policy had been defined by Premier Herriot in a note to A. I. Rykoff, President of the Council of the People's Commissars, as follows: [24]

The Government of the Republic wishes to reserve expressly the rights that French citizens possess through obligations contracted by Russia or its nationals [*ressortissants*] under the previous regimes and whose sanction is upheld by the general principles of law which remain for us the rule of international life.

Legation. A very old institution in the negotiation between states is

[20] *Ibid.*; *Annual Digest*, 1941–1942, Case no. 53.
[21] (1945) 324 U.S. 30; *American Journal of International Law*, vol. 39 (1945), p. 585; Hudson, *Cases on International Law* (1951), p. 308.
[22] In *Berizzi Bros. Co. v. S. S. Pesaro*, however, the Court allowed immunity to a merchant vessel owned by a foreign government, though the Department of State had refused to recognize such immunity. 271 U.S. 562. See also Hudson, *Cases* (1951), 309n.
[23] Oppenheim-Lauterpacht, *op. cit.*, p. 686.
[24] *Union of Soviet Socialist Republics v. Compagnie Ropit*, Sirey, *Recueil général des lois et des arrêts*, 1926, vol. II, p. 12; Hudson, *Cases* (1951), p. 105.

the so-called legation, of which there are many examples even in the earliest records of ancient nations. And it is interesting, indeed, that long before the advent of a systematic body of international law, ambassadors enjoyed special privileges and protection through the sanction of religious custom. The embassies of antiquity were not permanent but consisted of special missions sent by one monarch to another to negotiate treaties of war and peace. It was not until the thirteenth century that the first permanent legations began to appear in Europe.[25] It is of interest to note that Grotius did not think permanent legations necessary. History, however, has proved him wrong; for today diplomatic relations take place almost entirely through the medium of this institution. Legation has become the keystone in a greater community of nations.

The question of whether states have a "right of legation" has been until recently a matter of controversy among writers on international law.[26] Because diplomatic relations are necessary and of mutual advantage to all states, to send and receive public ministers is now generally regarded as a right under international law. It is obvious that the very existence of an international community makes it imperative that the nations which make up the community should have occasion to negotiate with one another regarding various points of common interest. According to a memorandum of the Department of State of the United States from the Under Secretary to the Attorney General on April 8, 1920: [27]

Every independent and full sovereign member of the family of nations possesses the right of legation, which is the right of a State to send and receive diplomatic envoys. This right has been accorded at times in a restricted form to Part-Sovereign and Semi-Sovereign States, and the exact restrictions upon the diplomatic activity of each being determined by the instrument defining their international position.

The right of legation is, however, discretionary, as no state is under any obligation either to send or to receive diplomatic agents. It should be noted also that the United Nations, as an international person *sui generis,* enjoys the right of legation, and the same was true of the League of Nations.

[25] Oppenheim-Lauterpacht, *op. cit.,* p. 688. The *responsales* maintained by the Popes at the courts of the Frankish kings and at Constantinople at an earlier date cannot be considered as the first examples of permanent legations, according to Oppenheim, as their work "had nothing to do with international affairs, but with those of the Church only."

[26] For complete treatment of the problems of modern diplomacy, see the following works: J. W. Foster, *The Practice of Diplomacy* (1906), and *A Century of American Diplomacy* (1911); E. Satow, *A Guide to Diplomatic Practice* (1932); G. H. Stuart, *American Diplomatic and Consular Practice* (1936).

[27] G. H. Hackworth, *Digest of International Law,* vol. IV, p. 393.

Diplomatic Envoys. Diplomatic representatives may be divided, in a general way, into two main classifications: one *ceremonial,* the other *political.* To the first category belong special representatives, who are sent by one state to another in connection with certain state celebrations, such as coronations and weddings. In the second group are all envoys whose function it is to represent the state in a political capacity in a foreign country or at some international institution or conference. The most important category, and the one with which we are concerned here, is that of the political envoys. Of these there are also two classifications: (1) those accredited to the governments of foreign nations or international institutions, and (2) those representing their own state at some international conference or congress. Diplomatic envoys accredited to a state or to an institution like the United Nations are again classified according to rank.

It was not until the sixteenth century, however, that the first classification of political envoys made its appearance. And by the middle of the seventeenth century, when permanent legations had come into fairly general practice, two classes of diplomats were recognized. The more important of these were the envoys extraordinary, or ambassadors, and those of the second class, envoys ordinary, called residents.[28] In the eighteenth century another classification was introduced, namely, ministers plenipotentiary, but the problem of precedence continued to cause disputes, especially among the great powers.

It was plain that this matter could be settled only by some sort of international understanding. Thus, when the powers assembled at Vienna, in 1815, it was decided that three classes of diplomatic envoys were to be established according to rank as follows: (1) *ambassadors,* (2) *ministers plenipotentiary and envoys extraordinary,* and (3) *chargés d'affaires.* At the Congress of Aix-la-Chapelle in 1818 a fourth class was added to rank between ministers plenipotentiary and chargés d'affaires, namely, *ministers resident.* These, then, are the four classes of diplomats generally recognized today. We might add, however, that papal legates or nuncios are classified in the rank of ambassadors. All the above must present their credentials to the head of state with the exception of the chargé d'affaires, who is accredited to the Minister of Foreign Affairs in the country to which he is sent.

All diplomatic envoys accredited to the same state form what is called the *diplomatic corps.* At the head of this body is the *doyen* or dean in the person of the papal nuncio or, if no such, the diplomat of longest service of the highest rank. Sometimes, a country may acquire a privileged posi-

[28] Oppenheim-Lauterpacht, *op. cit.,* p. 695.

tion for its representative by special treaty provisions.[29] Though the diplomatic corps is not a legally constituted body, it is nevertheless of great importance in that it watches over the privileges and honors due to diplomatic envoys of the various ranks.[30] The qualification and rank of a diplomatic representative are matters for each individual state to determine. This is to some degree conditioned, however, by the possibility that the country for which the envoy is intended might refuse his reception.

The usual practice is to ascertain beforehand that the person contemplated for appointment to a diplomatic mission is *persona grata* in the country to which he would be sent. This approval is in diplomatic language called the assignment of *agrément*. In 1885, A. M. Keiley was refused reception as American diplomatic envoy, first in Italy and later by the Austro-Hungarian government. In the latter case the attention of the United States was called to "the generally existing diplomatic practice to ask previously to any nomination of a foreign minister the *agrément* (consent) of the government to which he is accredited." [31]

The Diplomat's Credentials. It is required by the law of nations that diplomatic representatives possess certain credentials. Such is the *letter of credence.* This document identifies the public minister, designates his rank, and describes the general purpose of his mission. At the same time it asks that the diplomat be favorably received and that full credence be given to whatever he has to say in behalf of the country from which he comes. The letter of credence is addressed by the head of the state sending the diplomat to the head of the state receiving him.

If the envoy is of the rank of chargé d'affaires, such correspondence takes place between the foreign ministers of the states concerned. A letter of credence is sufficient authorization for any diplomat to perform his ordinary duties in connection with a permanent mission. But if extraordinary tasks, such as the negotiation of a treaty or convention, are to be done, a special document known as *full powers* is required. These are given in letters patent by the head of state and are either limited or unlimited full powers, as each case may require.[32] Through this document the foreign government is informed of the authority vested in the diplomat, and to what extent his action may be regarded as binding upon the state he represents. It should be noted, however, that commitments even under full powers may not be interpreted as binding upon a sovereign

[29] By the Treaty of Alliance between Great Britain and Egypt of Aug. 26, 1936, Egypt promised to consider the British ambassador as senior to all other diplomats accredited to Cairo.

[30] Oppenheim-Lauterpacht, *op. cit.,* p. 697.

[31] Moore, *op. cit.,* p. 481.

[32] Oppenheim-Lauterpacht, *op. cit.,* p. 699.

state, as the right to ratification in conformity with the prescribed constitutional processes is either expressly or tacitly reserved.

Right to Innocent Transit. It is an ancient rule, deduced from the
necessity of diplomatic intercourse between nations, that public ministers
shall have the right to pass freely through any country when on diplomatic
missions. Such freedom of transit has, nevertheless, on several occasions
been refused. In 1926, for example, the United States declined permission
of territorial transit to the Soviet diplomatic representative to Mexico. The
general rule, however, is not only to allow "innocent passage" to foreign
diplomats, but also to exempt such individuals from civil suits as they
pass through the state's jurisdiction in connection with their diplomatic
office. In the case of *Wilson v. Guzman Blanco* [33] a New York court held
that the Venezuelan minister to France was not subject to its jurisdiction
in respect to a civil claim while passing through its territory. This point
of view is given at least qualified support by a British court in *New Chile
Gold Mining Co. v. Blanco*.[34] In this case it was held that a writ might
not be served on a diplomatic representative of a friendly power.

The matter of innocent passage for foreign diplomats rarely presents
any difficulties in time of peace. But in time of war the situation is different. The following examples will serve to illustrate: On November 9, 1916,
an announcement was made by the government of Austria-Hungary, saying that Count Tarnowski had been appointed its ambassador to the
United States. The Count and his suite were scheduled to embark for
this country on a Dutch ship at the port of Rotterdam. But safe-conducts
were refused by both the British and French governments on the alleged
ground that Austro-Hungarian embassies in neutral capitals had engaged
in activities quite outside their diplomatic functions. The United States
protested the action of the two belligerent powers and pointed out that
the exchange of ambassadors is an inalienable right of sovereign states,
which cannot be denied, even in time of war. A month later, both the
British and French governments granted the necessary safe-conducts,
and the ambassador passed unmolested through the enemy's territory.[35]

When diplomatic relations are severed as a prelude to war, safe-
conducts are often required so that public ministers and consuls may
reach their homelands without interception by the enemy. Thus when the
United States decided to enter the war against Germany in 1917, arrangements were made for the departure of German diplomats and consuls on

[33] 56 N.Y. Super. Ct. 582 (1889).
[34] 4 T.L.R. 346 (1888); P. Cobbett, *Cases on International Law*, vol. I, p. 308. For
the opposite point of view, see J. Westlake, *International Law* (1910–1913), vol. I,
pp. 275 and 275–276n.
[35] Hackworth, *op. cit.*, pp. 462–463.

ɹ Norwegian ship. Permits were secured from the French and British governments for their safe-conduct from New York to Christiania.[36]

Privileges of Nondiplomatic Persons. There are certain classes of officials who by treaty are invested with privileges and immunities similar to those enjoyed by regular diplomatic agents. Among these are certain international officials, such as those of the United Nations, as well as representatives of the members of this Organization.[37] The details of these immunities are, however, to be left for final determination to recommendations of the UN Assembly or to special conventions.[38] It may be pointed out that, unlike the League Covenant, the Charter of the United Nations does not employ the phrase "diplomatic privileges and immunities" in this connection.[39] The First General Assembly in February, 1946, approved a convention on the privileges and immunities of the United Nations, and on April 11, 1949, the International Court of Justice handed down an advisory opinion in which the international personality of the United Nations was recognized. In view of this legal nature of the Organization, it would seem to follow that its officials abroad should be entitled to the same immunities as those of states. This position has been taken by American courts in several cases involving representatives to the United Nations.[40]

In the separation case of *Tsiang v. Tsiang*,[41] the defendant moved the summons and complaint be set aside on the ground of diplomatic immunity. The court went on to say: "The uncontrovertible facts here indicate that defendant is accredited to the United Nations as Ambassador Plenipotentiary and Permanent Representative of the Republic of China, and is in the United States as the permanent resident representative of

[36] *Ibid.*, p. 463.

[37] Art. 105 of the United Nations Charter provides that "the Organization shall enjoy in the territory of each of its Members such privileges and immunities as are necessary for the fulfillment of its purposes," and according to par. 2 of the same article, "representatives of the Members of the United Nations and officials of the Organization shall similarly enjoy such privileges and immunities as are necessary for the independent exercise of their functions in connection with the Organization."

[38] Art. 105, par. 3, of the Charter of the United Nations.

[39] Art. 7 of the Covenant of the League of Nations provided that "officials of the League when engaged on the business of the League shall enjoy diplomatic privileges and immunities."

[40] An act of Dec. 29, 1945 (59 Stat. L. 669) sets forth the privileges and immunities accorded by the United States to international organizations and officials. This law was made applicable to the United Nations by Executive Order of Feb. 19, 1946. It should be pointed out, however, that certain local American courts, in cases involving members of the United Nations Secretariat, have shown considerable reluctance in according immunities to such officials and employees. See especially *Westchester County v. Ranollo* (1946), 187 Misc. 777; 67 N.Y.S.2d 31. See also comment by L. Preuss in *American Journal of International Law*, vol. 41 (1947), pp. 555–578.

[41] *New York Law Journal*, vol. 121 (1949), p. 484; 194 Misc. 259; 86 N.Y.S.2d 556.

the Government of China. Furthermore, the unqualified representation made by the Department of State as to defendant's immunity from suit would, in and of itself, prevent any further examination into the question by this court (*Matter of United States of Mexico v. Schmuck*, 294 N.Y., 265; 293 N.Y., 264)." Diplomatic immunity of an ambassador is based on international comity.[42] The court then called attention to an agreement between the United Nations and the United States, regarding the status of representatives to the United Nations,[43] Section 15 of which provides that every person designated as a principal resident representative to the United Nations shall be entitled to the same diplomatic immunity as is accorded to diplomatic envoys accredited to the United States.[44] The court, therefore, concluded that both by reason of the special statute and the abundant case law, a United Nations diplomat is immune from process.

In *Friedberg v. Santa Cruz* [45] a civil suit was brought against the Chilean representative to the United Nations and his wife, arising out of an automobile accident in New York. The New York Superior Court, Appellate Division, Second Department, held that, under the United Nations Headquarters Agreement, approved by an act of the United States Congress, the defendant "is entitled to the same privileges and immunities in the territory of the United States as it accords to diplomatic envoys accredited to it," and hence sustained his plea of diplomatic immunity. As for the wife, she was included in the statutory group of "domestics" and thus entitled to the same immunity.

A Convention on Privileges and Immunities of the United Nations was approved by the First General Assembly on February 13, 1946,[46] and by 1950 accessions had been deposited by about thirty-five member states. The convention contains detailed provisions concerning such matters as the juridical personality of the United Nations; the immunity and inviolability of its property, its premises, and its archives; and exemption from taxation and customs duties.

With respect to the International Court of Justice, it is provided in Article 19 of the Statute that "the members of the Court, when engaged in the business of the Court, shall enjoy diplomatic privileges and immunities." A large number of other international organizations, by virtue of their constitutions, claim immunities for themselves and their officials,

[42] *The Schooner Exchange v. McFaddon*, 7 Cranch 116 (1812).
[43] 80th Cong., 1st Sess., Public Law 357, 1947, chap. 482; 61 Stat. L. 756, 762.
[44] Diplomatic immunity of a diplomatic envoy is based on international comity (*The Schooner Exchange v. McFaddon*, 7 Cranch 116; *Hannes v. Kingdom of Romania Monopolies Institute*, 260 App. Div. 189; *Curran v. City of N.Y.*, 191 Misc. 229).
[45] 86 N.Y.S. 2d 369; *American Journal of International Law*, vol. 43 (1949), p. 814.
[46] *United Nations Treaty Series*, vol. I, p. 15.

and in some countries national legislation has been enacted granting such privileges to international organizations of various kinds.[47]

National officials, aside from regular diplomatic representatives, are frequently granted certain privileges and immunities by treaties and conventions. This has been the case with respect to certain trade commissions acting in behalf of the Soviet government.[48] National officials who are delegates to various international organizations, such as the United Nations, or to international congresses and conferences, are usually given special immunities either by custom or by treaty.

[47] See especially the British Diplomatic Privileges (Extension) Acts of 1941, 1944, and 1946. In 1945 an act passed by the United States Congress extended certain privileges, exemptions, and immunities to international organizations, their officials and employees (Public Law 291).

[48] Oppenheim-Lauterpacht, *op. cit.*, p. 739.

CHAPTER 17

Diplomatic and Consular Agents

DIPLOMATIC ENVOYS

Diplomacy has been defined as the art and science of interstate representation and negotiation.[1] The same word has also been employed to express generically the whole complex of a state's foreign relations, i.e., the department of foreign affairs including its foreign representation. It is in this sense that one may speak of the merits of American diplomacy in a certain era, or of French and Russian diplomacy, etc. Finally, the term *diplomacy* is used to designate the profession itself, and one has come to view *la diplomatie* as a profession of the state in the same manner *the military* is so regarded.[2]

In 1693 Leibnitz published his *Codex juris gentium diplomaticus,* and Dumont in 1726 the *Corps universel diplomatique du droit des gens.* Both these works were collections of treaties and official documents, and the term *corps diplomatique* was here treated as equivalent to the *corps du droit des gens.* Later the diplomatic corps was differentiated from the general body of international law, and came to be the designation for the ensemble of foreign diplomats in a given country.

Today the term *diplomatist* or *diplomat* has a wider meaning. It is taken to include all public servants in the field of diplomatic relations, whether serving at home in the department of foreign affairs or as members of

[1] Sir Henry Wotton, a British diplomat of the seventeenth century, had this to say about the function of a diplomat: *"Legatus est vir bonus peregre missus ad mentiendum Reipublicae causa."* This epigram has remained to this day, perhaps not the most correct, but certainly the most famous definition of a diplomat. In English it would read something like this: "An ambassador is an honest man, sent to lie abroad for the good of his country."

[2] See Rivier, *Principes du droit des gens* (1896), vol. II, p. 432. The words *diplomacy* and *diplomat* are believed to derive from *diploma,* a document by which privilege is conferred and emanating from princes. The word *diploma,* according to Sir Ernest Satow, first came into use in England in the year 1645—*A Guide to Diplomatic Practice* (1932), vol. I, p. 3.

embassies and legations in foreign countries. Thus, strictly speaking, the head of the foreign department of a government is himself a diplomatist in the truest sense of that term, in that as a responsible statesman he conducts the foreign relations of his country. With the development of modern means of communication, the home office of foreign affairs has become even more important than formerly in the field of diplomacy. It is, of course, true that the minister of foreign affairs may be merely a political personage, but frequently he is an individual professionally trained in international law and diplomacy. Thus, when we speak of the diplomacy of a country as skillful or blundering, we have reference not merely to the work of diplomatic agents abroad, but rather to the direction of the nation's foreign department as a whole. It would be a mistake to put the blame for weak and unintelligent diplomacy on the agents in the field, when in fact the blunder is caused by the leadership at home in the direction of foreign relations.

The regulations of most countries make it clear that the principal duty of diplomatic and consular officers is to protect the interests of their state and nationals abroad. Having reference to the duties of an American Foreign Service officer, the Department of State has said that "he protects generally the interests of the United States in accordance with international law and protects, advises, and otherwise assists Americans resident or traveling abroad for business or other purposes." [3]

The Meaning of Protection. The protection of nationals and their interests abroad is based on a rule, which an American Secretary of State once termed "the correlative rights of allegiance and protection." [4] It is interesting to note, however, the *Foreign Service Regulations of the United States*, which provide, *inter alia*, that "diplomatic and consular officers may, upon request, assume temporarily the protection of foreign interests." [5] Similar provisions are found in the diplomatic and consular regulations of other countries, so that the general practice throughout the world in this regard seems to have no relationship to the medieval formula of *allegiance and protection*. Yet it is to this principle we must look for the rationale of a time-honored practice by which states lend protection to their nationals abroad.

The assumption by one state of the protection of the interests of another in the territory of a third state is best illustrated in time of war. In the present century the possibilities of indirect communication between belligerent states through this means has become so general and so extensively exploited as to constitute an important modification in the tradi-

[3] Department of State, *The American Foreign Service* (1942), p. 3.
[4] Fish to DeLong, no. 108, Sept. 19, 1871, Ms., Japan, Instructions, vol. 1.
[5] Department of State, *Foreign Service Regulations* (1946), chap. XII, sec. 4.

tional severance of relations between nations at war.[6] The practice illustrates a striking cohesiveness in modern international society even in times of conflict. Not so well known, but more numerous and no less significant, are the instances, in time of peace, when the protection of one state has been accorded the interests of another in the territory of a third power.

Inasmuch as the terminology relative to this practice is somewhat confusing, a word of explanation seems in order. The terms *good offices, representation,* and *protection* have often been used synonymously. Moore and Hackworth in their respective *Digests* have classified the temporary assumption of protection by one state of another's interest in a third under the general heading of "good offices." The difficulty seems to be, however, that this term has in recent years come to have several other meanings in diplomatic usage. It has often been employed in American practice "only to indicate the most informal and occasional type of protection of foreign interests." [7] The word "representation," though it has been frequently used as a generic term in this regard, is no less confusing, as it fails to distinguish between the "representation" of foreign interest, on the one hand, and "representation" of a state abroad through its own diplomatic and consular officers on the other hand. In making clear this very important distinction American Secretaries of State have frequently pointed out that in the so-called "representation" of foreign interests American diplomatic or consular officers do not, in a real sense, *represent* foreign governments.[8] The type of confusion which has resulted from the use of the term "representation" in this connection is illustrated by the following: "Representation of foreign interests usually ceases upon the direction of the unrepresented government. . . ." [9] In order to avoid such ambiguities, the latest edition of the *Foreign Service Regulations* describes the function of diplomatic and consular officers in connection with the affairs of a state other than their own, by the generic term "protection."

General Functions of Diplomatic Envoys. A distinction must, first of all, be made between the functions of those diplomats who represent their state in a temporary and ceremonial sense and the permanent political envoys attached to embassies and legations throughout the world. Included in the first group are such political envoys as represent the state in a "negotiatory" capacity at some international conference or congress. Their functions are at best temporary in nature and deserve no further

[6] William McHenry Franklin, *Protection of Foreign Interests, A Study in Diplomatic and Consular Practice* (1946), p. 2.
[7] *Ibid.*, pp. 3 and 175.
[8] *Ibid.*, p. 3.
[9] Quoted from Ms., General Instructions Consular, no. 177, Mar. 14, 1921, in Franklin, *op. cit.*, p. 4.

consideration here. It is those of the second category, the so-called "permanent" envoys, with which we shall now deal. Their functions can, in the main, be grouped under three headings: (1) negotiation, (2) observation, and (3) protection.[10]

In his capacity as negotiator, the envoy serves as the mouthpiece of his own state in the totality of its foreign relations and not merely with regard to the state to which he is accredited. But between the latter and his own government he is the "regular channel" of diplomatic communication. It is his task also to be, so to speak, the eyes and ears of his own country abroad, and thus to observe and report all facts and occurrences of significance to his government. Finally, a diplomatic representative is charged with the duty to protect the persons and properties of his compatriots and, as we have seen, under certain circumstances, similar interests of states other than his own. Though all states are compelled to observe certain minimum standards of international law in their treatment of aliens, it is for the municipal law of his home state to prescribe the limits within which an envoy may afford the necessary protection of his countrymen.[11]

Aside from the functions enumerated above, diplomatic agents may at times be expected to perform other duties in behalf of their own states, such as the registration of births, deaths, and marriages and the issuance of passports. In all cases, however, the home state must be careful not to order its diplomatic or consular agents to perform duties which according to law in the receiving country come within the exclusive jurisdiction of the local authorities. Above all, foreign diplomats must under all circumstances refrain from interference in the political and other domestic affairs of the state to which they are accredited. Though the history of international diplomacy is full of examples of such interference, it is nevertheless unacceptable under the law of nations.

The rights and duties which diplomats enjoy are derived from the rights and duties of the states they represent. It should be noted, therefore, that the privileges and immunities which diplomats enjoy abroad are granted by the municipal law of the receiving power in compliance with rights under international law belonging to all states. "Thus, a diplomatic envoy is not a subject but an object of international law, and is, in this regard, like any other individual." [12]

Diplomatic Immunity. It is incumbent upon every state not to violate the immunities to which diplomatic envoys are entitled under the law of nations. The protection of foreign diplomats, their official residence,

[10] Oppenheim-Lauterpacht, *International Law* (1947), vol. I, p. 703.
[11] *Ibid.*, p. 704.
[12] *Ibid.*, p. 706.

families, assistants, automobiles, papers, messengers, letters [13] and telegrams, etc., must find its expression not only through adequate preventive measures against violation, but in the proper punishment of offenders as well. Even after a diplomatic mission has been terminated, the archives of a foreign embassy or legation must not be disturbed by the local authorities, provided they have been properly sealed and entrusted to the protection of a third power.[14]

It is obvious that the immunities to which diplomats are entitled cannot prevent proper authorities from applying measures of personal restraint should such an individual be engaged in open violation of local ordinances and laws. If ambassador *X* of country *Y*, for example, should drive his automobile through the streets of our nation's capital at a speed of 90 miles per hour, he could, of course, be restrained and prevented from thus endangering public safety. It may be said, therefore, that a diplomat's personal inviolability is very largely conditioned upon the "correctness of his own conduct." [15] In *Dickinson v. Del Solar*,[16] the court said: "Diplomatic agents are not, in virtue of their privileges as such, immune from legal liability for any wrongful acts. The accurate statement is that they are not liable to be sued . . . unless they submit to the jurisdiction. Diplomatic privilege does not import immunity from legal liability, but only exemption from local jurisdiction."

The procedure in cases where a diplomat is guilty of a serious infraction of law is to ask his own government to terminate the mission by recall. This the offender's state is compelled to do under international law. If, on the other hand, a political offense is committed by a foreign diplomat, his person might be seized and turned over to the authorities of his own country. This may be done, however, only in a case of urgent danger. An example of such political crime was the notorious Gyllenborg-

[13] It is doubtful whether his official correspondence by mail can always escape examination in countries where such censorship is a general practice. "The State archives of every country doubtless possess, in the shape of intercepted dispatches, evidence that it was quite common in the eighteenth century, and there seems to be no reason to suppose that it has been altogether abandoned"—Satow, *op. cit.*, p. 252.

[14] Oppenheim-Lauterpacht, *op. cit.*, p. 708.

[15] E. Satow, *A Guide to Diplomatic Practice* (1922), vol. I, p. 252.

[16] [1930] 1 K.B. 376. In the case of *The Magdalena Steam Navigation Company v. Martin*, involving a suit against the minister plenipotentiary for the republics of Guatemala and New Granada for alleged nonpayment of debt, in which the defendant contended that he should be exempt from suit by reason of being a public minister, the court said: "We are of opinion that his plea is good, and that we are bound to give judgment in his favour. The great principle is to be found in Grotius *de Jure Belli et Pacis*, lib. 2, c. 18, s. 9, 'Omnis coactio abesse a legato debet.' He is to be left at liberty to devote himself body and soul to the business of his embassy. He does not owe even a temporary allegiance to the Sovereign to whom he is accredited, and he has at least as great privileges from suits as the Sovereign whom he represents." England. Court of the Queen's Bench, 2 Ellis & Ellis 94 (1859).

Goertz conspiracy of 1717 which had for its purpose, among other things, the deposition of George I of England. The conspiracy was exposed through a shipwreck off the Norwegian coast, and Gyllenborg, the Swedish ambassador to the Court of St. James, was arrested and his papers seized. Goertz, who had taken part in the conspiracy as a secret agent of Charles XII of Sweden, was soon thereafter arrested at Arnhem. Another such case was that of Prince Cellamare, who in 1715 was appointed ambassador extraordinary to the French Court by Philip V of Spain. Cellamare proceeded to organize a conspiracy against the French government which resulted in his arrest in 1718.[17]

Not only do diplomats enjoy the so-called *franchise de l'hôtel*, or immunity of domicile; they are also, as we have seen, exempt from criminal jurisdiction in the states to which they are accredited. Nor can any civil action be brought against a foreign diplomat in the courts of the receiving state. We should bear in mind that the rules regarding the immunity of diplomats are in no way different from those governing the immunity of heads of state. In both cases we must look for its derivation to the international personality of the state they represent. The rule that sovereigns and diplomats are exempt from civil jurisdiction is, however, subject to certain exceptions: (1) All cases in which such immunity is waived; and (2) cases where a diplomat or head of state as a plaintiff is made subject to a setoff or counterclaim. In *Norway v. Federal Sugar Refining Company*,[18] the court said:

> A sovereign State, generally speaking, is not obliged to go into court; but, if it seeks the assistance of the court, it would seem to be in accord with the best principles of modern law that it should be obliged to submit to the jurisdiction of the court in respect to any set-off or counterclaim properly assertable as a defense in a similar suit between private litigants.

This same principle would also hold in cases where diplomats are involved, as their immunity is neither more nor less than that of the states they represent. In the case *Taylor v. Best*,[19] the British court held that the secretary to the Belgian legation in London could not be sued for money deposited in his care as one of the directors of a commercial firm. But inasmuch as he had voluntarily submitted to the jurisdiction of the court, it was held he could not later claim his official privilege of diplomatic immunity.[20] A third exception is that the local courts have jurisdic-

[17] Satow, *A Guide to Diplomatic Practice*, pp. 256–257.
[18] 286 Fed. Cas. 188 (D.C.S.D.N.Y. 1923); M. O. Hudson, *Cases and Other Material on International Law* (1936), p. 543.
[19] 14 C.B. 487 (1854).
[20] C. G. Fenwick, *International Law* (1948), p. 470; see also John Bassett Moore, *Digest of International Law*, vol. IV, pp. 657–658.

tion over immovable property which diplomats may hold in their private capacity and, in most cases, over their private business ventures.

A foreign diplomat cannot be made to testify as a witness in a civil, criminal, or administrative court. But if he should elect to appear voluntarily, any court may make use of his testimony. Thus, when Guiteau was tried for the assassination of President Garfield, the Venezuelan minister to Washington, Comancho, was asked to give testimony for the prosecution, and did so on instructions from his own government.[21] But in 1856 the Dutch minister to the United States, Dubois, refused to be made a witness in another homicide case and was supported in this refusal by his government.[22] It should be noted that in the Guiteau case, the district attorney took occasion to point out that, as a foreign diplomat, Comancho was "entitled under the law governing diplomatic relations to be relieved from service by subpoena or sworn as a witness in any case." [23] There can be no doubt that the refusal of the Dutch diplomat to appear as a witness is in conformity with well-established principles of both law and practice. "A diplomatic representative cannot be compelled to testify, in the country of his sojourn, before any tribunal whatsoever. This right is regarded as appertaining to his office, not to his person, and is one of which he cannot divest himself except by the consent of his government." [24]

Diplomatic agents are likewise exempt from police regulations, as well as the payment of taxes, etc. International law does not claim, in behalf of diplomats, any exemption from the payment of customs duties. By comity, however, municipal laws in most countries provide for the free entry of such goods as are intended for a foreign diplomat's private use.

Diplomatic Asylum. Every state has the right under the law of nations to offer asylum to political refugees from other countries, i.e., a place of shelter, security, and protection within the jurisdictional area of the state. Whether this is an exterritorial right extending to embassies and legations abroad is doubtful.[25] It has been argued that this so-called right of asylum, within the precincts of a foreign embassy, follows as a corollary from the diplomat's right to immunity of domicile. But even as early as the days of Grotius, the right of asylum, in this sense, was questioned, and writers on international law in the seventeenth and eighteenth centuries tended to give the doctrine less and less sanction.[26] It seems clear, however, that, since the local police authorities may not, without permission, enter a foreign embassy or legation, temporary refuge can be afforded to anyone who enters within a diplomat's official residence. Such sanctuary could be

[21] Moore, *op. cit.*, pp. 644–645.   [22] *Ibid.*, p. 643.
[23] *Ibid.*, p. 645.   [24] *Ibid.*, p. 642.
[25] Fenwick, *op. cit.*, p. 472.
[26] George Grafton Wilson, *Handbook of International Law* (1939), p. 179.

only of a temporary nature, as the proper procedure would be to surrender the fugitive upon demand from the local authorities. The attitude of the United States on this matter is given expression in an Executive Order, dated December 1, 1932.[27] It runs in part as follows:

The affording of asylum is not within the purposes of a diplomatic mission.

The limited practice of legation asylum, which varies in the few states permitting it according to the nature of the emergency, the attitude of the government, the state of the public mind, the character of the fugitives, the nature of their offenses, and the legation in which asylum is sought, is in derogation of the local jurisdiction. It is but a permissive local custom practiced in a limited number of states where unstable political and social conditions are recurrent.

There is no law of asylum of general application in international law. Hence, where asylum is practiced, it is not a right of the legate state but rather a custom invoked or consented to by the territorial government in times of political instability.[28]

The United States in signing the Havana convention of 1928, by which the 21 American republics agreed to grant asylum to certain political offenders, reserved the right not to recognize the so-called "doctrine of asylum" as part of international law.[29] The terms of this convention were defined in a new accord signed at Montevideo on December 26, 1933,[30] Article 1 of which provides: "It shall not be lawful for the States to grant asylum in legations . . . to those accused of common offenses who may have been duly prosecuted or who may have been sentenced by ordinary courts of justice, nor to deserters of land and sea forces." Political asylum, according to Article 3 of the convention, is "an institution of humanitarian character" and is not subject to reciprocity, while the "judgment of political delinquency concerns the State which offers asylum." [31]

With respect to this question, three judgments [32] by The International Court of Justice in connection with the *Colombian-Peruvian Asylum*

[27] This Order was incorporated in the printed Instructions to Diplomatic Officers as par. 6 of chap. 7. G. H. Hackworth, *Digest of International Law*, vol. II, p. 623.

[28] While the practice is recognized in most Latin-American countries, it has never existed in the United States and has never been recognized as a right which could be claimed by refugees or granted by diplomatic missions.

[29] "The Delegation of the United States of America, in signing the present Convention, establishes an explicit reservation, placing on record that the United States does not recognize or subscribe to as part of international law the so-called doctrine of asylum"—M. O. Hudson, *International Legislation*, vol. IV, p. 2415.

[30] In order to avoid an implied recognition of the "doctrine of asylum" as a part of the public law of nations, the United States of America refrained from signing the Montevideo convention.

[31] Art. 2 of the convention.

[32] The two first judgments were handed down on Nov. 20 and 27, 1950, and the third on June 13, 1951.

Case [33] are of special importance. This action concerned a controversy between Colombia and Peru as to the status and disposition of Victor Raul Haya de la Torre, leader of the leftist *Alianza Popular Revolucionaria Americana*, who was given asylum in the Colombian Embassy in Lima on January 3, 1949. Diplomatic negotiations between the two countries over a period of many months proved unsuccessful, and the controversy was finally submitted to the International Court of Justice for settlement.

In its judgment of November 20, 1950, the Court held that Colombia's unilateral qualification of Haya de la Torre as a political offender was not binding on Peru; that Peru had failed to prove that the fugitive was any more than a political offender; and finally, that diplomatic asylum should be granted only under conditions of urgency, which had not been shown to exist in this case.[34] The question of the fugitive's surrender was not answered by the Court, as neither party had submitted this matter for settlement. Colombia at once sought to have the judgment interpreted by the Court with respect to this issue. But on November 27 this request was dismissed on the grounds that an interpretation cannot be made regarding a point which was not raised by the parties in their original submission of the case, nor can such action be initiated unless the parties are in dispute with respect to the judgment.[35]

On December 13, a new action was initiated asking the Court to decide what should be done with Haya de la Torre, as yet a fugitive within the Colombian Embassy in Lima. Accordingly on June 13, 1951, the Court handed down its third judgment in this case. By a vote of 13 to 1 the Court sustained the Colombian argument, which was to the effect that the asylum state was not bound to surrender the fugitive to the local authorities. It was pointed out, however, that diplomatic asylum, under the Havana convention of 1928, can afford a political offender only temporary shelter, during which time he must make other arrangements to secure his safety. The only method which the convention provides for termination of such asylum is departure of the fugitive from the country under a safe-conduct. But the Court had found in its first judgment of this case that such safe-conduct can be demanded from the territorial state only provided the asylum has been "regularly granted and maintained and if the territorial State has required that the refugee should be

---

[33] See *ICJ Reports*, 1950, p. 266; *American Journal of International Law*, vol. 45 (1951), p. 179; *ICJ Reports*, 1951, p. 71; *American Journal of International Law*, vol. 45 (1951), p. 781.

[34] See Note by Alona E. Evans regarding the judicial phase of this dispute in *American Journal of International Law*, vol. 45 (1951), p. 755. See also editorial comment concerning the same case by Herbert W. Briggs, *ibid.*, pp. 728–731.

[35] *ICJ Reports* (1950), p. 403.

sent out of the country." [36] Since in this case asylum had been granted irregularly and the territorial state had not required the fugitive's departure, the Court found that the convention was silent as to what action should be taken. "The silence of the Convention implies that it was intended to leave the adjustment of the consequences of this situation to decisions inspired by considerations of convenience or of simple political expediency." [37]

Though the Court held that since the asylum had been granted irregularly it should be terminated immediately, Colombia as the asylum state was under no obligation to surrender the political offender. To avoid apparent contradiction here the Court felt obliged to add that "surrender is not the only way of terminating asylum." [38] The Court went on to say that

it can be assumed that the Parties, now that their mutual legal relations have been made clear, will be able to find a practical and satisfactory solution by seeking guidance from those considerations of courtesy and good-neighbourliness which, in matters of asylum, have always held a prominent place in the relations between the Latin-American republics.[39]

Termination of Mission. A diplomatic mission may come to an end in a number of different ways.[40] Following are some of the more common situations which lead to its termination: (1) when the period of a diplomat's appointment expires; (2) when the object of a mission is attained; (3) by recall, owing to dissatisfaction either of the diplomat's own government or the government of the receiving state; (4) by the envoy's own resignation; (5) by the death of his own sovereign or of the sovereign of the state to which he is accredited; (6) when the government of the receiving state, for some reason, presents him with a passport without waiting for his recall, considering him no longer *persona grata*; and (7) when a mission is terminated as a result of a diplomat's change of rank. Whatever the causes leading to the termination of a mission, the diplomat remains in possession of the privileges and immunities appertaining to his office until he has had time to leave the country.

[36] *ICJ Reports* (1951), p. 80.   [37] *Ibid.*, p. 81.
[38] *Ibid.*
[39] *Ibid.*, p. 83. This *cause célèbre* of "legation asylum" was settled after a new interpretation of the asylum law had been voted by all South American countries. In 1953 at Buenos Aires, the Inter-American Judicial Committee approved a general convention of asylum, though Peru voted against it. An agreement was finally signed between Colombia and Peru, and in April, 1954, Victor Raul Haya de la Torre, who had been a voluntary prisoner in the Colombian Embassy in Lima for five years, was given a safe-conduct to Mexico City.
[40] Oppenheim-Lauterpacht list no fewer than 11 causes for the termination of diplomatic missions—*op. cit.*, pp. 727–728. See also Satow, *A Guide to Diplomatic Practice* (1922), vol, I, pp. 376–419; Wilson, *Handbook* (1936), pp. 185–187.

When a public minister is recalled, for whatever reason, it is accomplished by the following procedure: The diplomat in question, if of a rank higher than chargé d'affaires, receives from the head of his own state a *letter of recall* which is then presented to the head of the receiving state in solemn audience, and in exchange for which the so-called *lettre de récréance* is received terminating the mission. When the recall involves a diplomat of the rank of chargé d'affaires, the same process takes place but exclusively through the foreign ministers of the countries concerned. Frequently, however, when the agent is recalled from some distant post to be transferred elsewhere, he may take his departure before the letter of recall has had time to reach him. Under such circumstances, his successor will deliver the letter of recall along with his own letter of credence. The response to a letter of recall, by the head of state to which the diplomat in question was accredited, is a formal expression of regret at the diplomat's sudden departure, etc. If, on the other hand, hostile relations between states should lead to a rupture in normal diplomatic relations, the envoy does not ask for a farewell audience but returns to his own country without taking formal leave.[41]

In cases where a foreign envoy, after having been admitted to the diplomatic corps, behaves in such a way as to cause grave offense to the receiving state, the latter has often been induced to ask his recall. An exmaple of this kind in American history is the notorious case of Citizen Genêt. It was in the year 1792 that the French government appointed, as minister to the United States, Edmond C. Genêt. He arrived in Charleston in April, 1793, and instead of going on to Philadelphia to present his credentials to President Washington, proceeded to outfit privateers to prey upon British shipping in violation of American neutrality. He even went so far as to set up French consular prize courts whose function it was to condemn prizes captured by these privateers. When Genêt was remonstrated with to desist from these illegal activities, he expressed contempt for President Washington's opinions and questioned his authority. The result was that the United States through its representative in Paris asked for the recall of Citizen Genêt, which was at once granted.[42]

Another interesting case dates from 1846, when Jewett was the United States chargé d'affaires at Lima. In April of that year, the Peruvian Minister of Foreign Affairs, Soldan, took occasion to send Jewett a copy of the official paper, *Peruano*, containing a decree the object of which was to restrict intevention by foreign states in behalf of their nationals in Peru. In the course of some correspondence regarding this matter between Soldan and Jewett, the decree in question was characterized by the latter

[41] Satow, *A Guide to Diplomatic Practice* (1922), vol. I, pp. 379–380.
[42] Moore, *op. cit.*, pp. 485–487.

as "a compound of legal and moral deformities presenting to the vision no commendable lineament, but only gross and perverse obliquities." The upshot of the whole matter was Jewett's recall as chargé d'affaires to the Republic of Peru.[43] It was in this connection that the Secretary of State, James Buchanan, gave expression to the following principles concerning the relationship between the recall and the functions of diplomatic representatives: [44]

If diplomatic agents render themselves so unacceptable as to produce a request for their recall from the government to which they are accredited, the instances must be rare indeed in which such a request ought not to be granted. To refuse it would be to defeat the very purpose for which they are sent abroad, that of cultivation of friendly relations between independent nations. Perhaps no circumstance would justify such a refusal unless the national honor were involved in the question. . . .[45]

CONSULAR REPRESENTATIVES

Consular Officers. The consular institution is exceedingly old. It was known in ancient Phoenician cities centuries before Christ. But the consuls of antiquity had a status and duties very different from their counterparts of today. The main reason for this difference is to be found in the ancient conception of law, which was tribal and national rather than territorial. The idea of personal jurisdiction required that the law should follow the traveler wherever he went and that local law should have no application to foreigners. This concept is particularly well illustrated by the Roman *jus gentium*. This was also the chief reason why so many of the ancient treaties granted "exterritorial" jurisdiction to consuls, especially with regard to commercial matters.[46]

With the decline of the Ottoman Empire and the commercial development of Western Europe at the end of the Middle Ages, the consular institution underwent profound changes. The Christian states now began to appoint consuls on a reciprocal basis, and the function of the consular

---

[43] *Ibid.*, pp. 492–493.

[44] *Ibid.*, p. 494.

[45] In connection with a request by the United States in 1852 for the recall of the Nicaraguan minister Marcoleta, Secretary of State Webster wrote that "such a request can never be refused between Governments that desire to preserve amicable relations with each other; for a minister whose recall has been asked loses, by that fact alone, all capacity of usefulness. If previously unacceptable, he must become doubly so by being retained in office in opposition to a distinct wish expressed for his recall"—Moore, *op. cit.*, p. 499.

[46] See Wyndham A. Bewes, "Contractual Capacity in Commerce," *Transactions of the Grotius Society*, vol. 16, p. 14.

office became increasingly less judicial and more commercial. But the exterritorial rights which consuls enjoyed in former times were no longer their prerogative. The consular service of most states as we know it today is the product of national legislation in the nineteenth and twentieth centuries.

The consular service of a state is a branch of its foreign service, though it differs in a technical sense from the diplomatic service.[47] Generally speaking, the duties of diplomatic officers are of a political nature, while those of consuls are more strictly commercial. In practice, however, no hard and fast line can be drawn between them, as the functions of the two categories of officials cannot in every detail be completely separated.

Sometimes the term *consul* is used in a very broad sense to include all consular officers regardless of grade or classification, and sometimes a narrow definition of the term is employed to include only officers of a particular rank. In the main, however, consuls can be divided into two major classifications: (1) *consules missi,* who are the professional consuls, always subjects or citizens of the sending state, and devoting all their time to the consular office; (2) *consules electi,* who may or may not be subjects or citizens of the state they represent, and whose consular duties are auxiliary of their main duties or profession. Some states, such as France, appoint only professional consuls, but most countries are represented by both types.[48] It is natural enough that the professional consuls should enjoy greater authority and a more exalted social position than the nonprofessional type, though the general law of nations does not distinguish their status.[49]

Consuls have been classified into a number of grades as follows: consuls-general, consuls, deputy consuls-general, vice-consuls-general, deputy consuls, vice-consuls, consular agents, and in some countries consular archivists, attachés, chancellors, and clerks are included in the classification of consular officers.[50] No one state, however, has consular officers of all these grades in its service. In the United States, for example, it is stated in the *Regulations* of 1931 that "the term consular officer shall be deemed to include consuls general, consuls, vice-consuls, and consular agents, and none others. . . ."[51]

Consular agents are subservient to the diplomatic envoys of their home state. According to the municipal laws of almost every country, consuls are responsible to diplomatic agents in return for the latter's protection.

[47] Marcellus Donald A. R. von Redlich, *The Law of Nations* (1937), p. 394.
[48] Oppenheim-Lauterpacht, *op. cit.,* p. 744.
[49] *Ibid.,* p. 744.
[50] Von Redlich, *op. cit.,* p. 395.
[51] *United States Regulations, 1931,* sec. 20; 38 Stat. L. 806.

It should be noted, furthermore, that although consuls are accredited by the heads of their respective states, unlike diplomatic envoys they are not official representatives of one government to another. They are public agents sent to foreign ports and cities to promote the commercial and industrial interests of their country and to lend assistance to the nationals of their home state who may be traveling abroad.

Appointment of Consuls. There can be no doubt that every fully sovereign state is competent to appoint consuls. As to the states which are not fully sovereign, everything depends upon the special case.[52] The appointment of a consul takes place through a patent or commission, the so-called *lettre de provision,* and his reception in the country to which he is sent through the *exequatur.* The diplomatic envoy of the appointing state presents the *lettre de provision* to the Foreign Secretary of the receiving state for transfer to the head of state. The exequatur is given in reply, either as a separate document or by stamping the word exequatur across the patent itself. No state, however, is obliged to receive a consul within its jurisdiction. But the ties of modern commerce are so strong and the mutual advantages so great that in practice every state finds it to be good policy to admit consuls and in turn to send such agents abroad to promote its own trade and commerce.

Consular Functions. "Consuls are agents appointed by a State to watch over its commercial interests, and also to protect the interests of its merchants, its seamen, and its subjects generally, in some foreign place or country." [53]

With the vast improvement in communication and the expansion of trade in the last century and a half, the consular institution has acquired a greater importance than was the case in the more pedestrian world of an earlier age. Though the functions of consuls are, in general, to watch over and protect the commercial and business interests of the country they represent, many other duties have in recent times been added to their responsibility. Even though both the duties and the legal character of consuls are different from those of diplomatic agents, some nations have found it convenient to combine their functions in the same person. Thus a consul may at times be charged with both consular and diplomatic duties, and likewise a diplomat, with consular functions. In such cases, however, in order to avoid confusion, the person who is to act in both capacities is usually admitted by the receiving state through the formal presentation of a letter of credence as a diplomat, and at the same time a *lettre de provision,* asking an exequatur as consul.

[52] Oppenheim-Lauterpacht, *op. cit.,* p. 747.
[53] Cobbett, *Cases and Opinions on International Law,* 3d ed., vol. I, p. 310, quoted by Von Redlich in *op. cit.,* p. 411

In the United States, by Act of Congress in 1924,[54] and amended in 1931 and 1935, it is provided that

All appointments and promotions of Foreign Service officers shall be made by the President by and with the advice and consent of the Senate and such officers may be commissioned as diplomatic or consular officers or both: . . . *And provided further,* That all official acts of such officers . . . shall be performed under their respective commissions as secretaries or as consular officers.

A consul must be permitted to perform, within the district where he is stationed, any act which is authorized by treaty or sanctioned by immemorial custom. Among the functions generally so authorized and sanctioned are the following: (1) to authenticate copies and translations of official documents of the sending state; (2) to issue passports and affix visas thereto; (3) to register births, deaths, and marriages of the nationals of the appointing state; (4) to adjust disputes between nationals of the sending state within the consular district, and in innumerable ways assist such persons; (5) to protect the estates of deceased nationals of the sending state; (6) to visit and inspect vessels of the sending state and adjust matters pertaining to the internal order of such vessels; and (7) to take proper measures, in cases of disaster, to salvage ships and cargoes belonging to the sending state.[55]

All the functions which a consular officer may perform within his district in the receiving state are much too numerous to be listed here. It should be emphasized, however, that in no case may a consular officer use force to accomplish his mission. The case of *Emmet v. Lomakin* [56] involved the compulsory detention of a Russian national, Mrs. Kosenkina, within the Soviet Consulate in New York and a refusal on the part of the Russian consul to honor a write of habeas corpus, issued by a New York court, ordering her release. The court referred the question of Russian authority in this case to the Department of State, whose Legal Adviser replied as follows:

[54] Prior to the passage of this act, entitled "An Act for the reorganization and improvement of the Foreign Service of the United States, and for other purposes," (43 Stat. L. 140), the diplomatic and consular service of the United States consisted largely of two separate and distinct classes of officers. Appointment to one branch of the service did not qualify the appointees to serve in the other branch. This act is more popularly known as the Rogers Act.

[55] For a more extensive treatment of the duties of consuls see *Instructions,* issued by the Department of State of the United States. See also the Draft Convention of the Research in International Law, 1932, on the Legal Position and Functions of Consuls, *American Journal of International Law,* vol. 26 (supp., 1932), p. 195. Also Hudson, *Cases* (1951), p. 436.

[56] 84 N.Y.S.2d 562. See also *American Journal of International Law,* vol. 43 (1949), p. 381.

258 *Diplomatic Relations*

It is the view of the United States Government that there is no basis under international law or under any law of the United States for considering that Mrs. Kosenkina is in any manner subject to the control or authority of the Soviet Government so long as she remains in this country. The Department of State already has advised the Soviet Embassy that Mrs. Kosenkina will not be placed under control of any person against her own will. The Department has also advised the Soviet Embassy that although it recognizes the right of the Soviet Government, through its officials abroad to extend all proper assistance and protection to Soviet nationals, this right does not include authority to take charge of Soviet citizens in this country irrespective of their wishes.

Because of Mrs. Kosenkina's escape from the Soviet Consulate, no warrant of attachment to enforce the writ was ever issued. But the court expressed the conviction that "the Soviet Consul General was not entitled to diplomatic immunity so as to permit him to ignore the mandate of this court."

Though consular officers do not enjoy privileges and immunities comparable to the rights of diplomats, they nevertheless are granted, on a reciprocal basis, considerable latitude in this regard within the jurisdiction of a foreign state. In the case of *Thureau Dangin v. Paturau* [57] the Mauritius Supreme Court held that "consuls, although not entitled to the privilege of personal immunity enjoyed by the diplomatic service, are, nevertheless, according to international courtesy and usages, granted a certain protection when acting in their official capacity."

Immunities. The exercise of consular functions may at times encroach upon the jurisdiction of the receiving state and for this reason requires the latter's consent. The powers and rights of consular officers are usually set forth in reciprocal agreements between nations, but no such immunities as diplomats enjoy can, with respect to consuls, be said to repose in the general law of nations. Yet, certain jurisdictional immunities are in general practice accorded consuls. They are not, for example, liable in civil proceedings with respect to acts which they perform in their official capacity or which, according to the law of nations, fall within the scope of consular functions. [58]

According to Article 16 of the Havana convention of February 20, 1928: "Consuls are not subject to local jurisdiction for acts done in their official character and within the scope of their authority." While Article 17 of the same convention provides that "in respect to unofficial acts, consuls are subject, in civil as well as in criminal matters, to the jurisdiction of the State where they exercise their function." [59]

[57] *Mauritius Reports* (1949), p. 160. Also, *American Journal of International Law*, vol. 45 (1951), p. 384.
[58] Oppenheim-Lauterpacht, *op. cit.*, p. 753.
[59] For the text of the convention on consular agents, adopted at Havana on Feb. 20,

The consular offices and archives are at all times inviolable.

They shall under no circumstances be subjected to invasion by any authorities of any character within the country where such offices are located. Nor shall the authorities under any pretext make any examination or seizure of papers or other property deposited within the consular office. . . . No consular officer shall be required to produce official archives in court or testify as to their content.[60]

All consular officers and the employees of the consulate, provided they are not engaged in gainful occupations, in a private capacity, within the country of their station, are exempt from taxation. But unlike diplomatic agents, consular officers may be called upon to give testimony in criminal cases in the country where they are located. Due regard must be had, however, to the dignity and the duties of the consular office. The consulate of a foreign nation may not, under any circumstances, be used to afford asylum to fugitives from justice, though it has an undisputed right to display its country's arms and flag. "If a consular officer shall refuse to surrender a fugitive from justice on the lawful demand of the authorities of the territory, these authorities may . . . if necessary, enter the consular office to apprehend the fugitive." [61]

The immunities and privileges mentioned above are so frequently included in consular treaties and so generally observed in practice that they have become a part of the law which governs the consular relations between nations.

Termination of the Consular Office. Universally recognized reasons for the termination of a consular office are (1) the death of the consul; (2) the withdrawal of his exequatur, a matter completely within the discretion of the receiving state; and (3) the outbreak of war. But unlike a diplomatic mission, the consular office does not come to an end by reason of a change in leadership in either the appointing or the admitting state. "Neither a new patent nor a new *exequatur* is therefore necessary as a result of a new king coming to the throne or the election of a new president; nor in consequence of a change in the form of government, as from monarchy to republic." [62]

It is not altogether clear whether the consular office terminates when

---

1928, see Hudson, *International Legislation*, vol. IV, p. 2394. See also *Bigelow v. Princess Zizianoff, Gazette du palais*, May 4, 1928 (no. 125), and *Mazzucchi v. United States Consulate, Monitore dei tribunali* (1931), vol. 72, p. 621.

[60] Art. XIX of treaty signed June 5, 1928, and Feb. 25, 1929, between the United States and Norway. 47 Stat. L. 2135.

[61] Art. 8, sec. 5, United States–United Kingdom Consular Convention, Feb. 16, 1949. Department of State Press Release, 91 (1949); Hudson, *Cases* (1951), p. 436.

[62] Oppenheim-Lauterpacht, *op. cit.*, p. 756.

the district [63] to which he is assigned becomes part of another state through cession, annexation, or revolt. It would seem reasonable, however, to conclude that such state succession, by whatever method it comes about, would have the effect of rendering the consul's exequatur invalid and thus bring his mission to an end.

[63] The operation of each consul is confined to the district for which he is appointed, as agreed upon by the sending and receiving state. Consular districts usually coincide with provinces or other political subdivisions of the state to which they are sent.

CHAPTER 18

International Agreements

As we have already seen in an earlier chapter, custom and treaties are the most important sources of international law. But here again it would be a mistake to draw too sharp a line of distinction, for "treaties are a source the power of which derives from custom."[1] Not only does the validity of treaties repose in custom, but the multifarious nature of con- tractual agreements between states reflects to a considerable extent the history of international law and relations.

Many writers on legal theory have sought to draw an analogy between international agreements and contracts in municipal law, pointing out that treaties "derive their validity from the agreement of the parties."[2] Others contend that such changes and additions as treaties produce, with respect to the law of nations, are indicative of a process more akin to legislation. "The term *international legislation*," writes Judge Hudson, "would seem to describe quite usefully both the process and the product of the conscious effort to make additions to, or changes in, the law of nations."[3] It might be added also that in such great multilateral instru- ments as the League Covenant and the Charter of the United Nations some authorities have seen the beginnings of a world constitution.

Though international agreements are known by a variety of titles, such as treaties, conventions, pacts, acts, declarations, protocols, accords, ar- rangements, concordats, and *modi vivendi*, none of these terms has an absolutely fixed meaning. The more formal political agreements, however, are usually called *treaties* or *conventions*. Though these titles are often used synonymously, the latter seems more appropriate as a designation for agreements of a rather technical nature. The term *protocol* is generally used to designate a supplementary instrument to a treaty or convention. *Acts* and *declarations* are more frequently associated with international conferences and congresses. Examples here would be the Final Act of the

[1] Oppenheim-Lauterpacht, *International Law* (1947), vol. I, p. 27.
[2] Philip C. Jessup, *A Modern Law of Nations* (1948), p. 124.
[3] M. O. Hudson, *International Legislation*, vol. I (1919–1921), Introduction, p. xiii.

Congress of Vienna, 1815, and the Declaration of Paris in 1856. The basic instrument of an international body is usually called a *constitution* or a *statute*, such as the Constitution of the International Labor Organization, and the Statute of the International Court of Justice.[4] In this connection the terms *covenant* and *charter* have also been used, as in the Covenant of the League and the Charter of the United Nations.

For the sake of convenience, all international agreements are divided into two classes: (1) the so-called lawmaking or legislative treaties, and (2) treaties of contract. The first of these are concluded for the purpose of laying down general rules of conduct to which a large number of states subscribe, while the second category consists of bilateral arrangements concerning matters of special interests to the parties concerned. Treaties of the first group are likely to deal with matters of general concern, such as public health and morals, or communication and transit; while those of the second classification are confined to such problems as trade and commerce, financial and industrial concessions, and extradition of fugitives from justice. Notwithstanding the distinction, given above, between legislative and contract treaties, it may be said that all treaties are in principle lawmaking, "inasmuch as they lay down rules of conduct which the parties are bound to observe as law." [5]

The great multipartite treaties and conventions which have contributed so greatly to the general body of the modern law of nations were but little known before the nineteenth century. But in the last hundred and fifty years science and technology have transformed the physical environment and in so doing have brought about an ironic correlation between material progress and the interdependence of peoples. As a result, the "splendid isolationism" of former times began to give way under the impact of common problems, the solution of which proved impossible save through cooperation and compromise. "It was only when the changes wrought in nineteenth century international society came to be appreciated that the modern legislative movement began, and this may possibly be dated from the assembling of the International Telegraphic Conference at Paris in 1864." [6] In the years since then, the number of multilateral treaties of legislative significance has grown very large, dealing with a multitude of problems of international concern, unimagined by earlier generations. Thus it was no exaggeration for John Bassett Moore in 1907 to say that "of all the achievements of the past hundred years, the thing that is most

---

[4] See M. O. Hudson, *Cases on International Law* (1951), p. 443; also J. L. Brierly, *The Law of Nations* (1949), p. 229.

[5] Oppenheim-Lauterpacht, *op. cit.*, p. 794.

[6] Hudson, *International Legislation*. For a list of international conferences in the period between 1826 and 1907, see Simeon E. Baldwin, *American Journal of International Law*, vol. 1 (1907), appendix, p. 808.

remarkable, in the domain of international relations, has been the modification and improvement of international law by what may be called acts of international legislation." [7]

In spite of the disruptive forces of war and revolution in the present century, fantastic progress in science and the industrial arts has greatly enlarged the area of common concern and the corpus juris of nations.

The Treaty-making Power. The power to conclude international agreements has been described by some authors as a right of sovereign nations. It is perhaps more correct and certainly more logical to say that the treaty-making power is an attribute or capacity of international persons. But it will be remembered that though all states are international persons, all international persons are not states. A little later we shall have occasion to show that international persons who are not states may be parties to treaties.

In the case of *The S.S. Wimbledon,* decided by the Permanent Court of International Justice in 1923, it was held that the capacity "of entering into international engagements is an attribute of State sovereignty. . . ." [8] And according to Oppenheim, the making of treaties "is not a right belonging to a state in the technical meaning of the term, but a mere competence attaching to sovereignty." [9] Thus, we may say that all fully sovereign states are competent in the making of all kinds of international agreements, whereas dependent states possess a competence, in this regard, only to the extent of their sovereignty. It is, however, quite impossible to lay down a hard and fast rule defining the treaty-making capacity of all states that are not fully sovereign. "Everything depends upon the special case." [10]

Though independent states, under the law of nations, possess the capacity to enter into international agreements of all kinds and concerning objectives of an almost infinite variety, this competence may, in some cases, be limited by constitutional law. Yet, since the affairs of nations must be adjusted to the needs of the hour, a certain amount of flexibility in the treaty-making function is necessary.

Treaty-making Power and Procedure in the United States. Some of the most interesting and in many ways difficult problems concerning treaty making are associated with states of federal organization. And among these, the United States of America is undoubtedly the most important in the world today. Let us, therefore, take this country as an example in an effort to illustrate some of the problems in both international and consti-

[7] Quoted by Hudson, *International Legislation,* from *Proceedings of the American Society of International Law* (1907), p. 252.
[8] *PCIJ Publications,* ser. A, no. 1; Hudson, *Cases* (1936), p. 474.
[9] Oppenheim-Lauterpacht, *op. cit.,* p. 795.
[10] *Ibid.,* p. 796.

tutional law,[11] relative to the modification and restriction of the treaty-making power.

In the United States the sovereignty of the people finds expression simultaneously through two systems of government—federal and state. To speak of a divided sovereignty here is to confuse sovereignty with government. The two are obviously not synonymous. The United States is a federal republic, whose people are sovereign, and whose will and power is manifested at once both through the federal government and through the governments of the several states of the Union. Neither the Constitution of the United States is sovereign, nor those of the several states.[12] To argue that they are, is to confuse sovereignty and law. It should be noted that laws are only a manifestation of government, which in turn derives its power from the sovereignty of the people.

While the sovereignty of the American people is manifested internally through the medium of both federal and state government, in the nation's external relations it is expressed singly and solely through the government of the United States. Thus with respect to the treaty-making power the federal Constitution provides the the President "shall have Power, by and with the Advice and Consent of the Senate, to make treaties, provided two-thirds of the Senators present concur." [13] It further provides that "no State shall enter into any Treaty, Alliance, or Confederation;" [14] and that "no State shall, without the consent of Congress . . . enter into any Agreement or Compact with another State, or with a foreign Power." [15] Furthermore it is provided that "this Constitution and the Laws of the United States which shall be made in Pursuance thereof; and all Treaties made, or which shall be made, under the Authority of the United States, shall be the supreme Law of the Land; and the Judges of every State shall be bound thereby, any Thing in the Constitution or Laws of any State to the Contrary notwithstanding." [16] Accordingly, the courts have often referred to treaties as "the supreme law of the land."

In the famous case of *Missouri v. Holland*,[17] Justice Holmes wrote as

[11] In practically all countries making up the international community, constitutional provisions govern the treaty-making power and procedure.

[12] We are, of course, aware that in the United States three different points of view have, from time to time, been given expression with regard to this matter: first, that of the present author, namely, that sovereignty resides in the people; second, a strictly legalistic notion to the effect that the Constitution itself is sovereign; and finally, lip service has at times been given to the fantastic proposition that the several states of the Union are sovereign.

[13] Art. II, sec. 2, par. 2.

[14] Art. I, sec. 10, par. 1.

[15] Art. I, sec. 10, par. 3.

[16] Art. VI, par. 2. See G. H. Hackworth, *Digest of International Law*, vol. V, p. 24, concerning restriction on states set forth in Art. I, sec. 10, of the Constitution.

[17] 252 U.S. 416; 11 A.L.R. 984 (1920).

follows: "Acts of Congress are the supreme law of the land only when made in pursuance of the Constitution, while treaties are declared to be so when made under the authority of the United States." Thus, a treaty may go further in derogation of states' rights than can a federal statute, enacted in pursuance of the Constitution. In *Ware v. Hylton*,[18] decided by the Supreme Court in 1796, Justice Chase wrote: "It is the declared will of the people of the United States that any treaty made by the authority of the United States shall be superior to the constitution and laws of any individual State; and their will alone is to decide."

There can be no question that the treaty-making power resides in the people as a whole and that it is a function not of constitutional law but of sovereignty. Though this power is, indeed, restrained by the Constitution, no definitive consensus as to the limits of this restraint can be found either in theory or practice. One attempt at some sort of definition of the treaty-making limitations was made by John C. Calhoun when he said that the nation "can enter into no stipulation calculated to change the character of the Government, or to do that which can only be done by the Constitution-making power, or which is inconsistent with the nature and structure of the Government." [19]

The constitutional limitations upon the exercise of the treaty-making power in the United States are likewise summarized by Justice Field in *Geofroy v. Riggs* [20] as follows:

The treaty power, as expressed in the Constitution, is in terms unlimited except by those restraints which are found in that instrument. . . . It would not be contended that it extends so far as to authorize what the Constitution forbids or a change in the character of the government or in that of one of the States, or a cession of any portion of the territory of the latter without its consent. But with these exceptions, it is not perceived that there is any limit to the questions which can be adjusted touching any matter which is properly the subject of negotiations with a foreign country.

It should be clearly noted that the treaty-making power never did belong to the several states. Nor is it a power delegated under the Constitution to the federal government. But rather it is a power inherent in the sovereign Union of the people. In *United States v. Curtiss-Wright Export Coroporation*,[21] Justice Sutherland said: "As a result of the separation from Great Britain by the colonies, acting as a unit, the powers of external sovereignty passed from the Crown not to the colonies severally, but to the colonies in their collective and corporate capacity as the United States of America."

[18] 3 Dall. 199, 236. See also *Hamilton v. Eaton*, Fed. Cas. No. 5980 (1796).
[19] *Works*, vol. I, p. 204.
[20] 133 U.S. 258 (1890).   [21] 299 U.S. 304, 318 (1936).

Thus, that which is delegated under the Constitution is not the treaty-making power but the exercise of that power.[22] This distinction is indeed implied in the language of the Constitution, which proclaims as the supreme law of the land treaties made "under the authority of the United States" and laws made "in pursuance of" the Constitution.[23] It is concluded, therefore, that the authority of the United States does not derive from the Constitution, but that its exercise may be limited by that instrument.

Though there is no case on record in which a treaty, duly ratified, has been held unconstitutional, the possibility of such a decision cannot be avoided. It is not surprising, therefore, to find that many American jurists have delivered themselves of obiter dicta on this question from time to time. In *Downes v. Bidwell*[24] the court said that "a treaty which undertook to take away what the Constitution secured or to enlarge the Federal jurisdiction would be simply void." In the *Cherokee Tobacco*[25] case Justice Swayne wrote: "It need hardly be said that a treaty cannot change the Constitution or be held valid if it be in violation of that instrument."

It is highly unlikely that the Senate of the United States would give its advice and consent to the conclusion and ratification of a treaty by the President, if such a treaty were manifestly unconstitutional. And since the courts, in a period of over a century and a half, have never held a treaty so concluded and ratified to be in contravention of the Constitution, foreign states may safely rely upon the rule that once a treaty has been ratified it will stand.

Matters Pertaining to the States of the Union. A difficult question relating to the treaty-making power in the United States is presented when a treaty deals with matters which appear to be reserved to the states of the Union. In *Missouri v. Holland*,[26] it was argued that the federal statute,[27] enacted in pursuance of an international agreement for the protection of migratory birds, was unconstitutional and therefore could not be enforced in the state of Missouri. "The ground of the bill is that the statute is unconstitutional interference with the rights reserved to the states by the Tenth Amendment,[28] and that the acts of the defendant done and threatened under that authority invade the sovereign right of the

---

[22] See Hyde, *International Law* (1947), vol. II, pp. 1388–1389.
[23] *Ibid.*   [24] 182 U.S. 244, 370 (1901).
[25] 11 Wall. 616, 620 (1870).   [26] 252 U.S. 416 (1920).
[27] Migratory Bird Treaty Act of July 3, 1918, c. 128, 40 Stat. L. 755 (16 U.S.C.A., secs. 703–710).
[28] According to the Tenth Amendment: "The powers not delegated to the United States by the Constitution, nor prohibited by it to the States, are reserved to the States respectively, or to the people."

state and contravene its will manifested in statutes." A motion to dismiss had been sustained by the District Court on the ground that the act complained of was in fact constitutional. The state of Missouri then appealed the case to the United States Supreme Court. In writing the opinion for this Court, Justice Holmes said:

It is unnecessary to go into any details, because, as we have said, the question raised is the general one whether the treaty and statute are void as an interference with the rights reserved to the states.

To answer this question it is not enough to refer to the Tenth Amendment, reserving the powers not delegated to the United States, because by Article II, Section 2, the power to make treaties is delegated expressly, and by Article VI treaties made under the authority of the United States, along with the Constitution and laws of the United States made in pursuance thereof, are declared the supreme law of the land. If the treaty is valid there can be no dispute about the validity of the statute under Article I, Section 8, as a necessary and proper means to execute the powers of the Government. . . . We do not mean to imply that there are no qualifications to the treaty-making power; but they must be ascertained in a different way. It is obvious that there may be matters of sharpest exigency for the national well being that an act of Congress could not deal with but that a treaty followed by such an act could, and it is not to be lightly assumed that, in matters requiring national action, "a power which must belong to and reside somewhere in every civilized government" is not to be found.

It seems rather obvious that the general terms in which the treaty-making power is delegated to the United States precludes the application, in this connection, of the Tenth Amendment.[29] In an address before the American Society of International Law on April 10, 1907, Elihu Root took the position that the powers reserved to the states can have no effect on, or in any way limit, the treaty-making power delegated to the Federal government under the Constitution.

No State can say a treaty may grant to alien residents equality of treatment as to property but not as to education . . . or as to education but not as to property or religion. That would be substituting the mere will of a State for the judgment of the President and the Senate in exercising a power committed to them and prohibited to the States by the Constitution.[30]

A decision which might have been one of the most important from the point of view of American constitutional law, international law, and legal policy, had it been allowed to stand, was that handed down by the Dis-

[29] See James Parker Hall, in *Proceedings, Academy of Political Science,* vol. 7, no. 3, pt. 2, pp. 548–550.

[30] *American Society of International Law, Proceedings,* vol. 1 (1907), pp. 41, 54–55.

trict Court of Appeals, 2d District, on April 24, 1950.[31] In this case, *Sei Fujii v. California*, [32] the court held that the alien land law of California, which provides that aliens ineligible to citizenship shall not "acquire, possess, enjoy, use, cultivate, occupy, and transfer real property, or any interest therein," was in conflict with the Charter of the United Nations and therefore invalid—this, notwithstanding the fact that the constitutionality of the alien land law had previously been upheld by the Supreme Courts of both the state of California and the United States.

But under the constitution of California it is provided that any case before a District Court of Appeal may, by order of the state Supreme Court, be transferred to the latter for hearing.[33] This order may be made either before the judgment or within a certain number of days after it.[34] In the case of such transfer, however, the Supreme Court does not review the decision of the District Court of Appeal; it reviews instead the decision of the trial court.

A hearing in the case of *Sei Fujii* before the Supreme Court of California was granted on June 22, 1950. Arguments were heard and the case taken under advisement until April 17, 1952, when by a decision of four judges against three the alien land law was declared unconstitutional as a denial of equal protection of the laws.

With respect to the applicability of the United Nations Charter in this case, it was found that none of the provisions relied upon by the District Court of Appeal invalidated the land law. Attention was called to Marshall's opinion in *Foster v. Nielson*,[35] where a distinction is drawn between a self-executing and a non-self-executing treaty. In terms of this distinction, which seems to have a peculiarly important place in American constitutional law, it was found that the provisions of the United Nations Charter, relied upon by the District Court of Appeal, were not of a self-executing character.[36]

American courts have frequently said that treaties should be so construed as to "effect the apparent intention of the parties." In *Nielsen v. Johnson* [37] Justice Stone, in writing the Court's opinion, said: "When a

[31] For an able discussion of the *Fujii Case*, see Quincy Wright, "National Courts and Human Rights—The Fujii Case," *American Journal of International Law*, vol. 45 (1951), pp. 62–82.

[32] *American Journal of International Law*, vol. 44 (1950), p. 590.

[33] Art. VI, sec. 4c of the constitution of California.

[34] "When such an order of transfer is made, the opinion and decision of the District Court of Appeal is no more effective as a judgment than if it had not been rendered." See *Estate of Kent*, 6 Cal.2d 154, 156; 57 P.2d 901, 902 (1936).

[35] 2 Pet. 253, 314 (1829).

[36] For an excellent discussion of these points, see Editorial Comment by Charles Fairman, "Finis to Fujii," *American Journal of International Law*, vol. 46 (1952), pp. 682–690.

[37] 279 U.S. 47 (1929).

treaty provision fairly admits of two constructions, one restricting, the other enlarging, rights which may be claimed under it, the more liberal interpretation is to be preferred." Even more to the point here is the finding of the United States Supreme Court in *Asakura v. Seattle.*[38] Said Justice Butler, speaking for the Court: "Treaties are to be construed in a broad and liberal spirit and when two constructions are possible, one restrictive of rights that may be claimed under it, and the other favorable to them, the latter is preferred." [39]

At this point something needs to be said regarding the rather nebulous distinction between self-executing and non-self-executing treaties. Generally speaking, a self-executing treaty is one which by its own terms, or by reason of existing statutes, can furnish a rule of law enforceable in the courts; while a non-self-executing treaty is one which requires implementation by an executive or legislative agency in order to constitute a rule for courts or private individuals.[40]

It was established early in American history that treaties which required an appropriation or a charge on the revenues of the United States could not be enforced as law before Congressional implementation had been secured. But since, in this country, all money bills must originate in the House of Representatives, and since this body has no treaty-making functions under the Constitution, the question as to whether implementation in any such cases is mandatory upon the lower house of the Congress has never been finally settled. Though President Washington maintained that it was the duty of the House of Representatives to enact such legislation as might be necessary to implement any treaty, Jefferson took the contrary view.[41]

Thus, apart from the controversy as to whether the treaty-making power in the United States, under certain circumstances, may be extended to the lower house of the Congress, there is the question of whether such legislative implementation is mandatory. In 1796 the House of Representatives asserted its right to deliberate on any treaty sent to it for implementation in the manner of any other project of law.[42] But in spite of the fact that this position has been reiterated from time to time by the Con-

[38] 265 U.S. 332 (1924). See also *Jordan et al. v. Tashiro et al.* 278 U.S. 123, 127–130 (1928). Other cases upholding the same rule are *Valentine v. United States ex rel. Neidecker,* 299 U.S. 5, 10 (1936); *Bacardi Corporation of America v. Domenech, et al.,* 311 U.S. 150, 163 (1940); *In re Anderson's Estate,* 166 Iowa 617; 147 N.W. 1098, 1099 (1914); *Fischer v. Sklenor et al.,* 101 Nebr. 553, 571; 163 N.W. 861, 868 (1917).

[39] Also quoted by Wright in *op. cit.*

[40] Alona E. Evans, "Some Aspects of the Problems of Self-executing Treaties," *American Society of International Law, Proceedings,* 1951, p. 68.

[41] *Ibid.,* p. 69.

[42] *Ibid.*

gress, the general practice has been to regard the implementation of international agreements as a moral duty and as imperative to continued friendly relations with other states. The only notable exception to this rule is the case of the Reciprocity Treaty with Mexico of 1883, in which case Congress failed to provide the necessary enabling legislation.[43]

In order to give this question a broader base, some reference should be made to the practice in other lands. It is provided in the French Constitution of September 28, 1946, for example, that "diplomatic treaties duly ratified and published shall have the force of law even when they are contrary to internal French legislation; they shall require for their application no legislative acts other than those necessary to insure their ratification." [44] According to British practice, at the moment a treaty becomes binding internationally, it is also given legal effect internally, as enabling legislation is secured well in advance.[45] The same is true with respect to Belgium. In Switzerland, the acceptance of a treaty by the Federal Assembly not only has the effect of the assumption of a new international obligation on the part of the nation, but also confers upon its content the force of law, which is from that moment binding upon the officials and the citizens of the state.[46]

Treaties and the Charter of the United Nations. It is provided by the Charter of the United Nations that in case of conflict between obligations under the Charter and obligations under any other international agreement, those under the Charter shall prevail.[47] Thus it may be said that the Charter of the United Nations is the supreme law of the international community of states and therefore occupies a place with reference to treaties somewhat analogous to municipal constitutions in their relationship to statutory law. It has been pointed out that this article of the Charter is not only more precise but also more far-reaching than any corresponding provisions in the Covenant of the League of Nations.[48] This supremacy of the Charter over other treaties has the effect of rendering those international agreements which may be in conflict with its terms "void and unenforceable." [49] It is plain, therefore, that the Charter of the

---

[43] *Ibid.*, p. 70.
[44] Lawrence Preuss, "The Execution of Treaty Obligations through International Law—System of the United States and of Some Other Countries," *American Society of International Law, Proceedings*, 1951, p. 87.
[45] *Ibid.*, p. 86.
[46] For a complete discussion of this question, the reader is referred to Alona E. Evans and Lawrence Preuss from whose papers, given before the American Society of International Law at the annual meeting of Apr. 26–28, 1951, these fragments are drawn.
[47] Art. 103 of the Charter of the United Nations.
[48] Oppenheim-Lauterpacht, *op. cit.*, p. 806.
[49] *Ibid.*, p. 807.

United Nations constitutes a "higher law," limiting to a certain extent the contractual capacity of those states who are members of the Organization. It is assumed that the limitations imposed by the Charter upon the signatory states are known to the states who are not members of the United Nations and that therefore their rights are not thereby affected. Here a parallel may be drawn between the Charter and municipal constitutions, where the assumption is that, since constitutional limitations upon the treaty-making power in one of the contracting parties is known to the other, no reduction of rights takes place under the law of nations.

Article 102 of the Charter of the United Nations stipulates that "every treaty and every international agreement entered into by any member of the United Nations after the present Charter shall come into force shall as soon as possible be registered with the Secretariat and published by it." It should be noted that failure to register a treaty, as provided in Article 102, paragraph 1, of the Charter, does not have the effect of making the treaty void for all purposes,[50] but merely precludes its invocation "before any organ of the United Nations." [51] Inasmuch as the International Court of Justice is such an "organ," it is obvious that failure to register a treaty, as the Charter provides, might have important consequences. In cases where treaties are concluded between states who are members of the United Nations and states who are not, only the member states are required to register the instrument with the Secretariat.

Specialized Agencies. As we have indicated already, the treaty-making capacity is not confined to states but is an attribute of all international persons. The United Nations is itself such a person *sui generis* [52] and, indeed, is endowed with the capacity of entering into treaty arrangements of various kinds. The agreement relative to the United Nations headquarters is an example of how the United Nations became one of the contracting parties to a treaty.

According to Article 63, paragraph 1, of the Charter, "the Economic and Social Council may enter into agreements" with various specialized agencies, "subject to the approval of the General Assembly." Likewise, the Food and Agricultural Organization may "enter into agreements with other public international organizations for the maintenance of common services, for common arrangements in regard to recruitment, training, conditions of service, and other related matters, and for interchanges of staff." The World Health Organization may enter into agreements with

[50] Art. 18 of the League Covenant simply provided that every treaty be registered with the League Secretariat and published by it and that no "treaty or international engagement shall be binding until so registered."
[51] Art. 102, par. 2, of the Charter.
[52] See advisory opinion handed down by the International Court of Justice on Apr. 11, 1949; *ICJ Reports,* 1949, p. 174.

the United Nations and other intergovernmental organizations. It is provided, however, that such agreements are subject to approval by two-thirds majority of the Health Assembly.[53] According to the Constitution of the United Nations Educational Scientific and Cultural Organization, it is provided that agreements with other organizations may be made by the Director-General, subject to the approval of the Executive Board.[54]

Negotiation and Ratification of Treaties. Treaties may be negotiated directly by heads of state or by agents acting in their behalf. The Holy Alliance of 1815 was signed by the King of Prussia and the Emperors of Austria and Russia. President Wilson, "acting in his own name and by his own proper authority," negotiated and signed the Treaty of Versailles in 1919. As a rule bilateral agreements are signed by the Minister of Foreign Affairs of the country in which the negotiations are conducted and by a plenipotentiary of the other contracting party.[55] The nationality of the person who negotiates and signs a treaty seems unimportant. Citizens of the United States, for example, have more than once signed treaties in behalf of other nations.[56] No instance can be found, however, in which an alien has ever signed a treaty for the United States.[57]

Although treaties are concluded by authorized representatives upon the manifestation of mutual consent, the binding force of such agreements is generally suspended until ratification is given.[58] Even though the negotiation and signing of a treaty have been completed, there exists no compulsion in international law to follow such steps by ratification. As John Bassett Moore said in his dissenting opinion in the case of the *Mavrommatis Palestine Concessions*,[59] in 1924: "The doctrine that governments are bound to ratify whatever their plenipotentiaries, acting within the limits of their instructions may sign, and that treaties may therefore be regarded as legally operative and enforceable before they have been ratified, is obsolete, and lingers only as an echo from the past." It is true, of course, that in former times the plenipotentiaries of sovereigns were always endowed with full powers to make treaties so that no subsequent ratification was necessary.

Ratification of Treaties in the United States. With the substitution of popular sovereignty for absolutism in the internal regime of many na-

[53] Arts. 69 and 70 of the Constitution of the World Health Organization.

[54] Art. XI of the UNESCO Constitution.

[55] Hyde, *International Law* (1947), vol. II, p. 1419.

[56] An example would be the treaty between the United States and China of July 28, 1868, which was signed by Anson Burlingame, an American, in behalf of China. See *Malloy's Treaties*, vol. I, p. 234. Also Hyde, *International Law* (1947), vol. II, p. 1419n.

[57] Hyde, *International Law* (1947), vol. II, p. 1419.

[58] Oppenheim-Lauterpacht, *op. cit.*, p. 813.

[59] *PCIJ Publications*, ser. A, no. 2, 57.

tions, the twin steps of *signature* and *ratification* in treaty making became imperative. This is particularly true in a republic such as the United States, for it should be noted that though the power to make and ratify treaties is vested in the President, it is nevertheless subject to the advice and consent of the Senate. For this reason consultation in advance between the Chief Executive and the Senate relative to contemplated international agreements very frequently takes place.

While, . . . the President can, under the Constitution of the United States negotiate and sign treaties with foreign governments without the prior approval of the Senate or of Congress, treaties negotiated and signed by the Executive cannot be ratified or made effective on the part of the United States without the advice and consent of the Senate, two-thirds of the Senators present concurring. The Senate, therefore, has power to disapprove treaties negotiated and signed by the President or to advise and consent to ratification with or without amendments. If the Senate advises and consents to the ratification of a treaty without amendment the Executive is at liberty to proceed with the exchange of ratifications and promulgation of the treaty. If, on the other hand, the Senate advises and consents to ratification with amendments, it is necessary that the foreign government concerned agree to the amendments before a treaty can be ratified and put into effect.[60]

The Senate of the United States has on numerous occasions refused to approve the ratification of treaties or has introduced amendments and reservations of such proportions as to render the end product unacceptable to the other contracting parties or to the Executive of our own government. This was the case, for example, with the Treaty of Versailles in 1919.

There can be no doubt that any government has the right to refuse ratification of a treaty for good and sufficient reasons. But there are no fixed criteria as to what might constitute good and sufficient reasons in this connection. One thing, however, seems certain: there is no legal or even moral duty on the part of any state to ratify treaties negotiated and signed by its plenipotentiaries. In the great majority of cases, however, treaties which have been negotiated by duly accredited agents of the state are subsequently ratified. And it is considered that to refuse ratification under those circumstances is so serious a step that it "ought not to be taken lightly." [61] In any case, ratification must be unconditional, as modifications in the terms of a treaty cannot be unilaterally introduced at this stage. Conditional ratification would, in fact, constitute a new proposal, "which the other party or parties are free either to accept or reject." [62]

[60] The Under Secretary of State (Grew) to the Minister of Norway (Bryn), July 21, 1926, Ms. Department of State, file 711.00/149 in Hackworth, *op. cit.*, pp. 57–58.
[61] Brierly, *op. cit.*, p. 232.   [62] *Ibid.*, p. 233.

The rather common practice of making reservations at the time of signing is quite another matter. For as these reservations are known to the other parties, the signing and ratification, on their part, is regarded as tantamount to acceptance of the reservations.

Ratification by the parties to a treaty makes the instrument binding under the law of nations. There is some difference of opinion, however, as to whether a treaty, once ratified, is operative from the moment of ratification or from the day of signature. In the case of *Haver v. Yaker*[63] Justice Davis, writing the opinion for the United States Supreme Court, said: "It is undoubtedly true, as a principle of international law, that, as respects the rights of either government under it, a treaty is considered as concluded and binding from the date of its signature. In this regard the exchange of ratifications has a retroactive effect, confirming the treaty from its date."[64] "But," the Court continued, "a different rule prevails where the treaty operates on individual rights." In so far as those rights are concerned, the treaty is not considered as concluded until ratifications have been exchanged. The reason for this rule is to be found in the American Constitution itself, which provides in Article VI that "all Treaties made, or which shall be made, under the Authority of the United States, shall be the supreme Law of the Land." It is obvious that as "the supreme law of the land" a treaty may operate upon individual rights, but it must be remembered that it cannot become such a law without the consent of the United States Senate. And since ratification of a treaty by the President is conditioned upon the advice and consent of the Senate, it would seem to follow that a treaty cannot be made to operate upon individuals in the United States before an exchange of ratifications has been effected. This, substantially, was the reasoning in the *Yaker Case.*

Essentials of Validity. In order for treaties to be valid under the law of nations, the parties must first of all possess the necessary capacity to contract. That is to say, they must be recognized members of the community of nations and thus be endowed with international personality. Treaties, for example, which have been concluded from time to time with island tribes of the Pacific or with chieftains of darkest Africa have no legal standing in international law. In 1928, the Permanent Court of Arbitration, in the *Island of Palmas Case,*[65] held that

[63] 9 Wall. 32 (1869).

[64] The Harvard Draft Convention on the Law of Treaties rejects the rule of retroactivity which, according to the Reporter, " 'has no support today among writers on international law outside the United States.' It is unsupported by decisions of national courts in other countries, and finds only scant favor in those of international tribunals." See Hyde, *International Law* (1947), vol. II, p. 1453.

[65] J. B. Scott, *Hague Court Reports,* second series (1932), p. 84.

contracts between a State or a company such as the Dutch East India Company and native princes or chiefs of peoples not recognized as members of the community of nations, . . . are not, in the international sense, treaties or conventions capable of creating rights and obligations such as may, in international law, arise out of treaties.

The validity of agreements is also conditioned upon the full powers of agents to act in a treaty-making and ratifying capacity. As we have already seen, certain officials of the government have the power to make international commitments which are binding upon the state they represent, provided their action is duly authorized or within the capacity assigned to them under municipal law. If, however, these agents exceed their legal powers, the state cannot be bound.[66] But if certain benefits to the state whose agents performed the illegal action should result, it is the duty of such a state to make reparations or to restore matters to their former status. If, on the other hand, the illegal exercise of power on the part of the agent in question was such as should have been known by the other party, "there is no obligation upon the agent's state." [67]

Inasmuch as a treaty is a contract, mutual consent of the parties is required. "To constitute a legal agreement there must be a free offer and a free acceptance." [68] Yet, according to the present law, consent does not imply absence of conditions that would make a certain line of action almost inevitable. It can hardly be denied that treaties which terminate wars are often imposed by superior force, yet—in theory, at least—it is assumed that the vanquished is free to make a choice between the continuance of the contest of arms or submission to the terms imposed by the victor.

Though the law of nations tends to disregard the element of coercion in a situation where the choice is one of continuation in dubious battle or submission to a victorious power, the principle has nevertheless been challenged both in theory and in practice. Since war, as a means of national policy, is prohibited by the Charter of the United Nations and by the Pact of Paris, such challenges are not without bases in legal fact. Nor does freedom of consent exist in cases where an erroneous impression is created through the agency of fraud, or agreement to terms brought about as a result of personal intimidation of state agents.[69] Treaties, therefore, which have their origin in such situations must be regarded as illegal and without validity under the law of nations.

Finally, a treaty, in order to be valid, must not be in contravention of

---

[66] G. G. Wilson, *Handbook of International Law* (1939), p. 203.
[67] *Ibid.*
[68] Charles G. Fenwick, *International Law* (1948), p. 439.
[69] William Edward Hall, *A Treatise on International Law* (1924), p. 382.

generally recognized rules of international law. Treaties, for example, which should have for their purpose the exercise of proprietary rights in the open sea, the establishment or protection of the slave trade, or the recognition and encouragement of piracy would of course be without legal sanction and consequently void.

Treaty Interpretation. There are no technical rules in international law which can be applied in the interpretation of treaties. The so-called "canons of construction" usually employed are derived for the most part from general jurisprudence. It should be noted that various standards of interpretation are available, and that the contracting parties are free to make their own choice.[70] In a general way, the method of interpretation consists in finding a connection between the linguistic terms of a treaty and the objects to which they apply. This process, according to Hyde, "involves two steps. One is to ascertain what has been called the '*standard of interpretation*'; that is, the sense in which the various terms are employed. The other is to learn what are the *sources of interpretation*; that is, to find out where it is possible to turn for evidence of that sense." [71]

In the United States, the Supreme Court has from time to time laid down certain rules for the interpretation of treaties. In the case of *Geofroy v. Riggs* [72] the Court said:

It is a general principle of construction with respect to treaties that they shall be liberally construed, so as to carry out the apparent intention of the parties. . . . As they are contracts between independent nations, in their construction words are to be taken in their ordinary meaning, as understood in the public law of nations, and not in any artificial or special sense impressed upon them by local law, unless such restricted sense is clearly intended.

Again in *Tucker v. Alexandroff* [73] the same court laid down a broad basis for the interpretation of treaties in these words:

As treaties are solemn engagements entered into between independent nations for the common advancement of their interests and the interests of civilization, and as their main object is, not only to avoid war and secure a lasting and perpetual peace, but to promote a friendly feeling between the people of the two countries, they should be interpreted in that broad and liberal spirit which is calculated to make for the existence of a perpetual amity so far as it can be done without the sacrifice of individual rights or those principles of personal liberty which lie at the foundation of our jurisprudence.

Sometimes it is necessary to examine the history of negotiation in order to ascertain the intention of the parties to a treaty. The Permanent Court

[70] Hyde, *International Law* (1947), vol. II, p. 1468.
[71] *Ibid.* Italics added.   [72] 133 U.S. 258 (1890).
[73] 183 U.S. 424 (1902).

of International Justice has often affirmed the usefulness of resort to the *travaux préparatoires* in cases where the meaning and intention of the parties are obscure. It should, however, be resorted to only in instances where the treaty is not clear and when all the parties to the instrument in question have had a part in the preparatory work.[74]

Pacta Sunt Servanda. Since the days of Grotius, many writers have argued that the breach of any part of a treaty by one of its parties will have the effect *ipso facto* of releasing every other party from all its obligations. This doctrine, because of its impractical consequences if applied to the more important multilateral treaties of the present day, has never found support in practice and, according to Brierly, "ought equally to be rejected by legal theory." [75]

According to the principle *pacta sunt servanda,* the assumption is that states are bound to observe in good faith all international obligations assumed under solemn agreements with other nations. In the words of Cordell Hull before the Inter-American Conference for the Maintenance of Peace at Buenos Aires, 1936: "Observance of understandings, agreements and treaties between nations constitutes the foundation of international order." [76] The nature and extent of whatever duties are imposed upon a state by its treaty obligations can in no way be affected by municipal law. Concerning the *Treatment of Polish Nationals in Danzig,*[77] the Permanent Court of International Justice held in its advisory opinion of 1932 that "a State cannot adduce as against another State its own Constitution with a view to evading obligations incumbent upon it under international law or treaties in force." Likewise, in the *Free Zones Case* [78] the same court said: "It is certain that France cannot rely on her own legislation to limit the scope of her international obligations. . . ." Again in its advisory opinion concerning *Greco-Bulgarian Communities,*[79] the Permanent Court of International Justice said that "it is a generally accepted principle of international law that in the relations between Powers who are contracting Parties to a treaty, the provisions of municipal law cannot prevail over those of the treaty."

Regarding conflict between treaties and federal legislation, the courts of the United States have held that the most recent enactment in time shall prevail. In *United States v. Thompson* [80] the Supreme Court said on this

---

[74] Brierly, *op. cit.,* p. 235.
[75] *The Law of Nations* (1939), p. 236.
[76] Quoted from the *New York Times,* Dec. 6, 1936, by Hyde in *International Law* (1947), vol. II, p. 1454.
[77] PCIJ *Advisory Opinion,* Feb. 4, 1932, ser. A/B, no. 44, p. 24.
[78] PCIJ *Order,* Dec. 6, 1930, ser. A, no. 24, p. 12.
[79] PCIJ *Advisory Opinion,* July 31, 1930, ser. B, no. 17, p. 32.
[80] 258 Fed. 257, 268 (E.D. Ark. 1919).

point that "there is no principle of law more firmly established by the highest court of the land than that, while a treaty will supersede a prior act of Congress, an act of Congress may supersede a prior treaty. The latest expression controls, whether it be a treaty or an act of Congress." [81] While this is quite true as a matter of municipal law, it does not, however, follow that a treaty is repealed or abrogated, as far as international obligations are concerned, by a later statute. Said Secretary of State Hughes in 1923: [82]

A judicial determination that an act of Congress is to prevail over a treaty does not relieve the Government of the United States of the obligations established by a treaty. The distinction is often ignored between a rule of domestic law which is established by our legislative and judicial decisions and may be inconsistent with an existing Treaty, and the international obligation which a Treaty establishes. When this obligation is not performed a claim will inevitably be made to which the existence of merely domestic legislation does not constitute a defense and, if the claim seems to be well founded and other methods of settlement have not been availed of, the usual recourse is an arbitration in which international rules of action and obligations would be the subject of consideration.

Thus, a treaty still subsists as an international obligation even though it may not be enforceable by the administrative and judicial authorities. And let us repeat once more the well-established principle of American constitutional law that treaties which are duly ratified are, like acts of Congress, the supreme law of the land and therefore cannot be affected by any subsequent laws enacted by the legislatures of the several states of the Union. And let us also not forget that all responsibility with respect to treaty obligations under international law rests with the federal government in the United States, for only the federal Union has international personality, without which there could be no responsibility.

"The rule that compacts must be kept," writes Lauterpacht, "is certainly one of the bases of the legal relations between the members of any community. But at the same time the notion that in certain cases the law will refuse to continue to give effect to originally valid contracts is common to all systems of jurisprudence." [83]

Modification and Termination of Treaties. "The right of a State to

[81] In *Johnson v. Browne*, 205 U.S. 309, 321, it was said: "Repeals by implication are never favored, and a later treaty will not be regarded as repealing an earlier statute by implication, unless the two are absolutely incompatible and the statute cannot be enforced without antagonizing the treaty"—Hackworth, *op. cit.*, p. 191.

[82] The Secretary of State (Hughes) to the Secretary of the Treasury (Mellon), Feb. 19, 1923, Ms. Department of State, file 811.54341/4/.

[83] H. Lauterpacht, *The Function of Law in the International Community* (1933), p. 273.

terminate a treaty or to free itself from the obligation to heed the terms of such an instrument, must not be confused with its power to effect such an achievement." [84] According to a pronouncement by the Department of State through the American Ambassador to Japan: "Treaties can be lawfully modified or terminated only by processes prescribed or recognized or agreed upon by the parties to them." [85]

Generally speaking, treaties may be terminated by a number of different methods, among which the following are examples: (1) fulfillment of the terms of the treaty; (2) expiration of the period of time for which the treaty was concluded; (3) agreement of the parties; (4) conclusion of a new treaty which has the effect of abrogating an earlier agreement; (5) notice by one of the contracting parties in conformity with the terms of the treaty; (6) elimination of one of the parties or of the subject matter of the treaty; and (7) denouncement by one party and acquiescence by the other.[86]

Every legal system is confronted with a certain conflict between stability and change, which necessitates the constant adjustment of formal rights to principles of equity and justice. That this is no less true in international law than in any other branch of jurisprudence has long been recognized by the publicists. Even among the early Spanish writers, though they do not mention the doctrine as such, evidence of the *clausula rebus sic stantibus*, or principles strongly analogous to it, is found scattered throughout their pages. Victoria contested the validity of a law after certain changes had taken place in the original circumstances which gave rise to it, and Suarez argued that a law ought to be abandoned if "a greater benefit may be expected from its revocation, or greater danger or evil may be thus avoided." [87]

According to Grotius, a justification of the doctrine of *rebus sic stantibus* was to be found only in the intention of the parties,[88] while the great rationalist Pufendorf refused to sanction its application except in cases where it was expressly provided and when the only reason which motivated the promise no longer existed.[89] Continuing the lead of the classical jurists, modern publicists are neither precise nor unanimous in their definition of the famous *clausula*. They do not even agree as to whether the principle of *rebus sic stantibus* is to be regarded as an accepted rule of international law. Some reject it completely; others regard it merely

---

[84] Hyde, *International Law* (1947), vol. II, p. 1516.
[85] Department of State Press Release, Apr. 30, 1934, p. 245.
[86] Hackworth, *op. cit.*, p. 297.
[87] From *Tractatus de legibus ac deo legislatore*, book VI, chap. xxv, as quoted by Shyun Keq Shaw in *The Obsolescence of Treaties* (1939), p. 8n.
[88] *De jure belli ac pacis*, book II, chap. xvi, sec. 27.
[89] *De jure naturae et gentium*, book V, chap. xii, sec. 20.

as a political or moral maxim; while still others consider it no more than a principle *de lege ferenda.*[90]

A relatively recent attempt to restate the doctrine of *rebus sic stantibus* was made in the Draft Convention on the Law of Treaties by the Harvard Research in International Law as follows: [91]

(*a*) A treaty entered into with reference to the existence of a state of facts the continued existence of which was envisaged by the parties as a determining factor moving them to undertake the obligations stipulated, may be declared by a competent international tribunal or authority to have ceased when the state of facts has been essentially changed.

(*b*) Pending agreement by the parties upon and decision by a competent international tribunal or authority, the party which seeks such a declaration may provisionally suspend performance of its obligations under the treaty.

(*c*) A provisional suspension of performance by the party seeking such a declaration will not be justified definitively until a decision to this effect has been rendered by a competent international tribunal or authority.

There seems to be no case on record in which the *clausula* has been applied by both parties to a controversy. But in the *Free Zones Case*, the Permanent Court of International Justice had to consider an argument to the effect that the withdrawal of the customs lines by France in 1815 had made Geneva together with the "free zones" a single economic unit, and that this unit had been destroyed by the institution of Swiss federal customs in 1849. Therefore, the treaty of 1815 which provided for a withdrawal of customs lines, the French argued, had lapsed owing to a change of circumstances. The Court, however, held that it would be necessary to show that it was in *consideration* of the absence of customs duties at Geneva in 1815 that the "free zones" were established. That this was the case France was unable to prove.[92] Thus it would seem that to put an end to treaty obligations, something more than a mere change in circumstances is needed.

Brierly writes: [93]

As defined by the Permanent Court the doctrine of *rebus sic stantibus* is clearly a reasonable doctrine which it is right that international law should recognize. But as so defined it is a doctrine of limited scope which has little to do with the problem of obsolete or oppressive treaties, for which it is too often supposed to be the solution.

The controversy over this doctrine, it would seem, is less concerned with the fundamental question of its juridical validity than with the possi-

[90] Shaw, *op. cit.*, pp. 15–16.
[91] Art. 28, in *American Journal of International Law*, vol. 29 (1935), supplement.
[92] See Brierly, *op. cit.*, pp. 244–245.
[93] *Ibid.*, p. 247.

bility of its application. It has been suggested that, when a state has become convinced that its obligations under a treaty, because of a "vital change of circumstances," can no longer be met without serious detriment to itself, then a request for abrogation should be directed to the other party or parties to the agreement. Should such a request be refused, the next step would be to submit the controversy for adjudication by an international tribunal. If, through this process, it is found that the treaty in question has lost its legal reason for continued existence, and the party who benefits should refuse to abide by the judgment, it is only then that a unilateral abrogation may be justified.[94]

The Effect of War upon Treaties. The effect of war upon treaties is a question which has proved most perplexing to administrative authorities and courts alike, and on this subject the law is by no means settled. In the case of *Karnuth, Director of Immigration, et al. v. United States ex rel. Albro* [95] the Supreme Court said that "the authorities, as well as the practice of nations, present a great contrariety of views. The law on the subject is still in the making."

At various times the proposition has been advanced that the commencement of war automatically abrogates existing treaties between the belligerent states. After the conclusion of the Treaty of Ghent, Britain contended that the Americans, in consequence of the War of 1812, had lost all rights in the North Atlantic fisheries under the treaty of 1783. John Quincy Adams, then United States Minister at London, argued that the treaty of 1783 was not "one of those which by the common understanding and usage of civilized nations is or can be considered as annulled by a subsequent war between the same parties." Lord Bathurst replied: "To a position of this novel nature Great Britain can not accede. She knows of no exception to the rule that all treaties are put to an end by a subsequent war between the same parties." During the negotiations which followed the British never abandoned this position, by which ironically they were to be excluded from the Mississippi, the free and open navigation of which was granted to the subjects of Great Britain forever by the treaty Lord Bathurst set aside.[96]

A leading case on the question of the effect of war upon treaties is *Techt v. Hughes,*[97] in which the United States Court of Appeals said:

International law today does not preserve treaties or annul them, regardless of the effects produced. It deals with such problems pragmatically, preserving

[94] See Oppenheim-Lauterpacht, *op. cit.*, pp. 847–848.
[95] 279 U.S. 231, 236 (1929).
[96] Davis, *Treaty Notes*, Treaty Volume, 1776–1887, p. 1237, in John Bassett Moore, *Digest of International Law*, vol. V, p. 381.
[97] 229 N.Y. 222; 128 N.E. 185; 11 A.L.R. 166 (1920).

or annulling as the necessities of war exact. It establishes standards, but it does not fetter itself with rules. When it attempts to do more, it finds that there is neither unanimity of opinion nor uniformity of practice. . . . This does not mean, of course, that there are not some classes of treaties about which there is general agreement. Treaties of alliance fall. Treaties of boundary or cession, "dispositive" or "transitory" conventions, survive. . . . So, of course, do treaties which regulate the conduct of hostilities.

We may safely say, therefore, that those provisions which are compatible with hostilities survive, unless there are in the treaties themselves express provisions to the contrary, and those incompatible with the contest of arms must of course fall.

In other cases treaties may be suspended during the period of hostilities, and unless they include provisions to the contrary, such treaties will again come into operation *mutatis mutandis* upon the termination of the war. In *Society for the Propagation of the Gospel in Foreign Parts v. New Haven* [98] the Supreme Court of the United States said:

There may be treaties of such a nature, as to their object and import, as that war will put an end to them; but where treaties contemplate a permanent arrangement of territorial, and other national rights, or which, in their terms, are meant to provide for the event of an intervening war, it would be against every principle of just interpretation to hold them extinguished by the event of war. . . .
We think, therefore, that treaties stipulating for permanent rights and general arrangements, and professing to aim at perpetuity, and to deal with the case of war as well as of peace, do not cease on the occurrence of war, but are, at most, only suspended while it lasts; and unless they are waived by the parties, or new and repugnant stipulations are made, they revive in their operation at the return of peace.

The political procedure for the modification and termination of treaties is twofold: (1) by action of the parties themselves, and (2) by intervention of the international community as a whole. Every treaty may be terminated by the contracting parties, subject to their mutual consent. This rule can, of course, be modified by the parties to a treaty by simply inserting into the instrument itself provisions to that effect. In treaties of a territorial nature the intention of the parties is generally to create a permanent situation, and the understanding is therefore that they shall abide forever. In treaties of an executory nature, however, such as treaties of commerce, the common practice is to insert clauses with respect to their termination. "Denunciation or revision clauses are scarcely found in coercive or unilateral treaties." [99]

[98] 8 Wheat 464 (1823); Hudson, *Cases* (1951), p. 479.
[99] Shaw, *op. cit.*, p. 157.

In the interest of all nations, intervention by some international agency in the adjustment of treaties is undoubtedly necessary. It is clear that treaty enforcement requires the existence of some means by which international obligations can be adjusted if a vital change in circumstances has occurred. The Secretary General of the United Nations in a Report of 1950 had this to say: [100]

If a change in circumstances has occurred such as to justify the clause *rebus sic stantibus* being invoked, what procedure should be followed by the State invoking the clause in order to divest itself of its obligations?

The State invoking the said clause may not, it would seem, divest itself on its own authority alone. It should obtain the consent of the other Contracting Parties. Without such consent, it should secure recognition of the validity of its claim by a competent international organ such as one of the executive organs of the United Nations or the International Court of Justice.

As things now stand, international law is confronted with a serious conflict between the dynamics of a changing world and a search for stability in a legal regime. To allow each state to be its own judge as to what constitutes a "vital change in circumstances" and justifies renunciation of treaty obligations must inevitably lead to international anarchy. It is to be hoped, therefore, that to such a situation, the international community through its own institutions will provide the necessary alternative. For there can be no peace without justice, nor order without law.

[100] UN Doc. E/CN. 4/367, Apr. 7, 1950, pp. 36–38, 71.

CHAPTER **19**

Pacific Settlement of Disputes

In an earlier chapter,[1] concerning the rights and duties of states, we introduced the topic of "pacific settlement of disputes" and mentioned some of the agencies through which adjustments are effected for the sake of peace. Inasmuch as various means and procedures for the promotion of order and justice in the international community have gradually come into being, a more detailed treatment of their nature and function will be given here.

International disputes regardless of their origin tend to fall within either of two groups, one political, the other legal. Within the latter classification are to be found those international differences in which the disputants base their respective claims and contentions upon recognized principles of international law. All other controversies are usually regarded as of a political nature. Hence also the classification of justiciable and nonjusticiable disputes, which we shall seek to differentiate later in this chapter.

In a general way the problem of effecting peaceful settlement of disputes between nations admits of two alternative methods of approach. In the first place, the disputants may be induced to arrive at an amicable solution of their differences on their own accord, through diplomatic negotiations or the media of good offices, mediation, and conciliation.[2] In the second place, settlement may be effected through the agency of a third party, by arbitration or adjudication of the questions at issue.

Diplomatic Negotiation. The procedure most frequently employed in the peaceful adjustment of international disputes is that of direct negotiation by the parties concerned. The drastic nature of war as a means to resolve differences between nations is very largely responsible for the creation of a legal obligation to resort to negotiation before arms.[3] Indeed,

---

[1] Chap. 9.

[2] Art. 2 of the Convention for the Pacific Settlement of International Disputes, signed at The Hague in 1907, provides that, in case of serious disagreement or dispute, "before an appeal to arms," the powers agree to have recourse, as far as circumstances allow, to the good offices or mediation of one or more friendly states.

[3] Charles G. Fenwick, *International Law* (1948), p. 508.

most treaties regarding peaceful settlement recognize negotiation as a first step toward amicable adjustment of whatever differences may obtain in any given case. It is quite possible, however, that the effect of negotiation is simply to show that the contending parties are unable to arrive at a peaceful settlement through this means. In such a case war may result, but this is by no means certain, as there remain yet other methods through which a peaceful solution may be found.

Good Offices and Mediation. The terms *good offices* and *mediation* are sometimes confused, especially in diplomatic documents. It should be noted that, though the one frequently leads to the other, the two are not the same.

Good offices has reference to suggestions or advice tendered by a third power, not party to the dispute, and may sometimes lead to mediation. The purpose of good offices is merely to bring the disputants together in order that negotiations may take place and a peaceful adjustment of differences may be achieved. Good offices may also be the means of bringing armed conflict to an end. A familiar example in this regard is found in the circumstances which led to the termination of the Russo-Japanese War in 1905. It was the good offices of the President of the United States which induced the leaders of the belligerent nations, Russia and Japan, to open negotiations which were to culminate in the Peace of Portsmouth on September 5 of that year. With respect to good offices, it is important to notice that no direct intervention takes place by the third party. Its mission is confined to what may be called a catalytic action by which the desired reaction on the part of the disputants is induced.

Mediation, on the other hand, is more in the character of direct intervention on the part of a third party. The mediator assumes the role of a middleman and plays a leading part in the conduct of negotiations, acting always in a conciliatory capacity, and thus becomes the medium through which a settlement may be effected. Article 4 of the Hague Conventions of 1899 and 1907 for the Pacific Settlement of International Disputes defines mediation as follows: "The part of the mediator consists in reconciling the opposing claims and appeasing the feelings of resentment which may have arisen between the States at variance." [4] And according to Article 5 of the same Conventions: "The functions of the mediator are at an end when once it is declared, either by one of the parties to the dispute or by the mediator himself, that the means of reconciliation proposed by him are not accepted." [5] Thus it may be said that mediation is a consequence of the tender of good offices and, in addition, a manifestation of their exercise.[6]

[4] James Brown Scott, *The Hague Court Reports* (1916), p. xxxvii.
[5] *Ibid.*
[6] Charles Cheney Hyde, *International Law* (1947), vol. II, p. 1563.

The acceptance of good offices and mediation cannot have the effect of interrupting, delaying, or hindering mobilization and other measures of preparation for war, unless there is agreement to the contrary. Likewise, if such measures are taken after the commencement of hostilities, no interruption of military operations can occur in the absence of agreement to that effect.[7] Yet, the value of these remedies for peaceful settlement "be it before or after the parties have appealed to arms, cannot be overestimated."[8] Furthermore, the Hague conventions have invested these means of pacific settlement with a new importance by giving third states a legal right to make use of their good offices and mediation in order to make possible a pacific settlement.

The Dogger Bank Case. In the Dogger Bank incident of 1904 it is probable that war was averted between Great Britain and Russia through the means of French mediation, which resulted in agreement between the disputants to establish a commission of inquiry for the settlement of their differences.

The circumstances which led to the dispute between the two countries were briefly as follows: In the bleak days of October, 1904, while a Russian fleet lay coaling off the Norwegian coast, there were rumors of Japanese torpedo boats in the vicinity. It will be remembered that war was then in progress between Russia and Japan. As a consequence of these reports the Russian Baltic fleet departed for the Far East twenty-four hours earlier than scheduled. As the last division of the fleet, in the immediate charge of the admiral, was passing through a fogbound sea in the early hours of the morning, it came upon what later proved to be a fishing fleet out of Hull, England. The Russians, mistaking the British fishing vessels for Japanese torpedo boats, opened fire, with the result that one fishing boat was sunk and others damaged, and two fishermen were killed and six others injured.

To prevent disastrous consequences, the French government suggested resort to an international commission of inquiry, as provided for in the Hague Convention for Pacific Settlement of International Disputes of 1899. The suggestion was accepted by both parties and an agreement was signed on November 25, 1904, which invested a commission composed of admirals from the British, Russian, United States, French, and Austrian navies with authority to find the facts in dispute and fix responsibility. With regard to the scope of its jurisdiction the commission went beyond the provisions of the Hague convention and assumed functions that amounted to those of an arbitral tribunal.[9] Though the commission's

---

[7] Art. 7 of the Hague Convention for the Pacific Settlement of International Disputes.

[8] Oppenheim-Lauterpacht, *International Law* (1944), vol. II, p. 11.

[9] Fenwick, *op. cit.*, p. 511.

work was done under circumstances of extreme tension, its success created a new faith in mediation as a means to pacific settlement of international disputes. As a direct result of the experience in the *Dogger Bank case,* certain changes were incorporated in the second Hague convention on this subject in 1907. This convention provided that there were to be three neutrals instead of one on the commissions of inquiry. This provision, it was believed, would lend a greater degree of impartiality to the decisions.

Arbitration. During the medieval period arbitration had frequently been resorted to as a means to settlement of international disputes. But with the opening of the modern age, with its national states and consequent theories of sovereignty, it fell into disuse and was not revived again until the latter part of the nineteenth century. Indeed, this mode of peaceful settlement is frequently dated from the famous arbitration of the *Alabama* claims in 1872 between Great Britain and the United States. This was also the first occasion where the arbitrators sat as a court of law, but with direct representation of the parties to the dispute: Sir Alexander Cockburn, Lord Chief Justice of England, on behalf of Britain, and Charles Francis Adams for the United States. This became a precedent for the constitution of arbitration tribunals in the future.[10]

In contrast to mediation, which is primarily a diplomatic function, arbitration involves the application of law and judicial methods to the determination of disputes between nations.[11]

Its object is to displace war . . . as a means of obtaining national redress, by the judgements of international-judicial tribunals; just as private war between individuals, as a means of obtaining personal redress, has, in consequence of the development of law and order in civilized states, been supplanted by the processes of municipal courts.[12]

Arbitration was for a long time regarded as of purely voluntary nature, but by the end of the nineteenth century it had become general practice to include in treaties the so-called *clause compromissoire,* which is an *a priori* agreement by the parties to arbitrate whatever differences might arise in connection with such treaties. With the expansion of the arbitral clause into special treaties in the latter part of the nineteenth century and the establishment of the Permanent Court of Arbitration, this mode of settlement of disputes between nations became widely accepted. Today many nations have, by treaties, agreed to submit disputes to arbitration rather than resort to costly arms.

A *cause célèbre* in the field of international arbitration is the case of

[10] Sir Thomas Barclay, *New Methods of Adjusting International Disputes and the Future* (1917), p. 41.
[11] John Bassett Moore, *Digest of International Law,* vol. VII, p. 25.
[12] *Ibid.*

El Chamizal, which by a convention signed in Washington on December 5, 1910, was submitted for arbitration by the United States and Mexico.[13] The dispute was one concerning the boundary between the two countries which was first defined, by the Treaty of Guadalupe Hidalgo of 1848, as beginning in the Gulf of Mexico, 3 leagues from land, opposite the mouth of the Rio Grande, and running thence up the middle of the river, "following the deepest channel, where it has more than one, to the point where it strikes the southern boundary of New Mexico;" etc.[14] Later, in connection with the Gadsden Purchase, the treaty of 1853 provided that the fluvial boundary between the two republics should follow "the middle" of both the Rio Grande and the Colorado River. But the terms of either treaty failed to make clear what would happen to the location of the boundary in case the course of these rivers should change through a sudden process of avulsion, or through a gradual process of erosion and accretion.

In the following years considerable diplomatic correspondence took place as to the meaning and effect of the boundary treaties of 1848 and 1853. In this period the United States consistently took the position that the fluvial boundary was not a fixed line, but that it moved with the rivers through the gradual process of erosion and accretion. Mexico, on the other hand, contended for the fixed-line interpretation of the treaties, though often qualifying her arguments by admitting that a shift in the fluvial boundary could take place through slow and gradual alluvial action.

In 1884 a new convention was concluded by the United States and Mexico regarding the "boundary line between the two countries where it follows the bed of the Rio Grande and the Rio Colorado."[15] It was established by this convention that the dividing line should follow "the centre of the normal channel of the rivers named, notwithstanding any alterations in the banks or in the course of those rivers, provided that such alterations be effected by natural causes through the slow and gradual erosion and deposit of alluvium and not by the abandonment of an existing river bed and the opening of a new one."[16] At the time this convention was signed great alterations in the course of the Rio Grande had already taken place. It appears in fact that the river of 1852 and the river of 1884 had no points in common, except points of intersection. These alterations

[13] The actual arbitration took place in the City of El Paso, Texas, between May 15 and June 2, 1911. For text of the award, see *American Journal of International Law*, vol. 5 (1911), pp. 782–812.

[14] *Malloy's Treaties*, vol. 1, pp. 1109–1110.

[15] Preamble of the boundary convention of 1884. See *American Journal of International Law*, vol. 5 (1911), p. 798.

[16] Art. 1.

in the course of the river appeared at times to have been caused by a slow and gradual alluvial action, while at other times it was the result of a sudden and massive erosion. The latter process was apt to be associated with great floods such as those from 1864 to 1868. Yet there were no specific provisions in the treaty of 1884 which would make it retroactively applicable to these problems.

By the convention of 1889, the governments of the United States and Mexico created the "International Boundary Commission for the purpose of carrying out the principles contained in the Convention of 1884 and to avoid the difficulties occasioned by the changes which take place in the bed of the Rio Grande where it serves as the boundary between the two republics, and for other purposes. . . ." [17] At a session of the Boundary Commission in September, 1894, the Mexican Commissioner presented the papers in a case known as "El Chamizal No. 4." These included a complaint made by Pedro Ignacio Garcia, who alleged, in substance, that he had acquired some property formerly located on the south side of the Rio Grande and known as El Chamizal. But as a result of an abrupt and sudden change in the course of the river, the property in question was now on the north side of the Rio Grande and within the limits of El Paso, Texas. The claim was examined by the International Boundary Commission, and witnesses were heard with regard to the facts. But after consideration, no agreement could be reached as to the disposition of the land in question. It was a result of the Boundary Commission's failure to come to any agreement in this case that the convention of June 24, 1910, was concluded providing for the arbitration with which we are here concerned.

The specific question to be decided was "whether the international title to the Chamizal tract is in the United States of America or Mexico." [18] The Commission, after careful consideration of the convention of 1910, the written and oral arguments, as well as the documents presented by either side arrived at the following decision and award: (1) The boundary line as established by the treaties of 1848 and 1853 was not a fixed and invariable line. (2) The United States claim to title by prescription was unanimously rejected. (3) The treaty of 1884 was regarded as having retroactive effect with respect to any changes in the course of the Rio Grande since the survey of 1852. (4) The whole of the Chamizal tract, as defined by the convention of 1910, was found not to have been formed by slow and gradual erosion and deposit of alluvium within the meaning of Article 1 of the convention of 1884. (5) That portion of the disputed tract which had been formed in the period before the great flood of 1864 was

[17] *American Journal of International Law*, vol. 5 (1911), p. 791.
[18] Art. 3 of the Convention of 1910.

found to have been the result of slow and gradual erosion and deposit of alluvium within the meaning of the treaty of 1884.

The Commission then applied the principle laid down in *Nebraska v. Iowa*,[19] *mutatis mutandis*, to the present case: [20]

> The Presiding Commissioner and the Mexican Commissioner are of the opinion that the accretions which occurred in the Chamizal tract up to the time of the great flood of 1864 should be awarded to the United States of America, and that inasmuch as the changes which occurred in that year did not constitute slow and gradual erosion within the meaning of the Convention of 1884, the balance of the tract should be awarded to Mexico.

The American Commissioner filed a vigorous dissenting opinion which he concluded in the following words: "The present decision terminates nothing, settles nothing. It is simply an invitation for international litigation. It breathes the spirit of unconscious but nevertheless unauthorized compromise rather than of judicial determination."

On August 24, 1911, the United States refused to accept the award as valid or binding, on the grounds that the finding and award was vague, indeterminate, uncertain in its terms, and impossible of enforcement. Thus the dispute of El Chamizal remains unsettled to the present day.

Arbitral Procedure. It should be noted that arbitration and adjudication are procedures of settlement very closely allied, and that both may be categorized as of a judicial nature.[21] The arbitrator differs from the judge of a regular court in two respects: (1) he is chosen by the parties to the dispute, and (2) his judicial function ends with the termination of the case for which he is appointed.[22] The difference, therefore, between arbitration and adjudication is largely of an *institutional character*. Arbitration is the term used when the tribunal is selected by the parties in dispute. Its members are then called arbitrators, and the decision an arbitral award.[23] But when the organ is a permanent institution, functioning with unchanged composition in all cases within its competence, "its members are called judges and its decisions judgments.[24]

Articles 51 to 85 of the Hague convention of 1907, which deal with matters of procedure, set forth the steps to be taken by the parties preliminary to adjudication, the function of the tribunal and the manner in which cases may be presented. The controlling instrument in this regard

---

[19] 143 U.S. 359 (1892).
[20] G. H. Hackworth, *Digest of International Law*, vol. I, p. 414.
[21] See Hyde, *op. cit.*, p. 1581.
[22] J. L. Brierly, *The Law of Nations* (1949), p. 251.
[23] A. F. Ross, *A Textbook of International Law* (1947), p. 276.
[24] *Ibid.*

is the so-called *compromis*. Here the subject of the dispute is defined, and the conditions of arbitration set forth, as agreed by the parties.[25] According to Article 53 the Permanent Court is competent to settle the *compromis,* if the parties agree to have recourse to it for that purpose. The Court is similarly competent, even if the request for such settlement is made by only one of the parties to the dispute, in cases where agreement has proved impossible through means of ordinary diplomacy, with respect to [26]

1. A dispute covered by a general treaty of arbitration concluded or renewed after the present Convention has come into force, and providing for a *compromis* in all disputes and not either explicitly or implicitly excluding the settlement of the compromis from the competence of the Court. Recourse can not, however, be had to the Court if the other party declares that in its opinion the dispute does not belong to the category of disputes which can be submitted to compulsory arbitration, unless the treaty of arbitration confers upon the arbitration tribunal the power of deciding this preliminary question.

2. A dispute arising from contract debts claimed from one Power by another Power as due to its nationals, and for the settlement of which the offer of arbitration has been accepted. This arrangement is not applicable if acceptance is subject to the condition that the compromis should be settled in some other way.

In cases where a sovereign or chief of state is chosen as arbitrator, the procedure is determined by him.[27] In certain other cases the *compromis* may be settled by a commission consisting of five members.[28] And in such cases, unless there is agreement by the parties to the contrary, such commission also constitutes the arbitration tribunal.[29]

In Article 61 of the Convention it is provided that if the question as to what language is to be used has not been settled by the *compromis,* it shall be decided by the tribunal. The parties are also entitled to appoint special agents whose function it is to act as "intermediaries between themselves and the tribunal." [30] The disputants may also retain for themselves advocates to represent their interests, but the members of the Permanent Court may not act either as agents or counsel "except on behalf of the Power which appoints them members of the Court." [31]

As a general rule, arbitration procedure comprises two distinct phases: (1) written pleadings, and (2) oral discussions. The pleadings consist of certain communications by the respective agents to the members of the tribunal and to the opposite party of "cases, counter-cases, and, if neces-

---

[25] Art. 52.   [26] Art. 53.
[27] Art. 56.   [28] Art. 54.
[29] Art. 58.   [30] Art. 62.
[31] *Ibid.*

sary, of replies." To these are annexed all the papers and documents relating to the case. The discussions, on the other hand, consist in the oral presentation development before the tribunal of arguments by counsel for the respective parties to the dispute.[32]

After the close of the pleadings, the tribunal is entitled to refuse discussion of any new papers or documents which one of the parties may wish to submit without the consent of the other. In addition, the tribunal can require from the agents of the respective parties the production of all papers and can demand all necessary explanations. In case of refusal the tribunal takes note of it.[33] The agents and counsel are entitled to raise objections. But the tribunal has the final decision, so that these objections may not be made the subject for further discussion. The members of the tribunal are entitled to put questions to the agents and counsel of the parties and to ask for explanations on doubtful points. "Neither the questions put, nor the remarks made by members of the tribunal in the course of the discussions, can be regarded as an expression of opinion by the tribunal in general or by the members in particular." [34]

The tribunal considers its decisions in private, the proceedings remain secret, and all questions are decided by a majority.[35] The award must be accompanied by the reasons on which it is based, and contains the names of the arbitrators as well as the signature of the president and registrar of the Court.[36] Such an award, when duly pronounced and communicated to the agents of the parties, "settles the dispute definitively and without appeal." [37] Any dispute, however, which may arise between the parties as to the interpretation and execution of the award "shall, in the absence of an agreement to the contrary, be submitted to the tribunal which pronounced it." [38]

According to Article 83 of the convention:

The parties can reserve in the *compromis* the right to demand the revision of the award.

In this case and unless there be an agreement to the contrary, the demand must be addressed to the tribunal which pronounced the award. It can only be made on the ground of the discovery of some new fact calculated to exercise a decisive influence upon the award and which was unknown to the tribunal and to the party which demanded the revision at the time the discussion was closed.

Proceedings for revision can only be instituted by a decision of the tribunal expressly recording the existence of the new fact, recognizing in it the character described in the preceding paragraph, and declaring the demand admissible on this ground.

[32] Art. 63.
[34] Arts. 71 and 72.
[36] Art. 79.
[38] Art. 82.

[33] Arts. 67 and 69.
[35] Art. 78.
[37] Art. 81.

The compromis fixes the period within which the demand for revision must be made.

It is important to note that the award is not binding except on the parties in dispute. In questions which involve conventions to which powers other than those in dispute are parties, all signatories shall be informed by the disputants "in good time." Each of these powers has a right to intervene in the case. Should one or more avail themselves of this right, "the interpretation contained in the award is equally binding on them." [39]

In Chapter IV of the convention, certain provisions are made for arbitration by summary procedure, i.e., by proceedings which are short and simple as compared with those we have outlined above. Accordingly, in cases where the arbitration of a dispute admits of summary procedure, the following rules apply: [40]

Each of the parties in dispute appoints an arbitrator. The two arbitrators thus selected choose an umpire. If they do not agree on this point, each of them proposes two candidates taken from the general list of the members of the Permanent Court exclusive of the members appointed by either of the parties and not being nationals of either of them; which of the candidates thus proposed shall be the umpire is determined by lot.

The umpire presides over the tribunal, which gives its decisions by a majority of votes.

In the absence of any agreement to the contrary, the tribunal, as soon as it is formed, fixes the time within which the two parties must submit their respective cases for arbitration.[41] Each party is represented by an agent, who serves as an intermediary between the tribunal and the power by which he is appointed.[42] The proceedings are conducted exclusively in writing, though witnesses and experts may be called. The tribunal, on its part, has the right to demand oral explanations from the agents of the two parties, as well as from the witnesses and experts whose appearance it may consider useful.[43]

Though little is heard of the Permanent Court of Arbitration in recent years, this institution has continued to exist for more than half a century. And to the Court is attached the Bureau at The Hague and a permanent Council for purposes of administration. The usefulness of the Court, as a means to pacific settlement of international disputes, is evidenced by the fact that no less than 21 cases have to this day been settled through its agency.

[39] Art. 84.
[41] Art. 88.
[43] Art. 90.

[40] Art. 87.
[42] Art. 89.

The Court of Judicial Arbitration. It soon became apparent that both in structure and function, the Permanent Court of Arbitration left much to be desired. As we have already seen, the Court, in spite of its name, is not a permanently constituted body. Its only permanent feature is the panel of judges from which the Court's membership is drawn in each case which comes up for arbitration. The considerable, and perhaps very unwise, latitude which the contending parties have with respect to the choice of arbitrators should also be noted. In view of these and other shortcomings of the so-called Permanent Court of Arbitration, an attempt was made at the second Hague conference in 1907, not merely to revise and enlarge the convention of 1899, but to establish a wholly new body to be known as the Judicial Arbitration Court.[44] In contrast to a mere panel of judges, this Court was to meet in plenary session once a year, though a large part of its work would actually be done through a committee of three members called the "delegation." [45]

The unwillingness, however, on the part of many nations, represented at The Hague in 1907, to give up the prerogative of selecting their own judges in cases of arbitration prevented the establishment of a court of arbitral justice.

The International Prize Court. Aside from the abortive attempt to establish a court of arbitral justice, the second Hague conference of 1907 created an International Prize Court, to function as a court of appeal in prize cases heard before national courts. But the question of how the Court was to be constituted presented many difficulties, as the same problems which defeated the judicial arbitration court were encountered once more.

It was finally decided that 8 of the 15 judges were to be permanent representatives of the so-called great powers, while 7 would be rotated among the rest of the signatories, subject to certain rules which were based on the maritime interests of these states.[46] It is believed that since the smaller states had reason to expect considerable advantage to themselves from the establishment of such a court, they were willing to forgo equal representation.[47] As a result, the court was established by the twelfth convention of the conference, the first in the history of the world to establish a universal world tribunal.

That this convention was never ratified, and that the court accordingly failed to come into operation, was due to fears on the part of certain powers, especially Great Britain. These fears were inspired by a provision in the convention to the effect that the adjudication of the Court was to be based on the rules of international law, or if such were lacking, on the

[44] Hyde, *op. cit.*, p. 1613. [45] *Ibid.*, p. 1614.
[46] Ross, *op. cit.*, p. 292. [47] *Ibid.*

general principles of justice and equity. Inasmuch as well-defined principles of international prize law did not exist in 1907 any more than is the case today, it was feared that the discretionary powers contained in the above-mentioned provision would tend to give the court international legislative functions. It was in this connection, and at the initiative of Great Britain, that the London conference of 1908–1909 was called in an effort to codify the law of prize. As we have seen in an earlier chapter, the outcome of this conference was the so-called London Declaration of 1909—which, however, because of severe opposition in the House of Lords, was never ratified. Thus, the International Prize Court turned out to be nothing more than a stillborn child of the second conference at The Hague.

The Central American Court of Justice. A few weeks after the adjournment of the Hague Peace Conference of 1907, the Central American Court of Justice was established, with its seat at Cartago, Costa Rica.[48] Though this Court came to an end within a decade from the time it was founded, it constitutes an experiment in the domain of international justice worthy of notice here.

Article 1 of the Convention of 1907 provided that the Court should have obligatory competence in all controversies which might arise among its members[49] and in which their respective departments of foreign affairs should fail to reach an understanding. It was also provided that the Court should have jurisdiction in cases involving individuals, when local remedies had been exhausted and justice denied, and "by common accord" any case between individuals and the contracting parties could be submitted to the Court. By Article 22 of the convention, it was provided that the Court be given competence to determine its own jurisdiction, to interpret "Treaties and Conventions germane to the matter in dispute," and to apply "the principles of international law."[50] In the Court's entire period, 10 cases were actually adjudicated through its agency, and of these, 5 were brought by individuals.[51]

The convention of 1907 which created the Court contained no provision for extension. It provided only that it should remain in force "during the ten years counted from its last ratification."[52] Accordingly, on March 12, 1918, ten years after the date on which Guatemala had deposited her

---

[48] The Court was moved to San José when its building was destroyed by earthquake in 1910. There all later meetings were held until its dissolution ten years later.

[49] The members were Costa Rica, Guatemala, Honduras, Nicaragua, and El Salvador.

[50] Manley O. Hudson, *The Permanent Court of International Justice 1920–1942, A Treatise* (1943), p. 49.

[51] For a brief account of these cases, see *ibid.*, pp. 52–62.

[52] *Ibid.*, p. 65.

ratification, the convention of 1907 came to an end. On that date the archives and property of the Central American Court of Justice were handed over to the government of Costa Rica.

In appreciation of this short-lived experiment in international justice, Judge Manley O. Hudson comments as follows: [53] "This was the first international court in modern history to be endowed with continuing functions. . . . In a period of greater relative stability, a useful future for the court might have been possible."

A World Court of Justice. Nearly a quarter of a century was to pass after the establishment of the Permanent Court of Arbitration at The Hague before a world court of justice was to find its seat in that famous city the Netherlands. As we have indicated in an earlier chapter, it was provided in Article 14 of the Covenant of the League of Nations that such a Court should be established. Accordingly, on December 13, 1920, the Assembly of the League approved the Statute by which the Permanent Court of International Justice came into being. Actually, the Statute did not come into force until the Protocol of Signature had been ratified by a majority of the members of the League. This was accomplished by September 1, 1921,[54] and on February 15, 1922, the Court opened amid ceremonies of considerable solemnity.[55]

In 1929, a number of amendments were made to the original Statute of the Court, and these were submitted in a new protocol to the members for ratification.[56] The progress of ratification of the amending protocol was slow, however, and it was not until February 1, 1936, that the Secretary-General of the League, acting "by order and in the name of the Council" could inform the Registrar of the Court to the effect that the Revision Protocol had come into force that day.[57]

Though the Permanent Court of International Justice had thus been established in conformity with Article 14 of the Covenant, it was to function as an institution quite apart from the League. Because the Protocol of Signature had been signed and ratified as a separate instrument, membership of the Court, as to rights and obligations, was independent of membership in the League. The judges, 15 in number, were nominated by the national groups in the Court of Arbitration [58] and elected by the

[53] *Ibid.*, p. 70.   [54] See *ibid.*, p. 128.
[55] Sir Geoffrey Butler, *A Handbook to the League of Nations* (1928), p. 72.
[56] For a complete text of the revised Statute, see Hudson, *op. cit.*, p. 669 ff.
[57] *Ibid.*, p. 140.
[58] Art. 4 of the Statute provided: "In the case of Members of the League of Nations not represented in the Permanent Court of Arbitration, the list of candidates shall be drawn up by national groups appointed for this purpose by their Governments under the same conditions as those prescribed for members of the Permanent Court of Arbitration by Article XLIV of the Convention of The Hague of 1907 for the pacific settlement of international disputes."

Assembly and the Council. But after the judges had been thus elected by the League, they were under no obligations to that body, nor could the League remove them. The Court was open to the members of the League and to those states mentioned in the Annex to the Covenant.

The United States and the Permanent Court of Justice. One of the states mentioned in the Annex of the Covenant was the United States of America, and in 1923 the President submitted the Protocol of the Court with certain reservations to the Senate for ratification. It was not until January 27, 1926, that the Senate gave its advice and consent, with the following reservations: (1) The adherence of the United States to the Court was not to involve any legal relationship to the League of Nations or to the Treaty of Versailles. (2) The United States was to participate on an equal basis in the election of judges. (3) The United States should pay a fair share of the cost of the Court. (4) The United States may at any time withdraw its adherence to the Protocol, and the Statute of the Court should not be amended without the consent of the United States. (5) With respect to advisory opinions the parties concerned should be given the benefit of public hearings, and the Court should not, without the consent of the United States, "entertain any request for an advisory opinion touching any dispute or question in which the United States has or claims an interest." [59]

In September, 1926, a conference was held by the signatories to the Protocol in an effort to find means to satisfy the American reservations. In its Final Act the Conference suggested the conclusion of a special protocol which would include the United States and presented a preliminary draft of such an instrument. But the recommendations "were not received with favor by the Government of the United States, and for more than two years the negotiations were not pursued." [60]

A new effort was made in March, 1929, when a committee of jurists was appointed by the League Council to draft a protocol which included the so-called "Root formula," containing amendments which met the demands of the United States.[61] Accordingly, on December 9, of the same year, signatures were affixed on behalf of this country to (1) the Protocol of Signature of the Statute of the Court, (2) the Protocol of Accession of the

[59] 69th Cong., 1st Sess., S. Res. 5, *Congressional Record*, vol. 67, p. 2825.

[60] Hudson, *op. cit.*, p. 222.

[61] "Mr. Root's plan was fully formulated before he arrived in Geneva in March, 1929, and its fundamental purpose and nature had been discussed by him with various official persons in Washington before he sailed from the United States. The plan was discussed by the committee and various changes in detail were made, although the substance of it was not altered in the slightest"—Philip C. Jessup, *International Conciliation*, no. 273 (October, 1931), p. 598.

United States, and (3) the Protocol of Revision of the Statute of the Court.

For five years the Senate failed to act, but on January 29, 1935, it defeated a resolution proposed by the Committee on Foreign Relations to ratify the above-mentioned instruments. Notwithstanding the fact that the United States never joined the Permanent Court of International Justice, four of her famous sons served in a judicial capacity as members of the tribunal.[62]

The United Nations and Pacific Settlement of Disputes. As we have indicated earlier, Chapter VI of the Charter of the United Nations is especially devoted to the problem of pacific settlement of disputes. Section 1 of Article 33 provides as follows:

> The parties to any dispute, the continuance of which is likely to endanger the maintenance of international peace and security, shall, first of all, seek a solution by negotiation, enquiry, mediation, conciliation, arbitration, judicial settlement, resort to regional agencies or arrangements, or other peaceful means of their own choice.

It is understood that only in cases where settlement fails by the means enumerated above, shall the issue be brought before the Security Council or the General Assembly, and then only if the continuance of the dispute "is likely to endanger the maintenance of international peace and security." It might be pointed out that while the Paris Treaty for the Renunciation of War of 1928 provided that settlement of disputes should "never be sought except by pacific means," Article 33 of the Charter constitutes a *positive obligation* on the part of the members of the United Nations to seek a solution to serious disputes by pacific means.[63] It should also be noted that the Charter makes a distinction between those disputes and situations which are likely to endanger peace and security, if continued, and those of a less serious nature.[64] The agency designated by the Charter to determine whether a dispute is of such nature as to endanger the peace is the Security Council itself. Article 34 provides that "the Security Council may investigate any dispute, or situation which might lead to international friction or give rise to a dispute, in order to determine whether the continuance of the dispute or situation is likely to endanger the maintenance of international peace and security."

In practice the Security Council has not limited its powers of investigation to the extent prescribed in Article 34, but has rather sought to

[62] They were John Bassett Moore, Charles E. Hughes, Frank P. Kellogg, and Manley O. Hudson.

[63] See Leland M. Goodrich and Edvard Hambro, *Charter of the United Nations: Commentary and Documents* (1949), p. 237.

[64] *Ibid.,* p. 245.

discharge its duties in "accordance with the Purposes and Principles of the United Nations." [65] It is further provided that "any Member of the United Nations may bring any dispute, or any situation of the nature referred to in Article 34, to the attention of the Security Council or of the Assembly." [66] It will be remembered, however, that with respect to any *dispute* or *situation* referred to in Article 35, the Assembly and Council have unequal powers. While the General Assembly can discuss such matters, action can be taken only by the Security Council. And should the latter organ be engaged in the settlement of such dispute or situation, the Assembly may not even make recommendations in their regard.[67]

The procedure of determining whether a matter which is before the Security Council for consideration is a *dispute* or a *situation* has not yet been settled.[68] A logical distinction may nevertheless be made, and according to Goodrich and Hambro it is as follows:

A *dispute* can properly be considered as a disagreement or matter at issue between two or more states which has reached a stage at which the parties have formulated claims and counter-claims sufficiently definite to be passed upon by a court or other body set up for purposes of pacific settlement. A *situation*, by contrast, is a state of affairs which has not as yet assumed the nature of a conflict between parties but which may, though not necessarily, come to have that character.[69]

The Security Council may at any time make recommendation to the parties regarding appropriate procedures or methods of settlement of such disputes or situations as are mentioned in Article 33 of the Charter.[70] The Council, however, should take into consideration any procedure for peaceful settlement of the dispute which might already have been adopted by the parties.[71]

The International Court of Justice. As we have indicated earlier, one of the principal organs [72] of the United Nations is the International Court of Justice. Apart from certain minor modifications, the organization and powers of the present Court are very similar to those of its predecessor, the Permanent Court of International Justice. In the case of the present Court, however, the Statute has been made an "integral part" of the Charter of the United Nations.[73] Accordingly, "All Members of the United Nations are *ipso facto* parties to the Statute of the International Court

[65] Sec. 2, Art. 24. See also Goodrich and Hambro, *ibid.*, p. 245.
[66] Art. 35 of the Charter.   [67] See pp. 48–49.
[68] Goodrich and Hambro, *op. cit.*, p. 249.
[69] *Ibid.*, p. 249. Italics added.
[70] Art. 36, sec. 1.   [71] Art. 36, sec. 2, of the Charter.
[72] Art. 7, sec. 1, of the Charter.   [73] Art. 92 of the Charter.

of Justice." [74] The members of the new Court are elected by the General Assembly and the Security Council, from a list of persons nominated by the national groups in the Permanent Court of Arbitration.[75]

The competence and procedure of the International Court of Justice have been discussed in an earlier chapter, and in order to avoid unnecessary repetition, they will not be dealt with here. On the other hand, something needs be said concerning the function of the Court as an instrument for the settlement of international disputes. The remainder of the present chapter, therefore, will be devoted to an evaluation of the role the Court has played in this regard both before and after the revision of the Statute in 1945.

Evaluation of the Court in the Settlement of Disputes. In order to evaluate the contribution the International Court of Justice has made to the peaceful settlement of disputes since its establishment in 1922, it is necessary to consider its true place and function as an institution in the world community. It must indeed be admitted that in the total picture of international relations of the last thirty years, "the contribution of the Court to peace through the settlement of disputes does not loom large." [76] Yet, it cannot be denied that the Court, because of its greater political independence, is an improvement, from the standpoint of impartial justice, over tribunals of arbitration whose members are selected by the parties to the dispute. Considering the imperfect development of world organization, it would seem that the successes of the Court as an institution in providing legal remedies in disputes between nations are more remarkable than its failures.

Article 38 of the Statute provides that it is the function of the Court "to decide in accordance with international law such disputes as are submitted to it." But this species of law, it will be remembered, is of primitive development both in substance and sanctions as compared with municipal ordinances of internally sovereign states. The layman's unfamiliarity with this fact has led to a great deal of misunderstanding as to the nature and function of the International Court of Justice.

It must be clearly understood that the jurisdiction of the Court, in cases of international disputes, is in the final analysis based upon the consent of the parties. Such consent may be given by various means, of which the following are examples: (1) by a declaration recognizing as compulsory the jurisdiction of the Court, with or without limitations, under the "optional clause" of the Statute; [77] (2) by recognition of compulsory

[74] Art. 93, sec. 1, of the Charter.
[75] Art. 4, sec. 1, of the Statute of the Court.
[76] Oliver J. Lissitzyn, *The International Court of Justice,* United Nations Studies, no. 6, p. 98.
[77] See Art. 36 of the Statute of the Court.

jurisdiction of the Court by some other means with respect to existing or future disputes; and (3) by an express or tacit agreement between states to submit a particular dispute to the Court for judicial settlement. Proposals to invest the Court with obligatory jurisdiction were rejected no less vigorously in 1945 than in 1920, largely through the insistence of the larger states.

In the vanguard of opposition to compulsory jurisdiction at San Francisco were the United States and the Soviet Union. The unwillingness of the two most powerful states in the world to accept compulsory jurisdiction of the Court should have been clear evidence, even then, that the world was more than "one."

The reasons for the opposition to compulsory jurisdiction on the part of the United States and the Soviet Union explain to a great extent the position of the International Court of Justice in the present world. According to S. B. Krylov, former Soviet member of the present Court: "The U.S.S.R. was guided by the necessity of defending the interest of the socialist state, the United States was apprehensive of opposition in the Senate." [78] The Soviet position appears to derive from a theory that all law is an instrumentality of power in the hands of the ruling class, and that the basically opposed policies of the Soviet and the capitalist states are such as to make an impartial adjudication of disputes between them virtually impossible.[79] Accordingly, the Soviet Union has refused to subscribe to compulsory jurisdiction under the "optional clause" and has frequently opposed judicial means to resolve disputes with respect to treaty provisions.

The United States, on the other hand, by a declaration communicated to the Secretary-General of the United Nations of August 14, 1946, recognized as compulsory *ipso facto* the jurisdiction of the International Court of Justice. The jurisdiction thus conferred, however, is narrowly limited by reservations. These reservations provided, *inter alia*, that the declaration regarding compulsory jurisdiction

shall not apply to disputes with regard to matters which are essentially within the domestic jurisdiction of the United States of America as determined by the United States of America; or disputes arising under a multilateral treaty, unless (1) all parties to the treaty affected by the decision are also parties to the case before the Court, or (2) the United States of America specially agrees to jurisdiction.[80]

John Foster Dulles, who suggested these reservations to the Foreign

[78] For Russian sources, see Lissitzyn, *op. cit.*, p. 63n.
[79] *Ibid.*, p. 63.
[80] Manley O. Hudson, "The Twenty-fifth Year of the World Court," *American Journal of International Law*, vol. 41 (1947), p. 12.

Relations Committee of the Senate, argued that "it would be reckless to proceed precipitately." He also contended that the Court "has yet to win the confidence of the world community" and that "international law has not yet developed the scope and definiteness necessary to permit international disputes generally to be resolved by judicial rather than political tests." [81]

Notwithstanding these reservations, the United States in a letter to the Secretary-General of the United Nations was said to "look forward to a great development of the rule of law in international relations through a broad acceptance of the function of the Court in the spirit of the Charter." [82] Thus is illustrated how wide sometimes the discrepancy is between language and action in diplomacy.

It must indeed be admitted that the usefulness of the Court as an organ for peaceful settlement of international disputes is subject to severe limitations. This is so not only because of an iron curtain dividing the peoples of the earth but equally because certain conflicts cannot be terminated by judicial means. In the history of the Court, examples are not lacking to show that conflicts have persisted in spite of decisions in consequence of judicial proceedings with respect to the issues involved. In 1931, for example, the Permanent Court of International Justice held the proposed customs union between Austria and Germany illegal in terms of Austrian treaty obligations. Notwithstanding this decision, political agitation in both countries regarding this matter continued and was finally to culminate in the *Anschluss* of 1938. Likewise, an advisory opinion of the Court in 1931 to the effect that Lithuania was under no obligation to reopen railroad communication with Poland [83] was undone by Polish power politics seven years later.

At the very beginning of this chapter we took occasion to introduce the terms *justiciable* and *nonjusticiable* disputes, and at that point promised to differentiate between them. While no clear-cut distinction between the two types of disputes can, in fact, be made, an explanation is nevertheless in order.

According to Article 36 of the Statute of the International Court of Justice, disputes of a legal or justiciable nature are set forth as belonging to the following four categories: (1) those which concern the interpreta-

---

[81] Mr. Dulles also proposed to except "disputes where the law necessary for decision is not found in existing treaties and conventions to which the United States is a party and where there has not been prior agreement by the United States as to the applicable principles of international law." *Hearings before the Senate Committee on Foreign Relations on Compulsory Jurisdiction, International Court of Justice*, July 11, 12, and 15, 1946. See Lissitzyn, *op. cit.*, p. 65n.

[82] See Hudson, "The Twenty-fifth Year of the World Court."

[83] *PCIJ Publications*, ser. A/B, no. 42.

tion of a treaty; (2) any question of international law; (3) the existence of a fact which, if established, would constitute a breach of an international obligation; and (4) the nature or extent of the reparation to be made for the breach of an international obligation.[84]

In the years following the First World War, the distinction between justiciable and nonjusticiable disputes was abandoned in a number of treaties. A treaty between France and Luxembourg in 1927, for example, provided that "all disputes" between the contracting parties, "of whatever origin," which could not be settled by ordinary diplomacy should be submitted "for judgment either to the arbitral tribunal or to the Permanent Court of International Justice." [85] The so-called *Locarno formula,* apart from the categories enumerated in Article 13 of the League Covenant (which are the same as those in Article 36 of the Statute of the Court given above) defined as justiciable "All disputes of whatever kind . . . with regard to which the parties make a claim of right one against the other." [86]

It is perhaps quite correct to say that all disputes contain both legal and political elements in varying proportions. The question, therefore, of whether a given dispute is justiciable is, in terms of the present development of international law and organization, dependent on the view taken by the contending parties. "If they all feel that the dispute can be effectively terminated by the application of legal standards, it is 'legal,' but if at least one of them does not share this attitude, the dispute must be regarded as primarily 'political.'" [87]

During the period between the two great wars, at least thirty of the judgments and advisory opinions of the Court were related to the peace treaties ending the First World War. Though the Court had to function pretty much within the framework of the peace settlement, it nevertheless demonstrated considerable judicial independence. This was evidenced, for example, in the cases involving the rights of the German settlers in Poland, in which the judgments were favorable to the erstwhile enemy.

Even though the activity of the Court as an organ for the settlement of international disputes has not been of a spectacular nature, it would be difficult to deny that it has in a number of instances contributed to the relaxation of tension between nations. In the *Corfu Channel Case,*[88] in-

[84] Since these four categories were included in the Statute of the Permanent Court of International Justice (Art. 36), a number of postwar treaties also listed them among the disputes which were to be considered as justiciable.
[85] See Max Habicht, *Post-war Treaties for the Pacific Settlement of International Disputes* (1931), p. 975.
[86] *Ibid.*, p. 973.
[87] Lissitzyn, *op. cit.*, p. 74.
[88] *Corfu Channel Case*, Judgment of Apr. 9, 1949, *ICJ Reports*, p. 100.

volving a dispute between Great Britain and the People's Republic of Albania, the Court served to eliminate at least one symbol of the widening gulf between the Soviet world and the Atlantic powers. No veto could block the adjudication of the International Court of Justice.[89] "Nor did the judgment of the Court, on the whole unfavorable to Albania, become a butt of Communist propaganda and for accusations of imperialist bullying." [90]

The Court's major significance is to be found in its long-range effects, not only as an instrument for the settlement of international disputes, but also as a means to a clearer definition and refinement of the law of nations.

[89] Lissitzyn, *op. cit.*, p. 100.
[90] *Ibid.*

CHAPTER 20

Problems of Collective Security

THE GREAT SCHISM AND THE NORTH ATLANTIC TREATY ORGANIZATION

The existence of a world community, however primitive in development, is the underlying presumption upon which the present treatise is based. It was the special concern of the first five chapters and has been the recurring theme in others. It is in terms of this community that we have sought to understand the law of nations, not only as to its origin but also as to its nature and function.

No part of the human race has wholly escaped the cataclysmic effects of the technological revolution. Consequently the secular trend has been in the direction of a more complex administrative and legal organization in an effort to meet the needs of a world which is becoming more and more interdependent. The mental and emotional climate of these times, however, is, in many respects, unfavorable to effective international-legal organization and administration.

Opinion with respect to the United Nations and other international institutions is divided. Some contend that the present ideological conflict between the Soviet world and the West precludes the effectiveness of any such organization on a universal basis, while others argue that nothing short of world government backed by a central force can provide security and peace. Still others hold that the universal approach to the problem is essential and must be pursued in so far as it is possible, but being mindful also of the virility of modern nationalism, they would resort to regional consolidations within the general framework of the United Nations Organization.

The Failure of Collective Security. The failure of the League of Nations to preserve the peace resulted in the massive tragedy of a second world-wide conflict, while the scars of the first yet remained. Techno-logical advances in the present century created new engines of war, but a

305

superior policy in international relations with respect to economics and politics was lacking. Thus the necessary conditions for a more effective legal order were not allowed to develop.

The Second World War not only demonstrated the failure of collective security on a universal basis, but gave rise to many new problems. The instability of the present international situation is the result of a multitude of complex factors which are clearly beyond the scope of this treatise. It is obvious, however, that the legal structure and organization of regional systems cannot be fully understood except against the background of historic forces that shape the destinies of nations. It is the power politics of a world divided by conflicting ideologies which make collective security, on a universal basis, a precarious means to lasting peace.

Soviet Theory of International Law. International law in the view of Soviet legal theorists is of a character based on the class structure of society. "International public law is the sum-total of legal norms governing rights and duties of collectivities of the ruling classes—participants in international intercourse." [1]

Contemporary international law, according to the Soviet concept, may also be defined as *"a provisional inter-class law which aims to further the interests of organized national laboring classes in their common struggle for proletarian world supremacy."* [2] Its provisional nature is predicated upon the eventual and certain triumph of the proletarian revolution in every country. In this manner, then, international legal theory is accommodated to the political strategy of world revolution.

It would seem that the dichotomy which now exists between the Soviet world and the countries of the West, with respect to the theory of international law, would preclude any agreement which involves the application of international-legal norms. This may not, however, be the case. It is quite possible that a limited number of such norms could be applied in regard to problems of a nonpolitical or technical character such as the prevention of epidemics; preservation of monuments of antiquity and works of art; and postal, telegraphic, and aviation agreements.

It is clear that the genera of international law in communist jurisprudence emerge from the dialectical materialism of Marx and Lenin. To the Marxists, law is an organic phenomenon, reflecting the potential forces of labor. It can be understood only in terms of historical materialism, which teaches that economic forces are the real bases of all social phenomena. Thus, the nature of any legal system, according to Communist theory, is not determined by the rational processes of the mind or by

---

[1] Chakste, "Soviet Concepts of the State, International Law and Sovereignty," *American Journal of International Law*, vol. 43 (1949), p. 26.

[2] T. A. Taracouzio, *The Soviet Union and International Law* (1935), p. 12.

the idealism of universal justice, but is rooted in the economic factors of any social order. It would seem clear, therefore, that to understand fully the Soviet position regarding international law, one must take into account the philisophical basis of communism itself. The fact that students of this philosophy can point to numerous inconsistencies in the teachings of its great exponents, is, in this connection, of minor significance; for it cannot be maintained that new revelations must necessarily reduce the force of dogma. The application of "Soviet international law" during the so-called "transition period" [3] is dependent upon norms which can be laid down only as an expedient and temporary compromise between the Western conception and that of the Soviet world.

The Great Problem. It was the hope of the greater part of mankind that, by means of collective security under the Charter of the United Nations, the splendid resolutions of its Preamble could be translated into reality. But the bitter ideological conflict between the Soviet world and the countries of the West has obscured the luster of this hope by a tarnish of suspicion and fear. Thus the failure of the nations, following the Second World War, to create the necessary basis for collective security on a universal level and consequently a more effective legal order must be regarded as a notorious fact.

To ascribe the present dilemma wholly to the lack of international law and organization, however, would be to put the cart before the horse. The answer can be found only in the obvious lack of consensus with regard to the solution of important problems and issues. But such a consensus, in turn, is dependent upon a degree of world community not yet achieved. Thus the dichotomy in legal theory and practice between the "two worlds" must be regarded as no less a result than a cause of our difficulties.

To blame the United Nations for the unsuccessful resolution of this conflict is to misunderstand its powers under the Charter. The present Organization, like the League of Nations, is nothing more than an association of independent states, based on the "sovereign equality of all its Members." [4] One can, of course, argue on philosophical grounds that the present world is in *need* of a stronger organization than that provided by the Charter of the United Nations, but standing in the way of such a union of states is the particularism which modern nationalism has so greatly strengthened. There can be no doubt that even among the countries of the West the forces which unify are greatly outweighed by the

---

[3] The period which, according to Soviet theory, intervenes between the beginning of the Russian Communist Revolution in 1917 and the eventual triumph of communism in all the countries of the world.

[4] Art. 2, par. 1, of the Charter.

forces which divide their aspirations. But what of a "union now" among the English-speaking peoples? Surely, here is a common basis in culture and language, which many have argued is essential to the success of such a project. Yet, the lessons of recent history [5] lead us to the inescapable conclusion that, even here, the popular consensus would, at this moment, oppose political union. This is not to say that within the British Commonwealth of Nations or, indeed, in the whole of the English-speaking world the basic forces which unify are necessarily on the decline. On the contrary, as we have said in an earlier chapter, it seems clear that here, at least, there is a conscious realization that continued peace and friendly relations can best promote mutual advantage and secure common interests.

The North Atlantic Treaty Organization. Had the United Nations in the early years of its existence proved an effective instrument of collective security, the Atlantic Pact might never have come into being.[6] The failure of the UN in this respect should not be attributed to any serious fault in the organization itself. Rather it was due to the wilful refusal of the Soviet Union to cooperate in the implementation of the Charter. The great schism which developed between the Western nations and the Soviet world must be regarded as the main reason for the "cold war" and the consequent failure of collective security on a universal level.

The North Atlantic Treaty [7] was signed by 12 nations [8] on April 4, 1949, in the capital of the United States, and came into force on August 24 of the same year.[9] The main purposes of this arrangement, as set forth in its Preamble, are to preserve "peace and security" and to unite for "collective defense." The parties "are determined to safeguard the freedom, common heritage and civilization of their peoples, founded on the principles of democracy, individual liberty and the rule of law."

Two questions have been raised regarding the North Atlantic Treaty Organization: (1) Is it a system of collective security as contemplated by the Charter of the United Nations? (2) Is it, in the same sense, a

[5] Consider, for example, the Statute of Westminster of 1931 which gave full autonomous statehood to the British Dominions by removing the remnants of their former dependence upon the Imperial Parliament in London. Thus the movement which established the British Commonwealth was in the direction of less rather than more political unification of a large segment of the English-speaking world.

[6] Walter S. Surrey, "The Emerging Structure of Collective Security Arrangements: The North Atlantic Treaty," *American Society of International Law, Proceedings* (1950), p. 9.

[7] *American Journal of International Law*, vol. 43 (1949), Official Documents, pp. 159–162.

[8] Belgium, Canada, Denmark, France, Iceland, Italy, Luxembourg, the Netherlands, Norway, Portugal, United Kingdom, and the United States of America.

[9] Department of State Publication 3497, General Foreign Policy Series 10, June, 1949.

regional system? The answer to the first question, as is readily seen, is dependent upon what is understood by the term *collective security*. Some writers hold that collective security must be of a universal character to be worthy of the name. The present author takes exception to this view, holding that collective security may be achieved in different degrees and through different levels of organization.[10] But if a system of collective security is to be something more than an alliance under a different name, it must be open to any would-be participant and must not be directed against any specific power. It must be defensive rather than offensive in character. The North Atlantic Treaty, in a strictly legal sense, is not in conflict with these criteria of collective security, as far as internal organization is concerned. The first sentence of Article 10 of the treaty reads: "The Parties may, by unanimous agreement, invite any other European state in a position to further the principles of the treaty and to contribute to the security of the North Atlantic area to accede to this Treaty." [11]

But is the North Atlantic Pact a *regional* arrangement in the true sense of that term? It has been pointed out that regions are not necessarily confined to land areas, for oceans are links rather than barriers between nations.[12] Though this is true, it has no application here, since the Organization is not confined to North Atlantic powers but includes, aside from the French Algerian departments, such countries as Italy, Greece, and Turkey. Though the inclusion of new states tends to enhance the collective-security aspects of the system, its geographic regionalism is correspondingly destroyed. To maintain, therefore, that the North Atlantic Treaty Organization has a regional character is no less incorrect than to say it is not a system of collective security [13] with respect to its internal affairs. Externally, it is a system of self-defense, or an alliance.

Though the North Atlantic Treaty Organization is a system of collective security on a nonuniversal basis, it is not a regional system, and does not fall within the compass of Chapter VIII of the Charter of the United

[10] On this point, see Georg Schwarzenberger, *Power Politics, a Study of International Society* (1951), p. 493.

[11] Nevertheless, it is perhaps more accurate to say that regional or nonuniversal organizations such as the Organization of American States and the North Atlantic Treaty Organization are systems of collective security only with respect to their internal relations. But in so far as they are directed against other states and systems of states, they must be considered in the familiar category of military alliances.

[12] Schwarzenberger, *op. cit.*, p. 521.

[13] The idea that collective security and self-defense arrangements necessarily must fall into regional patterns is rapidly becoming obsolete. Geography, in so far as it is a space concept, has very little meaning in the modern world. It is common interests with respect to certain vital issues and problems rather than geographic regionalism, per se, which determine the association of nations. Regionalism occurs only when geography and vital interests coincide, and this is as yet sometimes the case.

Nations.[14] Since the primary intention of the treaty was to establish a system of collective self-defense, its legal basis under the Charter must be found in Article 51. It should be pointed out, however, that this is by no means a unanimous opinion, especially in the United States. This situation is partly due to conflicting, though authoritative, statements made before the Foreign Relations Committee of the Senate. Secretary Acheson told this committee that the treaty was based on Article 51 exclusively, whereas Ambassador Austin asserted that it was "not necessary to define the organization of the North Atlantic community as exclusively a regional arrangement, or as exclusively a group for collective self-defense, since activities under both Article 51 and Chapter VIII are comprehended in the Treaty." [15]

But was it not the intention of the parties to avoid making the North Atlantic Treaty Organization a regional arrangement as defined in Chapter VIII of the Charter? If it were such an arrangement or agency, it would not be able to undertake any enforcement action without previous authorization, except against an enemy state, as defined in Article 53, paragraph 2, of the Charter. The pact had to be based on Article 51 in order to give its signatories an amount of freedom of action which is comparable to that of the parties to the Eastern treaties of mutual assistance. The overriding consideration of the parties, it would seem, was to create a system of collective self-defense which would not be rendered impotent by the combination of Articles 53 and 27 of the Charter. The only way this could be done, without by-passing the Charter altogether, was to establish a system of collective self-defense in conformity with Article 51, rather than a regional arrangement or agency as provided for in Chapter VIII and rendered nugatory by Article 27 of the Charter.

The elements of collective self-defense, contemplated by the North Atlantic Treaty, are illustrated in Article 5 as follows:

> The Parties agree that an armed attack against one or more of them in Europe or North America shall be considered an attack against them all; and consequently they agree that, if such an armed attack occurs, each of them in exercise of the right of individual or collective self-defense recognized by Article 51 of the Charter of the United Nations, will assist the Party or Parties so attacked by taking forthwith, individually and in concert with the other Parties, such

[14] Cf. Mr. Bevin's remark before the British Parliament: "The Treaty is not a regional arrangement under Chapter VIII of the Charter." On the same point, Secretary Acheson testified before the Foreign Relations Committee of the United States Senate to the effect that the treaty was not a regional arrangement but one of collective self-defense based on Art. 51 of the Charter of the United Nations. See Heindel, Kalijarvi, and Wilcox, "The North Atlantic Treaty in the United States Senate," *American Journal of International Law*, vol. 43 (1949), p. 638 and p. 639n.

[15] *Ibid.*, p. 638.

action as it deems necessary, including the use of armed force, to restore and maintain the security of the North Atlantic area.

The organizational pattern of NATO has had a rather haphazard development. In the beginning it was planned merely as a regional alliance of self-defence in which the United States was again to function as the arsenal of the free nations. The main air strength and a substantial part of the naval power would also be provided by the United States along with Great Britain, while France would furnish the manpower on land.

Originally, the chief coordinating agency of the organization consisted of the North Atlantic Council, established in conformity with Article 9 of the treaty. Among the permanent agencies of the organization the most important is the Committee of Deputies of the Ministers of Defence, which was established at the Paris meeting of the North Atlantic Council in July, 1950. Its work was chiefly concerned with the coordination of military and economic matters. Prior to February, 1952, the seat of this committee was in London with an American as chairman.

A number of permanent agencies were added to the organization from time to time, such as the Joint Production Board, the Control Commodity Group, and the Defence Shipping Authority. As a result, by the middle of 1951 the structure of NATO had become much too complex for efficient administration. Accordingly, an agency with over-all authority was established known as the Temporary Council Committee, composed of the so-called "Three Wise Men"—W. Averell Harriman of the United States, Sir Edwin Plowden of the United Kingdom, and Jean Monnet of France. But as this reorganization was only partially satisfactory, more basic reforms were undertaken at the Lisbon meeting of the Atlantic Council in February, 1952.[16]

The reorganization of NATO in conformity with the Lisbon decision involved the creation of a Permanent Council with a Secretary General. The North Atlantic Council continues, however, to be the highest authority. After much debate, the permanent Headquarters of the North Atlantic Treaty Organization was finally established in Paris. This is logical enough, as the French capital is also the home of the Supreme Headquarters of the Atlantic Forces in Europe.

THE AMERICAN AND SOVIET SECURITY SYSTEMS

The grim realities of the postwar situation have made it clear that collective security on a universal basis must necessarily fail in the absence

[16] Karl Loewenstein, "The Union of Western Europe: Illusion and Reality II. An Appraisal of the Motives," *Columbia Law Review*, vol. 52 (1952), p. 222.

of genuine cooperation among the so-called "great powers." The cleavage between the Soviet world and the countries of the West has made the Security Council of the United Nations an unreliable instrument of collective security. This unhappy situation has led to new efforts along regional lines in order to achieve a measure of security in an age of power politics.

The Organization of American States. It is in the Western Hemisphere that the oldest regional security system is found. Its origin may be traced to the Panama Conference of 1826, called by Simon Bolivar, and to the adoption in that year of a "Treaty of Perpetual Union." But it was not until 1889 that James Gillespie Blaine called the first of a series of Conferences of American States, which has continued ever since. The Pan American Union was created at that time, though its legal status and function were not well defined until 1929.[17]

The roots of the Organization of American States are deeply lodged in history; but it cannot be denied that the growth of this regional system has been characterized by much wasted motion. As we have noted in an earlier chapter, many treaties were enacted which never came into force for lack of ratification or for other reasons. Innumerable conferences were held which were little more than social functions with few tangible results. There have been in the past many curious efforts by the American states to build what might be called a *separate* "league of nations," and to create a *special kind* of "international law." These movements in the history of inter-American relations were motivated by a common desire to live a life apart from the turbulent affairs of the rest of mankind. The isolationism of the Americas, however, seemed determined by geography, rather than by a close cultural affinity within the region itself. But in recent years, it has become clear that such attempts, by a segment of European culture, to build a separate world ran counter to the basic trends in international organization. At the Havana conference of 1929, therefore, these separatist ideas appear to have been defeated.[18]

The Charter of Bogota, which came into force with the deposit of ratification by the fourteenth state on December 13, 1951, not only gave to the inter-American system a treaty basis; but the resolution-supported Union of American Republics by this action was succeeded by the Organization of American States.

The Bogota Charter defines the American community as a "regional agency" within the United Nations, which is to be known henceforth as the Organization of American States. Its structure as set forth in the

---

[17] J. L. Kunz, "The Pan American Union in the Field of International Administration," *Iowa Law Review* (1945), p. 31.
[18] Clyde Eagleton, *International Government* (1948), p. 462.

Charter comprises the following six organs: (1) the Inter-American Conference, (2) the Meeting of Consultation of Ministers of Foreign Affairs, (3) the Council, (4) the Pan American Union, (5) the Specialized Conferences, and (6) the Specialized Organizations.

The only new name which appears in the reorganization is the Council, which is substantially the old Governing Board of the Pan American Union. It is composed of one representative from each member state and acts as a permanent executive committee of the Conference and the Meeting of Consultation. The Council also acts in a supervisory capacity with reference to the specialized agencies and facilitates and coordinates their activities. Article 52 of the Charter of Bogota provides that the Council is to serve provisionally as Organ of Consultation, in accordance with Article 12 of the Rio Treaty of 1947.[19]

American Regionalism and the United Nations. The American republics for more than half a century have been cooperating rather successfully through the Pan American Union. A regional system for collective security had come into being in the Western Hemisphere and was a going concern even before the establishment of the United Nations. It is not surprising, therefore, to find that the relation of the Inter-American System to the larger world organization was a subject of much discussion at San Francisco.

With respect to this problem, the Inter-American Conference on War and Peace, which met in Mexico City in 1945, had adopted the following resolution: [20]

The American Republics are determined to cooperate with one another and with other peace loving nations in the establishment of a General International Organization based upon law, justice, and equity.

The American Republics desire to make their full contribution, individually and by common action in and through the Inter-American System, effectively coordinating and harmonizing that System with the general international organization for the realization of the latter's objectives.

Regional arrangements for the promotion of peace and security among nations are not without precedent in the history of international organization. Under the Covenant of the League, regional combinations were recognized, such as the Little Entente and the Balkan Entente, as well as the Pacts of Locarno. A more ambitious project along the same line

---

[19] For complete treatment of the reorganization of the Union of American Republics under the Charter of Bogota, see Josef L. Kunz, "The Bogota Charter of the Organization of American States," *American Journal of International Law*, vol. 42 (1948), pp. 568–589.

[20] Resolution XXX, Inter-American Conference on Problems of War and Peace, Mexico City, 1945.

was Aristide Briand's proposal in 1930 for European Union.[21] Thus the recognition in the Charter of the United Nations of "the existence of regional arrangements or agencies for dealing with . . . matters relating to the maintenance of international peace and security"[22] is consonant with historic reality.

Though ultimate responsibility for the maintenance of peace rests with the Security Council of the United Nations, primary responsibility for the settlement of local disputes is left to regional agencies: "The Members of the United Nations entering into such arrangements or constituting such agencies shall make every effort to achieve pacific settlement of local disputes through such regional arrangements or by such regional agencies before referring them to the Security Council."[23]

But with respect to the preservation of peace and the protection of its peoples and institutions, the Organization of American States has an external as well as an internal purpose. According to the Act of Chapultepec: "The security and solidarity of the Continent are affected to the same extent by an act of aggression against any of the American States by a non-American State, as by an American State against one or more American States."[24] This aspect of the inter-American system is no less clearly illustrated in the Rio Pact, or, as it is officially known, the Inter-American Treaty of Reciprocal Assistance of 1947.[25] Article III, paragraph 1, of this treaty provides as follows:

The High Contracting Parties agree that an armed attack by any State against an American State shall be considered as an attack against all the American States and, consequently, each one of the said Contracting Parties undertakes to assist in meeting the attack in the exercise of the inherent right of individual and collective self-defense recognized by Article 51 of the Charter of the United Nations.[26]

Though recognizing the "inherent right of self-defense," Article 51 of the Charter makes it mandatory that "measures taken by Members in the exercise of this right . . . shall be immediately reported to the

[21] Leland M. Goodrich and Edvard Hambro, *Charter of the United Nations, Commentary and Documents* (1949), pp. 309–310.

[22] Art. 52, par. 1.

[23] Art. 52, par. 2.

[24] The Act of Chapultepec, Resolution 7, *Department of State Bulletin*, Mar. 4, 1945.

[25] Department of State Publication 3016, International Organization and Conference Series II, American Republics 1, *Inter-American Conferences for the Maintenance of Continental Peace and Security*, pp. 59 ff.

[26] Art. 51 provides that "nothing in the present Charter shall impair the inherent right of individual or collective self-defense if an armed attack occurs against a Member of the United Nations, until the Security Council has taken the measures necessary to maintain international peace and security. . . ."

Security Council and shall not in any way affect the authority and responsibility of the Security Council . . . to take at any time such action as it deems necessary. . . ."

The obligation under the Charter to notify the Security Council is recognized by Article V of the Rio Pact, which provides that

The High Contracting Parties shall immediately send to the Security Council of the United Nations, in conformity with Articles 51 and 54 of the Charter of the United Nations, complete information concerning the activities undertaken or in contemplation in the exercise of the right of self-defense or for the purpose of maintaining inter-American peace and security.[27]

With respect to enforcement action, it is provided in Article 53 of the Charter that

the Security Council shall, where appropriate, utilize such regional arrangements or agencies for enforcement action under its authority. But no enforcement action shall be taken under regional arrangements or by regional agencies without the authorization of the Security Council, with the exception of measures against any enemy state, as defined in paragraph 2.

The definition in paragraph 2 of the same Article is as follows: "The term enemy state as used in paragraph 1 of this Article applies to any state which during the Second World War has been an enemy of any signatory of the present Charter."

Thus it appears that, when Article 53 is taken together with Article 27 of the Charter,[28] it is possible for any one of the permanent members of the Security Council to block enforcement action under regional agreements, unless such action is taken against an enemy state, as provided by the exception clause in paragraph 1 and defined in paragraph 2 of Article 53.

But the Declaration in the Act of Chapultepec provided that

in case acts of aggression occur or there may be reason to believe that an aggression is being prepared by any other State against the integrity and inviolability of the territory, or against the sovereignty or political independence of an American State, the States signatory to this declaration will consult amongst themselves in order to agree upon measures it may be advisable to take.

[27] The language of Art. 54 runs as follows: "The Security Council shall at all times be kept fully informed of activities undertaken or in contemplation under regional arrangements or by regional agencies for the maintenance of international peace and security."

[28] Art. 27, pars. 2 and 3, provides: "Decisions of the Security Council on procedural matters shall be made by an affirmative vote of seven members. Decisions of the Security Council on all other matters shall be made by an affirmative vote of seven members including the concurring votes of the permanent members. . . ."

It was further provided in the same Declaration that any such "threats and acts of aggression" would be met by the application of various sanctions, including the "use of armed force." Under the heading of "recommendations," the Act of Chapultepec provided that an inter-American treaty should be concluded which would establish procedures whereby acts of aggression against any American state could be met by collective sanctions, including armed force.

The conflict between the Dumbarton Oaks–Yalta formula, upon which Articles 53 and 27 of the Charter were based, and the Act of Chapultepec became obvious at San Francisco. Unless something were done to resolve this situation, the collective-security system of the Americas would collapse under the veto. This impasse led to a new formula designed to save the inter-American security system, which is today embodied in Article 51 of the Charter of the United Nations. That article reads as follows:

Nothing in the present Charter shall impair the inherent right of individual or collective self-defense if an armed attack occurs against a Member of the United Nations, until the Security Council has taken the measures necessary to maintain international peace and security. Measures taken by Members in the exercise of this right of self-defense shall be immediately reported to the Security Council and shall not in any way affect the authority and responsibility of the Security Council under the present Charter to take at any time such action as it deems necessary in order to maintain or restore international peace and security.

In view of the difficulties yet standing in the way of collective security on a universal level, the importance of Article 51 of the Charter can hardly be overestimated. Without this formula of regional self-defense, any one of the permanent members of the Security Council would indeed have an unlimited right under the Charter to prevent any collective defense organization against its own possible aggression. It is significant to note that the Soviet Union was well aware of this loophole in the Charter and consented reluctantly to the inclusion of Article 51.[29]

The Rio Pact of 1947. The first collective security agreement to be made under Article 51 of the Charter of the United Nations was the Inter-American Treaty of Reciprocal Assistance of September 2, 1947.[30] As we have already seen, the Inter-American Conference on Problems of War and Peace, held in Mexico City in 1945, had recommended that the governments of the American republics, in accordance with their constitutional processes, should consider the conclusion of such an agreement in order to meet threats or acts of aggression. More than two years

[29] See John Foster Dulles, *War or Peace* (1950), pp. 90–91.
[30] Department of State Publication 3016, pp. 59 ff.

had elapsed since Chapultepec when the Inter-American Conference for the Maintenance of Peace and Security met in the Brazilian capital to draft the treaty, popularly known as the Rio Pact.

This instrument of "reciprocal assistance" is open to all American states, and by its terms the area of the Americas was charted to include both Greenland and Canada.[31] The region as delimited by Article IV of the pact extends from pole to pole and includes substantial parts of the high seas adjacent to the American continents. The treaty binds the members to participate in an "Organ of Consultation" which, in the event of aggression against any American state, by two-thirds majority could decide on what measures should be taken.[32] Such measures might include the severance of diplomatic and consular relations; partial or complete interruption of economic relations and all means of communications; and finally, the use of armed force.[33] Decisions with respect to these measures are "binding upon all the Signatory States" which have ratified the treaty, "with the sole exception that no State shall be required to use armed force without its consent." [34]

If the inviolability or the integrity of the territory or the sovereignty or political independence of any American State should be affected by an aggression which is not an armed attack or by an extra-continental or intra-continental conflict, or by any other fact or situation that might endanger the peace of America, the Organ of Consultation shall meet immediately in order to agree on the measures which must be taken . . . for the common defense and for the maintenance of the peace and security of the Continent.[35]

In case of conflict between two or more American states, the treaty provides, "without prejudice to the right of self-defense in conformity with Article 51 of the Charter of the United Nations," that the parties to the treaty meeting in consultation shall call upon the contending states to suspend hostilities and restore matters to the *status quo ante bellum.* "The rejection of the pacifying action will be considered in the determination of the aggressor and in the application of the measures which the consultative meeting may agree upon." [36]

In the history of inter-American relations, the Rio Pact was a significant step. Unlike the unilateral Monroe Doctrine, this treaty is a multilateral agreement of equal partners by which an integrated system of regional security has been established. It is significant, also, because it was the

---

[31] This in spite of the fact that neither Denmark (the sovereign of Greenland) nor the Dominion of Canada were parties to the pact.

[32] Art. XVII provides: "The Organ of Consultation shall take its decisions by a vote of two-thirds of the Signatory States which have ratified the Treaty."

[33] Art. VIII.   [34] Art. XX.

[35] Art. VI.   [36] Art. VII.

first such security pact to be made in pursuance of Article 51 of the Charter of the United Nations and thus became a precedent for other regional security arrangements to follow.

The Soviet System of Collective Security. Because of an unfortunate gap in the Charter, by which any of the permanent members of the Security Council can prevent the application of sanctions against itself or any other state, collective-security agreements have, as we have already seen, been negotiated on a regional or nonuniversal basis. The legal dichotomy between the Soviet world and the nations of the West, which was explored in the first part of this chapter, is no less evident in the approach of the "two worlds" to the problem of collective security. While the Western system is based on multilateral agreements, the Soviet organization has been established through a series of bilateral treaties.[37] These bilateral agreements not only involve the Soviet Union and her satellites directly, by establishing the lines that lead to Moscow, but these lines are crossed, like a spider's web, by similar treaties linking *inter se* the "people's democracies." Thus the bilateral form of these treaties in no way constitutes an impediment to the complete integration of the Soviet system. With the elimination of seven Yugoslav treaties, which have now been denounced, the framework of organization consists of 17 instruments of mutual assistance. To these should be added the Soviet–Outer Mongolian Treaty of Mar. 12, 1936, and the Soviet-Chinese Treaty of Feb. 14, 1950.

The bilateral treaties of the Soviet system are ostensibly directed against Germany and so find legal sanction under Article 107 of the Charter of the United Nations.[38] But as Kulski has pointed out, the language of the various agreements is general enough to make possible the application of sanctions against states other than those who were enemies in the Second World War, as provided by Article 107 and the exception clause in Article 53 of the Charter of the United Nations.[39]

Article 3 of the Soviet-Czechoslovak treaty reads as follows: [40]

[37] "On Mar. 31, 1949, the Soviet Union was bound by treaties of mutual assistance with the following states: Czechoslovakia (Dec. 12, 1943), Yugoslavia (Apr. 11, 1945), Poland (Apr. 21, 1945), Rumania (Feb. 4, 1948), Hungary (Feb. 18, 1948), Bulgaria (Mar. 18, 1948), and Finland (Apr. 6, 1948)"—W. W. Kulski, "The Soviet System of Collective Security Compared with the Western System," *American Journal of International Law*, vol. 44 (1950), p. 454.

[38] This article reads as follows: "Nothing in the present Charter shall invalidate or preclude action, in relation to any state which during the Second World War has been an enemy of any signatory to the present Charter, taken or authorized as a result of that war by the Governments having responsibility for such action."

[39] Kulski, *op. cit.*, pp. 455–456.

[40] For English text of treaties in the Soviet-European system, see Department of State, *Documents and State Papers*, vol. 1, no. 4 (1948), pp. 227–249, and vol. 1, nos. 12 and 13 (1949), pp. 681–689 and 727.

Affirming their pre-war policy and mutual assistance, expressed in the treaty signed at Prague on May 16, 1935, the High Contracting Parties, in case one of them in the period after the war should become involved in military action with Germany, which might resume its policy of *"Drang nach Osten,"* or with any other State which might join with Germany directly or in any other form in such a war, engage to extend immediately to the other Contracting Party thus involved in military action all manner of military and other support and assistance at its disposal.

It is significant that none of the Soviet treaties contains a reservation clause, such as is found in all the Western security arrangements, to the effect that the Security Council of the United Nations is to be notified of any action taken under a given agreement and that such action is to be terminated as soon as the Security Council takes measures necessary to restore peace and security. The parties, under the Soviet agreements, pledge each other unconditional assistance without any reference to the controlling powers of the Security Council.[41] If the Soviet treaties could be said to have application only to Germany, notification, of the type mandatory under Article 51, would not be required. But in so far as the Soviet treaties are directed against states other than Germany or any other "enemy state" as defined above, these treaties can find no legal basis in either Article 53 or Article 107 of the Charter.

The Brussels and Atlantic pacts give as the *casus foederis* an "armed attack" by a third power against any of the contracting parties, using the very language of Article 51 of the United Nations Charter. The Soviet agreements do not conform to this restrictive terminology. Three of them use the term "war," five refer to "aggression," six to "attack," and ten to "an aggressive policy." [42] In view of the extremely loose and general language employed in the treaties of the Soviet system, it is difficult to see how their terms can be accommodated under the provisions of Article 107 of the Charter of the United Nations. According to this article, only a "state which during the Second World War has been an enemy of any signatory to the present Charter" can be made the object of such action as is contemplated by the Soviet security arrangements. Yet, a typical formula employed in a number of the East-European treaties is illustrated by the following: [43]

Should one of the High Contracting Parties become the object of aggression on the part of Germany, or any other country which would unite with Germany directly or in some other form, the other High Contracting Party shall immediately afford the other Party military and other assistance with all the means at its disposal.

[41] See Kulski, *op. cit.*, p. 461. [42] *Ibid.*, pp. 460–461.
[43] Art. 2 of the Polish-Bulgarian Treaty. See Kulski, *op. cit.*, p. 456.

Clearly, such an arrangement can be brought into conformity with the Charter only as a measure of self-defense under Article 51. But this interpretation would, of course, require notification to the Security Council as specifically provided in that article.

Even though the Soviet security sphere is based on a series of bilateral treaties, the striking uniformity in the pattern of these arrangements gives the whole the practical effect of a regional system of collective security, but without legal standing under the Charter of the United Nations.

TOWARD A UNITED EUROPE

The idea of a European Union, as we have seen in an earlier chapter, can be traced to certain proposals and projects advocated by famous men hundreds of years ago. But it was not until the nineteenth century that a European Union in a regional or continental sense gained widespread support, especially among the liberal intelligentsia.[44]

Among the advocates of European unification at the present time there are two schools of thought. One of these may be called the "federalists" and the other the "functionalists." Both agree that, for the present, European unification must of necessity be confined to the nations outside the Russian orbit, but they differ sharply as to the proper method of approach. The federalists would proceed at once to the creation of a federal union with limited sovereignty, whereas the functionalists take the position that economic integration is a necessary prerequisite to the establishment of an effective political community.

The Western European Union. The Treaty of Economic, Social and Cultural Collaboration and Collective Self-Defense, signed at Brussels on March 17, 1948, established the Western European Union. This treaty differs in important respects from the Inter-American Treaty of Reciprocal Assistance in that it provides for social, economic and cultural cooperation.[45] The most important element of the treaty, however, is collective self-defense. Article IV provides that if any of the contracting parties [46] is made the object of "armed attack in Europe," the other signatories, in accordance with the provisions of Article 51 of the Charter of the United Nations, shall "afford the party so attacked all military and other aid and assistance in their power." Thus, technically at least, the Brussels treaty

---

[44] See Pierre Renouvin, "Les idées et les projets d'union européenne au XIXe siècle," *Conciliation internationale*, no. 6 (1931), pp. 27–47. See also Richard Coudenhove-Kalergi, *Pan Europa* (1923), and P. Hutchinson, *The United States of Europe* (1929).

[45] Arts. I–III. For text, see *Department of State Bulletin*, vol. 18, no. 462 (May 9, 1948), pp. 600–602.

[46] Great Britain, France, Belgium, the Netherlands, and Luxembourg.

is not one of military alliance per se, but like the Rio Pact, it is rather an instrument of collective self-defense in strict conformity with the Charter of the United Nations.[47]

Unlike corresponding provisions in the Rio Pact, the five powers of the Western European Union are pledged to settle all international disputes "only by peaceful means." [48] Article VIII of the treaty provides that the parties will settle all disputes falling within the scope of Article 36, paragraph 2, of the Statute of the International Court of Justice [49] by referring such disputes to the Court for adjudication, and all other disputes to conciliation.[50]

The treaty also provides for a Consultative Council so organized "as to be able to exercise its functions continuously." [51] This Council may be convened at the request of any one of the contracting parties in order to consult regarding "any situation which may constitute a threat to peace. . . ." [52] Provision is also made for consultations "with regard to the attitude to be adopted and the steps to be taken in the case of a renewal by Germany of an aggressive policy," [53] a provision which tends to give to the agreement a broader conformity with the Charter of the United Nations.[54] By agreement of the parties, other states may be invited to accede to the treaty,[55] which was to enter into force on the date of deposit of the last instrument of ratification and to remain in force for fifty years.[56]

The Council of Europe. On August 10, 1949, Édouard Herriot of France opened the first session of the Consultative Assembly of the Council of Europe. This international event of high importance was made possible as a result of a series of formal agreements between the five powers who in the spring of 1948 had signed the Brussels treaty. In October, 1948, the Brussels treaty Consultative Council appointed a committee "to consider and report to Governments on the steps to be taken towards securing a greater measure of unity between European countries." [57] In March, 1949, as a result of the work of this committee, invitations were sent to Denmark, Ireland, Italy, Norway, and Sweden to meet with the five Brussels treaty signatories to draft a constitution for the Council of Europe. By the middle of April of the same year, diplomatic representatives of 10 countries had met in London and were able to submit a draft

---

[47] Art. 51. But in reality, the element of military alliance cannot be denied.
[48] Art. VIII of the treaty.
[49] The so-called "optional clause of compulsory jurisdiction."
[50] Art. VIII of the treaty.
[51] Art. VII.
[52] *Ibid.*
[53] Art. VII.
[54] *Ibid.*
[55] Art. IX.
[56] Art. X.
[57] Council of Europe, *Procedure of the Consultative Assembly* (1953), p. 7.

statute for the consideration of their respective governments. On May 5, 1949, the Foreign Ministers of the 10 countries,[58] meeting in London, signed the Statute of the Council of Europe. The Statute itself represented a stage in international relations never before achieved. Its most essential and unprecedented provision was that each member state should send representatives to a deliberative Assembly which was, in fact, a parliament, though that term was never used. Herriot, in his inaugural address to the Assembly, said: "We merely desire to associate ourselves in order to defend these two great acquisitions of human civilization: freedom and law." [59]

As a condition for membership in the Council of Europe every state must accept the principles of individual freedom, political liberty, and the rule of law as the basis of its internal policy. Although in May, 1949, only 10 nations signed the Statute, other countries have since joined the Council of Europe so that the total membership in March, 1955, was 14.[60]

The Council of Europe consists of the Committee of Ministers, the Consultative Assembly, and the Secretariat. Ordinary sessions of the Consultative Assembly are held once a year in the new House of Europe in Strasbourg, and the representatives are elected by the parliaments of the participating states. It is provided in the Statute that the representatives "shall enjoy in the territories of its Members such privileges and immunities as are reasonably necessary for the fulfilment of their functions." [61]

The European Coal and Steel Community. On April 18, 1951, the Treaty Constituting a Coal and Steel Community was signed in Paris by the representatives of six participating states.[62] This was done in pursuance of a plan proposed by the French Foreign Minister, Robert Schuman, on May 9, 1950. The Schuman Plan rests on two basic assumptions: (1) that agreement between basic industries with respect to trans-national policies is a necessary prerequisite to the removal of trade barriers, and (2) that no regional economic integration in Europe is possible without the inclusion of Western Germany. The plan was designed to create an economic partnership between France and Germany by pooling the steel and coal production of both countries.

The constitution of the Coal and Steel Community as finally established comprises a Council of Ministers, which includes a Minister from each

[58] These countries were the Kingdom of Belgium, the Kingdom of Denmark, the French Republic, the Irish Republic, the Italian Republic, the Grand Duchy of Luxembourg, the Kingdom of the Netherlands, the Kingdom of Norway, the Kingdom of Sweden, and the United Kingdom of Great Britain and Northern Ireland.
[59] Council of Europe, *op. cit.*, p. 8.
[60] These are Belgium, Denmark, France, Germany, Greece, Iceland, Italy, Luxembourg, Netherlands, Norway, Saar, Sweden, Turkey, and the United Kingdom.
[61] Art. 40 of the Statute.
[62] France, West Germany, Italy, Belgium, the Netherlands, and Luxembourg.

participating state; a High Authority of nine members, and an Assembly of 78 representatives chosen by the national parliaments. The High Authority, established at Luxembourg, is the executive and administrative body. It operates by majority vote, has its own staff, and although it consults with the Council of Ministers, it is, for the purposes of the Coal and Steel Community, largely a supranational body. Decisions of the High Authority are binding on enterprises and individuals and are enforced by the member states. Finally, a Court of Justice was established to adjudicate such controversies as may arise in connection with the operation of any agency of the Coal and Steel Community. Cases may be brought before the Court relating to such matters as the violation of a treaty, lack of jurisdiction on the part of some agency of the Community, or any other action *ultra vires*. But the Court may not pass upon the validity of any economic appraisal with respect to which the High Authority may have acted in a given case.

Since August 10, 1952, when the High Authority first began operations, Germany, Belgium, France, Italy, Luxembourg, and the Netherlands have welded together in coal and steel their basic economic destinies. Great progress has been made toward the goals which Schuman set for the Community when he first outlined the famous plan on May 9, 1950. Since then the institutions of the Community have been constructed, its foreign relations have been established, and common markets for coal, iron ore, scrap iron, and steel have been achieved.[63] The Coal and Steel Community was intended to teach by example the benefits of even limited economic unity. It was also designed to start the training of "a group of European officials whose loyalty was wider than national loyalty; whose horizons were wider than national horizons. Finally, it was to provide a symbol and a center around which new loyalties could group themselves." [64] It was to be the living sign of a future Europe pointing the way to the solution of other problems.

The European Defense Community. As we have said, the Coal and Steel Community was intended only as a beginning. The next step, however, came sooner than had been expected. While the Coal and Steel treaty was in the process of being negotiated, the Communists struck in Korea. This attack, and the fear that Europe might be next, focused attention on the pitiful state of its defenses. It soon became apparent that the participation of German forces would be vitally necessary to the creation of an effective military force in Western Europe. France, which opposed any revival of a German national army, drew on the example of the

[63] *Europe Today and Tomorrow*, International Bulletin of the European Movement, no. 30 (September, 1953), p. 14.

[64] *Department of State Bulletin*, vol. 30, no. 762 (Feb. 1, 1954), p. 140.

Schuman Plan to meet this problem. Thus, in the fall of 1950, René Pleven proposed the creation of a European army which would integrate the forces of the states who are members of the Coal and Steel Community. Accordingly, the draft treaty for the European Defense Community was signed by representatives of the six states in May, 1952.[65]

The idea of a European army was even more radical than that of the Coal and Steel Community. It dealt with more vital issues, charged with deep-seated loyalties and antagonisms and impinging directly on individual citizens who must serve in the military forces or who must make financial sacrifices for their support. In view of these facts it is not surprising that the powers granted to the Defense Community are relatively less than those under the Coal and Steel Treaty. It was clear, therefore, that before very long it would be necessary to expand the powers of the Defense Community, but in view of its vital nature and activity, this expansion would not be possible unless its institutions were ultimately given a broader and more democratic base.

A European Political Community. On the invitation of its Council of Ministers, the Coal and Steel Assembly, on September 15, 1952, created an Ad Hoc Assembly for the purpose of constituting a European Political Authority.[66] The Ad Hoc Assembly, which held its first meeting on September 15, 1952, adopted the same Bureau and procedure as the Coal and Steel Assembly. It comprises the 78 Representatives of the Coal and Steel Assembly, of whom 41 were also Representatives to the Consultative Assembly, together with 9 others who were members of the Consultative Assembly but not of the Coal and Steel Assembly. In addition, 13 others, who were members of the Consultative Assembly but nationals of countries not represented in the Coal and Steel Community, were invited to participate as observers. These were distributed as follows: the United Kingdom, 3; Greece, Sweden, and Turkey, 2 each; Denmark, Iceland, Ireland, and Norway, 1 each. These observers could take part in the debates but had no right to vote. The main accomplishment of this meeting of the Ad Hoc Assembly was the creation of a Constitutional Committee of 26 members. This Committee met in Paris from December 15 to 20, 1952, where a report was made containing a draft treaty for a European Political Community.[67]

In terms of the Preamble to this draft treaty, the peoples of the Federal Republic of Germany, the Kingdom of Belgium, the French Republic, the Italian Republic, the Grand Duchy of Luxembourg, and the Kingdom of

[65] *Ibid.*, p. 141.
[66] Council of Europe, *op. cit.*, p. 35.
[67] *Ibid.*, p. 36.

the Netherlands resolve to substitute for their national rivalries a fusion of essential interests by creating institutions capable of giving guidance to a common destiny. According to Article 1: "The present Treaty sets up a *European Community* of a supranational character. The Community is founded upon a union of peoples and States, upon respect for their personality and upon equal rights and duties for all. It shall be indissoluble." [68]

The institutions of the Community as outlined in Article 9 of the draft treaty are to include a Parliament, an Executive Council, a Council of National Ministers, an Economic and Social Council, and a Court of Justice. All member states of the Council of Europe will be free to join this political organization. The draft statute allows for and encourages the forging of the closest ties with these countries, and particularly with the United Kingdom. Space does not permit an analysis of the detailed provisions set forth in the 101 articles of the draft treaty. Suffice it to say that this treaty constitutes the first attempt to build in Europe a greater political community on which the whole future of that remarkable continent and the sacred values of our Western heritage will depend.

OTHER CONSOLIDATIONS AND THE UNITING FOR PEACE RESOLUTIONS

In this chapter we have endeavored to show that, in an age of power politics and resurgent nationalism, collective security on a universal basis is extremely difficult of attainment. The relative impotence of the United Nations in the face of an extremely dangerous international situation is not so much the result of defects in the legal structure and the rules of procedure of the organization as it is due to the absence of a sufficiently well developed world community. This is not to say that the unanimity rule, with respect to the "big five" in the Security Council, is not recognized as a major defect in the Charter. On the contrary, the so-called veto, because of its excessive use by the Soviet Union, has proved to be one of the great stumbling blocks to effective action on the part of the United Nations. It was for this reason that a significant effort was made in 1950 to strengthen the hand of the Assembly in the matter of safeguarding peace and security among the nations.

Uniting for Peace. At its 302nd plenary meeting on November 3, 1950, the United Nations General Assembly adopted certain resolutions in an effort to make collective action more effective. The resolutions are three

[68] Draft Treaty Embodying the Statute of the European Community, *Information and Official Documents of the Constitutional Committee* (October, 1952–April, 1953), p. 59.

in number and recognize that the principal function of the United Nations is that of maintaining peace and security in conformity with the Charter.[69] It is pointed out that failure on the part "of the Security Council to discharge its responsibilities on behalf of all the Member States . . . does not relieve Member States of their obligations or the United Nations of its responsibility under the Charter to maintain international peace and security."

It is resolved that if the Security Council, because of lack of unanimity of the permanent members, fails to exercise its primary responsibility, the General Assembly shall consider the matter and make recommendations to the member states with respect to whatever collective measures may be required to handle the situation. A Peace Observation Commission and a Collective Measures Committee were established, and recommendations were made to all governments and authorities to assist in their functions. The rules of procedure of the General Assembly were amended in several important respects in order to make this body a more effective instrument for the maintenance of peace and security.

Resolution C recommends to the permanent members of the Security Council that:

(*a*) They meet and discuss, collectively or otherwise, and, if necessary, with other States concerned, all problems which are likely to threaten international peace and hamper the activities of the United Nations, with a view to their resolving fundamental differences and reaching agreement in accordance with the spirit and letter of the Charter;

(*b*) They advise the General Assembly and, when it is not in session, the Members of the United Nations, as soon as appropriate, of the results of their consultations.

The real significance of the Uniting for Peace Resolutions is difficult to assay at the present time. If they are indicative of a trend in the direction of strengthening the General Assembly in matters involving peace and security, their importance may be of lasting value. It is rather significant that these resolutions were adopted by the overwhelming majority of 52 to 5 votes in the General Assembly. The five who voted against the resolutions were all of the Soviet bloc, while India and Argentina abstained from voting. The action has been called the most momentous ever taken by the General Assembly. But in the meantime, as we have indicated, new techniques have been evolved by which it is hoped that a safe equilibrium can be maintained between nations, that the forces of antagonism can be contained, and that peace can be preserved in our time. The new means to this end are the regional systems of collective

[69] UN General Assembly, Fifth Session, UN Doc. A/1481, Nov. 4, 1950.

security described above and other such groupings which have so far been omitted from our discussion. Among the latter arrangements are the Australia–New Zealand–United States of America Security Treaty of September 1, 1951; [70] the Arab League of March 22, 1945; [71] and the Mutual Defense Assistance Agreement between the United States of America and Japan of March 8, 1954; [72] as well as the American Japanese Security Act of 1951.[73]

ANZUS. The first of these agreements is often referred to as ANZUS. Its formal organization consists of a Council of Foreign Ministers or their deputies, whose job it is to consider matters relative to the implementation of the treaty. For this purpose, the Council is able to meet any time.[74] Pending the development of a more comprehensive system of regional security in the Pacific area and the development by the United Nations of more effective means to maintain international peace and security, the Council is authorized to maintain a consultative relationship with states, regional organizations, associations of states, or other authorities in the Pacific area in a position to further the purposes of the treaty and promote security in the area.[75]

The Arab League. A political result of two great wars in this century was the national independence of nations who had long been submerged in the sprawling Turkish Empire, which, itself, was little more than a geographic expression, allowed to exist under the servitudes imposed by the imperialistic powers of Europe. Not only was political independence of the various nations of the Near and Middle East the prerequisite to voluntary union, but such a union became necessary to preserve that independence.

Accordingly, upon the initiative of Egypt, exploratory conversations in an effort to establish some sort of unity among the Arab states were begun in September, 1944. The result of these deliberations was the establishment of the Arab League by a treaty signed in Cairo, March 22, 1945.[76] The organization machinery of the League consists of a Council, a permanent Secretariat, and a number of committees concerning such matters

[70] For text, see *American Journal of International Law*, vol. 46 (1952), supplement, pp. 93–95.

[71] See M. Khadduri, "The Arab League as a Regional Arrangement," *American Journal of International Law*, vol. 40 (1946), p. 756; the same author, "Towards an Arab Union: The League of Arab States," *Political Science Review*, vol. 40 (1946), p. 90.

[72] For text, see *Department of State Bulletin*, vol. 30, no. 771 (Apr. 5, 1954), pp. 520–523.

[73] For text, see *American Journal of International Law*, vol. 46 (1952), supplement, p. 91.

[74] Art. 7 of the treaty.

[75] Art. 8 of the treaty.

[76] See Khadduri, "The Arab League as a Regional Arrangement" and "Towards an Arab Union: The League of Arab States."

as nationality, passports, extradition, execution of judgments, social welfare, and health. With respect to internal disputes, not involving sovereignty and territorial independence, the decisions of the Council are final. This body is also to determine what measures should be taken to repel aggression.

On April 13, 1950, a Joint Defense and Economic Cooperation Treaty [77] between the states of the Arab League was drawn up in Cairo and came into effect by deposit of the last ratification in April, 1952. Article 2 of this treaty provides for collective self-defense in conformity with Article 6 of the Arab League Pact and Article 51 of the Charter of the United Nations.

Though this Joint Defense and Economic Cooperation Treaty has many features which resemble a military alliance, it is certainly no more so than the Organization of American States, the North Atlantic Treaty Organization, or the Soviet system of mutual assistance. It is a regional system, organized for the purpose of economic and cultural cooperation as well as for collective self-defense. Article 11 states that "no provision of this Treaty shall in any way affect, or is intended to affect, any of the rights and obligations devolving upon the Contracting States" under the Charter of the United Nations. The Arab League, like the other regional systems, is the result of a deep desire for some measure of security in an unstable world—a security which the United Nations so far has been unable to provide.

The Mutual Defense Assistance Agreement between the United States and Japan of 1954. This treaty is modeled after similar agreements between the United States and many other nations participating in the mutual-security program. It provides the basis for the grant of assistance pursuant to the mutual-security legislation of the United States.[78] The agreement also contemplates the establishment of an American military-assistance advisory group to operate under the direction and control of the American ambassador to Japan. Nothing in this agreement alters or in any way modifies the security treaty between the United States and Japan which was signed in Washington on September 8, 1951. This latter treaty, which came into force on April 28, 1952,[79] gives the United States the right to dispose land, air, and sea forces in and about Japan. "Such forces may be utilized to contribute to the maintenance of international peace and security in the Far East and to the security of Japan against armed attack from without, including assistance given at the express re-

[77] For the text of this treaty see unofficial translation from the Arabic in *The Middle East Journal*, vol. 6 (1952), pp. 238–240.

[78] The Mutual Security Act of 1951, as amended, or any acts supplementary, amendatory, or successory thereto.

[79] 82d Cong., 2d Sess., S. Ex. D.

quest of the Japanese government to put down large-scale internal riots and disturbances in Japan, caused through instigation or intervention by an outside power or powers." [80]

Other agreements of mutual defense to which the United States is a party are the Mutual Defense Treaty with the Philippines of 1952; the Defense Agreement with Spain of 1953; the United States–Korean Defense Treaty of 1953; and the Southeast Asia Collective Defense Treaty signed in Manila on September 8, 1954, by representatives of the United States, Great Britain, France, Australia, New Zealand, the Philippines, Pakistan, and Thailand.

Such then is the picture, in rather rough outlines, of the various measures which have been taken by many nations in order to protect their security in a divided world of power politics. It is true that, in a strictly legal sense, most of these security arrangements are within the provisions of the Charter of the United Nations. But unless the universal Organization is invigorated and greatly strengthened, these combinations of mutual security are, in many respects, no different from ordinary military alliances. On the other hand, it is possible that we are approaching the end of an era in world history which in retrospect might be called "the Age of Nationalism" and that in the new atomic times which lie ahead we shall see further consolidations of nations into larger regions, which for a variety of purposes may overlap each other. Thus geographical boundaries may tend to fade away in the bright sunlight of common interests.

[80] Art. 1 of the security treaty.

PART FIVE

Hostile Relations Between Nations

CHAPTER 21

The Nature of War and Its Law

From the days of Grotius, whose great opus was inspired by the outrages of an irrational conflict which lasted for thirty years, to the opening of the present century, the so-called law of war has been a major preoccupation of international-legal publicists. Treatises on the law of nations were according to standard practice divided into two parts—one concerning war, the other peace. Indeed, the emphasis upon the law of war in the standard texts before 1914 has left the widespread impression among laymen that these rules are both synonymous and coextensive with the law of nations. The cynical attitude, therefore, which today is so common with respect to the importance of international law is very largely the product of a misplaced emphasis in the literature of this subject.

"Law," according to Jackson H. Ralston, "suggests peace, order, regularity, the result of sound reasoning when laid down by the authority of men, universality within the realm it covers, approved methods of conducting affairs to which it relates." [1] But the social institution of war can be defined in terms of its properties, which are force and violence, destruction and disorder. Thus to speak of a law of war is in itself a contradiction in terms, as obviously there can be no law of disorder. Never was the ancient aphorism *inter arma silent leges* more obviously logical or more profoundly true than it is today. It is, indeed, debatable whether the laws of war and neutrality as embodied in existing conventions are of any significance at all beyond that of historical interest.

The present rules of military necessity are a logical result of "total war" in which the line of separation between military and nonmilitary groups has become more and more nebulous. The confusion is worse confounded by the present inability to separate war from peace. The principle of a "just war" had been a keystone in the system of Grotius, but by the end of the nineteenth century the term had practically disappeared from the vocabulary of publicists. Though self-defense seemed an obvious

[1] *A Quest for International Order* (1941), p. 77.

ground for "just war," who could separate in every case a defensive action, in anticipation of attack, from aggression itself?

The confusion to which we have alluded above is the result of a discrepancy between the existing law and the manner in which modern war is conducted. Thus, *de jure belli* has in our day been largely supplanted by the German maxim *Kriegsraison geht vor Kriegsmanier*. It is ironic, indeed, that Samuel von Pufendorf, the great rationalist of the seventeenth century, should yet be heard proclaiming his doctrine of total war.

The Nature of Modern War. It will not be necessary to recount the numerous technological inventions, or to describe the industrial processes which have made possible the fantastic innovations in the art and science of war. It is sufficient to note that the technological revolution has given rise to new methods, the effect of which has been to separate the existing law from the frightening realities of modern war.

Modern warfare has indeed undergone a horizontal expansion, with the result that it is no longer possible to confine belligerent operations to the armies in the field or to the ships at sea; or to differentiate between combatants and noncombatants. With modern aircraft and guided missiles, the theater of war has been made to include virtually all territories of belligerent states. There has also been a vertical expansion of war, the effect of which has been to make the factory and transportation worker no less important than the soldier at the front. Thus it has come about that great industrial and transportation centers with teeming populations are today considered legitimate objectives for total destruction. It may be said, therefore, that armed conflict between nations in our time tends to become total war in that whole populations are involved directly in the struggle along with all their territories. But it is a somber fact that against the massive concussion waves and atomic radiation at Hiroshima and Nagasaki there was no defense, nor could a place be found in which to hide.

The right to self-help through the agency of war, when all other means of redress have failed, has in the past been regarded as a prerogative of state sovereignty. It has generally been considered the supreme sanction under the law of nations—the *ultima ratio*, or final argument, in a controversy between states. Yet, the admission that a state may use force to ensure compliance with its will has been referred to as "the most dramatic weakness of traditional international law." [2]

The institution of war has undergone vast changes, not only as regards the manner of its prosecution, but also as to its legal standing under the law of nations. The increased destructiveness of war—a fact so frightfully demonstrated in the present century—has given rise to new developments

[2] Philip C. Jessup, *A Modern Law of Nations* (1948), p. 157.

in international organization designed to limit the use of force in disputes between states. But before going on to see what these limitations are, it is necessary to define and, if possible, distinguish *war* and *peace*.

Public war has been defined as "a condition of armed hostility between States."[3] It is, according to Oppenheim, "a contention between two or more States through their armed forces, . . . a fact recognised, and with regard to many points regulated, but not established, by International Law."[4] Unilateral acts of force do not constitute war in a legal sense, unless such acts are met with armed retaliation. Though an ultimatum or a declaration of war sometimes precedes the commencement of hostilities, these formalities are by no means necessary as a prelude to legal war.[5] According to Hall: "Previous declaration . . . is an empty formality unless the enemy must be given time and opportunity to put himself in a state of defense, and it is needless to say that no one asserts such quixotism to be obligatory."[6]

During the Middle Ages notice of intended war was always given, often through heralds or by letters of defiance. Whether the practice had its origin in chivalry or in the Roman *jus fetiale* is not known. In modern times, however, writers on international law have given only sporadic support to the proposition that a formal notice of hostilities must precede the employment of arms and that the legality of the conflict is conditioned upon such a declaration. Indeed, if recent practice is to be our guide in this matter, the inevitable conclusion must be that this ancient custom has now been virtually abandoned, and that the legality of public war is independent of a formal declaration of hostilities.[7]

It should be noted that the use of force in international relations may not in every case produce a condition of public war. In this age of power politics, the diplomacy of great nations is often accompanied by use of

[3] C. C. Hyde, *International Law* (1947), p. 1686.

[4] Oppenheim-Lauterpacht, *International Law* (1947), vol. II, p. 166.

[5] On Oct. 3, 1935, the Italian army crossed the Ethiopian frontier without a declaration of war having been made. A report of a committee of the League of Nations Council, submitted four days later, found that the Italian government had resorted to war in violation of Art. 12 of the Covenant. The report stated that it was not necessary that war should have been formally declared in order for Art. 16 to be applicable. See *League of Nations Official Journal* (1935), p. 1225; also G. H. Hackworth, *Digest of International Law*, vol. VI, p. 169.

[6] *A Treatise on International Law* (1924), p. 444.

[7] War between China and Japan opened with the so-called "Mukden incident" on Sept. 18, 1931, without formal declaration. On Sept. 1, 1939, the *Wehrmacht* crossed the Polish frontier without a declaration of war. The Russian army entered Poland on Sept. 17, 1939, and Finland on Nov. 30 of the same year. In neither case was the invasion preceded by a formal declaration of war. The same was true in the case of the German invasion of Denmark and Norway on Apr. 9, 1940, and the infamous attack without warning on the American naval base at Pearl Harbor on Dec. 7, 1941. These are only a few examples of a fairly general practice.

force, short of actual war. With the discovery of new media of mass communication, language has become a powerful weapon in what is known as *ideological warfare.* The experience of this century tends to show that war, because of its total nature and its capacity for destruction of human and material resources, has reached the point of greatly diminishing returns. It is not without significance that a German housewife, when informed of the fact that there was still rationing in England, exclaimed incredulously: "I was under the impression that the British were on the side of the victors?" Thus, it may well be that we are approaching the point where war has lost much of its former usefulness as a human institution. It may be getting out of hand to such a degree that victory is no longer possible in a real sense and that mutual destruction of the belligerents becomes inevitable. This is not to say that war is likely to be relegated to the museum of antiquities very soon. In the first place, many problems to which war heretofore has been an answer still exist. Secondly, nationalism and the principle of sovereignty are great forces in the world. Thirdly, international organization is as yet imperfectly developed, and gives no promise in the immediate future, at least, of serving as an effective substitute for arms and men in disputes between nations.

The most remarkable fact of our age is the fantastic advance which has been made in the industrial arts. For this is the matrix of social-economic and political dynamics, the symptoms of which are wars and revolutions. But paradoxically as it may seem, the science and engineering which made possible atomic weapons and total war may soon make war itself obsolete. There is considerable evidence, even now, that the institution of war is undergoing changes in techniques, the implications of which are as yet but vaguely appreciated. The new methods may involve psychological and ideological warfare—a struggle for the minds of men. Thus the application of force may be greatly controlled in order to avoid total destruction and the ashes of an empty victory.

Legal Limitations upon the Right to Wage War. In all cases where an international delict had been committed and no redress could be obtained through peaceful means, the principle of self-help has generally been recognized. The right of states to make war is based in the main upon the theory of sovereignty and upon its corollary, which is that no authority exists above the state through whose agency a dispute can be finally settled. For this reason, as we have indicated above, a very considerable part of the law of nations has been concerned with rules and regulations governing the conduct of war. In the next section of this chapter, an attempt will be made to summarize some of the most important of these rules, but first let us consider how in this century the right to make war has itself been subjected to certain very significant limitations.

It was apparent by 1920 that the old right to make war had become greatly restricted.[8] The Covenant of the League of Nations provided in Article 10 that the organization should "undertake to respect and preserve" the territorial integrity and political independence "of all Members of the League." It further proclaimed the principle that all war or threat of war, "whether immediately affecting any of the members of the League or not," should be declared "a matter of concern to the whole League," whose chief responsibility it should be to maintain peace between nations.[9] It was declared to be "the friendly right" of each member of the League to bring to the attention of the Assembly or of the Council any circumstance whatever affecting international relations, that might endanger the peace of the world.

The next important step in the limitation of the right to self-help was taken in 1928 through the instrumentality of the Treaty for the Renunciation of War, popularly known as the Kellogg-Briand Pact. This treaty had its origin in a proposal by Briand that France and the United States should mutually renounce war as an instrument of national policy. The message of the French Foreign Minister to the American people was delivered on April 6, 1927, the tenth anniversary of the entrance of the United States into the First World War. At first it received very little notice in the United States, and it was largely through the efforts of private individuals that the State Department was prodded into action. A counterproposal was at length made by Secretary Kellogg to the effect that the agreement should be broadened to seek the approval of other nations. This was done, and ultimately no less than 65 states became signatories of the Pact of Paris. In the language of this treaty: [10]

The High Contracting Parties solemnly declare in the names of their respective peoples that they condemn recourse to war for the solution of international controversies, and renounce it as an instrument of national policy in their relations with one another.

The High Contracting Parties agree that the settlement or solution of all disputes or conflicts of whatever nature or of whatever origin they may be, which may rise among them, shall never be sought except by pacific means.

One of the most significant features of the Pact of Paris is that "it contains no clause of limitation, no provision for determination or denunciation." [11] It was to last for all time. This is of special interest, as in recent times treaties without a limitation clause are extremely rare.

[8] C. G. Fenwick, *International Law* (1948), p. 542.
[9] Art. 11 of the Covenant.
[10] Arts. I and II of the Treaty for the Renunciation of War, signed at Paris, Aug. 27, 1928. For French text, see D. H. Miller, *The Peace Pact of Paris* (1928), p. 246.
[11] *Ibid.*, p. 146.

As a multilateral pact, still in force, it is a part of the general law of nations, and by its terms practically every nation in the world is pledged not to resort to war as an instrument of its national policy. Though the text of the treaty made no reference to the right of self-defense, a qualification in this regard was included in identical notes addressed by Secretary Kellogg to all the states invited to sign the instrument.[12] According to the notes, there is nothing in the American draft of the antiwar treaty which "restricts or impairs in any way the right of self-defense." This right, it was pointed out, is "inherent in every sovereign state and implicit in every treaty." All nations are free, regardless of treaty provisions, to defend themselves and alone are "competent to decide whether circumstances require recourse to war in self-defense. It is clear that with a qualification as broad as this, the Pact of Paris cannot have the effect of making war as such illegal under international law. But, on the other hand, it cannot be denied that the right to make war, formerly regarded as a sovereign prerogative of states, has by the terms of this treaty been severely restricted.[13]

There can be no doubt that the Pact of Paris has the effect of limiting, in a very real sense, the right of the signatory powers to make war. But as experience has shown, no amount of legislation can of itself reduce the propensity to crime. This is no less true in international than in municipal relations.

The Charter of the United Nations is the latest milestone on the way to legal regulation of the use of armed force.[14] Article 2, paragraph 4, provides that "all Members shall refrain in their international relations from the threat or use of force against the territorial integrity or political independence of any state, or in any other manner inconsistent with the purposes of the United Nations." This provision is of special significance when taken in conjunction with paragraph 1 of the same article which states that "the Organization is based on the principle of the sovereign equality of all its Members." From this it follows that the regulations of the threat or use of force is not under the Charter regarded as inconsistent with the sovereign equality of states. Thus a resort to war can no longer be justified on the basis of the old concept of absolute sovereignty.[15] It is further provided that "all Members shall settle their international disputes by peaceful means in such a manner that international peace

---

[12] Fenwick, *op. cit.*, p. 234.

[13] An antiwar treaty of nonaggression and conciliation was signed by certain American republics at Rio de Janeiro on Oct. 10, 1933. This treaty is also known as the "Saavedra Lamas Treaty." In this treaty, as well, wars of aggression are renounced. It stipulates that territorial arrangements which are not obtained by pacific means shall not be accorded recognition. Hackworth, *op. cit.*, p. 9.

[14] Jessup, *op. cit.*, p. 158.   [15] *Ibid.*, p. 159.

and security, and justice, are not endangered." [16] This provision clearly implies that in international disputes certain alternatives to war are now available for their peaceful settlement.

With respect to the problem of war, the United Nations has taken important steps to supplement the provisions of the Charter, such as the Resolution of December 13, 1946, which was unanimously adopted by the General Assembly affirming "the principles of international law recognized by the Charter of the Nurnberg Tribunal" [17] as well as the judgment itself. Though the Charter of the United Nations severely restricts the use of force in international relations, it would be incorrect to draw the conclusion that resort to arms under all circumstances is prohibited by its terms. Article 2, paragraph 4, merely provides that force shall not be used in any "manner inconsistent with the Purposes of the United Nations." It is obvious, of course, that the use of armed force under the direction of the Security Council is free of such inconsistency.[18] Article 46 of the Charter provides that "plans for the application of armed force shall be made by the Security Council with the assistance of the Military Staff Committees." Neither does the Charter deny the validity of the ancient principle of self-defense. As we have already seen in the preceding chapter, nothing in the Charter impairs "the inherent right of individual and collective self-defense if an armed attack occurs against a Member of the United Nations, until the Security Council has taken the measures necessary to maintain international peace and security." [19]

It should be noted, however, that to recognize the principle of self-defense is one thing, but to determine under what precise conditions armed action for this purpose may be undertaken is quite another. Perhaps the criteria laid down by Daniel Webster in connection with the *Caroline* Affair, to which we have had reference earlier, will suffice. Action in self-defense, according to the American Secretary, should be confined to cases in which the "necessity of that self-defense is instant, overwhelming, and leaving no choice of means, and no moment for deliberation." [20] But what of "preventive action"? It was argued before the Nuremberg Tribunal that the German invasion of Norway on April 9, 1940, was made necessary in order to forestall an Allied attack, and that the action, therefore, was of a "preventive character." [21] But on this point the Tribunal said: "It must be remembered that preventive action in foreign territory is justified only in case of an instant and overwhelming

[16] Art. 2, par. 3, of the United Nations Charter.
[17] *Journal of the General Assembly*, no. 58, supp. A-A/P. V./55, p. 485. The international-legal significance of the war-crimes trials will be discussed in a later chapter.
[18] Jessup, *op. cit.*, p. 163.   [19] Art. 51.
[20] John Bassett Moore, *Digest of International Law*, vol. II, p. 412.
[21] Georg Schwarzenberger, *International Law* (1949), vol. I, p. 264.

necessity for self-defense, leaving no choice of means, and no moment of deliberation." [22] In the opinion of the Tribunal, no such compelling necessity existed in the case of Germany's armed attack upon Norway. There can be no doubt that under international law as it now stands, aggressive war is illegal. This fact, however, does not of itself render inoperative the existing rules of war. "Violations of the laws and customs of war," writes Schwarzenberger, "are war crimes both under international customary law and under Article 6 (*b*) of the Tribunal's Charter. There is no differentiation in this respect between States which act as aggressors or in self-defense." [23]

Thus it may be said that the limitations upon the use of force imposed by such instruments as the Pact of Paris and the Charters of the Nuremberg Tribunal and the United Nations, as well as the Resolution adopted by the General Assembly in 1946, tend to affirm rather than deny the existence of *jus belli*.[24] The doubts which may arise concerning the reality of a law of war may very well be ascribed to the paradox that such a concept presents to a logical mind, and the apparent difficulty—if not the impossibility—of keeping war in this atomic age within the limits of such a law.

A Summary of Certain Rules of Belligerent Operations. The main substance of the law of war is to be found in a series of conventions which have been subscribed to by a large number of states in the last hundred years. Many of the provisions contained in these treaties are now hopelessly obsolete and badly in need of revision. Yet it is not without profit to survey for a moment this curious legal structure, even though its underpinnings have been greatly weakened by the revolutionary techniques of modern war.

The more important multilateral treaties relating to the conduct of war which have been concluded since the middle of the last century may be enumerated and summarized as follows:

1. *The Declaration of Paris Concerning Naval War* was signed on April 16, 1856, by seven states, and later adhered to by nearly all the maritime nations of the world. The substance of the declaration is contained in the following four points: (*a*) privateering is and remains abolished; (*b*) the neutral flag covers enemy's goods, with the exception of contraband of war; (*c*) neutral goods, with the exception of contraband of war, are not liable to capture under enemy's flag; (*d*) blockades, in order to be binding, must be effective—*i.e.*, maintained by a force sufficient really to prevent access to the coast of the enemy.

[22] *Ibid.*
[23] *Ibid.*, p. 265.
[24] *Journal of the General Assembly*, no. 58, supp. A-A/P. V./55, p. 485.

2. *The Geneva Convention for the Amelioration of the Condition of Wounded Soldiers in Land Armies* was signed on August 22, 1864, by nine states, and later acceded to by practically every civilized nation in the world. On July 6, 1906, a new Geneva convention was signed by 35 states and in course of time was adhered to by others. The Geneva principles were adapted by convention X at the second Hague conference to maritime warfare.

3. *The Declaration of St. Petersburg* prohibited the use of projectiles under 400 grams which are either explosive or charged with inflammable substances. It was signed on December 11, 1868, by 17 states.

4. *The Convention of 1899 Concerning the Laws of War on Land* was enacted by the first Hague Peace conference and had its origin in Francis Lieber's *Instructions for the Government of Armies of the United States in the Field,* which had been published during the American War between the States. It was later revised and is now embodied in convention IV of the second Hague Peace conference of 1907, Article 2 of which contains what is known as the "general participation clause," providing that the regulations included in the agreement shall not be binding in the event a power not a party to the convention takes part in the war. The effect of this clause was, of course, to render the convention impotent even during the days of the First World War, because the required number of ratifications had not at that time been deposited, and the German government argued that for this reason the Hague convention of 1907 was without legal force.

5. *The Hague Declaration Concerning Expanding Bullets* was adopted by the first Hague conference and signed on July 29, 1899. It was subscribed to by 15 Powers and prohibited the use of the so-called dumdum bullets, which because of their peculiar make created severe wounds by expansion within the human body. These bullets had been made by the British in the arsenal of Dum-Dum near Calcutta. During the First World War each side charged the other with the use of these bullets.

6. *The Hague Declaration Concerning Projectiles and Explosives Dropped from Balloons* was also adopted by the first Hague conference and signed on July 29, 1899. Though it was renewed by the second Hague conference of 1907, only a few countries had deposited ratifications at the outbreak of the First World War.

7. *The Hague Declaration Concerning Projectiles Diffusing Asphyxiating and Deleterious Gases* was signed on July 29, 1899, by 16 states. Though it was renewed at the second Hague conference of 1907, its violation during the First World War was notorious. After the war, however, the use of poisonous gases and other types of chemical weapons was for-

bidden by Article 171 of the Versailles treaty as well as by a number of other treaties.[25]

8. *The Hague Convention of 1899 for the Adaptation of the Principles of the Geneva Convention to Sea Warfare* was replaced by Convention X of the second Peace Conference of 1907.

9. *The Hague Convention of 1907 Concerning the Opening of Hostilities.* By this instrument the contracting parties agreed that "hostilities between them must not commence without a previous and unequivocal warning, which shall take the form either of a declaration of war, giving reasons, or of an ultimatum with a conditional declaration of war." [26]

10. *The Hague Convention of 1907 Concerning the Status of Enemy Merchantmen at the Outbreak of War.* This convention concerns merchant vessels in enemy ports or at sea at the outbreak of hostilities. In the days before the Crimean War (1854), it had been the general practice to confiscate all enemy vessels in the ports of the belligerents, but since then this so-called *right of angary* has been abandoned. The custom has been to allow a reasonable time of grace for such ships to depart in peace, and this is supported by the provision of the Hague convention. With respect to enemy merchantmen at sea, the convention provides that they may be captured but not confiscated. During the First World War, however, the convention was frequently violated, and in 1925 it was denounced by Great Britain.[27]

11. *The Hague Convention of 1907 Concerning the Conversion of Merchantmen into Men-of-war.* By this convention it was provided that no converted merchant vessel can have the status of a warship unless made a public ship of the state whose flag it flies, and unless it carries the external markings of a warship. The ship must be listed as a man-of-war and her commander must be a commissioned officer in the navy of the state in question. During the two world wars converted merchantmen were frequently employed.

12. *The Hague Convention of 1907 Concerning Automatic Submarine Contact Mines.* This convention prohibits the laying of unanchored automatic contact mines unless so constructed as to become harmless in the space of an hour. It also forbids the laying of anchored automatic contact mines which do not become harmless as soon as they break loose from their anchorage. There were other provisions with respect to laying such mines off the coasts of the belligerents and in the paths of friendly commerce. During both the First and Second World Wars this convention was generally and flagrantly violated.

[25] The United States is not a party to any antigas convention.
[26] Convention III, Art. 1.
[27] Oppenheim-Lauterpacht, *op. cit.*, p. 266.

13. *The Hague Convention of 1907 Concerning Bombardment by Naval Forces*. This convention forbids the bombardment of undefended ports, though military installations may be destroyed with no responsibility attaching to whatever incidental damage may be done to such towns in course of the bombardment. In case of bombardment all reasonable care must be taken not to damage religious and cultural buildings and monuments. In all cases due warning must be given the authorities of the town before the bombardment, and if the place is taken by assault no pillage may be allowed. This convention was notoriously violated during both world wars.

14. *The Hague Convention Concerning the Right of Capture in Maritime War*. This convention provided that coastal fishing vessels, ships carrying mail, as well as ships of the belligerents which are engaged in philanthropic or scientific work were to be immune from capture. This, like so many of the other conventions, was generally violated during both the First and Second World Wars.

With respect to the development in the law of war since the First World War the following may be mentioned:

1. *The Protocol of 1925 Concerning the Use of Asphyxiating, Poisonous, and other Gases*. This protocol has now been ratified by more than 40 states, including all the great powers of Europe.[28] In this connection it is interesting to note that Article 39 of the Draft Convention of the Preparatory Commission on Disarmament of 1930 affirmed the prohibition of gas warfare. Likewise in 1938, the League of Nations passed a resolution stating that the use of toxic gases as a weapon of war is illegal under the law of nations.

2. *The Geneva Convention of 1929 Concerning the Treatment of the Sick and Wounded and of the Prisoners of War*. This convention, among other things, forbids reprisals against prisoners of war.

3. *The London Protocol of 1936 Relating to the Use of Submarines*. This protocol provided that submarines may not sink merchant vessels without regard for the safety of their crews. This was in conformity with Part IV of the London Naval Treaty of 1930. Needless to say, observance of this protocol during the Second World War was the exception rather than the rule.

Finally, at the Geneva Conference of 1949, the great majority of the nations of the world signed a Final Act for the Protection of War Victims. To this Act were attached four conventions concerning (1) the amelioration of the conditions of wounded and sick of armies in the field; (2) the amelioration of wounded and sick members of naval forces; (3) the treatment of prisoners of war; and (4) the protection of civilians in war.

[28] The United States, however, is not party to the Protocol.

Article 2 of each of these conventions includes the following provisions.[29]

The present Convention shall apply to all cases of declared war or of any other armed conflict which may arise between two or more of the High Contracting Parties, even if the state of war is not recognized by any of them.

The Convention shall also apply to all cases of partial or total occupation of the territory of a High Contracting Party, even if the said occupation meets with no armed resistance.

Although one of the Powers in conflict may not be a party to the present Convention, the Powers who are parties thereto shall remain bound by it in their mutual relations. They shall furthermore be bound by the Convention in relation to the said Power, if the latter accepts and applies the provisions thereof.

With this brief reference to some of the more important conventions comprising the law of war, we shall turn without further comment to a consideration of the effects of war upon various phases of the relations between belligerent states.

General Effects of the Outbreak of War. Because of the interdependence of nations in the modern world, the outbreak of war in any quarter of the globe is bound to have ramified effects throughout the whole of the international community. The industry and commerce of all nations are immediately affected, and certain rights and obligations at once devolve upon the so-called neutral powers. Even individuals, subjects or citizens of neutral states, who find themselves by chance within the boundaries of belligerent states, acquire with respect to the opposing power, the character of an enemy.[30] But the consequences of armed conflict are, of course, more particularly felt by the belligerents themselves. Yet it would not be correct to maintain that war puts an end *ipso facto* to all legal relations between the parties.[31]

The most obvious and immediate effect of the outbreak of war is the rupture of diplomatic relations, though this may have taken place before the actual commencement of armed conflict. The diplomatic envoys in such cases are either recalled by their own government or are asked to leave by the state in which they are resident. In any case they are entitled to full diplomatic immunity and must be allowed to depart in peace. The embassy or legation of the country whose diplomats have thus departed is usually entrusted to the care of some third power, and the archives are placed under seals. Consular activities of the belligerents likewise come to an end, and the archives of consulates are usually left

[29] *United Nations Treaty Series*, vol. 75, p. 32.
[30] Oppenheim-Lauterpacht, *op. cit.*, p. 243.
[31] *Ibid.*

in charge of consuls of friendly and neutral states. But since consular agents do not enjoy diplomatic immunity under the general law of nations, the question of whether they must be allowed to leave the country freely and without molestation remains, at the present time, unsettled. The practice in both the First and Second World Wars leads to the conclusion that many nations do not consider consuls entitled to any such immunities, as their departure at the outbreak of hostilities was often prevented by the belligerents.

With the advent of total war the relationships between belligerent states and enemy nationals has undergone considerable change from the practice generally regarded as lawful in the nineteenth century. As the line of demarcation between civilian and military groups became more and more uncertain, a relapse into the tribal conception of war became inevitable. For this reason, civilians of enemy nationality who are living within the jurisdiction of a belligerent state may, indeed, be subject to internment and their property may be confiscated.[32] With respect to contracts in force between the subjects of belligerent states, it is clearly within the power of such states to determine to what extent such arrangements may continue in force during the period of hostilities. Regarding such matters, municipal legislation in the form of "trading with the enemy" acts usually define the rights and duties of nationals in time of war. In cases of private claims growing out of such interruption of contractual arrangements, settlements are often made possible through mixed arbitral tribunals as provided for in the treaties of peace.

The Effect of War upon Private Citizens and Subjects. The effects of war cannot be confined to the public relations of states. To allow normal intercourse between private persons and corporations located in the territories of belligerents would, indeed, be inconsistent with the very nature of war. The overriding consideration here is the location within belligerent territory of such individuals—a fact which might make of them a source of military information to the enemy, should unrestricted communication be allowed. Furthermore, commercial intercourse between the nationals of belligerents might have the effect of adding to the resources and thus the warmaking potential of the opposing party. On this point Justice Story wrote in the case of *The Julia*: [33]

It would seem a necessary result of a state of war to suspend all negotiations and intercourse between the subjects of the belligerent nations. By the war every subject is placed in hostility to the adverse party. He is bound by every effort of his own to assist his own government, and to counteract the measures of its enemy. Every aid, therefore, by personal communication, or by other

[32] Georg Schwarzenberger, *A Manual of International Law* (1950), p. 80.
[33] 8 Cranch, 181, 194 (1814).

intercourse, which shall take off the pressure of the war, or foster the resources, or encrease the comforts of the public enemy, is strictly inhibited.

The question of whether or not suspension of intercourse between belligerent nationals follows as an automatic consequence of war, was answered by Justice Davis in *United States v. Lane*.[34] Writing for the Supreme Court, Justice Davis said that, "by a universally recognized principle of public law, commercial intercourse between states at war with each other, is interdicted. It needs no special declaration on the part of the sovereign to accomplish this result, for it follows from the very nature of war that trading between the belligerents should cease." From this it must be inferred that all commerce with the enemy is made unlawful by the fact of war, and that no special legislation in this matter is necessary. In *Kershaw v. Kelsey*,[35] Justice Gray wrote as follows:

The result is, that the law of nations, as judicially declared, prohibits all intercourse between citizens of the two belligerents which is inconsistent with the state of war between their countries; and that this includes any act of voluntary submission to the enemy, or receiving his protection; as well as any act or contract which tends to increase his resources; and every kind of trading or commercial dealing or intercourse, whether by transmission of money or goods, or orders for the delivery of either, between the two countries, directly or indirectly, or through the intervention of third persons or partnerships, or by contracts in any form looking to or involving such transmission, or by insurances upon trade with or by the enemy.

Belligerent nations may, of course, enact special legislation for the purpose of prohibiting or regulating commercial relations between their own nationals and those of enemy states. Illustrative of such enactments are "trading with the enemy" acts both in Britain and the United States at the time of the First World War. In the American law of October 6, 1917, the words "to trade" were given the following definition: [36]

(*a*) Pay, satisfy, compromise, or give security for the payment or satisfaction of any debt or obligation.

(*b*) Draw, accept, pay, present for acceptance or payment, or indorse any negotiable instrument or chose in action.

(*c*) Enter into, carry on, complete, or perform any contract, agreement, or obligation.

(*d*) Buy or sell, loan or extend credit, trade in, deal with, exchange, transmit, transfer, assign, or otherwise dispose of, or receive any form of property.

(*e*) To have any form of business or commercial communication or intercourse with.

[34] 8 Wall. 185, 195 (1868).
[35] 100 Mass. 561 (1868).
[36] Hackworth, *op. cit.*, p. 318.

Enemy Aliens. The general practice in former times upon the outbreak of armed hostilities, was to detain all enemy aliens as prisoners of war. Later, however, especially in the eighteenth century, a large number of treaties were concluded by which such aliens were given a reasonable period of time to leave the country. As a result of these treaties a new rule evolved to the effect that enemy aliens must be given a certain period of grace in which to depart without molestation or hindrance by the authorities. It may be fairly safe to say that, according to customary international law, nationals of the enemy who are not in a position to supply the authorities of their own country with information of military value must be allowed to depart in peace.[37] If, on the other hand, such enemy aliens are officers or members of the reserves of the armed forces of the opposing belligerents, they may be prevented from leaving by being made prisoners of war.

Whether an enemy alien has *persona standi in judicio* is a question which at the present time is somewhat unsettled. The old rule in this respect was that the outbreak of war *ipso facto* disqualified aliens of enemy nationality from taking or defending proceedings in the courts.[38] In recent years, however, the principle that enemy aliens are *ex lege* has pretty much gone into discard. This is particularly true on the continent of Europe, though in Great Britain and the United States the rule still survives with certain exceptions.[39] It has been a matter of debate among publicists whether England and the United States, in view of Section II, Article 23 (*h*), of the Hague convention of 1907, would not be compelled to change their municipal laws on this point. By this article it is expressly forbidden "to declare abolished, suspended, or inadmissible in a Court of law the rights and action of the nationals of the hostile party." Such a construction of Article 23 (*h*) was, however, repudiated by Great Britain in 1911, but it should be said that the exception to the British rule was such as to affect only nonresident enemy aliens and not even all those in some instances.[40]

In the United States, judicial opinion with regard to this matter tended to resemble the English. Chief Justice Kent of New York declared in *Clarke v. Morey* [41] that "according to the law of nations, an alien who comes to reside in a foreign country is entitled, so long as he conducts himself peaceably, to continue to reside there under the public protection and until the territorial sovereign expresses the will to order him away. Prior to that event he was said to be entitled to maintain an action." If the alien in question is resident in enemy territory the situation is different. In such a case the courts will not be open to him. But it is his pres-

[37] Oppenheim-Lauterpacht, *op. cit.*, p. 247.
[38] *Ibid.*, p. 250.   [39] *Ibid.*
[40] *Ibid.*, p. 251.   [41] 10 Johns. 69 (1813).

ence in the territory of the opposing belligerent rather than his national character which in such cases is decisive. It should be noted, however, that certain penalties which ordinarily would follow from the failure to initiate proceedings within a certain time do not in such cases apply. The statute of limitations, for example, does not operate against such individuals while they are being deprived of the use of judicial remedies.

The right of belligerent nations to control the activities of enemy aliens within their jurisdiction cannot be questioned, and the purpose of restrictive measures taken against such persons is the prevention of benefits to the enemy.[42] The law of nations does not prescribe the procedure to be followed, but it seems clear that in all such cases the belligerents must observe those elementary principles of justice which forbid cruel and inhuman treatment. The authority for proceeding against dangerous enemy aliens in the United States is the Alien Enemy Act of 1798 as amended in 1918.[43] This law provides that "natives, citizens, denizens or subjects" of any foreign country at war with the United States may be "apprehended, restrained, secured and removed as alien enemies." This statute is brought into effect by public proclamation of the President.[44]

Under English law there is no statutory basis for the control of enemy aliens in time of war. In this field the royal prerogative is still unlimited.[45] The internment of enemy aliens is considered an act of state not justiciable by the courts and may also be based on the rights of belligerents under the law of nations.[46] In *Netz v. Chuter Ede*,[47] which concerned a German national who was interned in 1940 and who was challenging a compulsory deportation order, the court held that Netz was an enemy alien, and that the act complained of was an act of state and as such nonjusticiable; while in *Rex v. Bottrill, ex parte Kuechenmeister* [48] a writ of *habeas corpus* was denied by the Court of Appeal because the applicant was an enemy alien.

In the United States the courts have followed essentially the same line of reasoning. In all cases dealing with internments and deportations of enemy aliens, the only question which has been considered justiciable

---

[42] "Every belligerent State possesses the inherent right to take such steps as it may deem necessary for the control of all persons whose conduct or presence appears dangerous to its safety. In strict law enemy subjects located or resident in hostile territory may be detained, interned in designated localities, or expelled from the country." (Rules of Land Warfare, U.S. Army, 1917, no. 25.) See also War Department Rules of Land Warfare, 1940, no. 20.

[43] Michael Brandon, "Legal Control over Resident Enemy Aliens in time of War in the United States and in the United Kingdom," *American Journal of International Law,* vol. 44 (1950), p. 383.

[44] *Ibid.*

[45] *Ibid.*, p. 384.

[46] *Ibid.*

[47] 1 All E. R. 628 (1946).

[48] 2 All E. R. 434 (1946).

is the determination of the status of such individuals under the Alien Enemy Act and the Presidential proclamations. In *Minotto v. Bradley* [49] it was held that an enemy alien arrested under the Alien Enemy Act could not contend that he had been deprived of liberty without due process of law. In 1948 the Supreme Court of the United States in *Ludecke v. Watkins* [50] denied a writ of *habeas corpus* to a German enemy alien detained for deportation, because he was regarded as dangerous to the public peace and safety. The Court further held in this case that the war powers of the President were not exhausted even though active hostilities had ceased. Four Justices dissented, however, holding that the technicalities of the "fictional war" should be without application in such cases. The outstanding fact in cases of this kind both in the United States and the United Kingdom is the tendency on the part of the courts to refrain from judicial inquiry into acts taken with respect to enemy aliens in time of war. The general practice in both countries has been for the courts to cooperate with the executive branch of the government in these matters.

Enemy Property and Economic Warfare. According to the old rule, private as well as public property located within the jurisdiction of belligerents could be confiscated in time of war. It had likewise been the practice of opposing belligerents to annul all public and private debts. But as treaties were concluded for the safe withdrawal not only of enemy persons but of their property as well, a new rule gradually evolved to the effect that private property could not be confiscated by the belligerents, nor could the debts owed to enemy subjects be annulled as a consequence of the outbreak of armed conflict.[51] Though there is no case of such confiscation during the whole of the nineteenth century, it is a matter of controversy whether this practice can be said to have created a binding rule of international law. In any case it would most certainly not apply to public property, such as funds and implements of war or even such private property as would be of obvious use to the enemy in the prosecution of the war.

The total nature of modern war would seem to demand that the economic as well as the military potential of the enemy should so far as possible be destroyed. Thus the confiscation of enemy property within the jurisdiction of a nation at war can be justified as incidental to the fundamental right of weakening the adversary by all means available. The right, therefore, of a belligerent to confiscate public property belonging to the enemy is, indeed, believed to exist—limited, perhaps, by certain rules which expediency and custom may dictate. Assets thus confiscated may be used to satisfy, in whole or in part, such pecuniary claims

[49] 252 Fed. 600 (1918).　　　　[50] 335 U.S. 160 (1948).
[51] Oppenheim-Lauterpacht, *op. cit.*, p. 260.

as might exist against the alien enemy. Whether the same right obtains with respect to private property in the hands of enemy aliens at the outbreak of war has been a matter of controversy among writers and jurists.

According to Oppenheim: "The rule that private property on land is not liable to confiscation guided the policy of the belligerents in the early days of the First World War." [52] This policy, however, was soon abandoned as the belligerents in both the First and Second World Wars added economic warfare to the general contest of arms. Both in the United States and Britain an Alien Property Custodian was created under the aegis of Trading with the Enemy Acts, and a bilateral policy was initiated by which all enemy property became liable either to blocking or vesting.[53] In order to illustrate more particularly the operation of such measures, let us consider for a moment what was done in this regard in the United States during the Second World War.

Even before the United States became a belligerent, unprecedented and all-embracing freezing controls over foreign-owned property were imposed by the American government. Although the freezing regulations are couched in highly technical language [54] and proscribe certain categories of specified transactions, the general effect of the whole procedure was to "freeze" or "block" all assets within the United States belonging to the countries designated in the orders. After such assets were frozen, they could not be transferred, withdrawn, or otherwise dealt with, except pursuant to a Treasury license. The blocking of foreign owned property was of such proportions that by June 14, 1941, it approximated an aggregate value of 8 billion dollars.[55]

Until the United States became a belligerent in the Second World War, no authority existed for the seizure, or vesting, [56] of the assets of foreign nationals. Only the blocking power was exemplified by the freezing orders. But when the United States actually entered the war the provisions of the Trading with the Enemy Act which authorized the seizure of enemy

[52] *Op. cit.*, p. 262.

[53] The bases for blocking were either (1) residence in enemy or enemy-occupied territory, or (2) inclusion in the British Statutory List and the American Proclaimed List of Certain Blocked Nationals. The latter might include, and did to a very large extent include, neutrals and nationals of friendly nations who continued to do business with the enemy. Vesting, on the other hand, applied to interests owned or controlled, directly or indirectly, by enemy nationals.

[54] The technical language of the freezing regulations is, in part, due to the fact that they were issued under a Statute, sec. 5(b) of the Trading with the Enemy Act as amended, which was designed for other purposes.

[55] *Census of Foreign-owned Assets in the United States*, Treasury Department, 1945.

[56] The terms *vesting* and *seizure* are synonymous under United States law relating to the Trading with the Enemy Act. In both cases, the title to the property is taken by the United States. In *blocking* the private owner retains the title, though as long as the assets remain blocked he has no effective control over them.

property became at once effective. In short order Section 5 (*b*) of this Act was amended so as to authorize the vesting of property owned by foreign nationals.

The Effect of War upon Contracts. In general, it may be said that contracts between persons who are separated by the line of war are determined as to their validity by municipal law and that this principle, within limits not yet clearly defined, is recognized by the law of nations.[57] In the opinion of American courts, international law is not concerned with the location of the contracting parties so much as with the necessity of prohibiting communication between them.[58] It is reasonable to assume that they likewise would regard as illegal any contract the performance of which would make imperative such communication in time of war. "If a contract necessitates communication between the territories of opposing belligerents, its continuance would be incompatible with the state of war. Numerous agreements are of such a kind, and consequently appear to suffer dissolution when war ensues." [59]

The Supreme Court of the United States has held that war makes it impossible for an individual to create a lawful agency within the territory of the enemy. It is, of course, quite possible that the government of a belligerent may itself act to prevent the conclusion of such contracts and to annul those already in effect. This would of itself remove the necessity of any judicial inquiry respecting the effect of war upon the particular relationship involved. By the Trading with the Enemy Act of October 6, 1917, it is forbidden not only to enter into contractual agreements with persons in enemy territory, but also to perform contracts already in existence between persons within the United States and those within the jurisdiction of the enemy.

Civil War. A civil war is never solemnly declared, but "when the party in rebellion occupy and hold in a hostile manner a certain portion of territory; have declared their independence; have cast off their allegiance; have organized armies; have commenced hostilities against their former sovereign, the world acknowledges them as belligerents, and the contest a war." [60] Armed insurrection against the government of any state by a portion of its population may, or may not, in time acquire the legal status of a belligerent action. As we have seen in an earlier chapter, such a status is dependent upon the recognition of belligerency. A frequent method by which such recognition is accorded an insurgent community by a foreign state is a declaration of neutrality. The parent state may rec-

[57] Oppenheim-Lauterpacht, *op. cit.*, p. 257.
[58] Hyde, *op. cit.*, vol. III, pp. 1706–1707.
[59] *Ibid.*, p. 1707.
[60] *Prize Cases*, 2 Black 635 (1862); Moore, *op. cit.*, vol. I, p. 190.

ognize the belligerent status of a revolting group by certain acts which imply the existence of a state of war or by a formal declaration. In either case foreign states are justified in according belligerent recognition to both parties in a civil conflict. The British proclamation of neutrality of May 14, 1861, by which the belligerency of the Confederate States of America was recognized, was justified by President Lincoln's proclamation of April 19 of the same year initiating a blockade of Confederate ports.

It is important to note that the principal effect resulting from the recognition of belligerent status in civil conflict is to render operative the laws of war in the same manner as if the armed contest were in fact between two or more independent states. In this connection the United States Supreme Court in *Ford v. Surget*[61] had this to say:

> To the Confederate army was, however, conceded, in the interest of humanity, and to prevent the cruelties of reprisals and retaliation, such belligerent rights as belonged under the laws of nations to the armies of independent governments engaged in war against each other—that concession placing the soldiers and officers of the rebel army, as to all matters directly connected with the mode of prosecuting the war, "on the footing of those engaged in lawful war," and exempting "them from liability for acts of legitimate warfare."

That the rights and obligations which follow as a consequence of recognition of belligerency are confined solely to military operations is well established by the general law of nations. This principle has also been reiterated in numerous decisions by the Supreme Court of the United States.[62] It should be clearly understood, therefore, that the adoption of rules of war by both belligerents in a civil conflict does not in any way imply an engagement extending beyond the limits of these rules. Nor does a recognition of belligerency prevent the legitimate government from trying the leaders of the rebellion for high treason and from treating them accordingly, unless they are included in a general amnesty.[63]

Bellum Justum and *Bellum Legale*. In the days before the First World War the right to self-help on the part of independent states was widely recognized both in theory and practice. In those days war was regarded not only as a means to enforce certain rights of sovereign states but as an effective method of changing international law itself. These views were justified by many publicists because there existed no international tribunal with compulsory jurisdiction, nor any organ of international legislation in the true sense of the term.[64] The fact that modern war is rapidly getting

---

[61] 92 U.S. 594 (1878).

[62] See *Prize Cases*, 2 Black 635 (1862); *Williams v. Bruffy*, 96 U.S. 176 (1877).

[63] Moore, *op. cit.*, vol. VII, p. 159.

[64] Josef L. Kunz, "Bellum Justum and Bellum Legale," *American Journal of International Law*, vol. 45 (1951), p. 528.

out of hand as a workable institution is chiefly responsible for a new trend in the works of modern publicists—a trend away from the purely positivist doctrine of the nineteenth century. The positivists had argued that to make war under all circumstances is a fundamental right of sovereign states. But with the rapid development of international organization and law in this age, alternative means are made available in the resolution of disputes between nations. It is the exigencies of our time which require a drastic revision in both the theory and practice of international relations if the treasures of our culture are to be made safe for coming generations. Thus it is that many of our best scholars both in science and letters are beginning to look to the past experience of mankind for some measure of wisdom and the road to a better life.

The doctrine of differentiation between a just and unjust war can be traced to ancient times. It was a significant part of the Roman *jus fetiale*. In the Middle Ages it was intrinsic to Christian theology, through which avenue it entered the modern law of nations. With the separation of international law from theology in the eighteenth century the notion of a *bellum justum* was left behind. But whereas the intrinsic justice of the cause was the heart of the classic doctrine of a just war, the main emphasis at the present time is on security and peace, both of which are inseparable. Hence the first aim in the United Nations Charter is "to save succeeding generations from the scourge of war," and the first purpose of Article 1 of the Charter is to "maintain peace and security." It may be said, therefore, that the new distinction is not one between just and unjust wars, but rather between wars which are legal and those which are not legal. This generation has chosen to place its faith in legal norms rather than in the precepts of theology and ethics. Yet, is it not reasonable to assume that the case of civilization would be strengthened by a combination of all these?

CHAPTER 22

Neutrality in Relation to Existing Law

THE EVOLUTION OF THE LAW OF NEUTRALITY

In the history of ancient nations no evidence can be found that the principle of neutrality was ever recognized either in theory or practice. It was not until near the end of the Middle Ages that a number of treaties were concluded between European princes stipulating that in time of war no aid whatever should be given by any one of them to the enemies of the other. The development of neutrality, as a principle recognized by the law of nations, is a by-product of the theory of sovereignty and is associated with modern times and the rise of national states. It is not surprising, however, to find that the new techniques of warfare, which the ingenuity of modern man has perfected, should also have had their effect upon the traditional rules of neutrality. In this chapter we shall trace the evolution of this concept in order to arrive at a definition of its contemporary nature, as well as test its validity against the background of the existing framework of collective security.

The Evolution of Traditional Neutrality. Though Grotius did not use the term *neutrality,* the seventeenth chapter of the third book of his *De jure belli ac pacis* was devoted to a brief discussion of this concept under the title: *De his qui in bello medii sunt.* Here he gave expression to two general rules which were to govern the conduct of nonbelligerent states with respect to nations at war: [1]

It is the duty of those who stand apart from war to do nothing which may strengthen the side whose cause is unjust, or which may hinder the movements of him who is carrying on a just war, and, in a doubtful case, to act alike to both sides, in permitting transit, in supplying provisions to the respective armies, and in not assisting persons besieged.

The definition of neutrality as a legal concept, however, did not find

[1] *De jure belli ac pacis,* book III, chap. xvii.

354

precise expression until the latter half of the eighteenth century. A considerable departure from the Grotian concept is found in the works of Vattel, who wrote in 1758 that "neutral nations, during a war, are those who take no one's part, remaining friends common to both parties, and not favoring the armies of one of them to the prejudice of the other." [2] But the Italian jurist Galiani was perhaps the first to give a clear and precise exposition of neutrality and to provide the legal form it retained to the days of the First World War. Galiani draws a distinction between the law of neutrality and a moral or legal evaluation of the war, and he points out that no duty can possibly derive from the latter which would impel a nation to enter the war. Yet, he recognizes that under certain conditions a moral duty may require such intervention.[3]

The theoretical development with respect to the principle of neutrality in the latter part of the eighteenth century was paralleled by certain developments in international relations for which it was to some degree a justification. By the Armed Neutrality Declaration of 1780, the maritime nations of northern Europe, under the leadership of Russia, maintained that neutral ships made free goods except for contraband of war. This principle had also been recognized by the treaty of 1778 between the United States and France and by later treaties to which the United States became a party.[4] In 1856 these same principles were incorporated into the Declaration of Paris.

The law of neutrality, as it was shaped in the late eighteenth century and allowed to grow throughout the nineteenth, owes a great deal to the influence of the United States.[5] It was in the interest of the young republic to stand aloof from the contentions of the Old World—to engage in friendly commerce without the entanglement of alliance and possible involvement in war.

At the outbreak of war between England and France in 1793, Edmond C. Genêt, the French minister to the United States, as we have already seen, asserted the right to outfit and commission privateers, and even

---

[2] *Droit des gens*, vol. III, p. 103.

[3] *De' doveri de' principi neutrali* (1782), vol. I, pp. 36, 42 ff.

[4] Treaties with the Netherlands in 1782, with Sweden in 1783, and with Prussia in 1785 contained such provisions. See C. C. Hyde, *International Law* (1947), vol. III, p. 2225.

[5] "The policy of the United States in 1793," says one of the greatest of English writers on international law, "constitutes an epoch in the development of the usages of neutrality. There can be no doubt that it was intended and believed to give effect to the obligations then incumbent upon neutrals. But it represented by far the most advanced existing opinions as to what those obligations were; and in some points it even went further than authoritative international custom has up to the present day advanced. In the main, however, it is identical with the standard of conduct which is now adopted by the community of nations." Quoted by Charles F. Phillips and J. V. Garland in *The American Neutrality Problem* (1939), p. 89.

went so far as to set up prize courts in connection with the French consulates in the United States. As might well be expected, his action led to vigorous protests by the American government.[6] Events such as this, along with a unique geographical position, caused the United States to turn its face from the machinations of European chancelleries to pursue a course of neutrality [7] and isolation that was to last to the end of the nineteenth century and the war with Spain.

The development of the rules of neutrality during the nineteenth century was due in the main to three factors. First among these, as we have indicated above, was the attitude of the United States.[8] As a second factor we might mention the permanent neutralization of Belgium and Switzerland, and as a third, the Declaration of Paris of 1856,[9] which stipulated that free ships make free goods, that neutral goods on enemy vessels cannot be appropriated, and finally that blockades to be legal must be effective.

The Second Hague Conference of 1907. At the second Hague peace conference of 1907, two conventions were concluded with respect to neutrality: convention V, conferring the rights and duties of neutral powers and persons in war on land; and convention XIII, regarding the rights and duties of neutral states in naval war. Inasmuch as the new techniques of warfare in the present century have rendered these conventions to some extent obsolete, only a very brief summary of some of their provisions will be attempted here.

The first Article of convention V states unequivocally that "the territory of neutral Powers is inviolable." Thus neutrality was established in international law with a recognized status which the belligerents were bound to observe.[10] But a duty is also imposed upon the neutral state to punish unneutral acts committed within its territory,[11] and if the application of force is necessary to prevent violation of neutrality, it cannot be regarded as a hostile act.[12]

It is incumbent upon the neutral state to intern members of the belligerents' armed forces who may be found within its territory and, in the absence of "a special convention to the contrary," to supply the interned with food, clothing, and such relief as may be "required by humanity." [13]

[6] See communication to Gênet, June 5, 1793, *American State Papers, Foreign Relations*, vol. I, p. 150.

[7] The first Neutrality Act was passed by the Congress in June, 1794.

[8] Oppenheim-Lauterpacht, *International Law* (1944), vol. II, p. 495.

[9] *Ibid.*, p. 496.

[10] James Brown Scott, *The Hague Peace Conferences of 1899 and 1907* (1909), vol. I., pp. 543–544.

[11] Art. 5 of Convention V.

[12] Art. 10.

[13] Arts. 11, 12.

But at the conclusion of peace the cost borne by the neutral in connection with such internment shall be made good. A neutral power which receives escaped prisoners of war shall leave them at liberty. But if they are allowed to remain within the territory of the neutral state, a special place of residence may be assigned to them.[14]

A neutral power may authorize the passage through its territory of the sick and wounded belonging to the belligerent armies, but great care must be taken to prevent the transportation of military personnel and materials of war.[15] Further evidence of the humanitarian emphasis of this section is the provision in Article 15 to the effect that the Geneva convention shall apply to the sick and wounded who may be interned in a neutral country.

The chief importance of Article 16 lies in its definition of what constitutes a *neutral*, and, indeed, without such a definition it would be impossible to fix neutral rights and duties.[16] In the language of the convention, a neutral is the national of a state not taking part in the war, and he cannot avail himself of his neutrality if he commits hostile acts against a belligerent, or acts in his favor, particularly if he takes service in the armed forces of one or the other of the parties at war.

Convention XIII, as we have noted above, concerns the rights and duties of neutral powers in naval war. Article I of this convention states that "belligerents are bound to respect the sovereign rights of neutral Powers and to abstain, in neutral territory or neutral waters, from any act which would, if knowingly permitted by any Power, constitute a violation of neutrality." Any act of hostility, "including capture and the exercise of the right of search, committed by belligerent war-ships in the territorial waters of a neutral Power, constitutes a violation of neutrality and is strictly forbidden." [17] It is further provided in Article 3 of this convention that when a ship has been captured in the territorial waters of a neutral power, this neutral power must employ, if the prize is still within its jurisdiction, all means at its disposal to release the prize with its own officers and crew and intern the prize crew. A neutral power is not bound, however, "to prevent the export or transit, for the use of either belligerent, of arms, ammunition, or, in general, of anything which could be of use to an army or fleet." [18] Nor is the neutrality of a power affected by the passage through its territorial waters of warships or prizes belonging to the belligerents.[19] But a neutral nation must use the means at its disposal to prevent the fitting and arming of any vessel within its jurisdiction which it has

---

[14] Art. 13.
[15] Art. 14.
[16] Scott, *op. cit.*, p. 551.
[17] Art. 2.
[18] Art. 7.
[19] Art. 10. See *Altmark* case, p. 369.

reason to believe may be used in hostile operations against a friendly power.[20]

In the absence of special provisions to the contrary in local law, belligerent warships are not permitted to remain in the ports, roadsteads, or territorial waters of a neutral power for more than twenty-four hours, except in certain cases covered in the convention.[21] If a power which has been informed of the outbreak of war learns that a belligerent warship is within its ports or territorial waters, it must notify such a ship to depart within twenty-four hours or within the time prescribed by local regulations. Such a ship may not prolong its stay in a neutral port beyond the permissible time except on account of damage or stress of weather. "It must depart as soon as the cause of delay is at an end." [22] When warships belonging to both belligerents are simultaneously within a neutral port or roadstead, a period of not less than twenty-four hours must elapse between their departures, and the order of departure is determined by the order of arrival. A belligerent warship may not leave a neutral port or roadstead until twenty-four hours after the departure of a merchant ship flying the flag of its adversary.[23] While in neutral ports, belligerent warships may carry out only such repairs as are absolutely necessary to make them seaworthy. The neutral power shall decide what repairs are necessary, and these must be carried out with the least possible delay.[24]

According to Article 21, a prize may be brought into a neutral port only for reasons of unseaworthiness, stress of weather, or want of fuel or provisions. It must leave as soon as the circumstances which justified its entry are at an end. Should such a prize refuse to leave upon the order of a neutral state, the latter may then release the ship in the hands of its own crew and intern the prize crew. A neutral power, according to Article 22, must release a prize which is brought into any of its ports under circumstances other than those given in Article 21. If, upon notification by the neutral power, a belligerent ship of war does not leave, measures may be taken by the authorities of the neutral state to render the ship incapable of taking the sea for the duration of the war. In such cases, the commanding officer of the belligerent ship must facilitate the action of the neutral. The officers and crews of such ships are detained by the neutral state and subjected to such restrictions as is required to ensure their incapacity for belligerent action of any kind.[25]

The exercise by a neutral power of its rights under this convention can under no circumstance be considered as an unfriendly act by any of the

[20] Art. 8.

[21] Art. 12.

[22] Arts. 13 and 14.

[23] Art. 16.

[24] Art. 17.

[25] Art. 24.

belligerents who have accepted the article relating thereto.[26] But in this convention, as in so many other international agreements, a vast loophole was provided which was to contribute to its impotence. Article 28 provided that "the present Convention does not apply except between the contracting Powers, and then only if all the belligerents are parties to the Convention."

The London Declaration. The second Peace Conference at The Hague was followed by the London Naval Conference of 1908–1909, which was a further attempt to codify the law of neutrality. Though it is true that the Declaration of London was never ratified, it nevertheless constituted a clear statement of the then recognized principles of international law.[27] Thus it may be regarded as a supplement to the Thirteenth Hague convention, which we have summarized above. It repeats the Declaration of Paris of 1856 concerning the test of legal blockade,[28] and sets forth in detail the rules for enforcement of such blockade with regard to the rights of neutrals. Contraband of war was divided into two categories, one of which was denominated "absolute contraband," and the other as "conditional contraband." [29] Articles which are not susceptible to use in war may not, however, be declared contraband,[30] and of these an enumeration is found in Articles 28 and 29 of the declaration.

Chapter IV of the Declaration of London deals with the destruction of prizes. Article 48 provides that a neutral vessel which has been captured may not be destroyed, "but must be taken into such port as is proper for the determination there of all questions concerning the validity of the capture." If, however, compliance with this provision would endanger the safety of the captor or the success of his operations, the prize may be destroyed.[31] But before the vessel is sunk all persons on board must be placed in safety, and such of the ship's papers as are of importance to the determination of the validity of the capture must be taken on board the warship. If the capture of a neutral vessel is subsequently found invalid, even though the act of destruction was held to be justifiable, the captor must pay compensation to the interested parties.[32]

Article 56 stipulates that transfer by the belligerents of any of their vessels to a neutral flag is void in the following cases: (1) if the transfer has been made during a voyage or in a blockaded port; (2) if a right to repurchase or recover the vessel is reserved to the vendor; and (3) if the requirements of the municipal law governing the right to fly the flag under which the vessel is sailing have not been fulfilled.

[26] Art. 26.
[27] Preliminary Provisions of the Declaration of London.
[28] Art. 2.
[29] Arts. 22 and 24 respectively.
[30] Art. 27.
[31] Art. 49.
[32] Arts. 50 and 52.

Chapter VI of the declaration has to do with the determination of "enemy character" as regards both ships and goods. According to Article 57, the neutral or enemy character of a vessel is determined by the flag which it is entitled to fly, while the status of goods found on board an enemy vessel is determined by the neutral or enemy character of its owner.[33] The absence of proof, however, that the goods found on enemy vessels are in fact neutral leaves the presumption that they belong to the enemy. With respect to visit and search, it is provided in Article 61 of the declaration that neutral vessels under national convoy are exempt from search. But forcible resistance to the legitimate exercise of the right of stoppage, search, and capture involves in all cases the condemnation of the vessel, as well as the cargo.

Contraband of War. In the very conception of contraband two essential elements are involved: (1) the nature of the goods, and (2) an enemy destination.[34] For centuries the notion of contraband had been familiar to statesmen and jurists, and it was generally considered to comprise the following three categories: (1) absolute contraband, (2) conditional contraband, and (3) noncontraband. In the Declaration of Paris in 1856 the term *contraband* had been used but not defined. The abortive Declaration of London attempted to classify contraband according to the above categories and to list the articles in each. But an "escape clause" was provided by which goods could easily be shifted from one category to another.[35]

The law of nations requires that the captor of neutral property on the high seas prove before a prize court that the alleged contraband had an enemy destination when seized. In the case of absolute contraband it is necessary only to prove that the goods had as their destination any point within enemy-controlled territory, while in the case of conditional contraband it must be shown in addition that the goods are destined for the use of the armed forces or the government of the enemy. The original basis upon which the classification of absolute and conditional contraband rests is the distinction between combatants and noncombatants. But as we have already indicated, the line of demarcation between these two groups has become exceedingly blurred under the impact of total war. As might be expected, therefore, the tendency during the two world wars was to enlarge the list of absolute contraband to cover almost all goods which might be of even the slightest use to the enemy. In this connection, the principle of continuous voyage played an important part in causing

---

[33] Art. 58.

[34] Herbert W. Briggs, *The Law of Nations, Cases, Documents, and Notes* (1952), p. 1040.

[35] *Ibid.*

goods to be transferred from the category of conditional to that of absolute contraband.

The Doctrine of Continuous Voyage. In general, according to international law, goods which are destined to a neutral port cannot be regarded as contraband of war.[36] But in recent times this law has been greatly modified by the doctrine of continuous voyage.

It has been observed that if a nation at war cannot get such goods as it needs through its own ports, either because it is a landlocked country or because its ports have been made useless by an effective blockade, it will endeavor to procure them from adjacent and friendly states. Thus during the First World War, Germany, whose ports were blockaded by the British, was able nevertheless to make use of certain neutral countries in the procurement of vast quantities of goods useful to her war effort. In order to cope with this situation the British expanded the list of contraband to include all goods whose ultimate destination she believed to be enemy territory, even though such goods were ostensibly bound for a neutral port such as Copenhagen. In other words, the doctrine of continuous voyage was applied to the transportation of goods from their port of origin to their ultimate destination. However, the seizure of such goods may not take place within neutral territory but must in all cases be carried out on the high seas.

Blockade. Blockade has been defined as "the blocking by men-of-war of the approach to the enemy coast, or a part of it, for the purpose of preventing ingress and egress of vessels or aircraft of all nations."[37] The institution of blockade dates from the late sixteenth and early seventeenth century, when the Dutch government declared the ports of Flanders, then under the control of Spain, to be blockaded.[38] The object of blockade, like that of contraband, is to cripple the commerce of the enemy—a measure of war which in our time is of the greatest importance. But in blockade it is the ship which is the main object of capture, while in contraband it is the cargo.[39] The tests of legality are (1) notification,[40] and (2) effectiveness. It must be carried out by men-of-war, as the mere laying of mines or obstructing of the entrance to harbors by sunken ships, though such means may be more effective in actually preventing ingress and egress, are not equivalent to blockade in a legal sense.[41]

[36] P. H. Winfield, *The Foundations and the Future of International Law* (1942), p. 89.

[37] Oppenheim-Lauterpacht, *op. cit.* p. 628.

[38] *Ibid.*, p. 629.　　　　　　　　[39] Winfield, *op. cit.*, p. 90.

[40] Art. 14 of the Declaration of London provides: "The liability of a neutral vessel to capture for breach of blockade is contingent on her knowledge, actual or presumptive, of the blockade."

[41] In 1861, during the American War between the States, the harbor of Charleston was blocked by sunken ships laden with stones. During the First World War the

With respect to the scope of blockade, paragraph 26 of the *Instructions for the Navy of the United States Governing Maritime Warfare*, dated June 30, 1917, provides that "a blockade must be limited to the ports and coasts belonging to or occupied by the enemy" and "must not bar access to neutral ports or coasts." [42]

Visit and Search. It is quite clear that, according to the law of nations as it now stands, belligerent powers have the right to visit and search neutral vessels on the open sea. If upon examination it is found that the neutral ship is carrying contraband of war, it may be taken to a harbor of the belligerent nation. The same is true in the case of ships which may have made attempts to run the blockade. In each case the matter will be settled by the prize courts of the belligerent who has made the capture of such ships. Though the prize courts are bound by the municipal laws of their own states, it should be clearly understood that no state is thereby absolved from responsibility under international law.

These are some of the more important rules which according to the present law should govern the relationships between belligerent and neutral states. But unfortunately, because of the exigencies of warfare in this age, the rights of neutrals have had to give way under the inexorable pressure of the power of belligerents. As late as 1936, the London protocol, which was ratified by a number of states including Great Britain, Germany, and France, made it unlawful for submarines to sink a merchant vessel without first taking measures for the safety of passengers and crew. These provisions, however, were set aside very early in the Second World War.

In the remaining part of this chapter we shall examine more closely the law of neutrality under conditions of total war and under the impact of collective security.

NEUTRALITY, TOTAL WAR, AND COLLECTIVE SECURITY

The conditions of belligerent operations in the First World War bore little relationship to those contemplated in the codifications of 1907 and 1909. The relative freedom of the seas which both the Hague conventions

---

harbor of Zeebrügge was blocked by the British by means of sunken ships filled with cement. Though such means of obstruction to the commerce of the enemy is legal, it is nevertheless not blockade. For this reason, if a ship should succeed in gaining entrance to the port in spite of such obstruction, it could not be held for violation of the rules of blockade. It is incumbent upon the belligerents to notify the neutral nations of the danger to navigation which such blocking of the channel or entrance to an enemy port would produce. Notification here is no less imperative than in the case of blockade.

[42] G. H. Hackworth, *Digest of International Law*, vol. VII, p. 119.

and the Declaration of London had conceded to neutral nations came to an end with unrestricted submarine warfare and the use of floating mines. Vast areas of the high seas were declared "prohibited zones," and neutral navigation was permitted only under the most stringent conditions.

England's blockade of German ports during the First World War led to a situation very similar to that which prevailed during the Napoleonic Wars. Naval superiority enabled Great Britain to divert much of the neutral trade away from Germany—in fact, to make the neutrals her economic allies.[43] She extended the list of contraband to include food and cotton, and she "rationed" such neutrals as Holland and the Scandinavian countries on the ground that much of the goods they imported were really destined for Germany. The effectiveness of England's blockading fleet was evidenced by Germany's frantic appeal to the United States, a historic champion of the rights of neutrals, to help maintain the "freedom of the seas." But more convincing than such appeals was the British interference with American commerce on the high seas, a practice which caused President Wilson to send a number of sharp notes to England. The United States complained especially because British cruisers, rather than searching ships on the high seas at the time of visit, took them into port for a more elaborate investigation. The British, on the other hand, justified this procedure on grounds of military necessity, as well as on historic practice.[44]

The difficulties which arose from the practice of diverting neutral ships for search in belligerent ports finally led to the adoption in 1916 of the so-called navicert system. *Navicerts* are certificates issued by a diplomatic or consular representative of the belligerent states in neutral countries. A neutral vessel on the high seas in possession of such a document, when encountered by a warship of the belligerent whose representative has issued the navicert, is allowed to proceed without being taken to port for search.[45]

That captured neutral vessels may not generally be sunk, burned, or otherwise destroyed is a well-established rule of international law.[46] According to Article 48 of the Declaration of London, captured neutral vessels may not be destroyed but must be taken to port for action by a prize court. But Article 49 of the same declaration provides that if the

[43] J. Salwyn Schapiro, *Modern and Contemporary European History* (1940), p. 730.
[44] The British notes in reply to the American protest pointed out that ships had been taken into port for search as long ago as the American War between the States. The same practice had been followed in the Russo-Japanese War and in the Second Balkan War. See Oppenheim-Lauterpacht, *op. cit.*, pp. 713–714.
[45] The navicert system was again adopted two months after the outbreak of war in 1939 and used on a large scale during the Second World War.
[46] Oppenheim-Lauterpacht, *op. cit.*, p. 723.

taking of a vessel into the port of a prize court involves great danger to the safety of the captor and the success of his operations, the vessel may be destroyed provided it is otherwise liable to condemnation. It should, of course, be noted that the Declaration of London was never ratified and is therefore not legally binding. During the First World War the Allied and Associated Powers refrained from intentionally destroying neutral ships, whereas "the Central Powers, on the other hand, are believed to have sunk no less than 1716" neutral vessels.[47]

Violations of the existing law of neutrality became even more general in the Second World War. Extensive use of aircraft, more efficient submarines, and greatly improved wireless communication, as well as an increased emphasis on economic warfare with a longer list of contraband, made the position of neutrals virtually untenable. Thus the desperate nature of modern war has had the effect of enlarging the rights of the belligerents while correspondingly reducing those of the neutral states. This development is certainly true in fact if not in law. The rules of visit, search, and seizure lost their meaning when any neutral ship might be sunk without warning or brought into a belligerent port even before any attempt had been made to run the blockade. Aside from all this, the ever-increasing interdependence of nations, the advent of total war, and finally, the twice-repeated experiment of collective security in this century has generally undermined the legal structure of neutrality.

Departure from Traditional Neutrality in the United States. At the outbreak of the First World War, the United States issued a neutrality proclamation in the firm hope that entanglement in the European conflict could be avoided. But as the seaborne trade of this nation found itself between the Scylla of unrestricted submarine warfare and the Charybdis of extensive blockade, the question of whether neutrality was the best course to follow became debatable. President Wilson, who in the beginning had exhorted the people of the United States to remain neutral both in thought and action, at length came to the conclusion that this "is a war against all nations" and that the "German submarine warfare against commerce is a war against mankind." [48] Thus traditional neutrality was abandoned for a policy of taking sides in order "to vindicate the principles of peace and justice in the life of the world as against selfish and autocratic power and to set up amongst the really free and self-governed peoples such a concert of purpose and of action as will henceforth insure the observance of those principles."

This was indeed a notable departure from the traditional policy of the United States. But it was evidence of a lesson learned, namely, that

[47] *Ibid.*, p. 725.
[48] War Message to the Congress of the United States on Apr. 2, 1917.

neutrality is an attribute of war rather than of law. That is to say, the enjoyment of neutral rights is dependent upon the nature of war to a much greater degree than upon the provisions in the so-called law of neutrality. Furthermore, the affinity between war and neutrality is one of inverse relationship, so that with an increase in the former, a corresponding decrease in the latter tends to occur. Thus as war expands both vertically and horizontally, the position of the neutral becomes more and more untenable. From a legal point of view, the right to self-preservation claimed by the belligerents tends to take precedence over whatever rights the neutral states may claim under existing law. This tendency is further reinforced by a return in our time to the ancient concept of *bellum justum*.

With the establishment of the League of Nations the principle of neutrality was abandoned and instead was established the principle of collective responsibility, under which each state had the duty "not to be impartial in a war." [49] It should, nevertheless, be clearly understood that whatever legal restrictions the collective-security arrangement under the Covenant placed upon the contracting parties, they did not apply to powers which stood outside the League. [50]

Though the United States was never a member of the League of Nations, it could not escape the effects of the new legal climate which the Covenant had produced. American as well as European jurists were sharply divided on the issue of neutrality. Some argued in the Wilsonian manner that neutrality was simply a manifestation of the refusal or the incapacity to distinguish between right and wrong. Earnest attempts were made to renounce war as an instrument of national policy and give legal sanction only to wars of self-defense. Furthermore, there was the certain knowledge that, if war should come again, the position of the neutral would be even more precarious than it had been during the last conflict.

What is the neutral to do in this new situation? The only way he has been able to maintain his rights in the past was to fight for them. . . . The old [law] of neutrality would have to be entirely rebuilt if used in the next war; and even then it could be maintained only by the combined strength of the neutrals against the belligerents. Times have changed! [51]

In opposition to this view, it was argued that, in a sea of war, islands of peace could indeed be made to exist through neutrality, which would have

[49] Clyde Eagleton, *Analysis of the Problem of War* (1937), p. 93.
[50] A large number of jurists argued, however, that the Kellogg-Briand Pact of 1928 definitely restricted the status of neutrality with respect to states which might otherwise have claimed exemption from such restrictions by virtue of the fact that they were not members of the League of Nations.
[51] Eagleton, *op. cit.*, p. 92.

the function of preserving law and an orderly civilization until peace should return once more. "Sanctions," according to the protagonists of this point of view, was nothing more than a euphemistic expression for war.[52]

Though the United States had rejected the Covenant of the League of Nations, it was not unaffected by the fortunes of this instrument of collective security. Thus, when it became apparent that the League would fail in keeping the peace, the American people looked with nostalgia to the old days of isolation and neutrality. This sentiment was reflected in the so-called neutrality legislation of the 1930s. But the neutrality acts of that decade were evidence of an abandonment of the traditional freedom-of-the-seas policy. The chief provisions of the first Neutrality Act of August 31, 1935, illustrates this point: An embargo was imposed with respect to shipments of "arms, ammunition, and implements of war"[53] to belligerent nations. It provided furthermore that American citizens could not travel on any vessel of a belligerent nation except at their own risk. The act, however, did not provide for the contingency of civil war. Accordingly, in January, 1937, a special resolution was rushed through Congress to take care of the unforeseen situation of the war in Spain. This addendum effectively cut off supplies to the loyalists, while in the meantime the insurgents were plentifully supplied by the Axis powers, and in this manner the civil war in Spain was allowed to continue to its bitter end.

An even more complete abandonment of neutral rights and the principle of the "freedom of the seas," which for more than a century had been the very keystone of American foreign policy, is evidenced in the act of May, 1937. In addition to the stipulations contained in the previous legislation, it vested in the President the authority to forbid the export of any goods to the belligerents except on a cash-and-carry basis. The President did not, however, make use of this power, and in 1939 the act was allowed to expire. Though it may be said that this legislation was evidence of an isolationist trend in American policy, it would be an error to maintain that it constituted a return to traditional neutrality. It may be said, therefore, that as the time bomb of the Second World War approached the hour of explosion, the United States was far more concerned about keeping out of the conflict than about insisting upon the neutral rights to which it might be entitled under the law of nations.

Neutrality and the Doctrine of Necessity. In the foregoing material of

---

[52] See Georg Cohn, *Neo-neutrality*, and Borchard and Lage, *Neutrality for the United States*, for able expositions of this point of view.

[53] These were later defined by the President to include airplanes, various chemicals, armored vehicles, but not cotton, oil, scrap iron, trucks, etc. See Phillips and Garland, *op. cit.*, p. 132.

this chapter we have pointed to the conflicting interests which must always exist in time of war between belligerent and neutral nations. Furthermore, we have indicated that this conflict has been enhanced by a more extensive employment of economic warfare. In the course of this conflict, the belligerents have come to rely more and more upon the doctrine of necessity for the sake of self-preservation, while the neutral nations have continued, with diminishing success, to claim certain rights under international law in order to continue their business as usual. It should be noted that it was the resistance of neutrals to the pretentions of the belligerents which in the first place gave rise to what we have called the traditional law of neutrality.

Inasmuch as experience in both the First and the Second World Wars seems to indicate a triumph of military necessity over the rights of neutrals, a brief consideration of this topic seems in order. The plea of military necessity is far from new in international jurisprudence. It was used by the British in the War of 1812 and doubtless could be traced to a much earlier origin. One of the leading cases concerning military necessity, however, is that of *The Curlew, Magnet and Others*.[54] The ships involved had been seized by the British and taken to the port of Halifax, where a petition was presented by the military and naval authorities asking leave to requisition some of the ships and part of the cargoes pending jurisdiction in the case. It was argued in support of the petition that such action was required by circumstances of urgent necessity. Dr. Croke of the Prize Court, in upholding the validity of the plea, declared that "there are certain cases of necessity, in which the right of self-defense, the first law of nature and of nations, supersedes all inferior rights, and dispenses with the usual modes of proceeding."

The same question again presented itself during the First World War in the case of *The Zamora*.[55] Here the facts were as follows: On April 8, 1915, the *Zamora*, a Swedish ship, on her way from New York to Stockholm with a cargo of grain and copper, was stopped by British cruisers between the Faroe and Shetland Islands, taken to Barrow-in-Furness, and in due course placed in the hands of the marshal of the Prize Court. On appeal the case came before the Judicial Committee of the Privy Council. The lower court had held that it was within the power and prerogative of the Crown to order the requisition of neutral property. Though this decision was reversed in the court of the last instance, Lord Parker in writing the opinion of the Court said:

A belligerent Power has by international law the right to requisition vessels

[54] Stewart's *Vice-Admiralty Reports* (Nova Scotia), p. 312.
[55] [1916] 2 A.C. 77; M. O. Hudson, *Cases and Other Material on International Law* (1936), pp. 1402 ff.

or goods in the custody of its Prize Court pending a decision of the question whether they should be condemned or released, but such right is subject to certain limitations. *First*, the vessel or goods in question must be urgently required for use in connection with the defense of the realm, the prosecution of the war, or other matters involving national security. *Secondly*, there must be a real question to be tried, so that it would be improper to order an immediate release. And *thirdly*, the right must be enforced by application to the Prize Court, which must determine judicially whether, under the particular circumstances of the case, the right is exercisable. . . .

The opinion in the case of *The Zamora* was reaffirmed by the same Court in the case of *The Canton*.[56] Similar action was taken by French and German authorities during the war, and its legality was not questioned by the prize courts.[57] It should be noted, however, that in order to justify a departure from "the usual modes of proceeding" the court must be confronted with clear proof that circumstances of military necessity do in fact exist.

The question has also been raised as to whether a plea of military necessity may justify the seizure and destruction of neutral property temporarily within the territory of a belligerent state. In this regard the famous *Duclair* Incident of the Franco-Prussian War of 1870 is called to mind. During the siege of Rouen, the Germans captured and sank a number of English colliers in the river Seine in order to prevent French gunboats from coming to the aid of the city. In defending the action, Prince Bismark said that [58] "the measure in question, however exceptional in its nature, did not overstep the bounds of international warlike usage." He pointed to a pressing danger which, even in time of peace, would justify the employment or destruction of foreign property under reservation of indemnification.

The seizure of neutral property temporarily within the territory of a belligerent is also recognized by the Hague rules. Article 19, paragraph 1, of the fifth Hague convention, on Rights and Duties of Neutral Powers and Persons in War on Land, provides that "railway material coming from the territory of neutral powers, whether it be the property of the said powers or of companies or private persons, and recognizable as such, shall not be requisitioned or utilized by a belligerent except where and to the extent that is abolutely necessary. It shall be sent back as soon as possible to the country of origin." [59] It is provided, however, in paragraph 3 of the same article, that "compensation shall be paid by one party or

[56] *Prize Cases*, edited by E. C. M. Trehern and A. W. Grant, vol. II, pp. 264–268.
[57] Burleigh Cushing Rodick, *The Doctrine of Necessity in International Law* (1928), p. 101.
[58] *British and Foreign State Papers*, vol. 61 (1870–1871), pp. 580–581.
[59] Scott, *op. cit.*, vol. II, p. 411.

the other in proportion to the material used, and to the period of usage."

The argument of military necessity has also been advanced in sinking of neutral vessels on the open sea. It was a plea advanced by England in the Napoleonic Wars, by the Central Powers during the First World War, and by both belligerents in the Second World War. It would seem, with the development of aircraft, radio, and radar, as well as the increased importance of economic warfare, that the plea of military necessity has been greatly strengthened.

The plea of urgent necessity has on various occasions been employed by belligerents as a justification for military action within the territorial waters of neutral states. In the case of *The Ryeshitelni*, during the Russo-Japanese War, it was argued by Japan that Chinese incapacity to perform her neutral duties created a situation so dangerous as to justify the capture of the Russian ship within the Chinese port of Chefoo.[60] A similar case during the First World War was that of the German cruiser *Dresden* which in March of 1915 sought refuge in Cumberland Bay, within the territorial waters of Chile. The *Dresden* was given orders by the Chilean government to leave within twenty-four hours, but refused to do so. After five days a British squadron appeared in the bay and ordered the surrender of the German warship, which was refused, and the *Dresden* was sunk by its own crew. The Chilean government protested the violation of its neutrality. While Great Britain offered an apology, it was pointed out that in view of repeated abuses of Chilean neutrality by German vessels and the apparent inability of Chile to enforce its neutral obligations, the British action was not without justification.[61]

The most celebrated case of this kind during the Second World War was that of the *Altmark*. The main facts were as follows: On February 16, 1940, the British destroyer *Cossack* forced the German naval auxiliary *Altmark* into a Norwegian fiord and removed more than 300 prisoners from aboard the German vessel. The British government and some international lawyers [62] charged that Norway had failed in its duties and that it should not have allowed the *Altmark* to transport prisoners along its coast. The British view of the incident was briefly as follows: (1) The German use of Norwegian territorial waters to avoid capture amounted to warlike operations within these waters. (2) The passage of the *Altmark* was illegal, as was the transport of prisoners. It was Norway's duty, therefore, to release the prisoners or at least order the German vessel

---

[60] Rodick, *op. cit.*, p. 111.
[61] *Ibid.*, p. 112.
[62] See C. H. M. Waldock, "The Release of the Altmark's Prisoners," *The British Year Book of International Law*, vol. 24 (1947), pp. 216–238.

to leave the neutral waters. (3) Norway had the power and opportunity to prevent the *Altmark*'s abuse of its territorial waters but refused to do so. The United Kingdom, therefore, became entitled to enter those waters in order to enforce international law and thus prevent serious prejudice to its interests.[63] In other words, it was argued that Norway's failure to meet its obligations as a neutral created a situation so prejudicial to British interest that the subsequent action of H.M.S. *Cossack* could be justified on the grounds of necessity.

Whether Norway was actually guilty of breach of neutrality in the *Altmark* incident is an academic question on which there is as yet no unanimous agreement. The view taken by the Norwegian government has been summarized as follows: [64]

(*a*) The *Altmark*, being a German warship, was immune from search, so that Norway's only right was to verify her identity and status from her papers, as was done by the first Norwegian torpedo-boat on 14 February.

(*b*) There is nothing in international law prohibiting a belligerent from conveying prisoners through neutral territorial waters if the passage itself is legal. Accordingly, if the *Altmark*'s passage was in itself legal, Norway was not concerned to inquire whether she had prisoners on board.

(*c*) The *Altmark* did not touch at any Norwegian port but was throughout merely making passage. As neither Hague Convention No. XIII of 1907 nor the Norwegian Neutrality Regulations of 1938 contained any express time-limit for mere passage, no obligation arose for the *Altmark* to leave territorial waters after 24 hours so that her passage was in itself legal.

(*d*) As Norway had not failed in the discharge of its obligations under the law of neutrality, no ground existed for the British action in its territorial waters.

To what extent the so-called "doctrine of necessity" can be regarded as a general principle of international law is difficult to determine. The main justification for the doctrine, as we have indicated, is the fundamental right of states to self-preservation. An examination of the authorities indicates that the doctrine of necessity as a legal principle must always

---

[63] *Ibid.*, p. 220.

[64] *Ibid.* According to Charles Cheney Hyde, Norway "lacked the right to search a public belligerent vessel such as the *Altmark* whose immunity from the local jurisdiction embraced immunity from search"—*op. cit.*, p. 2339. Edwin Borchard of Yale University argued concerning this case that "as a public ship the *Altmark* was free from visit and inspection except possibly to verify her conformity with Norway's neutrality regulations." He also points out that, during the Franco-Prussian war, "a French war vessel entered the Firth of Forth with German prisoners on board, whereupon the German Consul at Leith asked Great Britain to release the prisoners in accordance with Britain's alleged neutral duty. The British government replied that the French warship was privileged to enter and to remain for a limited time, that the prisoners on board did not become free, that while on board they were under French jurisdiction, and that the neutral authorities had no right to interfere with them"—*American Journal of International Law*, vol. 34 (1940), pp. 292–294.

be subject to numerous limitations, among which the following have been suggested: (1) it should be confined to circumstances in which its use is sanctioned by the law in advance; (2) it should be confined strictly to the defense of acknowledged rights; (3) it should be confined to cases in which the need to defend the state actually exists; (4) the employment of extralegal force must be commensurate with the particular circumstances of the case; (5) the danger must be imminent and overwhelming, and an opportunity lacking for other means of defense.[65]

Neutrality and Collective Security. In the final stages of the First World War, a great movement began among the nations to secure the future against repetition of so great a tragedy. The result, as we have seen in an earlier chapter, was the establishment of the League of Nations with the hope that the precarious balance of power could be replaced by a more effective system of collective security. The early proclamations to this end were filled with idealistic expressions regarding the ultimate nature of the "brave new world." One cannot escape the conclusion, upon reading again the famous Fourteen Points of Woodrow Wilson, that the reorganization of the international order which the American President had in mind was very different indeed from that which was eventually realized under the Covenant of the League. Much of the language in this instrument of collective security was vague and uncertain. From the text of Article 16, for example, it was impossible to determine what the legal status of neutrality was—whether it should be abandoned, or be kept and strengthened.[66] Confusion on this point was made no less when Switzerland, whose perpetual neutrality is guaranteed by the powers, was admitted to the League without reservations.[67] In a declaration of February 13, 1920, the Council of the League of Nations pointed out that the position of Switzerland was indeed exceptional and stressed that neutrality in a general sense was not compatible with the system created by the Covenant.[68] The very exception in the Swiss case seems to corroborate the notion that neutrality could have no legal standing within the League of Nations. It is indeed difficult to see how, in view of its theoretical basis and its nature, neutrality can on the whole be reconciled with the principle of collective security.[69]

There can be little doubt that we are experiencing a period of transition as far as the law of neutrality is concerned. This is due not only to the attempts in the last thirty years to substitute for individual neutrality col-

[65] See Rodick, *op. cit.*, pp. 119–120.   [66] Cohn, *op. cit.*, p. 48.
[67] *Ibid.*, p. 49.   [68] *Ibid.*
[69] On the other hand, it was argued that the reservationless admittance of Switzerland to the League, notwithstanding her authorized neutrality (Art. 435, Treaty of Versailles), was in itself proof that these two situations were not mutually exclusive. See Cohn, *op. cit.*, p. 49.

lective responsibility for keeping the peace, but perhaps even more, as we have already suggested, to the new methods of warfare. However, the conclusion should not be drawn from this statement that the violation of neutral rights, so notorious in the two great wars of this century, is in itself evidence of a changing law. On this point, Commissioner Nielsen in his dissenting opinion in the case of the *Oriental Navigation Company* [70] wrote in part as follows:

> Of course, custom, practice, and changed conditions have their effect on international law as well as on domestic law. However, it need not be observed that a violation of law is not equivalent to a modification or abolition of law. The fact that new instrumentalities of warfare make it inconvenient for a belligerent in control of the sea in a given locality to act in conformity with established rules of law does not *ipso facto* result in a change of the law or justify disregard for the law. . . . A belligerent cannot make law to suit his convenience. An international tribunal cannot undertake to formulate rules with respect to the exercise of belligerent rights, or to decide a case in the light of speculations with regard to future developments of the law, thought to be foreshadowed by derogations of international law which unhappily occur in times of war. Members of the League of Nations doubtless have entered into certain obligations under Article 16 of the Covenant of the League, but it must not necessarily be presumed that they must carry out their contractual obligations in violation of international law. It should rather be assumed that any action taken in fulfillment of such obligations will be executed in a manner consistent with the law. In the agony of great international conflict, resort may be had to expedients to circumvent law, but the law remains.

CONCLUSION

In the foregoing an attempt has been made to indicate the gradual development of the law of neutrality and to outline its basic substance in terms of the codifications of The Hague and London. As we have indicated earlier, it was the establishment of an international prize court by the second Peace Conference at The Hague which brought into sharp focus the indefinite character of the law of prize. This was a matter of great concern to the maritime nations—particularly Great Britain—and resulted, therefore, in the London Naval Conference of 1908–1909. After two months of deliberation, the famous Declaration of London was signed, and the signatory powers agreed that the rules contained therein represented, in the main, "the generally recognized principles of international law." This *disposition préliminaire* was the more significant for the fact that the declaration was the product of the ablest international lawyers of that day. "The *Institut de droit international* itself could not have

[70] *American Journal of International Law*, vol. 23 (1929), p. 437.

mustered a greater array of talent." [71] Yet, as we have already seen, the declaration was never ratified by a single state.

This, very largely, was the condition of the law of neutrality which was to face its first test in the war of 1914–1918. It was an expression of the law as understood in the nineteenth century. The basic principles recognized were nonintervention and impartiality, and these in turn were related to the then prevailing notions of sovereignty, but in reality not based upon them.[72] The laws of neutrality have suffered two massive blows in the present century, from which they may never recover. The first of these is occasioned by the ramified interests of interdependent nations and the coming of total war; while the second is caused by the substitution of collective security in international legal relations for the independent action of sovereign states. It may be concluded, therefore, that under such circumstances, nations must continue to lose their independence, and as a result neutrality can have no meaning either in fact or in law.

[71] Philip C. Jessup, Preface to the third volume of *Neutrality, Its History, Economics and Law.*
[72] Cohn, *op. cit.,* p. 40.

CHAPTER 23

The Law of Military Occupation

In the whole area of the law of war, the rules and regulations which govern military occupation are perhaps the most highly developed. Yet, this law as it exists today is of relatively recent origin. It was the custom in former times to consider occupied territory as property of the controlling state, who was regarded as having full rights over both the land and its inhabitants. It was not until the latter half of the eighteenth century that a legal distinction was made between military occupation as such and the acquisition of territory through conquest and subjugation. The consequences of this distinction, however, were not apparent in international law until long after the Napoleonic Wars.[1] Indeed, the whole of the nineteenth century was needed to develop the law of military occupation as it is today.

The Legal Nature of Occupation. Perhaps the most important principle of law, incident to military occupation, is that such occupation does not of itself displace or transfer sovereignty.[2] Though the occupying power is entitled to certain rights for purposes of military control over the occupied territory, sovereignty is not acquired until it is ceded by treaty or relinquished through subjugation, i.e., the destruction by force of the local sovereign, as in the case of the South African Republic and the Orange Free State at the end of the Boer War. Occupation affects neither the nationality of the inhabitants of the occupied territory nor their allegiance.[3] In *De Jager v. Attorney General of Natal* it was held that

[1] Though Vattel had given the matter some attention, the first author to deduce the legal consequences of the distinction between occupation and acquisition of territory was Heffter in a treatise entitled *Das europaeische Voelkerrecht der Gegenwart*, published in 1844. See Oppenheim-Lauterpacht, *International Law* (1944), vol. II, p. 338.

[2] Sir Arnold Duncan McNair, *Legal Effects of War* (1948), p. 320.

[3] In the nineteenth century, however, there was, especially in Anglo-American jurisprudence, the notion of "temporary allegiance." This principle found its first expression in *United States v. Hayward* (2 Dall. 485) where Justice Story declared that by the military occupation of Castine, Maine, by the British, the inhabitants as a consequence passed under temporary allegiance to the British government. This prin-

"the protection of a State does not cease merely because the State forces, for strategical or other reasons, are temporarily withdrawn, so that the enemy for the time exercises the rights of an army of occupation." [4] The rights and duties of the occupying power fall within the ambit of military administration, and according to international law, not even temporary changes may be made in the laws and government of the occupied country, except as might be required to maintain order and secure the safety of the occupation. Article 43 of the Hague regulations makes it incumbent upon the occupant to "take all steps in his power to re-establish and insure, as far as possible, public order and safety, while respecting, unless absolutely prevented, the laws in force in the country." It may be said, therefore, that the belligerent "has the right of exercising such control, and such control only, within the occupied territory, as is required for his safety and the success of his operations. But the measure and range of military necessity in particular cases can only be determined by the circumstances of those cases." [5]

Though during the early part of the nineteenth century the notion of "temporary allegiance" to the occupying power had found some favor in Anglo-American jurisprudence, it had to be abandoned at the turn of the century as incompatible with the Hague regulations. Article 45 of the regulations annexed to convention IV of 1907 provides that the population in occupied territory cannot be compelled to swear allegiance to any hostile power. A provision very similar to Article 45 had originally been drafted at the Brussels conference of 1874 and was restated in the Oxford Manual prepared for the Institute of International Law in 1880. [6] Furthermore, the unequivocal statements in the Hague regulations of 1899, which were repeated without further discussion in 1907, could not be reconciled with the notion that the inhabitants of occupied territory owed any allegiance whatever to the power of occupation. It is likewise stipulated by the Geneva convention of 1949 that an individual who has committed an offence against the occupying power is not to be regarded by the courts of the occupant as a national of that state. Thus, it would appear that the inhabitant of the occupied territory owes no allegiance to the occupying power.

---

ciple, though followed in subsequent decisions of the Supreme Court of the United States, was somewhat qualified in 1830, when it was suggested that the occupation of James Island and Charleston by the British in 1780 did not "annihilate" the allegiance of the inhabitants to the state of South Carolina.

[4] [1907] A.C. 326; M. O. Hudson, *Cases and Other Materials on International Law* (1936), pp. 1060–1062.

[5] W. E. Hall, *International Law*, 8th ed. by Higgins (1924), p. 559.

[6] Major Richard R. Baxter, "The Duty of Obedience to the Belligerent Occupant," *The British Year Book of International Law*, vol. 27 (1950), pp. 238–239.

According to the *Rules of Land Warfare* of the War Department of the United States, occupation is a "question of fact." It is a result of hostile invasion by which the authority of the invading power has been substituted for that of the "legitimate government" of the territory in question. Invasion must not be confused with occupation, though it precedes it and frequently coincides with it. Nor is occupation to be considered equivalent to conquest. It is essentially of a provisional nature, and sovereignty is not vested in the occupying power. Furthermore, occupation must be effective; that is, the organized resistance must have been overcome and the invading forces must be in a position to establish law and order. "It is immaterial by what methods the authority is exercised, whether by fixed garrisons or flying columns, small or large forces." [7] According to Article 42 of the regulations annexed to the convention respecting the rules and regulations of land warfare signed at The Hague in 1907: "Territory is considered occupied when it is actually placed under the authority of the hostile army. The occupation extends only to the territory where such authority has been established and can be exercised." [8]

Administration of Occupied Territory. Though sovereignty in a *de jure* sense is not acquired through the mere agency of occupation, it cannot be denied that *de facto* power rests with the occupying authority. By virtue of undisputed control over the territory in question, the occupant enjoys both the right and the duty to take whatever measures are necessary to maintain order and public safety.[9] In this respect a considerable latitude is allowed the occupant, whose first consideration must be the security of his position and the safety of his forces. As a matter of practical expediency, local institutions of law and government might be utilized by the occupant in the exercise of his authority. But more often, perhaps, the necessary control is better achieved through decrees emanating from the high command. Generally speaking, therefore, the government of occupied territory tends to be one of martial law.

But as we have already seen, the power of the occupant is to some degree limited by the law of nations. The inhabitants of occupied territory may not, for example, be compelled to take an oath of allegiance to the occupying state, or be made to serve in its armed forces. On the other hand, the occupant may demand that the inhabitants assume a "neutral attitude" and desist from any action which may endanger the safety of his forces. In accordance with Article 49 of the Hague regulations, contributions may be levied in occupied territories "for the needs of the army or

[7] G. H. Hackworth, *Digest of International Law*, vol. VI, pp. 388–389.
[8] Hackworth, *ibid.*, p. 388; 36 Stat. L. 2277, 2306.
[9] C. C. Hyde, *International Law* (1947), vol. III, p. 1882.

of the administration of the territory in question." [10] It is also within the right of the occupying power to demand various services from the inhabitants such as the construction of roads, buildings, and bridges. In this connection the phrase, "taking part in the operations of war" from Article 52 of the Hague regulations has become somewhat controversial. Many writers argue that the meaning of this article is to exclude projects such as roads and fortifications, or anything which could be classified in the category of "military preparations." In practice, however, there has been a tendency on the part of belligerents to distinguish between *military operations* on the one hand, and *military preparations* on the other. Thus during both the First and Second World Wars the populations of occupied territories were extensively used as labor on military projects, especially by the Germans. In view of the exigencies of modern war, it is doubtful that this state of affairs could be greatly changed by a mere clarification of Article 52 of the Hague regulations. Here again, military necessity seems to outweigh all other considerations.

Whatever the law regarding the employment of the inhabitants in occupied territory may be, it is quite certain that it does not countenance their deportation for such purpose to the country of the occupant. Though the Germans in both world wars resorted to this expedient, its practice can be regarded in no other light than as a flagrant violation of international law.

Some authorities affirm, while others deny, the proposition that the inhabitants of occupied territory are under a moral as well as a legal duty to refrain from doing anything which would render the position of the occupant less secure. The theory that international law creates an obligation of obedience is supported for the most part by Continental writers, but even among them a disquieting realization prevails that the duties of the inhabitants of occupied territory are a result of force rather than law.[11]

The Legal Status of "War Treason." There can be no doubt that the inhabitants of occupied territory are under compulsion to obey the occupation authority. But the duty of the population in this respect has no foundation in international law. Attempts have nevertheless been made to create such a norm through the ingenious concept of *Kriegsverrat* or "war treason." This term has been defined as hostile acts committed by persons other than members of the armed forces properly identified as such.[12] The history of *Kriegsverrat* may be traced back to medieval

---

[10] Regarding this matter, the Nuremberg Tribunal of 1946 held that "under the rules of war, the economy of an occupied country can only be required to bear the expenses of the occupation, and these should not be greater than the economy of the country can reasonably be expected to bear"—Cmd. 6964 (1946), p. 53.

[11] Baxter, *op. cit.*, p. 243.   [12] *Ibid.*, p. 244.

Germanic law. But as a technical term in modern jurisprudence, it appeared first in General Order No. 100, *Instructions for the Government of Armies of the United States in the Field*, prepared by Dr. Francis Lieber in 1862 and 1863. Article 90 of the *Instructions* defined a "war traitor" as "a person in a place or district under martial law who, unauthorized by the military command, gives information of any kind to the enemy, or holds intercourse with him." A distinction between this kind of treason and the ordinary domestic variety was also made by General Halleck, who in 1863 wrote the commanding officer of the Union Army in Tennessee defining "military treason" as hostile acts against an army of occupation.

Ever since Lieber's *Instructions* of 1863 "war treason" has been treated in military manuals. In the current *Rules of Land Warfare* for the United States Army, the very same provisions as those found in Articles 91, 92, and 95 of General Order No. 100 are to be found.[13]

Though it is clear that the occupant of hostile territory has a right to take whatever measures are necessary to safeguard his position, any action against him by the inhabitants can scarcely be said to constitute treason. This is so because the population of occupied territory owes no allegiance to the occupying state. The history of military occupation during and after the Second World War indicates that very little reliance was placed on the concept of "war treason." The Germans, to be sure, did sometimes make use of special tribunals for *Kriegsverrat*, an offence they defined as "all actions detrimental to the Army of Occupation." [14] Generally, it may be said that the concept of "war treason" has fallen into disuse. Not even the occupation of Germany following the Second World War has served to create a category of acts which could be regarded as "treasonable" to the occupying powers. The practice has been for the occupant to list those actions which he regards as dangerous to his security and thus deserving of punishment. It is significant in this connection that, though the United States Ordinance No. I of Military Government in Germany lists some forty acts as punishable because of the danger to the occupant, "war treason" is not among them.[15]

The Legal Status of War Rebellion. Though the history of "war rebellion" pretty much parallels that of "war treason," it has proved somewhat less controversial. In a pamphlet on *Guerrilla Parties Considered with Reference to the Laws and Usages of War*, Dr. Francis Lieber defined

[13] See pars. 207, 208, and 210 of Field Manual 27–10, Oct. 1, 1940. References to the concept of "war treason" are also found in the *British Manual of Military Law* as well as in the German *Kriegsbrauch im Landkriege*.

[14] Baxter, *op. cit.*, p. 251.

[15] *Military Government Gazette, Germany, United States Zone*, Issue A, June 1, 1946, p. 57.

a "war rebel" as a "renewer of war within an occupied territory." It is in this sense that the term is understood today.[16] It has reference to uprisings by armed groups within the population in occupied territory, and as such differs from "war treason" or individual acts of sabotage. The concept of "war rebellion" found its way from Lieber's pamphlet into the writings of Bluntschli [17] and so became a part of European jurisprudence.[18] The question of whether "war rebellion" constitutes a violation of legal duties imposed upon the population in occupied territory is as yet a matter of controversy. This point was raised at the Brussels conference of 1874 but proved at that time an insoluble problem. There was a strong feeling, especially on the part of the smaller states, that a *levée en masse*, or general uprising of the population, in occupied territory should not be prohibited by positive international law. It was not until the Hague conference of 1899 that the matter again came up for discussion. A member of the British technical delegation attempted a compromise by introducing a formula to the effect that nothing in the convention should be so construed as to preclude the population of an invaded country from offering by all lawful means the most energetic and patriotic resistance to the invader. But the proposal was soon withdrawn because of the strenuous objections from Germany and Russia.[19]

Concerning the legality of armed uprisings in occupied territory, there is considerable disagreement among authorities. To some it is a serious violation of international law, while to others such revolution is regarded not only as a right but as a duty.[20]

The *levée en masse* has in recent years been supplanted by more subtle tactics of resistance. The occupant is now more likely to be faced with guerrilla warfare, individual armed attacks, and sabotage, rather than open rebellion. But underground movements of this sort can hardly be regarded as in the category of "war rebellion." Resistance to military occupation by the local population is likely to follow as a logical consequence of total war and of the intimacy of association which exists in this age between the individual citizen and his political society.

As to the question of whether international law imposes upon the inhabitants of occupied territory the duty of obedience to the occupant, the answer is not as yet definitive. The very terms "war treason" and "war rebellion" are in themselves indicative of origins which must be

[16] Baxter, *op. cit.*, p. 253.
[17] *Das moderne Volkerrecht der civilisirten Staaten* (1868).
[18] Baxter, *op. cit.*, p. 253.
[19] J. B. Scott, *The Proceedings of the Hague Peace Conference of 1899*, pp. 550–555.
[20] See Baxter, *op. cit.*, pp. 254–255.

found in municipal rather than in international law. It may be of significance that in the Geneva Civilians Convention of 1949 [21] no mention is
made of either "war treason" or "war rebellion." The hostile acts of the
inhabitants of occupied territory are described as "espionage," "sabotage,"
or as "activity hostile to the security of the Occupying Power." The tentative conclusion may be drawn, therefore, that in terms of both the positive
law of nations and the general practice of states there is little to support
the proposition that a legal duty exists compelling obedience on the part
of the population in occupied territory to the power of occupation. Thus,
in the final analysis, obedience to the power of occupation will depend
upon the superior force of the occupant rather than upon the tenets of
the law of nations.

Military Occupation and the Transfer of Property. Generally speaking,
text writers have confined their treatment of war booty to the problems
of the battlefield. The Hague and Geneva conventions have been cited
regarding the most obvious forms of misconduct, such as pillage and the
robbing of prisoners. Far less has been said concerning the taking of
property in connection with military occupation, and the many problems
which arise when the whole economy of an occupied country is subjected
to the demands of total war.[22] "International law," wrote Jacob Robinson
in 1945, "was no more prepared for the dynamics of the present war than
was the Maginot school of military strategy. International lawyers had
given little serious thought to the legal problems which total war would
bring." [23]

Concerning the right of requisition by an army of occupation and the
duty of compensation, Article 53 of the Hague regulations of 1907 distinguishes between public and private property: [24]

> An army of occupation can only take possession of cash, funds, and realizable
> securities which are strictly the property of the State, depots of arms, means of
> transport, stores and supplies, and, generally, all movable property belonging
> to the State which may be used for the operations of the war.
>
> All appliances, whether on land, at sea, or in the air, adapted for the trans-
> mission of news, or for the transport of persons or things, exclusive of cases
> governed by naval law, depots of arms and, generally, all kinds of munitions of
> war, may be seized, even if they belong to private individuals, but must be re-
> stored and compensation fixed when peace is made.

[21] Department of State Publication 3938, General Foreign Policy Series 34, August,
1950.
[22] H. A. Smith, "Booty of War," *The British Year Book of International Law*, vol.
23 (1946), p. 227.
[23] J. Robinson, "Transfer of Property in Enemy Occupied Territory," *American
Journal of International Law*, vol. 39 (1945), p. 216.
[24] James Brown Scott (ed.), *The Reports of the Hague Conferences of 1899 and
1907*, p. 520.

The occupying state, however, is to be regarded only as an administrator of public buildings, real estate, and forests in the occupied territory.[25] The actual title to such property does not transfer through the medium of mere occupation.[26] The right of the occupying state is confined to the temporary control of the property and the use of its products. Rents and taxes may also be collected by the power in occupation, and receipts given for the payment of such rents and taxes are regarded as valid against any future claims.

It would appear that almost everything which is of use to the belligerent in his war effort may be seized without regard to its public or private ownership. The difference between the two paragraphs of Article 53, however, is that in the case of private property compensation must be fixed when peace has been restored. It is obvious that the significance of this distinction for purposes of compensation is much less today than it was in 1907. This is so because according to the holdings of prize courts, the real test of ownership lies in the power of disposition and control.[27] The greatly increased government control over resources, especially in time of war, has in a very real sense reduced the distinction between private and public property. Furthermore, in a socialist economy the presumed distinction between the two paragraphs of Article 53 can have no meaning whatever.

According to Article 56 of the Hague regulations, the property of communes, i.e., municipalities,[28] of religious, charitable, and educational institutions, and of arts and science, even when owned by the state, is to be treated as private property. It is provided in paragraph 2 of the same article that "all seizure or destruction of, or wilful damage to, institutions of this character, historic monuments, works of art and science, is forbidden, and should be made the subject of legal proceedings." It is furthermore provided in Article 50 of the regulations that "no general penalty, pecuniary or otherwise, shall be inflicted upon the population on account of the acts of individuals for which they cannot be regarded as jointly and severally responsible." But the destruction of the library of Louvain

[25] Art. 55 of the Hague Regulations; Scott, *loc. cit.*
[26] But the Supreme Court of the United States in 1815 held that "although acquisitions made during war are not considered as permanent until confirmed by treaty, yet to every commercial and belligerent purpose they are considered as a part of the domain of the conqueror, so long as he retains the possession and government of them"—*Thirty Hogsheads of Sugar v. Boyle*, 9 Cranch 191 (1815).
[27] This is especially true of British prize courts. See Smith, *op. cit.*, p. 231.
[28] It may not have been the intention to grant the highly preferential treatment of Art. 56 to all types of property owned by municipalities, simply on the basis of ownership. Military installations, for example, and all other property susceptible to military use, but owned by municipalities, would not enjoy protection under Art. 56. See William M. Franklin, "Municipal Property under Belligerent Occupation," *American Journal of International Law*, vol. 38 (1944), pp. 383–396.

on August 25, 1914, was defended by the Germans as lawful reprisal against the population of that city, who, it was alleged, had fired on German troops. This contention, however, was denied by the subsequent peace treaty. Article 247 of the Treaty of Versailles stipulated:

> Germany undertakes to furnish to the University of Louvain, within three months after a request made by it and transmitted through the intervention of the Reparation Commission, manuscripts, incunabula, printed books, maps and objects of collection corresponding in number and value to those destroyed in the burning by Germany of the Library of Louvain.

German Practice During the Second World War. As the German army moved across the continent of Europe like an avalanche, a unique plan of military occupation was put into effect. The plan had been systematically worked out long before the outbreak of the war and contemplated a new economic and political order designed to provide for "the Greater German Reich a maximum of security, and to the German people a maximum of consumption of goods in order to increase their welfare." [29] Only a few examples from the history of German occupation will be given here in order to illustrate by what ingenious means this master plan was put into operation.

In the first place, forced contributions were made in all occupied countries far in excess of the actual costs of occupation, and without regard to the resources of the occupied countries. [30] These things were done in direct violation of Articles 49 and 52 of the Hague convention. The strategy behind the German economic penetration in Europe was designed to establish links strong enough to hold even in case of military failure. [31] The following were some of the methods employed by the *Reich* in its illegal seizure of private property: (1) the confiscation, without compensation, of property belonging to persons in these categories: (*a*) those who had left the country, (*b*) those belonging to the ruling family, (*c*) those who were regarded as promoting the Allied

[29] The Royal Institute of International Affairs, *Europe under Hitler*, p. 5, quoting Dr. Funk's own writings.

[30] The following figures are in reichsmarks:

Annual occupation charges		Per capita annual cost
Norway	660,000,000	226
Denmark	276,000,000	73
Holland	443,000,000	51
Belgium	443,000,000	49
France	7,300,000,000	174

Anyone familiar with the economies of the countries listed cannot help noticing the flagrant disregard for the capacity to pay as determined by the resources of the occupied countries (see *ibid.*, p. 28).

[31] Robinson, *op. cit.*, p. 219n.

cause, (*d*) Jews, and (*e*) citizens of annexed territories; (2) the seizure of holdings in banks and private safety deposit vaults; (3) the so-called "aryanization" of property by which the Jews were subjected to wholesale robbery; (4) the "trusteeship device" by means of which both individual and corporate enterprises were assigned, in trust, to German firms instead of being confiscated outright; (5) forced sales of domestic and foreign holdings through various means of coercion, and the auctioning of private art collections and securities in a quasi-legal manner.[32]

The Taking of Hostages. In ancient times the practice of taking hostages as a precaution against disorder in occupied territory was widespread. In the period of their imperial expansion the Romans made use of hostages to ensure compliance with their decrees, and the sons of tributary princes often lived in Rome over extended periods for purposes of "education." [33] Hostages have been used frequently to ensure the observance of treaty commitments, to secure the payments of international debts, and for various other reasons. In the year A.D. 999, for example, hostages were given by the people of Iceland to the Norwegian king Olav Tryggvason to ensure a promise that they would become Christians. In more recent times hostages have been taken for various purposes, such as for the ensurance of treaty performance; for guaranteeing the payment of requisitions; for the protection and return of individuals held by the enemy; for purposes of reprisal; and for the maintenance of order in occupied territory.[34]

During the First World War the practice of "prophylactic reprisals" became widespread. This took the form of compulsory detention of prominent civilians in occupied territory, who were made to stand on bridges to prevent their bombardment and to ride on trains to discourage their derailment by the local population. This illegal practice assumed large proportions, especially during the occupation of Belgium in 1914.[35]

Though the taking of hostages is of ancient origin, and in spite of the fact that the practice survived the nineteenth century, it received no direct treatment in the Hague conventions. But in the war manuals of several of the great powers the employment of hostages for various purposes is still regarded as valid in time of international hostilities.[36] The

---

[32] See *ibid.*, pp. 219–220.

[33] Hammer and Salvin, "The Taking of Hostages in Theory and Practice," *American Journal of International Law*, vol. 38 (1944), p. 20.

[34] *Ibid.*, p. 21.

[35] The taking of hostages for such purposes had precedents both in the Franco-Prussian War of 1870 and in the Boer War of 1899, but by the end of the nineteenth century the practice had been generally condemned by publicists as illegal under the law of nations.

[36] "Of the western European powers only the French were unrealistic enough to call the taking of hostages obsolete." Hammer and Salvin, *op. cit.*, p. 23.

main arguments which have been advanced in favor of the practice of taking hostages have centered around its alleged effectiveness. According to Oppenheim, "it seems doubtful . . . whether even the most humane commanders will always be able to dispense with this measure, since it alone has proved effective." [37] But is it not equally doubtful that the widespread use of hostages and their illegal [38] treatment by the Germans during the Second World War contributed significantly to the lessening of sabotage against the occupation in most of the countries of Europe? Indeed, the infamous treatment and mass killing of hostages in which the Germans engaged was such as to bring it prominently within the category of a war crime,[39] for which some of the more prominent leaders of the *Reich* were to be held accountable at Nuremberg.

Though it may be admitted, under conditions of military occupation, that "the authority of the legitimate power" has "passed into the hands of the occupant," such power is not without its legal limitations. As we have already seen, no general penalty may be inflicted on the population on account of acts of individuals.[40] It is also of significance, in this connection, that the International Military Tribunal in its judgment at Nuremberg saw fit to quote at some length from the preamble to the Hague Convention Respecting the Laws and Customs of War on Land, of which we shall repeat the following: [41]

Until a more complete code of the laws of war has been issued, the high contracting parties deem it expedient to declare that, in cases not included in the Regulations adopted by them, the inhabitants and the belligerents remain under the protection and the rule of the principles of the law of nations, as they result from the usages established among civilized peoples, from the laws of humanity, and from the dictates of the public conscience.

[37] Oppenheim-Lauterpacht, *op. cit.*, p. 461.
[38] As far back as the Spanish theologian Victoria, objections were raised to the killing of hostages. Both Grotius and Vattel reiterated this point. The English War Manual states that hostages are to suffer captivity but not death, and according to the American General Staff, "when a hostage is accepted, he is treated as a prisoner of war." See Hammer and Salvin, *op. cit.*, p. 25. See also in this connection, the *List*, or *Southeast*, or *Hostages Case*. A careful report of that case will be found in vol. VIII of the United Nations War Crimes Commission's *Law Reports of Trials of War Criminals*.
[39] Art. 6(*b*) of the Charter of the International Military Tribunal at Nuremberg provides that "ill-treatment . . . of civilian population of or in occupied territory . . . killing of hostages . . . wanton destruction of cities, towns or villages" shall be a war crime. This, of course, is merely declaratory of the existing laws of war as expressed in Art. 46 of the Hague declaration, which states: "Family honor and rights, the lives of persons and private property, as well as religious convictions and practices must be respected." See Lord Wright, "The Killing of Hostages as a War Crime," *The British Year Book of International Law*, vol. XXV (1948), p. 298.
[40] Scott, The Reports of the Hague Conferences of 1899 and 1907, p. 519.
[41] *Ibid.*, p. 509.

Though it has been said that "the Hague Conventions were strangely silent on the subject," [42] the language of the preamble, cited above, as well as that of Articles 46 and 50 would seem broad enough to include within its compass the legal status of the general treatment of hostages. As a matter of fact, the International Military Tribunal has held that Article 46 of the convention was in itself applicable and sufficient.[43] This article provides that "family honor and rights, individual life, and private property . . . must be respected." [44]

Certain Problems in Connection with Friendly Occupation. Up to this point our concern has been with military occupation, the only type for which provisions are made in the regulations annexed to the Hague convention IV. Some authors have classified occupation into three more categories as follows: (1) *hostile occupation,* which is defined as military government in territory completely and unconditionally surrendered; (2) *pacific occupation,* i.e., military occupation of a neutral or friendly country for the sake of its "protection" in time of war; and (3) *peaceful occupation,* which is the occupation of military bases and installations in friendly countries in time of peace.[45] The author of the present treatise finds this classification somewhat confusing and will therefore be content to speak only in terms of *military or hostile occupation* (discussed above) and *friendly occupation,* to which the remainder of this chapter will be devoted.

The occupation is friendly when the armed forces of one state are located within the territory of another state with the latter's free and full consent. This type of occupation can take place (1) when the two states are allies or cobelligerents, as were England and the United States during the Second World War; and (2) when neither state is a belligerent, as in the present occupation of certain military bases in the Philippines and in Britain by the United States. In cases where cobelligerent territory is liberated by the troops of a third power, the consequent occupation must be considered as of a friendly nature. In such cases the rights of the occupant, until control is surrendered to the rightful sovereign, are probably the same as those generally accorded under international law.[46] It is possible, however, that these rights may have been modified by existing treaties between the cobelligerents in question, i.e., before the government

---

[42] See Hammer and Salvin, *op. cit.,* p. 23.
[43] Wright, *op. cit.,* p. 302.
[44] Scott, *The Reports of the Hague Conferences of 1899 and 1907,* p. 519.
[45] William G. Downey, Jr., "Revision of the Rules of Warfare," *American Society of International Law Proceedings* (1949), pp. 102 ff. See also Herbert W. Briggs, *The Law of Nations* (1952), p. 1024.
[46] Hyde, *op. cit.,* p. 1909.

of one or the other of them had become impotent by reason of the enemy's occupation, or through the agency of a government-in-exile.

The friendly presence of members of the military establishment of one state within the territory of another has, from time to time, given rise to certain jurisdictional problems. The main question is whether the local courts have jurisdiction in cases involving members of the foreign armed forces, or whether such jurisdiction is exclusive with the courts-martial of those forces. Although this question is not, as yet, free from controversy, the majority opinion [47] seems to be that "a foreign army permitted to march through a friendly country, or to be stationed in it, by permission of its government or sovereign, is exempt from the civil and criminal jurisdiction of the place. . . ." [48]

In cases where friendly occupation can be anticipated, the general practice is to define by treaty the rights of the occupant regarding questions of civil and criminal jurisdiction. Such agreements may then be implemented by statutes in the country where the visiting forces are to be stationed. During the Second World War, for example, the British Parliament passed "an Act to give effect to an agreement recorded in notes exchanged between His Majesty's Government in the United Kingdom and the Government of the USA." [49] This legislation is also frequently referred to as the "United States of America (Visiting Forces) Act of 1942." [50] It provided complete exemption for members of the armed forces of the United States, located in the British Isles, from criminal jurisdiction in the local courts, and it recognized in all such cases the full competence of the American courts-martial. A proviso to Section 1 of the act, however, stipulates that the United States may waive its right to exclusive jurisdiction in any particular case.[51]

The treatment with respect to immunity in criminal jurisdiction of other Allied forces located in Britain during the war was far less generous than that accorded those of the United States. The legislation governing this

[47] "Most modern British and American authorities deal with the question and recognize the existence of some such rule. French, German, and Italian writers on international law recognize the rule too"—M. E. Bathurst, "Jurisdiction over Friendly Foreign Armed Forces: The American Law," *The British Year Book of International Law*, vol. XXIII (1946), pp. 338–341.

[48] *Coleman v. Tennessee*, 97 U.S. 509, 515; also *Dow v. Johnson*, 100 U.S. 158, 165. See also *The Schooner Exchange v. McFaddon*, 7 Cranch 116.

[49] 5 & 6 Geo. VI, c. 31.

[50] Archibald King, "Further Developments Concerning Jurisdiction over Friendly Foreign Armed Forces," *American Journal of International Law*, vol. 40 (1946), p. 263.

[51] Such a waiver was made by the United States Command in Britain, in only one case, as far as this author knows. In that instance it was done in order to facilitate a joint trial of an American by name Hulten and an Englishwoman named Jones, who together murdered a cabdriver.

matter in relations with other nations is found in the Visiting Forces (British Commonwealth) Act of 1933,[52] and in the Allied Forces Act of 1940,[53] and the Orders in Council issued for their implementation. The Allied Forces Act allowed jurisdiction of Allied military courts only "in matters concerning discipline and internal administration." [54] These legislative provisions clearly denied to the forces of Allied nations other than those of the United States any exemption from the criminal jurisdiction of the local courts.[55] It has been pointed out that the rights conceded under these statutes to the visiting forces were less than those which would ordinarily be allowed under international law, and less even than those which have been said to exist by the highest court in the British Empire.[56] In *Chung Chi Cheung v. The King* [57] the Judicial Committee of the Privy Council held that China had a prior right to try a sailor for murder on board a Chinese public vessel in the territorial waters of the British Crown Colony of Hong Kong, unless such right should be waived by the Chinese government. In this case Justice Taschereau went on to say:

If the receiving Sovereign is presumed to waive his jurisdiction as to members of the crew of a foreign ship, can it not be said that the same presumption exists as to land troops visiting a foreign country?

This view, I think, has been implicitly accepted by the Judicial Committee, and is in accordance with the doctrine of the authors, the practice followed by the nations of the world and by the Supreme Court of the United States.

[52] 23 Geo. V, c. 6.

[53] 3 & 4 Geo. VI, c. 51.

[54] Allied Forces Act, 1940, sec. 1 (1).

[55] In a series of jurisdictional agreements concluded between the British government and most of the governments-in-exile, it was provided that members of the armed forces of those governments should be subject to trial in the local courts for offenses against the criminal law of the United Kingdom. Art. 2 of the Anglo-Czechoslovak agreement of Oct. 25, 1940, whose terms appear in similar form in agreements with other governments-in-exile, provided that "acts or omissions constituting offenses against the law of the United Kingdom . . . shall be liable to be tried by the civil courts in the United Kingdom." G. P. Barton, "Foreign Armed Forces: Immunity from Criminal Jurisdiction," *The British Year Book of International Law*, vol. 27 (1950), p. 197.

[56] *Chung Chi Cheung v. The King*, [1939] A.C. 160, cited by King in *op. cit.*, p. 264. According to Egon Schwelb: "The position of the Allied Forces does not, in some respects, come up to the rules of international law regarding extra-territoriality even in that restricted sense in which it is recognized even by those writers who are not in favour of extensive extra-territoriality." (*The Czechoslovak Yearbook of International Law*, 1942, p. 169.) Furthermore, when the debate on the Allied Forces bill was under way in the House of Commons, the Attorney General of England saw fit to make the following statement: "I quite agree with the honorable gentleman that these foreign governments might say, 'You do not in this bill go as far as international law.'" (King, *op. cit.*, p. 264.).

[57] [1939] A.C. 160; Briggs, *op. cit.*, pp. 303–308.

The government of the United States, however, was able to make favorable agreements with a number of states, aside from Great Britain, by which immunity with respect to criminal jurisdiction was granted its forces stationed in those countries.[58] But to argue that these agreements are declaratory of existing norms in international law is, of course, to invite dissent, and for good reason, as such a conclusion is probably incorrect. "Where a series of international agreements make uniform arrangements on a given subject, it is not easy to decide whether they consecrate by formal recognition a generally accepted principle of international law or whether they constitute a deviation therefrom." [59]

The Mixed Courts of Egypt have developed a body of case law which tends to show that whatever jurisdictional immunity exists in terms of the general law, in cases involving the armed forces of friendly occupation, such immunity cannot be said to exist without definable limitations. In *Triandafilou v. Ministère Public* [60] the offense charged had been committed while the accused was on duty. It was held, therefore, that the offender was immune from jurisdiction by the local courts, on the ground that even if no general rule could be said to exist in international law granting a blanket immunity to members of visiting forces, a residual principle would seem to dictate that such immunity must be granted in all cases where the offence was committed when *ex facie* the accused was on duty.[61] The Supreme Court of Brazil in the case of *In re Gilbert* [62] decided that the local courts had no jurisdiction, as the offence had been committed within the limits of a camp occupied by the forces of the United States. The accused was an American marine on sentry duty who had shot and killed a Brazilian citizen who had attempted to enter the Admiral Ingram Camp at Recife.

The Attitude of the United States. When the British Parliament enacted the United States of America (Visiting Forces) Act of 1942, it was done, as we have seen, in pursuance of an agreement granting jurisdictional immunity to American forces stationed in the British Isles. Neither the agreement nor the legislation, however, was made contingent upon any guarantee of reciprocity with respect to the treatment, in this regard,

[58] With Belgium (with respect to the Belgian Congo), Agreement of Aug. 4, 1943; with Canada, Exchange of Notes dated Dec. 27, 1943, Feb. 10, 1944, and Mar. 9, 1944; with China, Agreement of May 21, 1943; with Egypt, agreement of Mar. 2, 1943; with India, Agreement of Sept. 29 and Oct. 10, 1942; and with New Zealand, Exchange of Notes dated Dec. 11, 1942, and Mar. 23, 1943.

[59] Barton, *op. cit.*, p. 231.

[60] *Annual Digest* (1943–1945), supplementary volume, Case no. 86.

[61] In this connection see also *Ministère Public v. Tsoukharis, Annual Digest* (1943–1945), Case no. 40; and *Malero Manuel v. Ministère Public, Annual Digest* (1934–1945), Case no. 42.

[62] Reported by Barton in *op. cit.*, p. 229.

by the United States of British armed forces stationed in this country.[63] When later, the American government was asked by the British if similar arrangements could be made for their armed forces within the jurisdiction of the United States, assurance was given that such immunity would indeed be granted. It was pointed out by the American government, however, that no legislation in this regard would be necessary in the United States, for the following reasons: Though the jurisdiction of the United States within its own territory is ordinarily absolute and exclusive, it is limited by international law as regards the armed forces of friendly nations who with the consent of the United States may be located within its territory. The leading case in American as well as international law supporting this point of view is *The Schooner Exchange v. McFaddon.*[64] The case came before the Supreme Court of the United States in 1812 on appeal from a sentence of the Circuit Court for the District of Pennsylvania. It involved the question of whether or not a public vessel of a friendly power could, in any way, be brought under local jurisdiction while in an American port for supplies and repairs. In the course of his judgment in this case, Chief Justice Marshall said:

A third case in which a sovereign is understood to cede a portion of his territorial jurisdiction is, where he allows the troops of a foreign prince to pass through his dominions.

In such case, without any express declaration waiving jurisdiction over the army to which this right of passage has been granted, the sovereign who should attempt to exercise it would certainly be considered as violating his faith. By exercising it, the purpose for which the free passage was granted would be defeated, and a portion of the military force of a foreign independent nation would be diverted from those national objects and duties to which it was applicable, and would be withdrawn from the control of the sovereign whose power and whose safety might greatly depend on retaining the exclusive command and disposition of his force. The grant of a free passage therefore implies a waiver of all jurisdiction over the troops during their passage, and permits the foreign general to use that discipline, and to inflict those punishments which the government of his army may require.

In *Republic of Panama v. Schwartzfiger,*[65] the Supreme Court of Panama said in a case involving an American soldier: "It is a principle of International Law that the armed forces of one State, when crossing the territory of another friendly country, with the acquiescence of the latter, are subject, not to the jurisdiction of the territorial sovereign, but to that of the officers and superior authorities of its own command." The same court also went on to say that the members of "those forces when acting

---

[63] Bathurst, *op. cit.*, p. 338.   [64] 7 Cranch 116 (1812).
[65] *Annual Digest* (1927–1928), Case no. 114 (1925).

in the name of or on behalf of the Government of the United States, are subject to the authority and jurisdiction to which they belong, and not to our national authorities; nor to both simultaneously, because such a double jurisdiction is contrary to law."

The qualification, "when acting in the name of or on behalf of the Government of the United States," has been interpreted by some as narrowing the rule to those cases where the wrong had been committed in line of duty.[66] This point, however, is ably discussed by Archibald King,[67] who concludes

that the general principle is abundantly established by reason, authority, and precedent, that the personnel of the armed forces of Nation A, in Nation B by the latter's invitation or consent, are subject to the exclusive jurisdiction of their own courts-martial and exempt from that of the courts of B, unless such exemption be waived. That principle has already been expressly recognized by several of the United Nations.

We may safely say that the position of the United States is to admit immunity of jurisdiction in criminal cases as far as visiting armed forces of friendly nations are concerned. This principle is recognized, in this country, as part of the common law of nations and therefore part of the municipal law of the United States.[68] Because of a firm judicial tradition established by a series of precedents which assumes the existence of such jurisdiction under international law, it was not deemed necessary to enact special substantive legislation on this matter. The Congress did pass an act, however, dealing with procedure in which it was provided that arrests could be made by American civil as well as military authorities and the offenders surrendered to the foreign commands concerned. It also empowers the federal courts in the United States to compel the attendance of witnesses before foreign service tribunals sitting in the United States. Immunity is assured to the tribunals as well as to the witnesses, and provisions are made for the imprisonment of offenders sentenced by the foreign tribunals in institutions maintained by the United States for the detention of prisoners.

RECENT DEVELOPMENTS

The law of military occupation as it stood at the outbreak of the Second World War was to a very large extent based on custom and usage and to

[66] See Barton, *op. cit.,* p. 219.

[67] "Jurisdiction over Friendly Foreign Armed Forces," *American Journal of International Law,* vol. 36 (1942), pp. 539 ff.

[68] *The Paquete Habana and The Lola,* 175 U.S. 677 (1900); Briggs, *op. cit.,* p. 30–33.

a lesser degree on convention. As in other branches of the law of war, little had been done to adjust its norms to new problems and situations. In general, it may be said that this branch of the law, as it existed at the beginning of the Second World War, was based on the assumption that occupation was of a temporary nature and it did not contemplate interference with the constitutional process or other permanent aspects of life in the occupied country.[69] The Allied occupation of Germany and Japan, however, aimed at certain objectives not envisaged by the existing law of military occupation.

Allied Occupation of Germany. Following unconditional surrender of Germany and Japan, a long period of military occupation was deemed necessary by the victorious Allies in order to insure against a revival of militarism and aggressive war.[70] Germany was partitioned for purposes of occupation, though outright annexation was disclaimed by the Allied declaration of June 5, 1945. The legal situation with respect to the German occupation seems to fit into no previous precedent and therefore presents a curious problem not yet resolved. "Precedents of military occupations abound. World War II was overrich in the most diverse types of occupations. But no one of these well-recognized types exactly fits the case." [71] It is different from the occupation of Japan, for in that case certain conditions with regard to the position of the Emperor were accepted by the Allies. Thus the occupation of Japan has its basis in an international agreement.[72] This was not the case in Germany. The legal basis for occupation of Germany rests on conquest. The conqueror has the right to annex the conquered state but may take other measures. Germany was not annexed but was divided into eastern and western zones of occupation by the Soviet Union and the Western Allies respectively. The occupying powers were competent to bind Germany in the same sense that a *de facto* government can bind a state. The renunciation of annexation was not intended to limit the powers which could be exercised during the period of occupation.[73] The Occupation Statute for Germany provided, *inter alia,* for disarmament and demilitarization; controls in regard to the Ruhr; restitution, reparations, decartelization, and control over foreign affairs.

---

[69] Pitman B. Potter, "Legal Bases and Character of Military Occupation in Germany and Japan," *American Journal of International Law,* vol. 43 (1949), p. 323.

[70] France–United Kingdom–United States Occupation Statute for Germany, approved at Washington, Apr. 8, 1949, and entered into force on Sept. 21 of the same year. *Department of State Bulletin,* vol. 20, no. 511 (Apr. 17, 1949), p. 500.

[71] Josef L. Kunz, "The Status of Occupied Germany under International Law: A Legal Dilemma," *The Western Political Quarterly,* vol. 3, no. 4 (December, 1950), p. 539.

[72] *Ibid.*

[73] Quincy Wright, "The Status of Germany and the Peace Proclamation," *American Journal of International Law,* vol. 46 (1952), p. 305.

Reserved to the occupation forces of the Allies, furthermore, were control over foreign trade and exchange; over displaced persons and refugees; and over internal affairs necessary to ensure the use of funds, food, and other supplies in such manner as to reduce to a minimum the need for external assistance to Germany. In addition to the powers enumerated in paragraph 2 of the Statute, the occupation authorities reserved the right to resume full control over all German affairs if it should be found necessary to the preservation of democratic government in Germany.

The unique and unprecedented situation created by the unconditional surrender of the German armed forces in 1945, and by the political developments since that time led to the establishment in the Western zone of the Federal Republic of Germany in 1949. A month thereafter, the so-called German Democratic Republic was proclaimed in the Soviet sector. The state of war which had existed between the United States and Germany since December 11, 1941, was terminated by joint resolution of the Congress on October 19, 1951.[74] On May 26, 1952, contractual agreements were signed between the Western Allies and the Federal Republic of Germany, the most important of which is the Convention on Relations. Though this was not a peace treaty, it brought to an end the Occupation Statute. Henceforth the three powers of the West—the United States, France, and England—are to conduct their relations with the Federal Republic through ambassadors. Limited rights, however, are retained by the three powers, such as the right to station troops in Germany for the defense both of the Federal Republic itself and of their own position in Berlin. These forces, however, are not to be regarded as an army of occupation, but rather as military assistance to the Federal Republic.[75] In case of danger to their armed forces, the three powers may take whatever action is necessary to secure their own safety. The Federal Republic on its part agrees to cooperate to the greatest extent in the promotion of political, cultural, and economic reconstruction. Thus, the reserved rights of the Allies are not to be regarded as an infringement of sovereignty, but rather as restrictions upon its practical exercise. In this way it is possible to integrate the Federal Republic in a European Community on the basis of equality.[76]

The Treaty of Peace with Japan. This treaty was signed at San Francisco on September 8, 1951, and came into force on April 28, 1952.[77] By this treaty the state of war between Japan and each of the Allied powers is terminated, and the full sovereignty of the Japanese people over Japan

[74] 82d Cong., 1st Sess., Public Law 181 (H. J. Res. 289); 65 Stat. L. 451.
[75] C. G. Fenwick, "The Contractual Agreements with the Federal Republic of Germany," *American Journal of International Law,* vol. 46 (1952), p. 701.
[76] *Ibid.,* p. 702.   [77] 82d Cong., 2d Sess., S. Ex. A.

and its territorial waters is recognized.[78] Japan recognizes the independence of Korea and renounces all right, title, and claim to Formosa, the Kurile Islands, and that portion of Sakhalin which was acquired by the Treaty of Portsmouth on September 5, 1905.[79] It is also provided that all occupation forces of the Allied powers are to be withdrawn from Japan as soon as possible after the treaty comes into force. However, nothing in this provision shall prevent the stationing or retention of foreign armed forces in Japan in consequence of bilateral or multilateral agreements between one or more of the Allied powers, on the one hand, and Japan on the other.[80] By the terms of this treaty, Japan also agrees to accept the judgments of the International Military Tribunal for the Far East and other Allied war-crimes courts both within and outside Japan. The power to grant clemency, to reduce sentences, and to parole in cases of convicted war criminals may not be exercised except on the decision of the government which imposed the sentence and upon the recommendation of Japan.[81]

Agreement Concerning NATO Forces. This agreement between the members of the North Atlantic Treaty Organization, signed in London on June 19, 1951, and entered into force August 23, 1953,[82] has reference to the status of forces and civilian components of the contracting parties when stationed outside their own territory but within that of a member state. According to its terms it is the duty of a force and its civilian component to respect the laws of the receiving state and to refrain from any activity inconsistent with the spirit of the agreement, particularly from any political activity within the receiving state. It is provided, however, that the military authorities of the sending state shall have the primary right to exercise jurisdiction over a member of a force or of a civilian component in relation to "(1) offences solely against the property or security of that State, or offences solely against the person or property of another member of the force or civilian component of that State or of a dependent; (2) offences arising out of any act or omission done in the performance of official duty." [83]

In cases where loss of or damage to property occurs, no claims are to be made by any of the contracting parties if such damage or loss is sustained in connection with the operation of the North Atlantic Treaty. Members of a force or civilian component of the sending state are exempt from taxation within the receiving state on salaries or movable property. With respect to incomes from profitable enterprise aside from official

---

[78] Art. 1 of the peace treaty. [79] Art. 2 of the treaty.
[80] Art. 6. [81] Art. 11.
[82] 82d Cong., 2d Sess., S. Ex. T.; Department of State Publication 5307, Treaties and Other International Acts Series 2846.
[83] Art. VII, 3(a) of the agreement.

duties within the receiving state, exemption from taxation may not, however, be allowed.

United States–United Kingdom Mutual-Defense Agreement. The Mutual Defense Assistance Agreement between the United States of America and the United Kingdom of Great Britain and Northern Ireland was signed in Washington, January 27, 1950, and came into force the same day.[84] In Article 1 of this agreement it is recognized that "economic recovery is essential to international peace and security" and must be given clear priority. To this end it was provided that the contracting parties should furnish each other such assistance as would best promote the integrated defense of the North Atlantic area. Subject to the provision of the necessary appropriations, the government of the United Kingdom is to make available to the government of the United States sterling for the administrative expenditures within the United Kingdom in connection with assistance given by the United States. Goods belonging to the government of the United States are to be free from export or import duties in the United Kingdom.[85] Each party agrees to receive personnel of the other within its territory and to allow such personnel to operate as part of the embassy and under the direction and control of the chief of diplomatic mission of the government they are serving.[86] It is further provided that upon notification by the American ambassador in the United Kingdom, such privileges and immunities as are enjoyed by members of the American Embassy will also be accorded any other personnel of the United States with comparable rank.[87]

These examples of international agreements for the promotion of national security and mutual assistance are illustrative of new tendencies in international relations. Though the world is divided by opposing ideologies and the polarization of power, individual members of each power group are being forced into closer cooperation. Under the pressure of the "cold war," vast sectors of the national interest which traditionally

---

[84] Department of State Press Release 88, Jan. 27, 1950; *Department of State Bulletin,* vol. 22, no. 554 (Feb. 13, 1950), p. 253. Similar agreements were signed the same day with Belgium, Denmark, France, Italy, Luxembourg, the Netherlands, and Norway (Press Releases 83–87, 89, 90, Jan. 27, 1950), *Department of State Bulletin,* vol. 22, no. 553 (Feb. 6, 1950), pp. 200–211; no. 554 (Feb. 13, 1950), pp. 247–253; no. 555 (Feb. 20, 1950), pp. 293–295. On Jan. 26, 1950, the signing of a mutual-assistance agreement with the Republic of Korea under the terms of the Mutual Defense Assistance Act of 1949 was announced by the Department of State. The agreement went into force on signature. *American Journal of International Law,* vol. 43 (1949), supplement, p. 159.

[85] Art. VIII of the agreement.   [86] Art. IX, pars. 1 and 2.

[87] Art. IX, par. 3. It was understood that the government of the United States, in making the notifications referred to in par. 3 of Art. IX, would bear in mind the desirability of restricting, so far as practicable, the number of officials for whom full diplomatic privileges would be requested (Annex J to the agreement).

were reserved to the self-determination of sovereign states are now yielding to the need for cooperation. Political cooperation must perforce be extended to the military and economic fields, as defense in our time is no less total than war itself.[88] But cooperation, rather than being a legal term definable in law, is a pragmatic conduct pattern adopted by states for the attainment of mutual benefits of a political, economic, and military nature.[89] It may be said, therefore, that the concept of sovereignty has suffered a devaluation within each of the two power blocks in the "cold war," and the legal premises of the sovereign equality of states, therefore, must be regarded as little more than a pious fiction. The law of nations, as yet, has failed to become attuned to the new techniques in international relations presented by the pragmatic conduct pattern of wider cooperation between states. "To fill this gap appears to be an important objective of the science of international law." [90]

[88] Karl Loewenstein, "Sovereignty and International Co-operation," *American Journal of International Law,* vol. 48 (1954), p. 225.
[89] *Ibid.,* p. 243.
[90] *Ibid.,* p. 244.

CHAPTER 24

War Crimes

At an earlier stage in this treatise, we had occasion to refer to the postwar trials of war criminals and promised a fuller treatment of this topic in a later chapter. Accordingly, we shall now explore the nature and significance of the proceedings at Nuremberg in somewhat greater detail.

It is perhaps because of its controversial nature that the adjudication of war crimes both in Germany and in Japan [1] has been so sparingly treated by contemporary text writers. But if we are the first to "burst into that silent sea," it is because of a strong conviction that these judicial actions, even with all their shortcomings, constitute important contributions to the defense of the human race against its most dangerous enemy—the perverted genius of man.[2] The trials are significant, furthermore, because they point certain trends in the development of international law, not the least important of which is the return to earlier precepts through a certain fusion of law and morality. Justice Robert H. Jackson, Chief Prosecutor for the United States, said in his opening statement: "It is not necessary among the ruins of this ancient and beautiful city, with untold numbers of its civilian inhabitants still buried in its rubble, to argue the proposition that to start or wage a war of aggression has the moral qualities of the worst of crimes."

A New Conception. Prior to the First World War, it was the frequent practice of belligerents to include in the treaties of peace an amnesty clause by which immunity was granted to persons of both sides who had been guilty of violating the rules and customs of war. Even in the absence

---

[1] In 1948, an International Military Tribunal for the Far East was set up by the Supreme Commander for the Allied Powers having its seat in Tokyo. In the course of its proceedings some twenty-five accused persons were convicted after a trial which lasted from June, 1946, to Feb., 1948. See S. Horwitz, "The Tokyo Trial," in *International Conciliation,* no. 465 (November, 1950).

[2] It is urged that the student, in order to balance the point of view expressed in this chapter, read *Politics, Trials and Errors* by Lord Hankey (1950). In this book, the Right Hon. Lord Hankey argues with great sincerity that the war-crimes trials both of Nuremberg and Tokyo had no bases either in law or in justice. For the same point of view, see also R. T. Paget, *Manstein, His Campaigns and His Trial.* (1951).

of any such treaty provisions, amnesty was generally regarded as one of the legal effects of a treaty of peace. The immunity thus granted did not, however, extend to civil suits or to any criminal action which might be brought regarding matters not directly connected with the conduct of war.[3] The principle of immunity could have validity only in cases where *respondeat superior* could be demonstrated.

A notable departure from this practice is clearly discernible in the Treaty of Versailles, which provided in Article 227 that the German Emperor should be brought before an international criminal tribunal to answer "for a supreme offense against international morality and the sanctity of treaties." It was further provided, in the same article, that "if the accused is recognized to be guilty, it will be the duty of this tribunal to fix the punishment which it considers should be imposed." Germany, in terms of the treaty, also acknowledged the right of the Allied and Associated Powers to bring before military tribunals other "persons accused of having committed acts in violation of the laws and customs of war."[4] In this connection, the German government was pledged to furnish the documents and information "necessary to insure the full knowledge of the incriminating acts, the discovery of the offenders and the just appreciation of responsibility."[5]

Though these provisions of the Versailles treaty never came into operation,[6] their historical significance in the development of international law should not be underestimated. It might be said that the portion of the Versailles treaty dealing with war crimes and their punishment has contributed to the conversion of certain precepts of international morality into norms of law by providing legal sanctions for violations of the rules of morality.[7]

The Washington Naval Treaty of 1922, though it was never ratified,

[3] See Charles G. Fenwick, *International Law* (1948), p. 668.

[4] Art. 228 of the Treaty of Versailles.

[5] Arts. 228, 230 of the Treaty of Versailles.

[6] International criminal prosecution of the German offenders of the First World War proved impossible. In the first place, the Dutch government refused the surrender of the former Kaiser, who had in the meantime found asylum in the Netherlands. Secondly, great difficulties presented themselves in connection with the apprehension of designated members of the German armed forces. Furthermore, there were certain legal difficulties such as the defense of the accused that they had acted not on their own initiative but in obedience to higher authority. The alleged crimes, it was argued, were not of an individual nature but were acts of state. In addition to this there was the question of the *ex post facto* nature of the provisions of the treaty, as it was believed that the general law of nations did not sanction individual responsibility in cases of this kind. The result was that the Allied and Associated Powers finally yielded to the German request that the accused persons be tried in German courts. But that which was looked upon as a crime by the Allies, the German courts frequently regarded as a patriotic service to the nation.

[7] See Hans Kelsen, *Principles of International Law* (1952), p. 132.

included a provision to the effect that any person violating its rules should be deemed to have committed an offense against the laws of war and be liable to trial and punishment "as for an act of piracy." [8] Though the rule was limited to the terms of the treaty, it nevertheless embodied a very important principle, namely, that any person found guilty of its violation could not escape punishment simply by contending that it was an act of state.

War Criminals Are Warned. At various times during the course of the Second World War, the Allies let it be known that one of their principal war aims would be the punishment of war criminals.[9] On October 7, 1942, a simultaneous declaration was made by the President of the United States and the Lord Chancellor of Great Britain to the effect that "named criminals wanted for war crimes should be caught and handed over at the time of, and as a condition of, the Armistice, with the right to require the delivery of others as soon as the supplementary investigations are complete. . . ." It was further proposed in the same declaration "to set up with the least possible delay a United Nations Commission for the Investigation of War Crimes." On October 20, 1943, in conformity with this declaration, the United Nations War Crimes Commission, consisting of 17 representatives of the Allied governments, was set up. In addition, national offices were established by the various member governments whose job it was to collect evidence and submit charges to the United Nations Commission, who would then determine whether the evidence was sufficient to constitute *prima facie* a war crimes case.[10]

The next step was the Moscow Declaration of November 1, 1943. According to its provisions, German officers and men as well as members of the Nazi party who were responsible for, or had taken even a consenting part in, the atrocities, massacres, and executions were to be sent back to the countries in which their abominable deeds were done, there to be judged and punished. It was added, however, that this should not in any way prejudice the disposition of the "major criminals whose offences have no particular geographical location and who will be punished by a joint decision of the Governments of the Allies." [11]

[8] This, of course, would mean that the offender could be brought to trial by the civil or military authorities of any power within whose jurisdiction he might be found.

[9] An example of this was the Inter-Allied Declaration signed at St. James's Palace in London on Jan. 13, 1942, by the government representatives of nine occupied countries in which the signatories placed "among their principal war aims the punishment through the channel of organized justice, of those guilty of or responsible for these crimes, whether they have ordered them, perpetrated them or participated in them." See M. W. Mouton, "War Crimes and International Law," *Grotius annuaire international,* 1940–1946, p. 40.   [10] *Ibid.,* p. 41.

[11] For the complete text of the Moscow Declaration, see *Department of State Bulletin,* vol. 9, p. 310.

The Establishment of the Nuremberg Tribunal. On August 8, 1945, the government of the United Kingdom of Great Britain and Northern Ireland, the government of the United States of America, the provisional government of the French Republic, and the government of the Union of Soviet Socialist Republics entered into an "Agreement for the Prosecution and Punishment of the Major War Criminals of the European Axis." [12] Article 5 contained an invitation to other members of the United Nations to adhere to the agreement, and no less than 19 states eventually did so.[13] In this way a total of 23 nations with a combined population of 900 million joined in a legal process by presenting a common indictment against the war criminals before a single tribunal.[14] Annexed to the London agreement was the Charter setting forth not only the procedure but the law governing the trial of the defendants.[15] With respect to the constitution of the Tribunal, the Charter provided that it should consist of one judge and one alternate from each of the four powers.[16] At the same time a committee consisting of the chief prosecutors was charged with the preparation of the indictment and the presentation of the evidence in accordance with the law as set forth in the Charter.[17]

The International Military Tribunal was the result of a choice between alternative methods of procedure against the war criminals in 1945. There was always the possibility of doing nothing at all, or, on the other hand, of taking action in an *ad hoc* manner through national military courts against those who had violated the laws and customs of war. The latter course, had it been adopted, would not have been without sanction in international law.[18] Of course, a tribunal composed of jurists from the so-called "neutral" nations might have been constituted to sit in judgment of the war criminals; and finally, as was done after the First World War, the whole matter could have been left to the offending nations themselves.

[12] *Department of State Bulletin,* vol. 13 (1945), p. 222; *Trial of War Criminals,* Department of State Publication 2420 (1945), p. 13.

[13] Australia, Belgium, Czechoslovakia, Denmark, Ethiopia, Greece, Haiti, Honduras, India, Luxembourg, the Netherlands, New Zealand, Norway, Panama, Paraguay, Poland, Uruguay, Venezuela, and Yugoslavia.

[14] Peter Calvocoressi, *Nuremberg, the Acts, the Law and the Consequences* (1948), p. 16.

[15] "The Charter, in its contents, is substantive criminal law and procedural criminal law at the same time"—Hans Ehard, "The Nuremberg Trial against the Major War Criminals and International Law," *American Journal of International Law,* vol. 43 (1948), p. 226.

[16] The United States of America, the United Kingdom of Great Britain and Northern Ireland, the French Republic, and the Union of Soviet Socialist Republics.

[17] Arts. 6–10.

[18] Basically, the International Military Tribunal was an innovation only in a procedural sense. "Each victor had the right, long established and frequently exercised, of trying war criminals before an *ad hoc* military tribunal of its own creation"—Calvocoressi, *op. cit.,* p. 16.)

With respect to the first of the two last alternatives it might be asked: Who were the neutrals? As regards the second, the world was in no mood for an encore of the judicial comedy at Leipzig.[19]

Nuremberg, a city nearly one thousand years old, had long been famous for its architecture and many-towered walls, and in the days of Hitler for the September festival of the National Socialist party. It had been the home of Durer and Hans Sachs no less than of the infamous Julius Streicher and a bit of barbarism known as the "Nuremberg Decrees." But it was for none of these reasons that this ancient city was chosen as the seat of the International Military Tribunal in 1945. It happened that its commodious Palace of Justice had escaped serious damage during the aerial bombardments and therefore offered the best facilities for the conduct of the trial. Though the Tribunal had held its first public meeting in Berlin on October 18, 1945, it soon removed to Nuremberg, where the famous trial opened on November 20 and was continued until October 1, 1946.

The Procedure. Though it is quite true that, as a last act of war, summary procedure could have been taken against the war criminals and that this, indeed, would have met the needs of the case, it was strongly felt in 1945 that the Allies must put their victory to better use. It was hoped, therefore, that two things could be accomplished through the agency of the International Military Tribunal: (1) a just punishment of the guilty, and (2) the affirmation of a rule of law. Summary action on the part of the victors rather than resort to the more laborious process of international adjudication might well have satisfied the first of these objectives, but as *surely not* the second.

As we have seen in an earlier chapter, it is required under the law of nations that aliens, when subjected to criminal proceedings by any state or groups of states, may not be constrained to suffer a denial of justice. It was in conformity with this principle that Article 13 of the Charter provided certain procedural safeguards for the defendants at Nuremberg. Each was allowed a period of thirty days before the commencement of his trial to study the indictment and prepare his case. Ample opportunity was provided for the engagement of defense counsel and for the procurement of witnesses and documentary evidence, as well as the privilege to examine all documents submitted by the prosecution.[20] Under these

---

[19] Following the First World War the trial and punishment of war criminals had been left to the Germans. Two and a half years transpired following the armistice before the war-crimes trial at Leipzig finally opened on May 23, 1921. Of the 896 accused by the Allies, only 12 were actually tried, and of these only 6 were convicted. See Sheldon Glueck, *War Criminals, Their Prosecution and Punishment* (1944), p. 28.

[20] Quincy Wright, "The Law of the Nuremberg Trial," *American Journal of International Law,* vol. 41 (1947), p. 52.

rules of procedure, the defendants were given the right, furthermore, to address motions, applications, and other requests to the Tribunal. The accused were informed by the presiding judge, General Nikitchenko, at the very first session of the court that a special clerk had been appointed "to advise the defendants of their right and to take instructions from them personally as to their choice of counsel, and generally to see that their rights of defense are made known to them." [21]

With respect to the Tribunal's procedure, it should be pointed out that the rules of evidence under common law were not applied.[22] This, of course, was in conformity with the practice of criminal courts in continental Europe and of international tribunals generally. It should be noted also that the procedure which was finally adopted by the International Military Tribunal represented the reconciliation of widely divergent legal principles and traditions. Great Britain and the United States represented the common-law procedure, while France and the Soviet Union both use variations of what is generally known as the Continental system. But between the French and Soviet practices there are also significant differences. Both, to be sure, are of Roman origin, but French procedure has its roots in the law of the Western Empire, whereas Soviet practice derives largely from the judicial system of the Eastern Empire, which came to Russia by way of Byzantium.

Another matter with caused much difficulty was a fundamental cleavage with respect to the general theory of criminal jurisprudence which soon became apparent between the Soviet and Anglo-American systems. In Russian procedure, chief reliance is placed on the tribunal to develop the facts, whereas in Anglo-American practice this task is entrusted to the zeal and self-interest of the adversaries, a method which the Soviet jurist rejects and derides as the "contest theory." [23] A more basic cause for conflict between the Soviet and the Western legal systems, however, stems from opposing theories regarding the relationship of the judiciary to the state. As we have noted earlier, according to Soviet theory the judicial apparatus is an organ of state power—a means in the hands of the ruling class to safeguard its interests. In the Western countries, on the other hand, the judiciary is regarded primarily as the law-interpreting agency of the government, which in theory, at least, is supposed to be independent of class interests. While the Soviet authorities accept, in general, the binding force of international law, they are nevertheless unwilling to

[21] Quoted in *ibid.*

[22] "It has never been contended that those rules of evidence are required by international law"—*ibid.*, p. 53.

[23] Report of Robert H. Jackson, United States Representative to the International Conference on Military Trials, London, 1945, p. vi, Department of State Publication 3080, International Organization and Conference Series II.

submit to the mass of customary law deduced from the practice of Western states. Thus, having reference to the London agreement, Justice Jackson was constrained to observe: "With dissimilar backgrounds in both penal law and international law it is less surprising that clashes developed at the Conference than that they could be reconciled." [24]

Definitions of Crimes and the Law of the Charter. The most serious disagreement between the Western nations and the Soviet Union at London concerned the definition of crimes. The Soviet delegation, perhaps for reasons which have become clearer since, sought to define certain acts as crimes only when committed by the Nazis. The United States strongly contended that criminality could not be made dependent upon who committed the act but "that international crimes could only be defined in broad terms applicable to statesmen of any nation guilty of the proscribed conduct." [25] When it became clear that the United States would not "recede from its position even if it meant the failure of the Conference," the Soviet delegation at length agreed to a "generic definition acceptable to all." [26]

The vast catalogue of crimes of which the defendants at Nuremberg stood accused was, as it appeared in the Charter, divided into three categories as follows: [27]

(*a*) *Crimes against Peace:* namely, planning, preparation, initiation or waging of a war of aggression, or a war in violation of international treaties, agreements or assurances, participation in a Common Plan or Conspiracy for the accomplishment of any of the foregoing;

(*b*) *War Crimes:* namely, violations of the laws or customs of war. Such violations shall include, but not be limited to, murder, ill-treatment or deportation to slave labor or for any other purpose of civilian population of or in occupied territory, murder or ill-treatment of prisoners of war or persons on the seas, killing of hostages, plunder of public or private property, wanton destruction of cities, towns or villages, or devastation not justified by military necessity;

(*c*) *Crimes against Humanity:* namely, murder, extermination, enslavement, deportation, and other inhumane acts committed against any civilian population, before or during the war, or persecutions on political, racial, or religious grounds in execution of or in connection with any crime within the jurisdiction of the Tribunal, whether or not in violation of domestic law of the country where perpetrated.

It was also provided that the official position of the defendants, whether as heads of state or in any other responsible capacity, should not in itself constitute mitigation of punishment, nor could the plea of "superior order"

[24] *Ibid.*   [25] *Ibid*, p. viii.
[26] *Ibid.*
[27] *Trial of the Major War Criminals before the International Military Tribunal,* Nuremberg, Nov. 14, 1945–Oct. 1, 1946, p. 11.

be so regarded. In cases where organizations were declared to be of a criminal nature, their members were to be treated as collectively responsible and accordingly punished. This same principle was embodied in the Allied Control Council Law No. 10 [28] for minor war criminals, together with a provision for their surrender to the liberated countries as provided by the Moscow declaration.[29]

The legal principles set forth at Nuremberg, no less than their wide acceptance,[30] constitute a significant step in the development of international criminal law. The Charter itself may be regarded as something of a landmark not only in the establishment of a substantive code defining crimes, but also as an instrument establishing a procedure for their prosecution before an international tribunal. In the opinion of Justice Jackson:[31]

It carries the conception of crime against the society of nations far beyond its former state and to a point which probably will not be exceeded, either through revision in principle or through restatement, in the foreseeable future. There is debate as to whether its provisions introduce innovations or whether they merely make explicit and unambiguous what was previously implicit in international law.

The Great Controversy. Though the Nuremberg Charter was the law which governed the prosecutions, it was not, in the view of the Tribunal, the result of an arbitrary exercise of power on the part of the victorious states. It was rather an expression of international law existing at the time of the Tribunal's creation, and to that extent a significant contribution toward the codification of that law. The novelty, it was contended, was not so much in the creation of new law as in the special application of legal norms already in existence. But it was precisely the attempt on the part of the Allied powers to prove that the London agreement and the Charter of the International Military Tribunal were but declaratory of the present law that has given rise to one of the most controversial features of the war-crimes trials at Nuremberg. Inasmuch as powerful arguments have been advanced to the effect that the law set forth in the Charter of the International Military Tribunal was of an *ex post facto*

---

[28] The various military tribunals which were created under Control Council Law No. 10 of Dec. 20, 1945, sat at Nuremberg from 1946 to 1949. The reports are published in *Trials of War Criminals before the Nuremberg Military Tribunals.*

[29] Mouton, *op. cit.,* p. 43. In a resolution adopted by the United Nations Assembly on Feb. 13, 1946, it was recommended that the member states should apply the principles of the Moscow declaration in their adjudication of war crimes.

[30] The principles of the Nuremberg trial have been given general approval by the General Assembly of the United Nations.

[31] From the Preface of Justice Jackson's Report on the London Conference establishing the International Military Tribunal, 1945, Department of State Publication 3080, p. viii.

nature, it becomes necessary to explore this question more closely. International law as it existed in 1945 will be discussed, therefore, with special reference to the three groups of offences which were declared criminal under the Charter. These were, as we have already noted, *crimes against peace, war crimes,* and *crimes against humanity.*

Crimes against Peace. As we have indicated earlier, the sources of international law are found in treaties and custom, in general principles of justice, in the works of publicists, and in juristic analyses.[32] The law of nations resembles in its development the characteristics of the common law, upon which rests the jurisprudential systems in the greater part of the English-speaking world. This sort of law has a gradual development through the agency of immemorial custom, and when at length it becomes expedient to do so, its main principles may be reduced to writing, as in published codes and legislative enactments. It should be noted, however, that such enactments, though they may serve as evidence of what the law is, are not *necessary* to the determination of legal norms.[33]

The Charter of the International Military Tribunal may be said to constitute an attempt on the part of its framers to reduce to writing certain principles of international law derived from existing treaties and custom.[34] Yet it can be argued, as indeed it has been, that such codification may not correctly express the custom or interpret the treaties upon which the law of nations is based. This question was carefully considered by the judges at Nuremberg, and their conclusions in this regard were, as we have already seen, to the effect that the Charter was no more than declaratory of the existing law. It was emphasized that the development of international custom was of such nature as strongly to favor the contention that aggressive war must be regarded as criminal under the existing law of nations.

In the days of the Spanish theologian Victoria, it was a custom to differentiate between kinds of war and to speak of armed conflict between nations in categories of just and unjust, lawful and unlawful war. In later times, however, the right to make war came to be regarded as an inalienable attribute of sovereignty.[35] It was especially during the eighteenth and nineteenth centuries that the so-called "right of self-help"

[32] See Art. 38 of the Statute of the International Court of Justice.

[33] Calvocoressi, *op. cit.,* p. 32.

[34] Art. 38 of the Statute of the International Court of Justice provides as follows: "The Court, whose function is to decide in accordance with international law such disputes as are submitted to it, shall apply:
"*a.* international conventions, whether general or particular, establishing rules expressly recognized by the contesting states;
"*b.* international custom, as evidence of a general practice accepted as law;
"*c.* The general principles of law recognized by civilized nations; . . ."

[35] Calvocoressi, *op. cit.,* p. 33.

gained its greatest favor as one of the fundamental rights of states. But with the first Peace conference at The Hague in 1899 the validity of this concept of sovereign rights was to lose some of the certain ground upon which it had rested for several hundred years, for the Convention for the Pacific Settlement of International Disputes required that, in all cases of conflict, the first recourse should be to mediation in an effort to achieve peaceful settlement. Though a similar convention was signed in 1907 at The Hague, little progress was made toward the outlawry of war for many years. The next step in this direction was a draft Treaty of Mutual Assistance sponsored by the League of Nations in 1923, which provided (Art. 1) "that aggressive war is an international crime," and the parties would "undertake that no one of them will be guilty of its commission." [36]

In the Preamble of the Geneva Protocol of 1924, a war of aggression was declared to be in violation of the solidarity of the international community, and as such to constitute "an international crime." It further stated that the contracting parties were "desirous of facilitating the complete application of the system provided in the Covenant of the League of Nations of the pacific settlement of disputes between the States and of ensuring the repression of international crimes." [37] In 1927, at the eighth General Assembly of the League of Nations, it was unanimously resolved that a war of aggression should be regarded as an international crime.[38] In 1928 at the Sixth Pan-American Conference, held in Havana, the 21 American republics unanimously declared that a "war of aggression constitutes an international crime against the human species." [39] Likewise, the International Conference of American States on Conciliation and Arbitration, which met in Washington in December of the same year, signed a general convention which in its preamble expressed a desire "to demonstrate that the condemnation of war as an instrument of national policy in their mutual relations . . . constitutes one of the fundamental bases of inter-American relations. . . ." [40] In 1933, the Anti-War Treaty of Non-Aggression and Conciliation was signed in Rio de Janeiro "to the end of condemning wars of aggression and territorial acquisitions that may be obtained by armed conquest. . . ." [41] In addition to these

[36] *League of Nations Official Journal, Records of the Fourth Assembly* (special supplement no. 13, 1923), p. 403.

[37] *League of Nations Official Journal, Records of the Fifth Assembly* (special supplement no. 23, 1924), p. 498.

[38] *League of Nations Official Journal, Records of the Eighth Ordinary Session of the Assembly* (special supplement no. 54, 1927), pp. 155–156.

[39] *Foreign Relations*, Department of State Publication (1928), p. 13.

[40] *Bulletin of the Pan American Union*, vol. 63 (1929), p. 114.

[41] *Treaties, Conventions, International Acts, Protocols, and Agreements between the United States and Other Powers*, vol. IV (1938), p. 4793; 75th Cong., 3d Sess., S. Doc. 134.

there are, of course, a large number of treaties of "mutual guarantee" which could be listed. The Non-Aggression Pacts which Russia and later Germany entered into with their neighbors, in spite of the bad faith which is associated with them, would come within the category of treaties which renounce war as an accepted means of national policy.

It has been argued that such pacts, declarations, and resolutions as those listed above, though many never reached the stage of ratification and therefore cannot be classified as law, nevertheless constitute powerful evidence of existing custom among the nations of the world; furthermore, that this custom has given rise to a juristic climate in which a war of aggression not only is unjust and illegal but is also, in its very nature, criminal.[42]

The Pact of Paris of 1928, which was almost universally ratified, leaves no doubt as to the illegality of a war of aggression. The High Contracting Parties to this treaty solemnly condemned recourse to war for the solution of international controversies and renounced it as an instrument of national policy in their relations with one another.[43] And they agreed that "the settlement or solution of all disputes or conflicts of whatever nature or of whatever origin they may be, which may arise among them, shall never be sought except by pacific means."[44] But even though a war of aggression must be regarded as illegal under existing treaty law, it does not follow from this alone that it is also an international crime. Such a conclusion can be arrived at only through inference—which, to be sure, is greatly reinforced by custom. But this is so only if, in the light of such custom, an act of aggression by one state against another can be regarded as an international crime. On this point, there is grave disagreement among the authorities.

It is argued, for example, that "unratified protocols cannot be cited to show acceptance of their provisions" and that resolutions of international conferences "have no binding effect unless and until they are sanctioned by subsequent national or international action; and treaties of nonaggression that are flagrantly disregarded when it becomes expedient to do so can not be relied upon as evidence to prove the evolution of an international custom outlawing aggression."[45] According to Schwarzenberger: "Draft treaties and unratified conventions are legally non-existent, and the question of the legal effects of resolutions of the Assembly of the League of Nations—even if unanimously adopted—is highly controversial."[46] But as the same author has accurately pointed out, "the con-

[42] Sheldon Glueck, *The Nuremberg Trial and Aggressive War* (1946), p. 34.
[43] Art. 1.   [44] Art. 2.
[45] George A. Finch, "The Nuremberg Trial and International Law," *American Journal of International Law*, vol. 41 (1947), p. 26.
[46] *International Law* (1949), vol. I, p. 318.

sent on the part of States to resolutions, accepted with the necessary unanimity or majority, might at least have the effect of the recognition of a situation, on which the State concerned might not go back or such consent might even amount to an undertaking of a contractual character." [47] Thus, in the case of the *Monastery of Saint-Naoum* [48] the Permanent Court of International Justice held that a unanimous resolution of the Assembly of the League of Nations of October 2, 1921, was binding upon the disputants whose votes had been cast in its favor. In the case of the *Railway Traffic between Lithuania and Poland* [49] the same Court held that the two states were bound by their acceptance of a Resolution of the Council of the League of Nations. Likewise, in the case of the *German Minority in Upper Silesia* [50] it was held that the compromise between both parties as recorded in a Council Resolution, unanimously adopted with the concurrence of the disputants, was legally binding. It would seem, therefore, that the legal effect of resolutions both of the Assembly and of the Council of the League of Nations, if unanimously adopted, rather than being controversial, is well established. We are inclined toward the opinion of Sir Frederick Pollock, who wrote long ago: "As among men, so among nations, the opinions and usages of the leading members of a community tend to form an authoritative example for the whole." [51]

Having reference to the criminal character of aggressive war, Sir Hartley Shawcross, Chief Counsel for Great Britain at the Nuremberg trials, said: [52]

The future of international law, and indeed, of the world itself, depends on its application in a much wider sphere, in particular, in that of safeguarding the peace of the world. . . . If this be an innovation, it is an innovation which we are prepared to defend and to justify, but it is not an innovation which creates a new crime. International Law had already, before the Charter was adopted, constituted aggressive war a criminal act.

Concerning the criminal nature of aggressive war, Justice Jackson, Chief Prosecutor for the United States, had this to say: [53]

Any resort to war—to any kind of a war—is a resort to means that are in-

---

[47] *Ibid.*, p. 539.
[48] *PCIJ Publications*, ser. B, no. 9; Manley O. Hudson, ed., *World Court Reports*, vol. I, p. 392.
[49] *PCIJ Publications* (1931), ser. A/B, no. 42, p. 116.
[50] *PCIJ Publications* (1931), ser. A/B, no. 40, p. 16.
[51] F. Pollock, "The Sources of International Law," *Columbia Law Review*, (1902) pp. 511–512.
[52] Excerpt from a larger quotation from the Record of the Trial by Quincy Wright in *op. cit.*, p. 65.
[53] *The Nurnberg Case as Presented by Robert H. Jackson Together with Other Documents* (1947), p. 84.

herently criminal. War inevitably is a course of killings, assaults, deprivations of liberty, and destruction of property. An honestly defensive war is, of course, legal and saves those lawfully conducting it from criminality. But inherently criminal acts cannot be defended by showing that those who committed them were engaged in a war, when war itself is illegal.

With respect to that portion of the indictment which charged the defendants with *crimes against peace*, it is unnecessary to engage in further elaboration. As to whether a war of aggression constitutes an international crime, there is as yet no unanimous opinion among legal scholars. It may be premature, therefore, to assert with finality that the Charter of the International Military Tribunal, with respect to its criminal categories, is definitive of the law of nations. Yet, we are inclined to agree with Lord Wright that "the pressure of necessity stimulates the impact of natural law and of moral ideas and converts them into rules of law deliberately and overtly recognized by the consensus of civilized mankind." [54]

War Crimes. Counts 3 and 4 of the indictment charged the defendants with war crimes and crimes against humanity. It remains, therefore, to consider these two categories with respect to the then existing law. The category of war crimes, as defined in Article 6 (*b*) of the Charter,[55] is based for the most part on the Hague convention of 1907 and on the Geneva convention of 1927. Thus, the provisions of the Charter must be regarded, once more, as a restatement of the existing law rather than as a new attempt at legislation. It seems clear that the open violation of existing conventions which constitute the law of war must be regarded in the category of international crimes. "That violations of these provisions constituted crimes for which the guilty individuals were punishable," said the Tribunal, "is too well settled to admit of argument." The laws and customs of war, including those of military occupation, are clear enough. "They are enacted in national legislation, codified in military manuals, incorporated in binding international conventions, and affirmed by the immemorial practice of states. . . ." [56] Though it may be argued that certain portions of this law are rendered obsolete as a consequence of new methods of warfare, such a contention cannot serve as justification for adding crime to war as an instrument of national policy.

The evidence regarding the commission of war crimes by the Germans during the Second World War was, in the language of the Tribunal, "overwhelming in its volume and its details." [57] In the face of the Hague and Geneva conventions, the ancient formula *nullum crimen sine lege*

---

[54] "War Crimes under International Law," *Law Quarterly Review*, vol. 62 (1946), pp. 40, 51.
[55] See p. 402.
[56] Finch, *op. cit.*, p. 21.
[57] Calvocoressi, *op. cit.*, p. 47.

could find no application. On this point there seems to be general agreement, as war crimes are universally recognized as punishable under the law of nations. Objections to the effect that it is illegal to prosecute military and naval officers—who, it is contended, have merely been following orders of their superiors—are unsupported both in law and in practice. No one may commit with impunity a crime which constitutes a violation of the laws and customs of war on the plea of *respondeat superior*.[58] The application of this rule in any case is limited by a consideration of the justice of the charge in each instance.[59] Moreover, it is well to remember that the maxim *respondeat superior* is a twin-edged blade which cuts in both directions. Whenever it is succesfully invoked by a subordinate, "the liability for the commission of the crime is not extinguished but is tranferred to the superior who issued the order."[60] Were it not so, it is obvious that to punish anyone for the violation of the rules and law of war would be impossible in cases where the head of state could not be apprehended.

It is not necessary to recite here the long catalogue of crimes against the laws and usages of war of which the defendants at Nuremberg stood accused. It is sufficient to observe that they were on a scale more vast than any which the long history of mankind has a record. They were perpetrated in all the countries under German occupation and on the high seas, and they were attended by every circumstance of cruelty and horror. On the part of the accused, there was no serious defense apart from the argument that the occupied territories had been incorporated into the Greater German *Reich* and that within this area only German law was valid. This contention was rejected for two reasons: (1) because throughout the entire German occupation there had always been some unsubjugated army in the field within the area over which Germany claimed control, and (2) because, since the conquest had been made through the agency of aggressive, i.e., unlawful, war, it was not entitled to recognition. In support of this point the Pact of Paris may be cited as well as the now famous "Stimson Doctrine"[61] of 1932 which was made in its pursuance. Also the resolution of the League of Nations Assembly of the same year which (1) "proclaimed the binding nature of the Covenant and the Pact of Paris," and (2) "declared: 'that it is incumbent upon the members of the League of Nations not to recognize any situation, treaty,

[58] Finch, *loc. cit.*
[59] *Ibid.*   [60] *Ibid.*
[61] Secretary Stimson's identical notes to China and Japan of Jan. 7, 1932, read in part as follows: "The American Government . . . does not intend to recognize any situation, treaty, or agreement which may be brought about by means contrary to the covenants and obligations of the Pact of Paris of August 27, 1928, to which treaty both China and Japan, as well as the United States, are parties."

or arrangement which may be brought about by means contrary to the Covenant of the League of Nations or the Pact of Paris.' " [62]

The Legality of the Tribunal. The right of the Allies to prosecute individual offenders against the laws and customs of war rests firmly on customary law and must therefore be regarded as uncontested. Objection was raised, nevertheless, to the Tribunal's international character. This objection is based upon the universally recognized principle that there are limits to the criminal jurisdiction of every state. But there can be no doubt that any state has the right to create special tribunals to prosecute persons in its custody who have committed war crimes. It is believed, furthermore, that this right to jurisdiction is broad enough to cover the powers of the Tribunal under the Charter.[63] It would seem reasonable that if each of the parties to the Charter could individually create such a tribunal, they would have the legal right to create an international tribunal and exercise the jurisdiction jointly.[64] In the language of the Tribunal: [65]

The Signatory Powers created this Tribunal, defined the law it was to administer, and made regulations for the proper conduct of the Trial. In doing so, they have done together what any of them might have done singly, for it is not to be doubted that any nation has the right thus to set up special courts to administer law.

But there is yet another ground upon which the establishment and jurisdiction of the International Military Tribunal may be justified, namely, the condominium through which the sovereignty over Germany was jointly exercised by the occupying powers. "The making of the Charter," said the Tribunal, "was the exercise of the sovereign legislative power by the countries to which the German Reich unconditionally surrendered; and the undoubted right of these countries to legislate for the occupied territories had been recognized by the civilized world." [66] There can be no question that under international law any state or combination of states may acquire sovereignty over subjugated territory by a declaration of annexation, provided such declaration is generally recognized by other states. The Declaration of Berlin [67] of June 5, 1945, was

[62] Quoted by Samuel Flagg Bemis in *A Diplomatic History of the United States* (1950), p. 815.
[63] Quincy Wright, *op. cit.*, p. 49.
[64] *Ibid.* On this point, Major Willard B. Cowles, while attached to the Judge Advocate General's Department of the United States Army, wrote: "A military tribunal with mixed inter-allied personnel may properly be established by the commanding general of cooperating cobelligerent forces"—"Trial of War Criminals by Military Tribunals," *American Bar Association Journal*, vol. 30 (1944), p. 330.
[65] Judgment, p. 216.   [66] *Ibid.*
[67] By this declaration the four Allied powers assumed "supreme authority with

so recognized, not only by the United Nations, but by neutral states as well. It would seem logical that powers which are in a position to annex a territory, as were the Allies in this case, also would have the right to exercise sovereignty over the same territory for certain purposes through the agency of condominium, which in fact they did. We conclude, therefore, that no question of *ex post facto* law or procedure was involved with respect to count 3 of the indictment at Nuremberg.

Crimes against Humanity. These were defined in Article 6(*c*) of the Charter.[68] They were listed as constituting one of the three criminal categories within the jurisdiction of the Military Tribunal, and in this sense they stand in juxtaposition to "crimes against peace" and "war crimes." But within the meaning of the Charter, there is a certain overlapping of all three of these concepts. A war crime may also be a crime against humanity, and both may at times be inseparable from crimes against peace. The element which is new here is not the notion that offences against the "laws of humanity" may take place, but rather the designation of such crimes by a technical term, specifically defined, as in Article 6(*c*) of the Charter.

The Hague Convention IV of 1907, which, as we have seen, is an instrument concerned with war crimes in the narrower sense, recalls in its Preamble that the contracting parties are "animated by the desire to serve," even in war, "the interests of humanity and the ever-progressive needs of civilization." The parties declare, *inter alia*, that "the inhabitants and belligerents remain under the protection and governance of the principles of the law of nations, derived from the usages established among civilized peoples, from the laws of humanity, and from the dictates of the public conscience." Thus, the "interests of humanity" are here conceived as being served by the laws and customs of war, and the "laws of Humanity" as one of the sources of international law.[69]

In January, 1919, the Preliminary Peace Conference at Paris created a Commission on Responsibilities of 15 members to make an inquiry concerning the responsibility for the First World War. The report which the Commission returned in March of the same year stated, in Chapter II, that "in spite of the explicit regulations, of established customs, and of the clear dictates of humanity, Germany and her allies have piled outrage upon outrage." It was the Commission's conclusion that the war had been

---

respect to Germany, including all the powers possessed by the German Government, the High Command, and any state, municipal, or local government or authority." The declaration did not, however, contemplate permanent annexation.

[68] See p. 402.

[69] Egon Schwelb, "Crimes against Humanity," *The British Year Book of International Law,* vol. XXIII (1946), p. 180.

prosecuted by "the Central Empires together with their allies, Turkey and Bulgaria, by barbarous or illegitimate methods in violation of the established laws and customs of war and the elementary laws of humanity" and that "all persons belonging to enemy countries . . . who have been guilty of offences against the laws and customs of war or the laws of humanity, are liable to criminal prosecution." [70]

It should be emphasized that the Commission of Responsibilities of 1919 actually did make a distinction between ordinary war crimes and crimes against humanity, in a manner not unlike the classification of these offenses in Article 6, Sections (*b*) and (*c*), of the London Charter.[71] Yet, in the peace which ended the First World War, no mention is made of the "laws of humanity."

The next important attempt to consign crimes against humanity to a special, technical category of violations came with the Charter of the International Military Tribunal in 1945. In Article 6 (*c*) crimes against humanity are defined as

murder, extermination, enslavement, deportation, and other inhumane acts committed against any civilian population, before or during the war, or persecutions on political, racial, or religious grounds in execution of or in connection with any crime within the jurisdiction of the Tribunal, whether or not in violation of the domestic law of the country where perpetrated.

It will be remembered that the English, French, and Russian texts of the Charter were equally authoritative, but it soon developed that they were not completely identical. Because of the discrepancy in the texts, the so-called Berlin Protocol of October 6, 1945, was added.[72] In this document the parties declared that the meaning and intention of the London agreement and the Charter required that the semicolon in the English and French texts should be changed to a comma. This change in punctuation is of considerable significance in that it brings the qualifying phrase, "in execution of or in connection with any crime within the jurisdiction of the tribunal," to bear upon the whole of Article 6 (*c*). This, indeed, would imply a rather important restriction on both the concept

[70] *Violation of the Laws and Customs of War. Report of Majority and Dissenting Reports of American and Japanese Members of the Commission on Responsibilities* (Conference of Paris, 1919), Carnegie Endowment for International Peace, Division of International Law, Pamphlet 32.

[71] Schwelb, *op. cit.* Annex I to the Report of the 1919 Commission actually contained a summary of the infractions which had been committed by both the authorities and the troops of the Central powers and their allies in violation of the laws and customs of war and the laws of humanity (*Tableau sommaire des infractions commises par les autorités et les troupes des empires centraux et de leurs alliés en violation des lois et coutumes de la guerre et des lois de l'humanité*).

[72] For complete text, see Department of State Publication 2461, ser. 472 (1946), p. 45.

and the scope of crimes against humanity.[73] This is clearly illustrated in a general statement by the Nuremberg Tribunal concerning crimes against humanity. The Court said: [74]

To constitute crimes against humanity, the acts relied on before the outbreak of war must have been in execution of, or in connection with, any crime within the jurisdiction of the Tribunal. The Tribunal is of the opinion that revolting and horrible as many of these crimes were, it has not been satisfactorily proved that they were done in execution of, or in connection with, any such crime. The Tribunal cannot, therefore, make a general declaration that the acts before 1939 were crimes against humanity within the meaning of the Charter, but from the beginning of the war in 1939 war crimes were committed on a vast scale, which were also crimes against humanity; and in so far as the inhumane acts charged in the Indictment, and committed after the beginning of the war did not constitute war crimes, they were all committed in execution of, or in connection with, the aggressive war, and therefore constituted crimes against humanity.

The conclusion to be drawn from this statement is that, in the opinion of the Tribunal, all crimes enumerated in Article 6 (*c*) of the Charter could be considered as crimes against humanity only when they were committed in execution of or in connection with a crime against peace or a war crime. The Court had no difficulty, however, in assuming that war crimes and crimes against humanity in the narrow sense of the Charter were also crimes under the customary law of nations at the time the acts were committed. It was, therefore, unnecessary on the part of the Tribunal to devote as much discussion to this category as was given to crimes against peace.

War Crimes and the United Nations. On November 21, 1947, the General Assembly of the United Nations adopted a resolution affirming the principles of international law recognized by the Charter and the judgment at Nuremberg. Later, in 1950, under General Assembly resolution 177 (II), paragraph (*a*), the International Law Commission was directed to "formulate the principles of international law recognized in the Charter of the Nurnberg Tribunal and in the judgment of the Tribunal." Accordingly, during its second session, June 5 to July 29, 1950, the following seven principles were formulated: [75]

I. Any person who commits an act which constitutes a crime under international law is responsible therefor and liable to punishment.

II. The fact that international law does not impose a penalty for an act

[73] See Schwelb, *op. cit.*, p. 195.
[74] Cmd. 6964, p. 65.
[75] *American Journal of International Law*, supplement to vol. 44 (1950), pp. 125–134.

which constitutes a crime under international law does not relieve the person who committed the act from responsibilty under international law.

III. The fact that a person who committed an act which constitutes a crime under international law acted as Head of State or responsible Government official does not relieve him from responsibilty under international law.

IV. The fact that a person acted pursuant to order of his Government or of a superior does not relieve him from responsibility under international law, provided a moral choice was in fact possible for him.

V. Any person charged with a crime under international law has the right to a fair trial on the facts and law.

VI. The crimes hereinafter set out are punishable as crimes under international law:

a. Crimes against peace:

(i) Planning, preparation, initiation or waging of a war of aggression or a war in violation of international treaties, agreements or assurances;

(ii) Participation in a common plan or conspiracy for the accomplishment of any of the acts mentioned under (i).

b. War crimes:

Violations of the laws or customs of war which include, but are not limited to, murder, ill-treatment or deportation to slave-labour or for any other purpose of civilian population of or in occupied territory, murder or ill-treatment of prisoners of war or persons on the seas, killing of hostages, plunder of public or private property, wanton destruction of cities, towns, or villages, or devastation not justified by military necessity.

c. Crimes against humanity:

Murder, extermination, enslavement, deportation and other inhuman acts done against any civilian population, or persecutions on political, racial, or religious grounds, when such acts are done or such persecutions are carried on in execution of or in connection with any crime against peace or any war crime.

VII. Complicity in the commission of a crime against peace, a war crime, or a crime against humanity as set forth in Principle VI is a crime under international law.

The Meaning of Nuremberg. Before closing this chapter, a word should be added concerning the argument we have advanced. Though there can be little doubt that the Nuremberg trial marks an important step in the development of international criminal law, "a single landmark of justice and honor does not make a world of peace." [76] International law is still limited by international politics, and the advance of each is dependent on the other. But it is important that the difference between legal and political methods in international affairs should be clearly understood. The prevention of war is a political task, but the violation

[76] Henry L. Stimson, "The Nuremberg Trial: Landmark in Law," *Foreign Affairs*, vol. 25 (1947), p. 188.

of the peace through aggressive war is a criminal responsibility. "But in the judgment of Nuremberg there is affirmed the central principle of peace —that the man who makes or plans to make aggressive war is a criminal. A standard has been raised" to which all nations must repair; "for it is only as this standard is accepted, supported and enforced that we can move onward" [77] to a new day of friendly relations among the peoples of the world under the protection of universal law.

[77] *Ibid.*, p. 189.

PART SIX

The Individual in International Law

CHAPTER 25

The Legal Position of the Individual

With the triumph of positivism in the nineteenth century, the emphasis in international legal theory became less on the position of the individual in the world community, and more on that of the state. According to the orthodox positivists, only states are subjects of international law, while individual persons are its objects. This means that with respect to the law of nations the individual has no legal standing; that he lacks juridical personality and has neither rights nor obligations except with reference to his own state. While it is an established principle in international law that an alien is entitled to protection in accordance with minimum standards of civilization, the traditional theory assigns this right not to the individual in question but to the state of which he is a citizen or subject. In claims cases, international tribunals have held that established nationality with regard to the claimant is a condition for jurisdiction. With respect to the Calvo clause, it has been held that an individual may not sign away the right to appeal to his state for protection, as this would have the effect of reducing the rights of his own state under international law. That is to say, in the case of a denial of justice amounting to a violation of international law, the individual has no capacity in a juridical sense to vindicate the rules violated. This right and capacity, according to the "object theory of the individual," are exclusive with the state.

The Failure of Positivism. The extreme positivist position regarding the status of the individual under the law of nations has in recent years been subjected to sharp criticism, in the first place on the grounds that it is both illogical and immoral, and in the second place because it is inconsistent with the practice of international-legal relations. Among the better-known critics of the so-called object theory is Hans Kelsen, who has eloquently pointed out that all law is essentially the regulation of human conduct: "For a duty which would not be the duty of a man to behave in a certain way would not be a legal duty; a responsibility which would not

419

consist in a sanction executed by men and directed against men would not be a legal responsibility." [1]

In connection with the criminal character of aggressive war, the Nuremberg Tribunal made the following observation regarding the position of the individual in international law: [2]

That international law imposes duties and liabilities upon individuals as well as upon states has long been recognized. . . . Individuals can be punished for violations of international law. Crimes against international law are committed by men, not by abstract entities, and only by punishing individuals who commit such crimes can the provisions of international law be enforced.

It has been argued that individuals are frequently, in practice, subject to both rights and duties conferred and imposed upon them directly, indirectly, or derivatively by the law of nations. For these reasons it is maintained by a number of critics of the positivist position that individuals are in fact subjects of international law. It is contended that the object theory is based not upon practice but upon faulty premises regarding the nature of the state and the general theory of international law.

The contention by the orthodox positivists that only states can be subjects of international law, became, at the opening of the twentieth century, more and more irreconcilable with the factual experience of nations. As early as 1906, the German subjective [3] positivist, Von Liszt, was able to discern in the regulations of certain international bodies, such as the European Danube Commission, the faint beginnings of an international-legal personality for the individual. The abortive attempt to establish an international prize court in 1907, and the Washington treaty of the same year which brought into being the Central American Court of Justice, further weakened the position of the extreme positivists. Even Heilborn, who is credited with the formulation of the so-called "object theory" in 1896, was compelled to revise his earlier position with respect to the international-legal status of the individual.

It was not until after the First World War, however, that the subjective positivists began to recognize a wide variety of situations in which international law seemed to act directly upon the individual. Thus, they began

---

[1] *Principles of International Law* (1952), p. 97.

[2] Cmd. 6964 (1946), p. 41.

[3] The subjective positivists are so called because they postulate a subjective factor of will or consent on the part of states as a juridical basis for obligation under international law. This school of jurists stands in opposition to eclectic positivism which bases obligation under the law not only upon the subjective factor of consent, but also upon certain objective factors such as reason, juridical and moral hypotheses, principles, or norms. Yet a third group of jurists may be distinguished from the subjective and eclectic positivists, namely, the objective positivists who base legal obligation upon objective factors alone.

to regard the individual person not only as an object, but as "the final end, a beneficiary, and a *potential subject* of international law." [4] In practice, the juridical position of the individual was enhanced by the claims cases which were brought before the Mixed Arbitral Tribunals after the First World War and by international adjudications under conventions such as the German-Polish Railways Agreement of 1921 [5] and the German-Polish Convention of 1922. Treaties protecting minorities and the inhabitants of mandated territories were regarded as conferring rights directly upon individuals, and individual responsibility came to be recognized in cases of piracy, violation of blockades, and violation of customary and conventional rules concerning the slave trade. Following the Second World War, as we have seen in the preceding chapter, individual persons were held responsible for such violations under international law as crimes against peace, war crimes, and crimes against humanity.

It would seem clear that as a mere object of international law, the individual cannot be its final end, its beneficiary and potential subject. "For the technical term 'object' refers in law to means and not to ends; to things and not to persons; to passive and not to active entities." [6] But the subject positivists do not regard the individual as the final end of the law of nations merely because he is an object of the rights and duties of states. Rather, he is assigned this status as a natural person, for as such he is the ultimate unit of human society and accordingly a subject of all law. The fact that a large number of publicists recognize in numerous situations this capacity in the individual raises the question: Why should he not be generally regarded as having personality in terms of international law? Yet, the subjective positivists have always maintained that, in a strictly legal sense, the individual is always an object and never a subject of the law of nations. They argue that though the individual is the final end of that law, his juridical relationship to it can be realized only through his relationship to the state; furthermore, that "the designation of the individual as a potential subject of this law refers to a future contingency and not to a present fact." [7]

Nationality. The legal relationship which exists between an individual and the state, by which the former owes allegiance and the latter pro-

[4] George Manner, "The Object Theory of the Individual in International Law," *American Journal of International Law,* vol. 46 (1952), p. 433. Italics added.

[5] In 1928, the Permanent Court of International Justice held that this agreement had direct application to individuals. The Court said: "According to its contents, the object of the *Beamtenabkommen* is to create a special legal regime governing the relations between the Polish Railways Administration and the Danzig officials, workmen and employees who have passed into the permanent service of the Polish Administration"—*PCIJ Publications,* ser. B, no. 15; M. O. Hudson, *World Court Reports,* vol. II, p. 237.

[6] Manner, *op. cit.,* p. 438.   [7] *Ibid.,* p. 437.

tection, is known as *nationality*. The law of nationality has gained in importance in recent years, and the term *national* has acquired a generic connotation that includes both *citizens* and *subjects*.[8] Yet a state may have nationals who do not enjoy the status of citizens. The British Nationality Act of 1948, Section 13, distinguishes between British subjects who are citizens of the United Kingdom and colonies and those who are subjects without such citizenship.[9]

In the United States, according to the Immigration and Nationality Act of 1952,[10] it is provided that the following shall be nationals and citizens of the United States at birth:

(1) A person born in the United States, and subject to the jurisdiction thereof;

(2) a person born in the United States to a member of an Indian, Eskimo, Aleutian, or other aboriginal tribe: *Provided,* That the granting of citizenship under this subsection shall not in any manner impair or otherwise affect the right of such person to tribal or other property;

(3) a person born outside the United States and its outlying possessions of parents both of whom are citizens of the United States and one of whom has had a residence in the United States or one of its outlying possessions prior to the birth of such person;

(4) a person born outside of the United States and its outlying possessions of parents one of whom is a citizen of the United States who has been physically present in the United States or one of its outlying possessions for a continuous period of one year prior to the birth of such person, and the other of whom is a national, but not a citizen of the United States;

(5) a person born in an outlying possession of the United States of parents one of whom is a citizen of the United States who has been physically present in the United States or one of its outlying possessions for a continuous period of one year at any time prior to the birth of such person;

(6) a person of unknown parentage found in the United States while under the age of five years, until shown, prior to his attaining the age of twenty-one years, not to have been born in the United States;

(7) a person born outside the geographical limits of the United States and its outlying possessions of parents one of whom is an alien, and the other a citizen of the United States who, prior to the birth of such person, was physically present in the United States or its outlying possessions for a period or periods totaling not less than ten years, at least five of which were after attaining the age of fourteen years: *Provided,* That any periods of honorable service in the Armed Forces of the United States by such citizen parent may be included in computing the physical presence requirements of this paragraph."

[8] C. G. Fenwick, *International Law* (1948), p. 253.
[9] Manley O. Hudson, *Cases and Other Materials on International Law* (1951), p. 137.
[10] 82d Cong., 2d Sess., Public Law 414 (H.R. 5678); 66 Stat. L. 163.

Nationals but not citizens of the United States are defined in Section 308 of the Nationality Act of 1952 as follows:

"Unless otherwise provided. . . . the following shall be nationals, but not citizens, of the United States at birth:

(1) A person born in an outlying possession of the United States on or after the date of formal acquisition of such possessions;

(2) A person born outside the United States and its outlying possessions of parents both of whom are nationals, but not citizens, of the United States, and have had residence in the United States, or one of its outlying possessions prior to the birth of such person; and

(3) A person of unknown parentage found in an outlying possession of the United States while under the age of five years, until shown, prior to his attaining the age of twenty-one years, not to have been born in such outlying possession."

According to the Hague convention of April 12, 1930, it is provided that each state shall determine under its own laws who are its nationals. "This law shall be recognized by other States in so far as it is consistent with international conventions, international custom, and the principles of law generally recognized with regard to nationality." It further provides that "any question as to whether a person possesses the nationality of a particular State shall be determined in accordance with the law of that State." [11] In the case of *Stoeck v. Public Trustee*,[12] the court decided that "there is not and cannot be such an individual as a German national according to English law," if he is not already so regarded under the municipal law of Germany. But according to the Permanent Court of International Justice in the case of the *Nationality Decrees issued in Tunis and Morocco* [13] in 1923, the discretion in matters of nationality which ordinarily belongs to the state may, under certain circumstances, be restricted by international obligations. "In such a case, jurisdiction which, in principle, belongs solely to the State, is limited by rules of international law." Inasmuch as the terms "citizen," "subject," and "person within the jurisdiction of the state" are often used in different meanings, the word "national" has been introduced to designate those whose legal relationship to the state is such as to require service in return for protection.[14]

---

[11] 179 *League of Nations Treaty Series*, p. 89.

[12] [1921] 2 Ch. 67.

[13] *PCIJ Publications*, ser. B, no. 4; Hudson, *World Court Reports*, Vol. I, p. 143.

[14] According to *Black's Law Dictionary*, nationality is "that quality or character which arises from the fact of a person's belonging to a nation or state." In *Falla-Nataf and Brothers v. Germany*, the Mixed Arbitral Tribunal of 1927 held that "the expression *ressortissants* appearing in Article 297e of the Treaty of Versailles is not restricted to nationals of a State, but the expression includes equally all those who, by any juridical relation other than nationality proper, belong to a State" (*Recueil des decisions*, vol. 7, p. 653).

How Nationality Is Acquired. Even though the determination of nationality is a matter solely within the province of the state, the principal modes by which such a status is acquired and lost are not without interest to the theory of international law.

In spite of numerous attempts to codify the law of nationality, there still exists a wide variety of opinion among legal experts, not only with respect to the proper solution of conflicting claims, but also regarding the correct basis for the determination of the law itself. In former times, when people were compelled by the hazards of travel to live and die in the land of their fathers, these problems were of minor consequence. But in the present age, with its amazing progress in the development of transportation and resultant mobility of populations, the whole question of nationality has acquired a new importance.

Generally speaking, nationality is acquired through either of two avenues. The one is based on *jus soli*; the other, on *jus sanguinis*. According to *jus soli*, nationality is determined by birth within the territorial jurisdiction of a given state, without regard to the status of the parents. This principle, which is of feudal origin, became part of the common law of England and thus is generally applied throughout the English-speaking world.[15] The fourteenth Amendment to the Constitution of the United States, in conformity with the principle of *jus soli*, provides that "all persons born or naturalized in the United States, and subject to the jurisdiction thereof, are citizens of the United States and of the state wherein they reside." The same rule is followed in British law.[16]

According to the principle of *jus sanguinis*, the nationality of an individual is determined by that of his parents. The Congress of the United States as early as 1790 enacted a law which provided that "the children of citizens of the United States that may be born beyond the sea, or out of the limits of the United States, shall be considered as natural born citizens."[17] This legislation, however, was superseded by later enactments.[18] The governing law at the moment, in the United States, is the Nationality Act of 1952,[19] which, as we have seen, makes a distinction between persons who are nationals *and citizens* of the United States and those who are nationals *but not citizens*.

Though the acquisition of nationality through birth is by far the most common, there are other means by which citizenship may be attained. Of these the most important is *naturalization*, a process which requires

[15] A number of Latin-American states also adhere to this principle for the determination of nationality. See Fenwick, *op. cit.*, p. 254.
[16] 4 & 5 Geo. V, c. 17.
[17] 1 Stat. L. 103.
[18] 1 Stat. L. 445 (1795); 2 Stat. L. 155 (1802).
[19] 66 Stat. L 163.

compliance with certain legal requirements as determined by municipal law. In the United States, it has been held that in all naturalization proceedings the existing law must be strictly construed, and that compliance with its every detail is imperative. "Naturalization," said the court *In re Pezzi*, "is a matter of favor, and not of right, and requires strict compliance with the acts of Congress." [20] The granting of citizenship by means of naturalization is, generally speaking, a function of the courts, though in recent years there has been a discernible trend in this country toward administrative participation.[21]

Other modes by which nationality is acquired are those of *redintegration, subjugation,* and *cession.* The first of these involves the resumption of citizenship on the part of persons who for some reason may have lost the nationality of their native land or of the country of previous naturalization. Subjugation and cession have reference to the transfer of territories, and accordingly of the nationality of the inhabitants, from one state to another.

Expatriation. The loss of nationality, no less than its acquisition, is a matter within the province of each individual state to regulate. Yet, it is of interest to the theory of international law to take notice of the various grounds upon which any person may lose his nationality.

Generally speaking, the loss of citizenship takes place in ways corresponding to those in which it is acquired. This generalization, however, is subject to certain exceptions. A national of the United States, according to the Nationality Act of 1952, loses his citizenship by becoming naturalized in a foreign state, either upon his own application or through the naturalization of a parent having legal custody of such a person.[22] In

---

[20] 29 F.2d 999 (1928). In the case of *United States v. Ginsberg*, 243 U.S. 472 (1917), the Supreme Court said: "An alien who seeks political rights as a member of this nation can rightfully obtain them only upon terms and conditions specified by Congress. Courts are without authority to sanction changes or modifications; their duty is rigidly to enforce the legislative will in respect of a matter so vital to the public welfare. . . . No alien has the slightest right to naturalization, unless all statutory requirements are complied with."

[21] Naturalization in the United States is conferred upon all District Courts in the nation, upon District Courts of the United States for the Territories of Hawaii and Alaska, for the District of Columbia, and for Puerto Rico, the District Court of the Virgin Islands of the United States, and the District Court of Guam [Sec. 310(*a*) of the Nationality Act of 1952; 66 Stat. L. 163], and upon courts of record in any state or territory. But see also H. B. Hazard, "The Trend toward Administrative Naturalization," *American Political Science Review,* vol. 21 (1927), p. 342. It should be noted also that on numerous occasions individual aliens have been naturalized by special acts of the Congress of the United States (39 Stat. L. 1495, 1588; 41 Stat. L. 1449, 1463).

[22] It is further provided, however, that nationality shall not be lost by any person under this section as the result of the naturalization of a parent or parents while such person is under the age of twenty-one years, or as the result of a naturalization ob-

certain cases mere residence abroad over an extended period may result in the loss of citizenship. According to the act of 1952, a person who has become an American citizen through the process of naturalization loses his nationality by [23]

(1) having a continuous residence for three years in the territory of a foreign state of which he was formerly a national or in which the place of his birth is situated, except as provided in section 353 of this title, whether such residence commenced before or after the effective date of this Act;

(2) having a continuous residence for five years in any other foreign state or states, except as provided in sections 353 and 354 of this title, whether such residence commenced before or after the effective date of this Act.

The right of expatriation was declared by the Congress of the United States in a joint resolution of July 27, 1868, to be "natural and inherent" in all people.[24] "For a century past," said the United States delegate to the Hague Codification Conference of 1930, "it has been the policy of my country that the right of expatriation is an inherent and natural right of all persons. . . . It is a principle of the rights of man and of the liberty of the human race." [25] According to the laws of a great many states, nationality is lost as a consequence of naturalization in a foreign country.[26] But this is by no means universally true, as some states do not recognize the right of expatriation—*nemo potest exuere patriam*.

Dual Nationality. Inasmuch as individual states are free to determine for themselves the conditions of nationality, it is quite possible that two or more states may claim the same person as their citizen. This can take place through a variety of ways, and a person may possess dual nationality without his own knowledge. As we have seen already, the nationality of most people is determined either by their place of birth (*jus soli*) or by the nationality of the parents (*jus sanguinis*). Thus anyone born or naturalized within the United States, and subject to the jurisdiction thereof, is a citizen of the United States. But the native-born, if his parents are aliens, may also be regarded as possessing the nationality of his parents in conformity with the principle of *jus sanguinis;* and in the case of the

---

tained on behalf of a person under twenty-one years of age by a parent, guardian, or duly authorized agent, unless such person shall fail to enter the United States to establish a permanent residence prior to his twenty-fifth birthday (sec. 349).

[23] Sec. 352(*a*).

[24] 15 Stat. L. 223; reenacted in Rev. Stat., secs. 1999, 2000, 2001.

[25] Conference for the Codification of International Law, *Acts*, vol. II, Minutes of the First Committee, League of Nations Publication C. 351 (a). M. 145 (a). 1930. V, pp. 44, 69–70, 78, 80–81, 275–276; G. H. Hackworth, *Digest of International Law*, vol. II, p. 162.

[26] The Polish Constitution of Mar. 17, 1921, provided (Art. 87) that "a Polish citizen may not be at the same time a citizen of another state." See Hudson, *Cases and Other Materials on International Law*, p. 191n.

naturalized citizen, as already noted, the nationality of his former state may persist, through a denial of expatriation.

Dual nationality may likewise result from marriage. Thus if an American woman marries an Englishman, she would, according to British law, acquire British nationality; yet she would not, since the enactment of the Cable Act,[27] cease to be a citizen of the United States. Because of the general confusion and considerable hardship in connection with the nationality of married women, this subject was taken up by the League of Nations Committee of Experts for the Progressive Codification of International Law, and a draft convention was submitted in 1926. The rule was here laid down that a married woman should not lose the citizenship of her original state unless by the laws of her husband's country she should acquire his nationality; likewise, that if her husband's nationality should change during their married life, she should not lose his former nationality unless she acquired his new nationality.[28] This formula was accepted by the Conference on Codification of International Law, held at The Hague in 1930, with the further provision that the naturalization of the husband, during marriage, should have no effect upon the nationality of the wife without her consent. A provision was also added concerning the recovery of the wife's nationality upon the dissolution of marriage.[29] The inconveniences and hardships resulting from dual nationality were greatly aggravated as a result of the First World War, and this was perhaps one of the reasons why the Hague Codification Conference of 1930 included this question on its agenda. The Permanent Court of International Justice, in an advisory opinion concerning the *Acquisition of Polish Nationality*, had observed in 1923 that only by means of international conventions could a "desirable result" be achieved with regard to the problem of conflicting allegiances which would necessarily follow from the structure of international customary law.[30] "The doctrine of double allegiance," says Moore, "though often criticised as unphilosophical, is not an invention of jurists, but is the logical result of the concurrent operation of two different laws." [31]

[27] According to this Act of September, 1922, "A woman citizen of the United States shall not cease to be a citizen of the United States by reason of her marriage after the passage of this Act, unless she makes a formal renunciation of her citizenship before a court having jurisdiction over naturalization of aliens: *Provided*, that any woman citizen who marries an alien ineligible to citizenship shall cease to be a citizen of the United States"—42 Stat. L. 1021.

[28] For text, see *American Journal of International Law*, vol. 23 (1929), spec. supplement 121. For comparison see also Harvard Draft, Art. 19.

[29] Convention on Certain Questions Relating to the Conflict of Nationality Laws, Arts. 8–11. *American Journal of International Law*, vol. 24 (1930), supplement, 192. See also Fenwick, *op. cit.*, pp. 160–162

[30] Georg Schwarzenberger, *International Law* (1949), vol. I, p. 163.

[31] John Bassett Moore, *Digest of International Law*, vol. III, p. 518.

428   *The Individual in International Law*

With respect to persons of dual nationality there is a generally recognized rule of international law. It is to the effect that an individual so encumbered, when residing in either of the two countries of which he is a national, is subject to the jurisdiction of the state of domicile.[32]

Stateless Persons. It is, of course, quite possible that a person may be without any nationality, in which case he is referred to as a *stateless person*. In the case of *Stoeck v. Public Trustee*,[33] a question was raised as to the legal possibility of a condition of statelessness. On this point the court found conflicting opinions among the authorities on international law but went on to answer the question as follows:

> After all the question of what State a person belongs to must ultimately be decided by the municipal law of the State to which he claims to belong or to which it is alleged that he belongs; and, if no State exists according to the municipal law of which a given individual is its national, it is difficult to see to what State he can belong, how he can be other than a stateless person, or why an international lawyer or any one else should close his eyes to such a possibility.

If, as the court suggested in this case, there was doubt as to the existence of a legal category of statelessness in 1921, such an attitude must be ascribed to the yet strong influence of the subjective positivists upon the theory of international law. For, as we have seen, according to this school of thought the individual can have no legal position under the law of nations. But the fact of his stateless condition is not denied.[34] It is precisely this lack of bond between the individual and the state which places him, in terms of positivist theory, outside the pale of international law— but also, it must be remembered, outside the protection of any state as well. It is this latter fact which renders the position of a stateless person most precarious.

It is very difficult for stateless persons to obtain passports for travel, which for the improvement of their position might prove desirable. In 1922, in order to afford relief to Russian refugees in this situation, the "Nansen passport" was devised by the League of Nations. The Nansen documents, unlike the ordinary passports, did not confer the right of reentry without a special authorization. In 1933, however, a Convention on the International Status of Refugees bound the contracting parties to include in such certificates a formula permitting both departure and return.[35]

[32] Hackworth, *op. cit.*, vol. III, p. 354.

[33] Great Britain, Chancery Division, 1921 (2 Ch. 67).

[34] "All individuals who have lost their original nationality without having acquired another are, in fact, destitute of nationality"—Oppenheim-Lauterpacht, *International Law* (1947), vol. I, p. 610.

[35] P. E. Corbett, *Law and Society in the Relations of States* (1951), p. 166.

As a consequence of the Second World War, the problem of refugees and stateless persons was greatly aggravated, and it was in order to alleviate this situation that an agreement for the issue of travel documents to refugees was signed in London on October 14, 1946, by the representatives of 15 nations.[36] This agreement, which came into force on January 13, 1947, makes certificates of the Nansen type available to numerous displaced persons not included in earlier agreements and unable to obtain national passports.

Statelessness and the International Law Commission. At its very first session in 1949, the International Law Commission selected "nationality including statelessness" as a topic for codification.[37] On August 11, 1950, a resolution was adopted by the Economic and Social Council in which the Commission was requested to prepare at the earliest possible date a draft convention or conventions for the elimination of statelessness. In response to this request, the International Law Commission at its third session of 1951 decided to initiate work on this project, and Manley O. Hudson of the United States was appointed special rapporteur.[38]

At length, two draft conventions were prepared by the International Law Commissions and submitted, through the Secretary-General of the United Nations, to the Economic and Social Council. One is entitled Draft Convention on the Elimination of Future Statelessness, and the other Draft Convention on the Reduction of Future Statelessness. The Preambles of both instruments call attention to the fact that the Universal Declaration of Human Rights proclaims that "everyone has the right to a nationality"; furthermore, that the problem of statelessness is such as to require cooperative action between the member states and the United Nations in order to bring about a satisfactory solution. It is also recognized that statelessness is often productive of friction between states and that nationality is a condition for the enjoyment of certain rights under international law.

The Draft Convention on the Reduction of Future Statelessness is the more conservative of the two. It provides (Art. 1) that a child who would otherwise be stateless shall acquire at birth the nationality of the party in whose territory it is born. This, of course, is simply a recognition of the principle of *jus soli*. But it is also provided that, for purposes of Article 1, any person born on board a vessel at sea shall have the nationality of the state whose flag the vessel flies. If such birth takes place on board an

[36] The United States was represented at this conference but did not sign the agreement.

[37] See the report of the Commission covering the work of its first session, *Official Records of the General Assembly, Fourth Session,* supp. 10, UN Doc. A/925.

[38] See the report of the Commission covering the work of its third session, *Official Records of the General Assembly, Sixth Session,* supp. 9, UN Doc. A/1858, par. 85.

aircraft, nationality is to be that of the place where the aircraft is registered.[39] Loss of nationality in consequence of marriage, termination of
marriage, or adoption is to be conditioned upon the acquisition of a new
nationality.[40] Nor shall renunciation result in the loss of nationality unless
the person thereby acquires another nationality.[41] Persons shall not lose
their nationality, so as to become stateless, on the ground of departure,
stay abroad, or failure to register or on any other similar ground.[42] No
person is to be deprived of his nationality on racial, ethnical, religious, or
political grounds, nor shall the transfer of territory automatically result
in the loss of nationality on the part of the inhabitants.

We have cited these provisions of the draft convention, not as an
illustration of what the law is at the present moment, but rather to indicate what the International Law Commission thinks it ought to be. As the
student can readily see, some of the provisions of the draft are already
recognized in American law, whereas others are not. Though the Draft
Convention on the Reduction of Future Statelessness is to some extent
within the classification of *de lege ferenda,* it is nevertheless illustrative
of a conscious effort to provide international solutions to a problem
hitherto regarded as within the exclusive province of municipal law.

Extradition. Inasmuch as the jurisdiction of states is territorial in nature, it is quite possible for an offender against the laws of any country
to avoid punishment, at least for a time, by escaping into the territory of
another jurisdiction. In such cases, however, the common interest of
nations in the preservation of law and order has led to a certain amount
of international cooperation for the promotion of justice. Extradition,
which is the return or surrender by one state to another of a fugitive from
justice, is an example of such cooperation. It is a well-recognized principle
of international law that a state not only may expel an alien offender
against its own laws, but may also surrender a person accused of crime
in another country upon the latter's request. Extradition has long been
recognized in international law. In 1625 Grotius wrote:[43]

> Since it is not customary for states to permit another state to enter its terri-
> tory under arms for the sake of administering punishment, nor is it expedient,
> it follows that the state where the offender sojourns ought to do one of two
> things: Either on demand it should punish the guilty party, or it should turn
> him over for trial to the state making the demand.

Though extradition is recognized as a principle of the general law of

[39] Art. 3 of the Draft Convention on the Reduction of Future Statelessness.
[40] Art. 5 of the draft.
[41] Art. 6.
[42] Art. 6(3).
[43] *De jure belli ac pacis,* book II, chap. xxi, sec. 4.

nations,[44] it is in the present day more frequently governed by specific treaty provisions. The modern system of international agreements regarding extradition had its beginning in the middle of the nineteenth century. Since then, the United States has entered into extradition treaties with a number of other states, and the practice has been not to allow extradition except in accordance with such treaties.[45] Extradition treaties are generally of two types: (1) the older or classical type, which lists the offenses which are extraditable, and (2) the modern treaty, which contains no such listing of offenses but provides in a general way for extradition in all cases where the offense is punishable in both the states concerned.

It was under a treaty of the latter type that the celebrated case of Gerhart Eisler arose before the Bow Street Magistrate's Court in London on May 27, 1949.[46] The facts were briefly as follows: Gerhart Eisler, an alien communist in the United States, while at liberty on bail pending decisions on appeals from criminal conviction, departed illegally from New York by stowing away on the Polish liner *Batory*. The *Batory's* first port of call was Southampton, and the American government sent a request to the British authorities for Eisler's arrest, detention, and extradition to the United States. Though Eisler had been convicted of two crimes [47] in the United States, neither was listed as an extraditable offense in the extradition treaty with Great Britain.[48] The United States based its application for extradition on the fact that Eisler had been convicted of perjury in connection with his application to leave the country. But according to English law such an offense did not constitute perjury, as the false statements which were alleged to have been made, and for which Eisler had been convicted, were not, according to the interpretation of the English court, made in connection with a judicial proceeding.[49] Accordingly, extradition was denied, and Eisler discharged from custody.

[44] See *In re Daniel Washburn*, 4 Johns. Ch. 106; 8 Am. Dec. 548 (1819). Also *In re Doelitzsch, Annual Digest* (1923–24), Case no. 156.

[45] It is true that a person by name Arguelles was surrendered to Spain in 1864 in the absence of extradition treaty; see *Wharton's Digest of International Law*, vol. 2, pp. 746 ff. But this case should be regarded as exceptional.

[46] George A. Finch, "The Eisler Extradition Case," *American Journal of International Law*, vol. 43 (1949), p. 487.

[47] Eisler had been convicted for contempt of Congress because he refused to testify before the Committee on Un-American Activities of the House of Representatives; also for making false statements in connection with application for permission to leave the United States.

[48] Treaty of Dec. 22, 1931, which came into force on June 24, 1935. *Department of State Treaty Series*, no. 849; *Treaty Information Bulletin*, June, 1935, p. 12.

[49] The crime of perjury under the common law can be committed only in the course of a suit or judicial proceeding. This is pretty much the case in England. In the United States, however, the definition of perjury has been extended by statutory law to include any false statements in connection with various nonjudicial and administrative proceedings, affidavits, and depositions.

The decision in this case hinged on the different meaning of perjury in English and American law. Somewhat similar is the *Case of Blackmer*,[50] which involved a request by the United States to France for the extradition of Blackmer for "false swearing" in connection with his income-tax returns. Perjury was not found by the French court to have been involved in this case, and extradition was therefore denied. As we have seen, in order for a crime to be extraditable it must either be included in the extradition treaty, or must be regarded as a crime under the laws of both contracting parties.

The prompt release of Eisler on the ground that he was not charged with an extraditable offense made it unnecessary for the English court to consider whether the offense for which extradition was asked constituted a political crime. It is pretty well established that, in the absence of provisions to the contrary, no extradition treaty is to be interpreted in such a way as to require the surrender of a person charged with a crime which is of a political nature.[51]

There seems to be no recognized principle in international law which requires the surrender of persons who have returned to their own country after committing crimes abroad. It is, of course, possible that the surrender of nationals in such cases could be included in the stipulations of treaties. It has become fairly general practice, especially in Europe and Latin America, to include in extradition treaties a special clause excluding the extradition of nationals. The British countries and the United States, however, surrender their nationals to each other under the same conditions as nonnationals.[52] The main reason for this difference in practice lies in the fact that a crime committed abroad is considered in most European and Latin-American countries as an offense against the laws of the homeland. Under the common-law principles of British nations, however, the priority of jurisdiction is given to the state in whose territory the crime was committed.

It has sometimes been argued that extradition is a matter of reciprocity. In the case of Henry Phillips Ames, whose extradition was asked by the Mexican government in 1928, the Secretary of State of the United States informed the Mexican ambassador in Washington that the extradition of Ames would not be granted except on conditions of reciprocity.[53] The same action was taken by the Department of State in the case of Severiano Riojas in 1939.[54] Generally speaking, extradition treaties between the

[50] France, Court of Paris, *Chambre des Mises en Accusation* (1928); Hudson, *Cases* (1936), p. 953.
[51] See *In re Castioni* [1891] 1 Q.B. 149.
[52] Corbett, *op cit.*, p. 175.
[53] Hackworth, *op. cit.*, vol. IV, pp. 60–61.
[54] *Ibid.*, p. 61.

United States and other powers contain lists of offenses which are extraditable. Though this is the general rule, a notable exception is provided in the Montevideo Convention on Extradition of 1933,[55] to which the United States is a party. This convention provides that extradition may be demanded if the offense "constitutes a crime and is punishable under the laws of the demanding and surrendering states with a minimum penalty of imprisonment for one year." [56]

During the Second World War, as the ring narrowed around the Axis powers, there was some reason to believe that the leaders of those powers who were guilty of various international crimes might seek refuge in neutral territory. In a statement of July 30, 1943, President Roosevelt expressed the hope that "no neutral will permit its territory to be used as a place of refuge or otherwise assist such persons in any effort to escape their just deserts." [57] The Tripartite Conference, in its "Declaration of German Atrocities," signed in Moscow on October 30, 1943, announced that the signatory powers would pursue the guilty persons "to the uttermost ends of the earth and will deliver them to their accusers in order that justice may be done." As the Nazi leaders were captured within belligerent territory, their pursuit into neutral territory, as announced in the Moscow Declaration, did not prove to be necessary.

There can be little doubt that in this age of rapid transportation, by which a criminal may remove himself far from the scene of his crime, a closer cooperation in the administration of justice is more vital than ever. This is necessary for the protection of human society against those who would violate its laws with impunity. On the other hand, it is no less important that the individual person be protected against cruel and unjust treatment by the group. In both cases, the best results are likely to come from greater cooperation among the nations.

[55] *American Journal of International Law,* vol. 28 (1934), supp., p. 65.
[56] Art. 1 of the convention.
[57] *Department of State Bulletin,* vol. 9, p. 62.

CHAPTER 26

Human Rights

The problem of human rights in a world community is greatly aggravated by hostile relations among the peoples of the earth. Indeed, the curtailment and sometimes total dislodgement of individual liberty, in countries where for a time it found a precarious foothold, must be regarded as one of the unfortunate by-products of war. Perhaps the most notorious effects of wars and revolutions in our time are found in the new gospel of power, in the leviathan state, and in the flagrant disregard for individual rights. Widespread tyranny has aggravated the refugee problem as hundreds of thousands of displaced persons press upon the gates of the Western nations where some measure of freedom yet remains.

The idea that the individual is endowed with certain fundamental and inalienable rights is, indeed, much older than the modern state. It was familiar to the peoples of antiquity and played an important part not only in the theological system of the Middle Ages, but in modern political theory as well. The struggle for the rights of man was vigorously pursued during the Age of Reason and was associated with important revolutions against absolutism in some of the Western nations. But the triumph of positivism and the rise of a new totalitarianism in our time have conspired to undermine the rights of the individual. Even in the Western democracies there is often a remarkable discrepancy between "constitutional guarantees" and actual practice. The true state of affairs in this regard can be ascertained only when one considers to what extent the abstract norms recited in constitutions are made concrete in simple statutes, administrative ordinances and regulations, private contracts, and judicial decisions.[1]

Publicists have at times expressed the view that certain fundamental rights exist under the law of nations which have application to the individual and to the whole of mankind. "Such rights have been said to comprise the rights of life, liberty, freedom of religion and conscience, and

[1] Josef L. Kunz, "The United Nations Declaration of Human Rights," *American Journal of International Law,* vol. 43 (1949), p. 320.

the like." [2] It is, to say the least, doubtful whether this view is descriptive of the actual practice of states.[3] Yet, in "the field of human rights as in other actual problems of international law it is necessary to avoid the Scylla of a pessimistic cynicism and the Charybdis of mere wishful thinking and superficial optimism." [4]

The increasing complexity of international relations with which this generation is confronted has demonstrated the need for a broader approach in international-legal theory than that which is provided by the extreme positivists of the nineteenth century. It had been the great purpose of the philosophical radicals [5] to destroy the juristic rationalism of the eighteenth century and to seek a basis in "reality" for the development of legal norms. Such utilitarian philosophers as Jeremy Bentham and John Austin argued vigorously against the natural-law doctrine, which in their day had entered a final period of decadence, and which even in its most creative phases they had really failed to understand.[6] Though this is not the place to embark upon an exhaustive analysis of the various doctrines of natural law in its relationship to later positivism, a certain orientation regarding these aspects of legal theory may be of some value in locating the juristic position of the individual in the community of nations.

The Classical Origins of Natural Law. In ancient Greek philosophy, natural law was invoked in a brave and precocious attempt to find harmony in conflict and reason in chaos. "What each thing is when fully developed," writes Aristotle, "we call its nature, whether we are speaking of a man, a horse, or a family." [7] Thus, the classical conception of natural law was the harmony found in the whole of nature at the point where each of its parts had reached the highest degree of development.[8] It was this conception which, according to Julius Stone, "yielded the famous distinction between natural and conventional justice." [9] The significant impact of Greek intellectualism upon the Roman world is clearly reflected in the following excerpt from the famous jurist Cicero: [10]

There is in fact a true law namely right reason, which is in accordance with nature, applies to all men and is unchangeable and eternal. . . . It will not

[2] Oppenheim-Lauterpacht, *International Law,* vol. I (1947), p. 583.
[3] *Ibid.*
[4] Kunz, *op. cit.,* p. 320.
[5] See Elie Halévy, *The Growth of Philosophic Radicalism;* also Julius Stone, *The Province and Function of Law* (1950), pp. 224–225.
[6] Stone, *op. cit.,* p. 270.
[7] *Politics* (Benjamin Jowett's translation) in *On Man and the Universe,* ed. by L. R. Loomis (Classics Club, 1943), p. 251.
[8] See Stone, *op. cit.,* p. 216.
[9] *Ibid.,* p. 216.
[10] From *De Officiis,* quoted by Stone, in *ibid.,* p. 216.

lay down one rule at Rome and another at Athens, nor will it be one rule today and another tomorrow. But there will be one law eternal and unchangeable binding at all times and upon all peoples.

In a jurisprudential sense, ideas of this kind became vastly more important with the Romans than had been the case in Greece, where a *corpus juris* never came into being as a separate entity from the rest of the social and political order. This difference was partly due to the fact that among the Greeks there never developed a professional lawyer class, whereas through the efforts of jurisconsults and praetors Roman law reached a high degree of refinement.

In the writings of St. Thomas Aquinas, both reason and natural law are used to support the authority of the Church, while at the opening of the modern age, natural law played a major part in the formulation of the first principles of public international law.[11] But if natural law could be used to affirm and support existing institutions, it can also be employed to undermine and overthrow their existing structures. In periods when the social and political order is relatively stable, natural law is often used to maintain the *status quo*. But as change continues to take place in certain areas of a culture and existing institutions become obsolete, natural law may indeed function as an instrument of revolution. Its employment in the latter sense is illustrated by certain events in the late eighteenth century—in America by the Declaration of Independence and in France by the Declaration of the Rights of Man. Yet, no sooner are reforms achieved than natural-law doctrines are invoked to protect established institutions and to prevent even the most gradual mutation in their structure and function. This dual role of natural law has been clearly evident since the days of the Reformation. It seemed reasonable enough that if St. Thomas Aquinas could marshal the doctrines of natural law to support the position of the Roman Church, so could the Protestant jurists and theologians use the same precepts to overthrow its authority.

The Pursuit of Happiness. By the end of the eighteenth century, natural law had lost much of the creative force which had distinguished its earlier career. Its separation from theology was by this time complete, but a growing agreement as to its detailed rules was to no small extent responsible for the loss of its intellectual dynamism and the increased stress on the immutability of its nature. Christian Wolff, as early as 1750, tells us that since "the nature and essence of man are immutable and necessary, it follows that natural obligation is also unchangable." But in spite of the stagnant condition of natural law in the eighteenth century, there were in this period ambitious attempts to provide a rational basis

[11] See p. 69.

for positive law.[12] This tendency was reflected not only in the works of publicists, but in contemporary legislation as well. But as regards the individual, perhaps the most important aspect of natural-law theory toward the end of the eighteenth century is its preoccupation with the pursuit of human happiness. "We hold these truths to be self-evident," wrote Jefferson in the famous declaration, "that all men are . . . endowed by their Creator with inherent and inalienable rights; that among these are life, liberty, and the pursuit of happiness. . . ." According to Julius Stone: "This was entirely to be expected, since the utilitarian theory of ethics was already making good headway. When the theory broke through into jurisprudence with Bentham it was not entirely a novelty. Ample authority could be vouched for it from the works of 18th century natural lawyers." [13]

Emmerich de Vattel, who was the greatest authority on international law in the eighteenth century, finds in natural law the rules which can best guide man to the great end, which is "to obtain the most perfect happiness of which he is capable."

The restatement of natural law in terms of human happiness has not been confined to theoretical speculations, for, as we have already indicated, it was to play a major part in the formulation of the political ideals which motivated both the French and American Revolutions. As Stone has so significantly pointed out: [14]

Changes in the content of "natural law" point to a profound truth, too often ignored by easy cynics. . . . Its very assertion, especially in its explosive phase, is a vindication of the claim of an ideal justice to criticise what is laid down by those who wield power. It is a reminder that positive law in the last resort must sustain criticism by other than its own standards, if it is not to degenerate into the commands of naked power.

Before ending this brief survey, one more observation regarding the utility of natural law in the promotion of human rights may be made, namely, that in the future and with respect to the community of nations, human rights can best be secured by the employment of all available means, both legal and political. Doctrines of natural law, of reason and justice, must be used along with the more concrete enactments of positive law. In the words of Professor Lauterpacht: "The law of nature must supply, as it has done in the past, much of the spiritual basis and much of the political inspiration of that elevation of the rights of man to a legal plane superior to the will of sovereign States." [15] But as the same author

[12] See Stone, *op. cit.*, p. 231.   [13] *Ibid.*, p. 232.
[14] *Ibid.*, p. 234.
[15] H. Lauterpacht *International Law and Human Rights* (1950), p. 126.

correctly points out: "The law of nature is in no sense a substitute for positive law; it cannot by itself supply the solution of the problem of the rights of man." For whenever "the law of nature is treated as an alternative to changes in existing law it ceases, on balance, to be a beneficent force and becomes a check upon progress." [16]

Human Rights and the United Nations Charter. In the language of the Preamble to the Charter, the peoples of the United Nations are

determined to save succeeding generations from the scourge of war, which twice in our lifetime has brought untold sorrow to mankind, and to reaffirm faith in fundamental human rights, in the dignity and worth of the human person, in the equal rights of men and women and of nations large and small, and to establish conditions under which justice and respect for obligations arising from treaties and other sources of international law can be maintained, and to promote social progress and better standards of life in larger freedom.

It is, of course, clear that while the Preamble is an integral part of the Charter, it does not set forth concretely the basic obligations of the members of the organization. Nevertheless, its purpose is to state in general terms the reason and intent of the most important single document in international legislation. It must therefore be regarded as a vital part of the existing law of nations.

In a Declaration by the United Nations of January 1, 1942, it was recognized that victory over the Axis powers was necessary "to defend life, liberty, independence and religious freedom, and to preserve human rights and justice in their own lands as well as in other lands." It had been the hope that an Allied victory not only would result in the liberation of the occupied countries, but would secure a lasting peace, and to mankind a larger freedom. Attempts had been made at San Francisco to incorporate in the Charter an International Bill of Rights, which would set forth in more specific terms the sentiments contained in the Preamble. Even though the main objective of these efforts was not attained, numerous articles in the Charter are designed to promote the rights of man under the law of nations.

Among the purposes of the United Nations is the achievement of international cooperation in solving problems of an "economic, social, cultural, or humanitarian character, and in promoting and encouraging respect for human rights and for fundamental freedoms for all without distinction as to race, sex, language, or religion." [17] In this connection, it is also provided in Article 13 of the Charter that the General Assembly shall initiate studies and make recommendations for the purpose of "promoting international

[16] *Ibid.*
[17] Art. 1, sec. 3, United Nations Charter.

cooperation in the economic, social, cultural, educational and health fields, and assisting in the realization of human rights and fundamental freedoms for all without distinction as to race, sex, language, or religion." Further emphasis upon the individual person as distinguished from the state is found in Article 55, which stipulates that the United Nations shall promote "higher standards of living, full employment, and conditions of economic and social progress and development," as well as "universal respect for, and observance of, human rights and fundamental freedoms for all without distinction as to race, sex, language, or religion." For the achievement of these ends, all the members of the United Nations are pledged "to take joint and separate action in cooperation with the Organization." [18] Among the functions of the Economic and Social Council is that of making recommendations "for the purpose of promoting respect for, and observance of, human rights and fundamental freedoms for all." [19] Among the objectives of the International Trusteeship System, as set forth in Chapter XII, Article 76, of the Charter, are "to promote the political, economic, social, and educational advancement of the inhabitants of the trust territories," and again to "encourage respect for human rights and for fundamental freedoms for all without distinction as to race, sex, language, or religion, and to encourage recognition of the interdependence of the peoples of the world."

A careful reading of the material in the preceding paragraph will reveal a remarkable and consistent restraint in the wording of the several parts of the Charter concerning human rights. It had been suggested by some of the delegates at San Francisco that it should be the function of the United Nations not only to "promote" and "encourage," but also to "protect" the fundamental rights of man. This proposal was rejected, however, on the grounds that it would impose upon the Organization duties and functions which only individual states are competent to perform. It should be noted also that the agencies which are entrusted with the "promotion" of human rights are precisely those which are lacking in executive power. These agencies are the Assembly and the Economic and Social Council, both of which under the terms of the Charter are deprived of any executive or legislative power of binding force. The Security Council, the only organ of the United Nations having such power, is without jurisdiction in matters of human rights—except, of course, in cases where violations of these rights constitute a danger to world peace and security.[20] But in spite of the cautious language of the Charter regarding the matter of human rights, it should not be surmised that the provisions

[18] Art. 56 of the Charter.
[19] Art. 62, sec. 2, of the Charter.
[20] Lauterpacht, *op. cit.*, p. 147.

of this important international legislation are without legal force. According to Lauterpacht: [21]

These provisions are no mere embellishment of a historic document, they were not the result of an afterthought or an accident of drafting. They were adopted, with deliberation and after prolonged discussion before and during the San Francisco Conference, as part of the philosophy of the new international system and as a most compelling lesson of the experience of the inadequacies and dangers of the old.

The Universal Declaration of Human Rights. It was in pursuance of such provisions of the United Nations Charter as we have discussed above that the General Assembly, on December 10, 1948, unanimously adopted the Universal Declaration of Human Rights. Its 30 articles set forth in clear and precise language certain inalienable rights of the individual in the economic, social, and cultural fields, as well as personal and civil rights. Among these are the right to life, liberty, and security of person; to freedom from arbitrary arrest; to a fair trial; to privacy; to freedom of movement and residence; to social security; to work; to education; to nationality; to freedom of thought and conscience; to freedom of worship; to freedom of expression and of peaceful assembly; to take part in the government of one's own country; to hold public office; to seek and be granted asylum; and to own property. The Assembly proclaimed these rights as "a common standard of achievement for all peoples and all nations" and called upon the member states, the Secretary-General, and the specialized agencies to aid in their dissemination throughout the world.

As to the real value and importance of this Declaration there is divided opinion. But one thing is certain: it cannot be regarded as part of the existing law, binding upon all states and governments.[22] More properly, perhaps, it may be compared to a surveyor's stake pointing the direction of a future highway. In his Report to the General Assembly in 1948, the Secretary-General voiced the opinion that "this Declaration, the first attempt in history to write a 'Bill of Rights' for the whole world, is an important first step in the direction of implementing the general pledges of the Charter concerning human rights."

[21] *Ibid.,* p. 147.

[22] On this point, the delegate from the United States (Mrs. Roosevelt) said: "In giving our approval to the declaration today, it is of primary importance that we keep clearly in mind the basic character of the document. It is not a treaty; it is not an international agreement. It is not and does not purport to be a statement of law or a legal obligation. It is a declaration of basic principles of human rights and freedoms, to be stamped with the approval of the General Assembly by a formal vote of its members, and to serve as a common standard of achievement for all peoples of all nations." *State Department Bulletin,* vol. 19, no. 494 (Dec. 19, 1948), p. 751.

Though it may be readily admitted that the Declaration of Human Rights is not in itself a legal document involving legal obligations, it may nevertheless be of considerable importance as a landmark in the development of the law of nations. Its future value in this respect, however, is dependent upon the degree to which its principles can find support in public opinion. For it is only when so supported that the ideals expressed in this famous document will crystalize into norms of binding law. In the meantime, the General Assembly proclaims this Universal Declaration of Human Rights as

a common standard of achievement for all peoples and all nations, to the end that every individual and every organ of society, keeping this Declaration constantly in mind, shall strive by teaching and education to promote respect for these rights and freedoms and by progressive measures, national and international, to secure their universal and effective recognition and observance, both among the peoples of Member States themselves and among the peoples of territories under their jurisdiction.

A United Nations Bill of Rights. As early as 1947, the initial provisions for a Covenant on Human Rights were prepared. This instrument, unlike the Universal Declaration of 1948, was to be in the nature of a treaty and therefore legally binding upon the parties. Since then a number of draft conventions have been prepared, but up to the present time no agreement upon a final text has been reached.[23] In accordance with a decision of the Paris session of the General Assembly in 1952, the Commission on Human Rights is now engaged in the drafting of two covenants instead of a single text—one to be called a Covenant on Civil and Political Rights and the other entitled a Covenant on Economic, Social, and Cultural Rights.[24] This innovation was hit upon in order to avoid some of the difficulties encountered earlier, which had prevented a consensus of the parties. It was the opinion of many that such a separation of the main objectives would enable some countries to ratify at least one of the covenants at an early date.

The Covenant on Civil and Political Rights retains in its present language the basic elements of earlier drafts on this subject. These are well known in American law and include the rights to life; to protection against torture, slavery, and arbitrary arrest and detention; to fair trial by an impartial tribunal; to protection against *ex post facto laws;* to freedom of religion, expression, and assembly; and to equality before the law. The draft

[23] The first revision of the 1947 proposals was made by the Drafting Committee of the Commission on Human Rights in 1948. Later revisions were made in 1949, 1950, and 1952.
[24] James Simsarian, "Progress in Drafting Two Covenants on Human Rights in the United Nations," *American Journal of International Law* vol. 46 (1952), pp. 710–718.

Covenant on Economic, Social, and Cultural Rights contains provisions with respect to employment, conditions of work, trade unions, social security, the family, food, clothing, housing, health, education, science, and culture.

The present language of both covenants is such as to ensure that they are non-self-executing. Article 2 of the draft Covenant on Civil and Political Rights stipulates that in cases where the rights recognized in the covenant have not already been "provided for by existing legislative or other measures, each State undertakes to take the necessary steps, in accordance with its constitutional processes and with the provisions of this Covenant, to adopt such legislative or other measures as may be necessary to give effect to the rights recognized in this Covenant." In the same manner, Article 2 of the draft Covenant on Economic, Social, and Cultural Rights ensures the non-self-executing character of its provisions. It provides that each contracting party shall take steps "with a view to achieving progressively the full realization of the rights recognized in this Covenant by Legislative as well as by other means." Though the need for affirmative action is recognized in the phraseology of these provisions, it is clear that the terms of the two covenants cannot in themselves be enforced in the municipal courts but are in each case dependent for such enforcement upon some kind of enabling legislation.[25]

Inasmuch as at the present writing no further progress has been made with respect to a United Nations Bill of Rights, it is unnecessary to engage in a more extensive treatment here. It is enough merely to state that the whole matter of human rights is greatly in need of international-legal safeguards—a fact which is now becoming more and more widely recognized. But in the present community of internally sovereign states it is to be expected that progress along this line will be slow and painful.

The European Convention on Human Rights. While the instructions of the General Assembly of the United Nations of 1948 giving priority to the drafting of a Covenant on Human Rights have so far met with little success, more concrete results have been achieved on a regional level. This may perhaps be regarded as supporting evidence of the thesis we have maintained in earlier chapters of this treatise, namely, that in view of the imperfect development of a world community, universal declarations and resolutions are likely to be of an ephemeral nature lacking the permanence and stability of effective law. But in the meantime the problems persist, and the need for their solution becomes more and more pressing. Thus if the answer cannot be found on a universal level, regional remedies may find a profitable, though perhaps temporary, application.

[25] See *ibid.*, pp. 714–715.

It may be said, therefore, that a forward step was taken by the members of the Council of Europe in their signing at Rome on November 4, 1950, of a Convention for the Protection of Human Rights and Fundamental Freedoms.[26]

This convention must be regarded as pursuant to Article 1 of the Statute of the Council of Europe, which provides *inter alia* for "the maintenance and further realization of human rights and fundamental freedoms"; likewise, to Article 3 of the same Statute, which reads: "Every Member of the Council of Europe must accept the principles of the rule of law and of the enjoyment by all persons within its jurisdiction of human rights and fundamental freedoms, and collaborate sincerely and effectively in the realization of the aim of the Council as specified in Chapter I." Respect for human rights and fundamental freedoms is regarded as a first step to the closer integration of European states. Thus, in the Preamble to the Statute devotion is affirmed to the "spiritual and moral values" which are the common heritage of the peoples and "the true source of individual freedom, political liberty and the rule of law, principles which form the basis of all genuine democracy."

The original proposals of the Consultative Assembly of the Council of Europe listed for inclusion in the convention 10 rights already contained in the Universal Declaration of the United Nations. These were the following: security of person; exemption from slavery and servitude; freedom from arbitrary arrest, detention, or exile; freedom from arbitrary interference in private and family life, home, and correspondence; freedom of thought, conscience, and religion; freedom of opinion and expression; freedom of assembly; freedom of association; freedom to unite in trade unions; the right to marry and found a family. After considerable debate these proposals with minor verbal changes were included in the final text of the Covenant.

The next step was that of devising some machinery for the enforcement of the rights enumerated. In this connection the suggestion of the Consultative Assembly that a Commission on Human Rights be established was accepted. This Commission was to function as an international organ to which complaints could be made in cases where any of the member states should fail to secure to individuals such rights and freedoms as are defined in the convention. It was further provided that the

---

[26] This convention was signed by the governments of Belgium, Denmark, France, the German Federal Republic, Iceland, Ireland, Italy, Luxembourg, the Netherlands, Norway, the Saar, Turkey, and the United Kingdom. It was later signed in Paris on Nov. 28 of the same year by the governments of Greece and Sweden. These 15 nations constitute the total membership of the Council of Europe.

membership of the Commission should be equal to the number of the contracting parties and that no two of its members should be nationals of the same state.

What action should be taken in cases where friendly settlement of individual rights should fail constituted a major problem. The original proposals by the Consultative Assembly, in this connection, included the creation of a European Court on Human Rights, whose function it would be to adjudicate such infringements of the convention as could not be settled through the agency of the Commission. The judges are to be elected from lists of persons nominated by the member states, each party nominating three candidates, of whom at least two shall be its nationals. The jurisdiction of the Court may be accepted as compulsory through express declarations of the contracting parties. It is significant to note, however, that individuals as such do not have access to the Court, as cases can be brought only by the high contracting parties or by the Commission on Human Rights. But in spite of the failure to grant individuals direct access to the Court and the limitations placed upon the Commission in its executive powers, the creation of this machinery on a regional level for the protection of human rights must be regarded as a significant step forward. It goes far beyond the Universal Declaration of the United Nations in that it recognizes the need for legal remedies to vindicate the rights of man under the law of nations.[27]

A Turn in the Road. As we have already indicated, the concept of inherent and inalienable human rights had long constituted a substantial part of natural-law doctrines. It began in ancient times with the Stoics, and was later infused by the legal philosophy of Rome as well as by the Christian theology of the Middle Ages. In the eighteenth century these precepts were eloquently formulated both in Europe and America as a justification for revolution in the overthrow of despotism. But it was as though the explosive force of these doctrines in the latter days of the Age of Reason consumed, at once, their earlier vitality.

The nineteenth century saw the triumph of positivism, with the result that international-legal theory became increasingly preoccupied with rights and duties of the states, while the individual was consigned to the position of a mere object of the law of nations. During this period the monistic conception of the *Rechtsstaat* reached new stages of refinement as doctrines of rationalism, which had distinguished the development of international law in the last three hundred years, were gradually ob-

[27] For a more detailed discussion of the European Convention for the Protection of Human Rights, see A. H. Robertson in the *British Year Book of International Law*, vol. 27 (1950), pp. 145–163; also, H. Lauterpacht, *International Law and Human Rights*, (1950), pp. 435–463.

scured by the romantic adulation of the state. But a profound crisis in Western culture, manifested by wars and revolutions, has made our century the most turbulent in the entire history of the human race, and a new and frightful despotism has infested the earth. The rights of individuals, once regarded as sacred and inalienable, are in this age obscured by the shadow of a leviathan state. It is in the face of this clear and present danger to human freedom that new trends are discernible, not only in the writings of publicists but in the positive development of international law and organization as well.

Though it may be true that the conception of the corporate state, as an entity apart from its citizens, is incompatible with the realities of the modern world, its central position in the general structure of international law cannot be denied. Yet, under the inexorable pressure of necessity a large number of treaties for the protection of elementary human rights have been concluded from time to time. Among these are agreements relating to such matters as slavery and the slave trade; forced labor; the protection of refugees and stateless persons; the promotion of health and sanitation; better conditions of work; and similar topics. Here, it would seem, is evidence of an intimate connection between the individual and the law of nations. And, as we have suggested above, the repeated emphasis in the charter of the United Nations on "human rights and fundamental freedoms" must be regarded as indicative of a growing trend in this direction. It may, indeed, be said that we have come to a turn in the road, where legal theory must bend its course in conformity with new developments in the larger aspects of international relations.

The great wars of this century, the resurgence of despotism, and the startling advancements in science and technology are all situations which to each other bear a significant relationship and to all other things are the main causes of determination. As a consequence, neither the state nor the individual is likely to escape normative changes in relationship to international law. It might well be that the era of the nation state, as we have known it in the past five hundred years, is nearing an end. Thus, the increasing evidence of a revolt against positivism may find its best explanation in the present crisis of the state system.

A Selected Bibliography of International Law

International Law Digests

Annual Digest and Reports of Public International Law Cases, edited by
H. Lauterpacht and others, 12 vols., London: Butterworth (1919–   ).

Fontes juris gentium, edited by Viktor Bruns, 7 vols., Berlin: Heymanns.

Hackworth, Green H., *Digest of International Law,* 8 vols., Washington: GPO
(1940–1944).

Harvard Law School, "Research in International Law," in *American Journal of
International Law,* supplements for respective years.

Lapradelle, A. de, and J. P., Niboyet, *Répertoire de droit international,* 10 vols.,
Paris: Sirey (1929–1934).

Moore, John Bassett, *Digest of International Law,* 8 vols., Washington: GPO
(1906).

Strupp, Karl, *Woerterbuch des Voelkerrechts und der Diplomatie,* 3 vols.,
Berlin: De Gruyter (1924–1929).

Wharton, Francis, *Digest of the International Law of the United States,* 2d ed.,
3 vols., Washington: GPO (1887).

Cases and Reports

Bishop, William W., Jr., *International Law Cases and Materials,* New York:
Prentice-Hall (1953).

Briggs, Herbert W., *The Law of Nations: Cases, Documents and Notes,* 2d ed.,
New York: Appleton-Century-Crofts (1952).

Cobbett, Pitt, *Cases on International Law,* London: Sweet and Maxwell (1947).

Dickinson, E. D., *Cases and Materials on International Law,* Brooklyn: Foundation Press (1950).

———, *Cases and Other Readings on the Law of Nations,* New York: McGraw-
Hill (1929).

Fenwick, Charles G., *Cases on International Law,* 2d ed., Chicago: Callaghan
(1951).

Green, L. C., *International Law through the Cases,* New York: Praeger (1951).

Hambro, Edvard, *The Case Law of the International Court,* Leyden: Sijthoff
(1952).

Hudson, Manley O., *Cases on International Law,* 3d ed., St. Paul, Minn.: West
(1951).

———, *World Court Reports,* 4 vols., New York: Carnegie Endowment (1934–
1943).

International Court of Justice, *Reports of Judgments, Advisory Opinions and
Orders* (annual volumes since 1947), Leyden: Sijthoff.

Lapradelle, A. de, *Causes célèbres du droit des gens,* 5 vols., Paris: Editions
internationales (1929–1931).

Lapradelle, A. de, and N. Politis, *Recueil des arbitrages internationaux*, 2 vols., Paris: Pedone (1905, 1923).

Lloyd's Reports of Prize Cases, 10 vols., London: Lloyd's (1915–1924 and 1940–1950).

Martens, Charles de, *Causes célèbres du droit des gens*, 2d ed., 5 vols., Leipzig: Brockhaus (1858–1861). *Nouvelles causes célèbres*, 2 vols. (1843).

Moore, John Bassett, *International Adjudications*, Ancient Series, vol. 2 (1936); Modern Series, 6 vols., New York: Oxford (1929–1933).

Permanent Court of International Justice Reports, ser. A, B, and A/B, Leyden: Sijthoff.

Prize Cases in the United States Supreme Court, 1789–1918, 3 vols., New York: Oxford (1923).

Reports of International Arbitral Awards, 1920–1941, 3 vols., New York: United Nations (1948–1949).

Roscoe, E. S., *Reports of Prize Cases, 1745–1859*, 2 vols., London: Stevens (1905).

Scott, James Brown, *Hague Court Reports*, New York: Oxford (1916). Second series (1932).

Sohn, Louis B., *Cases and Materials on World Law*, Brooklyn: Foundation Press (1950).

Stowell, Ellery C., *Consular Cases and Opinions*, Washington: Byrne (1909).

———, and Henry F. Munro, *International Cases*, 2 vols., Boston: Houghton Mifflin (1916).

Wilson, George Grafton, *Hague Arbitration Cases*, Boston: Ginn (1915).

Laws, Treaties and State Papers

American State Papers, *Documents, Legislative and Executive, of the Congress of the United States*, Washington: Gates and Seaton (1789–   ).

Annals of the Organization of American States (quarterly, 1949–   ).

Beckett, Sir W. Eric, *The North Atlantic Treaty, the Brussels Treaty and the Charter of the United Nations*, London: Stevens (1950).

British and Foreign State Papers, 1812, London: H.M. Stationery Office (1841–   ).

Committee to Frame a World Constitution, *Preliminary Draft of a World Constitution*, Chicago: University of Chicago Press (1948).

Deák, Francis, and Philip C. Jessup, *Neutrality Laws, Regulations and Treaties of Various Countries*, 2 vols., New York: Carnegie Endowment (1939).

Descamps, E. E. F., and Louis Renault, *Recueil international des traités du XIXe siècle*, Paris: Rousseau (1914).

——— and ———, *Recueil international des traités du XXe siècle*, 7 vols. (1901–1907), Paris: Rousseau (1904–1908).

Feller, A. H., and Manley O. Hudson, *Diplomatic and Consular Laws and Regulations of Various Countries*, 2 vols., New York: Carnegie Endowment (1933).

Flournoy, Richard W., and Manley O. Hudson, *Nationality Laws of Various Countries*, New York: Oxford (1929).

Great Britain, *Treaty Series*, London: H.M. Stationery Office (1892–   ).

Hudson, Manley O., *International Legislation, 1919–1945*, 9 vols., New York: Carnegie Endowment (1931–1950).

League of Nations Documents, Geneva: Secretariat of the League of Nations.

League of Nations Treaty Series, Geneva: Secretariat of the League of Nations.

MacMurray, John V. A., *Treaties and Agreements with and concerning China, 1894–1919,* 2 vols., New York: Oxford (1924).

Manning, William R., *Arbitration Treaties among the American Nations to the Close of the Year 1910,* New York: Oxford (1924).

Miller, Hunter, *Treaties and Other International Acts of the United States of America (1776–1863),* 8 vols., Washington: GPO.

Myers, Denys P., *Manual of Collections of Treaties and of Collections relating to Treaties,* Cambridge, Mass.: Harvard University Press (1922).

Répertoire général des traités et autres actes diplomatiques, 1895–1920, The Hague: Nijhoff (1926).

Scott, James Brown, *Hague Conventions and Declarations of 1899 and 1907,* 3d ed., New York: Oxford (1918).

Strupp, K., *Documents pour servir à l'histoire du droit des gens,* 5 vols., Berlin: Sack (1923).

Systematic Survey of Treaties for the Pacific Settlement of International Disputes, New York: United Nations (1948).

Systematic Survey of Treaties for the Pacific Settlement of International Disputes 1928–1948, Secretariat of the United Nations (1949).

Treaties and Conventions Concluded between the United States of America and Other Powers, Notes by J. C. Bancroft Davis, Washington: GPO (1873).

United Nations Treaty Series, Secretariat of the United Nations.

United States Executive Agreement Series, 1929–1945, Washington: GPO.

United States Naval War College and M. O. Hudson, *International Law Documents,* Vol. XLVI (1948–1949), Washington: GPO (1950).

United States Treaties and Other International Acts Series, 1946–   , Washington: GPO.

United States Treaty Series, Washington: GPO (1908–   ).

Wilson, Robert R., *The International Law Standard in Treaties of the United States,* Cambridge, Mass.: Harvard University Press (1953).

General Treatises

Americano, Jorge, *The New Foundation of International Law,* New York: Macmillan (1947).

Bluntschli, J. C., *Das moderne Voelkerrecht der civilisirten Staaten,* 3d ed., Noerdlingen: Beck (1878).

Bonfils, Henry, *Manuel de droit international public,* 7th ed., Paris: Rousseau (1914).

Brierly, J. L., *Law of Nations,* 4th ed., New York: Oxford (1949).

————, *The Outlook for International Law,* New York: Oxford (1944).

Briggs, Herbert W., *The Progressive Development of International Law,* Istanbul: I. A. Matbaasi (1947).

Bustamante, A. S. de, *Derecho internacional publico,* 5 vols., Havana: Carasa (1933–1938).

Butler, Geoffrey, and Simon Maccoby, *The Development of International Law,* London: Longmans (1928).

Calvo, Carlos, *Droit international théorique et pratique,* 5th ed., 6 vols., Paris: Rousseau (1896).

Castanos, Stelios, *Critique du droit international public moderne,* Paris: Sirey (1953).

Castberg, Frede, *Folkerett,* Oslo: I. G. Lindkvist (1948).

Classics of International Law, edited by James Brown Scott. Publications of the Carnegie Endowment for International Peace:

Ayala, Balthazar, *De jure et officiis bellicis et disciplina militari,* edited by John Westlake, 2 vols., Washington (1912).

Belli, Pierino, *De re militari et bello,* 2 vols., Oxford (1936).

Bynkershoek, Cornelius van, *De dominio maris,* New York (1923).

———, *De foro legatorum,* Oxford (1946).

———, *Quaestionum juris pubilici libri duo,* 2 vols., Oxford (1930).

Gentili, Alberico, *Hispanicae advocationis libri duo,* 2 vols., New York (1921).

———, *De jure belli libri tres,* 2 vols., Oxford (1933).

———, *De legationibus libri tres,* 2 vols., New York (1924).

Grotius, Hugo, *De jure belli ac pacis libri tres,* Vol. I, Washington (1913); Vol. 2, Oxford (1925).

———, *De jure praedae commentarius,* 2 vols., Oxford (1950).

Legnano, Giovanni da, *De bello, de repraesaliis et de duello,* edited by T. Erskine Holland, Oxford (1917).

Pufendorf, Samuel, *Elementorum jurisprudentiae universalis libri duo,* 2 vols., Oxford (1931).

———, *De jure naturae et gentium libri octo,* 2 vols., Oxford (1934).

———, *De officio hominis et civis juxta legem naturalem libri duo,* 2 vols., New York (1927).

Rachel, Samuel, *De jure naturae et gentium dissertationes,* edited by Ludwig von Bar, 2 vols., Washington (1916).

Suarez, Francisco, *Selections from three works,* 2 vols., Oxford (1944).

Textor, Johann Wolfgang, *Synopsis juris gentium,* edited by Ludwig von Bar, 2 vols., Washington (1916).

Vattel, E. de, *Le Droit des gens,* 3 vols., Washington (1916).

Vitoria, Franciscus de, *Relectiones theologicae: De indis et de jure belli,* edited by Ernest Nys, Washington (1917).

Wheaton, Henry, *Elements of International Law* (reproduction of Dana's edition of 1866), edited by G. G. Wilson, Oxford (1936).

Wolff, Christian von, *Jus gentium methodo scientifica pertractatum,* 2 vols., Oxford (1934).

Zouche, Richard, *Juris et judicii fecialis, sive juris inter gentes, et quaestionum de eodem explicatio,* edited by Erskine Holland, 2 vols., Washington (1911).

Davis, George B., *Elements of International Law,* 4th ed., New York: Harper (1916).

Dickinson, Edwin D., *Law and Peace,* Philadelphia: University of Pennsylvania Press (1951).

Diena, G., *Principi di diritto internazionale,* 2d ed., 2 vols., Naples: Pierro (1914, 1917); 3d ed., Vol. 1 (1930).

Fenwick, Charles G., *International Law,* 3d ed., New York: Appleton-Century-Crofts (1948).

Fiore, Pasquale, *Il diritto internazionale codificato,* 5th ed., Turin (1915); English translation by Edwin M. Borchard, New York (1918).

Grob, Fritz, *The Relativity of War and Peace,* New Haven: Yale University Press (1949).

Guggenheim, Paul, *Lehrbuch des Voelkerrechts*, Basel: Verlag fuer Recht und Gesellschaft (1947–1951).

Hall, William E., *Treatise on International Law*, 4th ed (1895); 8th ed., by Higgins, New York: Oxford (1924).

Halleck, Henry W., *International Law*, 4th ed., 2 vols., London: Paul (1908).

Heffter, August Wilhelm, *Das europaeische Voelkerrecht der Gegenwart*, 8th ed., Berlin: Mueller (1888).

Hershey, Amos S., *Essentials of International Public Law and Organization*, rev. ed., New York: Macmillan (1927).

Hurst, Sir Cecil J. B., *International Law*, London: Stevens (1950).

Hyde, Charles Cheney, *International Law Chiefly as Interpreted and Applied by the United States*, 3 vols., Boston: Little, Brown (1947).

Jessup, Philip C., *A Modern Law of Nations—An Introduction*, New York: Macmillan (1948).

Keeton, G. W., and G. Schwarzenberger, *Making International Law Work*, London: Stevens (1946).

Kelsen, Hans, *Principles of International Law*, New York: Rinehart & Co. (1952).

———, *Recent Trends in the Law of the United Nations*, London: Stevens (1951).

Kuhn, Arthur K., *Pathways in International Law*, New York: Macmillan (1953).

Lawrence, Thomas J., *Principles of International Law*, 7th ed., Boston: Heath (1925).

Liszt, Franz von, *Das Voelkerrecht*, 12th ed., Berlin: Springer (1925).

Louter, J. de, *Le Droit international public positif*, 2 vols., New York: Oxford (1920).

Martens, G. F. de, *Précis du droit des gens moderne de l'Europe*, 2 vols., Paris: Guillaumin (1864).

Nussbaum, Arthur, *A Concise History of the Law of Nations*, New York: Macmillan (1954).

Nys, Ernest, *Droit international*, 2d ed., 3 vols., Paris: Rivière (1912).

Oppenheim, L., *International Law*, 7th ed. by H. Lauterpacht, New York: Longmans. Vol. I (1947) and Vol. II (1944).

Phillimore, Robert, *Commentaries upon International Law*, 3d ed., 4 vols., London: Butterworth (1879–1889).

Potter, Pitman B., *An Introduction to the Study of International Organization*, 5th ed., New York: Appleton-Century-Crofts (1948).

Ross, A., *A Text-Book of International Law*, London: Longmans (1947).

Rousseau, Charles, *Droit international public*, Paris: Sirey (1953).

———, *Principes généraux du droit international public*, Paris: Pedone (1944).

Scelle, Georges, *Précis de droit des gens*, 2 vols., Paris: Sirey (1932, 1934).

Schwarzenberger, Georg, *International Law*, 2d ed., Vol. 1, London: Stevens (1949).

———, *A Manual of International Law*, New York: Praeger (1951).

Seagle, William, *The History of Law*, New York: Tudor Publishing Co. (1948).

Stockton, Charles H., *Manual of International Law for the Use of Naval Officers*, 2d ed., Annapolis: Naval Institute (1921).

Stone, Julius, *The Province and Function of Law*, Cambridge, Mass.: Harvard University Press (1950).

Stowell, Ellery C., *International Law,* New York: Holt (1931).

Strupp, Karl, *Eléments du droit international public,* 2d ed., 3 vols., Paris: Éditions internationales (1930).

United Nations Secretary-General, *Survey of International Law in Relation to the Work of Codification of the International Law Commission,* New York (1949).

Verdross, Alfred, *Die Verfassung der Voelkerrechtsgemeinschaft,* Vienna (1926).

Walker, Thomas Alfred, *History of the Law of Nations,* Vol. 1, New York: Cambridge (1899).

Westlake, John, *International Law,* 2d ed., 2 vols., New York: Cambridge (1910, 1913).

Wheaton, Henry, *History of the Law of Nations,* New York: Gould, Banks (1845).

Wilson, George Grafton, *Handbook of International Law,* 3d ed., St. Paul, Minn.: West (1939).

Woolsey, Theodore Dwight, *Introduction to the Study of International Law,* 6th ed., New York: Scribner (1897).

Special Works

Allen, Eleanor Wyllys, *The Position of Foreign States before National Courts, Chiefly in Continental Europe,* New York: Macmillan (1933).

Ball, Margaret M., *The Problem of Inter-American Organization,* Stanford, Calif.: Stanford University Press (1944).

Borchard, Edwin M., *Diplomatic Protection of Citizens Abroad,* New York: Banks (1915).

Brüel, Erik, *International Straits,* 2 vols., London: Sweet & Maxwell (1947).

Camara, José Sette, *The Ratification of International Treaties,* Toronto: Ontario Publishing Co. (1949).

Carlston, Kenneth S., *The Process of International Arbitration,* New York: Columbia University Press (1946).

Castrén, Erik, *Succession in International Law,* Helsinki: A. Kirjakauppa (1950).

Chen Ti-Chiang, *The International Law of Recognition,* edited by L. C. Green, London: Stevens (1951).

Colbert, Evelyn Speryer, *Retaliation in International Law,* New York: King's Crown (1948).

Colombos, C. J., *Law of Prize,* 3d ed., London: Longmans (1949).

Cooper, John C., *The Right to Fly,* New York: Holt (1947).

Corwin, Edward S., *The Constitution and World Organization,* Princeton, N. J.: Princeton University Press (1944).

Crosswell, McCormic Carol, *Protection of International Personnel Abroad,* New York: Oceana Publications (1952).

Dickinson, Edwin D., *The Equality of States in International Law,* Cambridge, Mass.: Harvard University Press (1920).

Drost, Pieter N., *Human Rights as Legal Rights,* New York: H. H. Bentler (1951).

Dunn, F. S., *The Protection of Nationals,* Baltimore: Johns Hopkins Press (1932).

Eagleton, Clyde, *The Responsibility of States in International Law*, New York: New York University Press (1928).

Feilchenfeld, Ernest H., *Public Debts and State Succession*, New York: Macmillan (1931).

Feller, A. H., *The Mexican Claims Commission, 1923–1934*, New York: Macmillan (1935).

Fleming, Denna Frank, *The United States and the World Court*, New York: Doubleday, Doran (1945).

Flory, William E. S., *Prisoner of War*, Washington: American Council on Public Affairs (1942).

Franklin, William McHenry, *Protection of Foreign Interests*, Washington: GPO (1946).

Freeman, Alwyn V., *The International Responsibility of States for Denial of Justice*, New York: Longmans (1938).

Freeman, Harrop, *Coercion of States: in International Organization*, Philadelphia: The Pacifist Research Bureau (1944).

Garner, James W., *International Law and the World War*, 2 vols., New York: Longmans (1920).

———, *Prize Law during the World War*, New York: Macmillan (1927).

Gathings, James A., *International Law and American Treatment of Alien Enemy Property*, Washington: American Council of Public Affairs (1940).

Gidel, Gilbert, *Le Droit international public de la mer*, 3 vols., Paris: Sirey (1923–24).

Glueck, Sheldon, *The Nuremberg Trial and Aggressive War*, New York: Knopf (1946).

———, *War Criminals: Their Prosecution and Punishment*, New York: Knopf (1944).

Goodrich, Leland M., and Edvard Hambro, *Charter of the United Nations*, 2d ed., Boston: World Peace Foundation (1949).

Graper, Doris Appel, *The Development of the Law of Belligerent Occupation, 1863–1914*, New York: Columbia University Press (1949).

Gunst, Dietrich W., *Der Begriff der Souveraenitaet im modernen Voelkerrecht*, Hildesheim: R. Oppermann (1953).

Hall, Duncan H., *Mandates, Dependencies, and Trusteeships*, New York: Carnegie Endowment (1948).

Higgins, A. Pearce, *The Hague Peace Conferences*, New York: Cambridge (1909).

——— and C. J. Colombos, *International Law of the Sea*, New York: Longmans (1943).

Hill, Norman, *Claims to Territory in International Law and Relations*, New York: Oxford (1945).

———, *Immunities and Privileges of International Officials. The Experience of the League of Nations*, New York: Carnegie Endowment (1947).

Hudson, Manley O., *The Permanent Court of International Justice, 1920–1942*, New York: Macmillan (1943).

International Tribunals, Washington: Carnegie Endowment and Brookings Institution (1944).

Jessup, Philip C., *Law of Territorial Waters and Maritime Jurisdiction*, New York: Jennings (1927).

Jones, J. Mervyn, *Full Powers and Ratification*, New York: Cambridge (1946).

Jones, S. B., *Boundary-making*, New York: Carnegie Endowment (1945).

Kansas, Sidney, *United States Immigration Exclusion and Deportation, and Citizenship of the United States of America*, 3d ed., New York: Matthew Bender Co. (1948).

Keelor, Frances, *American Arbitration*, New York: Harper (1948).

———— and Martin Demke, *Arbitration in International Controversy*, New York (1944).

Keeton, G. W., *Development of Exterritoriality in China*, 2 vols., London (1928).

Kelsen, Hans, *The Law of the United Nations*, London: Stevens (1950).

Kunz, J. L., *Kriegsrecht und Neutralitaetsrecht*, Vienna: Springer (1935).

Lachs, Manfred, *War Crimes*, London: Stevens (1945).

Ladas, Stephen K., *International Protection of Industrial Property*, Cambridge, Mass.: Harvard University Press (1930).

Langer, Robert, *Seizure of Territory*, Princeton, N. J.: Princeton University Press (1947).

Lauterpacht, H., *Function of Law in the International Community*, New York: Oxford (1933).

————, *An International Bill of the Rights of Man*, New York: Columbia University Press (1945).

————, *International Law and Human Rights*, London: Stevens & Sons (1950)

————, *Private Law Sources and Analogies in International Law*, New York: Longmans (1927).

————, *Recognition in International Law*, New York: Cambridge (1947).

Leonard, L. L., *International Regulation of Fisheries*, New York: Carnegie Endowment (1944).

McClure, Wallace, *International Executive Agreements*, New York: Columbia University Press (1941).

McFee, William, *The Law of the Sea*, Philadelphia: Lippincott (1950).

Maclaurin, John, *The United Nations and Power Politics*, New York: Harper (no date).

McNair, Arnold D., *Law of Treaties--British Practice and Opinions*, New York: Columbia University Press (1938).

————, *Legal Effects of War*, 3d ed., New York: Cambridge University Press (1948).

Masterson, William E., *Jurisdiction in Marginal Seas*, New York: Macmillan (1929).

Moore, John Bassett, *Extradition and Interstate Rendition*, 2 vols., Boston: Boston Book (1891).

Mouton, M. W., *The Continental Shelf*, The Hague: M. Nijhoff (1952).

Nielsen, Fred K., *International Law Applied to Reclamations*, Washington: Byrne (1933).

Northrop, F. S. C., *The Taming of the Nations*, New York: Macmillan (1952).

Padelford, Norman J., *International Law and Diplomacy in the Spanish Civil Strife*, New York: Macmillan (1939).

Pastuhov, Vladimir D., *A Guide to the Practice of International Conferences*, New York: Carnegie Endowment (1945).

Politis, Nicolas, *La Morale internationale*, New York: Brentano (1944).

Ralston, Jackson H., *Law and Procedure of International Tribunals*, rev. ed., Stanford, Calif.: Stanford University Press (1926).

Reid, Helen Dwight, *International Servitudes in Law and Practice*, Chicago: University of Chicago Press (1932).

Reinsch, Paul S., *International Public Unions*, Boston: Ginn (1911).

Riesenfeld, S. A., *Protection of Coastal Fisheries under International Law*, New York: Carnegie Endowment (1942).

Rodick, Burleigh Cushing, *The Doctrine of Necessity in International Law*, New York: Columbia University Press (1928).

Roth, Andreas H., *The Minimum Standard of International Law, Applied to Aliens*, Leyden: Sijthoff (1950).

Sandifer, D. V., *Evidence before International Tribunals*, Chicago: Foundation Press (1939).

Satow, Ernest M., *A Guide to Diplomatic Practice*, 3d ed., London: Longmans (1932).

Scelle, Georges, *Les Fondateurs du droit international*, Paris: Giard & Brière (1904).

Shawcross, C. N., and K. M. Beaumont, *Air Law*, London: Butterworth (1945).

Smith, H. A., *The Crisis in the International Law of Nations*, London: Stevens (1947).

———, *The Law and Custom of the Sea*, London: Stevens (1948).

Sörensen, Max, *Les Sources du droit international. Etude sur la jurisprudence de la Cour Permanente de Justice Internationale*, Copenhagen: E. Munksgaard (1946).

Spaight, J. M., *Air Power and War Rights*, 3d ed., London: Longmans (1947).

Stone, Julius, *The Atlantic Charter—New Worlds for Old*, Sydney: Current Book Distributors (1945).

Stowell, Ellery C., *Intervention in International Law*, Washington: Byrne (1921).

Stuart, Graham H., *American Diplomatic and Consular Practice*, New York: Appleton-Century-Crofts (1936).

Taracouzio, T. A., *The Soviet Union and International Law*, New York: Macmillan (1935).

United Nations Secretariat, *Historical Survey of the Question of International Criminal Jurisdiction*, New York (1948).

United Nations War Crimes Commission, *History of the United Nations War Crimes Commission and the Development of the Laws of War*, London: H.M. Stationery Office (1948).

Vyshinsky, Andrei J., *The Law of the Soviet State*, New York: Macmillan (1948).

Whiteman, Marjorie, *Damages in International Law*, 3 vols., Washington: GPO (1937–1943).

Wilson, Robert R., *The International Standard in Treaties of the United States*, Cambridge, Mass.: Harvard University Press (1953).

Wright, Quincy, *Mandates under the League of Nations*, Chicago: University of Chicago Press (1930).

———, *A Study of War*, 2 vols., Chicago: University of Chicago Press (1942).

Periodicals

Académie de Droit International, Recueil des cours (1923–   ), Paris.

The American Journal of International Law (1907–   ), Washington.
American Society of International Law, Proceedings (1907–   ), Washington.
Annuaire de l'Institut de Droit International (1877–   ), Brussels.
Annuaire suisse de droit international (1944–   ), Zurich.
Archiv des Voelkerrechts (1948), Tübingen.
British Year Book of International Law (1920–   ), London.
Grotius annuaire international (1913–   ), The Hague.
The Grotius Society: Transactions (1916–   ), London.
Hague, Académie de Droit International, Recueil de cours (1923–   ), The Hague.
Inter-American Juridical Yearbook (1948–   ), Washington.
International Conciliation, Washington: Carnegie Endowment.
International Law Association, Reports (1873–   ), London.
International Law Quarterly (1947–   ), London.
International Organization (1947–   ), Boston: World Peace Foundation.
Journal of Air Law (1930–   ), Chicago.
Journal of the Society of Comparative Legislation and International Law (1896–1920).
League of Nations Official Journal (1920–1946), Geneva.
Nordisk Tidsskrift for international Ret (1930–   ), Copenhagen.
Revista argentina de derecho internacional (1920–1922, 1938–   ), Buenos Aires.
Revista de derecho internacional (1922–   ), Havana.
Revista peruana de derecho internacional (1941–   ), Lima.
Revue de droit international (de Lapradelle, 1927–   ), Paris.
Revue de droit international et de législation comparée (1869–1939), Brussels.
Revue de droit international, de sciences diplomatiques et politiques (1923–   ), Geneva.
Revue égyptienne de droit international (1945–   ), Alexandria.
Revue général de droit international public (1894–   ), Paris.
Revue internationale française du droit de gens, Paris.
Rivista di diritto internazionale (1906–1943), Rome.
United Nations Bulletin, New York.
United States Department of State Bulletin, Washington.
United States Foreign Relations, Washington.
United States, Naval War College, International Law Situations (1901–   ), Washington.
Zeitschrift fuer auslaendisches öffentliches Recht und Völkerrecht (1929–   ), Brunswick.
Zeitschrift fuer internationales Recht (1891–1937), Kiel.
Zeitschrift fuer oeffentliches Recht (1914–   ), Vienna.
Zeitschrift fuer Voelkerrecht (1913–1944), Breslau.

Index

Aaland Islands, 112
Abbé Grégoire, 29–30
Absolute sovereignty, 69
Accretion, 169, 182
Acheson, Secretary Dean, 310
Acquisition, derivative, 178–180
  by prescription, 182
Acquisition of Polish Nationality, 427
Act of Berlin (1885), 173
Act of Chapultepec, 314–316
Actions *in rem*, 211
Acts, of Congress, 265
  of state, 134
Ad Hoc Assembly, 324
Adams, Charles Francis, 287
Adams, John Quincy, 281
Adélie Land, French claim to, 175
Adriatic Sea, 185, 187
Adverse possession, 180
Advocatio hispanica, 187
Aerial circulation over high seas, 191
Aerial Navigation Convention (1919), 44, 214
Aerial transportation, 215
Aeronautics, science of, 225
Africa, 274
  partition of, 169
Age of Nationalism, 30, 329
Age of Reason, 434
Aggression, 24
Aggressive wars, responsibility for starting, 132
Air Navigation Commission, 220
Air Navigation Convention of 1919, 193
Airspace, 167, 213, 225
  sovereignty in, 168
Aix-la-Chapelle, Congress of (1818), 237
  Court of Appeal, 235
  Declaration of 1818, 32
  Protocol of, 31*n*.
Aksionariornoye Obchestvo v. James S. Sagor & Co., 106
Alabama claims, 36, 129, 152, 287
Albania, 304
Alexander VI, Pope, 185

Alguacil mayor, 118
Alianza Popular Revolucionaria Americana, 251
Alien Enemy Act of 1798, 348
Alien land law of California, 268
Aliens, property custodian, 350
  protection of, 138
    judicial, 145
  treatment of, 137–138
Allegiance, temporary, 375
Allied and Associated Powers, 41, 113, 156, 364, 397
Allied Control Council Law No. 10, 403
Allied Forces Act of 1940, 387
Allied military courts, 387
Allies, 177, 392
  government of, 398
Alluvial action, 183
Alluvion, 182
Alsace-Lorraine, 41
Altmark, 369
Alverstone, Lord, 64
Amalfi, Italy, 197
America, commerce, 363
  Constitution, 274
  constitutional law, 267, 278
  continents, 317
  foreign policy, 366
  government, 356, 389
  Great Lakes, 163
  jurists, 266
  legislation, 210
  people, sovereignty of, 264
  policy of isolationist trend in, 366
  regionalism, 313
  republics, 194, 313
  and violation, of neutrality, 253
    of territory, 124
American-Danish negotiations, 179
American Foreign Service officer, duties of, 244
American Institute of International Law, 122
American-Japanese Security Act (1951), 327